Commuter Airlines of the United States

New York's FIRST AIRBOAT COMMUTER!

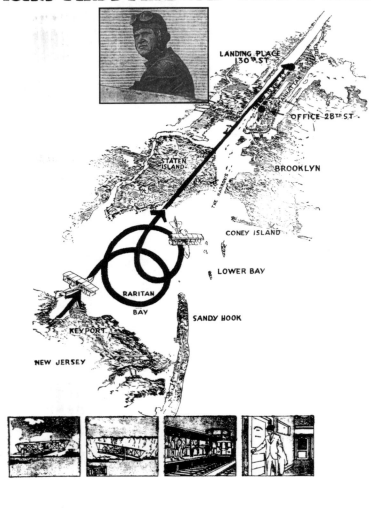

As early as 1913, Alfred W. Lawson claimed fame as the first person to fly his own aircraft between his home in New Jersey and upper Manhattan. In Chicago, Harold McCormick had preceded Lawson as an aerial commuter, but he had hired both the aircraft and the pilot to do so. (Reset from *The World Magazine*, November 16, 1913.)

Commuter Airlines of the United States

R. E. G. Davies and I. E. Quastler

Foreword by George Haddaway

Smithsonian Institution Press

Washington and London

Editor and typesetter: Peter Strupp/Princeton Editorial Associates
Production editor: Therese Boyd/Initial Cap Editorial Services
Designer: Alan Carter

Library of Congress Cataloging-in-Publication Data
Davies, R. E. G. (Ronald Edward George)
    Commuter Airlines of the United States / R.E.G. Davies and I.E. Quastler; foreword
by George Haddaway.
        p.   cm.
    Includes bibliographical references and index.
    ISBN 1-56098-404-X
    1. Local service airlines—United States—History.   2. Local service airlines—
Government policy—United States.   I. Quastler, I. E.   II. Title.
HE9785.D38   1994
387.7′42′0973—dc20

                                                                                              94-19849
                                                                                                    CIP
British Library Cataloguing-in-Publication Data is available.

Manufactured in the United States of America

00 99 98 97 96 95 94   5 4 3 2 1

♾ The paper used in this publication meets the minimum requirements of the
American National Standard for Permanence of Paper for Printed Library Materials
Z39.48-1984.

The tabular material in Part III and Appendix 1 has been directly reproduced from
camera-ready copy prepared by the authors.

Contents

III REGIONAL TABULATIONS OF COMMUTER AIRLINES   325

APPENDIXES   443

Foreword

Back yonder, before newspapers evolved into syndicated factories, the more perspicacious publishers usually assigned coverage of aviation to one specific reporter designated the "aviation editor." By the late 1930s, about the time Adolf Hitler was proving that his objectives as set forth in *Mein Kampf* were not to be laughed at, there were enough aviation scribes around to justify the formation of the Aviation Writers Association, an idea proposed by the spirited and erudite Devon Francis of the Associated Press.

At the organization's first annual news conference I asked Francis why he had picked aviation as his main journalistic pursuit. He replied that there was no other contemporary area of human endeavor as "dynamic or as colorful" as aviation. "There is," he said, "adventure and high drama in it; besides, it reflects human progress far more than any other activity in today's dangerous and uncertain world."

His perceptive remarks went into my diary and flashed through my mind when I read the manuscript of *Commuter Airlines of the United States*, a timely sequel to Ron Davies's delightful *Rebels and Reformers of the Airways*, a volume that revealed Davies's penchant for seeking out uninhibited and maverick characters ever ready to pounce upon any opportunity to get into the airline business.

Of equal significance is the timeliness of the new volume's appearance—at a time when once again the trunk airlines are downsizing, abandoning the communities that desperately need air accessibility.

It was back in 1980 that Davies and Dr. I. E. Quastler first talked about writing a definitive history of this unique and poorly documented segment of U.S. commercial aviation, complete with informative charts and statistical information heretofore hard to come by.

The authors realized that to complete such a project would require a lot of plowing in wet mud, that it would be a challenge to write about such a complex mélange of untested route structures and diverse, trial-and-error operating conditions with no set standards of equipment or procedures, all under the direction of a mix of personalities from taxi pilots on one end of the experience spectrum to astute businessmen on the other. Nevertheless they identified a need and filled it.

More than forty years ago *Flight Magazine* vigorously editorialized and campaigned politically (pro bono publico) for the "feeders" to be developed as an essential element in domestic air transportation. The major airlines dominated the system. How could the trunks be called a bona fide transportation system while serving only two hundred markets? In fact they constituted a true monopoly, in cahoots with the cities they served.

The magazine's lone wolf campaign to establish new short-haul services into the smaller communities took root, became a prairie fire, and stirred up Congress, where small town constituencies far outnumbered and outfought the big boys—a lesson wisely applied by today's surviving commuters.

Davies and Quastler's very readable seminal volume of long-ignored history reminds us that so-called commuter operators have been around for a long time, that they have actually been in business since shortly after the end of World War I. Before the outbreak of World War II the persistent talk of creating "feeder" lines was put on hold. At the war's end, some fifteen companies, mainly originating in air taxi or fixed base operations, acquired temporary Certificates of Convenience and Necessity over the vehement protests of the trunks.

Even with the assurance of federal subsidy, the newcomers, restricted by experimental certificates with no long-term guarantees, had trouble finding risk capital. When the Civil Aeronautics Board (CAB) ignored their justifiable petitions for permanent certificates, the extent of small-town political clout was again demonstrated when Congress ordered the CAB to rouse itself from its lethargy and award permanent certificates. Local airlines were no longer bastard members of the clan.

The locals justified federal subsidy payments as subsidy to the towns receiving air service, not to the companies, thus establishing a precedent valuable to the commuter lines. The locals became junior trunks, many doing quite well as the majors continued to drop low-density points. The locals finally disappeared as a second-level system because of growth, mergers, bankruptcy, sell-outs, and the natural vicissitudes of deregulation. As a result the doors opened once again for the traditional professionals of short haul to develop, many to be recognized by the big brothers as an essential segment of scheduled air transport, even as partners rather than poor relations. So we can believe that aviation pioneering is far from dead.

This previously neglected chapter of domestic air transportation history makes good reading because the authors have removed the wraps from the idiosyncratic wheeler-dealers who fly on the periphery of high-density air transport. The case histories of the major players in this diverse society are so well written, so vivid, that the protagonists of the drama come to life off the printed page. Do not be surprised if some of these colorful, uninhibited entrepreneurs are reborn some day in Broadway plays, with or without music. I speak with authority, for I am personally acquainted with most of these masters of risk. They have enriched my life.

Fact is, the authors have done such a good job I'm thinking about giving the book as a Christmas present to some very special friends. It's a great story. I would have written it myself but I was afraid nobody would believe it.

George Haddaway
Dallas, Texas

Preface

When, in December 1980, Imre Quastler informally suggested that we should jointly write a book on the history of the U.S. passenger commuter airlines, I did not demur. Thinking about this grand idea, I felt that Imre's specialized interest in this section of the industry, combined with my broader approach to the history of airlines in general, would be a good combination. Both of us were researchers and writers, and both of us in different ways came into contact with various companies and people.

At first, because I was about to move from California to Washington, D.C., I delayed my decision until I felt settled. Having moved, and after further correspondence and meetings with Imre, we shook hands on the project and began to prepare for action. I was, I think, swayed by the knowledge that, living in Washington, I would at least have access to the files and records of various federal agencies based in the nation's capital.

Little did I know—and neither, I think, did Imre know—what we had let ourselves in for. Both of us knew that the number of commuter airlines that had come and gone—mostly gone—was legion. Imre had done some studies and had written a couple of individual histories, and a chapter on this section of the industry in my *Airlines of the United States since 1914* had given me more problems than I care to think about. Nevertheless we set about the task in the summer of 1981 in good spirits.

Tracing the history and development of the commuter airlines was far from straightforward. No government agency or department had ever ordained (as in the case of the U.S. domestic trunk and local service categories of airline), "Let there be commuter airlines." Individual companies, responding to local specialized demands, had emerged, almost surreptitiously, from the vastness of the forty-eight states,

Alaska, Hawaii, and the Caribbean, from the army of fixed base operators that abounded in corners and crannies off the beaten track of the
airways. In the beginning, the Civil Aeronautics Board (CAB) was loath
to recognize them, and such recognition, when it existed at all, placed
them in categories such as "other" or "miscellaneous." The Federal
Aviation Agency (FAA) was content at first simply to ensure that the
scheduled air taxi operators obeyed the rules of navigation and instrumentation, complied with safety regulations, and generally behaved
themselves. In the early years, the FAA tried to keep records and ana-
lyze the situation, but the annual reports tended simply to provide lists
and to observe a few trends about numbers of companies and aircraft.

Not until 1969 did the CAB start to gather information about commuter airlines; for the first time, data on passenger traffic began to be
published. Like the FAA, however, it tended to regard the commuter
airlines as the poor relations of their larger and richer airline brethren,
and its regulation of them was halfhearted; thus, the board's passenger
data were often markedly incomplete.

During the 1960s and 1970s the commuter airlines developed their
own lobbying groups, such as the Association of Commuter Airlines and
the Commuter Airlines Association of America. Although their records
and occasional reports were useful to this historian, the ephemeral
nature of so many of the precariously supported and financed operators
did not lend itself to systematic chronology or narrative.

Compounding the problem was the authors' realization that, as in the
animal kingdom, there were many species within the major genus. Just
as a Kentucky Warbler differs in plumage and habits from a Connecticut
Warbler, a commuter airline from the Midwest or the Far West varies in
its methods of operation and market opportunities from a small airline
based on Long Island Sound. We therefore sought to distinguish among
the different types of airlines by dividing the United States and the
Puerto Rico–Virgin Islands area into thirteen geographical regions. In
addition to compiling a general history, we attempted to identify the
special characteristics of each of these areas and to review the individual carriers that met their air transport needs.

The emphasis is on the term "individual." Until the mid-1980s,
commuter airlines were never cast in a common mold. Almost without
exception, whether large or small, wildly ambitious or of limited aspiration, well-capitalized or with shoestring resources, all were invariably
founded by hardy individualists, many of them philosophically or even
psychologically opposed to regulations or bureaucracy of any sort. Rec-

ognizing too that certain individuals were trendsetters because they were able to combine their instincts for fulfilling a need with their ability to achieve results, we selected a number of airline personalities for special recognition, and their profiles constitute an important section of this book.

Today, much of the adventure and sense of pioneering has disappeared from the code-sharing commuter world. Since the advent of airline deregulation, the U.S. airline industry has undergone a metamorphosis that has seen the birth and early demise of airlines of considerable substance and no little fame, such as People Express. Great airlines, such as Pan American, Eastern, and Braniff, have succumbed to the changing and relatively unregulated airline environment, and many others, such as Western and Piedmont, have been absorbed into larger carriers. As this book goes to press the entire U.S. airline industry still faces severe problems, not least in terms of massive financial losses and staff layoffs. Commuter airlines, therefore, may seem unimportant by comparison.

But they have played their part, and their role continues to increase in importance in the 1990s. Collectively, more than one thousand airlines have provided connecting and feeder services to the mainline carriers and in doing so have served the American public well. Many of them were able to construct a flimsy route network based on links to small communities that the larger airlines no longer had any interest in serving, simply because they were separately too small to fit the traffic patterns served by large propeller or jet aircraft. While the big airlines turned their backs, the scheduled air taxis, later called the third-level airlines and finally commuter or even regional airlines, came to the rescue, filled the gap, and kept air transport alive in hundreds of small cities throughout the United States. Now the big airlines have come full circle, have realized that the aggregate of small community service was essential to their needs, have readopted the commuter airlines (by code-sharing and even ownership), and have thereby gone back to their roots as well as their routes.

Future generations may forget the largely undefined commuter airline industry that was somehow born during the 1950s, grew lustily and independently in the 1960s and 1970s, and was engulfed by the commuter lines' big brothers in the 1980s. But these commuter airlines deserve to be recognized for their efforts, and Imre and I hope that this book will go some way toward placing on record the unique collective achievement of a small army of true aviation pioneers.

R. E. G. Davies

My interest in commuter airlines goes back to the late 1960s, when my friend Tom Wilson, who had worked for Bonanza and Hughes Air West, first told me about the remarkable growth of this segment of the airline industry. Thereafter my level of interest increased rapidly, and soon I was quite fascinated by this new phenomenon. Before too long (and perhaps prematurely), I had presented several papers and had published an article on the subject. I also began to visit as many airports as possible, trying to record on slides the rapidly changing American commuter airline scene.

Not until the mid-1970s, however, did I begin to study individual airlines in detail, and to feel that I was understanding the industry. In about 1976 I started a history of one of the pioneer California carriers, Swift Aire Lines, of San Luis Obispo, which had prospered under the leadership of Charlie Wiswell. The result of many hours of interviewing different people in the company and of studying California Public Utilities Commission records, the book was published in March 1979, in time to celebrate Swift Aire's tenth anniversary. It was followed almost immediately by a history of Gary Adamson's Air Midwest, a book that subsequently was updated for the airline's twentieth anniversary celebrations in 1985. The latter book included a short history of Ray Ellis's Scheduled Skyways, a company that was in the process of being merged into Air Midwest.

These two books could perhaps be regarded as case histories of individual commuter airline development; the idea of writing a general history of the commuter airline industry as a whole had been germinating in my mind for some time before I mentioned it to Ron Davies in 1980. Although I knew that writing this book would be a challenge, I did not know just how difficult it would in fact turn out to be. As noted by Ron, the amount of systematically assembled information available about the industry has been remarkably small, and much of that which is available is not necessarily accurate or is incomplete. Building on this kind of treacherous base, writing the book turned out to be a most challenging—but ultimately rewarding—task.

I. E. Quastler

Acknowledgments

In a book such as this, the compilation of which has spanned a period of almost fourteen years, to acknowledge every person who assisted in any way would clearly be impossible. Scores, perhaps hundreds, of individuals contributed. They provided valuable information and factual data, either by reminiscence or experience, first- or second-hand, or by giving us literature and other printed matter that related to the countless commuter airlines that have otherwise failed to publish information about themselves.

First, among the many who deserve special thanks must be the willing volunteers who joined with the authors as area coordinators, collecting information on the airlines within the thirteen groups of states that were designated as distinct regions so as to take account of perceived differences in individual airline characteristics. Some of these voluntary pillars of strength devoted many hours of their time to traveling, telephoning, and typing during the periods of interviewing commuter airline operators. In particular Jim Thompson, of Columbus, Ohio, contributed a considerable percentage of the data contained in the tabulations for Area 9 (Midwest) and Area 1 (Alaska), in the latter case drawing on material gathered during his visits to the forty-ninth state. John Davis performed sterling work in Area 7 (Central) and Area 8 (Texas and Louisiana) and was also kind enough to help proofread and copyedit the historical narrative of the book. Bill Callahan dived enthusiastically into the intricacies of area 11 (Northeast), and Frank Koral anchored our work in Area 3 (Northwest). Peter Forman checked the data on Area 2 (Hawaii), Mike Marsh, aided and abetted by Al Minich, covered Area 5 (Rocky Mountains), and Terry Love did the same for Area 6 (North Central). Jerry Marlette added valuable information for Areas 6 and 9 (Midwest) and even donated his own valuable files and records to the cause. Various members of the Washington Airline Society, notably Roger Bentley and Dick Hurley, were also most generous in providing data from their own files.

To all these good folks—and to the countless others who, in turn, must have helped *them*—the authors take off their hats in grateful acknowledgment of a formidable collective undertaking, cheerfully accomplished, which will survive as a permanent reference for future scholars and historians.

Second, we must thank the publishers of and contributors to the several magazines that have devoted much of their space and interest to the affairs of the lowest stratum of the U.S. airline industry. Foremost must be George Haddaway, of *Flight Magazine* (sadly no longer published), who must take much credit for paying attention to the small airlines as early as the late 1950s (when other journals paid no attention to them at all). Ed Pickering, one of *Flight*'s authoritative writers, deserves to be recognized for his perception in recognizing what he called the third-level airlines. Although the term was to be superseded, his identification of the commuter operators as a distinct category of airline was almost clairvoyant, preceding full recognition by either the FAA or the CAB.

Subsequently, various magazines and periodicals have specialized in the commuter or regional airlines, as they became known. *Air Transport World*, in the good hands of Joe Murphy and later of Jim Woolsey, devoted a fair amount of space to the commuter airlines. Lou Davis has been a constant campaigner for their cause and a defender of their role in the scheme of airline things in general. As editor of *Commuter Air*, his was often the lone voice of the commuter airlines, while other prestigious publications concentrated on the great issues of deregulation and trunk airline problems. Kathryn B. Creedy, aviation industry journalist and co-founder, with Joe Murphy, of *Commuter-Regional Airline News*, has also given much help over the years, including access to copies of her many lectures on the state of the industry in the late 1980s and early 1990s.

The annual reports issued by the commuter airline industry itself have, of course, been energetically pursued, and our thanks are due to the various organizations that compiled this valuable historical record: the National Air Transportation Conference, the Commuter Airline Association of America, and its successor, the Regional Airlines Association.

Several directories, such as *JP Airlines Fleets*, *North American Aviation News*, Günter Endres's *World Airline Fleets Directory*, and the *Airline Handbook*, have also been invaluable sources of data. The ubiquitous *Official Airline Guide,* which has done its job so well since 1929, has not been found entirely wanting, publishing as it has the schedules of tiny airlines as well as grand ones (provided they supplied information regularly and reliably).

Third, we must thank the special people who are profiled in Part II of the book. They were most patient with the interviewing procedures, and generous in their lack of censorship when exercising editorial privileges. In addition to describing their personal involvement, they were also able to help the authors in other ways. Sometimes consciously, sometimes unconsciously, they were able to bring into sharp relief the sense of individualism that has been the constant thread of inspiration that developed a segment of the U.S. air transport industry before the computer-powered oligopoly took control during the deregulated 1980s.

Definition of Commuter Airlines

In this book, the reader must be alert to the real meanings and implications of the key terms "commuter" and "commuter airline." Because of the changing nature of our social behavior in the modern world, the meanings of both terms have undergone subtle and far-reaching modifications. This book is not about commuting by air; it is about those operations that became known as commuter airlines.

To Commute

The meaning of the verb "to commute" as applied to travel is of relatively recent origin, as is its derivative noun "commuter." Before the railways were built during the nineteenth century, leading to the development of mass travel behavior patterns, the predominantly agricultural population lived on the land and the growing nonagricultural communities lived in what today would be classified mainly as medium-size towns or cities and walked to work. Few people actually used a means of conveyance to travel regularly to and from their place of toil.

Then (and still today in a less frequent use of the term) to commute meant to interchange, usually in the sense of mitigation, for example, when a death sentence was commuted to one less severe.

The Commuter

As the pace of industrial expansion increased during the nineteenth and early twentieth centuries, towns and cities grew bigger, and railways began to provide easy access to areas of more spacious living in the suburbs. The rate and volume of the exodus from the inner cities grew as the commercial world changed from one centered on simple manufacturing and distribution processes into a complex one of administration in financial and service industries. Office workers began to predominate, and the railways developed intensive services for the growing army of "white-collar" workers. They began to provide discounted fares for multiple ticket purchases that eliminated the tiresome and time-consuming practice of standing in line at the ticket windows. The beneficiaries of this system became known as commuters because they made use of tickets of which the original face value had been commuted to a lesser amount. Interestingly, the term was not used in Great Britain for many years, and only recently have the "season ticket" holders acquiesced to the American terminology. Today commuters abound in every large city of the world, as do the commuter trains that serve them.

Air Commuting

As long ago as 1913, Harold McCormick of Chicago and Alfred W. Lawson (of Lawson Airline fame) used aircraft to travel to and from work, the latter claiming to be "New York's First Airboat Commuter." Many of the early airlines were located in populated areas and used the term loosely. As air transport developed, several of them included "commuter routes" in their networks, even though few passengers actually commuted, that is to say, traveled regularly day after day. But they were able to make the round trip in the same day, and the airline promoters felt justified in modifying the strict meaning of the term.

Commuter Airlines

Some airlines specialized in such operations and called themselves (or were called) commuter airlines. Examples were the Philadelphia Rapid Transit Service of 1926 and the frequent services operated between New York and Boston during the late 1930s by American Airlines and Northeast Airlines. When Kenneth G. Friedkin, founder of California's first intrastate carrier, Pacific Southwest Airlines (PSA) died, he was remembered as the father of the Los Angeles–San Francisco commuter airline business. The former Eastern Air Shuttle was always regarded as a "commuter" operation.

After World War II, however, high-frequency air service from outlying communities to urban centers began to expand. Opportunistic innovators identified specialist markets in the vicinity of large urban hubs. The clientele seldom traveled every day. Certainly little attention was given to the idea of commuting the price of the ticket: the airlines charged what the market would bear. But they began to be called commuter airlines nevertheless.

Official Recognition

At first—stemming from the manner in which the majority of the diminutive airlines evolved—they were called scheduled air taxi operators. The government agency charged with regulating the airline industry, the Civil Aeronautics Board (CAB), was inclined to disregard them. During the 1960s, as they grew in numbers and stature, the term "third-level airline" came into use, and they operated as airlines under the safety regulations of the Federal Aviation Agency (later the Federal Aviation Administration). But they felt this term to be degrading, even derogatory, and it was eventually superseded by the more preferable term "commuter airline." By the late 1960s they were so numerous and of such standing in the community that they were recognized as a special category by the CAB and were so regulated and so named until the Airline Deregulation Act of 1978. By then the term "commuter," as applied to the airlines, had also become an accepted term in marketing.

Commuter Aircraft

As in any other airline operational field, the commuter airlines have usually been highly selective in their choice of aircraft: the ideal airplane has been small enough to match the often slender traffic demand yet able to fly cheaply enough to permit operations under ideal conditions of fare structure and market demand. Some manufacturers recognized this trend and began to build specialized aircraft for the purpose. By a strange twist of language evolution, most commuter airlines are now in fact recognized as such because they operate commuter aircraft.

The Airlines in This Book

This book is not about all so-called commuter air routes and does not address the subject of operation on those routes operated by major airlines or by intrastate carriers such as PSA. Nor does it review the intensive services of airlines, such as the former Eastern Air Shuttle, that helped to pioneer "on the hour, every hour" service.

With minor exceptions that the reader will readily identify, the airlines in the book fall within the several definitions that have been applied by the CAB, which, as a matter of administrative convenience, has related them to the size of the aircraft used. In recent years, however, such limitations have often been disregarded as the full opportunities in a deregulated industry were put to advantage. On the other hand, the commuter airlines of today can no longer claim any special treatment. They are controlled and regulated in much the same manner as are the major airlines.

Such status is a measure of their achievement. In about thirty years they have matured from an unorganized collection of individual companies, which had to fight to gain legitimacy and to be recognized as airlines, into a class of operator that has collectively made up an essential segment of the U.S. airline industry, and without which hundreds of small communities in America would be without the privileges of air transport.

Part I

History of the Industry

Chapter 1

As It Was in the Beginning

Tracing a historical lineage often involves far more than a straightforward examination of the precise genealogy, and the exploration of airline history is no exception. Certainly, during air transport's infancy and adolescence, parallel instances can easily be identified in which aircraft of similar size, if not performance, were operating over routes similar to those of many of the commuter airlines today. Examples can be found during the interwar years of the use of the term "commuter" with the same broad connotation as it carries today. Although the parallels are not always direct, because the motivations of the key players and the competitive forces to which they reacted were far different, one common thread is woven through the decades: the routes were all short, at one time seldom exceeding one hundred miles. This short-haul characteristic has survived to this day, with only a modest increment in the average stage length.

But to identify all short-haul air routes automatically as commuter routes or commuter airline routes would be quite wrong. Until the early 1960s, short-haul route structures were not even classified into a separate category of airline, and much of this book examines the painstaking—and often painful—process by which official recognition of a distinct status for short-haul airlines, independent from those of trunk and local service airlines, was achieved.

The definitions themselves have changed. In the early 1920s, when the first airlines cautiously got their airplane floats wet (and their financial fingers burned), one hundred miles was considered to be a long range for an airplane carrying a passenger as well as a pilot. All the routes flown in the early 1920s would have been classified today as of the commuter type—on the basis of range, if not motivation.

In the early 1930s, typical ranges were still in the low hundreds, and even the Boeing 247s and Douglas DC-3s that ushered in a new era of air transport in the mid-1930s could not always be counted on to fly nonstop over the 800 miles from New York to Chicago. Today a 1,500-mile-range DC-9 is considered a short-haul airliner.

Aircraft size has undergone a similar shift in perception. When, no earlier than 1927, airlines in the United States began to carry passengers on a sustained basis and to provide such luxuries as seats (in the early mail planes, the passengers customarily sat on the mail sacks) even six-seat Travelairs were described as "giant air transports." When it was introduced, the fourteen-seat Ford Tri-Motor was truly the colossus of its time.

However, in spite of these problems in drawing broad comparisons, there are common denominators between the pioneer airline operators from the formative years of air transport and the commuter airlines that constitute their nearest modern counterparts. Both fall at the lowest end of the range of distances needing to be flown, and they also fly the smallest aircraft available for commercial purposes. This brief review of historical perspectives therefore attempts both to bring into focus the emergence of the commuter airlines as a group, and to explain how and why their phenomenal growth of the 1960s and 1970s came about as a feature of air transport development in the United States.

The Embryo Years

Curiously, the world's first scheduled airline, the 1914 St. Petersburg–Tampa Air Boat Line, would have fallen into the commuter airline category had it been operating today. Its one route was across Tampa Bay and it lasted for three months, flying Benoist flying boats on an eighteen-mile ferry service, able to carry one passenger on each flight in addition to the pilot. Most of the intrepid passengers were vacationers from New York and other northeastern cities, and they took the trip more as a novelty than as a means of getting from one place to another. They definitely were not commuters. But neither are most of the passengers who take the flight from the Massachusetts mainland to the island of Martha's Vineyard today.

Five years and a world war were to pass before any other airline, in any category, made its appearance anywhere in the world. At the close of hostilities, airlines emerged in almost every country in Europe, but strangely the people of the United States showed little enthusiasm for

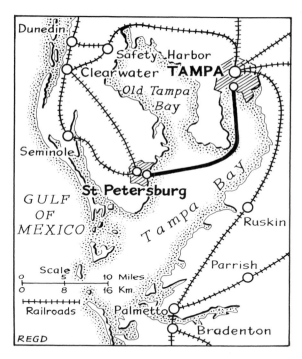

The St. Petersburg–Tampa Air Boat Line was operated for three months at the beginning of 1914. It was the world's first scheduled airline and could also be termed the world's first commuter airline. It did not carry commuter passengers, but it did carry 1,200 tourists, in much the same manner as some commuter airlines do today. The alternative routes were via a circuitous and slow railroad or an equally circuitous and poor road.

The St. Petersburg–Tampa Air Boat Line operated a tiny Benoist flying boat across Tampa Bay during the first three months of 1914. (Photo courtesy of Elliott Fansler.)

Syd Chaplin operated a Curtiss MF Seagull from San Pedro in the port of Los Angeles to Santa Catalina Island during the summer of 1919. His airline may even have carried the occasional commuter. (Photo courtesy of Randy Lieberman.)

taking to the air. Although there were some advocates for a nationwide system of air routes, the public was easily persuaded that flying was a dangerous pastime, and many former combat pilots encouraged this perception by their daredevil stunting on the barnstorming circuit.

Those pioneer innovators in the United States who did try to put the airplane to commercial use quickly discovered that the feasibility of doing so depended upon finding rare situations in which it was operationally competitive. The single-engined airplanes of the early 1920s were slow. A typical cruising speed was seventy or eighty miles per hour, hardly enough to demonstrate much of a time saving over surface transport, especially during a period when the railroads were accepted as the standard means of intercity transport. Aircraft were also unreliable, so that an acceptable degree of regularity or punctuality could seldom be achieved. But across short stretches of water, where the only competition was a relatively slow ferryboat or a circuitous and time-consuming road or rail journey, a floatplane or flying boat not only could save considerable time, but, in the event of an engine failure, also could alight on the water—an emergency procedure that was widely felt to be far safer than trying to find a flat field or other similar landing place.

Early passenger services before the passage of the 1925 Air Mail Act and the 1926 Air Commerce Act were therefore few in number and short in duration. Full credit should go to the Syd Chaplin Airline, promoted

The Syd Chaplin Airline operated for three months during the summer of 1919, carrying passengers from the Los Angeles area on the twenty-mile trip to Avalon, the resort on Santa Catalina Island. Various airlines have operated this route, with few interruptions, ever since; the postwar successor was to expand throughout California.

by the famous film actor's brother, which operated for three months beginning on 4 July 1919. The route was from San Pedro, in the port district of Los Angeles, to the resort city of Avalon, on Santa Catalina Island, and remarkably, with only a few interruptions, this route has been operated continuously ever since, usually by what we would today call commuter airlines. Almost all of Chaplin's clientele were pleasure-bent.

The longest-lived and certainly the most important of the early air ferry operations was Aeromarine Airways, which took over the Florida West Indies company in the fall of 1919, began service from Key West to Havana on 27 October 1920, and survived on this route and other routes

In 1925, Commuters Air Transport flew regularly between New York and Fire Island, using Curtiss flying boats. (Photo courtesy of Randy Lieberman.)

from Miami to the Bahamas until 1923. Aeromarine used a fleet of handsome Curtiss F-5L biplane flying boats, able to carry fourteen passengers in comparative luxury. Compared with most of the brave experimenters of the period—Aeromarine carried 9,200 passengers in 1922 alone—it was a giant trunk airline, the progenitor of the early Pan American Airways.

Another early airline, and one that came close to meeting the dictionary definition of a commuter airline (albeit one for very rich commuters), was the New York–Newport Air Service, started by the aircraft builder Grover Loening. Loening deployed his Air Yachts late in 1922 to carry a privileged stratum of society between the East River in New York City and the yacht clubs of Rhode Island. Even so, his was not a service for commuters as we know them today, and the service ended in July 1923 after a crash. But after a two-year interval, another airline, appropriately named Commuters Air Transport, operated a similar service from New York to Fire Island, on the Atlantic shore of Long Island.

Not until 1 March 1925 did an airline founded for the specific purpose operate an overland route on a scheduled basis. Ryan Airlines began a service using its own aircraft (or to be exact, the aircraft of other manufacturers, which Ryan had converted): first five-seat Standard biplanes, then eleven-seat Douglas Cloudsters similar to those that flew around the world in 1924. Ryan operated for exactly a year and carried 5,600 passengers on a 120-mile route from San Diego to Los Angeles. Subse-

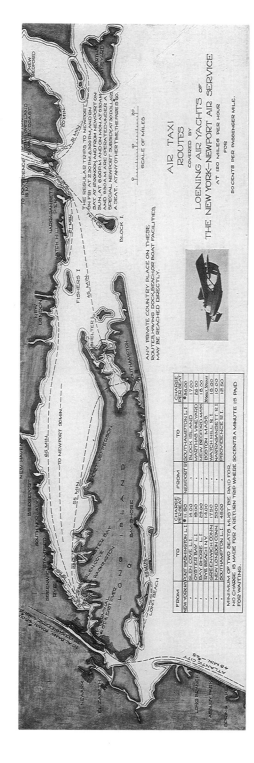

Grover Loening operated his Loening Air Yachts on an elite air service for an affluent clientele between New York and Newport, Rhode Island, in 1922 and 1923. (Courtesy of Carl Apollonio.)

quently, the company concentrated on building rather than operating aircraft, and one of its Broughams, specially converted by Charles Lindbergh, was to bring such fame to the Ryan company that its pioneering efforts in starting the first overland air route in the United States have almost been overlooked.

The Period of Infancy

During the early years of the Coolidge administration, a great deal of campaigning took place, both by privately financed lobbying groups and within government circles, for the United States to assert its role in the emerging world of commercial aviation. The existence of airlines in every country of Europe, even Albania, was considered degrading to the United States. The legislative machinery was therefore put in motion to set up a system by which financial encouragement could be given to innovative entrepreneurs to establish airlines. Echoing the direct or indirect subsidy arrangements then common in Europe, the "Kelly" Air Mail Act was passed on 2 February 1926, and, after the findings of the Coolidge-appointed Morrow Board were released, the Air Commerce Act was signed by the President on 20 May 1926. The act replaced no fewer than twenty-six separate state laws governing flying and provided the foundation for a formal regulatory system for the airlines.

Across the nation within the next year about a dozen small companies took advantage of the subsidy permitted by the Air Mail Act. Some had the financial backing of powerful interests. National Air Transport enjoyed the support of the Curtiss Airplane Company and was capitalized at $2,000,000—a fair-sized sum in those days, and ten times the starting capital of any of its contemporaries. Many airlines, however, were started by individuals, such as Walter Varney, Vern Gorst, Clifford Ball, or Charles Dickenson, whose approach to the business of commercial aviation could arguably be seen as a close historical parallel to that of the founders of the commuter airlines forty years later.

Although the main objective of the Kelly Act was to transfer the responsibility for carrying airmail from the United States Post Office (which had performed the task admirably from 1918 to 1927) to a private nationwide system, the horizons of almost all the first contract airmail carriers were quite limited. The Robertson Aircraft Corporation, for example, operated only from St. Louis to Chicago, and its airplanes stopped twice, at Springfield and Peoria, on the way. Northwest Airways, founded by Dickenson, operated only from the Twin Cities to Chicago, with three stops, but soon developed close interchange relationships—not with other airlines, but with the railroads. Cliff Ball stopped at Youngstown en route from Pittsburgh to Cleveland, and Bill Stout, who was to take over the Ford Motor Company mail contracts between Chicago and Detroit, started service on 2 August 1926 from Detroit to Grand Rapids, with a stop at Kalamazoo. Such itineraries were hardly segments of the main arteries of a nationwide network, although the principle of feeding traffic to and from the main intercity routes was a factor even then, as it certainly was with the post–World War II commuter airlines.

As more entrepreneurs applied for mail contracts, the pattern of local carriers, as opposed to national ones, continued. In Texas, two different companies operated short-haul routes from Dallas and Houston, and in Bill Stout's territory, another airline, the Thompson Aeronautical Corporation, began service on 17 July 1928 from Bay City, Michigan, to Chicago. It added a second route, from Bay City to Detroit and on to Cleveland across Lake Erie, on 1 April 1929. Thompson operated segments that averaged no more than fifty miles in length to link the medium-sized cities of Michigan, such as Flint, Pontiac, Lansing, and Battle Creek, with the major population centers of Chicago, Detroit, and Cleveland, operating a fleet of six four-seat Stinson Detroiters.

Air Commutation Fares

Yet it was Bill Stout who was in the vanguard of passenger air travel promotion and who was one of the few of the original mail contractors who from the start had a genuine interest in carrying passengers as a primary responsibility, rather than as fill-up loads for the subsidized airmail. His association with the Ford Motor Company was a priceless asset. Having sold his own Stout Metal Airplane construction business to Ford, which proceeded to develop the famous Ford Tri-Motor, Stout began carrying passengers in those aircraft. The Tri-Motor could carry up to sixteen passengers, about three times as many as the average single-engined general-purpose airplanes being built by such companies as Travel Air, Stearman, Stinson, and Waco.

The aircraft of this era, even the Ford Tri-Motor, could not be operated at a profit without subsidy, because not enough people could afford

Offices and Agencies

of

Stout Air Services, Inc.

In Detroit:

3-216 General Motors Building,
Telephone Empire 1690

Ford Airport,
Oakwood Blvd., Dearborn

In Grand Rapids:

Office Yellow Taxicab Co.,
Telephone 4633

Airport, South Madison Ave.,
Telephone 38-592

This 10-Ride Commutation Book

No. 241

IS THE PROPERTY OF

....

....

AND IS GOOD FOR TEN RIDES BY AIR BETWEEN DETROIT AND GRAND RAPIDS, SUBJECT TO THE TERMS AND CONDITIONS OUTLINED HEREIN

Received Payment

Date..

....
Stout Air Services, Inc.

Note:
Good for.................... *months*
from date of purchase.

Time Table

Summer 1926

Daily except Sunday
(*Subject to alteration without notice*)

DETROIT

Lv. 8:40 A. M......... †Statler Hotel.........Ar. 7:05 P. M.
Lv. 8:45 A. M......... †Book-Cadillac.........Ar. 7:00 P. M.
Lv. 9:00 A. M. Michigan Central Depot Ar. 6:45 P. M.
Lv. 9:30 A. M........... Ford Airport ....Ar. 6:15 P. M.

GRAND RAPIDS

Ar. 11:10 A. M..... *Grand Rapids Airport Lv. 4:35 P. M.
Ar. 11:30 A. M..... *Pantlind Hotel ....Lv. 4:15 P. M.

†Bus marked "Airport" leaves from Washington Blvd. entrance.

*Fast (or Daylight Saving) time. All times shown are Eastern Standard Time.

Through Connections with Michigan Central R. R. at Detroit

Lv. 6:00 P. M............ New York ....Ar. 9:30 A. M.
Ar. 8:45 A. M.............. Detroit ....Lv 7:10 P. M.
Lv. 9:30 A. M....... Detroit Airport ....Ar. 6:15 P. M.
Ar. 11:10 A. M....... *Grand Rapids..........Lv. 4:35 P. M.

*Fast, or Eastern Standard Time

Table of Passenger Fares Between Grand Rapids and Detroit

One Way - - - - - - - - - - - - -	$25.00
Round Trip - - - - - - - - - - - -	42.00
Ten Ride Book, per trip - - - - - - -	16.00

Transportation by car between Airport and Hotel included.

Be Sure to Make Your Reservations Early

Recognition of the practical possibilities of commuting by air was displayed by Stout Air Services, which, as early as 1926, issued a ten-ride commutation book that permitted discounted or commuted fares. (Courtesy of Stout Air Services.)

to pay the high fares necessary to enable the operators to break even, even with the subsidized mail loads. Occasionally, however, there were opportunities to achieve consistently high loads at high fares, especially on over-water routes. A classic example was in the Great Lakes area, where Stout and Thompson were exploring all the possibilities.

Over the years Bill Stout was a source of many good ideas in addition to his metal airplane design, even if his inventive and hyperactive mind did not always allow him to carry these through to their logical conclusions or to his own benefit. One of these ideas was the promotion of air travel on his route from Detroit to Grand Rapids by trying to persuade travelers to become regular air commuters. In the summer of 1926 Stout Air Services issued a pocket-sized ten-ride commutation book of airline tickets. The one-way price per ticket was $16.00, a substantial savings over the normal fare of $25.00 one way or $42.00 round trip. This was probably the first time that the idea of literally commuting by air had ever been seriously promoted.

To provide a glimpse of why extraordinary measures were needed to persuade people to travel by air, and to overcome their temptation to

save money by taking the train, some extracts from the Stout commutation book are revealing. Among the pieces of advice under the heading
"How to Get the Maximum Enjoyment Out of Your Flight" were such
items as the following: "The Pilot Always Banks the Plane when Turning
in the Air. . . . Take the turns naturally with the plane. Don't try to hold
the lower wing up with the muscles of the abdomen—it's unfair to
yourself and an unjust criticism of the pilot." Passengers were advised
to "put [their hands] out the window and feel the tremendous pressure"
so as to reassure themselves that the air indeed had density. "Under no
occasion," cautioned the instructions, "attempt to open the cabin door,
until the plane has come to a full stop." Of course the final section,
which stated "Our Motto is: Safety—First, Last, and Always," could
perhaps have been better phrased, at least the middle portion!

High-Density Air Routes

With the introduction during the latter half of the 1920s of the Ford
Tri-Motor and other trimotored equipment such as the Fokker F-10, air
transport in the United States finally released the brake and began to
move forward, albeit in low gear. The disciplines of market and traffic
analysis were as yet unknown, so it was by trial and error that the
airlines began to identify routes on which passenger demand justified
special attention to encourage patronage and growth. Following a long-
established gravity model which relates traffic potential to population
size and distance, these routes were mainly between pairs of large cities,
from 100 to 350 miles apart—just far enough for aircraft to provide
journey times comparable to or even better than those of the railroads.

Three areas in the United States met the necessary conditions, possessing urban population concentrations of several million persons separated by distances that took many hours to traverse by train but that
could be spanned in an hour or two by air. The Boston–New York–
Philadelphia–Baltimore–Washington ("Boswash") corridor, the San
Francisco–Los Angeles corridor, and the Great Lakes region centered on
Chicago and radiating to Milwaukee, Detroit, and Cleveland: all were
ready for airline development. Reference has already been made to the
activities of Bill Stout and Thompson Aeronautical in the Great Lakes
region. These air services never seem to have developed their full potential at the time, even though the over-water beeline flights had a signifi-

Though not in the same category as the modern commuter airline, the Ludington Line, catering to the densely traveled East Coast route in the early 1930s, was the forerunner of today's air shuttle services and commuter routes. (Photo courtesy of Randy Lieberman.)

cant advantage over circuitous rail and road journeys. In the other two corridors, however, the story was different.

On 21 July 1927, Jack L. Maddux, a car dealer from Los Angeles, started Ford Tri-Motor service from Los Angeles to San Diego, following in the air trails of Ryan Airlines. This venture was successful enough to encourage him to start twice-daily Ford service to San Francisco (using the Oakland airport), and by the time he sold out to Transcontinental Air Transport on 16 November 1929, he had built his fleet to fifteen Fords and had carried 40,000 passengers between Los Angeles and the Bay Area in one year.

In the Boswash corridor, the major airlines were American Airways (formerly Colonial Air Transport) and Eastern Air Transport. These had emerged from the frantic amalgamation process touched off by Charles Lindbergh's trans-Atlantic flight in May 1927, which had electrified the nation and prompted big business to enter the airline scene. The New York–Boston route was perhaps just too short, and the quality of the competing rail service perhaps just too good, to stimulate American to make special efforts. But on the New York–Washington segment, a newcomer prodded Eastern, the incumbent but hitherto apathetic airline, into action. In August 1929, a group of Philadelphia financiers launched a service using Ryan Broughams—the same type of aircraft that Lindbergh had used—and initially called itself the New York–Washington Air Line. It quickly became known as the Ludington Line. By choosing smaller aircraft such as the Lockheed Vega, the Consolidated Fleetster, and the Stinson Trimotor, it operated at a high frequency and at a higher speed than Eastern. Within two years, Ludington had carried 124,000 passengers and had forced Eastern to take extraordinary steps, namely to acquire the mail contract for the route from a postmaster general who, in turn, took equally extraordinary steps to provide it—a factor that was to contribute to his downfall in the notorious Air Mail Scandal of 1934. Without the mail contract, Ludington could not survive, but this early commuter-type airline had established the concept of every-hour on-the-hour service. In so doing, it demonstrated the basic principle that any successful transport organization must ensure that waiting for the next flight is better than seeking an alternative service.

In the chronicle of air services that started in response to the air fever that spread around the United States during the early 1930s, one more airline deserves mention. At least one hundred small companies attempted to operate almost exclusively local services, and their efforts were, almost without exception, of short duration, to provide a close parallel to the short longevity of most of the early postwar commuter airlines in the 1960s. Yet the one that stood out from the throng was Air Ferries, started by the always enterprising Vern Gorst, who provided an air ferry service—exactly according to its name—across San Francisco Bay for three years from 1 February 1930. In 1933 the equally enterprising Walter Varney took over the service and operated it until the Bay Bridge across San Francisco Bay opened in 1935.

Of all the early airlines Air Ferries came closest to being literally a commuter airline because it truly carried commuters on a regular basis. Even the postwar commuter airlines hardly ever carried daily commuters, the name being more a marketing term than a realistic description of function. The distance from San Francisco to Alameda on the eastern shore was only three miles and the trip took only six minutes in the Loening Air Yachts. The frequency of service was probably one of the highest ever achieved by any airline, reaching as many as fifty flights each way in a day. In 1930 no less than 60,000 passengers took advantage of the speed of the airplane over that of the ferryboat.

Air Ferries and the Wilmington-Catalina Airline, which inherited the 1919 Los Angeles–Avalon route, represented special cases in which the time saving compared to competing travel modes was significant. Airlines such as these were the ones that stood the best chance of survival. Gorst Air Transport, for example, operated Loenings across Puget Sound from June 1929, and even with a much smaller, almost precarious, traffic base, was able to keep going until 1935; in later years the route was even revived by others.

All the rest of the 1930–1933 aspirants failed to last more than a season or so, and many enjoyed a fleeting existence of only a few months. One at least deserves mention, if only because of its name. Commuters Air Service tried to offer such an amenity in the summer of 1932 on a route from Springfield, Massachusetts, to Hartford, Connecticut—a distance of only twenty-five miles. For it to succeed, the Massachusetts and Connecticut state authorities would have had to cooperate by closing the state border. Otherwise such a short distance would deny viability to any airline promoter, however hard he might have tried to make ends meet by operating expensive airplanes over a route that was doomed never to generate adequate revenues.

Toward Regulation

Following the 1934 Air Mail Scandal and after the reorganization of the air mail contract routes, stricter regulations forced out of business almost all the small airlines. In the three densely populated areas enumerated earlier, high-density routes such as San Francisco–Los Angeles in the west, New York–Boston and New York–Washington in the east, and Chicago-Detroit in the Midwest became segments of the extensive trunk line systems of United Air Lines, American Airlines, and Eastern Air Lines. The opening of the San Francisco Bay Bridge left Varney's Air Ferries stone dead. Of the small airlines that were not the fortunate recipients of mail contracts, even well-capitalized, aggressive, and enterprising companies such as Bowen Air Lines in Texas and Wedell-Williams in Louisiana were either forced out of business or compelled to merge with the incumbent airmail contractors.

Among the small short-haul independent operators, the sole survivor was the Wilmington-Catalina Airline. It seemed oddly out of place in the orderly list of airlines that eventually won the coveted "grandfather rights" Certificates of Public Convenience and Necessity in 1938, upon the formation of the Civil Aeronautics Authority (see Chapter 2). It traced its origin to 1932, when it took over the route to Avalon from Western Air Express, which had acquired it when it bought Pacific Marine Airways, which in turn had maintained the service started by Syd Chaplin in 1919. On 22 July 1941 it was renamed Catalina Air Transport, and it continued for another fourteen years until 13 September 1955. Other companies took over the resort route, which has thus become a unique thread linking the prewar and postwar commuter airline fraternities. But, as has already been mentioned, the over-water route was a special case. The competition was the ferryboat: very enjoyable, but also very time-consuming.

During the 1930s, the larger airlines built up the business in the California and New York–Washington air corridors, but the establishment of reliable air service from New York to Boston lagged behind, possibly because American Airlines regarded the segment as but the tail end of the more lucrative transcontinental route. Surprisingly, and notwithstanding the lesson of the bizarre Commuters Air Service in 1932, another company tried again in 1937. On 4 October of that year Airline Feeder System (AFS) started service from Springfield to New York (then served by Newark's airport) via Hartford, New Haven, and Bridgeport. Echoing Bill Stout's coupon books of 1926, this company tried to encourage the habit of traveling regularly by air by offering discounts. Operating Stinson Model A trimotors, and in a display of inspired marketing, AFS offered "for the first time in airline history a Commutation Ticket . . . which entitles any passenger to fly at rail fares." The regular fare from Springfield to Newark was $10.05 but the commutation fare was only $4.80. Unfortunately, such praiseworthy initiative did not reap its true reward, and service was discontinued in 1939. The route was taken over by Northeast Airlines, which used it to make a case for entering the postwar Boston–New York market, in competition with American Airlines.

Demography Is the Spur

An indirect thread that links the attempts to master this Northeast Corridor route to New England is the continued existence of a special demographic situation. On the one hand, it has defied the efforts of the certificated airlines to operate profitably—even the historic Eastern Air Lines Air Shuttle of 1960 was at best only marginally profitable. On the other hand, it has never seemed to provide the basis for a successful commuter airline, however enterprising. The potential market has always seemed to be present, but the cities are too close together or not quite populous enough to generate sufficient traffic over routes that are long enough to be economical to operate. Commuters Air Service could not make it, and neither could AFS. After World War II, Northeast Air-

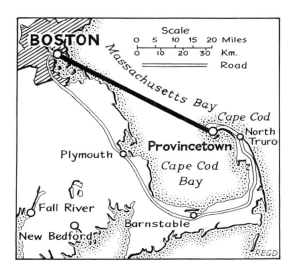

John C. Van Arsdale's Provincetown-Boston Airline took advantage of the peculiarities of local geography in eastern Massachusetts by offering a quick, short air trip instead of a meandering surface journey around Cape Cod Bay.

lines lost money heavily, and so, in the 1970s, did Air New England, a latter-day local service airline authorized by the Civil Aeronautics Board to operate a subsidized regional service.

Nevertheless, as with any form of transport, the demographics are the key to the market base. The Boswash corridor, about four hundred miles from end to end, contains seven urban concentrations, each with more than a million people. Four of them have more than three million, and New York itself is a giant hub of major international as well as domestic stature.

In this area too there has always been a peculiar geographical situation. The folks who live on the Cape Cod peninsula are relatively isolated from the remainder of Massachusetts, and the city of Provincetown, at the tip of the Cape, is especially isolated from Boston. The inhabitants have a choice of traveling 45 miles by sea across Massachusetts Bay or about 130 miles by land, starting off in precisely the opposite direction from that in which they wish to go.

Cape Cod was therefore an ideal area for entrepreneurial aviation people to show their mettle. Before World War II, Mayflower Airlines had started services in the area, serving also the islands of Nantucket and Martha's Vineyard, but it had been taken over by Northeast in 1945. This latter certificated airline was busy trying to make the grade as a trunk airline and was beginning to realize that short-haul services, even when operated by the ubiquitous and versatile DC-3, were heavy money-losers. Northeast chose to leave a gap in its system, from Provincetown to Boston, and it was here that a new airline found its niche.

In 1949, John C. Van Arsdale started service as the Provincetown-Boston Airline, the first postwar independent company with the specialized objective of providing service for the commuting businessman, shopper, or traveler wishing to connect with the nationwide air system. One or two other small companies had made brief, tentative appearances, but PBA, as it quickly became known, not only survived but prospered vigorously. Today it is acknowledged by its peers as the prototype of what were known first as scheduled air taxi operators, then as third-level carriers, and later as commuter airlines, before adopting, in recent years, the somewhat vague designation of regional airlines. The development of these enterprising companies, as an organized industry rather than as a small number of separate entities, is traced in the succeeding chapters of this book.

Chapter 2

The First Postwar Pioneers

This book is the history of what has come to be known as the commuter airline industry of the United States, a phenomenon of the post–World War II era. Commuter airlines have customarily operated scheduled services with equipment significantly smaller than that used by contemporary major airlines, because they have specialized in serving small cities and have emphasized the provision of high frequency rather than simply high capacity. They have concentrated on linking the nation's smaller cities and communities with major airlines through interchange connections at convenient large metropolitan airports.

As discussed in Chapter 1, for perhaps a decade after the infancy of sustained American passenger airline service in the 1920s, all airlines operated with what would be described today as small aircraft. Even the largest companies usually operated equipment that seated fewer than a dozen passengers. The 1926 Ford Tri-Motor, seating fourteen to sixteen people, was considered a large aircraft and was publicized as such. The individual companies had not yet begun to group themselves into distinctly different classes or levels of airlines, operating equipment that was dependent upon the traffic demand, which was usually directly proportional to the size of the cities served and inversely proportional to the distance between them.

The emergence of different classes of airlines began in the late 1920s, and more particularly in the 1930s, with the introduction of faster and/or larger aircraft to supersede the Ford Tri-Motor: the ten-seat Boeing 247, the fourteen-seat DC-2, and especially the twenty-one-seat DC-3. Such was the generally high level of operating costs that fares were consistently high—beyond the range of income of all but the most affluent travelers. Thus, only some of the airlines served routes with traffic densities that could justify the use of DC-3s.

Differences in equipment size according to airline category became more distinct after World War II. This trend coincided with the widespread adoption of four-engined airliners by the nation's largest "trunk" airlines, those serving the major cities. These companies began to standardize on such equipment, simultaneously retiring their smaller airliners, including the DC-3, which had been the dominant aircraft until the end of the war.

This trend toward adoption of larger aircraft by the industry leaders was a factor in establishing a new class of airline. In 1944, federal regulators decided that the national route network should be expanded to many smaller cities, and that such places would best be served by companies that specialized in this type of operation. Because of the small expected average loads, as well as the necessity of operating older equipment (since modern small airliners had not yet been produced), costs would be high and revenues low. From the start, therefore, there was general agreement in Washington that these operations would need to be subsidized. Between 1945 and 1950 about twenty newly established airlines were authorized to provide services to literally hundreds of smaller cities. Throughout much of their subsequent history, these companies were officially referred to as local service airlines. Later, as they grew in stature, they came to prefer the less deprecatory term "regional airlines." At first, most of them used small twin-engined aircraft, although some started with single-engined airplanes, until they were obliged to upgrade their equipment under pressure from federal regulators on safety grounds.

During this same period, the first tentative signs of a commuter airline industry began to appear. The predecessors of today's commuter airlines were the so-called air taxi operators. These companies originally were mainly fixed base operators, commonly involved in aircraft maintenance, flight training, and sales, but also providing nonscheduled flights, serving points that were not on trunk or local service airline maps. Sometimes they upgraded themselves, with special authorization from Washington, to a scheduled basis. Small though this group was, it did constitute another stratum of airline activity, and to put this important development into proper perspective the origins of the economic regulation of United States airlines should be discussed.

Federal Regulation of the Airlines Begins

In 1938, Congress passed legislation that, for the first time, placed U.S. scheduled airlines under federal economic regulation. The law created the Civil Aeronautics Authority, responsible for enforcing these regulations. Perhaps the most important new requirement was that a certificate from the authority was needed before a company could provide interstate scheduled air service. The authority also assumed far-reaching powers in regulating fares, routes, and business practices. Although federal *safety* regulations had been in force since the 1920s, this was the first time that direct federal *economic* regulations were imposed on the industry.

Under what became known as the "grandfather clause" of this act, all existing airlines—or, as they were widely known, carriers, a term surviving from the era of regulation-by-subsidy by the U.S. Post Office— that could demonstrate that they had provided continuous airmail service between 14 May 1938 and the effective date of the Act, 22 August 1938, automatically received Civil Aeronautics Authority Certificates of Public Convenience and Necessity. Twenty-three airlines were certificated in this way. Any company organized thereafter, however, would first need to submit to a rigorous examination before it could be certificated to provide service. Because of the limits of federal jurisdiction, these regulations did not apply to airlines operating solely within a single state (intrastate air carriers). As a matter of interest, between 1938 and the advent of airline deregulation in 1978, very few airlines (except the local service companies), and none in the largest (trunk) category, ever received that coveted certificate.

In 1940 the Civil Aeronautics Authority was reorganized and renamed the Civil Aeronautics Board (CAB), a name that it would retain until it passed out of existence on the last day of 1984. A branch of the CAB, the Civil Aeronautics Administration (CAA), was responsible for the safety regulation of the airlines.

When the Civil Aeronautics Authority was first established, it exempted all nonscheduled airlines, whether passenger or freight specialists and irrespective of size of equipment operated, from the need to obtain an economic operating certificate (but not from safety certification). After World War II this exemption opened the door for the establishment of many nonscheduled (charter) airlines by returning servicemen, particularly former air force and navy pilots with a flair for commerce. Soon there were far more airlines than could possibly be supported by the market, and only a few determined and astute "nonskeds" survived. Later this exempt category was narrowed, and most commercial operations, both scheduled and nonscheduled, became subject to more stringent CAB supervision and insistence upon strict observance of the regulations.

On 5 May 1947, the CAB adopted regulations for those charter air-lines that operated large equipment. It designated the nonscheduled airlines as irregular air carriers and distinguished between the large and the small. Small irregular carriers were defined as those that provided charter services with small aircraft; they would remain free of federal economic regulation. Popularly, they became known as air taxis. They were restricted to using aircraft with a gross takeoff weight (GTOW, the total weight of the airplane, including furnishings, crew, payload, and fuel) of no more than 10,000 pounds. On 5 October 1949, this limit was increased to 12,500 pounds, to conform to the standard that had been adopted in June 1949 by the CAB's safety division for distinguishing between small and large equipment.

The distinction between scheduled and nonscheduled operations was not always obvious. If a small irregular carrier met a steady demand for charter flights to a certain location at a regular time of day or on a regular day of the week, it would soon find itself operating a quasi-scheduled service. Were the service successful, the company might soon be of a mind to apply to the CAB for permission to operate regular scheduled services. Normally, this was done by applying for exemption authority, i.e., permission to operate scheduled flights without having to go through the lengthy, expensive process of obtaining a CAB certificate.

Early Postwar Commuter Operations

Pride of place as the first postwar commuter operator should go to Robert F. (Bob) Schoen, who founded Orcas Island Air Services to serve the San Juan Islands in Puget Sound in 1947. Using a Stinson Voyager, regular services began on 8 July of that year to link the islands with Bellingham on the mainland of Washington State. The airfields on the islands, if they could be so described, were invariably farmer's fields, leveled and cleared of debris. A 1926 Whippet two-door sedan served as the airport limousine. This pioneering service has, after several transfers of ownership and name changes, survived to the present day (see Area 3 of Part III).

Another early postwar scheduled service of this kind, using only small aircraft, was provided in New Mexico. Starting in 1948, Cutter-Carr Flying Service traveled the sixty miles between the atomic research city of Los Alamos and the nearest metropolitan center,

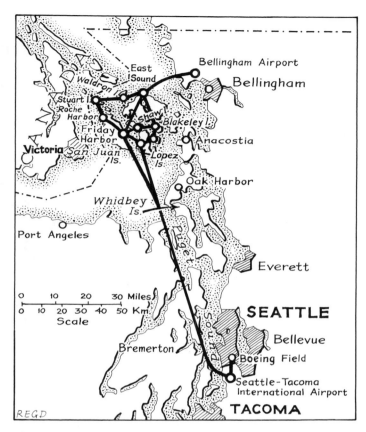

The Puget Sound area in northwestern Washington state was an ideal environment for commuter airline activity, linking especially the San Juan Islands with the mainland. This map shows the route network of Island Sky Ferries, which for several years during the 1960s maintained the interisland links and the routes to Seattle and Bellingham on the mainland.

Albuquerque, using Beech Bonanzas. By 1960 Cutter-Carr was often using a Beech Twin Bonanza, rather than the then customary single-engined equipment of the typical air taxi operator. In 1963 a new firm, Carco Air Service, took over the operation. Cutter-Carr and Carco did not, however, strictly qualify as commuter airlines, because their scheduled services were conducted under contract to the Atomic Energy Commission and were therefore not available to the general public. Carco operated this route on contract until 1970, when the current operator, Ross Aviation, took over.

An ideal situation for operating a "third-level" network was in Puget Sound, linking San Juan Islands with Seattle. This Cessna 150 coming in to land vividly illustrates the meaning of an "unprepared strip" in the immediate postwar years. (Photo courtesy of Roy Franklin.)

Both the air and the ground equipment of the commuter airlines were of different breeds, compared with those of the trunk airlines. This Island Sky Ferries Stinson-108 Voyager's status was matched by the 1941 De Soto airport limousine, which replaced the vintage Whippet. (Photo courtesy of Roy Franklin.)

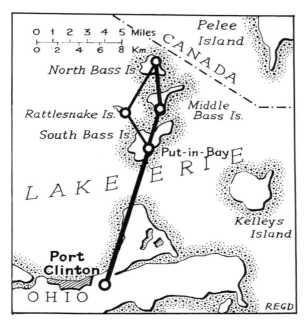

One of the most unusual of the noncertificated airlines was Island Air Lines of Port Clinton, Ohio. The mileage of its routes was counted in single figures, the airfields it used were just grass or dirt fields, and its aircraft were venerable Ford Tri-Motors that had first taken to the air in 1930. Yet it was a genuine commuter airline, carrying commuters and, uniquely, acting as an aerial school bus service.

Before 1949, at least three other companies provided scheduled operations of the type that later became known as commuter. One was Chalk's Flying Service, which flew Grumman amphibians between Miami and several islands in the Bahamas. It has claimed—erroneously—to be the oldest airline in the United States, but its prewar record of scheduled operations was intermittent. This firm continued to operate as Chalk's International Airline until its sale on 30 November 1989. Intrastate scheduled operations with small equipment, beyond the jurisdiction of the CAB, included Island Air Lines, which flew, among other aircraft, Ford Tri-Motors from Port Clinton, Ohio, to several islands in Lake Erie, and South Central Air Transport, which briefly operated a fairly extensive network of routes in Arkansas with Cessna T-50s in the late 1940s.

Occasionally, circumstances arose to provide a regular clientele in sufficient numbers to justify larger aircraft. Island Airlines, for example, operated Ford Tri-Motors from Port Clinton, Ohio, to the Bass Islands in Lake Erie. (Photo courtesy of the Roger Bentley collection.)

The CAB Experimental Exemption of 1949

On 5 October 1949 the CAB made a decision that had far-reaching consequences for what was eventually to become the commuter airline industry. It ruled that it would, experimentally, exclude from its economic controls all companies that wished to operate scheduled interstate services with small equipment, defined as aircraft with a GTOW of 12,500 pounds or less. Thereafter such companies could freely enter and leave the business, fly any route (except as noted subsequently), add and delete cities at will, and charge fares as they saw fit. In short, this segment of the scheduled airline business was largely deregulated many years before the well-known Airline Deregulation Act of 1978. Each company, however, still had to be certificated by the CAA. This ruling may have been made so that the CAB would not be burdened with a large number of requests for exemption authority from potential scheduled air taxi operators. Though constituting only a tiny fraction of the total national airline industry, measured by passengers carried or passenger-miles flown, such cases could have added substantially to the workload of the CAB, the staff of which numbered only about eight hundred—a modest size compared to that of most federal agencies. The board may also have reasoned that the small communities involved would benefit from the resulting freedom and flexibility bestowed upon the newcomers. Whatever the reasoning, this exemption ruling laid the foundation for the eventual development of the American commuter airline industry.

With their small equipment, the new airlines could pose little threat to the economic health of the certificated carriers. Nevertheless, to reassure the latter, several restrictions were placed on such exempt operators. They were not allowed, for example, to serve any route flown by a certificated airline, and they also were ineligible to carry mail.

No technical or other justification for the 12,500-pound level has ever been officially stated. One rumor has it that, in an effort to seek a rational figure that would protect the major scheduled airlines from incursion, someone at the CAB suggested "half a DC-3," the maximum GTOW of which at the time was 25,000 pounds. This explanation is open to doubt, however, because it was the CAA, not the economic branch of the board, that first used the 12,500-pound figure in place of 10,000 pounds. The former figure was probably chosen because it was a convenient natural break in the range of weights between the small and large aircraft that were commonly available for commercial use in the late 1940s.

Not long after the exemption ruling, the CAB became involved in an interesting case dealing with the previously mentioned Provincetown-Boston Airline (PBA). Organized by John C. Van Arsdale, this airline came into being in the classic pattern of pioneer commuters. Soon after World War II, at Marston Mills, Massachusetts, Van Arsdale had started Cape Cod Flying Service primarily as a pilot training school for veterans. In 1948 a branch of this school opened at the new airport at Provincetown, a resort city on the tip of Cape Cod; in the following year, it offered a charter service on the forty-five-mile route from Provincetown to Boston. The trip took about thirty minutes, compared with almost four hours via a circuitous land route. Because of the success of these charters, the owner obtained a certificate from the state of Massachusetts and established regular scheduled service on 30 November 1949 with a Cessna UC-78 Bobcat. During its first month, PBA carried 103 passengers at a one-way fare of $8.50 per person. For some years thereafter these scheduled operations were carried out every summer, but eventually year-round services were inaugurated.

Less than a year after Provincetown-Boston scheduled flights began, the company became involved in a dispute with the CAB. Because his airline connected two points within Massachusetts and did not compete with a certificated carrier, Van Arsdale believed he was not subject to CAB regulations. In due course, however, he was visited by an investigator from the board who told him that he was in violation of the Civil Aeronautics Act. One reason was that some of his passengers were connecting at Boston for flights to other states; therefore PBA was engaging in unauthorized interstate commerce. Another problem, apparently involving several branches of the Washington bureaucracy, was that the route crossed Massachusetts Bay, and that a good part of it was therefore beyond the then internationally accepted territorial limit of the United States, extending three marine leagues (a little more than ten miles) from land. PBA was therefore leaving and reentering both the state of Massachusetts and the United States on each trip, and such operations came under the jurisdiction of the CAB and even, to stretch the point at issue, the State Department. In the fall of 1950 the board issued a cease and desist order, telling Van Arsdale to stop his flights unless he received authority from the CAB. Van Arsdale complied, and he was then issued an exemption to engage in interstate transportation without the need to obtain a certificate.

Slow Early Growth

Liberal though the CAB's 1949 exemption ruling was, it did not lead to an immediate rush to establish new scheduled airlines. A major reason was that the selection of flying equipment available at the time was very limited. The most widely available aircraft within the statutory weight limit of 12,500 pounds was the twin-engined Beech Model 18. More than seven thousand had been constructed since 1937, mainly as the military C-45 during World War II. The civilian versions could carry only about seven or eight passengers, had a correspondingly limited freight capacity, and were expensive to maintain. The Beech 18 was also handicapped by being regarded as an aging aircraft of prewar vintage, although, starting in 1947, Beech did deliver a few craft of the updated airliner version (the D18CT), some of which went to companies that later became local service airlines. Reliable though it may have been, passengers looked upon it as out of date, and so did the embryo commuter airlines, who hesitated to rush to buy hundreds of Beech 18s in the same manner that their larger contemporaries had rushed to buy war-surplus C-46s and C-47s.

Another aircraft that qualified under the 12,500-pound rule was the British twin-engined de Havilland DH-104 Dove, able to carry up to eleven passengers. The first Dove had flown on 25 September 1945, and thereafter 544 were produced. Equipped with its original Gipsy Queen engines, it had a reputation for being expensive to maintain. Nevertheless, the Beech 18 and the Dove were the biggest twin-engined aircraft that were suitable and available in fairly large numbers until the 1960s. The Dove's larger cousin, the four-engined, seventeen-seat Heron, was also built, but only in small numbers. With a fortunate (or contrived to be so) listed GTOW of 12,499 pounds, it just scraped in under the exemption regulations.

Some other twin-engined aircraft designed for executive or private use were also pressed into service by the early commuter airlines. These included the four-seat Piper Apache, introduced in 1954, and the slightly larger Piper Aztec, first produced in 1959. The five- to seven-seat Aero Commander 520 and 560, more elegant in appearance and more comfortable in cabin design, were also used by some early commuter airlines. Such types were not, however, designed for the rigors of flying day in, day out, for up to two thousand hours per year, not to mention enduring rough treatment by the clientele in typical commuter service. But they had to be used for lack of better alternatives, even though maintenance costs were high.

Supplementing these "first-line" twin-engined commuter flagships, a variety of single-engined airplanes were also flown by early scheduled small aircraft operators. This pattern of aircraft selection, trying to improvise with aircraft designed for private and executive use, was to repeat itself in later generations and would not really end until the advent of a new generation of commuter aircraft in the 1980s.

There were several reasons, other than aircraft inadequacy, why the scheduled small carrier industry grew slowly after 1949. One important factor was that the CAB was in the midst of establishing subsidy-supported local service airlines that also specialized in small-community service. These companies were expanding rapidly and thus severely limited the number of potential routes available to the embryo commuter airlines. Also, the great majority of ordinary people could still not afford the high airline fares prevalent at the time, even though average personal income levels were increasing rapidly. Air travel was largely the privilege of businessmen, the otherwise affluent, or passengers (such as politicians) who did not pay their own fares; coach fares on scheduled routes had only just been introduced by Capital Airlines in 1948. Finally, any apprehension there may have been about flying applied particularly to small aircraft. Despite all these limitations, however, by the early 1950s the stage had been set for the future growth of the U.S. commuter airline industry.

The CAB Part 298 Exemption and FAA Part 135 Regulation of Scheduled Air Taxis

Effective 20 February 1952, after several years of experience with the experimental exemption ruling, the CAB decided to formalize this policy as Part 298 of its economic regulations. The majority of such Part 298 operators were expected to act primarily as traffic feeders to the certificated carriers, and new policies now allowed standard interline agreements (such as those for the transfer of luggage) to be established with the latter. The small irregular carriers were now officially renamed air taxi operators, and those that provided scheduled services were prefixed "scheduled." Part 298 maintained the provision that scheduled air taxis were not allowed to operate over certificated routes, and it barred them completely from Alaska, Hawaii, and other U.S. territories. The formal adoption of Part 298 helped to remove the most pressing questions about the immediate future of such operations. Nevertheless, it was adopted on a "temporary" basis, subject to periodic review, a decision no doubt reflecting a justifiable degree of caution as the regulatory authorities ventured into previously uncharted airways.

In the early 1960s, the Federal Aviation Agency (FAA, later the Federal Aviation Administration), which had been created in 1959 to take over the nation's air safety regulations after studies had revealed serious deficiencies in the old system under the CAA, began to pay more attention to this growing industry. It also adopted the term "scheduled air taxi operator," thereby recognizing a new category of scheduled firms that would become known later as commuter airlines.

In 1964 the FAA adopted Part 135, the first operating-maintenance regulations specifically applied to commercial (air taxi) operators of equipment with GTOWs of 12,500 pounds or less. Part 135 regulated such considerations as minimum pilot qualifications, maximum hours between engine overhauls, administrative procedures, and even the basic organizational structure of the airline. New air taxi aircraft now also had to adhere to Federal Aviation Regulations Part 23, which included upgraded minimum standards of construction and installed equipment.

In 1964 the FAA began to collect data on scheduled air taxi operators, to provide the first systematic record of these operations, which hitherto had been included only sporadically by the CAB under the amorphous term "other airlines"—when their existence was admitted at all. The FAA publication *Scheduled Air Taxi Operators as of November, 1965* listed twelve companies on 1 January 1964, and by 1 July there were fifteen. With the appearance of this annual publication it became possible, for the first time, to follow some of the changes that were occurring within this emerging industry, even though the qualifications of some companies were questionable, since certain reporting airlines took a broad view of the definition of the word "scheduled."

Pioneering Role Models

During the 1950s and into the early 1960s, several pioneer commuter airlines were formed, a few of which were to play important roles in the history of the industry. Perhaps the earliest of these was Scheduled Skyways, founded by Raymond J. Ellis. In September 1953, it began to operate between the university town of Fayetteville, Arkansas, and the state capital at Little Rock. Initially its main clientele consisted of faculty members traveling to and from Little Rock to teach extension courses. In terms of equipment and type of service, Scheduled Skyways was a good example of an early commuter airline. In common with many pioneers, it was the outgrowth of a fixed base operation, in a situation in which regular and sustained demand for air taxi services on a single route eventually led to scheduled flights. When service began, Scheduled Skyways provided the only flights on its route, and it used single-engined equipment. One of the classic examples of a small operator identifying an opportunity, this airline may well have been the nation's oldest surviving commuter airline, by the strict definition of the term, before it was absorbed by Air Midwest in 1985.

In Colorado, Aspen Airways played a pioneering role, connecting the winter sports resort town of Aspen with the state capital, Denver, the biggest city serving the Rockies and an important airline hub. The company dated back to 1953, when Aspen Airways Air Taxi was founded to cater almost exclusively to skiers, and it initially provided service with small equipment. In 1955, under new ownership, the company received permission from the Colorado Public Utilities Commission to provide scheduled service, and it began such flights with Twin Beechcraft.

By 1962, business was so good that the traffic demand warranted larger aircraft, and the company decided to operate Douglas DC-3s. Because of Aspen's high altitude (7,850 feet) and restricted approaches to the mountain-fringed airfield, the DC-3s were equipped with auxiliary jet power for takeoffs. The adoption of aircraft with more than 12,500 pounds GTOW required a special CAB certificate, obtained in June 1967. Although the DC-3s and the certificate put Aspen outside the ranks of commuter airlines, as defined in Washington, it regained that status after the airlines were deregulated in 1978. In 1990 Aspen Airways was sold to the holding company that owns Air Wisconsin, and some of its routes were sold to Mesa Airlines.

Another early example was TAG Airlines (formerly Taxi Air Group), developed largely by Ross Miller, which found a niche in the air transport arena by flying primarily between the Detroit City Airport and Cleveland's Burke Lakefront Airport. Both fields were served by local service airlines, but not on a turnaround shuttle basis, nor during the convenient morning and evening rush hours. Frequent intercity service was provided by trunk and local service airlines, but only from the main airports situated on the outer fringes of the two cities. Detroit City and Burke Lakefront airports are considered downtown fields (although Detroit's is six miles from the city center), and TAG's frequent shuttle services made it possible for business travelers to avoid long drives to and from the metropolitan outskirts. The company claimed that downtown-to-downtown travelers could save three and a half hours by using TAG, and this considerable advantage permitted Miller to charge $14.00 one way against the scheduled airlines' $10.00. In 1965 TAG boarded a record 84,000 passengers, and at that time it was carrying over half of the passengers flown by the whole scheduled air taxi industry. Thereafter, however, problems with the pilots' union and a new competitor on the Detroit-Cleveland route led to a decline in traffic.

TAG had started service in 1956, initially operating de Havilland of Canada Otters and Beavers between the downtowns of Toledo and Cleveland. However, flights had to be suspended during the winter months because of ice. The company was not profitable, and it was sold

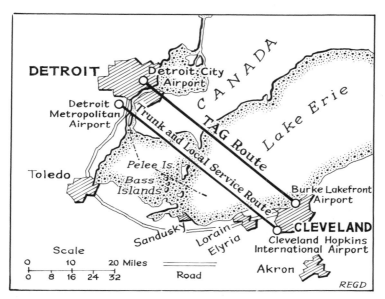

Ross Miller, from Toledo, realized that the certificated airlines were not providing a good intercity service between two of the three largest cities in the U.S. Great Lakes region. The services were offered only on segments of through routes from Chicago to the east coast, the airports were on the edges of the urban areas, and the surface route alternative was a long diversion. Miller started TAG Airlines between downtown airports and was so successful that he was considered as a special case by the CAB.

TAG Airlines operated a short-cut route across Lake Erie between downtown airports. This billboard advertisement tells the whole story. (Photo courtesy of Ross Miller.)

TAG's earliest aircraft were the rugged de Havilland Aircraft of Canada DH-2 Beaver (left) and the DHC-3 Otter (right), pictured here on the ramp at Toledo in the late 1950s. (Photo courtesy of Ross Miller.)

to Miller and a friend in July 1957. Miller bought two eight-passenger de Havilland Doves and then switched to the Cleveland-Detroit route. Later brief route expansions included Rockford and Chicago, Illinois (at downtown Meigs Field), Akron and Columbus, Ohio, and Pittsburgh, Pennsylvania. Although TAG went out of business early in 1970, after a tragic crash into Lake Erie, its bread and butter downtown Cleveland-Detroit route has continued to be operated by other companies to this day.

On 1 August 1957, Reading Aviation Service began scheduled flights from Reading, Pennsylvania, to Newark, New Jersey (serving New York City), initially with a Beech 18. It had been founded by Alfred Bertolet, a fixed base operator, who echoed Ross Miller's marketing strategy by providing well-timed flights in a market poorly served by the certificated carriers. Linking as it did a small city with a nearby major metropolitan area, Reading provided the kind of service that later became standard in the commuter industry, and it was therefore one of the first true commuter airlines to operate in the United States. In May 1968, and now under the leadership of Art Horst, Reading Aviation merged with Air Taxi Company, which was operating scheduled service from Red Bank and Princeton, New Jersey, to New York City's three airports under the name Suburban Air Lines. The latter name was adopted for all sched-

Reading Aviation Service operated de Havilland DH-104 Doves on short routes in eastern Pennsylvania and into New York in the late 1950s. (Photo courtesy of Art Horst.)

uled services, steady expansion followed, and the company is still in business as one of the USAir Express (formerly Allegheny Commuter) family.

Apache Airlines received its FAA air taxi certificate in November 1957 and began operating scheduled routes in Arizona soon thereafter. Its early aircraft included Beech 18s and Twin Bonanzas, and a few years later de Havilland Doves were adopted. By mid-1959 it was serving Phoenix, Tucson, Ft. Huachuca, and Nogales. For a while it dominated the Phoenix-Tucson market by offering high-frequency service—as opposed to the sometimes uncertain en route services offered by the American, Frontier, and Continental Airlines itineraries. By 1967 it was offering an hourly frequency from 7 A.M. to 10 P.M. Such participation in a rapidly growing, high-traffic-density market, however, was short-lived, and the company went out of business late in 1970, partly because of the construction of an interstate freeway link.

Joseph C. Whitney's National Executive Flight Service began scheduled service with Aero Commanders on 20 June 1960 on the route from Boston to the resort island of Martha's Vineyard. During the next two years the network expanded to Hyannis and Nantucket Island, Massachusetts, and New York's La Guardia airport. On 1 December 1964, a Florida division was established, to balance seasonal utilization of personnel and equipment, using single-engined Piper Cherokee Sixes between Sarasota and Tampa. In 1964 the company began to acquire de Havilland Doves and subsequently expanded to several points in Maine. In January 1967, the operations were renamed Executive Airlines.

Among the early aircraft used by the scheduled air taxi operators was the Beech 18, which was in plentiful supply from war surplus stock. Seen are (top) one of Command Airways, at Dutchess County Airport, Poughkeepsie, New York, and (center) one of MacAire at La Guardia Airport, focal point of many small airlines in the latter 1960s. At bottom is a Catalina Air Lines Grumman Goose, a sturdy amphibian that maintained regular service from the California mainland to the resort city of Avalon. (Collection of R. E. G. Davies.)

During the late 1960s, the smallest of the operators used the equipment that had served them well in their scheduled air taxi role. These pictures show (top) a Piper Aztec of GCS Flying Service at Galion, Ohio; (center) a Piper Cherokee of Pilgrim Airlines at New London, Connecticut; and (bottom) a Cessna 206 of Chatham Aviation, about to take off from New York's La Guardia Airport en route to Morristown, New Jersey. (Collection of R. E. G. Davies.)

The following year the Florida division was expanded considerably, and Yankee Airlines, of Pittsfield, Massachusetts, was acquired. By 1969 Executive was the country's largest commuter airline, operating, among other aircraft, twelve nineteen-passenger Twin Otters and eight fifteen-passenger Beech 99s; however, in 1971 it filed for Chapter 11 bankruptcy and in 1973 it went out of business.

The early pioneers also included Joe Fugere's Pilgrim Airlines, which began service in 1962 with two Piper Apaches from New London/Groton, Connecticut, to New York's Idlewild (now John F. Kennedy) Airport, at a $14.50 one-way fare. Once again this was a case of seized opportunity. The surface alternative route was circuitous and time-consuming, threading its way through dense traffic zones on the Connecticut shore of Long Island Sound and in the New York metropolitan area. Traffic was brisk, so that the Apaches were replaced by Beech 18s after only about three months. By 1964 Pilgrim was carrying over 11,000 passengers per year.

The Hagerstown Commuter was established by Dick Henson as a subsidiary of Henson Aviation, a fixed base operation. It began scheduled services on 23 April 1962, initially using an eight-passenger Beech 18 and smaller backup aircraft between Hagerstown, Maryland, and Washington National Airport. Operating as it did in a highly traveled region, The Hagerstown Commuter received widespread attention, and it was one of the earliest airlines, if not the first, to adopt the name "commuter" in its marketing. Renamed Henson Airlines, it became a subsidiary of Piedmont Aviation, later absorbed by the USAir Group, and was allocated a role covering a far more extensive sphere of influence than is common for a commuter airline. Both Apache and Henson were later to play pioneering roles in a particular aspect of the commuter airline industry, as explained in the next chapter.

The Third Level—*Flight Magazine* Coins a Term

Starting in August 1961, an influential series of articles about the emerging commuter airline industry appeared in *Flight Magazine*, George Haddaway's Dallas-based magazine, directed toward private, executive, and commercial users of small aircraft. Written by E. H. Pickering, the eight-part series was entitled "Needed: A Third Level of Air Service." The author felt that the local service airlines—those that could be termed, in deference to the first-line trunk airlines, the second level—were rapidly growing out of their original role of serving small communities and were becoming airlines of substance, with interests in intercity links between metropolitan areas. He felt that the nation needed a new type of airline that would specialize in serving the smaller points, and that would bring the benefits of aviation to a far larger percentage of the population than was presently being served. Pickering visualized the industry using some of the newer light twin-engined executive aircraft then becoming available, such as the Twin Bonanza and the Aero Commander. He outlined various ways in which such operators could keep down their costs and subsidy needs.

Pickering also described some major characteristics of the half dozen or so such carriers then in operation and in the process coined the term "third-level airlines," recognizing that the trunk airlines were clearly the first level and the local service airlines constituted the second level. The articles were so well received that the magazine had to reprint them for more general distribution. These creative articles inspired widespread interest in this newest, and now rapidly evolving, section of the American scheduled airline industry. Pickering, who has since died, deserves special credit for having provided a rational basis of definition, and then for furnishing one. By the summer of 1962 the CAB was already using the term "third-level" in its Hi-Plains Airways case, one of many board-reviewed cases involving decisions on the selection of an airline according to its status.

The Term "Commuter Airlines" and Other Developments in the Early 1960s

By the early 1960s the term "commuter airlines" was starting to come into general use. This label was eagerly promoted by the industry as preferable to such terms as "scheduled air taxi" or "third-level airline." According to some sources, it was used because so many of the passengers were on one-day business trips. The term "commuter flights" has been used for decades by airlines operating on such heavily traveled short-haul routes as Boston–New York–Washington and San Francisco–Los Angeles. In common usage, however, the term "commuter" usually refers to someone who travels to and from work on a daily basis. Yet, as mentioned in Chapter 1, only a minuscule portion of commuter airline passengers have ever literally been commuters, and the term is most realistically seen as a product of airline marketing. The media soon adopted the name, and by the mid-1960s it was becoming the standard way of referring to the industry even though the term "third level" also continued to be used until the late 1970s. By then, the path of progress having taken yet another course, some of the affected airlines were rejecting the term "commuter" as they claimed membership in the regional airline fraternity.

The new term was given added legitimacy by the formation, in 1963, of the Association of Commuter Airlines (ACA), organized by several airlines to promote the industry. Originally there were only six members, but by 1968 membership had grown to thirty-six. Soon it was lobbying for the extension of the CAB's Part 298 temporary exemption and for the right of commuter lines to carry mail. It was also urging manufacturers, some of whom were associate members, to produce aircraft specifically to meet the industry's needs.

In 1964 a new aircraft engine was introduced: the PT6, a light turboprop of 579 horsepower, built by Pratt & Whitney Canada (later United Aircraft of Canada). It was matched to the size of aircraft that would be ideal for commuter airline operations, and it would play an important role in the upgrading process of small aircraft development. One of the great advantages of turbine engines over their piston predecessors was that they weighed much less per equivalent horsepower, and the engine weight saved could therefore be replaced by extra payload. The PT6 would thus allow the production of airplanes that still weighed in within the 12,500-pound limit but that featured greater passenger and cargo capacities than piston-engined aircraft of the same size. Two revolutionary commuter aircraft utilizing this engine were soon to appear: the DHC-6 Twin Otter and the Beech 99 (see Chapter 3).

Commuter Airlines in 1964

Information gleaned from the July 1964 issue of the *Official Airline Guide (OAG)*, the standard information source for airline schedules and fares, provides some insights into the nature of the early commuter industry. Twenty scheduled air taxi operators were listed. This number compared to only fifteen listed by the FAA on the same date, and the discrepancy tends to throw some doubt on the completeness of the

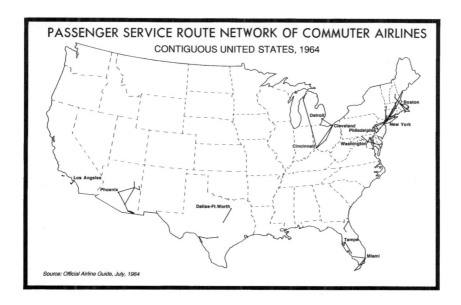

PASSENGER SERVICE ROUTE NETWORK OF COMMUTER AIRLINES
CONTIGUOUS UNITED STATES, 1964

Source: Official Airline Guide, July, 1964

federal data, especially considering the fact that the *OAG* was quite conservative about which commuter airlines it would list. Companies such as Yankee Airlines (serving Massachusetts and New York), American Air Taxi (Florida), Airtransit (Arizona), and even Wild Goose Airlines (Texas) were typical entries, and routes were quite scattered. Large sections of the country, however, such as the northwestern states and all of the southeast except Florida, were conspicuously without any commuter services that the *OAG* was willing to list.

Such a sporadic geographic pattern seemed to reflect individual cases of opportunism, of entrepreneurs identifying situations with the best economic opportunities—and these, more often than not, involved concentration on selected large cities. The twenty *OAG* companies of 1964 served about 4,700 route-miles.

By this time the main characteristics of the growing industry had been established and could be defined with some precision. For the most part, commuter airlines provided connecting flights to smaller cities, some of which had previously enjoyed (and a few of which still retained) trunk or local airline service. All of these airlines operated small aircraft of 12,500 or fewer pounds GTOW. Most of these were twin-engined, but sometimes schedules were maintained with single-engined aircraft. Commuter airlines were invariably owned, managed, and operated by latter-day pioneers, men whose qualifications varied from those of the ex-professional, typically from an established airline, to those of the enterprising fixed base operator, with the occasional inexperienced entrepreneur or enthusiastic amateur adding variety. Since even the ex-professional was often a specialist and inexperienced in administration and management, the commuter industry turnover rate was high. Nevertheless, as it was almost totally free from the shackles of federal economic regulations, this segment of the U.S. airline industry seemed to face few limitations on its future growth and success. For those pioneers who participated in this exploratory stage in the development of a well-defined commuter airline industry, the era must have been one of great expectation, charged with unprecedented optimism.

Chapter 3

The First Commuter Airline Boom

The American commuter airline industry underwent almost explosive growth between 1965 and 1968. The FAA's *Scheduled Air Taxi Operators as of November, 1968* listed only 15 companies in operation in the contiguous United States on 1 July 1964. By 1 November 1965, the number stood at 69, and by 1 November 1968 the total had increased to an astonishing 228. During the four-year period, the number of aircraft listed as operated by the commuter or scheduled air taxi operators increased from 83 to 1,272. Of the latter figure, 814 were multiengined piston aircraft, 318 were single-engined piston airplanes, and 12 were twin-engined turboprops. Given these numbers, 1965–1968 can justly be described as the first boom period in the history of the industry.

The increase in the number of companies was matched by growth in the level of traffic. There had obviously been a dormant demand for service and, in a clear cause-and-effect relationship, an enterprising group of willing entrepreneurs rose to the occasion. No traffic data are available for 1965, but *Time* magazine estimated the number of commuter airline passengers as one million in 1966—though this vague number could have been little more than an informed guess. The following year the volume approximately doubled to around two million, and *Time* estimated traffic in 1968 at three million. No systematically collected statistical data on the industry, except for aircraft numbers, are available until 1969, and the first full year when such traffic data were collected was 1970.

Initially, the boom was unevenly distributed. A November 1965 route map published by the FAA revealed a pattern similar to that of the previous year—a high concentration in the northeastern states, plus a new concentration in California. The northeastern routes predictably radiated from the main metropolitan—areas: Boston, New York, Phila-

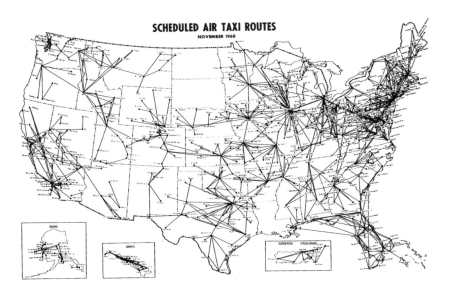

SCHEDULED AIR TAXI ROUTES
NOVEMBER 1968

delphia, and Washington—and those in California similarly focused on the large Los Angeles and San Francisco metropolitan areas and adjacent regions. Few routes were operated in much of the rest of the country, and at the extreme, there were none at all in the southeastern states, except in Florida. Such a distribution was explained partly by the uneven yet somewhat compensating distribution of local service networks. In the southeast, for example, Southern Airways and Piedmont Aviation provided widespread service, and even trunk airlines such as Eastern and Delta continued to serve many small cities in the region.

By November 1968, on the other hand, the situation had changed substantially. The FAA map (above) showed that almost all parts of the country enjoyed commuter airline service. As before, the network was densest in the northeast, but it was also impressive in many other areas. By this time almost all large metropolitan areas were the hubs of fairly extensive commuter networks. Where this occurred at medium-sized metropolitan centers, such as Des Moines, Wichita, or Oklahoma City, most of the routes were largely or exclusively for the transportation of mail.

A second map of commuter airlines in 1968, derived from schedules in the *Official Airline Guide* (*OAG*) (page 47), showed a somewhat different geographic pattern. There were far fewer routes than on the FAA map, partly because the all-cargo and mail-only airlines are not included in the *OAG*, which was also quite selective in the choice of

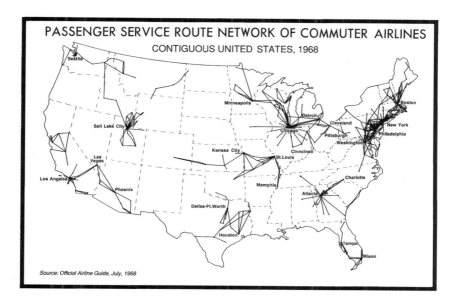

PASSENGER SERVICE ROUTE NETWORK OF COMMUTER AIRLINES
CONTIGUOUS UNITED STATES, 1968

Source: Official Airline Guide, July, 1968

passenger-carrying commuter airlines that it agreed to include. This map may be seen, therefore, as depicting the country's more important commuter passenger routes. There was a distinct concentration in the northeast, and network growth had been impressive, with 33,163 route-miles, compared to 4,703 four years earlier.

This explosive growth did not occur without problems. The corporate turnover rate was high; there were periods when almost as many companies were leaving the industry as were entering it. On the other hand, some prospered, to the extent that mergers and acquisitions were made, albeit often overambitiously. But the net gain, by every measure of statistical comparison, was substantial, and by 1968 this newest segment of the scheduled airline industry was clearly here to stay.

The Causes of the Boom

There were several major reasons for the acceleration of growth in the mid- to late 1960s. Most important, perhaps, was the appearance of several new and efficient aircraft types, all qualifying under the 12,500-pound rule, that helped to revolutionize the industry. Piston and turbo-prop aircraft alike were involved. Although the turboprops were the

The de Havilland Aircraft of Canada DHC-6 Twin Otter made an outstanding contribution to the progress of the scheduled air taxi, or "third-level," airlines, providing nineteen seats and qualifying under the 12,500-pound GTOW rule. (Collection of R. E. G. Davies.)

largest and fastest and received the most media attention, the piston-engined machines accounted for a much higher percentage of the new aircraft and did the bulk of the work.

Two outstanding new turboprop aircraft were both powered by Pratt & Whitney Canada PT6 engines. The de Havilland Aircraft of Canada DHC-6 Twin Otter could carry up to twenty passengers and still meet the gross takeoff weight (GTOW) limitation imposed by the CAB. In the United States, however, it was usually fitted with nineteen or fewer seats, because under FAA regulations no flight attendant was required on aircraft with fewer than twenty passenger seats. (In practice, a few airlines provided an attendant anyway.)

The Twin Otter had originally been built as the latest member of a family of bush-type aircraft designed to operate into the Canadian north-lands and in other areas where flying conditions were difficult and airfields unpaved, with surfaces of grass, dirt, or gravel. Short takeoff and landing capability was an essential feature of its performance. By fortuitous timing, the Twin Otter also came into widespread use as a commuter airliner and was particularly favored by companies with

First off the mark with the ubiquitous Twin Otter was Joe Fugere's Pilgrim Airlines. (Photo courtesy of Joe Fugere.)

short routes. It first flew on 20 May 1965, and deliveries of the original series 1 model began in July 1966. Only five series 1 Twin Otters were built, to be followed by the somewhat modified series 100. Sales of the latter totalled 110 aircraft, many sold to small air taxi companies or to third-level airlines around the world. The first series 200 model, with increased baggage space in a longer nose section, was delivered in April 1968. By November of that year, 73 aircraft of this sturdy Canadian type were already being operated by commuter airlines in the United States.

Illustrating the efficiency of this new breed of aircraft, the 26 June 1968 issue of the British magazine *Aeroplane* noted that, within one year, the potential direct operating costs per seat-mile for a one-hundred-mile commuter airline stage length (route segment) had fallen from 6.0 cents for a one-pilot Beech 18 to 3.3 cents for a two-pilot Twin Otter. Such a reduction in operating costs alone was sufficient to spark a minor revolution, and the Twin Otter played a critical role in the development of the United States commuter airline industry.

Unlike the Twin Otter, the Beech Aircraft Corporation 99 was developed specifically for commuter airline use. A lengthened, turboprop variant of the Beech Queen Air, designed originally as an executive airplane but modified as an airliner, the Beech 99 could carry fifteen passengers and a crew of two. It was certified by the FAA on 2 May 1968 for a GTOW of 10,400 pounds. The first Beech 99 cruised at about 250 miles per hour, but in March 1969 a new model, the 99A, was

Though slightly smaller, the Cessna 402 rivaled the Piper Navajo as one of the best of the latter-day piston-engined airplanes used by the commuter airlines. This picture shows one of the Provincetown-Boston Airline's fleet, based in Naples, Florida. (Photo courtesy of the Roger Bentley collection.)

introduced. Carrying a more powerful version of the PT6 engine, the 99A was designed for operations at high altitude and out of hot weather airports; it also had a faster rate of climb than the original 99 and cruised at 284 miles per hour. Another variant, the B99, with still more powerful PT6s and a GTOW of 10,900 pounds, was introduced in April 1972.

The Beech 99 was considerably faster than the Twin Otter and was therefore well suited for companies with relatively long stage lengths. On the other hand, the Twin Otter's extra four seats provided more revenue potential. The Beech, having been derived from an executive aircraft design (one with a low typical annual utilization of less than one thousand hours), could not always withstand the rigors of more intensive use and the more varied (and usually less fastidious) clientele of the commuter airlines, and it was therefore the more expensive aircraft to maintain. Neither the Twin Otter nor the Beech 99 was pressurized.

Among new twin-engined piston aircraft, the Cessna 402 had been designed for air cargo and air taxi use and was widely adopted by the new small airlines. The prototype Cessna 401, the business version of the 402, first flew on 26 August 1965. The first customer delivery of a 402 took place in November 1966, and sales were soon brisk. The commuter version could carry up to eight passengers and a crew of two. The 402A model, with a longer nose for additional baggage, was introduced in 1969 and was well received.

The prototype Piper Navajo flew on 30 September 1964, and deliveries began on 30 March 1967. The early commuter version, with 310-horsepower Lycoming engines, could carry up to six passengers and a crew of two. The Navajo Chieftain, of which first deliveries were made

Among the small piston-engined aircraft used for commuter airline work was the Piper Navajo. This one, of Swift Aire, is seen taxiing at San Jose, California. (Photo courtesy of the Roger Bentley collection.)

in 1973, was a modification of the original model, with its fuselage lengthened by two feet, and it could seat up to eight passengers. With improved 350-horsepower engines, it was particularly favored by many commuter airlines.

Certain regulatory changes also contributed to the industry's explosive growth after 1964. In 1965 the CAB made the Part 298 exemption permanent and removed the restriction that barred commuter lines from routes flown by certificated carriers in the contiguous United States, with the minor exception of a few routes flown by certificated helicopter airlines (all of which eventually went out of business). The Board also authorized the commuters to carry mail, but only on a subsidy-free basis between noncertificated points, unless an exemption were granted. This soon led to the development of a network of third-level air mail routes radiating from the main U.S. Post Office hub cities.

State, as opposed to federal, economic regulation of commuter carriers remained in effect in a few places. Most states, however, had chosen to regulate these airlines either minimally or not at all. This apparent laxity was a function of geography rather than negligence or apathy on the part of state authorities. Few states were large enough to warrant systematic intrastate airline organization, and most of those that were large enough were sparsely populated. Two notable exceptions were California and Texas, where the Public Utilities Commission (PUC) and the Texas Aeronautics Commission, respectively, exercised considerable control.

Another development favoring growth was the increasing momentum in the abandonment of unprofitable trunk and, especially, local service routes serving small communities. In 1959 the CAB had adopted its "use it or lose it" policy, which stated that if a subsidized community could not generate at least five passenger boardings per day, or 1,800 per year, the board might allow the service to be abandoned. This policy was put into effect during the early 1960s, and by June 1967 101 cities, mostly on local service networks, had lost their certificated air service. Although these communities could not be served profitably by the larger carriers, many offered promising opportunities for route development by the commuter airlines, whose aircraft were better sized for the market demand.

In the 1960s the CAB also pursued a policy of airport consolidation under which separately subsidized scheduled services to two or more cities that were located near each other were consolidated at one of those cities. North Central air service to Appleton, Wisconsin, for example, was terminated in favor of nearby Oshkosh, and Pacific Air Lines flights to San Luis Obispo, California, were discontinued in favor of Santa Maria, about thirty-five miles to the south. Both Appleton and San Luis Obispo subsequently—and even consequently—became the operating bases for important commuter airlines.

Suspension-Substitution Agreements

In a development perhaps even more important, though less publicized, than the "use it or lose it" ruling and airport consolidation, the CAB began to favor suspension-substitution agreements. Under this policy, a commuter airline and a certificated carrier could jointly propose that the former be allowed to replace the latter at a small city. If the CAB approved, the larger carrier was allowed to suspend service temporarily at that city and the commuter airline was permitted to provide substitute service. Meanwhile, the certificated airline remained responsible for the "quality and quantity" (the CAB's words) of air service to the community. Should the commuter airline prove unable to provide satisfactory service, the trunk or local service airline was obliged to reenter that market. This device and the discipline applied to its application derived from one of the original obligations mandated by the CAB in 1938: a route certificate included the requirement to serve a city, as well as the privilege of doing so. But if the commuter airline could prove its worth in serving a city, the trunk or local service airline would eventually be allowed to delete (permanently omit) the point from its network.

The first such agreement was approved in September 1964. It involved the small city of Douglas, Arizona, which had been served once a day, and unprofitably, by American Airlines four-engined DC-6s for some years. American had tried since 1953 to terminate service in favor of a local service airline but could not win CAB support. Finally, on 21 September 1964, the board approved a plan for American to suspend service at Douglas for three years and to be replaced by Apache Airlines (which was already serving Douglas); the latter was to provide substitute service on the route Douglas-Tucson-Phoenix. A contract, under which American subsidized Apache at $26 per flight, was soon implemented; the *OAG* for June 1965 showed only Apache serving Douglas, offering four flights per day to Tucson, three of which continued on to Phoenix. The CAB extended American Airlines' suspension at Douglas for three additional years in 1967, and again in 1970, when Apache went out of business, to be replaced by Cochise Airlines.

Rather surprisingly, bearing in mind the mutual convenience offered to operators and consumers alike, the Apache-American agreement was the only example of suspension-substitution for three years. Yet such agreements were gradually perceived as a useful way to relieve certificated carriers of the onus of serving weak markets. Thus, on 13 October 1967, the Board ruled that Henson Aviation of Hagerstown, Maryland, would be allowed to take over Allegheny's sixty-seven-mile route from Hagerstown to the Baltimore-Washington Friendship Airport. The CAB instructed Allegheny to guarantee that Henson would at least cover its total expenses for the first two years. Replacement service began on 15 November. Initially Henson provided five round trips on weekdays and two on weekends, its Beech Queen Airs and later its Beech 99s replacing a single daily Allegheny F-27 flight. In its first year Henson carried 11,313 passengers, compared to 5,429 for Allegheny during its last year, and became the Allegheny Commuter.

Such an increase provided proof positive that, for journeys of the length and time offered by commuter airlines, the traveling public was prepared to pay a reasonable price for having more frequent and more conveniently timed service. Accordingly, the CAB thereafter approved, with increasing frequency, additional suspension-substitution agreements. On 1 July 1968, it allowed Pocono Airlines of Hazelton, Pennsylvania, to replace Allegheny on the Hazelton-Newark route. On the same day, it authorized Combs Airways temporarily to replace Frontier Airlines at Glendive and Sidney, Montana, while the airports were being upgraded to accommodate Frontier's Convair 580s. The CAB ordered

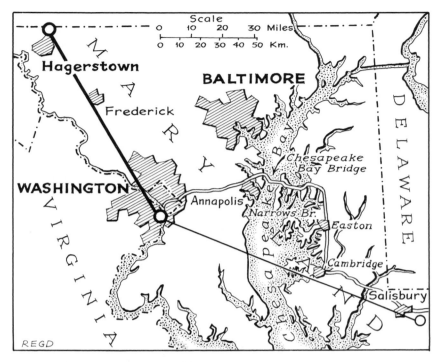

Henson Aviation was a flourishing fixed base operator in the Washington, D.C., area. Dick Henson saw a good opportunity to serve a small city on a short route that was uneconomical for the local service airline and in 1962 established The Hagerstown Commuter, the first time the word was used for a scheduled air taxi or "third-level" route.

Allegheny to guarantee Pocono a break-even operation for the first two years of the contract, but required no subsidy for Combs. Frontier resumed service at Glendive on 1 June 1969.

On 8 October 1968, Roy Clark's Pennsylvania Commuter Airlines was allowed to replace Eastern Air Lines at Lancaster, Pennsylvania, with a subsidy not to exceed $55,000 annually. Later that month Gary Adamson's Aviation Services (later Air Midwest) replaced Frontier at Dodge City, Kansas, but with no monetary support required. As time went on, the CAB specified financial support for commuters in ever fewer cases and finally ceased to require it altogether. By 1969 the number of such "temporary suspensions" had become a flood, with Eastern (e.g., at Rome and Waycross, Georgia), Northeast (e.g., at Rockland and Bar Harbor, Maine), and Allegheny (e.g., at Danville, Illinois, and Mansfield,

Ohio) among the most active trunk and local service airline participants in suspension-substitution agreements.

In two cases, the CAB allowed a commuter airline to provide service to supplement, rather than to replace, that offered by a local service airline on a certificated route. Combs Airways provided a second daily round trip between Cody, Wyoming, and Billings, Montana (approved in 1968), and from Billings to Lewistown, Montana (approved in 1969), where Frontier's certificate required it to offer at least two round trips daily. In the Cody case, Frontier provided ground services and financial support to Combs.

The Allegheny Commuter System

Observing closely the success of its 1967 partnership with Dick Henson between Hagerstown, Maryland, and Washington, Allegheny Airlines actively explored the full development of suspension-substitution agreements, and in the process the widely acclaimed Allegheny Commuter idea was born. This involved a special partnership between Allegheny Airlines (renamed USAir in 1979) and a number of small uncertificated airlines whereby the latter operated their aircraft in close association with Allegheny and invariably painted them in Allegheny Commuter colors. This arrangement had actually started with the original Henson Aviation case, and the same pattern was followed in all subsequent replacement agreements involving Allegheny.

In several other important respects, Allegheny Commuter agreements were different from those normally provided under CAB procedures. The commuter flights were published in the Allegheny Airlines timetables and were integrated into Allegheny's computer reservations system under its AL two-letter identifier code. Importantly, favorable joint fares were offered from the replacement city to all points on the Allegheny Airlines network. The commuter lines were also given access to Allegheny's ramp, waiting room, and ticket counter space at major connecting airports. As stated earlier, the CAB at first required Allegheny to guarantee a break-even operation for two years.

With this type of arrangement, all parties involved were usually better off. Allegheny was able to abandon many money-losing services to small cities yet retain their feeder value and its own market identity there. Because appropriately small aircraft were used, the affected cities received more frequent and convenient air service, and traffic usually

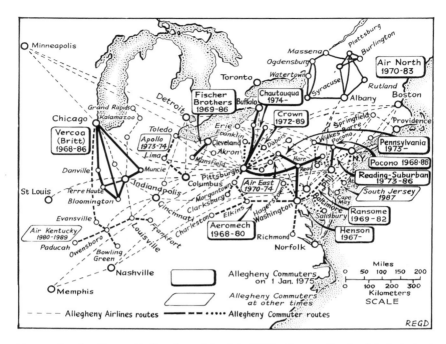

Except for the Metro Air Service of the late 1960s, the small scheduled air taxi operators were invariably independent. When Dick Henson established The Hagerstown Commuter, however, he made an agreement in 1967 for connecting service and joint ticketing with Les Barnes of Allegheny Airlines. This arrangement was so successful that it became the pilot operation for a widespread organization of partner companies that combined to form the Allegheny Commuter airline system.

increased accordingly, often dramatically. The advantage for the federal government was that subsidy payments declined. For the commuter airlines, with their small aircraft and their nonunion wage scales, these smaller cities usually proved profitable, and normally accounted for the bulk of or even all of their traffic.

The second Allegheny Commuter was Pocono Airlines, which replaced Allegheny at several locations, including on the Wilkes-Barre/Scranton to Newark route. In this case a competing third-level airline, Altair, complained to the CAB about the use of Allegheny Commuter titles and its two-letter code, claiming that these practices were "likely to cause public confusion," i.e., that they would lead a passenger to believe that he or she would be flying on Allegheny Airlines rather than on a commuter line. The board made an informal investigation of the complaint but took no action. Later the CAB routinely authorized re-placements with the understanding that the Allegheny trademark and code would be used. The Altair complaint, remarkably similar to objec-tions to code-sharing that would appear in the 1980s (see Chapter 7), was the harbinger of a more widespread future controversy.

One vital element that ensured this program's success was that Alle-gheny was able to convince its pilots to accept such agreements, even though members of the Air Line Pilots Association (ALPA) were being replaced by nonunion commuter crews. Union resistance was appar-ently not a factor because Allegheny's jet airliner fleet and route net-work were growing rapidly, and pilots were assured that no union jobs were threatened by the program.

A map in the issue of *Allegheny Commuter* magazine dated 1 August 1970 showed eleven cities with substitute service. Eventually, Allegheny concluded such arrangements with about a dozen companies. As addi-tional members were welcomed into the "club," one or two departed, and the exact number fluctuated with time. In providing feeder traffic at so many points and by taking Allegheny Airlines out of many an unprofitable market, the commuter program contributed in no small way toward Allegheny's success, in 1974, in becoming the first local service airline to dispense completely with federal subsidies.

With one minor exception, and for reasons that are difficult to fathom, the Allegheny Commuter innovation was not copied by other airlines for a long time. Not until the 1980s did strong, formal ties between commuter and major airlines become so familiar a part of the scene that the names of individual commuter airlines became subordi-nated to those of the major or national airlines (as the trunks and local service companies became known) on a nationwide basis.

The Post Office Increases Use of Commuter Airlines

In 1966, after the CAB's prohibition against the carrying of mail by commuter lines was lifted, the U.S. Post Office began to use them to handle airmail and first class letters. Specifically, it began an experimen-tal program to decrease the delivery times of such letters by awarding contracts to third-level airlines to provide service to smaller cities. This policy was instituted in conjunction with the introduction of the Post Office's sectional center idea.

This Piper Apache carried the mail for the SMB Stage Lines under contract to the U.S. Post Office to serve many of the smaller communities in Missouri and other midwestern states. (Photo courtesy of the Roger Bentley collection.)

In the first year of the program, the Post Office awarded eleven route contracts, worth $187,000, to the small companies. Some of the earliest operations utilized single-engined equipment, but the Post Office soon canceled those contracts and insisted on the use of twin-engined aircraft equipped for instrument flight rules operations. The following year there were 80 such routes, worth $3.5 million in post office contracts, and by December 1968 the number had grown to 150 mail routes, operated by forty-two companies. The largest mail carrier, with forty-five routes, was the quaintly named Sedalia-Marshall-Boonville Stage Lines (SMB), which until September 1967 had specialized in operating highway post offices. SMB's route network soon extended from the Canadian border to southern Texas, and from Wyoming to the eastern border of Ohio. By mid-1969 the planned route network was essentially complete, with 225 routes that generated $10 million in annual revenues.

In 1968 over one-half of the third-level airlines' mail-carrying fleet consisted of Beech 18s, with Piper Aztecs second in the ranking. A few airlines carried passengers as well as mail, but many carried just mail. By some measures of growth, such as numbers of aircraft operated and route-miles flown in scheduled service, mail carriage was a substantial factor in the commuter airline boom of 1965–1968.

The Major Airlines Take Notice

By 1965 the commuter airlines' main role within the national air network was clearly to act as traffic feeders to the larger airlines. Most commuter passengers transferred to or from certificated airline flights, usually at the twenty-five or so busiest airports in the nation, and this still remains the leading commuter airline function. In this role commuter airlines sometimes developed hub-and-spoke networks, and they thus presaged the development and later consolidation of such route networks by larger companies, superseding the traditional line and grid networks, after airline deregulation in 1978.

During the later 1960s, as the feeder role of the commuter airlines grew, the traffic patterns that evolved began to attract the attention of

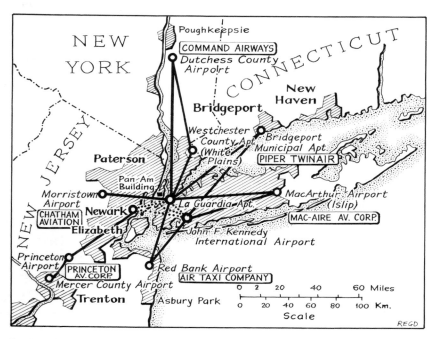

During the late 1960s—long before the terms "computerized reservation system" and "code-sharing" came into fashion—American Airlines devised the Metro Air Service. The assembly of small air taxi companies provided connections from the outlying regions of the great New York megalopolis, easing the anguish of air travelers, who could otherwise reach the main airports by either bridge or tunnel, but invariably by a circuitous route that was time-consuming and aggravating. The three airports were also connected by the helicopters of New York Airways in association with Pan American Airways.

major airline managements. Some recognized particularly the great potential value of extending air transport to a wider cross section and a larger percentage of the American population. In a few cases, such as with United Air Lines and Trans World Airlines (TWA), special programs were established to improve interchange with third-level airlines and nonscheduled air taxis. TWA, for example, instituted its Piper Twinair project to encourage trunk–air taxi traffic interchange at six major cities in its system. As a rule, this project involved charter flights to cities within two hundred miles of the air hub, but it also included a scheduled feeder service between Bridgeport, Connecticut, and New York's John F. Kennedy Airport, a route whose characteristics closely paralleled those of Pilgrim's Groton/New London-based operations across Long Island Sound. For a short time, beginning in September 1965, American Airlines sponsored the Metro Air Service program, a name under which several commuter airlines (including Air Taxi Company, Chatham Aviation, Princeton Aviation, Mac-Aire Aviation, and Mid-Hudson Airlines) flew into New York and fed traffic to American. Northeast and American also advertised connecting agreements with commuter lines. But many other larger airlines barely acknowledged the existence of the diminutive newcomers, and, with the exception of Allegheny, even the most cooperative trunks and locals were reluctant to accept them as full partners. The contested and much-debated issue of joint fares illustrates this point.

Joint Fares and Interline Agreements

Many of the small noncertificated airlines benefited from interline ticketing, baggage, and freight agreements with the larger carriers. Under these arrangements, commuter airlines were able to use standard ticket stock and to issue tickets that included both the commuter and trunk or local service segments of interline trips, whereas formerly the passenger had to purchase two separate tickets. Passengers were also allowed to check their baggage onto commuter aircraft for transfer to the larger carrier at the connecting hub, and viceversa. Freight interline agreements were established as well. By early 1968, about fifty commuter companies had interline agreements with one or more of the major carriers.

Although joint ticketing was relatively easily agreed upon, the commuter airlines were not successful in their efforts to negotiate joint fares, i.e., those applying to trips requiring the use of two or more carriers. Under such cooperative arrangements, the cost of the joint fare is less than if two tickets are bought separately, each company normally absorbing a portion of the lower ticket revenue in the interest of generating more traffic. The decrease in revenue per passenger-mile flown is compensated for by increased load factors and consequently higher revenue per aircraft mile. Certificated airlines had customarily offered such fares for trips involving the use of another certificated company. Not until 1968, however, did the CAB even permit joint fares between certificated airlines and scheduled air taxi operators, except at suspension-substitution points.

The certificated airlines showed no enthusiasm for joint fares with their commuter brethren. Most felt that the latter were too inexperienced or managerially weak to handle such complex arrangements. In addition, if for any reason, a flight did not go smoothly on the commuter segment of a joint-fare journey, it was felt that the major carrier might be blamed by the customer. Because of such doubts, no joint fares with commuter airlines, other than at suspension-substitution points, were established before 1970.

Important New Companies Join the Commuter Airline Ranks

The 1965–1968 boom inspired the formation of several companies that were soon to become prominent among commuter airlines. Collectively, they serve to illustrate some of the functions, problems, and special characteristics of an emerging industry in transition from cautious infancy to confident adolescence.

Air Wisconsin began operations on 23 August 1965 with four daily round trips on the single route from Appleton, Wisconsin, to Chicago's O'Hare airport, using two nine-seat de Havilland Doves. The company was organized by the citizens of Appleton and neighboring cities after being told that they would lose their subsidized service by North Central Airlines, which would instead serve them (under the CAB's airport consolidation program) via nearby Oshkosh. By assiduously cultivating its home market of about 185,000 people in the Fox River Valley around Appleton, Air Wisconsin saw its traffic grow from 600 passenger boardings in the first month to more than 11,000 per month four years later, with 80 percent of the passengers connecting with major airline flights.

The company soon became one of the most successful and influential members of the industry, rapidly expanding into additional markets. Air Wisconsin remained a commuter airline (though it preferred to rank itself higher) until well into the 1980s, eventually operating as a unit of United Express. By that time its greatly increased revenues had placed it, by CAB ground rules, into a new ("national") category of air carrier.

As was often the case in the early stages of the commuter airline industry, Air Midwest was the outgrowth of an air charter business. In this case, the co-founder and president, Gary Adamson, initially focused on air ambulance and air mortuary services. In April 1965, with only elementary knowledge of the airline business, he decided to offer scheduled service with a single-engined Cessna 206 from Wichita to Salina, Kansas, after Central Airlines had dropped the eighty-mile route. Later Air Midwest moved on to twin-engined Cessna 402s, to fifteen-seat Beech 99s, and then to ever larger turboprop equipment, eventually becoming one of the largest commuter companies, with a network that stretched halfway across the nation.

Although short-lived, Commuter Airlines probably received more media attention than any of its contemporaries. Founded by Paul G. Delman, a World War II bomber pilot, it was organized in 1964 at Sioux City, Iowa, and from the start was publicly owned through the sale of $2.75 million in common stock. Scheduled service began in November of the following year, connecting Ames and Marshalltown, Iowa, with O'Hare Airport, Chicago, using nine-seat Beech Queen Airs, of which type it eventually had a fleet of eleven, before switching to Beech 99s in 1968.

This initial route system proved unsuccessful, so in 1967 Delman decided to move to Chicago to develop a hub-and-spoke network radiating from that metropolis to medium-sized cities within three hundred miles, including Madison, Wisconsin; Muncie, Indiana; and the Illinois cities of Peoria, Rockford, and Springfield, while continuing service to Ames and Marshalltown. By September 1967, Commuter Airlines was carrying about five thousand passengers per month, and it was soon claiming to be the largest third-level airline.

The Chicago hub included O'Hare, where 75 percent of the incoming passengers transferred to other airlines, and Meigs Field, located in downtown Chicago on the Lake Michigan waterfront, which was more convenient for some Chicago-bound travelers. In 1968 it became the second commuter airline (after Ross Miller's pioneering TAG Airlines) to offer downtown-to-downtown services, with routes from Meigs Field to the Detroit City Airport (a seventy-minute flight) and to Cleveland's Burke Lakefront Airport (ninety minutes). Services to Meigs were also provided from Springfield, Milwaukee, Peoria, and several other points. These flights to downtown Chicago, aimed at business travelers, were even advertised in such prominent and prestigious publications as *Time, Newsweek,* and the *Wall Street Journal.* One full-page advertisement neatly headlined the theme: "The superjets miss the city [of Chicago] by 23 miles. Commuter Airlines is much more accurate." In 1968 the company spent $75,000 for promotion, a very high figure for the industry.

Commuter Airlines was the first third-level company to develop an extensive hub-and-spoke passenger network focused on a major metropolitan airport. The related idea of a whole network focusing on a downtown airport is unique, on this scale, in the industry's history. Delman also claimed that his company was the first in its category to be publicly owned, to have central and computerized reservation systems, and to include a route development department. It was also the first user of the Beech 99, and Delman probably played a role in that aircraft's development. He proposed airline franchising, with Commuter Airlines providing managerial guidance to other potential operators. Delman was certainly a good publicist, not only for his own company but for the whole third-level industry.

With such promising ideas and with all the qualities necessary for it to serve as a pacesetting role model for the industry, Commuter Airlines seemed destined for success. But unfortunately, like many other non-certificated companies, it was undercapitalized, and its expansion, fueled by undue optimism, was too rapid. After a change of management, it went out of business in May 1970, to end an eventful but all too brief episode in the formative years of commuter airline development.

The three airlines just described exemplified some of the many and varied facets of an industry still feeling its way and seeking a definable identity, but they were not typical. The flavor of the typical commuter airline of the mid-1960s was well captured in a report compiled by one of the coauthors of this book. After a 1966 tour of the United States on behalf of a British aircraft manufacturer, R. E. G. Davies tried to summarize the main characteristics of the sixteen companies he visited. He found that the typical owner had been a fixed base operator for many years and operated only one or two scheduled routes, started within the past four years in response to a regular demand for charter flights. Services were usually timed at the beginning and end of each business day, and sometimes they took traffic from the larger airlines because of the better timing of flights. He classified the types of commuter airline routes into five categories: suburban, satellite-hub, linear, special geographic situation, and special social situation. The typical passenger paid the rather high rate of twelve to twenty cents per mile, but was willing to do so because of the convenience and because on short trips the absolute fare was low.

Davies made some additional comments about the typical operator, who tended to do his own airframe overhauls, but not major engine work. "In general, his approach to operating costs is empirical, and unrelated to long-term planning." He was also described as self-reliant, enterprising and ruggedly independent, and usually possessing limited access to capital. Davies thought this last problem would be ameliorated if the FAA and CAB changed their policies toward the industry. There was much interest in several planned turboprop aircraft that would ideally cruise at 250 miles per hour, have a three-hundred-mile range, seat up to twenty passengers, and sell for a maximum of $300,000.

Industry Group Activities

During the mid-1960s two groups represented the interests of the industry. One was the Association of Commuter Airlines (ACA), discussed previously, whose membership comprised some of the largest companies. The other was the National Air Taxi Conference (NATC), formed in the early 1960s, whose ranks included mostly nonscheduled operators, but which had a committee devoted to the interests of scheduled air taxi firms. Early in 1968 the NATC was renamed the National Air Transportation Conference (since many members strongly disliked the term "air taxi") and was reorganized, with the scheduled operations committee expanded and renamed the airline division; there were also charter and mail-cargo divisions.

The twenty- to thirty-member ACA appears to have been the more active of the two groups, vigorously promoting its views, especially to the CAB and the FAA. It wanted these agencies to recognize commuter airlines as a distinct branch of aviation, with "rules to assure responsible management," and for the commuter airlines to be disassociated from air taxi operators—in short, to be considered as "legitimate members of the scheduled airline industry." Thus, late in 1966, it passed a resolution asking the CAB not to refer to scheduled carriers as air taxi operators, a term that it felt to be disparaging. The ACA's goals, as summarized by one aviation publication, were to "help promote high standards of safety and to promote recognition, as a true part of the U.S. airline network, of operators flying aircraft under 12,500 pounds in scheduled service."

In October 1967 leaders of the ACA had a shirtsleeve meeting with all five members of the CAB. They made four requests. The board was asked to appoint a staff member to act as a liaison officer to the commuter industry. The leaders also thought that the board should require traffic and route reports from all carriers and should study the need for legislation that would give some route protection to commuter airlines. Such limited protection should not necessarily require a normal CAB certificate, as the process of obtaining one was expensive, costing at least $25,000. The ACA asked the board to establish a classification for scheduled third-level companies that would clearly distinguish them from air taxi operators. It saw no need for the CAB to raise the 12,500-pound limit and said that its members were not interested in receiving subsidies. Later it also took the position that the CAB should require liability insurance of at least $75,000 per passenger. Such was the success of this lobbying effort that toward the end of 1968 the CAB was circulating proposed amendments to Part 298 that included most of these suggestions.

Many ACA airlines were also members of the NATC, an organization of about 250 members, of which perhaps 50 to 60 were commuter airlines. One of the NATC's strengths was that it had negotiated blanket interline agreements with the trunk and local service airlines for all of its members.

The NATC adopted several positions that were similar to those of the ACA. In 1967, for example, it petitioned the CAB to require third-level airlines to file their schedules with the board, stating that this practice would lead to "increased acceptability and use by the certificated carriers and the public." In the following year it favored more federal data collection, a mandatory minimum level of insurance coverage, tighter FAA licensing, and the requirement for CAB "letters of registration" (a simplified form of certification).

During one period, both the ACA and the NATC had petitions before the CAB asking that commuter airlines be regulated. As a trade periodical observed in September 1968, most members thought that "real stability" could come only with CAB regulation. The board, however, was reluctant to comply, as it felt that the industry had developed very well within its nonregulated environment. It also probably viewed certification essentially as a protective device for the established companies to prevent the emergence of new competitors. One spokesman went so far as to accuse the industry of fuzzy thinking: "They want freedom to develop routes, but then they want freedom from competition."

Both the ACA and the NATC felt that the industry needed a catchy new name. There was little support for "scheduled air taxi" or "third-level airline," the names that were then in most common use but that were considered to be self-derogatory and an invitation to satirical comment, if not outright criticism. By 1968, when the CAB was thinking about adopting the ponderous term "scheduled small aircraft operators," the NATC was recommending "commuter air carriers." At the same time the ACA was suggesting either "commuter airlines" or "scheduled local air carriers" (and that the local service airlines be renamed the "regionals"). For the moment, however, the CAB, apparently determined to ignore reality, refused to adopt any name that stressed the airline nature of scheduled air taxi operators.

In December 1968, the two trade organizations voted to merge. The resulting group was called the National Air Transportation Conferences (still NATC). Its first president was Thomas S. Miles, a former military pilot who had subsequently been a travel agent.

Profitability Proves Elusive

Despite the commuter airlines' outstanding growth and superficial indications of success, few were profitable. The 7 September 1968 issue of *Business Week*, for example, quoted one owner as saying that, of the two hundred or so commuter airlines, fewer than ten were profitable. Another owner said that "nobody flying more than three routes is making a red cent." One magazine estimated that less than 5 percent of the commuter airlines were operating in the black. At about the same time the ACA claimed that few, if any, of its members were able to show regular profits. Continued growth without consistent profits does not make sense, yet new investors were constantly entering the industry to replace those going out of business. How could this phenomenon be explained?

Eternal optimism about the prospects for long-term future profits, stemming from expected continuous traffic growth, may have been the single most powerful reason for the continued enthusiasm among investors. Many aviation observers and commentators, including those in the financial community, considered that the commuter airlines had good prospects, apparently speculating that even if profits were unachievable now, they would eventually appear. Rapidly growing demand and the assumed eventual demise of inefficient competitors were the two elements that, in due course, were expected to provide a firm foundation for a comfortable return on investment. This course of events was confidently predicted by many respected industry consultants. Forecasts of high growth were accepted, and investors seemed to have been swept along on a wave of optimism.

On a more personal level, one rooted in human psychology, some entrepreneurs seemed to have been captivated by the prospect of achieving presidential status in the exciting world of airlines, however modest that niche might be. Could it not lead to greater opportunities in the upper echelons of the industry? This aspiration led them to work like beavers to raise capital and to keep their companies going even when the going got rough. Many labored intensively for little or no salary in first establishing and then trying to sustain their airlines. Many hopeless enterprises stayed in business longer than business sense—or even common sense—dictated. Often these forlorn efforts were a reflection of desperation, as people who had invested their lives' savings in unsuccessful commuter airlines worked on simply to try to salvage their investments, risking bankruptcy in the vain hope of performing a minor miracle.

The industry's early history also suggests that many entrepreneurs entered the industry believing, somewhat arrogantly, that on routes that attracted substantial volumes of traffic they could drive their competitors out of business by offering superior service, utilizing better marketing, or competing on the basis of rates and service. Once such exclusivity was theirs, they reasoned, they could reap substantial benefits from localized route monopolies. These individuals apparently did not realize that, with few curbs on new entrants in an unregulated industry in which the main resources (aircraft) can easily be moved around, any attempt to create such monopolies would simply attract new competitors into the markets.

Another reason why so much money went into such an unprofitable industry was the lack of accurate financial information. In the commuter airline industry, few companies were public corporations and therefore obliged to report financial results or even to reveal in the most general terms the condition of their financial health. Optimistic aspirants wishing to join the commuter airline ranks could imagine all kinds of successes for themselves, based on hearsay rather than on the record.

Consistent financial losses, overt or covert, were thus a serious problem for the adolescent commuter airline industry. Given this condition, the high growth rate of the mid-1960s could not possibly be sustained for very long. In a classic example of survival of the fittest, the weaker members eventually would have to drop out.

Changing Relations With the FAA

During this formative period, the FAA instituted new regulations for the air taxi industry. The need for a change had become more urgent as new high-capacity turboprop aircraft began to appear. These types, with advances in structural design and light turbine engines, made it quite possible to carry up to twenty passengers under regulations that the FAA had designed to apply to small airplanes with, at most, eleven passenger seats. One aviation writer succinctly remarked that the FAA had never intended an unassisted pilot to be able to fly twenty passengers without radar and without the need to file a flight plan. By the end of 1966 the FAA was deep into plans to tighten its Part 135 operations and maintenance regulations for air taxis. One change under consideration was the requirement that two pilots be aboard all aircraft capable of carrying more than a fixed number (perhaps nine) of passengers.

Along similar lines, there was considerable debate within the FAA as to how the larger aircraft that were nevertheless within the 12,500-pound weight limit should be certificated. Many thought that some Federal Aviation Regulations Part 25 (transport category) rules should be imposed on those Part 23 (general aviation) airplanes that were capable of carrying large numbers of people. The main point of contention revolved around the single-engined capability of these airplanes during climbout.

As the FAA began to reexamine its regulations, it first added special conditions to the certification of new turbine-powered aircraft such as the Twin Otter and the Beech 99. The latter has sometimes been called the first new airliner to be certificated specifically as a commuter aircraft, even though its original design (as the Beech Queen Air) had been for another purpose.

Several companies that operated under FAA regulations governing small airlines were based in the Caribbean. Prinair operated dozens of flights per day from San Juan, Puerto Rico, to the Virgin Islands with the four-engined de Havilland DH-124 Heron (top). The Virgin Island Seaplane Shuttle preserved the heritage of the flying boat, inheriting pioneer Charlie Blair's routes and introducing the Grumman Mallard, pictured here (bottom) taxiing up the ramp at Roadtown, British Virgin Islands, 1983. (Collection of R. E. G. Davies.)

These new conditions, which applied particularly to flight performance and vulnerability to crashes, were incorporated into Special Federal Aviation Regulation 23, issued in December 1968. They applied to aircraft within the 12,500-pound limit that could carry ten or more passengers. Thus, for example, newly certificated airplanes had to be able to take off with a full load after an engine failure at or above takeoff speed.

In 1968 the first report questioning commuter airline safety came to the attention of the media. The National Transportation Safety Board had urged the FAA to take concerted and speedy action to improve the scheduled air taxi safety record. The report was embarrassing, for such questioning could inspire the kind of publicity that no industry or company wanted to receive—least of all one that had so many other problems to solve.

The stage was thus set for a number of possible additional changes in the safety regulation of the industry. Ironically, however, the resultant rules did not appear until after the first commuter airline boom—the intensity of which had made such rule-making necessary in the first place by creating a new operating environment—had ended.

Problems of the Late 1960s

Three major problems faced the commuter airline industry in the latter part of the 1960s. First was the question of access into major airports through the air traffic control system, and the related concern about increasing airport congestion. Second, the OAG was not listing the commuter airlines satisfactorily. Third, the Air Line Pilots Association was unhappy about the prospect of an increasing number of cities being served by noncertificated airlines employing nonunion pilots.

As mentioned earlier, the late 1960s were a time of worsening congestion for the nation's airports and airways, and the FAA had to consider, for the first time, whether or not to limit access to a few of the busiest airports. One option seriously considered was to restrict or even to ban general aviation from these locations; because the FAA still classified commuter airlines as a segment of general aviation, this option threatened the very heart of the industry.

Predictably, the NATC and ACA both campaigned actively against such a policy. The ACA, for example, petitioned the CAB to grant air carrier status to commuter airlines. Others argued that short runways, to be used only by general aviation and thus by the commuter airlines, should be constructed parallel to the main runways, wherever feasible, at the crowded hubs. Such a runway was, in fact, opened at New York's La Guardia airport in August 1968, but it was less than one thousand feet long and could be used by very few commuter aircraft. More practically, the FAA began to allow small aircraft to make routine intersection arrivals and departures (i.e., those using only a portion of the main runway), thus increasing frequency and thereby total airport capacity.

Eventually the problem of airport crowding led to a rationing (slot) system at four of the busiest airports (New York's La Guardia and Kennedy, Chicago's O'Hare, and Washington's National), where a fixed number of instrument flight rules takeoffs and landings were allocated per hour. Although commuter aircraft were included in the slot system, the limitation on flights thus imposed (e.g., ten operations per hour at O'Hare) was a major concern.

The (*OAG*) continued to restrict the inclusion of commuter airline schedules, requiring proof of regular service and even monthly affidavits to that effect. Even then, such schedules were segregated at the end of the city pair listings, following all nonstop and connecting services by the major airlines. This was a severe disadvantage, as apparently few travel agents or reservations employees looked all the way through the listings.

The *OAG* was the airline industry's most important channel for conveying flight information to the public, and the commuter companies considered better coverage to be vital. To illustrate this need, one company reported a 60 percent loss of traffic in one month when its listings were mistakenly omitted from the *OAG*. For its part, worried about the poor regularity and punctuality of many commuter airlines, passenger reluctance to and annoyance at flying unexpectedly in small aircraft, and the frequent demise of commuter airlines that had nonetheless sent in their affidavits, the *OAG* was unwilling to comply. The question of access to this publication would remain a sore point until the early 1980s.

ALPA was seriously concerned about the growth of the commuter airlines. In particular, ALPA's leadership disliked the increasing number of suspension-substitution agreements and reacted by attempting to include protection against any resulting job losses in some of its contracts (so-called scope clauses). Such resistance threatened the future expansion of these agreements.

Other Developments, 1965–1968

Despite the many bankruptcies and other problems during the boom period, a few companies went public between 1965 and 1968. In spite of sporadic failures, the industry was beginning to show signs of resilience, even permanence. In some cases, commuter airlines even started to appear attractive as investments, and Trans East, Wright, Commuter, and Skymark, for example, sold stock successfully. In the case of Sun Airlines of Missouri, however, serious questions about the attempted stock sales, including charges of stock watering, were raised. Sun was banned from selling stock in its home state, and the enterprise, which even operated a few scheduled services with Learjets, quickly went into the record books as a boom-and-bust case study. On the whole, however, the fact that financial wheeling and dealing was taking place at all indicated that the industry was beginning to develop from a precocious infant into an irrepressible adolescent.

In 1967 aircraft manufacturers started to offer planning assistance to the commuter airlines. Beech offered management consulting services, including assistance with economic and route analyses, and also advice on such matters as standardized accounting procedures and the preparation of uniform financial statements. The following year Piper announced computer programs for the Aztec, Navajo, and its planned (but stillborn) Pocono aircraft, by means of which potential operators could project direct operating costs for depreciation, crews, maintenance, fuel, and landing fees. Piper found that the two most common errors committed by commuter airline aspirants were failures to conduct an adequate market study and to assess operating costs accurately. Several consulting firms, such as Systems Analysis and Research Corporation, also began offering their services to the industry.

Although commuter airlines had long supplemented their revenues by carrying cargo on passenger flights, a few all-cargo commuter airlines made their first appearance at about this time. Cherokee Airlines began to operate from Los Angeles International Airport in April 1967. Formed as a part of Tri-Aviation, a fixed base operator at Fullerton, California, its first scheduled route was Los Angeles–San Diego, operated with two single-engined Cherokee Sixes, each of which had 110 cubic feet of cargo space and could carry about 1,300 pounds of freight. In 1968 Cherokee ordered three of the much larger, boxlike Skyvans, produced by Short Brothers in Northern Ireland. Powered by two Garrett AiResearch turboprop engines, the Skyvan had a capacity of 780 cubic feet and could lift 4,600 pounds; and it went into service on 15 August 1968. Most of Cherokee's business was in handling goods for freight forwarders, but for a short time it had a contract to handle much of United Air Lines' Los Angeles–San Diego air cargo business. It ceased operating in the early 1970s, simply because the operating costs always exceeded the fluctuating cargo revenues.

In 1966 Del-Air (Delaware Air Freight Company, a subsidiary of Summit Aviation) began scheduled runs from the Greater Wilmington Airport at New Castle, Delaware, to various points in Delaware and New Jersey. Initially it used a Cessna 172 and three Cessna 206s, all single-engined aircraft, and later it also operated Beech 18s and Cessna 402s. In 1970 it received the first of nine Skyvans, before moving on to even larger aircraft, such as Convair 580s. Del-Air changed its name to Summit Airlines in 1974 and continued in operation until 1988.

As the decade of the 1960s drew to a close, the commuter airlines had collectively developed into an identifiable segment of the U.S. airline industry. Yet the individual commuter airlines were more often than not still vigorously independent, with no defined leadership except an unofficial hierarchy of respected elders who served as ad hoc advisors and campaigners for operating and commercial rights or privileges that, as yet, were still controversial. And further controversy was ahead.

Chapter 4

The Economic Shakeout

For several years immediately following the boom period of 1965–1968, the commuter airlines went through a severe economic crisis. In 1969 most were suffering substantial losses; many services could not be maintained and the weaker companies ceased to exist. There were also many mergers—the primary intent of which was often simply to decrease or eliminate the level and intensity of competition. In 1969, for example, Golden West Airlines was formed by the merger of four California commuter lines (Cable Commuter, Aero Commuter, Skymark, and Catalina Airlines). For the first time the number of firms going out of business began to exceed the number of new entrants into the field by a substantial margin.

The deteriorating fortunes of the commuter airlines attracted comment. In a thoughtful article in the May 1970, issue of *Interavia*, the Swiss aviation periodical, P. L. Cronbach asserted that the third-level industry suffered from overoptimism, financial losses, and difficulties in borrowing money. Of the approximately thirty California companies, not one had achieved break-even status, and he concluded that "the industry faces a difficult financial future," as fares and load factors were too low, the companies were too small, and much of their equipment needed replacement. Cronbach suggested that the industry's proud disdain of subsidies might have to change.

A similar sentiment was echoed in an article entitled "Why Not Subsidy for Third Levels?" by Robert Burkhardt in the June 1972, issue of *Airline Management*. Burkhardt mentioned that, early in 1972, the CAB had discussed such a possibility, but that neither the local service nor the commuter carriers had favored the proposal. He felt, however, that the industry might need subsidies to survive, for most of the "200 odd air taxi companies trying to operate regularly scheduled services are in trouble."

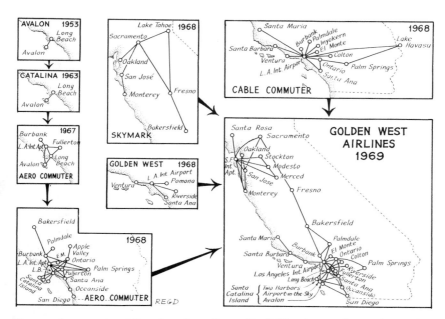

Scores of commuter airlines have been formed in California, usually supplementing trunk and regional route networks, but sometimes replacing them. This map shows the development of Golden West Airlines, which operated until the 1980s.

The most intense period of bankruptcies, mergers, and companies otherwise leaving the industry began early in 1969 and continued for approximately a year. In November 1968, the FAA listed 240 commuter airlines, but by September 1969 the number had decreased by more than a hundred, to 138 (see table). Where there was enough traffic demand, the network gaps left by airline casualties were soon filled through expanded service by the survivors or by new commuter airlines that felt they could do the job more efficiently. In other cases, however, commuter service had simply not been economically feasible from the start, and the network gaps remained.

When this painful adjustment to overexpansion had been completed, the number of companies began to stabilize in the early 1970s. From a broader perspective, however, the industry's turnover rate continued to be high and would remain so until the mid-1980s. The apparent stability did no more than reflect the rough balance between the number of new entrants and casualties. After 1972 the number of companies began to increase slowly.

Commuter Airlines, 1968–1972

	Companies	Aircraft	Passengers (in millions)
1968	240	1,272	3.0
1969	138	864	4.1
1970	140	741	4.3
1971	127	743	4.7
1972	142	751	5.3

In 1969 commuter airlines were estimated to be serving about 200 airports that lacked certificated airline service, but by 1970 that number had dropped to 152 (out of more than 300 airports served in total by commuter lines); however, by 1972 this trend had reversed again, and the estimate was about 250 airports. The total number of aircraft in the commuter fleet decreased from 1,272 in 1968 to 751 in 1972, but during the same period the number of large turbine-powered aircraft increased from 122 to 175. Many of the older aircraft that were retired had not been contributing much to the airlines' total productivity, and the general slump in the industry thus had some positive effects, by imposing stricter operating disciplines.

The shape and content of the commuter airline industry were, in fact, undergoing a fundamental change. Despite the considerable economic instability and the decrease in the number of companies and aircraft, most indicators of industry size actually continued to show an increase. The number of commuter airline passengers, for example, rose from an estimated 3.0 million in 1968 to 5.3 million in 1972. In short, by 1972 about 40 percent fewer commuter airlines, with 40 percent fewer aircraft, were carrying 77 percent more people than they had in 1968.

A map of commuter airline passenger routes in 1972, derived from schedules in the *Official Airline Guide (OAG)*, also illustrates the continued growth of the industry. Between 1968 and 1972 the number of route-miles in the contiguous United States served by the most important passenger-carrying commuter lines (those listed in the *OAG*) increased from about 33,000 to almost 44,000. As before, the routes served tended to be especially concentrated in the northeastern states, around Chicago, in California, and in Florida. Elsewhere, commuter passenger services were available in most of the larger cities of the nation in 1972, and many distinct hub patterns are evident.

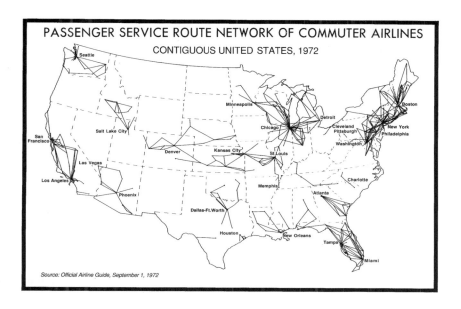

PASSENGER SERVICE ROUTE NETWORK OF COMMUTER AIRLINES
CONTIGUOUS UNITED STATES, 1972

Source: Official Airline Guide, September 1, 1972

The FAA Sponsors a Study

In November 1970, the FAA published a study, *The U.S. Commuter Airline Industry—Its Current Status and Future.* Carried out by the firm of Waldo and Edwards, Inc., it made some useful generalizations about the industry as it stood in 1969–1970. It found that the average stage length of forty of the fifty-six passenger carriers studied was less than one hundred miles, and that the average stage length of eleven of those forty was less than fifty miles. During this period the average passenger on the top fifty commuter airlines flew ninety-one miles and paid the high rate of 17 cents per mile (over twice the average fare on the major airlines). Thirty-two companies offered only cargo or mail service.

The study gave additional evidence of the high corporate turnover rate in 1969–1970. The authors found that the 1 May 1969 issue of the *OAG* listed ninety-eight commuter airlines. Eighteen months later (November 1970) only fifty-seven of these were still in the publication, but thirty-nine new carriers were listed, for a total of ninety-six. This stability in the number of firms listed implied that the large decrease in the number of commuter airlines in 1969–1970 was mostly accounted for by small, newer firms, whose schedules were often excluded from the *OAG*.

Waldo and Edwards identified a high degree of concentration in the industry, estimating that, in the last half of 1969, the top fifty commuter airlines accounted for about 90 percent of the industry's available seat-miles, whereas the top twenty-five accounted for 75 percent, and the top ten fully 53 percent. Of the 894 city pairs studied, 441 produced an average of only one passenger per day, 269 produced five or more passengers, 195 produced ten or more, and only 95 produced twenty or more. Such low traffic levels went a long way toward explaining the high casualty rate among commuter airlines.

The authors also found considerable geographic concentration of traffic. About 19 percent of U.S.-flag commuter passenger traffic occurred in the Puerto Rico–Virgin Islands area (where Prinair was the leading carrier), 14 percent was in Southern California (where Golden West was the leader), and 8 percent took place in the Massachusetts-Maine area (Executive Airlines). A CAB study of about the same period confirmed this high degree of geographic concentration: 82 percent of the passengers on the fifty largest commuter airlines traveled to or from the twenty-two leading air traffic hubs in the United States and Puerto Rico.

Perhaps the most important revelation of the Waldo and Edwards report was that the passenger commuter airlines had a load factor (the percentage of seats occupied by revenue passengers) of only 32 percent in 1969, and that they needed a load factor of 47 percent to break even. This severe shortfall had led to an operating loss of more than $28 million in that year. Because of the operating losses and many bankruptcies, the report noted that the financial community was now wary of investment in commuter airlines.

In comparison, by 1988 the average load factor was 40 percent, and the industry's break-even load factor was 44 percent. These figures show a relative consistency in some aspects of the commuter airlines over time (albeit in the negative sense), despite the many developments that affected the industry after the late 1960s.

CAB Recognition and Regulation

In 1969, reacting to pressures from the industry and possibly to a widespread impression in the aviation community that the commuter airlines were going their own way in an almost anarchic manner, the CAB took action. The Part 298 economic regulations were amended so that all air taxi operators (scheduled and nonscheduled) had to register with the board by 1 July 1969 and renew their registrations annually thereafter. The new regulations distinguished between air taxis performing scheduled services and all others. The former were now called "commuter air carriers" and were defined as firms operating at least five round trips per week with small equipment (maximum of 12,500 pounds) between two or more points and publishing timetables to describe the locations and schedules of their services. Alternatively, they were defined as scheduled airlines operating small aircraft that transported mail under contract with the Post Office. Commuter air carriers were also required to carry liability insurance and to file both quarterly traffic reports and their schedules. These rules represented the first adoption of the term "commuter" by a federal government agency.

The new requirements resulted in 177 applications for registration from scheduled air taxis, of which 13 were from mail-only carriers. Thereafter the CAB supplemented the FAA as a regulatory agency, and incidentally as an important data source, for the industry. As in the past, however, commuter airlines remained exempt from most CAB regulations, including the requirement to obtain the time-honored Certificate of Public Convenience and Necessity, still the vital document needed by all other airlines.

Seeking Commuter Airline Certification

Several proposals were put forth between 1969 and 1972 for CAB certification of commuter airlines. The main impetus came from the industry itself; some companies regarded certification as a way to provide stability and prestige and as a device to avoid some of the rigors of competition. In 1969, for example, Prinair asked the CAB for a certificate, primarily to protect its routes from incursions by other commuter airlines in the Caribbean. Another reason to support such a policy was that it would open the possibility of subsidies.

A number of proposals for commuter airline certification were introduced in Congress. In 1970, such legislation was proposed by Senator James B. Pearson of Kansas, who was deeply interested in the problems of maintaining air service to small cities. The bill called for the establishment of a "new class of limited air carriers" regulated by the CAB "to permit [their] growth, expansion and stability." The board would determine the size of aircraft allowed, make sure that little or no subsidy would be required, and see to it that there would be no "wasteful or destructive" competition with the major airlines. Pearson's proposal was meant to "allow the Board sufficient flexibility to ensure that, as traffic needs [changed], there [would] always be a class of dependable carriers to serve small communities with frequency and adequacy at a cost the public [could] afford."

In the following year the Commuter Air Carrier Act of 1971 was introduced in both houses of Congress. Hearings were held to determine if the public interest required "route protection" for those wishing to operate under a CAB "commuter certificate." The Limited Air Carrier Act of 1971 called for the issuance of "limited air transportation certificates" to certain commuter airlines without the finding that "the public convenience and necessity" required a normal certificate. In the next year the Commuter Air Carrier Act of 1972 was introduced in the House. None of these proposals, however, got very far in the legislative process.

This lack of progress may have been related to the CAB's general opposition to commuter airline certification. It explicitly rejected the idea during its Part 298 gross takeoff weight (GTOW) limit investigation in 1972. The board viewed certification as an "inappropriate regulatory framework," reasoning that the type of service commuter lines provided without subsidy could not successfully be provided by certificated carriers, even with subsidy. This was because the CAB, no doubt recalling similar situations with local service airlines, believed that the high risk faced in small-city service required a degree of flexibility unattainable under a system calling for certification.

Earlier, in April 1971, the CAB's Bureau of Operating Rights (BOR) had issued a brief stating that, in short-haul markets, air transport gave only limited benefits versus surface transport and that the question of where to provide such service should be left to the marketplace. The board as a whole seems to have concluded that commuter airlines provided good economical service to small cities even in their unregulated form. No doubt it also wished to avoid the additional workload and bureaucratic red tape, not to mention extra staff, that regulation would inevitably entail. The sheer number of commuter airlines, coupled with the continual stream of new entrants replacing or supplementing the incumbents, would have imposed a severe burden on the CAB's personnel.

Although the principle of commuter airline certification was not widely supported, the CAB did award certificates to a few airlines that wished to operate with equipment exceeding the 12,500-pound limit.

Two such companies were TAG Airlines and Wright Airlines, both operating between the downtown airports at Detroit and Cleveland. In 1969, the Board gave TAG a five-year certificate on that route, and it issued Wright a similar temporary certificate about two years later. The CAB felt that both situations were special cases, not to be taken as precedents for widespread commuter airline certification. In fact, TAG went out of business before it could put such larger aircraft into service.

Commuter Airline Subsidies

The question of commuter airline subsidies was closely linked to that of certification. Under laws in effect in the early 1970s, only CAB-certificated airlines were eligible to receive federal subsidies. This issue was vital to a few commuter airlines, especially to those providing replacement services where demand was weak or where the cost of service was high. The enthusiasm that had stimulated the applications for replacements now came face to face with harsh economic realities. Operating small aircraft at acceptable fares to points with low traffic demand was all too often economically impossible, and even commuter airlines with low overheads could not break even, much less make a profit.

Though wary of giving subsidies to the commuter airlines, the CAB was not as adamant over the issue as it was over the principle of certification. It appreciated the airlines' dilemma and was ready to listen to reasonable suggestions for a solution.

As a result, several proposals were made to the board. The most active airline on this question was Air Midwest, which was interested in replacing Frontier Airlines at a few small cities in western Kansas where demand for air service was limited and the operating costs were high, especially in winter. Because these small communities were classified as isolated (that is, they were a considerable distance from hub airports, and road and rail transport services were few and far between), government policy favored continuation of service.

By the early 1970s Air Midwest had developed two subsidy proposals. The first, named Progressive Aid for Rural Transportation (PART), called primarily for federal subsidies to help purchase equipment, as the acquisition of aircraft was a major financial problem for small airlines. PART, in turn, had been influenced by an earlier Department of Transportation (DOT)–National Aeronautics and Space Administration

(NASA) recommendation that the government should sponsor demonstration studies of small-airplane services with subsidy in low-density, short-haul markets. The second proposal was simple and direct. It called for the concerned local service airline (Frontier) to subsidize the commuter. Neither of these proposals was successful.

After the BOR had recommended a contract system (with contracts to be awarded via competitive bidding) to provide service to small cities, a bill was introduced in the Senate to enable the CAB to conduct a three-year experiment with such a system. In April 1972, a Senate subcommittee held hearings on this issue, but again there were no concrete results.

Then, in September, 1972, Secor Browne, chairman of the CAB, delivered a speech in Wichita, Kansas, indicating that the board was interested in a possible experimental program of third-level subsidies, particularly for small, isolated communities. His proposal also included a bidding system whereby the carrier bidding for the lowest amount of subsidy would be awarded a contract to provide service for a certain period to a city qualifying under the criteria to be laid down. Browne mentioned a total of $2 million as possibly being enough to fund the experiment. Constructive and positive though his speech was, it led to some complaints within the industry that it did not propose route protection or permanent certification for commuter airlines.

Funding for such an experiment would require congressional support, the main hope lying in the probability that this type of program would considerably reduce subsidies to the airline industry as a whole if commuter air carriers replaced local service airlines at small cities. This prospect gave the industry hope that subsidy legislation might soon be passed. But Browne's speech did not lead to any immediate CAB or congressional initiatives toward such a program, partly because many CAB staff members remained adamantly opposed to third-level subsidies.

Replacement Agreements Continue

Although progress was slow on the major issues of certification and subsidy, the industry continued to benefit from CAB approval of suspension-substitution agreements. Local service operators were keen to make such arrangements with third-level airlines, now asserting their new official status as commuter air carriers. The locals' attitude reflected their accelerating retirement of small propeller-driven aircraft types in favor of larger jet equipment. They were themselves moving into a new era, upgrading their role to that of "regionals," a self-bestowed term that soon gained popular acceptance. They did this by moving into more densely traveled intercity routes, an operating environment the CAB had never intended for them originally and one that the trunks were not very willing to concede. But these "second-level" airlines eagerly sought the routes so as to reduce subsidy requirements, and with these changes they became less well suited to fly into the very communities they had been created to serve.

Even the trunk airlines continued to serve some small cities. Early in 1969, for example, Eastern Air Lines was still flying to such places as Bowling Green, Kentucky (population 36,000), and Ocala, Florida (population 23,000). Eastern's eagerness to remove these cities from its route map was attributable to the large losses suffered there and the company's plans to drop all propeller-driven Convair 440s by the middle of 1969. Another trunk airline with many small cities on its route map was Northeast, serving New England, whose network resembled that of a local service airline more than a trunk airline. And United Air Lines was still providing extensive local service in the San Joaquin Valley of California. These firms were, understandably, even more eager than those in local service to abandon smaller cities to the upstart commuter lines. (There were, as always, exceptions. For example, old-fashioned sentiment and ready sources of capital had a great deal to do with Delta's extended tenure in Monroe, Louisiana.)

The CAB was quite willing to promote such commuter air carrier substitutions, seeing this trend as an opportunity to rationalize the national airline map into more clearly defined strata. Between September 1964 and October 1970, it approved suspension-substitution agreements with local service airlines at thirty-nine points, and with trunk airlines at twenty-six places.

The most impressive group of such agreements continued to involve Allegheny Airlines. Under the visionary leadership of Leslie O. Barnes, Allegheny systematically dropped unprofitable cities in favor of its associated Allegheny Commuter carriers. In 1969 *Airline Management and Marketing* quoted Barnes's two key criteria for ensuring the success of his program: "First, you have to remember that communities have a personality, and second, your pilots must be clued in." Each city's leadership had to be convinced that a substitution was in its best interest, and the pilots involved had to be assured that their future job prospects would improve as Allegheny bought larger jets to serve higher-density routes, even as the propeller-driven airplanes used to serve the small cities were phased out. Between August 1970 and the end of 1972, the number of cities served exclusively by Allegheny Commuters increased from eleven to twenty-five.

In November 1969, Allegheny Airlines turned over its Washington-Philadelphia route to a new affiliate, Ransome Airlines. This was the first major role for a commuter airline in transporting passengers over short distances between a pair of large metropolises; it was a role that would greatly expand in the future. Ransome was flying the same route as the Philadelphia Rapid Transit line of 1926 and the Ludington Line of the early 1930s. Both had been pioneers in providing air service in a densely traveled air corridor.

The addition of this type of short-haul route, one linking two major cities, completed the list of the five main types of routes that are operated by commuter airlines to this day. Their leading function remains to connect the smaller cities of a region with one or more nearby metropolitan centers. Their other functions are to provide flights from suburban locations to the leading airports within a few of the largest metropolitan areas, such as Ontario, California, to Los Angeles International Airport; to supplement flights of the larger airlines between the largest hubs and some nearby medium-sized cities, such as Chicago to Madison, Wisconsin ("filling the holes in the schedule"); and, in a few cases, to provide service to downtown airports, rather than to the main air terminus, such as from Springfield, Illinois, to Chicago's Meigs Field.

Local Service Airlines Seek Protection

In an apparent paradox, even while the number of suspension-substitution agreements was increasing, the local service airlines were simultaneously discussing the feasibility of seeking CAB protection from commuter air carriers. Some of the locals disliked the competition they were experiencing from the commuter airlines and wanted the CAB to remove the irritant by banning them from routes shared with the locals.

Thus, in the winter of 1971–1972 ten local service airlines petitioned the CAB for route protection both for the petitioners and for existing commuter airlines. The latter provision was presumably added to pre-

vent an avalanche of opposition from the third-level industry. The petitioners thought that a CAB "competitive service authorization" should
be required for commuter airlines that wished to serve routes already
flown by themselves or by the established commuter airlines, and that
such an authorization should be granted only if none of the existing
carriers objected.

In making this petition, the local service airlines stressed that the
commuter lines had far outgrown their original stature as small-scale
companies, incapable of competing effectively with the certificated
airlines. In support of their case, they cited the board's own 1969
finding that commuter airlines controlled at least 30 percent of the
traffic where they were directly competitive with the locals. On
1 July 1971, they were competing on a nonstop basis in 109 city pairs
also served by the local service carriers. Clearly the latter were
worried that the commuters would pose even more formidable
competition in the future. Whether intentionally or not, the local
service airlines refrained from observing that they themselves had
set the example by encroaching upon the preserves of the trunk
airlines and that history was now simply repeating itself. However, to
remain consistent with its views on similar matters in the past and
because of its obligation to stimulate competition, the CAB was not
keen to comply with the petitioner's request. Such an action would,
in its view, interfere with what it considered to be a successful experiment in unregulated air service. Thus the local service airlines' suggestion came to naught, and the commuter airlines achieved a minor
victory.

Local Service Small-Aircraft Services

The commuter airlines were not alone in operating scheduled services
with small equipment. Several local service carriers decided to experiment with small-plane schedules, apparently feeling that this type of
service should not necessarily be left by default to the lower orders of
the airline industry. With the exception of that of Frontier Airlines,
however, all of these experiments were short-lived.

West Coast Airlines had been the first to start such an operation, in
August 1966, when it wet-leased (i.e., leased with fuel, crew, and maintenance provided by the owner) Piper Aztecs from Eugene Aviation

Service to operate its route between Eugene and Roseburg, Oregon. When the FAA objected to the wet-leasing arrangement, West Coast crews began to fly the aircraft. In 1967 the company put the Piper Navajo into service and added two more routes. West Coast used the term "Miniliners" for these services, but after it merged with Pacific Air Lines and Bonanza Air Lines in the Air West amalgamation, the small airplane services were withdrawn in January 1970.

In February 1970, Texas International Airlines (TIA) began an experimental service to a few cities, using two Beech 99s. Initial maintenance problems were eventually overcome, and by mid-1971 TIA was operating five Beech 99s. At about this time the aircraft were modified to carry an additional 500 pounds, primarily to increase baggage capacity. In mid-1971 TIA also agreed to lease five new Swearingen Metroliners to replace the Beech 99s, but this arrangement did not materialize and the whole experiment was abandoned in 1972.

Early in 1972 Ozark Airlines began to use de Havilland Twin Otters between Springfield, Illinois, and Meigs Field in downtown Chicago. This operation was started in competition with a similar service provided by a commuter airline, Air Illinois. Ozark's services lasted only for approximately one year, after which they were terminated because of financial losses. These losses were, in part, the result of relatively high crew salaries, for Ozark's pilot contract did not include provisions for proportionately lower wages for flying such small aircraft.

After a six-month experience with substitute flights by Apache Airlines at seven points in North Dakota and Minnesota, Frontier Airlines decided to operate these services itself late in 1970, initially using a leased Twin Otter. Such small aircraft services were later expanded, so that by December 1971 the company was operating two Twin Otters and two Beech 99s. In 1972 and 1973 Frontier disposed of its Beech 99s, but it continued to operate Twin Otters successfully on a number of routes until June 1981.

However, such experiments by local service airlines with commuter-type operations were mostly unsuccessful. Major problems included their relatively high union wage rates, the negative image and unpopularity of small propeller-driven aircraft in local service, and the operational and commercial incompatibility of small aircraft in companies with administrative structures oriented to much larger equipment. Thus, the evidence accumulated to show that such services were best offered by small-equipment specialists.

Joint Fares with Major Airlines

A breakthrough in commuter airline marketing occurred during the early 1970s—a development that, a few years earlier, would have been dismissed as an impossible dream. For the first time (other than in suspension-substitution agreements), bilateral joint fares were established with major carriers. In 1970 American Airlines filed an application with the CAB to offer joint fares with Air Wisconsin. Passengers with joint fare tickets would, for example, save $7.00 on the Appleton-Chicago segment of a trip to New York or Washington, with American absorbing $5.00 of that amount and Air Wisconsin $2.00. This was the first joint fare agreement between a major airline and an independent commuter airline, and for a time remained an isolated case, related to localized competition and in no way setting a precedent at that time.

In 1972, with support from the National Air Transportation Conferences, the commuter airline industry started a major drive for more joint fares, asking the CAB to require the larger airlines to offer them in all commuter markets. This action was seen as tantamount to recognition of commuter airlines as a "legitimate part of the system."

In a related matter, on 11 June 1972, as a result of its massive Domestic Passenger Fare Investigation, the CAB ordered joint fares to be applied between all points in the contiguous United States served by *certificated* airlines. Previously, they had only been offered on a voluntary basis. The commuter airline industry, however, was not included in this order. In fact, its lobbyists had committed a major blunder in not even asking to be included in the Domestic Passenger Fare Investigation, and the number of voluntary joint fares agreed upon between the commuter carriers and the major airlines increased only slowly.

New Commuter Aircraft

Several new or improved commuter aircraft were introduced between 1969 and 1972. One important model to enter service was a successor to the now well-established de Havilland Aircraft of Canada DHC-6 Twin Otter, the Dash 300 series (DHC-6-300). This airplane differed from earlier types by retaining the additional baggage capacity of the 1968 Dash 200 model while substituting a more powerful version of the PT6 turbine engine. The DHC-6-300 first entered revenue service in May 1969, and it sold in even better numbers than earlier models.

A small and efficient nine-seat aircraft introduced in the late 1960s was the British Britten-Norman BN-2 Islander. This one is seen taking off at St. Thomas, Virgin Islands. (Collection of R. E. G. Davies.)

The British nine-seat Britten-Norman BN-2 Islander was certificated by the FAA in December 1967. It was inexpensive (costing only about $80,000 with avionics), and eleven Islanders were in service in the United States by the end of 1969. A year later this aircraft was followed by the stretched BN-2A Mk. III Trislander, an ungainly looking but effective eighteen-seat variant with the third engine mounted in the vertical tail section. A small number of these craft eventually entered U.S. service.

The nineteen-seat twin turboprop Handley Page Jetstream was produced in the United Kingdom. This promising pressurized airliner, with French Astazou XIV engines and six-foot stand-up headroom, was first flown on 18 August 1967, and deliveries began in 1969. One or two may have been put into service briefly by Cal-State Airlines, but these and other Jetstreams languished in storage when the Handley Page company ceased operations. Eventually the Jetstreams were used by several companies, but this entrant into the commuter airline arena was not an initial success. The design and construction, however, were sound, and, quite remarkably, the aircraft was successfully resurrected about a decade later, with different engines, as the British Aerospace Jetstream 31.

There was even some discussion about the introduction of commuter aircraft powered by pure jet engines, rather than turboprops. United

Though first flown in England in 1967, the Handley Page Jetstream did not win an extensive market until much later, when, after being reengined, it was sold as the British Aerospace Jetstream 31. This one is pictured at San Francisco in 1980. (Photo courtesy of the Roger Bentley collection.)

Aircraft of Canada, for example, studied a three-engined, twenty-four-passenger jet aircraft and concluded that it would be economically viable. In the United Kingdom, de Havilland was promoting its DH-126 (later the HS 136) twin jet with between twenty-six and forty seats. In the United States, Beech was studying the feasibility of no less than three possible commuterliners, powered by Garrett fanjets, with capacities ranging from twenty-six to forty-four passengers. However, none of these proposed aircraft was ever produced.

City-Center Service Becomes a Key Issue

In 1969–1970, interest in air services between city-center airports (sometimes called metroflight services), which had been building throughout the decade, peaked. Because of its apparent promise for providing convenient service and relieving congestion at conventional airports, the DOT, the FAA, and other government agencies supported the idea. One major problem, however, was that appropriate equipment still remained to be developed. Therefore these agencies, as well as aerospace firms, gave attention to designs for short takeoff and landing (STOL) and vertical takeoff and landing (VTOL) aircraft, which would operate within a whole network of city-center STOLports—those airports with short runways of perhaps 1,500 to 2,000 feet. With appropriate onboard and ground navigation equipment, such operations could take place at low altitudes, perhaps at less than three thousand feet, without interfering with the existing air traffic control system. Implementing this idea therefore could add substantially to the nation's air traffic capacity.

Such services would be offered between large cities that were located at most 500 miles apart, and preferably over shorter distances of 200 to 350 miles. Significantly, about 50 percent of U.S. air passenger traffic consists of trips of less than five hundred miles, such as journeys within the Los Angeles–San Francisco, California corridor or the Boston–New York–Philadelphia–Washington "Boswash" concentration, where more of the total journey time was then and still is spent on the ground than in the air. Potential STOL routes were determined by estimating the time saved on the airport-to-downtown segment of the total journey, based on the proximity of the STOL field to the city center. The reduction or elimination of this segment of the trip would compensate for the slower speed of the STOL aircraft in comparison to the jet aircraft used between conventional airports. The media were intrigued by the potential of such services for relieving overcrowded conventional airports and for speeding journey times, and the idea received much public attention.

The FAA was deeply interested in the concept, partly because congestion had reached record levels at many of the nation's major airports during the years before the first wide-bodied jets were introduced to relieve the strain. It sponsored several studies of potential STOL and VTOL operations. In one such study the agency projected, rather unrealistically, that if about twenty of the largest American cities had city-center STOLports, 90 to 95 percent of passengers traveling up to five hundred miles would use the STOL airlines. It foresaw the eventual development of fifty- to sixty-seat aircraft for such services, to be operated by commuter airlines under a CAB exemption to use equipment weighing more than 12,500 pounds. Late in 1969 the DOT recommended an almost immediate start for experimental air services of this type. The National Aeronautics and Space Administration was also interested in constructing experimental STOL aircraft, planning at one time to invest up to $100 million in the new technology.

In 1970 the FAA established a Commuter and V/STOL Air Carrier Branch to determine an exact definition for STOL and coordinate such activities as STOLport feasibility studies and projects to demonstrate the practicability of STOL and VTOL operations. There were proposals for such demonstrations in the Atlanta and Los Angeles areas. Oscar Bakke, chief planner for the FAA and a strong supporter of city-center air services, felt that the commuter air carriers should try to start them with existing equipment, perhaps using the DHC-6 Twin Otter—even though it hardly fell within the fifty- to sixty-seat category. He thought that these airlines were well suited to pioneer the concept and to demonstrate its potential in part because their small aircraft were less likely to generate opposition than those that might be used by the larger companies.

The CAB was also involved in plans for a STOL-VTOL network in the northeastern states. This involvement was closely related to the area's chronic air traffic congestion problems. Early in 1970 a board examiner strongly recommended metroflight services, especially in the Boston–Washington–New York corridor.

The commuter airlines were not the only ones interested in the STOL idea. The idea attracted the attention of some trunk airlines, and because of the importance of its shuttle services in the highly urbanized Boswash corridor, Eastern Air Lines was particularly active. It worked with the McDonnell Douglas Corporation to demonstrate the capability of a sixty-four-seat, French-built STOL Breguet 941. Designated the McDonnell Douglas 188 in the United States, this was a four-engined turboprop that could cruise at 270 miles per hour, take off in one thousand feet, and land in five hundred—true STOL performance. It arrived in Washington, D.C., in September, 1968 for a series of demonstration flights. American Airlines was also interested.

But a whole series of problems was associated with the STOL concept. Most fundamentally, many of its promoters failed to recognize (or chose deliberately to ignore) that it was an entirely new type of transport system, separate from any other, and not simply one that called for flying a special breed of aircraft. The STOLport, air traffic control, and equipment requirements for such services would be substantial and costly. The construction of a whole network of downtown STOLports in the largest cities would be politically difficult and enormously expensive, in part because of high land values. The special performance aircraft required would be expensive both to purchase and to operate. The extra power needed to provide their superb takeoff and landing performance would have to be traded off for lower efficiency during the cruise.

The environmental problems inherent in such a system were probably even greater deterrents to progress. In the Los Angeles area, plans for STOLports at the Los Angeles Dodgers baseball park and the Anaheim sports stadium were blocked by resistance from nearby residents. A grandiose plan to build an airport above the downtown Los Angeles railroad station remained just that. The same was true for a floating STOLport project, complete with 1,800-foot runway, recommended for Manhattan and presented as a major solution to New York's air traffic problems. Everyone thought that STOL or VTOL was a wonderful idea, but no one wanted it in his or her own backyard.

The idea of using special STOL runways, parallel to the main ones, at La Guardia and Washington National airports was considered, and much of the success of the program depended upon receiving FAA permission to fly direct (as opposed to using airways routes) with freedom of altitude as well as itinerary, so as to reduce block-to-block times (often defined as the time from "doors shut to doors open") to a minimum. But this operational procedure proved less feasible than expected.

Finally, and perhaps most ominously, two early pilot projects failed to turn in encouraging results. The McDonnell Douglas 188 was not successful because of unacceptable economics and marginal operational feasibility. And, after a one-year study simulating the use of various aircraft on the Washington–New York route, American Airlines concluded that there was no foreseeable use for intercity services using STOL turboprops and found that such operations would be highly risky financially.

Altogether, little real progress in STOL was ever achieved, and eventually the whole idea was shelved. High aircraft operating costs coinciding with a large increase in oil prices, together with environmental incompatibility and technical and regulatory obstacles, fortunately killed the vision of STOL before too great an investment had been made.

Nevertheless, in 1972 one experiment, albeit on a modest scale, in downtown-to-downtown air service in the northeast was implemented. The previous year the Grumman Corporation had made a full engineering study of a water-borne metroflight system centered on New York City. The shore of the East River in Manhattan was chosen as the best location for a New York terminal. The project was effectively the rejuvenation—or disinterment—of an old idea originally launched by Grumman back in the late 1930s, when it had introduced the Grumman Goose as a commuter seaplane for wealthy businessmen living on Long Island.

Four commuter airlines had previously expressed an interest in providing New York–Philadelphia city-center seaplane service, but little progress had been made. Then, in July 1972, Downtown Airlines began

Philadelphia–New York service, using a five-seat Piper Aztec equipped with floats and flying from Pier 8 on the East River, near Wall Street in lower Manhattan, to Penn's Landing on the Delaware River in downtown Philadelphia. The one-way fare was $25, compared to $21 first class and $17 coach on the regular airlines. On 6 August 1973, Downtown began service five times a day in each direction with Twin Otters equipped with floats. Late in 1974 the service was extended to Buzzard Point, near downtown Washington, D.C.

However, this innovative service proved to be unremunerative and was discontinued in mid-1975. A part of the problem, no doubt, was the short distances between the cities, which were also well connected by road, rail, and conventional air services. The well-paid executives who must have constituted most of the traffic probably also disliked the cramped conditions in an Aztec or a Twin Otter, preferring Amtrak or the various air shuttle services, which, despite somewhat austere on-board amenities, had proven records of reliability and were effectively institutionalized.

FAA Regulations and Questions of Commuter Safety

The number of commuter air carrier safety regulations increased during this period as the FAA took steps to tighten industry standards, in response to a perception by many groups and individuals that current policies were inadequate. Notably, late in 1969 the FAA changed its Part 135 regulations. These were the operational and maintenance standards required of commuter airlines and air taxi operators using aircraft with GTOWs of 12,500 pounds or less; the FAA now sought to bring them more closely into line with those of the certificated airlines. The new regulations required (1) two pilots for all aircraft with ten or more passenger seats; (2) a flight attendant for aircraft with twenty or more passenger seats; (3) under instrument flight rules, the minimum pilot qualifying time to be increased from 500 to 1,200 hours; (4) tightening of maximum pilot duty times; (5) passengers to be informed of the safety features of the aircraft; (6) the companies to prepare manuals for the FAA covering their maintenance and operating procedures; and (7) certain defects and malfunctions to be reported to the agency.

Despite such changes, the FAA's regulations and the general safety record of the commuter industry periodically came under attack, both from the media and from within the aviation community. For example, during a special National Transportation Safety Board investigation of commuter airline and air taxi safety, both the Air Line Pilots Association (ALPA) and the Flight Safety Foundation (FSF) attacked the FAA's Part 135 regulations. An FSF representative stated that the overall safety record among commuter airlines was not very good. He claimed that the FAA's general aviation offices, which monitored commuter airline activities, were not sufficiently staffed for adequate surveillance. He saw the need for regulations that were even more closely aligned with those applied to the certificated airlines, with such rules enforced by FAA commuter industry specialists. He also expressed a common viewpoint in saying that "until such time as the CAB provides economic regulations to permit growth without disastrous competition, industry-wide safety and a financially sound commuter airline system will be difficult to achieve." Never reluctant to dramatize any problem, the spokesman from ALPA called commuter accident statistics "horrifying" and said that they "cry for immediate remedial action." He added that the "most serious dilemma facing [commuter airlines] at this time is the lack of reliable, economic and highly productive aircraft," and that if subsidies were needed to guarantee high safety levels, then the government should consider providing them.

Such criticisms of the commuter airline industry, drawing strength from media publicity that was disproportional to the magnitude of the problem, continued for many years. Like a bad case of chickenpox, the visible evidence was more dramatic than the underlying condition, but the scars were to remain for many years.

Other Developments

During these years a second local service company, Mohawk Airlines, tried to establish a commuter feeder network based on the Allegheny Commuter model. The first agreement for "Mohawk Commuter" service was made with Northern Airways (later Air North) and involved several communities in the upper reaches of New York state. Eventually two more companies, Executive Airlines and Command Airways, became Mohawk Commuters. Although shown in Mohawk timetables, they retained their individual identities.

In contrast with Allegheny's success, however, the program soon ran into trouble. Specifically, it contributed to a protracted strike by

Mohawk's main line pilots, who strongly objected to nonunion third-level pilots replacing ALPA members. The strike in turn was a factor in weakening Mohawk's ability to survive, and it did so only by being absorbed into Allegheny Airlines—ironically the very role model for Mohawk's innovative but ultimately unsuccessful experiment.

A number of proposals for commuter airline franchising, somewhat in the manner of many fast food chains, were advanced in the late 1960s and early 1970s. In 1970, International Sky Cab was formed. The Sky Cab concept was to give nascent commuter airlines a strong identity and provide management help via the parent firm. Franchisees would also receive assistance with group insurance, aircraft leasing, and reservations. The cost for a franchise was quoted as between $6,000 and $15,000, plus eight percent of the gross annual revenues. As far as is known to the authors, International Sky Cab launched only two operations, one in Puerto Rico and the other in central Florida, both of which were short-lived.

The Airspur Corporation, which started operations late in 1969, planned no less than a national network of up to one hundred associated commuter airlines, some owned and others franchised. Airspur would provide uniformity in such areas as financial practices, administration, marketing, aircraft purchases, and maintenance. Within a short time the company had acquired three commuter airlines: Tradewinds Airlines of Puerto Rico (renamed Airspur Caribbean), Metro Air Service (renamed Airspur–New York), and Newport Aero. Perhaps because of its attempt to buy the Jetstream production line from the Handley Page liquidators, as well as its overly grandiose plans, Airspur went out of business within a year without starting any franchised operations.

The End of the 12,500-Pound Limitation

In January 1970, with encouragement from the commuter airline industry as a whole, the CAB began to investigate whether or not the 12,500-pound GTOW limit was still desirable. There was disagreement on details, but widespread support existed for the idea of replacing the current weight ceiling by a passenger or payload capacity limit. Most suggestions were for an upper limit of between twenty and thirty passengers. Proponents of the shift claimed that, if the old weight restriction were lifted, aircraft could be equipped with additional avionics,

After the CAB modified its 12,500-pound GTOW limitation, one aircraft that seemed to offer much promise was (top) the twenty-six-seat Nord 262 (shown in the modified Mohawk 298 version), which was used during the 1970s and 1980s by Ransome Airlines. The trusty old Douglas DC-3 (bottom) also gained a new lease on life, as it could carry thirty passengers and land on short, often poorly paved, strips. (Collection of R. E. G. Davies.)

baggage space, and fuel capacity, and that this change would also permit such amenities as pressurization, stand-up headroom, lavatories, and air conditioning without the need to reduce payload. Under the 12,500-pound weight rule there had always been a tendency to provide payload capacity at the expense of amenities and fuel (thus reducing range and coming close to jeopardizing safety), in a sometimes desperate effort to maximize revenue.

In mid-1971 the BOR issued a brief on this question. It urged the board to allow commuter airlines to operate aircraft with up to thirty seats and to permit a revenue payload of up to 7,500 pounds. The latter would allow an aircraft to carry a full load of passengers and up to 1,500 pounds of freight. The bureau stated that "the concept of a weight limitation is undesirable because it encourages manufacturers to allocate the limited available weight to revenue-producing seats rather than to passenger comfort factors or to fuel capacity." A thirty-passenger limit was said to fit neatly between, on the one hand, the twenty seats available in the largest contemporary commuter aircraft weighing 12,500 pounds or less (the Twin Otter and Metroliner, which were usually operated with nineteen seats) and, on the other hand, the forty-seat F-27, the smallest aircraft then in widespread use by local service airlines. The BOR felt that a thirty-passenger limit would improve the viability of the commuter airlines without seriously affecting the financial health of the locals.

On 19 July 1972, the CAB adopted the BOR's recommendation. Among other sequels to the decision, the veteran Douglas DC-3, a classic airliner that could seat thirty passengers in comfort, thus became available to the commuter industry, as did the much newer twenty-six to twenty-nine-seat French-built pressurized turboprop, the Nord 262. The board said it hoped that the new limits would give manufacturers an incentive to produce aircraft that were ideally suited to commuter airlines. Yet many manufacturers doubted that this would be the case, because a new thirty-passenger aircraft would have to be certificated under the FAA's more stringent regulations for airplanes weighing more than 12,500 pounds—that agency having retained the previous weight limit to distinguish between small and large aircraft in its safety regulations. A thirty-seat aircraft would also cost about $1.5 million, which was more than most commuter lines could afford. Some years were to pass before the actual impact of the CAB's weight ruling would become clear.

Chapter 5

The Last Years
before Deregulation

In the five years before airline deregulation took effect in 1978, commuter air carriers continued to be the fastest growing segment of the U.S. scheduled airline industry. Traffic almost doubled, increasing from 5.7 million passengers in 1973 to a little more than 11 million in 1978, at an average annual rate of about 10 percent, versus close to 7 percent for the major airlines. Similarly, the average annual growth rate for cargo carried by the commuter airlines was about 30 percent, compared to only 5 percent for the major airlines.

This traffic growth was accompanied by a rapid geographical expansion of the network. During the same five-year period, the number of route-miles in the contiguous United States served by those commuter airlines listed in the *Official Airline Guide* (*OAG*) almost doubled, from 43,825 to 83,278.

As in earlier years, the most intense areas for commuter airline routes were in the northeastern seaboard states and in California, but substantial networks also focused on other large metropolitan areas, such as Chicago, Denver, and Dallas–Ft. Worth. For the first time, it became possible to take a trip from coast to coast entirely by commuter airlines—given enough money, time, and stamina. In fact, at least two well-publicized journeys of this type were made, one by a commuter airline pilot and another by a newspaper reporter.

These impressive increases occurred despite a continued high turnover rate of individual companies. Most newcomers left the industry after only a year or two, often via bankruptcy, and some lasted only a matter of days or weeks. Many other unprofitable firms lingered for several years as their owners tried desperately to survive or to find a buyer or merger partner. Occasionally the industry was shocked by the failure of a company that was perceived to be both well established and successful. Most of those that went out of business simply ran out of

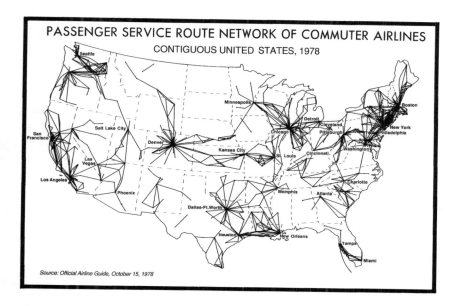

PASSENGER SERVICE ROUTE NETWORK OF COMMUTER AIRLINES
CONTIGUOUS UNITED STATES, 1978

Source: *Official Airline Guide, October 15, 1978*

money, as their business plans had been based on overly optimistic and inadequately researched traffic and revenue forecasts. Given this record, mere survival was tantamount to success. There have been few industries in American business history in which it was more difficult to make a reasonable profit. Commuter airlines, before deregulation, may go on record as one of the least profitable industries in the country's economic history, rivaling the interurban railroads of the early part of this century.

Despite the generally upward trend, 1975 was the first year in the industry's history when passenger traffic was actually lower than in the previous year. Closer inspection of the facts, however, reveals that this decrease was more institutional than real and was caused by a unique event in U.S. airline history. In 1974 Air New England, one of the largest air carriers at the third level, was elevated by the CAB to the ranks of the second level, the certificated local service airlines. This was the first—and the last—such promotion since the establishment of that category of air transport. Had Air New England been included, traffic in 1975 would actually have increased by a modest 2.3 percent, despite the fact that 1975 was a very tough year for all parts of American aviation.

Even while the commuter airline industry as a whole continued to grow, one segment was in sharp decline. In 1974 third-level air mail services reached their all-time high, with flights to about 250 points, gross payments of about $30 million per year, and the transport of 164 million pounds of mail. Then, in 1975, the United States Postal Service (as the Post Office had come to be known under legislation enacted in 1970) changed its policy of using commuter airlines to carry first class mail, shifting much of the traffic back to the highways. Between 1975 and 1976 the amount of mail carried by the commuter lines decreased from 75,000 to 49,000 tons, and the all-mail route mileage declined sharply. This trend continued, so that by the early 1980s the specialized network had almost disappeared.

Industry Concentration

As in earlier years, most commuter airline traffic continued to be concentrated among relatively few companies, although as many as 250 (including those outside the contiguous United States and those that carried only cargo or mail) were in service in any given year. Thus, in 1976—typical of the pre-deregulation period—the top fifty passenger carriers handled almost 86 percent of the traffic, and the top five alone accounted for 28 percent. The single biggest airline continued to be Prinair of Puerto Rico, which carried about 825,000 passengers. The second largest was Golden West Airlines, with almost 400,000 passengers.

As implied by these figures, many small operators were in service at any given time. Of the 176 passenger-carrying commuter air carriers registered with the CAB in 1976, 86 carried fewer than five thousand passengers that year. Assuming daily service, that amounted to only about fourteen passengers on the average day.

Similarly, a small number of routes accounted for a large proportion of the passengers. In 1976, just 25 of the 1,412 routes operated by commuter air carriers, or about 2 percent, accounted for 36.7 percent of the traffic. Four of the six busiest were in the Puerto Rico–Virgin Islands area, with San Juan–St. Thomas, dominated by Prinair, leading with about 350,000 passengers. The second-ranking route, also in Prinair's territory, connected Mayaguez and San Juan, two points in Puerto Rico. The third busiest route, and the leader within the contiguous United States, was Philadelphia-Washington, where Ransome was the largest carrier, with 166,000 passengers. The second highest-ranking continental route, and the sixth-ranked generally, was wholly within the greater Los Angeles metropolitan area, from Ontario to Los Angeles International Airport, with 131,000 passengers carried mainly by Golden West Airlines.

The four leading routes mentioned, incidentally, also illustrate the diversity of operations that now fell within the reach of commuter airlines. One was an interisland route, two were overland intercity routes, and one was an intracity route. All, however, had one common characteristic: they offered the advantages of speed and convenience over competing modes of transport.

Mail, cargo, and express traffic was also highly concentrated in a few companies. In 1976 the top five mail carriers handled about 44 percent of the traffic, led by Sedalia-Marshall-Boonville Stage Lines, with 14.5 percent of the total. The top five all-cargo airlines handled 56 percent of the freight. Federal Express, the first airline in the world to open a scheduled network devoted exclusively to the carriage of air express, was by far the largest in that category, accounting for fully 30 percent of the tons generated.

Further emphasizing the degree of operational concentration, in the mid-1970s about 77 percent of commuter airline routes were less than two hundred miles long, and most of the passengers traveled distances of about half that length. About three-quarters of the routes generated fewer than ten passengers per day. In contrast, at the same time 86 percent of local service airline routes were more than two hundred miles long, and 89 percent boarded more than ten passengers per day.

More Replacement Agreements

Early in 1974 the total number of CAB-approved replacement points, from certificated to commuter airlines, stood at fifty-three cities in twenty-one states, and commuter air carriers were providing 2,064 replacement flights per week. New agreements continued to be made, sometimes for the simultaneous transfer of several points. By 1976 commuter lines had replaced certificated airlines at sixty-five points.

The Allegheny Commuter network continued to maintain healthy growth, and in 1974 yearly ridership exceeded one million passengers for the first time, a level that persuaded Allegheny Airlines to appoint Robert A. Jenkins as Vice President–Allegheny Commuter Activities. His tasks were to select replacement airlines and to help in setting up operations. In 1974 Allegheny had agreements with twelve commuter lines, all under ten-year contracts. The concept continued to stress frequent schedules to convenient connections at Allegheny Airlines hubs, a strategy that allowed the commuter airlines to divert business effectively from their main competitor, the interstate highway system. A couple of these agreements had not worked out, but these were definitely exceptions to the rule. In 1978 the twelve Allegheny affiliates carried fully 17.8 percent of all U.S. commuter airline passengers.

The continued success of the Allegheny experiment can also be gauged by the fact that, by 1974, twenty-four of the twenty-five affected communities had generated more traffic after the commuter air carrier took over. In most cases traffic more than doubled, particularly because of the increased service frequency and the convenient timing of connecting flights.

Besides the routes serving these twenty-seven replacement communities, five Allegheny Commuter routes supplemented those of the parent firm. These tended to be short-haul segments between some of the largest cities on the northeast seaboard, such as from Philadelphia to Washington and to New York City.

Quite apart from the evidence of the statistical record, the Allegheny Commuter network (renamed USAir Express on 1 July 1989) consolidated the parent company's dominance of its catchment area, strengthening its grip on the market potential. It served as a model for others, as, fully a decade later, most of the trunk airlines indulged in a scramble for possession or control of those airlines not yet scooped up by the pioneering local service airline. Ironically, in the 1980s USAir lost some of its most important partners, including Ransome and Britt Airways. As is frequently the case, the groundbreakers were not always the ones that benefited most from their own innovations.

New Commuter Turboprops

All the new, larger commuter aircraft introduced in the last few years before airline deregulation were powered by turboprop engines, whose light weight added to the advantage of using relatively inexpensive kerosene rather than high-octane gasoline. The most important newcomers were the Swearingen Metroliner, the Nord 262 (and the related Mohawk 298), the Shorts SD-330, and the de Havilland Aircraft of Canada Dash 7.

Three new turboprop aircraft that entered service with the commuter airlines during the 1970s were (top) the Swearingen Metroliner, (center) the British Shorts SD-330, and (bottom) the de Havilland Aircraft of Canada Dash 7. (Collection of R. E. G. Davies.)

The first airplane to enter service after 1972 was the nineteen-seat Swearingen Metroliner, powered by two Garrett/AiResearch turboprop engines. The prototype first flew on 26 August 1969, and the Metro was certificated by the FAA in June 1970. With a cruising speed of more than 250 miles per hour and a pressurized cabin, it was especially well suited to companies that operated at high altitudes over long stage lengths. Although the cabin height was somewhat less than that found in most commuter aircraft in the same class, no other successful type was comparable in the three elements of speed, capacity, and comfort. The Swearingen Aircraft company encountered financial difficulties, however, thus setting back production, and it was left to Fairchild Industries to take over the project and restart production. The Metro was first placed into service by Commuter Airlines of Binghamton, New York, in March 1973. Although underpowered, it soon proved to be a valuable addition to commuter airline fleets, and after a rather slow start, it began to sell well.

The much improved Metro II was introduced in 1974. This version featured more advanced aircraft systems, full airline-standard instrumentation, larger windows, and an unusual jet-assisted takeoff unit for emergency power in case of engine failure during climbout. Powered by a pair of Garrett/AiResearch TPE-331 engines, each with 840 shaft horsepower, it had a cruising speed of just under three hundred miles per hour. The Metro II sold particularly well to airlines serving "hot and high" airports.

The twin-engined French turboprop, the pressurized twenty-six- to twenty-nine-seat Nord 262, with stand-up headroom and a lavatory, had won a design competition sponsored by the FAA and the Association of Local Transport Airlines for a feeder aircraft, back in the days when the need for the development of a "DC-3 replacement" was a popular theme. The prototype first flew in December 1962, and production models, powered by two 1,080-horsepower Turbomeca Bastan VI engines, entered U.S. service with Lake Central Airlines in 1965. This was, however, the only local service company ever to order the type, and the aircraft was not a big success, mainly because of a disappointing engine reliability record that resulted from the fact that it was underpowered and therefore always had to fly "flat out." It was also considered to be too small to be an effective DC-3 replacement.

When the thirty-seat limit was instituted in mid-1972, this aircraft seemed to be a good choice for some of the larger commuter airlines. Three 262s had, in fact, entered commuter service even before the new limit went into effect, under a CAB exemption authority granted in January 1972 to Ransome Airlines. Altair, one of the larger commuter air carriers, placed eight into service after 1972, and the Nord continued to serve the third-level airlines in limited numbers for many more useful years.

The Mohawk 298 (the name is derived from Part 298) was a modified Nord 262, developed by Allegheny Airlines for a network of commuter-type routes, where it replaced the larger Convair 580. The 298 was improved by replacing the original French Turbomecas with United Aircraft of Canada PT6A-45 turboprop engines. These provided greater speed and reduced fuel consumption. Nine aircraft were converted by Frakes Aviation of Texas for Allegheny, and the type was certificated by the FAA in October 1975. These nine, however, were the only 262s to be so converted.

Only one important new aircraft, the Shorts SD-330, was built in response to the CAB's enlarged Part 298 size limits. This boxlike, un-gainly-looking, but eminently practical aircraft, built by Short Brothers in Belfast, Northern Ireland, was an extensive thirty-seat modification of the earlier fifteen- to twenty-seat Skyvan. The industry affectionately remarked that the aircraft looked as if "they put wings on the box it came in." Powered by two 1,120-shaft-horsepower United Aircraft of Canada engines, the 330 cruised at about two hundred miles per hour. Equipped with thirty seats and a lavatory, the 6'6" cabin was high enough to allow adults to stand up. The Shorts SD-330 was not pres-surized, as the manufacturer believed that although commuter airlines and their clientele would have preferred this feature, the additional cost would have been excessive and neither the airline nor the customer would have been prepared to pay for it. The aircraft made its first flight on 22 August 1974, roughly two years after the Part 298 regulations were changed.

Command Airways of Poughkeepsie, New York, was the first to place the $1.4-million 330 into service in the United States, on 1 October 1976. The ugly duckling soon proved quite popular, as it customarily operated in areas of low elevation where pressurization was unimportant. It was designed to operate best on routes of up to about three hundred nautical miles, the essential decision having been made by the manufacturer to trade off additional range for maximum passenger capacity.

The largest aircraft to enter commuter airline service during this period was the de Havilland Aircraft of Canada DHC-7, or Dash 7, a pressurized fifty-seat, four-engined turboprop with short takeoff and landing (STOL) capability. Before airline deregulation, commuter air carriers needed CAB exemptions from the thirty-passenger limitation to operate an aircraft of this size, but the board was quite liberal in granting them. The prototype rolled out of the factory on 5 February 1975 and made its initial flight on 27 March. It first entered U.S. commercial service on 3 February 1978 with Rocky Mountain Airways. Eventually 114 Dash 7s were built, a comparatively modest output by the manufacturer's normal standards. They gained some popularity, particularly with the larger airlines whose traffic demand warranted the fifty-seat capacity. But the Dash 7's STOL capability was an expensive enhancement that was not a particular advantage for most companies, since the communities that could generate enough traffic to justify 50 seats were almost invariably served by modern airports with adequate runways. In addition, the STOL capability, by definition, implied excessive power, and this could not be reconciled with maximum cruising economy.

Several other fairly large twin-engined aircraft were used by the commuter airlines between 1973 and 1978. In 1973 Air South placed into service a twenty-one-seat Grumman Gulfstream, a modified version of the successful executive aircraft of that name, and the type was later used by a handful of other commuter airlines. This aircraft was even more overpowered in relation to its size than the Dash 7, and was more suited to the executive uses for which it was designed than for airline situations.

By the following year Air South was operating, under CAB exemption authority, three forty-passenger turboprop Fairchild F-27s, of the type already popular among the local service airlines. In October 1973, Air Illinois placed the Hawker Siddeley HS-748 into service. This forty-eight-seat twin turboprop aircraft was used on the busy route between Springfield, the state capital of Illinois, and Meigs Field in downtown Chicago. Because it operated only on intrastate flights, Air Illinois did not need a CAB exemption to use this aircraft. Other commuter operators of aircraft with more than thirty passenger seats included Pacific Airlines (Convair 240s), Marco Island Airways (Martin 4-0-4s), and Shawnee Airlines (F-27s).

Nevertheless, despite the increasing number of larger and apparently more attractive aircraft, the commuter airline fleets continued to be dominated by aircraft with nineteen or fewer seats. This was the partly because these did not require flight attendants, an additional expense that seemed to be superfluous in an operating environment in which few flights lasted more than an hour and most took much less time.

Commuter Airline Subsidies and Certification

In 1973 Air Midwest became the first commuter air carrier to receive federal subsidies when the company's proposal for a "flow-through" subsidy was approved and given a trial. As early as 1970 a CAB staff member had hinted at such a possibility when he said that the board was thinking about subsidizing commuter airlines indirectly through local service airlines, and that he could see no problem with viewing such support as a legitimate indirect expense of the certificated carrier.

Under this arrangement, a subsidy for replacement services at three western Kansas points continued to be paid to the certificated local service airline (Frontier), which, in turn, transferred or "flowed" the funds to the associated commuter airline. Thus Air Midwest could receive subsidies without the need for the prerequisite certification. The subsidy passed on to Air Midwest was substantially lower than that which Frontier had been receiving for these cities, and the innovation would thus appear to have been a wholly sensible experiment.

The CAB thought enough of this idea to authorize an experimental two-year program. Yet almost immediately it was challenged in the courts by the Air Line Pilots Association and the bus lobby, and just before the end of the two-year period the program was judged to be illegal. The courts reasoned that if direct subsidies to an uncertificated carrier were not allowed, then indirect subsidies, as in the flow-through program, were also illegal, as they were effectively an evasion of the law. This decision ended the eminently practical but apparently illegal flow-through experiment, but the need for commuter subsidies continued, and several years would pass before a solution to this problem was found.

Certification for the commuter airline industry, with full recognition by the CAB as a category of airline in its own right, remained an important issue. In 1973 the National Air Transportation Conferences had called for certification and route protection by the CAB. A bill to this effect was introduced into Congress by Representative Bob Wilson of California and co-sponsored by thirteen other congressmen as the Commuter Air Carrier Act of 1973. The act called for the "limited certification" of commuter airlines, a low-cost device that would give them such advantages as better access to interline agreements and the *OAG*. It would also make subsidies available and, it was claimed, give the industry "much needed identification," thereby making it easier to attract capital. The bill also offered limited route protection, which would keep commuter airline competitors off routes already served by other certif-icated commuter lines; it would not, however, protect the industry from competition by the certificated major airlines. Even though it was la-beled "limited," the foregoing description shows that the proposed bill was, in fact, fairly comprehensive.

As in earlier years, however, such proposed legislation did not get far, because the CAB, the Department of Transportation, and the executive branch were all firmly opposed to commuter certification. Coinciden-tally, and for different reasons, so were the large airlines and the Air Transport Association, which represented them.

A few commuter air carriers did achieve full CAB certification during this period. As mentioned earlier, the first was Air New England, one of the largest. In the early 1970s Delta Air Lines (which had acquired Northeast) and Allegheny Airlines (which had acquired Mohawk) were trying to abandon their small, unprofitable markets in New England. As a result, the CAB conducted its "New England Service Investigation." The board was not convinced that a network of several commuter air-lines would be a better choice than a single certificated airline, nor that the cost of certification would, in the long run, be disproportionate to the public benefit.

The CAB apparently was looking for a reasonable compromise. Air New England, the product of some delicate negotiations by Joe Whitney with concerned airline parties in the area, received a certificate, but not as a commuter airline. Rather, it became the first new local service company to be certificated since Ozark Airlines in 1950, and, in fact, proved to be the only commuter airline ever to be elevated to this status. But there were problems. As a certificated airline operating Fairchild FH-227s, Air New England had to operate under the FAA's more strin-gent Part 121 maintenance and operating regulations, and this compli-ance was costly. There were also questions about the quality of its management. In any event, the company was financially unsuccessful and went out of business in 1981.

The first company to be certificated as a commuter airline was Air Midwest. In this instance, Frontier Airlines was eager to abandon cer-tain small markets in Kansas and Colorado, and Air Midwest was inter-ested in taking them over. However, several routes were of such low traffic density that not even a commuter airline could earn an adequate income without subsidy. The flow-through experiment having been ruled illegal, Air Midwest decided that its only recourse was to seek certification. Late in 1976 its application was successful, and the CAB order in this case stated that Air Midwest was authorized to provide "regional feeder" service. The term "feeder" had to be included to make Air Midwest eligible, as the law was written, for the FAA's aircraft loan guarantee program.

Before the advent of deregulation, there were a few other cases of commuter airline certification. One was Cochise Airlines, formed in 1971, which served some unprofitable but isolated small points in Arizona. Early in 1978 Cochise was recommended for a certificate by a CAB law judge, and the airline received it soon thereafter. At about the same time, SkyWest Airlines of St. George, Utah, was also certificated. On 1 October 1978, Air Wisconsin began to operate under a subsidy-ineligible certificate as a "regional" airline, a term it preferred to "commuter." These companies could now benefit, among other things, from being listed as equals with the major airlines in the *OAG* and could negotiate joint fares with all other certificated airlines.

Joint Fares Proliferate

In the first half of the 1970s, the number of bilateral joint fare agreements between commuter and larger airlines increased rapidly. This change was partly the result of the increasing prestige that the commuter airlines were enjoying during this period. At first, Delta and Braniff were the most active trunk airlines in concluding such agreements, and by late 1974 Braniff alone had developed joint fares with eleven commuter lines. American, United, and TWA, which had been strongly opposed to such fares (even though American had pioneered the arrangement with Air Wisconsin in 1970; see Chapter 4), then began to relent. By 1978 joint fares had become so common that they no longer retained special status within the airline industry. In that year, for example, Golden West Airlines had such agreements with all the certificated companies serving Los Angeles International Airport.

For a commuter airline, obtaining a joint fare agreement with one large airline was often providential, for such an agreement could often be used as leverage to obtain additional joint fares with that company's competitors.

For some commuter airlines, however, this notable advance in obtaining selective joint fares was not enough. They lobbied instead for the regulators to mandate joint fares between them and the major airlines *on all routes*. However, such a step could be brought about only by Congress or, more likely, the CAB. This transformation of the industry was not achieved before airline deregulation was enacted into law in 1978.

Relations with the *Official Airline Guide*

Although most commuter airline schedules were now included in the *OAG*, the airlines' status within this publication—whose influence was so great that it was sometimes called air transportation's biggest marketing tool—remained a matter of considerable controversy. The fight for improved access was at first led by the Commuter Airline Association, a division of the National Air Transportation Associations, which had come into being in March 1974 through the merger of the National Air Transportation Conference and the National Aviation Trades Association (NATA).

One of the main points of contention was that the commuter airlines wished to list their interline connections (for trips involving an en route change of carrier) with certificated airlines. Except for Allegheny Commuter flights, only on-line commuter connections were printed at this time, and then only at the end of the city pair listings. As before, the industry ultimately wanted its flights (including connections) to be fully integrated with those of the larger airlines, and it even expressed a willingness to pay for such improved listings.

Yet the *OAG*'s publisher, the Reuben H. Donnelley Corporation, strongly resisted such pressure, stressing quite reasonably that because commuter airlines could (and often did) enter or leave a market at will, they were unreliable. The publisher also claimed that they lacked financial stability and had not been in business long enough to justify acceptance. Considering the industry as a whole, there was ample statistical evidence to support this view on all counts.

NATA asked for the CAB's help. Because the *OAG*'s major argument was that the commuter airlines were not required to maintain schedule reliability, NATA petitioned the CAB to publish schedule performance statistics. The publishers responded by asking the board to establish performance criteria for inclusion, so that purchasers of the guide could be guaranteed that what was printed in it was accurate. Because of the additional workload that such recordkeeping would entail, it was assumed that the CAB would not be likely to agree to this request. The commuter airlines also complained to the Federal Trade Commission, accusing the *OAG* of unfair trade practices. Finally, late in 1976 the airlines won a partial victory, as the publisher agreed to include single-plane and connecting schedules for commuter lines on a segregated basis, at the end of the city pair listings, while continuing to resist commuter airline pressure for other changes.

Formation of the Commuter Airline Association of America

In 1975 many commuter airlines, dissatisfied with the way their interests were being represented by the NATA, formed a new organization solely devoted to their interests. The Commuter Airline Association of America (CAAA) came into formal existence on 1 October 1975. The association was headquartered in Washington, D.C., and its first president was Thomas S. Miles, a man long associated with the industry. Within a few months the CAAA had more than a hundred members, and it soon became the main voice of the industry.

When first organized, it favored several changes to the way the industry was regulated, advocating commuter airline certification by the establishment of a separate class of CAB-certificated commuter carriers. It also favored new FAA operating regulations for the industry that were a compromise between Part 135 (for air taxi and commuter operators) and Part 121 (for certificated airlines).

On 6 January 1976, the CAAA met with the CAB and outlined a number of goals: equal status with the certificated airlines in the *OAG;* participation in the board's joint fare policy; regulation solely by the federal government (i.e., an end to economic regulation by states); and the encouragement of new aircraft development. It also wanted the government to make funds available for "commuter service airports," to find ways to reduce fuel costs, and to make it possible for commuter airlines to "become full participants in the nation's air transportation system at the earliest possible date." Some months later the organization was reported to be opposed to a proposed bidding system for awarding subsidies for small city service and to a possible fifty-five-seat limit for commuter airliners.

The First Fuel Crisis, 1973–1974

Late in 1973 the commuter airline industry was seriously affected by a problem entirely outside its control: the first fuel crisis of the 1970s, which lasted well into 1974. At this time several Arab nations, all members of the Organization of Petroleum Exporting Countries, cut off oil exports to the West, and fuel prices rose alarmingly. Geographically restricted though it was, the reverberations of this embargo throughout the world were alarming.

The fuel crisis was even more serious for the commuter lines than for the larger scheduled airlines, because the FAA still classified them as a segment of general aviation, and as such they could not buy fuel on long-term contracts or on a bulk basis. Without this cushion, fuel prices for the commuter airlines rose proportionately more than those for their certificated cousins. In many categories of general aviation (private, executive, or agricultural, for example), the operators simply reduced their work output. But the commuter airlines had an obligation to maintain public service and could not reduce or cancel flights without serious consequences to their reputations, or even their commercial viability. Because fuel always accounts for a considerable percentage of air transport direct operating costs, and because it is an especially large part of such costs on short-haul routes, this development had a major negative impact on the commuter airlines. For some of them, fuel purchases now represented more than 30 percent of their total operating costs, versus perhaps 15 percent before the crisis.

Despite the obvious cost problem, the fuel crisis had a positive economic impact on some segments of the airline industry. Because of the high price and reduced availability of gasoline, many highway business trips were diverted to the airlines. Thus, while the number of flights had to be cut, load factors often soared, and for some airlines the fuel crisis increased profitability. The ill wind from the Persian Gulf actually did bring some good.

Other Industry Developments

A good indicator of the growing importance of third-level airlines during the mid-1970s was that *Air Transport World,* perhaps the leading American aviation journal devoted solely to the airlines, named its first commuter airline editor, Danna K. Henderson. Regular monthly coverage began with the February 1976 issue.

During this period another local service airline began commuter-type services, starting them in conjunction with plans to retire its twin piston-engined Martin 4-0-4 aircraft. In a bold move to cut operating costs to small cities, Southern Airways ordered seven nineteen-seat Fairchild Metroliners, which began to replace the Martins in August 1977. The first four were used to provide Gadsden and Anniston, Alabama, and Athens and Moultrie-Thomasville, Georgia, with service to Atlanta. Later the Metros, which eventually numbered eight, were used to link small cities with Memphis and Nashville. But Southern experienced serious maintenance problems, and this program was discontinued in early 1980, at about the time when the airline merged with North Central Airliners to form Republic Airlines.

Allegheny Airlines also began to operate its own commuter division, as distinct from its long-standing policy of relying on commuter airlines to replace it at smaller points. For these operations, as mentioned earlier, it had ordered several Mohawk 298s, which began to be placed into service in November 1975. The first two were assigned to Williamsport, Pennsylvania, the base for Allegheny's commuter division, whence they provided service to Pittsburgh and Philadelphia. Later small aircraft operations were expanded to such cities as Bradford, Pennsylvania, and New Haven, Connecticut. Late in 1979 the company decided to cease these "Metro Express" services and to lease its Mohawk 298s to the two commuter airlines that would take over the routes.

Federal Express, under the leadership of Frederick W. Smith, Jr., began its all-cargo operations in April 1973. Smith had a new idea—rare in modern commercial aviation—and possessed the considerable financial resources to conduct the extensive tests necessary to prove its worth. He wanted to establish an overnight express package service, using a hub-and-spoke route system, centered on Little Rock, Arkansas, a point that is geographically quite central to the United States (although the idea was later actually implemented at Memphis, Tennessee). Smith based his plans on an idea tried by the postal authorities in India from 1949 to 1953. He would almost certainly have been unable to obtain a regular CAB certificate, that conservatively minded agency not being noted for supporting new ideas. Federal Express (or FedEx, as it came to be called) therefore started operations as an exempt all-cargo commuter airline and began to exploit a new field: exclusive overnight air express.

Initially FedEx used fanjet-powered Dassault Falcon 20s, aircraft that had originally been designed for executive use but that in this operation were modified with a strengthened floor, load restraining devices, and the addition of a large cargo door. The Falcon's payload was less than 7,500 pounds and thus qualified under the Part 298 exemption. FedEx later grew out of its commuter category and obtained a regular freight certificate, but the commuter airline exemption provided the opportunity by scheduled operations for it to establish itself beyond any doubt, so that the CAB had to face reality.

Fred Smith's airline is now recognized as one of the most successful firms to have been organized in the United States in the 1970s, and its new kind of service was soon copied by others. In due course, FedEx reversed a traditional trend. Air express, as a category of commercial load, grew at an astonishing rate, and on 1 August 1989 the company absorbed Flying Tigers, the largest and sole remaining scheduled air freight airline operating large equipment.

Effective on 1 December 1978, the FAA thoroughly revised its Part 135 regulations and in the process brought them more into line with CAB rules. Previously Part 135 rules had applied only to aircraft under the 12,500-pound gross takeoff weight limit. Now they applied to aircraft weighing more than 12,500 pounds but still under the thirty-seat or 7,500-pound payload limit. Commuter airlines were now required to establish continuous maintenance programs for all airplanes with ten or more passenger seats, and the aircraft had to be equipped with thunderstorm detection devices (radar). In the future, the pilot in command would almost invariably be required to have an air transport rating. A commercial license would no longer be enough. In effect, the new regulations imposed virtually the same maintenance, training, pilot proficiency, and equipment standards on commuter airlines operating aircraft with more than ten passenger seats as were required of the certificated airlines. These standards ensured that commuter airlines were subject to the same operational discipline and therefore as potentially safe as any other airlines—a status not always recognized by the press and public.

On the other hand, companies operating aircraft weighing more than 12,500 pounds, but still within the thirty-seat/7,500-pound limit, were no longer required to operate under the more intense and expensive Part 121 regulations of the larger airlines. With this change the FAA fell into line with the CAB in distinguishing between operators of large and small aircraft. The new Part 135 rules, in a rare case of unanimity, drew high praise from the commuters, the manufacturers, and the CAAA.

Chapter 6

Deregulation and Essential Air Service

The Airline Deregulation Act of 1978 was passed by Congress with wide bipartisan support. For those who had observed the industry for the many years during which little change had occurred, the enactment of this radical legislation was as revolutionary as it was unexpected, and the effect on the fortunes of some of the large airlines was devastating. When the act was signed into law by President Jimmy Carter on 24 October 1978, a new era in the history of the airlines of the United States began. Every aspect of the business was about to experience drastic changes, and deregulation even called for the eventual demise of the CAB itself.

The act had a profound impact on the American commuter airlines. The five years following its passage witnessed changes that were as far-reaching as any in the history of the industry. One result of the economic forces loosed by the legislation was that a second commuter airline boom occurred.

Several provisions of the act had a major impact. The permitted size limit of commuter aircraft was increased from thirty to fifty-five seats, and the maximum payload was increased from 7,500 pounds to 18,000 pounds. Companies whose entire fleets fell within these considerably expanded limits were not required to obtain a CAB certificate to enter the scheduled airline business, but they were, of course, still required to obtain an operating certificate from the FAA. This relaxation of the size regulations was an abrupt departure from precedent, bringing as it did a host of aircraft types in the forty- to fifty-seat class—from piston-engined Martins and Convair-Liners to the Rolls-Royce Dart–engined turboprops (F-27, BAe-748)—within the reach of the hitherto deprived commuter airlines.

In December 1979, the CAB further liberalized the passenger limit from fifty-five to sixty, a move specifically made to permit the sixty-seat

Japanese-built Nihon YS-11 turboprop to be used by the commuter airlines. This aircraft had previously been operated by airlines in east Asia and South America and by Piedmont Aviation and Hawaiian Airlines in the United States. The statutory freight payload limitation of 18,000 pounds remained unchanged.

Perhaps the most controversial part of the Airline Deregulation Act affecting commuter air carriers was the Essential Air Service (EAS) provision, under which all cities on the certificated airline networks at the date of enactment (including those where certificated service was "temporarily" suspended) were guaranteed air service for the next ten years, even if subsidy was necessary. This provision had been included primarily because of pressure from smaller communities that were naturally concerned about the possibility of losing their air service after deregulation—for the act made it much easier for certificated airlines to withdraw from less desirable cities and routes. The CAB was also directed to study the air traffic situation at all 137 cities that had been deleted from the certificated network since 1 July 1968, and to determine if they should be included in the EAS program.

The board was told to investigate those cities that might lose all service because of deregulation and to set a minimum level of service (the Essential Air Service) that should be guaranteed to them. It had one year within which to take this action. The CAB's review was to encompass 555 communities, of which 323 were in the contiguous United States and most of the rest were in Alaska; there were also a few communities in Hawaii, Puerto Rico, and U.S. overseas territories.

Under the formula devised by the CAB staff, the guaranteed minimum levels of service were expressed as a certain number of seats to be offered each day from the community to the nearest hub or, in a few cases, to two hubs. Although EAS procedures and the number of seats guaranteed to individual communities were subsequently modified, the basic principles of the guarantee have remained the same. When, on the last day of 1984, the CAB passed out of existence altogether, responsibility for the EAS program was transferred to the Department of Transportation (DOT).

An important related aspect of the new law was that certification was no longer required to qualify for subsidies. Under Section 419 (an amendment to the Federal Aviation Act of 1958), uncertificated commuter airlines became eligible, for the first time, for such aid. In a sharp change from earlier practice, subsidies were now to be awarded on the basis of competitive bids: the airline offering to provide an essential service for the lowest subsidy would be chosen as the official EAS carrier. It was further supposed (correctly) that at many cities airlines would offer to provide the essential service without subsidy. With this new procedure, the level of subsidies was predicted to decline substantially.

Because of the suitability of their small equipment, commuter airlines were expected to provide most of the services that were rated essential. In fact, by 1982, 91 percent of all points outside Alaska that were designated EAS cities were being served by commuter lines.

Several other aspects of the new law were worthy of note. In another departure from the earlier program, as set forth under Section 406 of the Federal Aviation Act of 1958, subsidies were now based on the needs of the communities involved, rather than on the financial needs of the airline serving them. There was a so-called "bumping provision," under which, after 1 January 1983, any carrier could file an application to replace an airline serving a city with EAS subsidies. The CAB decided that such an application would be granted only if the newcomer offered to provide the city or cities with substantially better service with the same level of subsidy, or the same service at a considerable reduction in subsidy. And, in a phrase familiar to airline veterans, before a commuter airline could be designated to supply EAS, it had to demonstrate to the CAB that it was "fit, willing, and able" to provide such service.

Under another provision of the law, uncertificated commuter airlines became eligible, for the first time, for aircraft loan guarantees, under which the federal government guaranteed that loans for aircraft purchases would be repaid to the banks. Because the airlines thereby gained the credit rating of the federal government, they could borrow money at very favorable interest rates. The regulations that applied to this program were published by the FAA in the *Federal Register* on 30 July 1979, and the first guarantee to a commuter airline was made in August of that year. During the first fiscal year in which commuter airlines were eligible for the guarantees, $50 million in guarantees was made available to the industry, and, for subsequent years, the amount was set at $100 million. The program was in effect for only a few years, however, and it was eliminated by Congress in mid-1983. The act also mandated the implementation of joint fares between commuter and certificated airlines, but this provision was strongly resisted by the major companies, as will be explained later.

Operating the Essential Air Service Program

Because the Airline Deregulation Act was not specific about many aspects of the EAS program, the CAB's staff worked hard for several months to establish procedures for its implementation. For example, Congress had specified only that the level of essential service would be no fewer than two round trips daily, five days per week, or the level of service in effect in 1977, whichever was less. The board thus had to address such additional basic questions as the definition of a reasonable level of essential service, the criteria to be used to measure community eligibility, how to process subsidy requests, and how to determine a fair level of subsidies. To help to answer such questions, the board held a series of regional meetings, which were also intended to inform the public about the program and to obtain the views of the communities involved.

In the meantime some major airlines had already filed to abandon service at certain cities, and the board found itself forced to make interim decisions about the level of service still required at these points and how to select replacement carriers. It also had to determine whether or not to require pressurized equipment and if cargo capacity should be considered a part of the EAS. Both of these questions were answered in the negative. In a move related to concerns about safety, an early decision was made to require two pilots on all aircraft.

As the conflicting interests of communities and commuter companies were frequently involved, such decisions could not be made without generating controversy. Some early decisions (such as those affecting Carlsbad and Hobbs, New Mexico), made in haste, created problems and were subsequently modified. Nevertheless, within a short time the CAB staff had the EAS program well in hand.

The level of air service determined essential by the board was based on historical data on the demand for air service and the traffic patterns in each community. The required service levels for each city were determined on a state-by-state basis. The first state figures, for Iowa, were issued on 17 September 1979. The other states and territories and Puerto Rico were then handled in quick succession. All this work was commendably carried out by a CAB staff of only thirty people.

For cities in the contiguous United States, the board usually called for at least two daily round trips (sometimes fewer on weekends) to a nearby hub, and occasionally for service to more than one hub. The number of seats required to be offered every day ranged from as few as six to as many as eighty each way. Eighty seats (at a 50 percent load factor) was the maximum because any city that enplaned more than forty passengers per day was assumed to be able to attract all the service it might require without subsidy. The actual service provided by the EAS carrier customarily exceeded the minimum required, because frequency of flights is a necessary element of successful short-haul air transport; indeed, in July 1981, 317 of the 323 EAS cities in the contiguous United States were receiving more service than the minimum levels guaranteed by the CAB.

As with all such subsidy-related matters, the EAS program increased the amount of CAB (later DOT) regulation of participating commuter airlines. This was an apparent paradox in an age of deregulation, but the age-old dictum of "he who pays the piper calls the tune" still held true. Specifically, service to EAS-designated cities could not be reduced below the essential level without due notice, and service could not be abandoned until a replacement carrier had been found. These conditions applied even if the EAS airline was a commuter carrier, and even if it was losing money. The board reasoned that the company had signed a contract to provide essential service and was bound by that contract, at least until a replacement could be found. Certificated airlines and commuter airlines receiving subsidies had to give at least ninety days' notice before reducing service below the EAS level, and unsubsidized commuter airlines that had been designated as EAS carriers had to give thirty days' notice. Taking advantage of their new freedoms under provisions that relaxed conditions of entry and egress, the certificated airlines applied to withdraw from smaller cities at an unprecedented rate soon after passage of the deregulation law, dropping service at 46 cities in the first year. This level compared to 172 cities (an average of 12 per year) that had lost their certificated service during the fourteen years since approval of the first suspension-substitution agreement in 1964.

The normal sequence of events was straightforward. When an airline announced that it would delete a city where it was providing the only certificated service, or if it wished to reduce service below the essential level, the CAB requested proposals from any company that was interested in providing the defined essential service, with detailed information as to how it would serve that point. The board then compared the various proposals and designated one company as the official EAS carrier; but if a replacement airline could not be found within ninety days, the incumbent certificated company was required to continue to serve that city. The airline was compensated, however, for any losses suffered

while continuing service beyond ninety days. If a commuter airline designated as the EAS carrier wanted to withdraw from that city at a later date,
it was also entitled to compensation if required to remain there for more
than ninety days if subsidized and more than thirty days if not subsidized.
Early in October 1979, the CAB was prolonging EAS service at twenty-six
cities, pending the appointment of suitable replacement airlines.

In some cases, the airlines were unanimous in refusing to serve a city
without subsidy. If the competing airlines were judged equally fit to
perform the service, the board normally chose the lowest bidder. When
they were not considered equal, it would make a judgment as to which
bid to accept based on other criteria. The lowest bidder was not always
chosen, especially if that company had no record of providing reliable
scheduled service.

The CAB occasionally erred in selecting a replacement carrier. A
notorious case involved Bakersfield, California, where Air Pacific was
chosen to replace United Air Lines on the route to San Francisco. Air
Pacific was able to meet its service obligation only on the first day, using
a fifty-seat de Havilland Aircraft of Canada Dash 7. During the next few
days the airline had to substitute a much smaller Twin Otter, because
"the carrier's only qualified Dash 7 captain had run out of flight time [for
the month]." Problems with replacement carriers continued for several
years at Bakersfield, involving a whole series of airlines. Eventually,
however, stable commuter airline service was achieved through code-
sharing affiliates of the major airlines (see Chapter 7).

Because of the rapid increase in the number of cities under this
program, subsidy payments to commuter airlines rose greatly after 1978.
By mid-1982, thirty-five companies were receiving subsidies to serve
about eighty cities. However, the government's airline subsidy bill as a
whole was decreasing, as commuter airlines with appropriately sized
equipment were taking over routes formerly served by local service
airlines. Federal subsidies, at $113.5 million for the fiscal year 1981,
decreased to $94.3 million in 1982. On 30 September 1983, the CAB's old
Section 406 subsidy program was terminated, and the companies still on
that program were transferred to the new program.

The Second Commuter Airline Boom

After deregulation, the commuter airlines experienced a sharp rise in
short-haul traffic between large metropolitan areas. This trend was
greatly accelerated by a second fuel crisis, early in 1979, which was a

deterrent to car drivers on intercity journeys because of inflated gasoline prices. The resulting steep fuel price increases made it expensive to use large aircraft on short hauls, where a significant proportion of the fuel consumption took place during taxiing, predeparture delays, and maneuvering, rather than actually flying between the cities. Consequently, certificated airline service frequencies on such important intercity routes as New York–Philadelphia and Chicago-Milwaukee (both about 100 miles) and Los Angeles–San Diego (120 miles) were cut sharply.

Commuter airlines moved in rapidly to fill this vacuum. Sometimes, as between Los Angeles and San Diego, far too many commuter seats were offered, and the glut of service resulted in low load factors and high financial losses. However, when the necessary adjustments were subsequently made, these routes proved to be an arena well suited to commuter airlines, where the new fifty-five- to sixty-seat aircraft size limits were appropriate.

The rapid increase in the number of EAS cities served by commuter airlines and their increasing relative importance in short-haul, high-density markets contributed to a substantial rise in commuter traffic after deregulation. Data published by the Regional Airline Association (RAA), the successor to the Commuter Airline association of America (CAAA) showed that the number of passengers enplaned rose from eleven million in 1978 to almost fourteen million in 1979, and then to almost fifteen million in 1980. In the first three years after passage of the act passenger enplanements grew by 34 percent, and cargo tonnage increased by 58 percent. Most of this increase was absorbed by existing companies, as the number of commuter airlines stabilized at an average of about 240 or so from 1978 into the early 1980s.

During the same period, the number of city pairs served by commuter airlines doubled to 3,000, and the aircraft fleet increased by almost 50 percent to about 1,750. Turbine-powered types accounted for close to 40 percent of the commuter fleet but about 70 percent of its seating capacity.

Traffic and network growth after deregulation was, in fact, so rapid that an aircraft shortage soon developed. Manufacturers were unable to cope with the demand, a sellers' market prevailed, and high prices were the inevitable outcome. This problem continued, to some degree, during the early 1980s.

CAB Certification and Fitness Hearings

Another way in which the new law led to increased regulation was that it required the CAB to determine the "fitness" of all commuter airlines.

New entrants were given priority in this process, as they were not allowed to enter the business at all until the board had determined that they were "fit, willing, and able" to do so. At these hearings the board examined the qualifications of the firm in terms of operations, credit-worthiness, and maintenance. Established commuter airlines could continue to operate, but as time went on they also had to submit to an examination for fitness, as CAB resources allowed. In 1983 the board completed its fitness hearings for these established companies. Formal certification of commuter airlines was still not required, but the fitness hearings were widely viewed as being so thorough that they amounted to almost the same thing.

The Airline Deregulation Act established a new way for commuter air carriers to become CAB-certificated. This involved the section of the law dealing with "dormant" routes, or routes that had been awarded to certificated airlines, but which they had declined to serve. On routes that had been dormant for at least six months, the CAB was authorized to issue the same type of certificate (a Section 401 certificate) under which trunk and local service airlines had been operating for many years to the first fit, willing, and able applicant. Many commuter airlines, including Golden West, Aspen, Mississippi Valley, and Colgan, obtained CAB certificates through this provision, and by mid-1980 twenty-nine commuter airlines had received Section 401 certificates.

Unfortunately for those wishing to carry out a strict statistical analysis, the CAB reports on commuter airline traffic did not include data for those airlines with Section 401 certificates. This is one reason why traffic data provided by the CAB and by the CAAA (or RAA) do not agree. The board was also not at all vigilant in collecting data from commuter airlines, and even some of the leading companies did not always bother to report quarterly traffic data. In the early 1980s, the CAB and the DOT finally began to enforce the requirement for commuter airlines to report their traffic data.

Certification and the fitness hearings helped to resolve the long-standing question of how commuter airlines would be listed in the *Official Airline Guide* (*OAG*). After seventeen years of disputes over policy, and five years in the courts, the *OAG* finally agreed that certificated commuter airlines and those the CAB had found fit would be listed on a nondiscriminatory basis, and the first such integrated listing was included in the 1 June 1981 issue. These carriers were required to adhere to their published schedules, and to change them only if the *OAG* had enough lead time (several months) to keep the publication accurate.

Thus, after many years of campaigning, the commuter airlines had finally achieved their long-sought legitimacy in the vital world of travel agencies—for which the *OAG* was the equivalent of the Authorized Version of the Bible.

Mandatory Joint Fares Are Resisted

One feature of the Airline Deregulation Act of 1978 proved to be especially unpopular with the trunk and local service airlines. This was the provision that specifically required joint fares with the commuter airlines, using the formula for the division of revenues that had been devised some years earlier by the CAB. This formula had favored the short-haul carriers, the local service airlines, and was often seen as a form of indirect subsidy to them.

The board made this part of the deregulation act effective on 22 January 1979, but it was concerned about the "inequitable division of revenue" involved. Thus the law stated that the CAB could allow this provision to expire on 1 January 1983 if it thought such an action was appropriate.

The certificated airlines pointed out that this provision was contrary to the whole spirit of deregulation. They argued that joint fare agreements should instead be concluded on the basis of voluntary negotiations between the affected airlines. Many CAB staff members also remained skeptical of the wisdom of the law. They pointed out that, in the then highly competitive air travel environment, it was doubtful that the larger airlines would be in any position to subsidize their commuter traffic feeders. Such was the level of concern that the CAB issued a proposal to eliminate all mandatory joint fares as of 22 January 1980. This was not implemented, but in February of that year the board granted a partial exemption from the joint fare formula to twelve airlines, ten of which were trunk carriers, allowing the division of fares to be made on the basis of voluntary agreements between the parties.

On 8 August 1980, American Airlines petitioned the board to eliminate all of the deregulation requirement for mandatory joint fares. American felt that, in the new deregulated environment, commuter airlines should have to bargain for such rates, and that it should offer them only when they benefited American. The CAB denied the petition.

These actions were followed by much discussion on joint fares among the commuter airlines, the CAB, and the large trunk line operators. The latter remained of the opinion that such joint fares should be based solely on the self-interests of the parties involved. This line of reasoning must have been convincing, because mandatory joint fares were eventually eliminated.

New Commuter Aircraft

With the second air commuter boom in full swing, manufacturers once again began to develop new aircraft for the industry. Three engine manufacturers were also working on new power plants, especially for several models in the thirty- to forty-seat capacity range, slated to fly in the mid-1980s, that would need turboprop engines with between 1,500 and 2,000 shaft horsepower.

In the United States, Beech produced the Beech C99, a modification of the earlier 99 model, with fifteen seats and more powerful engines, but retaining the unpressurized cabin of its forebear. The first deliveries, on 31 July 1981, were to Christman Air System of Pennsylvania and Sunbird Airlines of North Carolina. The market for this new $1.5-million aircraft fell short of expectations, however, and production was halted in 1986, after 76 C99s had been built.

Fairchild produced a new version of the Metro, the nineteen-seat Metro III. It featured more powerful engines, a wider wingspan, four-bladed propellers (which improved its performance in both range and capacity), and a modified landing gear. As had its predecessors, the Metro III sold well, and the Metro in all versions was the most common type of turbine-powered aircraft used by U.S. commuter airlines in 1982, with 153 aircraft accounting for 14.3 percent of the industry's seats.

With demand for aircraft rising rapidly, Piper also reentered the field and announced the production of two new models: the piston-powered T-1020, successor to the Navajo Chieftain, and the turboprop-powered T-1040, successor to the Cheyenne that retained the fuselage of the earlier craft. Neither model sold well, perhaps because both aircraft had only nine passenger seats and post-deregulation commuter airlines were seeking larger aircraft in response to their many new business opportunities. Another problem was that spare parts for Piper aircraft—and this applied also to those made by Beech—were reputedly difficult to obtain. As a matter of record, in 1982 the Piper Navajo and the Cessna 402 were still the most numerous types in commuter airline service, with 167 and

One turboprop aircraft from Beech was the Beech 99, which was faster than the Twin Otter and had greater range but fewer seats (fifteen versus nineteen). (Photo courtesy of the Roger Bentley collection.)

177, respectively. However, given their small size, each accounted for only about 3 percent of the industry's total seating capacity.

The United Kingdom produced two successful new commuter airliners. One was the unpressurized Shorts SD-360, a larger and improved version of the 330, with thirty-six seats and two uprated PT6A-65R engines, each capable of 1,424 horsepower. This aircraft, launched in mid-1980, was technically and aesthetically more satisfactory than the earlier box-shaped model, and it sold quite well.

The second contender was the British Aerospace Jetstream 31, a greatly improved nineteen-seat version of the Handley Page Jetstream of the late 1960s. With many desirable features, including pressurization, stand-up headroom, and two 940-horsepower Garrett/AiReseach TPE331-10 turboprops, it first flew on 18 March 1982 and received its FAA certificate on 30 November of that year. The initial U.S. customer was Atlantis Airlines of Florence, South Carolina, which received its first aircraft in July 1983. The Jetstream 31 sold very well in the United States, proving to be especially popular among the large commuter airlines. One reason why it was so successful is that it was the only nineteen-seat aircraft with stand-up headroom. Another factor contributing to its success was the generous financial terms offered by British Aerospace.

In 1979 the eighteen- to nineteen-seat, 230-mile-per-hour Embraer EMB-110 Bandeirante, powered by two 750-horsepower PT6A-34 engines, was introduced in the United States. This Brazilian-built aircraft

Whereas Canadian types such as the DHC-6 Twin Otter and the Dash 7 were local imports from just across the Canadian border, foreign aircraft from overseas became popular during the early 1980s. One such success from the Embraer factory in Brazil was the EMB-110 Bandeirante. (Collection of R. E. G. Davies.)

An unusual aircraft, seen occasionally in the 1980s, was the Australian-built GAF Nomad. This one was operated by Skybus Express in Alabama. (Photo courtesy of the Roger Bentley collection.)

Typical of the larger twin-engined turboprops was the Convair 580, previously piston-engined, but rejuvenated with Allison turboprop engines.

had been in service in South America and elsewhere for many years. Popularly called the Bandit (although "Bandeirante" in Portuguese actually means pioneer), it first flew in the United States early in 1979, for Wyoming Airlines, and proved very popular, so that by 1982 it was already the fourth leading type in commuter airline service, accounting for 8.5 percent of total seats offered.

Two other foreign-built aircraft were used by commuter airlines of the period, but neither was imported in large numbers. The Australian-built twelve- to eighteen-seat Government Aircraft Factories Nomad first flew in 1971 and was introduced to the United States in mid-1979 at the Reading Air Show. Another newcomer was the Spanish CASA C-212, a twenty-six-seater. Both turboprop types were used by only a handful of U.S. operators, with the C-212 the more successful of the two.

A few forty- to fifty-seat turboprop airliners, formerly used widely by the local service airlines, now began to find their way into the commuter ranks in increasing numbers, as the more liberal size regulations permitted the use of several types that had previously been disqualified. These included the turboprop versions of the veteran Convair-Liners, the 580, 600, and 640 series, accounting for 7.4 percent of commuter passenger capacity in 1982, as well as Fokker and Fairchild F-27s and Fairchild FH-227s, accounting for close to 6 percent.

Strengthening Relations between the
Commuter Airlines and Larger Airlines

Before 1978 and the Airline Deregulation Act, and with the notable exception of the Allegheny Commuters, third-level airlines normally worked closely with any local service, trunk, or international carrier that showed an interest. They were impartial in their choice of partners and acted as neutral feeders to any airline that was prepared to cooperate with them, however informally. After deregulation, however, much closer and more rigidly controlled relationships began to develop, with one commuter airline acting primarily or exclusively as a feeder for a single trunk or local service airline. In time this was to become the standard pattern, and such was the nature of the change that the members of a once proudly independent industry became little more than surrogates for the major airlines at small and medium-sized cities.

The first example of this new development, in 1980, involved rapidly expanding Air Florida. In a major policy decision, this company arranged for Air Miami to provide substitute "Air Florida Commuter" service, starting on 26 October, in a few small Florida markets. All of these routes had formerly been flown by Air Florida Douglas DC-9s and Boeing 737s and evidently had lost money because those craft were too big for the traffic demand. Air Miami operated twenty-six-seat CASA C-212s and fifteen-seat de Havilland DH-114 Herons. Initial service was to Ft. Myers, Miami, Marathon, and Tampa, and additional contracts were signed later with other commuter airlines. These contracts generated a good deal of controversy and will be discussed in more detail in the following chapter.

A less contentious early example of a strong relationship between a commuter airline and a major carrier involved Bar Harbor Airlines, based in Maine. Bar Harbor agreed to a close working relationship with Eastern Air Lines and to act primarily as its feeder. Some of the benefits of the relationship for Bar Harbor included lower fuel costs through access to Eastern's bulk rates, lower communications charges, and, most important, access to Eastern's computer reservations system. The last item led almost instantly to a substantial traffic increase for Bar Harbor. The ability to work in conjunction with Eastern's low discount fares also led to an increase in discretionary travel, to balance Bar Harbor's traditional reliance on business travel. Furthermore, Eastern guaranteed certain loans for the purchase of a few aircraft and provided free handling for Bar Harbor at Boston and New York's La Guardia airport. The arrangement did not, however, involve the use of Eastern's two-letter reservation code, nor were the aircraft painted in Eastern's colors.

On 1 June 1982, Ransome Airlines left the Allegheny Commuter system to become independent and moved toward a close working relationship with Delta Air Lines that included a renewable five-year agreement that admitted Ransome to the larger airline's reservation system. J. Dawson Ransome had long chafed under USAir's (formerly Allegheny Airlines) restrictions on its associated commuters, including the requirement that each new route had to be approved by the parent firm and that Ransome was not allowed to fly any route being served by USAir, no matter how poor the service. His was to be but the first of several commuter airlines that would leave the Allegheny Commuter system over the next few years, as explained in the next chapter.

Some Airlines Desert the Ranks

After deregulation, several commuter airlines decided to purchase aircraft with more than sixty seats, thereby leaving the commuter ranks and accepting the regulatory disadvantages of such a move in the interests of widened operational horizons. Empire Airlines of Utica, New York, and Altair Airlines of Philadelphia both ordered eighty-five-seat, twin-jet Fokker F-28s in the fall of 1979. Later Altair also decided to add DC-9s to its fleet, but it outgrew its strength by expanding and changing

An eighty-six-seat (some versions had more seats) British four-engined airliner, the British Aerospace BAe-146, came into service with a few of the larger commuter airlines in the early 1980s. (Photo courtesy of British Aerospace.)

its route network too quickly and went out of business in late 1982. Empire was more successful, operating the F-28s in partnership with its Fairchild Metros until it was purchased by Piedmont Aviation in 1985.

Other commuter air carriers that operated large equipment included Air Illinois, which ordered one BAC One-Eleven in 1982 to provide service from Chicago to Springfield, Decatur, and Champaign-Urbana in Illinois and to Evansville in Indiana. Early in 1983 Air Wisconsin received the first of several new 109-seat British Aerospace BAe-146s. After starting 146 service on 27 June of that year, Air Wisconsin ceased to be classified as a commuter airline, as the term is used in this book.

Safety, a Controllers' Strike, and Other Developments

Several other developments, of a widely varying nature, affected the commuter airline industry in the first few years after deregulation. These included the introduction of area navigation, the disruption caused by the air traffic controllers' strike of 1981, continued concerns over commuter airline safety, and even a somewhat controversial new name for the industry.

On 26 November 1980, Ransome Airlines began to use a three-dimensional area navigation system between Philadelphia and Washington's National Airport. This was the first instance of the employment of such technology in regular airline service, and it allowed the company's flights to follow a more direct path, saving twenty miles between airports, than did the conventional navigation systems. It also permitted flights to be made at lower than conventional altitudes, and so independently of the flow of larger aircraft operated by trunk and local service airlines, thus avoiding potentially costly delays. In effect, area navigation expanded airspace capacity. Used in conjunction with a microwave landing system, area navigation enabled Ransome's Dash 7s, with their short takeoff and landing capability, to use a portion of the cross runway (that between the threshold and the intersection with the main runway), thus freeing additional operating slots and avoiding delays at National Airport, which was often crowded to its saturation point at busy times. All of Ransome's Dash 7s were equipped to operate in this way.

The long-standing public debate over commuter airline safety continued in full force during the late 1970s and early 1980s. Once again, much to the industry's chagrin, well-publicized charges of poor safety standards had some validity for a few airlines. In 1979, for example, National Transportation Safety Board (NTSB) chairman James B. King announced that his board had found "examples of sleazy to nonexistent maintenance, weight and balance problems, and inadequate training for pilots." He added that investigations of recent accidents had found the recurrent themes of "deficient management and disregard for federal safety regulations." In the previous year, King claimed, commuter air carriers had had an accident rate more than six times higher than that of the certificated airlines.

Yet some allowance should have been made in passing such harsh judgments. Although there were some breaches of discipline, these were, as a rule, isolated cases. Indeed, following the imposition of tighter controls by the FAA, many such breaches were revealed in all strata of U.S. airline operations, not just at the commuter level. In fact, with considerable justification, the commuter airline industry has often complained of a double standard, in which its members have frequently been grounded by the FAA for the very same offenses that only led to fines, or even only a few words of reprimand, for the larger airlines.

The commuter safety issue continued to boil into 1980. By March this topic had been the subject of a two-day FAA symposium, a four-day NTSB hearing, and a hearing before the oversight subcommittee of the House Ways and Means Committee. In response to the increased level of concern, the FAA issued an emergency regulation to raise the time-in-type required for pilots. It also began to monitor commuter airline practices more closely. Some serious problems were found, and a few airlines were grounded; several subsequently went out of business. Given the perceived double standard, the commuter airline industry saw itself as an easy target for the FAA's politically motivated need to impress the public with its new "get tough" attitude.

Nevertheless, criticism of commuter airline safety continued. The general implication of much of this discussion was that commuter airlines should have as good a safety record as the major companies. However, given the more difficult operating environment of the commuter airlines, including their large numbers of takeoffs and landings on short-haul flights and the fact that 70 percent of commuter airports lacked sophisticated approach and landing aids, this goal was almost impossible to achieve. Almost by definition, the "third-level" airlines had to operate into many airfields and under conditions that were themselves arguably "third level." Offering a higher standard of service would have required, first of all, a significant improvement in the fields themselves. In the face of tighter regulation, costs would have soared, discussions on subsidy would have followed, and arguments would have raged over who was to pay for the higher standards demanded, not to mention the cost of upgrading the airports or of removing obstructions. Inevitably, some airlines would have had to withdraw service altogether. Finally, the safety issue was not helped by the rapidly increasing number of commuter pilots who were being hired by the major airlines, to be replaced by less experienced personnel.

In August 1981, the nation's air traffic controllers called a strike to seek better work rules and better pay, and thus greatly disrupted the operations of all U.S. airlines. This action was quickly followed by President Ronald Reagan's unprecedented decision to fire all the strikers. The unfortunate controllers, upon whom so much responsibility rested, received no support from anyone, least of all from the pilots, whom they had served so well. Because of the length of time required to train new controllers, the impact of the strike was to be felt for years. In the short run, it led to many canceled flights and delays. The commuter companies were hit especially hard, for the delays involved—often because of the imposition of flow control, under which the FAA held an aircraft on the ground until another airplane had left the air traffic system and thereby made space available—often doubled or tripled the time required to make short-haul flights. Although the most drastic impact was in some places ameliorated in a matter of weeks or months, the longer-term impact in decreased system capacity at certain locations (such as Chicago's O'Hare Airport) and in other operational limitations (such as area control and supervision) continued for years. The nation as a whole—not to mention the president—could count itself lucky that the airlines survived this period of reduced air traffic control without a major disaster.

About two years after the advent of deregulation, on 2 October 1980, the CAB changed the way in which it classified U.S. airlines. The old system of trunk, local service, and commuter (as well as other categories such as all-cargo and supplemental) airlines had been developed according to the functions of the carriers. As the scheduled airlines emerged from World War II, the different categories had been based on geographic function and reflected such criteria as the size of cities served, the length of routes, and the type and size of equipment operated. This last element, in fact, had been the basis for distinguishing between commuter and other airlines for many years. A commuter airline could not be considered as such if it normally operated aircraft larger than a certain size.

The new classification system was based strictly on the gross yearly revenue generated by the companies. The largest new airline category, the majors, included companies that grossed more than $1 billion per year. The list of majors at first corresponded closely to that of the earlier trunk airlines, although today it includes some newcomers, promoted from the minor leagues. Airlines that grossed between $75 million and $1 billion per year, the nationals, corresponded more loosely to the former local service, intrastate, territorial, supplemental, and all-cargo airlines. Finally, regional airlines were those that grossed less than $75 million per year. This category included most of the former commuter airlines, together with some small post-deregulation companies that operated large equipment, such as DC-9s. This regional category, in turn, was divided into large and small regionals, with $10 million in revenue as the separation point.

For commuter airlines, the new regional category was far less satisfactory than the older, functional definition. At its annual meeting in 1981, the CAAA voted only with considerable dissension to change its name to the Regional Airline Association. It was felt at the time that, despite great efforts to make the term "commuter airline" acceptable, its public image had become too negative and that a change was justified. Nevertheless, the name "commuter" continues to be widely used to this day by the public and the airline industry alike, although the term "regional" is now used loosely to describe almost any airline that does not fly coast to coast. In this book, the *functions* of the commuter airlines, irrespective of the CAB classification, have been adopted as the qualification for inclusion.

Chapter 7

The Code-Sharing Revolution

The mid- and late 1980s witnessed a continuation of many long-standing trends within the commuter airline industry. With the greater freedoms granted by deregulation, allowing larger airlines to leave many markets and stimulating competition and thereby market demand, passenger traffic increased sharply. This expansion was given fresh impetus by the introduction of several technically advanced airliners, most with between thirty and fifty seats. These aircraft were the first to be designed specifically for the commuter airlines, and they brought about a revolution in the industry. In contrast with earlier aircraft, which were usually modified corporate models, these newcomers were built to airliner standards to withstand the rigors of two thousand or more hours of utilization per year. With their greater size, more plentiful passenger amenities, and high dispatch reliability, they contributed substantially to the growth and improved image of the commuter airline industry.

The route network also grew rapidly. In 1986 this intricate web contained close to 155,000 route-miles in the contiguous United States, compared with 83,000 at the time of deregulation in 1978. Yet even this high figure understates the tremendous expansion that had taken place, for many routes were served by more than one commuter airline, a rare occurrence in 1978. Every large metropolitan area now had an array of feeder routes radiating in all directions, and not surprisingly, those cities used as hubs by the major airlines were especially prominent. Comparison with the 1978 map emphasizes dramatically the spectacular growth of commuter airlines and their inevitable influence upon the air traveling habits of the public. By the early 1990s commuter airlines served more than 850 cities, or more than the major and national airlines combined, reaching almost every corner of the nation.

Passenger traffic continued to grow impressively throughout the 1980s and into the 1990s. According to the Regional Airline Association

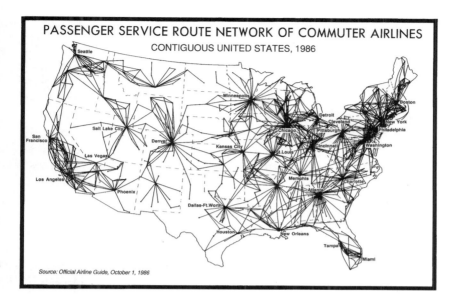

PASSENGER SERVICE ROUTE NETWORK OF COMMUTER AIRLINES
CONTIGUOUS UNITED STATES, 1986

Source: Official Airline Guide, October 1, 1986

(RAA), ridership increased from twenty-four million in 1984 to thirty-eight million in 1990. By the latter year, about 10 percent of passengers on major airlines connected to or from the commuter lines. The same years, however, saw the number of companies decline from 203 to 159. The industry was dominated, more than ever, by relatively few large firms; in 1988, for example, the fifty largest commuter airlines handled 95 percent of the traffic, whereas the sixty-three smallest had a mere 1 percent.

Background to Code-Sharing

The most far-reaching development during these years was the rapid diffusion of a practice that quickly and appropriately became known as code-sharing. Although not totally new to the industry, code-sharing had been rare before 1984. In the two years 1984–1985, however, it spread throughout the industry.

Superficially, code-sharing is a simple and apparently benign practice that would hardly seem to qualify as the catalyst for major changes for an entire industry. Code-sharing commuter airline flights are listed in the *Official Airline Guide* (*OAG*) and in computer reservation systems under the two-letter code of the major carrier with which the commuter airline is affiliated. This juxtaposition can give the impression that the whole air journey, including a short connecting flight, can be made on the major company's aircraft. Because most passengers prefer not to have to change airlines en route, access to and use of a major airline's code can thus give an affiliated commuter airline a significant competitive advantage. When this practice was combined with a CAB decision in November 1984 on how connecting flights were to be listed in computer reservation systems (as explained later in this chapter) and with preferential joint fares, the code-sharers' advantages were such that it was almost impossible for an independent commuter airline to compete. Therefore, the diffusion of code-sharing soon led to some fundamental changes in the industry.

To a limited extent, code-sharing had been practiced for many years. The first code-sharers were the Allegheny Commuters (see Chapters 3 and 4), which had been listed under the AL code since the first agreement with Allegheny Airlines in 1967. Allegheny Commuter flights were conspicuously marked in the *OAG* and in computer reservation systems as actually operated by commuter affiliates.

In October 1980, over a dozen years after Leslie O. Barnes first had the idea, code-sharing began to spread beyond the Allegheny Commuter network when Air Florida arranged for Air Miami, an air charter firm, to fly some of its low-traffic-density routes (see Chapter 6). The aircraft were painted in Air Florida colors and carried the "Air Florida Commuter" insignia. Unlike the Allegheny system, however, this arrangement no longer needed CAB approval, in the wake of airline deregulation in 1978. Perhaps to avoid possible legal problems, Air Florida wet-leased the CASA C-212 fleet (i.e., hired the crew as well as the aircraft), paying Air Miami a flat rate per trip regardless of the number of passengers carried. Much more controversially, the commuter flights were now listed in the *OAG* and in computer reservation systems under Air Florida's two-letter code, as if they were Air Florida flights.

Competing airlines claimed that this practice misled the public into thinking it would be taking an Air Florida flight in a jet, and that therefore such code-sharing constituted unfair competition. But they did not take the matter to the CAB, nor to the courts.

In February 1981, Air Florida entered into a second code-sharing contract, this time with Florida Airlines, for services to several cities. In the next few years additional contracts were made, with the airlines participating in the Air Florida Commuter system constantly changing. Early in 1984, for example, there were arrangements with Finair Express, Skyways of Ocala, and Gull Air. As Air Florida's financial health was deteriorating and as the affiliates were not strong competitors, these contracts did not severely affect rival commuter airlines. The threat of possible litigation never materialized, and the Air Florida commuter network was disbanded in May 1984.

In the last half of 1982 Pan American World Airways also made agreements to share its code with two airlines flying to some of its main international hubs. Pan Am wished simply to increase the number of domestic flights making convenient connections. The two earliest fixed-wing Pan Am code-sharers were Emerald Airlines in Texas and Empire Airlines in New York state, and others were added later. Certain flights of these airlines were listed in computer reservation systems and in the *OAG* under the designators of both Pan American and the affiliated firms. Although Emerald and Empire operated some commuter-sized aircraft, they also operated larger equipment and therefore did not strictly qualify as commuter airlines under the contemporary official definition. The other fixed-wing code-sharers operated only jet equipment.

The earliest use of code-sharing between major and commuter airlines, in the general pattern that would become standard, began in Houston late in 1983. Starting with the 15 September issue of the *OAG*, Royale Airlines' flights to that hub were listed under the CO code of Continental Airlines, and on 1 October Metro Airlines' flights to the same city began to use Eastern Airlines' EA designator. At this time, however, neither Metro nor Royale adopted the larger companies' color schemes or names.

On 17 October 1983, Combs Airways began to use Frontier Airlines' FL code, operating under Frontier Commuter signage and leasing nine of the larger company's Convair 580s without changing the color scheme. Frontier Commuter had been formed to feed traffic to the Denver hub from smaller cities that had been served by Frontier before deregulation, with initial service to Cheyenne, Laramie, Riverton, Rock Springs, and Montrose.

Late in 1983, in another precedent-setting move, Piedmont Aviation became the first large company to buy—as opposed to making an arrangement with—a commuter airline. It purchased one of the pioneer scheduled air taxi companies, Henson Aviation. Henson was highly respected by its peers, and it had been the original Allegheny Commuter. The owner, Dick Henson, agreed to sell his company to Piedmont, thus severing his relationship with USAir's Allegheny Commuter network. On 30 October 1983, the renamed Henson Airlines started to operate under Piedmont's PI designator. The company also adopted the Piedmont color scheme and began to call itself "The Piedmont Regional Airline."

From Piedmont's perspective, this arrangement had several advantages. Most important, it was a way to establish a stable feeder network and to maintain total, rather than partial, control. Henson's network was soon reoriented, notably to feed into Piedmont's expanding hub at Baltimore, and rapid expansion followed, northward as far as Vermont and southward to Georgia and Florida, as the direct result of the reorganized system. Curiously, USAir later bought Piedmont and thereby regained control over the Henson network, now almost unrecognizable from its original Allegheny Commuter shape and stature.

Life or Death with Code-Sharing

The preceding examples were the background to a general diffusion of code-sharing that gained momentum in 1984. The first agreement implemented that year was between Eastern and Metro Airlines and involved a feeder network for Eastern's hub at Atlanta. Under this ten-year contract, Metro established a subsidiary operation around Atlanta under the title Eastern Metro Express, using the Eastern Airlines color scheme and the EA code. Eastern Metro Express ordered new equipment, nineteen-seat British Aerospace Jetstream 31s, and began service on 2 April 1984.

From the start, this service was highly successful, and even Eastern was surprised at its rate of growth, from 7,000 passengers in April 1984 to 30,000 in March 1985. This success was highly publicized, and the operation was inevitably copied. In its breadth and scope, Eastern Metro Express may be considered the refined model of the code-sharing practice that quickly spread through most of the industry. It was also the first example of what was later occasionally called "create-a-feed," a practice by which a wholly new commuter airline was formed specifically to feed traffic to a major company at a hub. Other examples of this practice included Phoenix Airline Services starting a Republic Express feeder at Memphis, Air Midwest organizing an American Eagle network at Nashville, and WestAir (doing business as NPA, Inc.) starting a United Express airline in the Pacific Northwest.

Only one month later, on 1 May 1984, Delta Air Lines implemented a code-sharing agreement with Atlantic Southeast Airlines, which served the same Atlanta hub as Delta. Given the advantages of code-sharing, this response to the Eastern initiative was inevitable, for otherwise

Delta would have lost much feeder traffic to its competitor. A month later, on 1 June Delta also implemented such arrangements with Ransome Airlines to provide connecting traffic at the Philadelphia hub and with Rio Airways at Dallas–Ft. Worth. Delta did not (and still does not) require its Delta Connection affiliates to use the Delta color scheme or its name, although most other code-sharing agreements include such provisions.

As code-sharing spread, the CAB began to hear from parties as diverse as the giant United Airlines and the commuter airline Britt Airways, all objecting strongly to the practice. Early in 1984 the board ruled that United had to continue to show code-sharing connections in its Apollo reservation system, pending an investigation. That company had threatened to remove them, saying the practice led to the listing of single-carrier connections that actually did not exist. At about the same time, thirteen commuter airlines (including Britt, Provincetown-Boston Airlines, Horizon Air, Imperial Airlines, and Sun Aire) jointly filed a motion asking the CAB to halt this "biased and deceptive" practice. They claimed that code-sharing's objective was to deceive passengers into thinking they would be traveling on a single carrier for the whole trip. They wanted the board to rule that the commuter airlines' own designator had to be used.

One well-known objector was John C. Van Arsdale, founder of the pioneer Provincetown-Boston Airline (see Chapter 1). He echoed the widespread opinion that commuter code-sharers were representing themselves to the public as something they were not—a major airline—stating the following in a letter to the CAB on 3 March 1984: "I strongly believe that unless the Board takes a strong position against the continued franchising of commuters, we will see the demise of the independent commuter, the free enterprise system in our industry, and competition among commuter airlines." Prophetic though some of these words were, the board listened but did nothing to stop the practice, saying only, in the tradition of bureaucracies everywhere, that it would study the question further.

This highly controversial topic came up for discussion at the 1984 spring meeting of the RAA, which voted to condone code-sharing. The members were sharply divided on the issue, however, and the vote led to a deep rift within the organization.

Even as the controversy continued, several more airlines followed the trend. In October 1984, three major carriers, American Airlines, Northwest Airlines, and Republic Airlines, announced that they soon would begin code-sharing. American began to work with its first American Eagle partner, Metro Airlines, at its Dallas–Ft. Worth hub on 1 November. Metro, which was also using the Eastern code at Atlanta and Houston, thereby became the first commuter company to share codes with more than one major airline. The benefits of the new arrangement became almost instantly apparent, as Metro's traffic increased dramatically. A second American Eagle affiliate, Chaparral Airlines, began to feed traffic to Dallas–Ft. Worth from several additional cities in December. As American was such an important airline, this action led some observers to doubt if code-sharing could now be stopped and to become concerned about the future of the independent commuter airlines— even about the future of the industry itself.

On 1 December 1984, Mesaba Airlines became the first Northwest Orient Airlink partner, providing connections at the Minneapolis–St. Paul airport. Republic's feeder services began in 1985. The first of these was with Simmons Airlines, and in the process Republic purchased a 9 percent interest in this affiliate. A new airline in the "create-a-feed" mold of Eastern Metro Express, Republic Express, began to serve the Memphis hub on 31 May 1985. Later, Republic itself was to be absorbed by Northwest Airlines, bringing its code-sharing partners with it.

Wider Impacts

Until code-sharing came into general use, independent commuter airlines had customarily fed traffic at hub airports, freely interchanging passengers and freight with all major airlines. Usually several commuter airlines would serve the larger metropolitan areas, each company monopolizing a particular market or set of markets, and direct competition between commuter airlines had been unusual. The wider adoption of code-sharing, however, led to a significant increase in competition among commuter airlines, which now became essentially surrogates for the major carriers at the smaller cities.

This competition, in turn, was related to the fact that, after deregulation, the major airlines began rapidly to focus their operations on connecting hubs. Deregulation had made it possible to create new hubs literally overnight, as did United at Memphis (the hub was later discontinued), Continental when it completely reoriented its network around the Denver hub with one stroke in 1979, and Western at Salt Lake City in 1982. Such rapid changes would have been impossible in the days of glacial change before deregulation. Among the trunk airlines, only Delta and, to a lesser extent, Eastern already had real hub-and-spoke systems, both at Atlanta, before deregulation, and these were reinforced after 1978.

At cities where more than one major airline had a hub, the tendency was for each to form a close alliance there with a commuter airline, preferably one that had consolidated a strong local catchment area. These affiliates then established their own hub-and-spoke feeder networks from the metropolitan hub, often to the same outlying cities. Competition among commuter airlines where they were acting as surrogates for the major companies became common. On the other hand, at a smaller metropolitan airport used as a hub by only one major airline, the affiliated commuter company could now enjoy a near-monopoly on feeder traffic.

In this new pattern, the fate of the affiliate was inevitably tied closely to the decisions of its senior partner. If the major company decided to deactivate a hub (as Eastern did at Houston and Kansas City), or if it went out of business (like Braniff and Eastern), the affiliate would be deprived of its main traffic source. If it did not find a new partner at the existing metropolitan hub, it would have to either relocate to a new hub for its foster parent, revert to being an independent, or go out of business. In some cases commuter affiliates were released from their contracts with the majors because of nonperformance under agreements that allowed termination if schedule completion or on-time performance fell below a certain standard. This partnership pattern between commuter and major airline produced a situation in which the junior partner became so utterly dependent on its parent that few commuter airlines have survived the cancellation of a code-sharing contract.

On the other hand, code-sharing with a successful partner was not a guarantee of success. AVAir (formerly Air Virginia), for example, went bankrupt despite its affiliation as an American Eagle carrier. Rio Airways encountered financial difficulties, and eventually went out of business, despite its Delta affiliation, partly because it was unable to redeem funds owed to it when Braniff and Continental airlines both declared bankruptcy.

As code-sharing spread, its many additional advantages became clearer. Normally at the hub airport, the commuter airline could use the same concourse, reservation center, and ticket counter as its larger affiliate, thus greatly improving passenger interchange by consolidating these functions with its partner. There were substantial benefits in such activities as joint advertising and marketing. The management of many a commuter airline had hitherto relied largely on a combination of intuition and opportunism in running the company. They would now receive assistance in those elements of airline management that were commonly weak at a small company: planning, scheduling, market development, employee training, cost and revenue accounting, and passenger handling. Often there was the additional advantage of lower fuel prices through bulk purchases by the major airline, and sometimes direct financial help was available. Certainly, code-sharing with a major airline and adopting its name (as by becoming a Northwest Airlink or American Eagle carrier), could give name-recognition to a commuter company thereby enhancing its image, increasing its ability to attract passengers, and improving its channels for obtaining financing.

On the other side of the coin, several additional disadvantages of such close affiliations, from the point of view of the commuter airlines, also became clear. The most serious, in the eyes of some of the hardy entrepreneurs, was the loss of management independence. Code-sharing also usually led to the loss of corporate identity, the need to surrender an image that had been carefully nurtured for many years. The latter disadvantage, however, rested more on sentiment than on reality. One long-established industry pioneer commented: "At first I felt bad about losing my name on the side of the airplane; but I soon came to terms with that when the first code-sharing month's figures showed a traffic increase of 50 percent."

In the longer run, these arrangements could also lead to large increases in costs, notably when the major partner wanted its affiliates to adopt more modern, costly aircraft so as to minimize the discomfort to the passenger of changing from a jet to a commuter liner, a practice intended to provide "seamless service." Besides the greater debt-servicing cost of acquiring the aircraft, such a trend would lead to higher costs in pilot salaries (as pay scales vary sharply with the size of the aircraft), the need for more employees at stations and for more training to conform to the service standards of the major airline, and higher maintenance costs.

Another serious problem was that the affiliate became highly vulnerable to any problems affecting the major airline. Earnings would suffer if the commuter airline was forced to participate in deep-discount fare wars. Worst of all, income would virtually disappear if there were a strike or if the major airline went out of business. Interestingly, many of these disadvantages were the same ones that had been ascribed to the Allegheny Commuter concept fifteen years earlier.

The CAB Strengthens Code-Sharing

In the midst of these developments, the CAB issued a ruling that had the unintentional effect of greatly increasing the competitive advantages of code-sharing commuter airlines. In response to many complaints about unfair practices in the computer reservation process, which favored the airlines that owned the systems, the board ruled that henceforth all listings would have to be presented in a nondiscriminatory sequence. Now all nonstop and direct flights between each city pair (listed chronologically by time of departure, regardless of airline) were to be listed first, followed by on-line connections and finally by interline services. This ruling went into effect on 14 November 1984.

For commuter airlines the precedence given to on-line over interline connections was critical. Because code-sharing connecting flights are classified as on-line, these appeared on the computer screens before connections with independent commuter airlines or with competitive code-sharers. The latter, however, would have their own affiliates' flights, with which they would enjoy preferential listings. Only the independents were left out in the cold. In practice, the on-line connections would appear on the first computer screen, whereas interline connections would not appear until a second or later screen was called up by the operator. As about 80 percent of travel agency reservations are made from the first screen (and travel agencies account for most ticket sales), the independent airlines were now at a hopeless disadvantage.

Diffusion of Code-Sharing

The first half of 1985 was a critical period for those airlines that had still not entered into code-sharing contracts. Early that year eight independent commuter airlines asked the Department of Transportation (DOT), which had assumed some of the responsibilities of the CAB, to ban the practice. However, the DOT did not respond, and the case grew dimmer for those companies still struggling to survive as independents.

Finally, on 1 June, United Airlines, which had long been a leading foe of code-sharing, said that it would begin to allow three commuter airlines to use its UA designator. This move, combined with the DOT's inaction, effectively terminated efforts to stop code-sharing.

Top Twenty Commuter Airlines and Their Code-Sharing Partners, Listed in Descending Order of Passengers Carried (1988)

Airline	Affiliation
Metro Airlines	American-Eastern
WestAir	United
Henson Aviation	Piedmont-TWA
Atlantic Southeast	Delta
Simmons Airlines	American
Horizon Air	Alaska-Northwest
Comair	Delta
Bar Harbor Airlines	Continental-Eastern
Pan Am Express	Pan Am
Express Airlines One	Northwest
Wings West Airlines	American
SkyWest Airlines	Delta
Brockway Air	Piedmont
Aspen Airways	United
Air Midwest	Braniff-TWA
CCAir	Piedmont
Britt Airways	Continental
Jetstream International	Piedmont
Business Express	Delta
Rocky Mountain Airways	Continental

By the fall of 1985 all twelve major airlines had one or more partners, as did one national (formerly local service) carrier, Ozark Airlines. At this time there were forty-six such agreements, involving forty commuter airlines. This compared to only seven code-sharing relationships involving commuter airlines (excluding the Allegheny Commuters) that had been in effect at the end of 1983 and fourteen as late as 1 January 1985. These figures indicated that, without conscious intervention from any government agency (unless apathy could be interpreted as intervention by consent), a revolutionary transition had occurred. The number kept growing until, in September 1986, sixty-six contracts were in effect. Thereafter the number of contracts (but not the relative importance of code-sharing) declined somewhat because of mergers (such as the Northwest-Republic and TWA-Ozark combinations) and the sloughing off of some weak commuter airline partners. By the middle of 1987, no fewer than forty-five out of fifty, or 90 percent, of the largest commuter airlines were code-sharers.

For those airlines that could not or would not form a code-sharing alliance, the penalty was often severe. Air Wisconsin, for example, experienced substantial problems in 1985 because of its determination to remain independent. Although it had a close (but not a code-sharing) relationship with United, its traffic dropped by 8.5 percent in the first half of the year. The problem had actually begun in November 1984, when, because of the CAB ruling on computer reservation system listings, its interline connections (including those with United) began to disappear from the first screens of the systems. The severity of the problem was illustrated graphically at the corporate hometown of Appleton, Wisconsin, where Republic Airlines made substantial inroads. There could hardly have been a better illustration of an entrenched airline, even one with an excellent reputation and a solid market base, suffering in the new competitive environment. This problem cost Air Wisconsin twenty thousand passengers in the first half of 1985 and contributed to the company's only first-quarter loss in fifteen years. The experience was a sharp lesson to the aspiring airline, bringing it face-to-face with the realities of the marketplace, not to mention the power of larger corporations. Recognizing the futility of trying to stay independent, Air Wisconsin's management now helped to convince United to join the trend toward code-sharing. Starting in June 1986, Air Wisconsin flights began to be listed under the UA code, and traffic improved thereafter.

One of the most widely publicized cases of resisting code-sharing involved Britt Airways and its dynamic president, Bill Britt. He was vehemently against the practice, asserting that it would destroy a fine system of independent commuter airlines, organized to feed traffic to any connecting airline. These companies, Britt argued, had been built up, often at great risk and with commendable initiative, over twenty years or more of patient work. In a broader sense, therefore, he regarded the practice as an attack on the free enterprise system itself, and possibly even, un-American. Britt probably summarized the feelings of many pioneer commuter airline managers, unwillingly affected by code-sharing, when he complained, "When becoming a [code-sharer], the larger airline uses your assets, runs your schedules, determines your pricing, and decides what the feed schedules should be. The only thing a major partner wants is for the commuter [airline] to run its airplanes, its pilots, and its mechanics." After experiencing much traffic loss as an independent, Britt Airways, like Air Wisconsin, succumbed to the inevitable and became the Piedmont Commuter at the Dayton hub. Later, in December 1985, Britt sold his company to the post-deregulation star, People Express. Yet even then he continued to fight against code-sharing, lobbying both the DOT and Congress.

The Majors Buy In

The sale of Britt Airways illustrates another change that accompanied code-sharing. Starting in 1983, many major airlines began to buy equity shares in, or to acquire full ownership of, commuter airlines. The cases of Republic buying a share of Simmons Airlines and Piedmont purchasing Henson Airlines have already been mentioned. Other such moves included Pan American's acquisition of Ransome Airlines (renamed Pan Am Express) and American's purchase of the Nashville Eagle operation, formerly owned by Air Midwest.

Several major airlines went so far as to purchase commuter lines that were at the time code-sharing with other major airlines. The new owners would then break the existing code-sharing relationship and reorient the commuter route network to serve their own needs. Late in 1986, for example, Alaska Air bought Horizon Airlines, even though the latter was code-sharing with United. Shortly thereafter it left the United system and began using the AS code.

Thus, full ownership or an equity interest was sometimes obtained to protect the major airline's feeder network. In a broader sense, such purchases allowed the major airline to maximize the amount of traffic it controlled all the way from the point of origin to the destination, a desideratum of most transport organizations. Ownership of commuter airlines by the larger firms increased from one in 1983 (Henson) to twenty in 1990. By early 1989, fourteen of the thirty largest commuter airlines in the RAA were totally or partially owned by their affiliates in the ranks of the major and national airlines, and they accounted for more than half of the passengers carried by the industry.

The most conspicuous exception to this trend was United, whose arrangements with commuter airlines never involved actual purchase. This was the case because United had a clause in its pilot contract that would result in sharp wage increases for those pilots flying for any United-owned commuter airline.

With the expansion of code-sharing, many an airline name with a long and respected history had to be sacrificed to the new reality. To give up their identities for such names as Trans World Express and American Eagle must have been a bitter pill for many long-active commuter airline presidents and boards to swallow. A few hybrid titles, such as Eastern Air Midwest Express, were adopted, but usually old names had to give way in the interest of conforming to the corporate identity of the new owner. Thus, on 28 October 1986, "Air Wisconsin" began to be painted

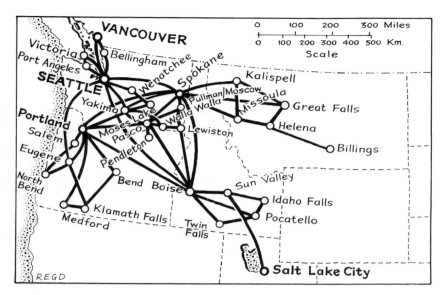

With the dissolution of the pre-deregulation airline organizational framework in full swing by the early 1980s, the commuter airlines were well positioned to replace the new major and national airlines on routes that were now defined as regional. Some of the new ones neatly fulfilled a need and grew rapidly, such as Horizon Airlines in the Pacific Northwest. As with some other airlines, history seemed to repeat itself, as Horizon's 1993 network was remarkably similar to that of West Coast Airlines thirty years previously. It was an important and valuable acquisition for Alaska Airlines in 1986.

out from the sides of aircraft in favor of "United Express," and in the same year Aspen Airways suffered the identical fate. The pattern continued at a quickening pace throughout the United States.

With the tremendous increase in code-sharing, by 1986 only between 15 and 20 percent of commuter industry traffic was estimated to remain unaligned, and this level remained more or less constant thereafter. Some of these independents were operating into medium-sized metropolitan areas that had not yet been chosen as hubs by any major company. For a long time Mesa Airlines was the largest of the independents (until it became a United Express carrier), feeding most of its traffic into such a city, Albuquerque. In other cases, some small independents still operated to cities that generated insufficient traffic to be of interest to larger code-sharing companies. Ironically, should good service by the independents cause traffic to these cities to increase significantly, their routes would become highly vulnerable to incursions by code-sharers. Clearly, the future for independent commuter airlines was not bright.

Major airlines also began to become more involved in managing their code-sharing partners. Sometimes the major airline's role was so dominant that the very necessity for separate commuter airline management was questionable. Late in 1987 Julius Maldutis of Salomon Brothers, an investment banking firm, repeated a term first used by Kingsley Morse of Command Airways at an RAA meeting in 1984. Referring to the code-sharing commuter airlines as "serfs," he pointed out to them, "You are being told where to fly, when to fly and, soon, what to fly." Going one step further, in 1987 American Airlines bought five of its seven American Eagle affiliates and gradually replaced the former presidents with its own personnel. Later some of these airlines were consolidated with each other, further simplifying the corporate structure.

Maldutis's statement may have been related to an announcement by the Texas Air Corporation, owner of Continental and Eastern airlines, that it had ordered sixteen (and optioned thirty-four) new forty-two-seat Franco-Italian ATR-42 airliners, which were to be distributed among the four Texas Air code-sharing partners. Shortly thereafter Texas Air announced that its affiliates would be standardizing on the ATR-42, the thirty-passenger Embraer Brasilia, and the nineteen-passenger Beech 1900. In time these three models were to replace the current fleet of three hundred commuter aircraft of no fewer than twenty-three different types. Texas Air also planned to standardize the customer service, uniforms, purchasing, maintenance, and pilot training of its affiliates. By about this time the company had centralized the management of its commuter airlines in Houston, with Neil F. Meehan as president of Texas Air's Regional Airline Division. All these moves were eminently sensible and indeed were soon emulated by others, but they were the antithesis of the original hopes and dreams of the rugged individualists who had created the commuter airline industry. As in the retail trade, the small shopkeeper could not match the operating economies of the supermarket next door.

In the midst of these developments, the country was experiencing a wave of mergers among the major airlines themselves. A few of these merger partners focused on the same hubs, raising the question of whether some affiliated commuter airlines would lose their partners after the mergers. Although a few were set adrift in this way, in most cases the duplicate routes were divided between the formerly competing commuter airlines. For example, when Northwest and Republic merged, the spoke cities of Northwest Orient Airlink and Republic Express, radiating from Minneapolis–St. Paul, were divided between them. The same happened at the St. Louis hub when TWA and Ozark merged, with the outlying cities divided between Trans World Express (Resort Air) and the former Ozark Midwest Air Lines (Air Midwest). In general, those commuter lines that had been affiliated with the senior merger partner retained the more attractive markets when the spoke cities were parceled out.

Somewhat anticlimactically, on 23 September 1985, the DOT issued its rules on "shared airline designation codes." These rules mandated full disclosure of such affiliations in computer reservation systems and in the *OAG*, where an asterisk denoted any service performed by a code-sharing commuter airline. The DOT also called for a study of the impacts of "marketing alliances" to identify their anticompetitive aspects, if any.

The results of that study were published approximately one year later. It was greeted with widespread ridicule within the airline industry when the independent research team that carried out the study concluded that there was "no clear indication that [commuter] carriers sharing the designator code of larger airlines enjoy a competitive advantage over . . . carriers that continue to operate independently," although the authors acknowledged that such closely related items as the availability of joint fares and the higher placement of on-line flights in computer reservation systems might give a competitive advantage to code-sharers. In retrospect, the academicians who carried out this work were very cautious in interpreting the limited data available to them, concluding that there was insufficient evidence to support the hypothesis that code-sharing carried a large competitive advantage and suggesting that the fears of the independent commuter airlines were greatly exaggerated. Although their conclusion may have been, on a selective basis, statistically supportable, it contradicted widespread evidence to the contrary and to many observers seemed to be short on common sense.

In the light of the apparent facts, two dissenting members of that team published their own paper on the subject. This contradictory report clearly demonstrated the competitive advantages of code-sharing and claimed that there were significant barriers to entry into the industry for any new firm without a code-sharing agreement—a fact that the Reagan administration did not wish to acknowledge.

The authors gave examples of independent commuter airlines that had been injured by the practice, having collected data on twenty-two feeder markets at nine hub airports where an independent commuter airline competed with a code-sharer. Between early 1985 and October 1986, the independents serving these competitive markets had reduced their flights by 80 percent while the code-sharers increased their departures by almost 15 percent. Eventually, the independents had to withdraw from seventeen of the twenty-two markets. These findings simply reinforced what had long been known about the power of code-sharing, and they called into question whether the DOT study team's conclusions had been dictated by the political motivations of an administration that had done nothing to stop the practice and needed retroactively to defend its actions.

Larger Commuter Airliners

The middle and later years of the 1980s witnessed the appearance of a series of new passenger commuter airliners. The traditional type, with the statutory maximum of nineteen seats required to dispense with a flight attendant, continued to account for most new airliner sales, but only one new aircraft, the Beech 1900, was of this size.

Instead, several "new-generation" turboprop aircraft with between thirty and forty-two passenger seats now made their debut, to bring another fundamental change to the commuter operators. These aircraft, whose very existence was largely an outcome of deregulation (the removal of the thirty-seat limitation), were appropriate for the code-sharing commuter airlines of the deregulation era. When they began to enter U.S. airline service in 1984, their impact on the economics and consumer appeal of the industry was significant. With their amenities and considerable ranges, they were well suited to the desire for "seamless service" and for the industry's increasing average stage length. Five aircraft in this size category were produced (although only four found customers in the United States), and the resulting competition for sales among the manufacturers created a buyer's market.

The one new nineteen-seater—an exception in the new wave—was the pressurized Beech 1900. It had been authorized in 1979 and first flew on 3 September 1982. The 1900 first went into service with Bar Harbor Airlines early in 1984, but the type at first sold only in moderate numbers. One deterrent to sales was that Beech did not match the favorable financing arrangements of its competitors. Equipped with two 1,100-

The Beech 1900, a nineteen-seat airliner, entered service in 1984. (Photo courtesy of the Roger Bentley collection.)

horsepower Pratt & Whitney Canada PT6A-65B engines, the 1900, though somewhat cramped inside, was—and still is—especially suitable for airlines that have to operate in hot weather and at high-altitude airports. It has a cruising speed of almost three hundred miles per hour, and a maximum takeoff weight of 16,600 pounds. Some 215 Beech 1900s, priced at about $3.3 million each, had been delivered by the end of 1990.

By far the best-selling pressurized nineteen-seater twin continued to be the Jetstream 31, built in the United Kingdom by British Aerospace. In mid-1987 an improved version of this aircraft, the Super Jetstream 31, was announced. With two 1,020-horsepower turboprop engines (versus 940 horsepower for the earlier version), a higher maximum takeoff weight, increased range, simpler wings, a higher and wider (but not longer) cabin, and lower cabin noise level, the Super 31 made its maiden flight on 18 April 1988. This aircraft is also well suited to the "hot and high" conditions often encountered in the western United States, and it seems to have been produced with this market foremost in mind. By the end of 1990 about 320 Jetstreams had been delivered worldwide, with the United States accounting for over 75 percent of the total.

The first of the larger new-generation airliners to enter service was the thirty-four-seat SAAB 340. It was originally built as a cooperative venture by SAAB of Sweden and Fairchild of the United States as the

Yet another foreign-built aircraft came into service in 1984: the thirty-four-seat Swedish SAAB 340. (Photo courtesy of SAAB.)

SF-340, but the partnership was dissolved on 1 November 1985, when Fairchild withdrew. Powered by two 1,735-horsepower General Electric CT7-5A2 turboprop engines, it has a cruising speed of about 280 miles per hour and a range of nine hundred miles with full payload. The first prototype 340 flew on 25 January 1983. The first American operator was Comair, a Delta Connection airline, which placed it into service in October 1984. Total deliveries by the end of 1990 (including the improved 340B) stood at 225. Among the other American commuter airlines to place this $5.7-million aircraft in service have been Air Midwest, Express Airlines One, Metroflight Airlines, and Bar Harbor Airlines.

The next airliner of this size class to enter service was the de Havilland Aircraft of Canada (which in 1986 became Boeing Canada) Dash 8, which first flew on 20 June 1983 and which entered U.S. service with Eastern Metro Express on 24 April 1985. The original twin-engined, thirty-six-seat Dash 8-100, powered by two Pratt & Whitney Canada PW120 two-thousand-horsepower turboprops, with four-blade Hamilton Standard propellers, had a maximum takeoff weight of 33,000 pounds, a cruise speed of about 310 miles per hour, and a maximum range exceeding 1,500 miles. The $5.5-million Dash 8-100 has sold well; through 1990, about 210 aircraft had been delivered. Among the other airlines to take delivery are Horizon Air, Henson Airlines, and Suburban Airlines. A stretched version, the Dash 8-300, is discussed later in this section.

The fastest of the larger new commuter passenger aircraft was the thirty-passenger EMB-120 Brasilia, built by Embraer at São José dos Campos, Brazil, with a cruising speed of 330 miles per hour. It was

The EMB-120 Brasilia, a new design for Embraer of Brazil, became very popular among the leading commuter airlines. (Collection of R. E. G. Davies.)

Largest of the airliners built specifically for regional operations was the Aérospatiale/Aeritalia ATR-42, able to carry forty-two passengers. (Photo courtesy of Avions de Transport Régional.)

powered by two Pratt & Whitney Canada PW118 turboprops, rated at 1,800 horsepower, and sold for a base price of $5.3 million. The first prototype flew on 27 July 1983, and the first customer delivery, to Atlantic Southeast Airlines, was in August 1985. By December 1990, 225 Brasilias had been delivered. EMB-120s are also operated by, among others, SkyWest, WestAir, and Comair. The Bandeirante established a foothold for the Brazilian aircraft industry in the United States; the Brasilia seems destined to consolidate that market position.

The largest of the new-generation aircraft in this size range was the forty-two-seat ATR-42, constructed as a joint venture by Aerospatiale of France and Aeritalia of Italy. It uses two Pratt & Whitney Canada 1,800-horsepower PW120 turboprops, has a maximum range exceeding one thousand miles, cruises at more than three hundred miles per hour, and has a maximum takeoff weight of 35,600 pounds. The type first flew on 16 August 1984, and its first U.S. delivery took place on 7 February 1986 to Command Airways, an American Eagle partner. By the end of 1990, deliveries totaled 187 aircraft; this number included orders by Pan Am Express, Simmons Airlines, and the Texas Air Corporation (for Continental Express and Eastern Express affiliates).

Two larger aircraft types have been designed with the commuter airline market partly in mind. Both are fifty-seat turboprops, but only one has been ordered in the United States. This is the Boeing Canada Dash 8-300, about eleven feet longer than the standard Dash 8, with a wider wingspan and strengthened landing gear. Powered by two 2,380-horsepower Pratt & Whitney Canada PW123 engines, it has a maximum takeoff weight of 41,400 pounds, cruises at about three hundred miles per hour, and has a maximum payload range of 575 miles. The prototype first flew on 15 May 1987, and initial revenue service commenced on 30 March 1989 for Time Air of Canada. Given its commonality with the earlier model, the 300 would appear to be a perfect successor aircraft for Dash 8-100 operators, whose traffic is outgrowing the earlier model. Through December 1990, forty-two aircraft had been delivered.

The other fifty-seat aircraft is the Fokker 50, based on the highly successful Fokker Friendship, which was in production for thirty years from 1957 until 1986. The Fokker 50 made its maiden flight on 13 February 1987 and was first delivered to Ansett Airlines of Australia in August of that year. Even though no sales have been recorded in the United States, it has done well in other countries, with well over one hundred sales, especially to national airlines and their subsidiaries in Europe.

Essential Air Service Survives

Early in 1984 there was much discussion in Washington about the adequacy and the future of the Essential Air Service (EAS) program. This increased attention was partly in response to the poor performance of EAS service at a few cities, particularly in California.

The Aviation Subcommittee of the House of Representatives held two days of hearings on this topic. On a positive note, CAB chairman Dan McKinnon reported that, in the forty-eight contiguous United States, the program had helped to reduce subsidies from $71.7 million at 202 cities in 1978 to $40 million at 104 cities in 1984. In Alaska, 190 points had been receiving $9.5 million in 1981, whereas only 50 points were receiving $5.5 million in subsidy in 1984. The subsidy per boarded passenger varied wildly, from a low of $5 at Stockton and Modesto, California, to a high of $836 at Blythe in the same state.

A wide variety of views were expressed by witnesses at this hearing. Some thought that the EAS program should not be extended beyond its scheduled termination date of 23 October 1988, whereas others claimed that the policy of stressing the low bid, by encouraging a minimum level of service, ensured a drastic erosion of traffic in the markets being served. Still others thought that the board should have the authority to terminate EAS at cities where traffic levels were disappointing and that states and communities should share in the funding of the program. The high level of airline fares at EAS cities was also criticized. Several subcommittee members were strongly in favor of phasing out the program.

A panel from the RAA presented the views of its members, alleging that the lack of proper airport facilities, and inadequate air navigation and landing approach aids were major factors in the rather low level of service reliability. They appealed for funds for improvements at EAS airports, although they realized that these were unlikely to be forthcoming as long as such projects had to meet the FAA's cost-benefit tests.

The general conclusion of the Aviation Subcommittee was that EAS was benefiting the public and should be continued, but that Congress should give the CAB and its DOT successor the necessary authority to enforce performance not only by the commuter airlines but also by the communities. The subcommittee also urged the CAB and DOT to try to foresee and prevent the kind of collapse of EAS service that had been experienced at several California points.

On 4 February 1985, the Reagan administration asked Congress to terminate the program, three years before it was due to expire. This move was part of an effort to eliminate federal transport subsidies, and more generally to decrease the federal budget deficit. The administration also cited low traffic volumes as a reason to support the change. Transportation Secretary Elizabeth Dole represented the administration's view when she suggested that if the air services were indeed vital to the cities, they should come up with ways to fund them. She also pointed out that about half of the subsidized points were within sixty miles of a major hub.

This effort to eliminate the EAS program, as well as several later ones by the Reagan administration, was not successful. Political support for the continuation of the program was especially strong in the West and Midwest and in Alaska, and Congress voted to maintain the subsidies. This continued support may, correctly or not, have validated the view of those who, somewhat cynically, regarded the program as a political pork barrel.

In mid-1987 three bills were introduced to extend the EAS program beyond its scheduled termination date, 1988. At that time there were ninety-seven subsidized cities outside Alaska, and about seventy of them were projected to lose air service completely if the subsidies were eliminated. Strong Congressional support was reported for a program that, in financial terms, had clearly been successful. Direct subsidies to the U.S. airline industry had declined from $109 million in 1981 to $27 million in 1986. Much of the reduction could be credited to the increasing role played by the commuter airlines. At the time the Airline Deregulation Act was passed in 1978, such airlines had served 35 percent of the designated EAS points outside Alaska, but by the end of 1986 the figure was 84 percent. On the other hand, there were still some very high subsidy levels. At thirty-six cities, for example, the per capita subsidy was higher than the average fare paid by the passengers.

Ultimately, the EAS program was extended by ten years to 30 September 1998 under amendments to the Airport and Airway Safety and Capacity Expansion Act of 1987. Reacting to some of the criticisms of the former program, the new law differed in many ways from the one that had brought the EAS into being. It was more specific regarding the qualifying criteria, which were sensibly tightened. Now, to receive subsidies, a city had to be located at least forty-five highway miles from a large or medium-size hub; this provision, however, disqualified only a few communities. All aircraft in EAS service had to have at least fifteen seats, except at cities boarding fewer than twelve passengers per day. With rare exceptions, the aircraft had to have twin engines and two pilots. The minimum level of service of two round trips per day was increased from five to six days per week. Whereas two-stop service to a hub had previously been allowed, only one stop was now permitted. The flights had to be well timed to make connections, and the fares could not be "excessive." If the aircraft operated regularly at altitudes higher than eight thousand feet, they had to be pressurized. Code-sharing commuter airlines were specifically encouraged to apply to provide essential service, and it was stated that "the air carrier whose code is being used . . . shall share responsibility with [the commuter airline] for the quality of service provided under such code to the public." The new program specified that a community's cargo needs also had to be met; the old one had not dealt with cargo at all.

This law also made it possible for communities to receive new or improved air service. Any state or local government could now apply for enhanced service at an EAS point, provided that it was willing to pay for 50 percent of the increase in costs involved. A local government unit, such as a city or a county, could also apply for such enhanced service, with 100 percent federal subsidy, provided that it was understood that all such subsidies would be eliminated, after an experimental two-year period, if traffic increases did not meet predetermined minimum levels. Under certain criteria, cities that had received certificated service in the past but had lost it before deregulation could now be added to the EAS network, provided that a government agency, a corporation, or an individual was willing to pay 25 percent of the required subsidy. Finally, if a city had been receiving subsidized service for at least two years and if traffic levels were low, the secretary of transportation could eliminate the subsidy if he or she thought that such a step was in the public interest.

The new provisions went into effect on 1 October 1988 and were expected to add between $10 and $15 million to the airline subsidy bill, which at that time was approximately $25 million per year. Congress, however, did not provide adequate funding for this expected cost increase. Therefore, in mid-1989 President George Bush had to sign a bill for an emergency supplemental appropriation of $6.6 million for EAS. This appropriation also had a provision, effective 1 October, for a subsidy cap of $300 per passenger in the contiguous United States. As a result, six cities were eliminated from the program.

Further changes were required when Congress appropriated only $30.6 million for the EAS program in its Department of Transportation Appropriations Bill for fiscal year 1990. Approximately $4 million more would have been required just to maintain services to existing cities.

The DOT therefore had to tighten its criteria under which a city could qualify for subsidy, an action that led to the elimination of twenty more cites. Now cities were dropped if they were less than seventy highway miles from a large or medium-size hub, less than fifty-five miles from a small hub, or less than forty-five miles from a nonhub that boarded one hundred or more passengers per day. A new subsidy ceiling of $200 per passenger was introduced at the same time; six of the twenty cities were eliminated because they exceeded this limit. After these changes, ninety cities in the contiguous United States and forty in Alaska were still subsidized.

These progressive cutbacks may well foreshadow the eventual end of the EAS program. Clearly, the whole concept of national subsidy for local air travel needs is seriously in question. If the program is eliminated, it is quite possible that state and local governments may try to step in to fill the void. Several states have considered implementing a subsidy program to maintain air services at small cities. South Dakota did implement a fairly extensive subsidized air network in 1990, but it was unsuccessful and the program was dropped after a short time.

Still Larger Jets and a Pilot Shortage

After 1983, continuing an earlier trend, several more commuter airlines adopted aircraft with more than sixty seats, including types previously associated with local service and trunk line operations. All, however, continued to operate primarily with small equipment. In 1984 Royale began to use a leased DC-9 on the Brownsville-Houston route; Pilgrim flew an F-28 between New York and Ottawa, Canada; and Britt acquired BAC One-Elevens for Evansville-Chicago service. In the same year Horizon bought a DC-9 for its Seattle–Boise–Sun Valley route and Cascade received two BAC One-Elevens to use in the same part of the country. In December 1984, Aspen Airways took delivery of its first British Aerospace 146, initially using it for its routes from Denver into the Rocky Mountain ski resorts, and in the following year Mid Pacific Airlines of Hawaii introduced F-28s.

In some respects, this trend echoed a similar development among the local service airlines, sparked by Mohawk's acquisition of BAC One-Elevens in 1965. But unlike the earlier program of equipment upgrading, most of these latter-day experiments were notably unsuccessful and short-lived. Horizon Air, for example, called its DC-9 an "economic disaster," and the same description applied to the Royale route in Texas.

Only the BAe-146 operation from Denver up to the mountain resorts was satisfactory, but this success derived as much from specialized performance—almost STOL airfield capability—as from size. Aspen's 146 operations were only marginally profitable.

In 1985 the industry began to face a major handicap: a high turnover rate among the approximately six thousand commuter airline pilots. This problem was directly related to greatly accelerated hiring by the major airlines, which by now were drawing nearly one-third of their new pilots from commuter airlines. The majors had formerly depended substantially on armed forces retirees to provide their flight deck crews; but as recruitment from these services diminished owing to the decline in retiree numbers, the commuter airlines provided a welcome reservoir for much-needed flying personnel. Retirement rates from the large airlines also accelerated, with the result that they hired 7,872 pilots in 1985, about three times the total hired in 1983. In 1985 alone the commuter airlines had to hire 3,046 pilots, indicating a yearly attrition rate of 50 percent, which was burdensome and very expensive. For some individual companies, pilot turnover that year exceeded 60 percent. Pilot hiring continued to increase, until in 1989 4,365 commuter airline pilots were hired, an all-time high; the following year the total dropped somewhat to 3,988.

Because of the high cost of training, the turnover issue quickly became a major economic problem. Pilot training costs for the commuter airline industry in 1985 were estimated at between $200 and $300 million; indirectly this was a form of subsidy to the large airlines, which were thus relieved of some of the expense of a complete training program.

The commuter companies responded by instituting a variety of programs to retain these employees. Pilots with Henson Airlines, for example, had to sign contracts stating that they would stay with the company for at least a year after completing their training or pay for the costs involved. This approach was not motivated simply by the high costs of training: in November and December 1985, Henson did not have enough pilots to fly a full schedule. Such contracts, however, are generally viewed as legally unenforceable. Other airlines began to pay bonuses to pilots who were upgraded to fly larger commuter aircraft. Nevertheless, the pilot turnover rate remained high.

Perhaps partly because the strong demand made it possible, commuter airline pilots joined unions at an unprecedented rate. In contrast to its modest recruitment record in earlier years, the Air Line Pilots Association (ALPA) made substantial inroads. In September 1987, *Air*

Transport World reported that pilots at three large commuter airlines had recently voted to be represented by ALPA, which was then the bargaining agent at nineteen companies. It was widely assumed that this trend was reinforced by code-sharing, which led to considerable contact between the union pilots of the majors and the nonunion pilots of the commuter airlines that shared their codes.

Commuter Airline Safety

The ever-present topic of commuter airline safety continued to stimulate much discussion and to receive media attention during the 1980s and into the 1990s. The airlines were roundly criticized from several sides on the safety issue, despite the fact that the general trend, with a few exceptions, was one of steady improvement. In fact, the year 1990 was the safest year on record for commuter airlines.

One thing the critics often failed to note was the great difference in accident rates between those commuter airlines operating relatively large equipment (more than thirty seats) under the FAA's Part 121 regulations and those operating under Part 135. In fact, Part 121 commuter airlines, which accounted for more than 40 percent of the commuter airline industry's traffic, had a better safety record during this period than did the major airlines. The critics also failed to take airline size into account—to distinguish between the very good safety record of the fifty largest commuter airlines and the much weaker record of the smaller ones.

Early in this period the issue was brought into media focus by an Air Illinois crash on 11 October 1983. A subsequent National Transportation Safety Board (NTSB) investigation uncovered problems of maintenance and inadequate record-keeping and also showed that some unprofessional habits had become deeply ingrained in the Air Illinois corporate culture. These findings led the NTSB to question the effectiveness of the FAA's surveillance of the industry as a whole, and they revealed that, to keep within its budget over the past few years, the agency had cut its staff by one hundred inspectors. Always eager for a sensational story, and always keen to pounce on a convenient scapegoat, the media paid a great deal of attention to the Air Illinois case.

This kind of publicity was reinforced, on 4 January 1986, by an internal report by the General Accounting Office (GAO). The subject was airline safety, and such was the report's perceived importance that the

Investigations and Oversight Subcommittee of the House of Representatives held hearings on it. These publicized the GAO's findings that commuter airlines were more dangerous than the larger companies; there was particular furor over the fact that airlines operating small equipment (aircraft with nine or fewer seats) had a fourteenfold higher accident rate than those operating aircraft with more than thirty seats. Both the GAO and the NTSB felt that the FAA had not done enough to ensure that small commuter airlines had sufficient reliability and systems redundancy to maintain high safety standards. Labor unions, led by ALPA, were critical of commuter airline safety as an element of their campaign against deregulation. They claimed that the pressures of competition in an unregulated environment were forcing companies to take unnecessary risks by practicing economies in maintenance and operating procedures that were potentially dangerous.

In response to this publicity, the secretary of transportation ordered the FAA to conduct "white glove" inspections of commuter airlines. The results partially confirmed previous suspicions. After eighteen months' work, by July 1985 the FAA had grounded sixteen companies. The inspectors concluded that some commuter airline managements had been strained by the growth of their companies. Often they could not produce documentary proof that the required maintenance and training work had been carried out. The agency also claimed that problems were especially likely to occur when companies were in financial trouble, although the general question of a correlation between safety and finance was, and still is, a hotly debated issue. The agency recommended that managements should periodically hire independent consultants to audit training and maintenance records.

The commuter airline industry predictably took a very different view of these groundings. It felt that they were, to some extent, politically motivated, intended to show the public that the FAA was doing its job properly. It was pointed out once again, and correctly, that commuter airlines had been grounded for the very same offenses for which the major airlines were only fined. Many of the grounded firms were not strong enough to recover financially from such an action and often had to go out of business even before their side of the story could be presented. Also noted was that many of the "infractions" were the result of subjective interpretations of the FAA's regulations, and that different regions of the FAA often interpreted the same rules in different ways. In 1986 the RAA called for the FAA to carry out its inspections, certifications, and enforcement proceedings on a national basis, to eliminate the problem of inconsistency in the interpretation of rules between regions.

Media coverage of the commuter airline safety issue varied according to the number of accidents occurring at any given time. Early in 1985, for example, a great deal of attention followed a rash of accidents. The year 1986, in contrast, was a safe one, and little attention was paid to the topic. Then a spate of eight accidents in the last quarter of 1987 and the first quarter of 1988 predictably led to renewed media exposure. This was followed by an announcement by the FAA that it had ordered special inspections of Part 135 operations to determine their compliance with safety regulations. The inspectors were told to investigate management practices, training programs, aircraft airworthiness, and record-keeping. About 20 percent of the 173 commuter airlines were to be inspected.

One stated reason for the inspections was to determine whether or not the FAA should encourage the major airlines to assume an active role in overseeing the operating and maintenance practices of their code-sharing partners. In 1988 the NTSB and Congress also suggested that the larger airlines should exert more control over their affiliates. The members of the commuter airline industry felt that such tightened control would be disastrous, claiming that the major airlines knew little or nothing about the specialized nature of commuter operations.

The question of whether or not the major airlines should be active in overseeing their affiliates on such matters as safety standards was a logical, although unforeseen, consequence of the trend toward code-sharing. Certainly the underlying reasons for what, on the surface, appeared to be widespread negligence were in need of urgent review. The traveling public, relying on the airlines for efficient service, always expects fares to be at a level it can afford and assumes that the aircraft in which it flies are safe. Regarding the fare level, the commuter airlines operate, almost by definition, over short routes, which are demonstrably more expensive to fly than longer ones. As for safety, they invariably operate into smaller airfields (other than their central hubs) and, in some parts of the West especially, these are often situated in difficult terrain. Because of the low levels of traffic, the aircraft operated are smaller, lighter, and therefore more vulnerable to the unexpected whims of the weather.

This is not to defend the commuter airlines that have broken the rules. But the public cannot have it both ways. If it requires the commuter airlines to achieve the impeccable safety record of the big carriers (which use superbly equipped aircraft, operate into immaculate airfields, and for much of the time fly at altitudes immune from weather disturbance), then it should be prepared to pay for the privilege. Additional requirements covering maintenance practices, flight training, and dispatch control are all costly. Extra expenditures have to be covered by increased revenues, i.e., higher fares. Higher fares mean less traffic. Less traffic leads to less service, and eventually—if the trend continues—to no service. And so the insistence on higher standards and the criticism of the commuter airlines, whose operations are specialized and arguably far more demanding than those of the larger airlines, should be expressed with a full appreciation of their operational circumstances. The inevitable economic consequences of controls could become so rigid as to strangle the industry.

The Propeller Image Problem

In the late 1980s the commuter airline industry was still trying to decide what to do about a major image problem that had existed for many years. No matter how modern were the industry's airplanes, the public tended to treat them as old-fashioned if they had propellers. Thus, a 1988 survey of travel agents in the Washington, D.C., area found that "the single largest deterrent [to] booking commuter travelers was the fact that it was a propeller-driven aircraft." In response the Regional Airline Public Affairs Council, an ad hoc organization consisting of representatives from the manufacturers, the media, and commuter airlines, was formed in 1987. It decided to produce a videotape and travel agent materials to argue the case for the modern turboprop airliner. After eighteen months, however, progress had been so slow that the group failed to generate enough additional financial support within the RAA to complete its mission.

Such an attitude constitutes an astonishing commentary on how improved technology can change entire aspects of accepted behavior. Just as a generation gap has evolved between those people who can drive with a manual gearshift car and those who only feel comfortable with an automatic transmission, today's air traveler, at least those travelers under fifty years of age, cannot remember when the major airlines used propeller aircraft as front-line equipment.

Once again, what does the public expect? Over short routes and into small airfields, jet airliners would be hopelessly uneconomical. There are simply no small jet airliners available today that can produce a level of seat-mile operating costs that would make it possible to break even, much less to make a profit. Many aircraft manufacturers have tried, and there have been isolated examples of an airline attempting to schedule a Learjet, a Falcon, or a Citation. Those that did usually withdrew the equipment as soon as they saw the fuel bill and compared it with the income from the flights. A fortune may await the manufacturer that can demonstrate sound and consistent profitability with a thirty- to fifty-seat airliner that can use landing strips of less than a mile.

Over the distances flown by commuter airlines, much of the competition comes from surface transport, so that fares have to be delicately set at a level the public can afford, on a perilous knife edge between acceptance and rejection. Speed is not a factor. Door-to-door, a jet aircraft can gain only a few minutes on a one-hundred-mile segment, and it could lose even this marginal advantage by a missed approach. The public is bemused by the promotion, without qualification, of speed as an advantage. Cars are sold on the basis of 120-mile-per-hour top speeds—without reference to the maximum fifty-five- to sixty-five-mile-per-hour speed limit. Similarly, fast jets are sold on the basis of a speed advantage over turboprops that can only be substantially proved over routes of more than two hundred miles in length—and these are in a distinct minority among commuter airlines.

The public's attitude toward air transport is unusually biased. It expects too much, partly in response to the high-powered promotion of the big airlines. The public does not discriminate. It expects luxury standards in a Jetstream or a Shorts SD-360. The same New Yorker who will tolerate straphanging on the subway and stand all the way on a suburban commuter rail line will complain bitterly because the airplane from White Plains to Albany has propellers. But if the commuter airline were to operate a jet and increase fares to cover its higher costs, the same commuter would be campaigning for a return of the Jetstream or the Shorts, propellers notwithstanding—and commenting on the fact that the new jet was only a few minutes quicker than the old turboprop.

Chapter 8

Prospects for the Future

A few comments about some possible future directions for the commuter airline industry seem appropriate. As a noted French philosopher observed, "forecasting is difficult, especially when it concerns the future." Technological predictions are relatively safe to make, at least in the short run, but predicting the future in terms of social changes and economics—not to mention forecasting the resultant traffic growth, which depends upon an almost infinite number of politicogeographic and socioeconomic variables—is highly risky. Even today, with decades of experience behind us, we simply know too little about the causal factors underlying such changes. Nevertheless, despite the risks, a few possibilities for the commuter airline industry between the early 1990s and the turn of the century should be discussed.

In 1989 the FAA offered some projections about future levels of ridership and aircraft needs. The agency predicted that U.S. enplanements (excluding Alaska, but including Hawaii, Puerto Rico, and the Virgin Islands) would more than triple between 1989 and 2001, for an average annual rate of growth of 6.9 percent over the twelve-year period. It also expected the commuter airline fleet to increase from 1,792 to 2,220 aircraft during the same time, and for the average trip length to increase from 180 to 212 miles. The number of aircraft operated with twenty to forty seats and with more than forty seats is expected to increase rapidly.

Future Aircraft

Plans are already well established for the production of a series of new airliners in the 1990s. Most of these aircraft are expected to be larger than the nineteen-seater standard of the past, because the major airlines want to upgrade the equipment of their code-sharing partners and also because the acquisition and operating costs of the new nineteen-seaters are increasing rapidly, partly because of new FAA certification requirements. Thus the typical new commuter aircraft of the 1990s is expected to have between thirty and sixty seats, to cruise at perhaps 350 miles per hour, to be pressurized for operations up to an altitude of about 25,000 feet, to offer amenities as close as possible to those of the large jets, and to have more baggage space than its predecessors.

One planned new airliner, and an exception to the generalizations just made, is the successor to the Metro III, which was produced for many years in the former Swearingen plant at San Antonio, Texas. The Metro III could no longer be produced after October 1991, when new, stiffer FAA regulations for certificating small airliners came into effect. A minimum-cost response to this problem, the Fairchild Metro 23, was announced in early 1991. This aircraft has essentially the same fuselage as the nineteen-passenger Metro III, but optionally will have the more powerful Garrett/AiResearch TPE331-12 engines, with 1,100 shaft horsepower. These engines will allow a rather high cruising speed of about 335 miles per hour.

The introduction of the Metro 23 is related to the fact that Fairchild filed for bankruptcy protection in February 1990. Before then the company had planned to produce the Metro V, a 320-mile-per-hour aircraft with stand-up headroom, but these plans were dropped because of financial difficulties and because the company claimed that, given the added cost, there was little demand for this feature. The evidence suggests, however, that the lack of stand-up headroom will make it unlikely that the code-sharers, who constitute the bulk of the U.S. commuter airline industry, will order the Metro 23. Most sales will probably come from smaller domestic firms and from third-world countries.

Because of the assumed strong demand for stand-up headroom, Beech is producing the 1900D, a modified Beech 1900. This nineteen-seater can also be regarded as case study of a relatively low-cost way to produce a new aircraft under the more stringent post-1991 certification regulations. The 1900D has seventy-one-inch stand-up headroom, expanded baggage capacity, and an optional lavatory and incorporates winglets for better "hot and high" operations. This $4- to $5-million aircraft is powered by two 1,280-horsepower Pratt & Whitney PT6A-67 engines and cruises at about 330 miles per hour. The first flight took place on 1 March 1990, and it was certificated early in 1991; deliveries began in the second half of 1991.

A much more radical aircraft, of unusual design, is the CBA-123, named the Vector. It is being built jointly by Embraer of Brazil and Fabrica Argentina de Materiales Aerospaciales of Cordoba, Argentina, and it will be certificated to the same Part 25 standards as the large jet airliners. The CBA-123 is a four-hundred-mile-per-hour, pressurized, nineteen-seat airliner equipped with two Garrett/AiResearch TPF351-20 two-thousand-horsepower turboprops and six-bladed propellers. The engines are of the rear-mounted (pusher) type, thus reviving an engine placement that has not been used for several decades. The craft is equipped with a galley and lavatory, although these amenities could be removed to make room for extra seats or extra legroom, at the customer's request. The first flight of the prototype was on 18 July 1990. By late 1990 the company had about 150 options to purchase the aircraft, but not a single firm sale. The main problem is the $6-million price tag, which is simply too high; in 1991 the company started a price reduction program to make the aircraft more appealing. Because of this problem, as well as financial difficulties at Embraer, it is not clear whether this model will, in fact, ever enter commercial service.

In mid-1989 British Aerospace announced plans for the new Jetstream 41, a twenty-nine-passenger version of its highly successful nineteen-passenger Jetstream 31. The aircraft, with a gross takeoff weight of 22,377 pounds, is a sixteen-foot stretch of the earlier model; a repositioned wing will also make possible an additional thirty-five cubic feet of baggage capacity. The Jetstream 41 is powered by two Garrett/AiResearch TPE331-14 engines, each rated at 1,500 horsepower, and cruises at somewhat over three hundred miles per hour. This new commuter aircraft is expected to cost $6 million when it enters service in the second half of 1992. Pan Am Express was the first company to place a firm order for Jetstream 41s when it ordered 10 early in 1990; a year later 114 orders and options had been received.

Another aircraft that will enter service in the 1990s is the pressurized, thirty- to thirty-three-seat Dornier 328. This high-winged, twin-turbo-prop successor to the Dornier 228 is powered by two 2,180-shaft-horse-power PW119B engines. It is designed to cruise at about 385 miles per hour, making it the fastest of the new generation of turboprops in the thirty-seater class. The first aircraft was rolled out in October 1991, and the initial delivery took place in October 1993. By early 1994 this German company had received forty-three orders and fifty options for the 328. The first U.S. customer was Horizon Air, which put the aircraft into service in February 1994.

A much larger future turboprop is the fifty-eight-passenger SAAB 2000, equipped with two 4,152-shaft-horsepower General Motors Allison GMA 2100 engines, and designed to cruise at 426 miles per hour. The go-ahead decision was made on 15 December 1988, construction of the prototype began early in 1990, and the first flight was made 26 March 1992. The SAAB 2000 was certificated on 22 March 1994, and deliveries to the airlines were scheduled for the summer of that year. American Airlines has taken an option on fifty for its affiliates. At the same time American placed fifty firm orders and fifty options for SAAB's improved 340B, at a cost of $8 million each. The contract for both aircraft types, worth a possible $1 billion, was described as the largest single order ever for commuter airliners. American's first 340B was delivered to its Nashville Eagle operation early in 1990.

The SAAB 2000 and the Dornier 328 are attempts to turn out fast turboprops that will produce shorter block-to-block times and that may even be able to replace older jets on stage lengths of up to five hundred miles. To what degree major airlines would be interested in making such substitutions is not clear, especially in view of the negative public perception of propellers. The other unanswered question is whether or not the great expense of pushing turboprops to higher speed will be cost-effective. To operate a turboprop at 400 miles per hour rather than 320 miles per hour takes twice as much horsepower and involves a much higher engine weight. Commuter airlines are interested in employing faster aircraft in the future, but are they prepared for the higher operational and acquisition costs that this trend will bring about?

This interest in higher speeds, together with designs that comply with the public image of what an airplane—any airplane—should look like and offer in amenities, has led to three separate proposals, first enunciated in 1988, for the construction of "regional" jets with sixty or fewer seats. The marketing advantage of acquiring jets for commuter airlines is neatly summarized in a statement by Larry Crawford, president and chief executive officer of Avitas, an aircraft appraisal company: "A commuter jet is perceived as consistent with the major airline's fleet. A turboprop aircraft, even though it may be equally or more modern than a jet, is seen by the uninitiated as antiquated by comparison." As an increasing number of aircraft decisions are made by the major code-sharing partners, this observation is one that must be taken seriously.

The three jets that have been proposed for the commuter airline markets of the 1990s are the Canadair Regional Jet (RJ), the Shorts FJX, and the Embraer EMB-145. The Shorts aircraft was the first to be announced, in March 1988. The proposal was for a forty-four- to forty-eight-seat airliner with two fanjet engines, projected to cost $14 million. However, the project was canceled when the Northern Ireland company was acquired by Canadair's parent firm, Bombardier.

The twin-engined Canadair airliner, with General Electric CF-34 turbines, is a variant of the company's successful Challenger business jet, has fifty seats and a cruising speed of 528 miles per hour, and costs $15 to $16 million. Canadair signed up a launch customer in 1988 when the European airline DLT (now Lufthansa CityLine) ordered six. The following year several additional orders were received. Toward the end of 1990 airlines had ordered and optioned about one hundred aircraft. Significantly, by then Canadair was no longer marketing the new jet primarily as a commuter airliner, but as a replacement for some of the older small aircraft of the major airlines, such as DC-9s, 737s, and F28s. It was also seeking a market niche for the Regional Jet in the 350- to 1,400-nautical-mile range, which is far longer than the typical commuter airline stage length. The first flight took place on 10 May 1991.

Embraer is building a stretched (by eighteen feet), redesigned, forty-five- to forty-eight-seat, four-hundred-mile-per-hour jet version of the Brasilia, with two Allison GMA-3007 turbofan engines. Originally, the engines were to be mounted ahead of and above the wing, but this configuration was later redesigned to a more standard under-wing arrangement. The EMB-145 will have a 70 percent commonality with the Brasilia, with obvious implied savings for airlines that operate both types. This jet is projected to sell for about $11 million; first deliveries were scheduled for 1993.

To what extent airliners such as the Regional Jet and the EMB-145 will actually be used by commuter airlines depends on demand, which itself will be related to future fuel costs and other cost considerations. Although they do have some advantages, it is not at all certain that jets will fit well into a commuter airline industry that is oriented to feeding traffic over relatively short distances to major airlines at hubs. In the early 1990s the average stage length for the commuter airline industry was about two hundred miles. The two jet manufacturers admit that their aircraft are best suited for routes of four hundred miles and more, although the builders of large turboprops claim that the figure should be closer to five hundred miles.

On the other hand, several major airlines are eager to improve the image of their affiliates, and nothing could be more effective in accomplishing this goal than adopting small jets. In addition, average stage lengths within the commuter airline industry have been increasing steadily, a trend that bodes well for the newcomers. Some of this increase has resulted from "hub raiding," whereby flights from a hub are offered to more distant spoke cities that have traditionally been served from another hub. This practice is also referred to as expanding the "catchment area" of a hub. Another possibility for using such jets (in an apparent return to former route patterns, predating the hub system) is for so-called point-to-point services, in which congested hub airports are avoided and commuter airline services are provided directly between two spoke cities. In the early 1990s SkyWest, Express Airlines One, and Continental Express, among others, were known to be interested in using such jets, or fast turboprops, for these two types of services. Overall, the proposals for small jets led to much discussion about the whole future direction of the code-sharing commuter airline industry.

To one of the coauthors, this future possibility contains a strong element of déja vu. During the late 1960s he was deeply involved in researching the market for a small jet airliner, aimed at the local service airline industry in the United States and many regional operations elsewhere in the world. The idea originated at de Havilland (U.K.) as the DH-126 project, a twenty-six-seat rear-engined jet, rather like a small DC-9. This aircraft developed, on the advice of dozens of airlines interviewed on world surveys that included most of the United States local and territorial airlines, into the thirty-six- to forty-four-seat Hawker Siddeley HS-136 (de Havilland having in the meantime been taken over by Hawker Siddeley Aviation). After many iterations and a further consolidation of the British aircraft industry, the project underwent a further metamorphosis to become the BAe-146, unrecognizable from the original DH-126 design.

The intriguing aspect of this little history is that the Shorts FJX appeared to have been designed to the almost identical specifications of the HS-136. At the time (1966) the airlines seemed to like it, but Hawker Siddeley would not take the risk of striking an entirely new note in aircraft procurement, preferring to concentrate on the HS-748 turboprop, which had already made its mark throughout the world.

The problems facing the small jet were exactly the same then as the ones that will face Canadair and Embraer or any other manufacturer today, except that the engines will be more efficient. The direct operating costs will still be higher than those for a similarly sized turboprop, and the speed advantage will not be demonstrably effective over stage lengths of less than two hundred miles. As will be observed at the end of this book, the similarity between the main commuter airline routes of today and the local service routes of yesteryear is quite remarkable. Time will tell if other circumstances have changed so as to make the RJ or EMB-145 any more acceptable today than the HS-136 was in 1966.

Oddly enough, in 1966 the jet configuration was a handicap. Airlines and the public alike were used to propellers and did not yet regard them as old-fashioned. Vickers (BAC) Viscounts and Lockheed Electras were still accepted as modern, competitive equipment. The identification of the turboprop engine as a symbol of inferiority, as opposed to a variant of the jet principle, is a phenomenon that should be corrected.

Foreign Aircraft Inventories

One trend that, from all known indications, seems to be a portent of the shape of things to come is that the majority of commuter airliners are now supplied by overseas manufacturers (see table). The Metro 23 and Beech 1900D are isolated examples of U.S.-built candidates for the market. A census of commuter aircraft today reveals that the dominant western suppliers are from Canada, Brazil, the United Kingdom, Germany, Spain, Sweden, France, Italy, and the Netherlands. Argentina, China, Czechoslovakia, Indonesia, and other countries may well be contenders for the market in the foreseeable future.

Lower production costs, sometimes (but not invariably) resulting from lower wage rates, do not wholly explain the competitive pricing offered by the foreign manufacturers. Piper and Cessna, traditional suppliers in the early years, never tried seriously to develop a good aircraft larger than the Piper Navajo or the Cessna 402, which were successful as executive and private aircraft but less so as commuter liners, although they possessed the characteristics and general specifications from which better aircraft could have been developed. Beech, which had customarily built aircraft larger than Cessna or Piper, never broke out of the small aircraft category, the nineteen-seat 1900D appearing to represent the limit of the company's aspirations. Fairchild may yet do well with the Metro 23, but it gave up a very promising market when it pulled out of the SF-340 program.

Top Ten Commuter Airlines and Their Flagships (1990)

Airline	Flagship airliner
Metro Airlines	SAAB 340
Henson Aviation	Dash 7
Simmons Airlines	ATR-42
Atlantic Southeast	Dash 7
Comair	SAAB 340
Britt Airways	ATR-42
Metroflight	SAAB 340
Pan Am Express	ATR-42
Business Express	SAAB 340
Nashville Eagle	SAAB 340

U.S. manufacturers turned their backs on the small airliner market in the 1970s, to concentrate on lucrative turbine-powered business aircraft at a time when the demand was strong. The predictable outcome has been that most commuter airliners placed into service today are foreign-built. U.S. manufacturers produce no airliner with more than nineteen seats, and both the nineteen-seaters, derived as they are from corporate models, are not designed specifically as airliners.

Such are the production costs for any modern aircraft that, at the very least, 250 aircraft have to be built to break even. The competition is so severe, and the market so fragmented among a number of suppliers, that the U.S. commuter airline market cannot alone justify the launching of a new design. Even the Metro 23 and the Beech 1900D may be feasible only because they were developed from existing designs.

The foreign manufacturers, on the other hand, often have a vigorous home market. These are usually small by comparison with that in the United States, but the markets in Brazil and Indonesia, for example, are not insignificant. Some of the manufacturers are also supported, sponsored, or subsidized, to a varying degree, by their own governments, in the interests of preserving or creating indigenous aviation industries. This approach is not as reprehensible as it may seem. It is a fact of the aircraft world's life, and the United States is no exception.

Additionally, the technological advantage formerly enjoyed by the United States has evaporated. Other countries, even those formerly categorized as part of the third world, have emulated the likes of Beech, Fairchild, or Cessna. Their products are at least as good and there is therefore little pressure in overseas markets to import aircraft from the United States, as was formerly the case. Thus, any U.S. manufacturer is largely dependent upon the domestic market—which, already inundated by products of the foreign competitors, is just not big enough. One compensation for the North American aircraft industry as a whole, however, is that all the small turboprop *engines* are made in the United States and Canada.

Overseas, the many manufacturers, except for the European Airbus consortium and those in the former Soviet Union, are resigned to the hard reality that they do not have the resources to build large airliners any more. Consequently, they have tailored their talents and their production lines to the smaller types and have become specialists in their development. Meanwhile, foreign airlines all over the world buy the big Boeing and McDonnell Douglas jets, and the United States buys the foreign commuter and regional types. It is perhaps a reasonable exchange, and one still weighted in favor of the United States.

Whither Independence?

Code-sharing is here to stay and current trends suggest that the practice will become ever more dominant, leaving little opportunity for the independent commuter airlines, which seem destined to be restricted to special markets with a purely local clientele, immune from interline entanglements because their specialized operations are incompatible with the higher cost structures of the code-sharers. Code-sharers already control over 90 percent of the commuter airline industry's traffic in the mid-1990s. This situation implies a diminished decision-making role for the remaining commuter airline presidents.

These trends will be mourned by traditionalists, but they will also bring increased stability to a segment of the industry whose record of maintaining continuity and balancing its budget has been notoriously precarious. Whether stability will bring long-term profits or not is unclear. Such an outcome would seem to depend on the role assigned by the major carriers to their affiliates. If the commuter divisions are used as "loss leaders" in competitive struggles for local market supremacy, the financial results will be easy to predict, but equally difficult to identify, as the accountants will find mysterious ways to obscure the real costs and revenues of the exclusively commuter routes.

What is clear, however, is that the stability of code-sharing has brought impressive short-term financial success to an industry that has historically been anything but profitable. For example, the operating profits of the publicly held commuter airlines tripled between 1983 and 1988, and during the same five-year period the net profits of this segment of the industry doubled. Many commuter airlines have gone public by selling stock; the fact that they have been able to do so is an excellent indicator of their increasingly positive image in the financial community.

In 1985 the Regional Airline Association estimated that all but seven of the fifty largest commuter airlines (which were then carrying 84 percent of the industry's traffic) were profitable. The stimulus to traffic growth provided by code-sharing and the ensuing stability were often cited as the main reasons. In the late 1980s one financial analyst went so far as to call commuter airlines a high-growth-rate industry with "outrageously strong" returns. These facts were succinctly outlined in an article in the 7 August 1989 issue of *Business Week* entitled "Small Planes, Tiny Towns, Big Bucks." This article also noted that the number of commuter airlines had declined, and that the industry is characterized today by fewer but stronger firms.

Is there a place for the independent commuter airline in the future? Restricted as most of them are by the dominant code-sharers to the smallest and least profitable markets, will they be forced to remain in a subservient role: to operate only on those few light-traffic-density routes where competition is irrelevant? On the other hand, should the costs of code-sharing commuter airlines continue to rise rapidly, the privileged code-sharers may be forced to abandon many current markets and to make way for the independents. Indeed, in the mid-1990s, costs for code-sharers seem to be rising rapidly, especially because of greatly increased overhead expenses forced on the commuter airlines by their major partners. There were indications that the major airlines were beginning to regard thirty-passenger aircraft as the smallest size acceptable for their affiliates. Were such a policy to become widespread, code-sharing commuter airlines would be forced to abandon many markets, unless subsidized by the parent affiliates. Presumably, they would then sell their nineteen-seat aircraft, which would become available at relatively low prices to potential new entrants, thus reviving the fortunes of the smaller independents. A new, rejuvenated commuter airline industry could emerge to write yet another chapter in the annals of U.S. air transport.

These new companies would, however, be faced with a host of problems, including securing access to hub airports, negotiating interline agreements and joint fares, and obtaining fair listings in computer res-

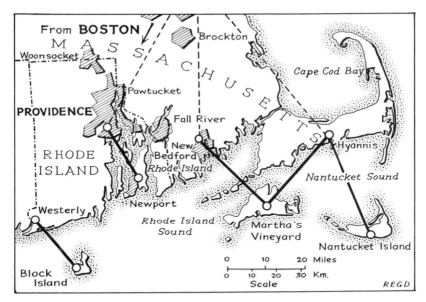

Small communities with small airstrips on offshore islands have been ideal locales for commuter airlines, whose mode of operation—smaller aircraft and higher frequencies at convenient times—has been preferable to that of the larger airlines. In New England, Martha's Vineyard, Nantucket Island, Block Island, and even Rhode Island have all received commuter airline service since the 1950s.

ervation systems and in the *Official Airline Guide*. These are, of course, the very problems that the independents face today, and which so far have proved insurmountable. Major airlines will continue to want to control as much of the traffic base, from origin to destination, as they can; thus, the appearance of these newcomers could perhaps even pave the way for an eventual second tier of low-cost code-sharers.

Another possible future role for the independents, as mentioned earlier, lies in bypassing existing hubs and providing point-to-point flights between large spoke cities. Reflecting a general increase in air travel and severe congestion at some hubs, the demand for such air service may be strong enough to make it viable. But here is the dilemma: the code-sharers would also move into these markets as they develop. Given the advantage of their marketing identification with major companies, they would have little difficulty in absorbing the bulk of such traffic. As has already happened in much larger operations, the established airlines can afford to observe events from the sidelines. If a new market fails, they lose nothing; if it succeeds, they jump on the bandwagon—and throw the incumbents off the tailgate.

On the other hand, there are airlines for which any kind of change, be it in aircraft performance, airport facilities, or reservations and operating procedures, seems to be ruled out by geographic and demographic factors that remain constant. Such an area is New England, where airway connections to the offshore islands were first started in the 1930s. Defiantly independent "mom-and-pop" businesses, such as Martha's Vineyard's Edgarton Airways (see Part III), have been continuously operating since shortly after World War II and will probably still be earning their keep in the year 2050.

Will History Repeat Itself?

Given these developments, the wider question is, "will history repeat itself?" In many respects, the commuter airlines of the 1960s and 1970s had already mirrored the progress of the local service airlines of the 1940s and 1950s. As the commuter airlines grew rapidly, they adopted ever larger aircraft, and regulations were changed to match an inexorable trend. When the local service airlines did this in the 1950s and 1960s, they grew out of their former operating environment and, in so doing, left the door open for the growth of the commuter airlines. As the current members of this latter group grow larger, as their aircraft increase in size, and as their employee wage levels begin to approach those of the major airlines, is it possible that yet another new category of airline will be established? Will we see the rise of a new third-level airline industry, using small equipment, employing a nonunion work force, and led by highly motivated individualists? Is it possible that the independent commuter airline, whose epitaph was pronounced in the late 1980s, will rise again?

One curious element of this fascinating chronology is that, in some areas, the wheel has already turned full circle. Long ago, before World War II, long before the CAB even had to consider the idea of putting airlines into categories, all routes, even the little ones, were operated by the trunk airlines. After World War II, and especially in the 1950s and 1960s, these little routes were transferred to the local service carriers. As these too grew more ambitious in the 1970s, they in turn handed the same routes over to the commuter airlines, whose nationwide route pattern in 1975 looked intriguingly similar to that of the local service airlines in 1965. Today the commuter airlines are affiliated with the major airlines, which cling protectively to their new offspring and, with the pressures of code-sharing, for better or for worse, threaten to obliterate their identity altogether. With the local service airlines now extinct and the commuter airlines largely mere surrogates, the major airlines have in effect reverted to their 1939 status, when the grandfather routes first outlined the regulated airline pattern and the U.S. air transport industry was controlled by a privileged oligarchy.

Part II

Profiles

If you have ever tried to beat off frozen snow from an airplane while a doctor is waiting, trying to keep someone alive, you don't have to be a genius to know the first building you better build is an aircraft hangar.

If you have ever had your heart slamming against your rib cage while you feel your way down at seventy miles per hour onto a black and unlighted cow pasture, there will be no doubt as to the value of runway lights.

If you have ever worked all night on a sick engine with frozen fingers and lockjaw from holding a flashlight in your mouth, you will automatically be making plans for a lighted and heated aircraft maintenance building.

If you have ever started out the first flight of the day with fuel gauges bobbing on empty and the closest fuel miles away across the waters on the mainland, you know you will mortgage your soul for a local fueling facility.

If you have tried to the last ounce of your strength and resolve to maintain an on-time flight schedule with aircraft mired axle-deep in mud or a blown tire from frozen ruts, or watched your few and precious passengers step in cow pies, you will know about drainage, hard-surfaced runways, and airfields that are for airplanes and people and not cattle.

And finally if you have ever experienced the joy of parents greeting a well and happy child when only nights before the same child was near death; seen the dignity and courage of a senior citizen on his last ride; experienced the thrill and wonderment of a first airplane rider, young or old—then you will begin to understand how it was with us.

—Roy Franklin

One of the great clichés, beloved of politicians, business tycoons, and evangelists alike, is that the strength of the country, the company, or the movement, lies in its people. Cliché or not, this homily carries much validity when applied to the evolution of the commuter airline industry as it is defined in this book. The assembly of diverse companies that gradually achieved some form of cohesion during the 1960s and 1970s took its shape as the commuter airline industry not because of a federally initiated plan, nor because of an organized effort by the incumbent trunk and local service airlines, but instead because of the perseverance of a collection of individuals.

The commuter airline industry as a whole somehow evolved from a host of disparate individual parts. And what parts they were! By their very nature, the small companies that somehow emerged from the community of fixed based operators and air taxi services confined their ambitions, as a rule, to meeting local needs within a small geographical area. Few of their founders needed to cooperate with others of the same bent. Each one had carved out a niche and was happy simply to be running a small business in his own backyard. They were true pioneers who possessed the individuality that is the hallmark of those who break new ground and must defy convention—and often the established regulations—to attain their objectives.

Such individuality, in the early days, characterized hardy souls who might have been equally happy prospecting for gold in the Yukon or building the Boulder Dam. An opportunity presented itself, an idea was born, and an embryo commuter airline emerged, invariably run almost single-handedly by its founder and owner. As time went on, however, the pioneering success was augmented and copied by others, not necessarily of the same rugged pioneering stock, but nevertheless innovators who adopted and adapted the original patterns to conform to new operational and marketing circumstances. Many of these second-generation commuter airline promoters brought into the industry the added elements of financial expertise and a recognition of the need for industry organization, both for advocating a joint cause and for beating a pathway through the almost impenetrable forests of bureaucracy and commercial rivalries.

Just as the history of the development of commuter airlines cannot be neatly tabulated as a calendar of sharply divided periods, the individual personalities of the industry's leaders cannot be similarly identified. Allowing for much overlapping of time, there was thus a third group of commuter operators who joined the throng during the latter years, particularly in the 1980s, when the pioneers ran into the rough waters of deregulation and had to absorb the crippling blows of code-sharing arrangements. During this last period, a few industry leaders appeared on the scene who not only navigated their way through the deregulated rapids but adapted themselves well to the new business environment and even profited from it.

Part II of this book therefore attempts to provide a cross section of these diverse personalities as a complement to the historical narrative in Part I. A true appreciation of the narrative is not possible without a familiarity with those who lived it. The authors selected twenty-two people who, in their opinion, have epitomized the pioneering and creative spirit that built this important segment of U.S. air transport. They were selected from all generations: the true innovators like Ross Miller, John Van Arsdale, and "Pappy" Chalk; the systematic developers like Dick Henson, J. Dawson Ransome, and Joe Whitney; and the successful expansionists like Bill Britt, George Pickett, and Milt Kuolt.

Just mentioning such fine people encourages the thought that other groups of names would have been just as representative. Ray Ellis, Bob Schoen, Roy Franklin, Pete Howe, Joe Fugere—all these, and a host of others, made their contributions and left a legacy to the hundreds of thousands, if not millions, of passengers to whom efficient air service was provided, not because of government or state direction, but because the spirit of free enterprise triumphed over restrictive handicaps and the "can do" spirit was translated into a public service.

The authors are also aware that some readers may feel that certain names have needlessly been omitted. The situation is somewhat akin to the selection of an all-star team: there are dozens of possible permutations. Much consultation took place with members of the commuter airline fraternity in an attempt to compile a list that was fairly balanced and that at least included most of the respected old-timers. The authors take full responsibility for their selection and regret that time and space did not allow for a longer listing. Indeed, if we had truly tried to do justice to all of the individuals scattered throughout the length and breadth of the fifty states who have paid their dues and given more than their share of dedication—and, let us admit, had more than a little fun in the process—this book would never have been finished.

Profile 1

Gary M. Adamson
Air Midwest

Not too many airlines started life as an aerial mortuary service. Not too many airlines actually persuaded the CAB to adopt a new formula for making subsidy payments. And few airlines, when trapped in the maw of code-sharing, were able to hedge their bets by a multiple partnership arrangement. Such a record could emerge only under the direction of a dynamic individual, one always ready to experiment and, if necessary, to resort to unorthodox practices. Such a man built and guided Air Midwest, which, during the period when fortune favored the brave, was one of the leading commuter airlines, even though its traffic base did not seem to justify such a status.

Gary Milton Adamson was born in 1936 in Wichita, Kansas, which likes to consider itself the "Aviation Capital of the World," and not surprisingly he soon developed an interest in aviation. When he was a child, both his parents learned to fly, and a close friend of the family was a stunt pilot. His father, Milton M. Adamson, worked at various times for Cessna and Boeing.

After graduating from Wichita's East High School, where he played football, Adamson enlisted in the army and became a paratrooper. Then he joined the elite Green Berets and trained as a medic, surmising that this knowledge might be useful later as he looked for a civilian job. In the army he became a close friend of Donald F. Beilman, also from Wichita, who would become both his business partner and his brother-in-law.

After Beilman left the army in 1958, he told Gary that there was a severe pilot shortage, and they both decided to seek their fortunes in the sky. Soon they were taking flying lessons, and eventually they received their private and commercial ratings. Then they sent applications to "about 95" airlines, but they quickly discovered that their qualifications fell far short of the minimum required and were forced to seek any job

Gary M. Adamson

that would pay the rent. Also in 1958, Adamson married the former Bernice Beilman, Donald's sister.

Until 1965, Adamson worked at wide variety of jobs, such as delivering bread and 7-Up, working on missile sites, and making deliveries for a drug wholesaler. As his father worked for Cessna, he was able to join the company's flying club to build up his experience, at a mere $4 per hour, in a Cessna 172. In 1963 he received his instrument rating.

Meanwhile, several events were taking place that would lead eventually to a career in aviation. In 1964 his father told Adamson that Cessna would soon be producing the Model 206, and that it had a large cargo door, designed to the specifications of a Minnesota funeral director so that a casket could easily be handled through it. Soon Adamson, his father, and Beilman were investigating the air mortuary business. A survey of local funeral directors encouraged optimism regarding the potential for profit. Therefore, on 7 May 1965, Aviation Services Incorporated (ASI) came into being. As the name implied, far more was foreseen for the young company than just air mortuary work, even at this early date.

Adamson, Beilman, and a friend, Calvin C. Hermann, each put up a third of the initial $6,000 investment, and almost immediately $3,500 was used as a down payment on a Cessna 206. Gary would manage the company, but all three would share in making major decisions. On 15 May 1965, ASI was certificated by the FAA.

But business was very slow. Soon it was decided to offer air ambulance service as well, and this line of work produced more revenue than the air mortuary business. Yet even then there was so little income that Adamson began to moonlight at a variety of jobs, including selling vacuum cleaners, driving an ambulance, and giving flying lessons. Luckily, Bernice was a nurse with a steady income; on some ambulance trips, she would go along to care for the patient. To save the company, Adamson had to borrow $400 from a bank, using his only substantial asset, an old Ford, as collateral.

In an attempt to stanch its losses, the company broadened its range of services. Regular passenger and freight charters were accepted, and Gary even began to carry skydivers in the 206.

Early in 1967 Central Airlines announced that it was dropping the eighty-mile intra-Kansas route from Salina to Wichita, and Adamson began to think of serving it. The charter business had improved, but the Cessna was still idle much of the time, and it could carry up to five passengers. After a few preparations, in April 1967 ASI became a scheduled airline. The first trip, northbound, was empty, but one passenger was carried on the return leg. Adamson himself, as ASI's only pilot, did the flying.

A few months later, a second route opened, from Wichita to Springfield, Missouri, but it averaged only about one passenger per trip. Just when ASI was about to go of business, a new opportunity arose.

In 1966, the U.S. Post Office began to award air mail routes to commuter airlines to speed up deliveries to smaller cities. Because of ASI's low fixed costs, it was the low bidder on no less than seven routes. One of these (from Dodge City, Kansas, to Pueblo, Colorado) called for a twin-engined airplane, and therefore a Cessna 402 was added to the company's growing fleet of 206s. ASI inaugurated several of the single-engined routes in October 1966, but the Post Office soon changed its policy and canceled all single-engined contracts.

Frontier Airlines was also serving Dodge City, and not only was it losing money on its route, but its veteran Douglas DC-3s were scheduled to be retired soon in favor of larger Convair 580s, a turboprop-engined type that the local airport could not handle. An agreement was worked out under which ASI would replace Frontier at Dodge City. Passenger response was highly favorable, and soon several other cities in western Kansas began to receive service by ASI's 206s.

With increasing passenger traffic, ASI brought in several new investors, and it ordered two new fifteen-seat Beech 99A turboprops. On

15 May 1969, the four-year-old company was renamed Air Midwest, added more routes, and was designated "The Official Flagship Airline of Kansas."

By November 1969, the company had nine aircraft (including six 402s), served fourteen cities, and had fifty-three employees. That year 16,600 passengers were carried, but Air Midwest lost $139,000 on revenues of $471,000.

To stay in business, in the early 1970s Adamson and Jim Pickett, his vice-president, devised a "flow-through" subsidy formula suitable for local, specialized needs that would, at the same time, be acceptable to the CAB. Air Midwest, like all commuter airlines, did not have a CAB certificate and was thus ineligible for federal subsidies. Under the flow-through arrangement, subsidies for three cities in western Kansas would continue to be paid to Frontier, which would then "flow" them to Air Midwest. The CAB was so impressed by this idea that it authorized a two-year experimental program, starting on 1 August 1973. Unfortunately, the legality of the arrangement was soon challenged in the courts by the bus lobby, and in June 1975 the program was judged to be illegal.

In the face of continuing losses, Adamsom decided to seek full certification from the CAB as an air carrier. In 1975, he sold the two Beech 99As and applied to be certificated at eight points in Kansas and Colorado, to replace Frontier. The CAB decided to allow Air Midwest to provide "regional feeder" service with small aircraft and Adamson chose the 285-mile-per-hour, seventeen-passenger Swearingen Metro II for the purpose. Air Midwest was the first carrier to be certificated as a commuter airline by the CAB.

Having received this confirmation of legitimacy, the company expanded rapidly; after the advent of airline deregulation in 1978 the number of opportunities for further growth greatly increased. Air Midwest expanded into New Mexico and Oklahoma and by July 1979 was flying to nineteen cities. Ten new Metroliners were delivered, and in 1980 three new thirty-seat SAAB 340 airliners were ordered from Sweden.

By 1982, Adamson had achieved the substantial reward that he had been seeking for so long, as Air Midwest earned a net profit of almost $2 million. For this achievement, he received *Air Transport World's* "Commuter/Regional Airline of the Year" award. In October he and Bernice went to Sweden to attend the rollout of the first 340 airliner and met the king of Sweden at the ceremonies.

In 1983 the Topeka *Daily Capital* named Gary Adamson "Kansan of the Year" and *Financial World* named Air Midwest one of the five hundred leading growth companies in America. By the end of 1983 the fleet consisted of twenty-four aircraft.

In September 1984, Air Midwest negotiated a merger with Scheduled Skyways, one of the oldest commuter airlines in the United States; the latter was considerably smaller than Air Midwest but possessed a route network adjacent to Air Midwest's. It was a natural partner and the merger took place in June 1985, several months after the inauguration of SAAB 340 service. Unfortunately, at about this time Republic Airlines, which had long worked with Scheduled Skyways at the growing traffic hub of Memphis, announced that it would in the future work with a new commuter airline that would fly under the Republic Express insignia. This decision was a severe blow to Adamson who, according to one analyst, had been left "holding the bag at Memphis, with a carrier with a lot of capacity and no one riding it." The year ended with a loss of about $3.5 million, an unfortunate reversal from the previous year.

By 1985 the commuter airline industry as a whole was in a state of flux as the code-sharing revolution intensified. Adamson arranged to become a feeder to Ozark Airlines at St. Louis, starting service on 1 October, and to Eastern Airlines at Kansas City, starting on 1 November. But Air Midwest had already lost much traffic to competing code-sharers. Adamson bluntly summed up the situation: "They're eating our lunch."

Most partnerships were between a single major carrier and a single commuter airline, but Air Midwest's relationship was not monogamous. With Ozark, Adamson established many new routes out of St. Louis as Ozark Midwest, using aircraft from the former Scheduled Skyways network, now rapidly shrinking. Later Ozark was merged into TWA, and Air Midwest flew under the Trans World Express insignia. At Kansas City Air Midwest, in a separate relationship, operated as Eastern Air Midwest Express.

To complicate matters further, Air Midwest was chosen to be the American Eagle carrier at American's newly established Nashville hub, starting on 1 April 1986. With three code-sharing operations, Air Midwest's traffic climbed to more than one million passengers annually. Losses were lower than in 1986, partly because of an employee pay cut and some pruning of the route network.

In the meantime, Robert Priddy, former vice-president at Atlantic Southeast Airlines, had bought a significant number of Air Midwest shares. He was placed on the board of directors in November 1987 and on 14 January 1988 was elected president. Adamson stood down from the presidency, commenting generously that if "Mr. Priddy can improve the security of (Air Midwest's employees), then I'm all for it." He remained as chairman of the board but no longer ran the everyday affairs of the airline.

Conditions have since changed rapidly at Air Midwest. On 15 September 1988, the code-sharing relationship with Eastern was discontinued, as the latter had stopped operating its Kansas City hub. This arrangement was replaced by a similar agreement with Braniff, but that carrier filed for bankruptcy on 28 September 1989. Air Midwest once again began to fly as an independent commuter airline into Kansas City, but substantial losses were sustained.

For about a year after leaving the presidency, Gary Adamson spent many hours on the golf links. But a man with so much energy cannot relax for very long, and in 1989 Gary and Bernice decided to strike out in a new direction: to build a new bed-and-breakfast on a golf course in Wichita.

Profile 2

Jerry C. Atkin
Skywest Airlines

By the time Jerry Atkin got into the commuter airline industry, many of the original pioneers (some of whom are profiled in this section of the book) were thinking about retiring. He can certainly be classified as being in the second wave of commuter operators who emerged in the 1970s, and some would say that, because of his comparative youth, he might almost be representative of a third era. He must qualify for inclusion in this book because during the past decade he has fashioned a route network that covers a considerable part of the United States west of Denver, one larger than the area covered by some of the local service airlines that flourished as the feeder airline segment of the air transport industry before his time.

The city of St. George, Utah, famous for a Mormon temple that towers above the roofs of the residential areas as a local landmark, is an unlikely spot to serve as the base of a far-flung airline. The region is not heavily populated, and the nearest big city, Las Vegas, is not exactly linked by community interest with St. George. But the distances in that part of the world are long, the climate is hot, and the terrain is arid, so that taking to the air is a natural impulse for travelers who over the years have sought an alternative to spending all day behind the wheel of a car. And so SkyWest Airlines was born at St. George, with no great ambition at first except to link the city with Salt Lake City to the north and Las Vegas to the south.

The airline's steady—the word "inexorable" comes to mind—growth has been carefully fashioned under the wise direction of Jerry Atkin, born at St. George on 27 February 1949. Unlike that of many of the pioneers, who were often born into aviation as sons of pilots or had been captivated by airplanes through early proximity to an airfield or to airline people, Atkin's education was relatively orthodox. He attended the local high school and spent two years at Dixie College, St. George,

Jerry C. Atkin

before attending the University of Utah at Salt Lake City, taking his B.S. in accounting and obtaining his MBA. Not for him the romantic apprenticeship of cleaning airplanes or sweeping hangar floors, hoping for a lucky break with a fixed base operator as a benefactor: Atkin started his career in 1972 as a certified public accountant with Elmer Fox & Co. in Salt Lake City.

Some might say, however, that he was predestined to become involved in the airline business, and that fate threw him and an airline into each other's arms. For in April 1972, the same year that he started work at his first job, his uncle, Ralph Atkin, founded SkyWest Airlines as a successor to Dixie Airlines, which had ceased its local operation. On 19 June of that year, SkyWest made its first scheduled flight, with a Piper Seneca, from St. George to Salt Lake City via Cedar City, on a thrice-weekly frequency. Business was steady if not spectacular, and in December 1973 the first of three Piper Navajo nine-seat Chieftains was leased to match the modestly increasing traffic; in May of the following year, two new routes were added from St. George to Las Vegas and to Page, Arizona.

Although SkyWest carried 11,887 passengers in 1974, the scheduled operation was not balancing its books. Atkin had been called in by his uncle in August 1974 as director of finance, and he soon had his work cut out for him, as the company faced a financial crisis. Confronting the problems head on—and with no false notions of seeking a way out by launching into an expansion program (as some airlines had done) in the hope of earning increased revenues from optimistic (and unrealistic) traffic forecasts—he raised $150,000 in fresh capital in October 1975.

The funds were used mostly for the less glamorous but financially sounder fixed base operations and contract work, and for trimming the scheduled operation in an effort to attain maximum efficiency with the current fleet. He restructured the company's debt, and within a year SkyWest had pulled itself up by its bootstraps, turning in a $15,000 profit for 1976 on $1 million of revenue, and with a grand total of thirty-five staff members. A profit margin of 1.5 percent was not one to make headlines in the *Wall Street Journal*, but SkyWest was afloat, and the direction of its fortunes was now under the level-headed control of Jerry Atkin.

Keeping the airline alive at this particular time was crucial, for the local service airlines, which had built up the feeder services of the United States with Beech 18s, Douglas DC-3s, and twin-engined turbo-props, were moving out as quickly as they could into the dizzy realms of jet operations. Putting aside the service obligations to small communities that had been their subsidized bread and butter throughout the 1950s and 1960s, the local airlines, or regionals, as they later preferred to be called, sought to transfer or to terminate airline service at small cities throughout the nation. The trend was especially prevalent in the Midwest and almost became a stampede in the West. Atkin and SkyWest were ready and waiting for such an opportunity, and although St. George, Utah, might not have been everybody's idea of the right place, the time was certainly right.

The first move took place in the summer of 1976. SkyWest began to work with the regional airline, Hughes Airwest, and obtained a Certificate of Public Convenience and Necessity from the CAB to offer a guaranteed service to link Cedar City and Page with the trunk lines at Las Vegas and Salt Lake City. On 15 August 1977, the CAB order became effective, and Hughes Airwest withdrew service entirely. SkyWest soon qualified for a mail subsidy, bought a fourth Navajo Chieftain, and doubled the frequency on its routes. In the spring of the following year, the acquisition of a fifth Chieftain confirmed that the airline was operating from a solid foundation of traffic demand that, even if it was not especially high in volume compared with some routes in California or in the East, was certainly regular and dependable.

During the next five years, SkyWest's progress in taking over routes that the local service (or even trunk) airlines wished to abandon became almost monotonous. Atkin methodically stepped in to fill the gaps as, one after another, the larger airlines erased from their route maps the small cities of the plateau country west of the Rocky Mountains. In preparation for such expansion, the first new Swearingen Metro II, with nineteen seats (double the capacity of the Chieftain) entered service in June 1979. Sensing that the opportunity was there for the taking, Skywest constructed a new hangar and company base at St. George and began to move from serving a localized catchment area within a two-hundred-mile radius around St. George to fashioning a network from the Canadian to the Mexican borders.

The first major extension was from Page to Phoenix, via Flagstaff, using a Navajo Chieftain released from the old routes by the arrival of the Metro II. After more of the Metros were acquired—by 1984, the fleet had grown to twelve—more segments were added in steady succession: to Pocatello, Idaho (previously served by Western Airlines or one of its affiliated companies for half a century), then to Frontier Airlines stations at Vernal, Utah, and Rock Springs, Wyoming. Assumption of a trans-Nevada service from Reno to Salt Lake City via Elko and Ely, served by United Airlines for many decades (even with Boeing 737s), was the next step. It was followed by further expansion in Idaho, to Twin Falls and Idaho Falls, taking over from Hughes Airwest again on a route that had originally been started by Zimmerly Air Lines and Empire Air Lines in 1946 and that had come to Hughes through West Coast Airlines, one of the group of carriers that became Airwest. To round off this pattern of populating the western skies with SkyWest airplanes, a Salt Lake City–Grand Junction, Colorado, route brought the number of states served to six.

The year 1984 was a watershed for Atkin and the airline that had seemingly come from nowhere to make its presence felt throughout the region once known as the Wild West. Already moving with the tide of route transfers made easier by the lifting of restrictions and regulatory pitfalls under the Airline Deregulation Act of 1978, SkyWest in that year chalked up two important events in its brief history. On 1 August 1984, it opened a route from Las Vegas to Palm Springs. This service was of a fundamentally different nature than the previous additions to its route map. The clientele was not the traditional blend of business and leisure travelers simply going from one place to another. This was a sophisticated market, linking the biggest gambling and good-time city in the United States to the one that epitomized luxurious and ostentatious standards of living, the home of film stars and celebrities. In short, SkyWest was stepping out.

Atkin then proceeded to consolidate his position in prestigious Palm Springs. On 30 September, only two months after opening his first counter at the airport there, he borrowed $7 million from the bank, added another $1 million from his own resources, and purchased Palm Springs–based Sun Aire Lines, complete with its fleet of twelve Swearingen Metro IIs, to bring his combined fleet to a round two dozen. This acquisition brought SkyWest Airlines into California, as Sun Aire specialized in linking the desert resort with its hub at Los Angeles, as well as with San Diego, Santa Barbara, Burbank, and Ontario, in addition to the Imperial Valley and Phoenix.

During the next two to three years, SkyWest integrated the two route systems, expanded to more big cities in California (San Francisco, Sacramento, and Fresno), and brought its Metro II fleet up to thirty-seven aircraft. But although the Swearingen product had served him well during the formative period of rapid route expansion, Atkin sought to retain flexibility—not to mention avoid the dangers, however remote, of being totally dependent on one aircraft supplier—by ordering, in 1985, a small fleet of Embraer 120 Brasilias. The Brasilia was the second craft from the Brazilian manufacturer that had made such an impressive entry into the commuter airline market with its Bandeirante, familiarly known all over the world as the Bandit.

By the time the first Brasilia was delivered, in December 1986, Atkin and SkyWest had already taken another giant stride in their corporate development. On 1 April of that year, a code-sharing agreement was worked out with Gerald Grinstein, now heading up Western Airlines. Skywest found itself doing business as Western Express, so as to identify more closely the association between the major and the regional airlines—as Western and SkyWest were now classified, respectively, under the post-deregulation terminology. This agreement was followed by an initial public stock offering, announced on 26 June 1986, which raised $12 million of fresh capital.

The first two Brasilias entered service on the Palm Springs–Los Angeles–San Diego route on 1 February 1987. Exactly two months later, in a nonhostile merger, Delta Air Lines bought Western Airlines, so that SkyWest was forced to change its identification markings once again, as it was now doing business as The Delta Connection. The Brasilia fleet was augmented to nine aircraft, and in March 1988 another state appeared on the SkyWest map, as the Montana cities of Great Falls, Butte, Billings, Helena, and Missoula came on line.

To peruse the SkyWest route network today is to realize at a glance the metamorphosis that has come about in the commuter airline industry during its eventful history of the past quarter century, as individual companies struggled to match their capabilities with changing market forces. Few would look at the SkyWest map and perceive it as a commuter network, and SkyWest serves a territory that is larger than that formerly covered by most of the local service airlines of the twenty or thirty years following World War II. It even embraces a geographical region larger than that allocated by the CAB in the prewar era as "grandfather" routes to airlines such as Western.

Such expansion has not, fortunately, gone to Atkin's head. Delusions of grandeur could so easily have been an ingredient in his planning process, tempting the ambitious airline president into rash decisions, such as ordering excessively large or even jet aircraft. The commuter airline industry is strewn with monuments to those who fell victim to such impetuosity. The secret of success, whether applied to the first, second, or third level of the airline business, has always been to match the flying equipment to the market demand through the proper combination of aircraft capacity and service frequency.

Under Jerry Atkin's wise direction, SkyWest has kept its course firm and true, its fleet of Metro IIs and Brasilias filling the western skies with an airline service well fitted to the needs of the market. But nobody's perfect. During the various transitions, since the key year of 1984, there has been a certain degree of wastage. Changes of affiliation and of flagship have demanded no fewer than seven different paint schemes for SkyWest airplanes. Such is the price of change in a changing world—but the price of paint is one that many an airline president would be only too glad to live with.

Profile 3

Captain Charles F. (Charlie) Blair
Antilles Air Boats

As author Robert Mikesh has observed, Charlie Blair could, in another age, have been recognized as one of America's aviation heroes. He did not perform his feats during the golden age of Lindbergh, Earhart, Hughes, or Post. Yet he did make some remarkable flights that were notable not only for their airmanship but also for their navigation and flight planning. In addition to a distinguished career as a globe-encircling airline pilot, he also founded a commuter airline of truly unique character.

Born in 1909, Blair made his first solo flight at the age of nineteen, and he was soon flying the mails on commercial air routes. He was already an experienced pilot at the outbreak of World War II, having served mainly with United Air Lines. However, the flying life for which he is best remembered began in 1941, when he joined American Export Airlines (AEA) as its chief pilot.

AEA had been founded by the shipping line American Export Lines, which tried to enter the airline world, possibly as insurance against competition on its North Atlantic routes. But because of U.S. legal restrictions, it was forced to sell its aviation component to American Airlines, under the control of which it became American Overseas Airlines (AOA) in 1945.

As AEA's chief pilot, Blair played a prominent role in introducing the Vought-Sikorsky VS-44 series of aircraft to the air transport industry. This fine flying boat is often forgotten in the annals of air transport history because its development and service coincided with World War II, and most of its operations were conducted under a cloak of secrecy. Blair flight-tested all of the three commercial VS-44s that came off the production line at Bridgeport—the last, in January 1942, just a month after the Japanese attack on Pearl Harbor.

The VS-44 was as large as the more famous Boeing 314. It carried forty passengers, compared to the latter's maximum of seventy for

Captain Charles F. (Charlie) Blair (photo courtesy of Bob Mikesh)

medium-haul routes, but it had trans-Atlantic range with as much pay-load as the Boeing. Blair achieved one of his many "firsts" by flying a VS-44 nonstop—i.e., without a refueling stop in Iceland, Greenland, Labrador, or Newfoundland—from the new flying boat base at Foynes, Ireland, to New York in June 1942. This remarkable crossing, unpublicized at the time because of wartime security, was achieved through judicious fuel management and selection of altitude, and was an indication of Blair's broad-based approach to the varied tasks confronting a transocean airline pilot.

Even when AEA became AOA in 1945 and abandoned these grand flying boats, Blair would still take time off from flying the Constellation and Stratocruiser landplanes to fly for his own enjoyment. In 1947 he flew the last VS-44 on a charter flight between Minneapolis and Iceland.

When Pan American Airways purchased AOA in 1950, he lost his position as chief pilot, but continued with "The World's Most Experienced Airline"—and it certainly was at that time—as one of its most experienced and respected pilots. But he was still seeking other opportunities for exercising his creative instincts for long-distance flying and his spirit of adventure in demonstrating his theories by example.

In January 1951, in his own North American P-51 Mustang, purchased from the famous Paul Mantz and renamed *Excalibur III* (all his personal aircraft were *Excaliburs*), Blair flew nonstop from New York to London in seven hours and forty-eight minutes, a record for piston-engined aircraft that still stands today. The wartime Mustang had already proved its worth by escorting bombers all the way from England to Berlin and back. Blair now inscribed its name indelibly in the aviation history books.

Blair must have loved the Mustang, and especially this one. He fitted it with extra tankage and, on 29 May 1951, flew it from Bardufoss, Norway, over the polar ice of the Arctic Ocean, nonstop to Fairbanks, Alaska. This was long before the technology of inertial navigation had been perfected. He proved his theory of navigation by taking "sunlines"—bearings on the sun from precalculated points. He made landfall across the northern coast of Alaska at Point Barrow, directly on course, and within one minute of his planned time. The flight took ten hours and twenty-seven minutes. This achievement in polar navigation also helped reveal the weakness of the detection and defense systems along America's northern border, a deficiency later remedied by the establishment of the well-known DEW line radar detection network.

By this time, Blair had made 435 Atlantic crossings with AEA, AOA, and Pan American (and was eventually to complete 1,600) and had achieved fame and honor among his peers. President Truman presented him with the coveted Harmon International Trophy for outstanding international achievement for 1951; he was made a colonel and later a brigadier-general of the U.S. Air Force; and he was awarded the Distinguished Flying Cross. His contribution to the science and art of aviation was thus acknowledged.

Blair retired from Pan American in 1969, having amassed 40,000 hours at the helm. This was the equivalent of spending more than three and a half years in the air, or an average of about one hour a day for his entire life. Such intensity betrayed an almost obsessive love of flying (a trait not uncommon among pilots), and so Blair's preretirement decision to form his own airline came as a surprise to no one.

He had already moved to St. Croix in the early 1960s. This former Danish possession in the Caribbean had been sold to the United States in 1917. Separated as St. Croix was from the Virgin Islands group by about forty miles, the journey from Christiansted, the biggest town on St. Croix, to Charlotte Amalie, on St. Thomas, took about four hours, either by boat or by airplane, because the airfields, especially at Christiansted, were out of town. To link the two harbors of Christiansted and Charlotte Amalie was an ideal venue for a flying boat operation. Blair's energies were galvanized. He could cut the four hours to thirty minutes, or less.

Blair would habitually commute from St. Croix to wherever Pan American needed his services, and because of his seniority he was able to arrange his periods of duty, time between duty, and vacation time. He was thus able to spend occasional long spells in St. Croix, and during one of these, in 1964, he bought a Grumman Goose ten-seat amphibian in Texas, had it reconditioned, and ferried it to St. Croix. On 1 February, he made the first scheduled flight from St. Croix to St. Thomas and thus began a unique air service. He called his airline Antilles Air Boats, but all the local Virgin Islanders just called it "the Goose."

At first there were no ramp installations at St. Croix, and so passengers were ferried from the Goose to the shore in a couple of sixteen-foot "Boston whalers"—an operation that sometimes encouraged the passengers to feel that a four-hour trip by other means was not such a bad deal.

During the first year, apart from Blair himself (who could have resigned from Pan Am but instead continued to work for another five years), Antilles Air Boats consisted of one plane, one pilot, five employees, and two small boats.

By the end of 1964, however, he had purchased a second Goose, and then a third in 1965. By 1971, he had fourteen of these sturdy aircraft, picking them up where he found them—he kept his eyes and ears open while flying the line with Pan Am. They came from places as far away as Paraguay, Tahiti, and Brazil; Alaska and Florida were particularly happy hunting grounds for Grumman Gooses. Blair also acquired a twenty-seat Catalina and two twenty-eight-seat Super-Catalinas.

These larger boats had one shortcoming: they could not be taxied up on the St. Croix ramp, which Blair had in the meantime built to save the passengers from the acrobatic indignity of stumbling into and out of the Boston whalers. Antilles Air Boats' ramp at St. Croix measured sixty-seven feet wide by hundred feet long, and it claimed that the structure was the smallest airport in the world.

The Goose was immensely popular. By the early 1970s, Blair and his staff were operating between thirty and forty flights a day between St. Croix and St. Thomas, and two or three to the unspoiled neighboring island of St. John. In October 1967, Antilles had expanded from St. Thomas to Fajardo, on the eastern tip of Puerto Rico, and it began flying directly from St. Croix to Fajardo in May 1968. In 1970, services began from St. Thomas to the Isla Grande Airport in the harbor at San Juan, Puerto Rico, where once again the amphibian Gooses would demonstrate downtown-to-downtown convenience, compared to out-of-town to out-of-town service by the landplanes.

The whole Antilles Air Boats operation was a success. The 93,000 paying passengers of 1967 grew to more than 200,000 in 1970, and the gross income exceeded $2 million. When Captain Charles Blair retired from Pan American in 1969, he must have felt that life had been good. For one thing, he had married glamorous movie star Maureen O'Hara, an event that is well remembered in St. Croix; for another, he had purchased one of his beloved old flying boats, a forty-three-seat Vought-Sikorsky VS-44.

He had obtained this on 22 January 1968 from Avalon Air Transport, a small airline operating between Los Angeles–Long Beach Harbor and Catalina Island, an offshore resort. Formerly the *Excambion*, Blair re-named it, according to his tradition, *Excalibur VII*, and operated it on the busy St. Croix–St. Thomas route for about a year. "Mother Goose," as the local residents affectionately called it, made about one thousand flights before it finished its career, quite literally, on the rocks. Blair managed to bring it to St. Thomas, and it was subsequently transferred to the Naval Air Museum at Pensacola, thence taken by barge on the Intracoastal Waterway to the custody of the Bradley Air Museum (now the New England Air Museum) in Bridgeport, Connecticut. Volunteers at Sikorsky Aircraft are restoring it to exhibit condition for the museum as the only surviving large U.S. commercial flying boat. (All these defining adjectives are indeed necessary: three Martin Mars are still in Canada, but these never operated commercially; several British ones are in museums, and one still flies occasionally.)

Not to be denied his adventurous trips down the memory lane of flying boat nostalgia, Charlie Blair tried again. This time, he journeyed twice to Sydney, Australia, where the last two remaining British S-25 Sandringhams (civil versions of the wartime Sunderlands) rested in quiet retirement at Rose Bay, the flying boat base that QANTAS and Imperial Airways had shared during the distant prewar years of the England-Australia flying boat service. One, named *Islander* by its last owner, Ansett Airlines, was ferried by Blair to the United States in 1974. The crew included Maureen O'Hara as an unpaid stewardess. Blair renamed the aircraft *Excalibur VIII*, although its sister ship, *Beachcomber*, which followed later, was renamed *Southern Cross* in a break from tradition.

On one historic occasion in 1977, Blair flew the *Southern Cross* to Great Britain and to Ireland, where it made some sightseeing tours and brought tears to the eyes of some of the citizenry in the Shannon River estuary, where they hailed Captain Charlie Blair as "the last to leave, and the first to come back."

All good things come to an end. On 2 September 1978, on a routine flight in a Grumman Goose from St. Croix to St. Thomas, Blair "lost" an engine and tried to fly the Goose on one, using the ground effect (taking advantage of the greater lift in the layer of air close to the surface). But the aircraft struck the water, cartwheeled, broke apart, and sank. Blair and three of the passengers drowned.

Already aware of the history of the maverick pilot-owner who had at times flaunted the letter of the law, if not the spirit of it, the National Transportation Safety Board threw the book at Antilles Air Boats. Citing falsified maintenance records, failure to brief passengers on survival procedures, and slack surveillance by the FAA itself, the official report found no mitigating circumstance for the crash, except the almost insulting conclusion that "the captain was trained properly for the flight."

It was a sad end to a brilliant career. Maureen O'Hara kept the airline going, using only more modern Grumman Mallards, for two more years. She then sold it to Resorts International, which planned to operate the airline in association with a casino business that it wished to start in the Virgin Islands. But permission from the authorities was not forthcoming, and Resorts shut the airline down immediately. After starting up again under a new owner, Antilles Air Boats ended its days on 10 September 1981.

Yet out of the ashes of the old one, a new company emerged, phoenixlike, using most of the former's equipment, facilities, and staff. Virgin Island Seaplane Shuttle's Mallards plied exactly the same routes as had Antilles Air Boats, until it too was, quite literally, devastated. Hurricane Hugo struck St. Croix head on on 16 September 1989, destroying everything in its path. The shuttle's fleet of Mallards was reduced to a pile of wreckage, and so was much of Maureen O'Hara's hillside home.

So ended the saga of the "Streetcar Line of the Virgin Islands." The unique service had been, for more than a decade, a tourist attraction as well as a local amenity. It provided service for vacationers and local commuters alike. As for Charlie Blair, he will be remembered long after other commuter airline personalities, innovative though they may have been, are forgotten. He was a great pilot, a pioneering man of action, and one of the airline industry's great characters, and he died with his boots on.

Profile 4

William C. (Bill) Britt
Britt Airways

A readiness to work hard, a love of aviation and flying, a willingness to take risks, and an independent spirit—these are the essential attributes of a successful commuter airline owner-operator. Bill Britt had all of these, but strongest was his spirit of independence. It has always guided and controlled his decisions to the exclusion of all other factors—and ultimately there was no compromise with this basic principle, in which he believed with an almost consuming passion.

Flying was always in his blood: his father had flown with Carl Spaatz in World War I. Born at Royal, Illinois, on 2 March 1927, and attending high school at nearby Ogden, Britt took his first airplane ride at the age of nine and started flying lessons at thirteen at the nearest city, Danville; he soloed at the age of sixteen. This simple statement hardly does justice to the achievement or the experience. Britt drove an old farm car on back roads from his home to the nearest interurban trolley stop on the route to Danville. "The conductor made a special stop so that I only had to walk 2½ miles to Danville Airport on Sunday to get in my flying lesson—I would then repeat this procedure to get back home."

In 1944 he joined the U.S. Navy and served on destroyers as a motor machinist's mate. Britt supplemented his love for flying with a respect for engines and machinery; in 1947, during his naval years, he attended the Spartan School of Aeronautics in Oklahoma and obtained a mechanic's license.

By 1948, Britt could thus not only fly 'em but also mend 'em. To move into the special world of the aviation fixed base operator was thus a natural sequel, and he worked for various companies in his home region for three years, serving a thorough apprenticeship. He learned quickly and well, and at the somewhat tender age of twenty-three (though no one has ever called Bill Britt tender) he started his own aviation business.

William C. (Bill) Britt

This was a risky undertaking at the time, and possibly the only truly uncalculated risk, with no knowledge of what the future might bring, that Britt ever took. But it was the one big risk that was to set the seal on a successful career that many would term almost flawless in its inexorable progress. For in 1950 he put his savings—a grand total of $53—plus a $500 loan and a broken-down Aeronca Champ that he owned into a crop-dusting operation. The Champ could carry 600 pounds of insecticide, and with this as almost his sole asset, apart from determination, he sought out all the local corn, soybean, and peanut farmers and was successful enough to be able to buy some J3 Piper Cubs.

The entry into crop spraying was not without its frustrations. Britt had missed one question on navigation when he took the test for his pilot's license, and by the time he retook the test he had already fitted out his airplane with the spray unit and could not therefore take the check ride. So he had to hire a qualified pilot; however, the man left after five days to work for an itinerant crop spraying outfit from Texas. Left with a thousand acres still to be sprayed under contract, Britt had to move quickly, not only to hire another pilot but also, as soon as the job was done, to make sure he could in the future do the job himself. In his subsequent twenty-five years of crop spraying, during which he always offered a money-back guarantee, he had to pay out less than $500.00.

In July 1956, after six years doing mostly crop dusting, Britt formed a full-fledged fixed base operation, Vercoa Air Service—so named because that was the sign that was already painted on the building. The shareholders were Britt and his wife Marilyn, and Raymond and Gayle Cramer; however, the latter couple soon sold their shares to the Britts so that Vercoa, as the company became known, became a one-family business.

Fixed base operators are known for their versatility in being able to take on almost any kind of operation in that all-embracing activity known as general aviation, and the Britts were no exception. After discovering that buying and selling aircraft was more profitable than operating them, they were aircraft brokers for quite a few years, though they did not neglect the flying part of Vercoa's responsibilities. Then, in 1964, an opportunity presented itself to carry explosives for the military; it was a lucrative contract that was to last for many years and provide a steady source of income. But carrying out this project required some effort and a little financial risk, as Britt had to acquire specialized aircraft. Typically, he found a solution that was practical, effective, and economical. He bought a twin-engined Beech C-45H (also called a Beech 18), by this time almost a vintage aircraft, and fitted it with cargo doors.

This old aircraft type, outmoded though it may have seemed to some, was to be the first of a fleet that grew to nine, such was its suitability for the mission in terms of performance and size. The twin Beeches carried explosive samples everywhere from Arizona to Kentucky, from Iowa to Florida. The average Beech 18 trip was 6,500 miles out and back to Danville, and the longest was 16,500 miles. Some made courier runs in Florida, from McDill Air Force Base to Tampa and other neighboring states, and up the Atlantic coast as far as Andrews Air Force Base near Washington. Britt also received the second air mail contract let for small aircraft, from Indianapolis to Charleston, South Carolina, via Cincinnati, and neatly coordinated this operation with the McDill courier operation at Norfolk, Virginia, so as to position the aircraft routinely back to Danville for maintenance.

In 1968, another opportunity presented itself, and Britt was able to put to good use the regular flying experience he had gained during the previous year or two. The local service carrier in the region was Lake Central Airlines. Handicapped by a network of routes, ordained by the CAB, that were all extremely short-haul, it had sought a solution in introducing the twenty-eight-seat Nord 262, a French-built turboprop. This aircraft had had its problems, not least because the FAA had reduced its gross takeoff weight (and therefore its carrying capacity) by 2,300 pounds. To meet an emergency capacity shortage on two routes between Indianapolis and Chicago, Lloyd Hartman of Lake Central sought assistance from Vercoa, which at first carried only excess baggage when needed on the whole route and later concentrated on carrying the total loads from Danville and Lafayette. Thus Britt had his first taste of operating a scheduled service, and he was in the right place at the right time when a chance came to do so permanently. At the time, he had a nine-seat Lockheed 12A. But he became disenchanted by passengers who referred to his little operation as the Amelia Earhart show, and so he replaced the Lockheed with the old faithful Beech C-45A, also with nine seats.

On 14 March 1968, Allegheny Airlines purchased Lake Central and quickly absorbed it into its route system. The new management decided to terminate service at some of the former Lake Central points where traffic levels were low. On 28 July Bill Britt bought a new Beech 99 turboprop, fitted with a modest twelve to fifteen seats, and started the first scheduled airline service by Vercoa on 7 October 1968, from Danville to Chicago. This operation was classified as an Allegheny Commuter airline, and it was the second (after Dick Henson's pioneering example) of this successful group of partnership agreements.

In November 1974, Vercoa moved its operating base from Danville to Terre Haute, Indiana, about fifty miles to the south, and shortly thereafter, in February 1975, changed its name to the more appropriate Britt Airlines, Inc., at the same time leasing two more Beech 99s. The Vercoa name, now superfluous, was still left on the building at Danville.

By this time, Britt had already demonstrated a healthy tendency toward independence. Between 1970 and 1972, he had operated the Vercoa Commuter, using a Volpar Beech 18, a modification of the aging aircraft that gave it a tricycle landing gear and a slightly more modern appearance. Britt had entered a market that Allegheny did not need or want, flying from Champaign and Decatur, Illinois, to Chicago's downtown airport at Meigs Field. Even though the operation was short-lived, he was honing his commuter airline skills.

Furthermore, he was becoming disenchanted with the Allegheny Commuter system. In later years, he was to reflect, somewhat bitterly, that from 1968 to 1973, "we were told where we could or could not fly, were not allowed to grow, and could not make any money." This went squarely against Britt's grain, and when his next chance came to expand, it was not with Allegheny.

During the 1970s, all the local service companies were moving to change not only their image as operators of secondary—and by implication inferior—airlines, but also their network patterns in conformity with their wish to upgrade equipment and to gain footholds in the more lucrative intercity routes, hitherto almost the exclusive privilege of the trunk airlines. As they gained new routes and retired their old fleets, the disposal of some of the less traveled routes was a natural sequel, and the latter half of the 1960s witnessed a steady procession of route transfer cases before the CAB.

One of the frequent applicants was Ozark Airlines of St. Louis, which began a steady program of route rationalization by terminating service at small communities, especially in northern Illinois. Contact with Britt as a candidate to take over the operations seemed almost predestined. Service began in July 1976 from Galesburg and Sterling to Chicago, and new routes under the Britt name followed, including Danville-Indianapolis and Bloomington-Indianapolis. Britt acquired more Beech 99s, building the fleet strength of this versatile turboprop to twelve.

More important than new routes or new aircraft, however was the fact that Britt had engineered this new expansion of his sphere of influence without the help of—and indeed in spite of his association with—the Allegheny Commuter organization. Because of what could be politely described as a conflict of interests, he avoided legal complications among Ozark, Allegheny, and himself by setting up a separate company, Britt Airways, to handle the Ozark partnership while Britt Airlines continued its relationship with Allegheny. Fortunately, the only point where the two Britt companies ever met was at Chicago, where the local staff had to wear two hats every now and again.

The process of local-service-to-commuter route transfer was accelerated in 1978 with the passing of the Airline Deregulation Act. The important Illinois cities of Peoria and Springfield and Evansville, Indiana, were added to the Britt Airways network, with a coincidental Ozark flight attendants' strike stimulating further traffic growth. The first of fourteen eighteen-seat Swearingen Metros joined the fleet late in 1978, and in September 1980 such was the booming momentum of the Britt business that three Fairchild FH-227s were purchased under the special provisions of Part 121 of the FAA regulations.

With most of his income and the greater part of his operation in the former Ozark territory but now completely independent, Britt took the important step on 26 April 1981 of disengaging himself from the Allegheny Commuter system, now under the control of the renamed USAir corporation, which was growing quickly and had also taken over Mohawk Airlines. He merged the two Britt companies under the Britt Airways name, winding up the Allegheny-connected operations. He had become disillusioned with the conditions imposed by the senior partner, believing that they stifled free enterprise on his part, and he disliked having to ask Big Brother if he wished to change a schedule, make a route modification, or upgrade equipment.

In 1979, feeling emancipated from a repressive system, Britt embarked on a spending spree, buying more forty-nine-seat FH-227s and forty-four-seat Fokker F-27s, the former from Air New England and others from sources in Europe and other parts of the world. By 1983, measured by the number of passengers carried in a year, Bill Britt had grown to be the biggest commuter airline operator in the contiguous United States. (Mid Pacific, in Hawaii, classified as a commuter airline, was the biggest of all in 1984). The astonishing period of sustained growth, from the time when Britt Airlines had been a relatively minor cog in the Allegheny Commuter wheel before its involvement with Ozark, had covered only seven years and had taken him to a position of eminence among his peers.

In 1984, less than a decade after he had taken over some Ozark routes with twelve-seat Beech 99s when that local service carrier expanded its Douglas DC-9 jet fleet, Britt purchased his own twin-jet aircraft, two British Aircraft Corporation BAC One-Elevens, each fitted with seventy-nine seats. One was put into service on the high-volume routes from the Chicago hub to Evansville, Cedar Rapids, and (for a short time) Champaign. The other was used for "Trump Charters" on behalf of Sterling Transportation, flying "high rollers" from Chicago and other points in the area to the casinos of Atlantic City. In 1985, one of the BAC One-Elevens was flying three round trips a day at an 85 percent load factor from Columbus, Ohio, to Orlando, Florida, carrying Disney World holidaymakers.

Apparently relenting for a time from his independent stand, Britt became associated with the Piedmont Commuter network in the fall of 1985. Under the benevolent leadership of Tom Davis, Piedmont had been one of the original local service airlines, and it had gradually moved up in the ranks to become one of the industry leaders; serving the thriving "silicon belt" of the North Carolina commuter industrial zone, it had prospered and expanded impressively. Britt prospered too, carrying 46,000 passengers to and from Dayton per month, using five Metroliners and a Fairchild F-27.

But by this time other storms were gathering, and these were beyond the control of Britt and, for that matter, of any of the commuter airline leaders. The idea that Allegheny Airlines had had many years pre-viously—to form a group of partnerships so as to feed traffic from the tertiary route system (the commuter airlines) into the secondary and thence the primary systems of the local service and trunk carriers—sud-denly took on new life during the mid-1980s. All the big trunk airlines discovered the benefits of code-sharing partnerships. In exchange for substantial assistance, particularly in booking reservations, provided by the major airlines, the commuter airlines would surrender much of their independence, even their perceived identities, by sharing the majors' two-letter codes in computerized reservation systems and often taking on the larger airlines' names as well. (See Chapter 7 for a more exten-sive discussion of code-sharing.)

There were considerable benefits to the arrangement on both sides. Indeed some commuter airline leaders, including many veterans—either grown tired of trying to make ends meet from year to year or simply deciding that, after a few successful years, the time had come to retire while on top—readily joined the ranks of such code-sharing partner-ships as American Eagle, United Express, or Northwest Airlink. Chicago was the focal point of Britt's empire, and it was there particularly that he came face to face with some formidable code-sharing competitors; he met them as well at St. Louis (Ozark and TWA), Indianapolis (USAir), and Dayton, although at the latter city he was himself in league with Piedmont, which had established a hub there.

Britt has often expressed himself forcefully on the subject of code-sharing, claiming that it will destroy the industry. His words, repeated by many as a synopsis of the problem, have, in many ways been pro-phetic: "When becoming a [code-sharer], the larger airline uses your assets, runs your schedules, determines your pricing, and decides what the feed schedules should be. The only thing a major partner wants is for the commuter [airline] to run its airplanes, its pilots, and its mechanics."

This was not Britt's way. On 23 December 1985, he took things into his own hands and sold Britt Airways to the star among the new post-deregulation airlines, People Express, for $36,500,000. At that time, he had 1,079 employees, of whom 276 were aircrew. He was carrying 123,000 passengers a month and had earned $90 million in gross reve-nues that year, with a fleet of forty-seven airplanes: two BAC One-Elev-ens, fourteen Fokker/Fairchild FH 227/27s, nineteen Metros, and twelve Beech 99s—all owned, not leased.

With this fleet, Britt Airways had become the third largest airline in number of flights, and the fifth largest in number of passengers, serving

Chicago's O'Hare Airport. Its route network covered a dense hub-and-spoke pattern, with connecting links throughout Illinois, Iowa, and Indiana and routes stretching to St. Louis, Detroit, Dayton, Louisville, and Memphis. The headquarters and base at Terre Haute was able to maintain the whole fleet, except the jet engines and propellers, and it also did contract work for other airlines. It was on the SABRE reservation system. Britt had no labor unions, but all employees participated in a profit-sharing program to which the company had contributed $8 million.

What happened subsequently to Britt Airways is another story, and Bill Britt had no part in it. People Express's star ceased to twinkle, and the airline went into decline, to be engulfed by Frank Lorenzo's Texas Air Corporation; the Britt name was perpetuated as one of the Continental Express commuter airline associates. The airline should have been a sound investment. During the whole of its existence under Bill's control, Britt Airways never lost money in any single month, and it never lost a passenger.

Profile 5

Arthur Burns (Pappy) Chalk and Dean Franklin
Chalk's Flying Service
(Chalk's International)

Arthur Burns Chalk used to claim that his was the world's oldest airline. Such an assertion depends entirely upon one's definition of an airline—and by any criterion the claim is, at best, questionable—but he certainly ranks as one of the pioneer commuter airline operators. He and his successors have operated between Florida and the Bahamas, with varying degrees of frequency and regularity, ever since 1919, the year in which air transport began to be recognized as a means of putting the airplane to commercial use.

"Pappy" Chalk, as he was always called, was born in 1889 and learned to fly in Paducah, Kentucky, in 1911, after working as a bicycle mechanic. When a barnstormer, no less a personality than the famous Tony Jannus, had asked him to replace a melted piston, he had been rewarded with flying lessons. During World War I, he flew for the Marine Corps, and after demobilization founded his small airline company in Miami in 1919. At that time no government agency existed to describe his operation, much less regulate it, but in fact it was the world's first air taxi operation, carrying passengers to a fixed destination at any time that could be mutually arranged.

For the next seventeen years Pappy Chalk's headquarters was a table under an umbrella on the seashore near the end of Flagler Street. This sufficed as the total organizational structure until 1936, when he erected a small building, hardly bigger than a hut—and strong rumor had it that the material for the building consisted of rocks collected from the seashore when nobody was looking.

His first aircraft were war-surplus Curtiss HS-2L amphibians. He described these aircraft as "overgrown Seagulls," and he modified them to carry four or five people. But in 1930 he acquired a Waco ASO. The aircraft, NC-654N, was registered to A. B. Chalk, 368 N.E. 57th Street, Miami, where he lived until he died on 26 May 1977.

Arthur Burns (Pappy) Chalk (photo courtesy of Dean Franklin)

The airline may well have owed its existence to prohibition. Through-out the fourteen-year period between the ratification of the Eighteenth Amendment, calling for prohibition, and its repeal by the Twenty-First Amendment, Chalk's Flying Service flew to Bimini, in the British-controlled Bahamas—almost within sight of Miami if one looked out from the top of a tall building. Bimini was temptingly within reach of thirsty Americans, and within a few months it became a desirable destination for all those who wished to take a legitimate swig or two of the hard stuff. Bimini meanwhile became a major gateway for illegitimate exports of hard liquor. Chalk was impartial. His Curtiss boats served everybody: the bootleggers, their customers, and even the customs men who did their best to keep an eye on things. Chalk was in the happy position of knowing that, although there were many who would have liked to stop his operation, there were far more who relied upon its continuance.

At the time, Chalk dominated the scene on the waterfront and monopolized the business of local charter flying. If anyone else flew, it was usually through his "agency," and Pappy was paid a percentage of the take.

Prohibition was repealed in 1933, and with it much of Chalk's regular traffic evaporated. So he set about finding a new source of traffic: big game fishermen who found the island of Bimini ideal as a base for their boats and wanted to be able to fly to and from them from the mainland.

The Waco was replaced by a Fairchild 71, which (except for a short-lived FC-2W2) made up the entire Chalk Flying Service fleet until 1940. (The Waco had been lost when, on an unusual contract in 1933, Chalk had flown his two-airplane fleet to Havana to take the Cuban dictator Gerardo Machado into exile. Unfortunately for Chalk, the opposing forces of Fulgencio Batista shot up the Waco, which had to be left in Havana harbor while he flew Machado to Nassau in the 71.)

During World War II, Chalk maintained intermittent service, when required and when permitted, with two Sikorsky S-38s, and he emerged after the conflict with his flying service still intact and augmented by a small fleet of Grumman Gooses. During the postwar return to normalcy, leisure travel recovered healthily, and he was able to reestablish himself as part of the Miami aviation scene.

By this time, Chalk had entered into a loose business association with Dean Franklin, a happy-go-lucky flier twenty-two years his junior who had arrived in Florida in 1936 with a patched-up Loening flying boat. Unsuccessful in making a living with it in the Florida Keys, he flew up the Chattahoochee River and on to the Ohio River, one of the few times in history when a barnstormer used a floatplane. He joined the Ferry Command in 1942, flew PBY-5s in Brazil for the Rubber Development Corporation, and, in 1944, accomplished the remarkable feat of flying a Grumman Goose across the Andes, from Manaus to Lima via Guajara Mirím, Cochabamba, and Arequipa. After the end of World War II, he once again joined forces with Chalk, bringing with him a Stinson SRH for which Pappy supplied the floats. He quickly became more than a pilot, mechanic, or assistant: he effectively shared the management of Chalk's Flying Service with Mrs. Chalk.

Miscellaneous aircraft came and went, but by 1947 Chalk's had turned to the sturdy amphibian products of Grumman, starting with four-seat Wigeons in 1947. During the same year, on 21 November, the company obtained its first certificate from the FAA, with special exemption from the CAB, as an irregular carrier. The certificate was renewed permanently on 18 July 1950, and during the ensuing decade the Wigeons and Gooses settled down to become a Miami institution, with visitors going to Chalk's Miami base at Watson Island at least to observe the operation, even if they did not patronize it.

Yet Chalk's suffered, as did so many Florida airlines big and small, from the intensely seasonal nature of the business. Miami seethed with visitors during the winter but was close to deserted during the summer. The Chalk's service was operated on demand, and the demand was spasmodic, hardly enough to make economic sense. In fact in 1955, the city of Miami tried to evict Chalk from Watson Island for nonpayment of rent on the property; but by this time Chalk had enough friends in influential places to support his claim for squatter's rights.

In October 1962, Chalk's Flying Service supplemented its revenue with some lucrative charters for the news media covering the Cuban missile crisis. Three Grumman Gooses were based temporarily at Great Inagua Island, southernmost of the Bahamas, and made formation flights on reconnaissance for the press. On one occasion, they came close to being shot down by U.S. aircraft from the base at Guantánamo Bay, when the photographer's telescopic lenses were mistaken for guns.

In 1964, at the age of seventy-five, Pappy Chalk retired. Dean Franklin bought his stock, i.e., the whole airline, in exchange for what amounted to a pension of $800 per month. At the time, the entire fleet consisted of one Wigeon. But Franklin had two Gooses in his own name, bought two more from a pilot friend, Paul Horvath, and augmented the fleet still further by purchasing five Grumman Mallards from Japan through the well-known aircraft trader Fred B. Ayer. Suddenly, Chalk's Flying Service was equipped with a fairly substantial inventory of good amphibians.

To put this mini-armada to good use, Franklin applied to the British government (this was before Bahamian independence) and obtained a "Route 9" certificate, which permitted him to fly to any point in the Bahamas from Miami, Palm Beach, Orlando, Tampa, and Fort Lauderdale. Moreover, this certificate included the rights to operate on a fixed schedule, as opposed to offering a series of on-demand or charter flights. Until this time, Chalk's had not been able to sell tickets to individuals; it had chartered the whole flight and the customers had split the price of the charter between them.

To celebrate its new status, Franklin changed the company's name to Chalk's International Airlines and added Cat Cay as an additional destination. For a short period during the 1970s, he also operated from West Palm Beach and Fort Lauderdale as Florida gateways and flew to Chub Cay and Walker's Cay. But Chalk's International Airlines' route network was otherwise little different from that of the old Flying Service. Franklin not only kept his head but also kept his extensive traffic rights in reserve, wisely conserving them until the demand increased and the competition desisted. In the event, the demand remained steady and the competition intensified, as many other commuter airlines jumped on the Bahamas bandwagon.

In 1972, almost forty years after undertaking its fateful charter to Havana, Chalk's flew there once again—under equally dramatic circumstances. One of its Grumman Gooses was hijacked by two armed men at the Walker's Island terminal. They forced the pilot, Jim Cothron, to take off at gunpoint. When he demurred, they shot him, fortunately not fatally. The copilot, Doug McKenzie, then had to fly the aircraft to Havana. Thereafter, no Chalk aircraft was ever allowed to take on enough fuel to fly nonstop to Cuba.

About two years after this incident, Franklin sold Chalk's International to Resorts International, a large corporation that owned, among other investments, hotels, casinos, restaurants, golf courses, and villas on Paradise Island, adjacent to New Providence Island and the Bahamas capital of Nassau. At this time, the fleet was honed down to five Mallards. These were fitted with turboprop engines, and plans were made to link the resort with Miami with its own air service.

During these changes of ownership, Arthur Burns Chalk reached another red-letter day in his life, exactly ten years after he had retired on his seventy-fifth birthday. On his eighty-fifth birthday, he made his last flight as a pilot, having been obliged, at FAA insistence, to surrender his license. He had flown 16,800 miles in the left-hand seat (or, in the early days, the only seat), but, as he reminded everyone, that figure only covered flights after 1925, when regulations demanded that he start to keep records.

Chalk was not able to enjoy much time as a retiree pilot. On 26 May 1977, he was killed when he fell out of a tree while pruning it, one of his favorite spare-time occupations at the home on 57th Street where he had lived throughout his career as an airline operator.

In recalling his partner, Dean Franklin said that, during the thirty-six years of their close association, they had never had an argument, although Mrs. Chalk "either liked you or she didn't." Franklin does not reveal the category to which he belonged.

Chalk was quite religious. A Seventh Day Adventist, he would not fly on Saturdays. But he relaxed this self-imposed limitation during later years when business was booming, on condition that 10 percent of the take "went to the Lord." Throughout the lifetime of his little company, he was never destitute, although there were some lean times. The injuries in the hijacking incident apart, no passenger or pilot had ever been hurt.

Chalk would have been aghast, had he survived another couple of years, to witness the financial quagmire into which his airline descended under its new management. Resorts International made grandiose plans, overreaching itself to such an extent that it lost $500,000 in 1979 and almost $1 million in 1980.

Eschewing caution and a belt-tightening policy, Resorts tried to stem the tide by introducing a fleet of twenty-eight-seat Grumman Albatrosses, converted to the G-111 commercial standard from the U.S. Navy HU-16 classification. The new craft were much bigger than the fourteen-seat Mallards, and Resorts' vain hope was to increase traffic, relying on what it saw as the magnetic attraction of Paradise Island. But the increases that did occur were not significant, and furthermore the Albatrosses had to carry a flight attendant, as they exceeded the FAA's nineteen-seat limit for an unattended cabin. And the noise level in the cabin was so high that the attendants had to pass around a note for the passengers to write in their choice of beverage.

In 1988, Donald Trump bought the airline, and he sold it a few months later to Merv Griffin. A new STOLport landing strip was built at Paradise Island to accommodate de Havilland Aircraft of Canada DHC Dash 7 forty-seat turboprops that operated under the name of Paradise Island Airways, actually an affiliate of Chalk's International.

This final chapter in the story of a "mom-and-pop" airline that, like the frog in Aesop's fable, inflated itself until it burst was none of Pappy Chalk's (or Dean Franklin's) doing. Chalk's International almost ceased to exist in 1989, but under new ownership it still survives, albeit with a little more conservatism in management. Perhaps the new owner, Seth Atwood of United Capital Corporation of Illinois/Atwood Enterprises, has taken note of Chalk's attitude toward finance. He never trusted the banks. He kept all his money at home, in rubber bands.

Profile 6

L. W. (Roy) Clark
Pennsylvania Airlines

If it can be said that a commuter airline president has paid his dues in coming up the hard way, then Roy Clark, who was fifty-three yeras old and had completed thirty-seven years of miscellaneous flying before he started his first commuter airline route, is free from debt. And in illustrating how a commuter airline operation can start almost on a hunch and by following a good example, his fortuitous journey to Reno in 1964 serves as an excellent case study of how to recognize an opportunity, seize it, and carry thought into action.

L. W. (Roy) Clark was born at Schenectady, New York, on 8 November 1911, in humble circumstances. He "peddled milk for four years in a horse and wagon until [he] was 15 years old" and took his first airplane ride when Vic Rickard, a barnstormer, flew into town, landed at the end of his street, and rewarded him for cleaning the machine. Clark entered Scotia High School in 1926 and learned to fly when, as a frequent visitor to Schenectady Airport, he met Sanford Liddle and once again was rewarded—to greater effect—for cleaning his airplane.

In 1930, Liddle bought a six-place Ryan Brougham from Parks Air College in St. Louis and flew it to Grosse Ile, Michigan, to fit it with pontoons, and thence to Lake Pleasant in the Adirondacks, site of Max Schmeling's training camp for the world heavyweight championship fight. Liddle and Clark barnstormed around the New York state lakes region for about three years, until they cracked up the Ryan in 1934.

Clark then rented a farmer's field near Schenectady, bought a Waco 10 for $500, and undertook a rather shaky career in freelance flying work in the Carolinas, much of it in the barnstorming tradition of the 1920s. He supplemented this by delivering cars to Florida, where he worked in hotels, rising from elevator boy to superintendent of services at the Blackstone Hotel. In 1936, he went to Goldsboro, North Carolina, and stayed for two years, earning $5.00 per week, plus room and board,

L. W. (Roy) Clark

and living in the home of Seymour Johnson, whose death in World War II led to Goldsboro Airport being named after him. Here he met Ace Vaughan, another barnstormer, with whom he joined forces to advertise Miami's Royal Palm Club over Miami Beach and at the racetracks by towing aerial banners behind a J-5 Travel Air. Clark and Vaughan were paid $40.00 per hour: half in cash and half in food, liquor, and other amenities.

Clark remembers some of the hazards of banner towing. Their first assignment was a banner that read "Rudy Vallee, Ted Lewis, 30 Beautiful Girls, Royal Palm Club, Now." The banner was so long that it drooped, leading the Civil Aeronautics Authority (CAA) to insist that it be shortened, and sparking a debate as to which words or letters should be cut. The issue was made more delicate by Ted Lewis's insistence that his name should be first.

In 1937, Clark moved to Raleigh, North Carolina, where he trained many civilian pilots from the local universities; this activity led to his selling the Travel Air and signing up as chief pilot for the Civilian Pilot Training Program. He progressed rapidly and by 1943 was a chief inspector for the CAA, assigned to Chicago. After World War II he was promoted to chief of the flight branch for the New York region, and in 1949 he became the supervising agent of the district office at Harrisburg, Pennsylvania.

Clark ended his career as a civil servant in May 1954, when he joined the L. B. Smith Aircraft Corporation to start a fixed base operation at the old Harrisburg Airport (now the Capital City Airport). He worked on salary and commission until 1968, when he approached L. B. Smith— during a game of golf in Florida—about the possibility of purchasing the business. Their verbal agreement was invalidated by the death of Smith shortly afterward, but his successor, Richard Jordan, nevertheless honored the agreement. (In 1970, the fixed base part of the L. B. Smith organization was spun off to become the Clark Aviation Corporation, which is still in existence.)

Opportunity had first knocked, quite by chance, a few years earlier, in the spring of 1964. Smith had a home in Reno, Nevada, and he had asked Clark to go there to look at some airplanes. Clark was delayed at Tucson and missed the connecting mainline flight to Reno. He heard that a nine-seat Beech 18 of Apache Airlines, the local scheduled third-level carrier, was about to leave for Phoenix and reasoned that the short hop would at least get him on his way. He was so impressed with what he saw on that flight that upon returning to Harrisburg he persuaded Smith to start a similar operation. He bought a Beech 18 from Hamilton Aircraft in Tucson, who rebuilt it with ten seats at a cost of $45,000.

On 15 April 1965, Clark started a scheduled service from Harrisburg to Washington as The Harrisburg Commuter. For a few months that fall, "The Airline with a Smile" made a stop in Baltimore, but this was dropped when Clark added a second Beech 18 in the spring of 1967, in favor of routes to State College, site of Pennsylvania State University, and to nearby Lancaster.

It was during this period of initial operations that Clark negotiated the complete ownership of the infant commuter airline. In 1969, he realized that he had to go it completely alone when he bought a Twin Otter for $175,000 and sold it the next day for $225,000. On 29 January 1970, the company was registered as Pennsylvania Commuter Airlines (PCA). However, such were the amicable relations between Clark and the L. B. Smith Corporation, that the latter agreed to finance the airline for a period of ten years. But Clark paid off the loan in two years, having done very well as a Cessna dealer.

Always a spontaneous, even impetuous, opportunist, Clark soon made his first move toward consolidating a territory in central Pennsylvania. He heard that Eastern Air Lines wished to terminate service at Lancaster, went to New York to negotiate a transfer, and signed an agreement with a guaranteed minimum income, for three years, for the

Lancaster-Washington route, replacing the Eastern Convair-Liner operation with a new PCA Beech 99.

In 1971, he started a route from State College to Pittsburgh with a Cessna 402, at the same time adding a nonstop Beech 18 flight from State College to Washington. Then, in an important development, Allegheny Airlines approached Clark to fly its route from Philipsburg (near State College) to Pittsburgh. Thus on 1 October 1973, PCA joined the Allegheny Commuter system. Clark paid Allegheny for reservation and passenger handling services at those stations handling PCA traffic.

Two years later, in 1975, another Allegheny Airlines partner, Air East, based at Johnstown, Pennsylvania, had a serious accident and closed down. PCA took over Air East's Altoona-Johnstown-Pittsburgh route (closely paralleling its own State College–Pittsburgh route) within five days.

Thereafter, Clark expanded steadily and strongly, purchasing three DHC-6 Twin Otters and two more Beech 99s during the period 1976–1978. At the end of 1978 he added another segment, Pittsburgh-Williamsport (previously an Allegheny route), operating French-built Nord 262s originally purchased by Lake Central Airlines and now designated Mohawk 298s after being reengined with Pratt & Whitney PT-6s.

Increasing the pace and intensity of its expansion, PCA leased four of Allegheny's eight Mohawks and moved into New York. Clark did not believe in half measures: services were started to all three airports—La Guardia, John F. Kennedy, and Newark—and Philadelphia was added for good measure. He also augmented his growing fleet with three Shorts SD-330s, that homely but eminently practical thirty-seat British airliner, built like a box with wings but flying economically over short routes. Clark soon liked them enough to buy three more. In May 1983, the Nords were retired, and by the end of the decade the fleet consisted of Beech 1900s (fifteen seats), Twin Otters (nineteen seats), and Shorts SD-330s (thirty seats).

In 1984, PCA moved into a new hangar-office complex, the largest at Harrisburg Airport, and Clark, at the age of seventy-three, began to hand over the reins to his son, William C. (Bill) Clark. He retired gracefully, to enjoy making the social rounds in his beloved XJ12 Jaguar. He died on 18 March 1987, leaving behind a legacy of commuter airline accomplishment in the classic style: serving small communities with quiet efficiency, linking with the national air network to provide an integrated service, and reaping a comfortable reward for hard work and sound judgment.

Profile 7

Raymond J. (Ray) Ellis
Scheduled Skyways

Scheduled Skyways is little known by most aviation historians, because it was small and, by conventional airline perspectives, far off the beaten track. However, this airline and its founder, Ray Ellis, deserve recognition as true pioneers of the commuter airline industry. Largely bypassed by the trunk airlines on both the transcontinental and north-south route axes, the relatively small population and few cities of Arkansas did not encourage airline service, even by the newly formed local service airlines of the postwar era.

This special demographic situation led to a special solution, one that would later be echoed in other states. The state university of Arkansas is not at the capital city of Little Rock, but rather 140 miles to the northwest at Fayetteville. Universities are typically populated by a faculty and staff who have a need to travel, and in the case of Arkansas this need was further stimulated by a satellite education program in the capital city. Cometh the hour, cometh the man: to meet a special need, a modestly sized fixed base operator in Fayetteville undertook a logical extension of his aviation business to begin one of the first scheduled air taxi services in the United States.

Raymond Jefferson Ellis was born at Adona, Arkansas, on 28 March 1905. His ancestors had originally settled in New England, and he can trace his lineage to John Ellis, who married Joanna Willis at Dorchester, Massachusetts, in 1650. The family then moved south, progressively to New Jersey, Virginia, North Carolina, and Georgia, and then westward to Mississippi and Arkansas.

In 1911 the Ellis family moved to Hugo, Oklahoma, and all of Ellis's formal education took place in that state. He graduated from Hugo High School and then went to Oklahoma A&M College (now Oklahoma State University), where he emphasized studies in business and education, played on the football team, and was a member of the student senate.

Raymond J. (Ray) Ellis

These early years gave no hint that some day he would play a pioneering role in commuter aviation.

After graduating in 1930, Ellis took a job as a high school science teacher in Haskell, Oklahoma. Besides teaching a full load of classes, he was in charge of the entire athletics program. The Great Depression had started, the local government had little money, and so he was paid not in cash but in county warrants, to be held until money was available or sold for cash at a discount. During the summers, Ellis worked for the Pure Oil Company in nearby Muskogee and played semiprofessional baseball. Because of its low salary, he resigned from his teaching job in 1933 and went to work full time for the oil company.

At Pure Oil Ellis began to develop an interest in flying. The company had an aviation department, based in Columbus, Ohio, and when one of the airplanes arrived at the Muskogee airport, he would often meet it and take the corporate official on a tour of local Pure Oil facilities. Occasionally he was invited to fly along on portions of the inspection trips, and from these experiences a strong interest in flying blossomed.

Ellis felt that he could advance his chances for promotion by learning to fly, so in 1937 he started to take lessons from L. L. Ruppert, airport manager at Hatbox Field in Muskogee. On 5 August 1937, he soloed in a J-2 Piper Cub, and he received his pilot's license on 8 August 1938, the same day that the Civil Aeronautics Act of 1938 went into effect. Not long thereafter he bought his first aircraft, a Waco 9 biplane. In 1939

Ellis married Sallye Margaret Chadwell of Muskogee, who was to be a vital partner to him in his later career in flying.

Faced with the threat of war in the late 1930s, the United States was taking steps to prepare for a possible armed conflict. One such measure was the formation of the Civilian Pilot Training Program (CPTP), which offered an introductory course for men who wanted to become military pilots. In 1940 one of Ellis's acquaintances, A. W. Hayes, was operating such a program in connection with the University of Arkansas at Fayetteville. The business was not doing well financially, and Ellis was persuaded to come to Fayetteville in September 1940 to take over the program for the fall semester. Partly because it was not very profitable, Hayes said that he would help Ellis through the first class and would then simply let him have the business at no cost.

Shortly after arriving, Ellis founded a fixed base operation, the Fayetteville Flying Service (FFS), which became the basis for all his future flying activities. With the onset of World War II, the CPTP became the War Training Service (later the College Training Detachment), and business picked up significantly. By the end of the war, about 3,000 pilots had been trained, and at its height FFS employed about fifty people and operated thirty-five aircraft. As the war wound down, however, this program was eliminated, and Ellis had to look for new business. In the late 1940s, such work included barnstorming trips, fire patrols for the state forest service, pilot training, charter trips for hunters, aircraft sales, and delivering thousands of chicks at a time for the rapidly expanding northwest Arkansas broiler chicken industry.

In the immediate postwar years, the CAB was engaged in establishing a number of new subsidized feeder (local service) airlines. Ellis and some business acquaintances were interested in obtaining a certificate for such an airline in the central United States. Sensing that experience in running an airline might give them a competitive edge in acquiring such a certificate, they started South Central Air Transport (SCAT), a scheduled Arkansas intrastate airline, in August 1946. All the SCAT routes radiated from the capital at Little Rock, serving such places as Fayetteville, El Dorado, Ft. Smith, and Hot Springs. To operate this service, they bought nine five-seat twin-engined Cessna UC-78 "Bamboo Bomber" military trainers, of which six were converted into civilian T-50s and three were cannibalized for parts. Because there were no lights or navigation aids, SCAT could operate only in daylight hours and under visual flight rules conditions, but despite this major handicap and the high maintenance costs of the aircraft, every effort was made to run the airline professionally. SCAT lasted for about eighteen months, until it became clear that the effort to obtain a certificate would not be successful.

In 1949, the University of Arkansas at Fayetteville started an evening continuing education program at Little Rock that led, eventually, to the formation of one of the earliest successful commuter airlines, Scheduled Skyways. These extension classes were taught by professors from the Fayetteville campus, and Ellis's FFS received a charter contract to take them to Little Rock in the late afternoon and to bring them back the next morning (as the Fayetteville airport still had no lights to allow them to come home at night). These "scheduled charters" usually accommodated between two and four faculty members in Cessna 170s, Stinson Voyagers, or a Cessna 195.

Eventually this operation became well known in Fayetteville, and FFS received an increasing number of inquiries from other people who wanted to take the flights to Little Rock. This expansion of the service was not possible under the existing insurance policy and would also have required the university's consent, but as there was an obvious demand, a compromise solution was found. In the future, the university would continue to pay the charter price if only professors were carried, but would receive a credit if regular passengers were also traveling.

Thus, on 1 September 1953—in time for the start of the fall semester—Scheduled Skyways' first scheduled (as opposed to regular charter) flight left Fayetteville (population 20,000) for Little Rock (population 100,000). Ellis himself was the pilot of the Cessna 195, and his three passengers were the president of the University of Arkansas, John Tyler Caldwell, its athletics director, John Barnhill, and a local businessman, Dwight Morris. From the start, three daily flights were offered each way, in the morning, at midday, and in the early evening. Thus began the third oldest successful commuter airline operation in the nation.* But Scheduled Skyways' early high frequency of service and its year-round operation may not have been matched anywhere. In the remaining months of 1953, 838 passengers were carried, and this number grew to 2,536 in 1954.

During the first year perhaps 60 percent of the passengers were from the university, but this percentage decreased steadily thereafter as de-

---

*The honor of first place goes to San Juan Airlines, which started service as the Orcas Island Air Service on 8 July 1947 and later operated as Island Sky Ferries. Second place goes to Provincetown-Boston Airlines, which began scheduled flights on 30 November 1949.

mand by the general public increased. The aircraft used on each flight varied with the number of passengers with reservations, and within a few years several twin-engined types such as the Piper Apache and Aztec were introduced. Business grew steadily because of the excellent, and often highly personal, service. The December 1961 issue of *Flight* quoted Ellis: "It's the service we give, and not the name of the airline or size of the plane, that attracts business." For example, when one regular passenger forgot his briefcase at the Fayetteville Airport, an airplane was sent especially to reunite him with his important papers. Quite often some of the better customers would be picked up or dropped off on request at the smaller cities between Fayetteville and Little Rock, such as Conway, Russellville, or Ft. Smith. Such privileges are no longer extended on today's frequent flyer programs! On one occasion an unaccompanied child listed for a flight from Little Rock turned out to be a baby just a few weeks old. By chance, one of the two other passengers that day was a pediatrician, Dr. LeMon Clark, and the other was John Tyler Caldwell, president of the University. In good humor, they agreed to take care of the baby during the flight, and made delivery to the waiting grandparents in Fayetteville.

When Central Airlines applied to come to Fayetteville in 1954, Ellis took a farsighted attitude and supported the application. He went as far as to fly members of the Chamber of Commerce to the CAB hearings at his own expense, reasoning that the additional service would broaden the market, and that as people became more used to the idea of flying, the increased air-mindedness would actually help Scheduled Skyways. Although the number of Scheduled Skyways passengers declined slightly in 1955, the first full year of Central service, it increased again to 2,891 in the following year. From the start, the scheduled flights were profitable, but the other activities of the FFS, such as flying lessons and aircraft sales, were more so, and these continued to provided the bulk of the family income.

Incidentally, during these years the Ellises lived in the FFS hangar at the Fayetteville Airport. This was a classic "mom-and-pop" airline, with Ray directing the operations but with Sallye Margaret also very important to the company's success. An article in the *Tulsa Sunday World* in 1969 noted that she "manages their office, greets travelers, handles reservations, dispenses information, keeps financial records, and shares in overall management duties." Ellis made sure that Scheduled Skyways had an outstanding record for reliability. In its first eight years only one flight was canceled for mechanical reasons, and delays from this cause totaled less than twelve hours.

Scheduled Skyways operations during the Ellis years were never large, as the population base in Arkansas was not large by national standards. But the years that followed saw generally steady growth. Passenger boardings increased from 3,000 in 1957 to almost 9,000 in 1969. Between 1953 and 1971 the load factor averaged an impressive 60.5 percent, as the size of the aircraft was neatly matched to the number of passengers. Eventually, twin-engined aircraft were used, starting with a four-passenger Piper Apache in 1958 and ending with the seven-passenger Piper Navajo, which was introduced in 1968 and was the largest aircraft used by Scheduled Skyways while Ellis owned the company. For a short time, he tried to establish a route from Fayetteville to Tulsa, but the centerpiece of the airline's route map remained the single, original 140-mile route to Little Rock. In the early 1960s 75 percent of the traffic flew between these two points, and the rest of the passengers connected to or from other airline flights at Little Rock.

In 1970 Ellis began to think of retiring, as he was already more than sixty-five years old. Several potential buyers investigated the property, including Fred Smith of Federal Express, who was interested in buying an established company as a nucleus for his planned air express services. He was not interested in the passenger operations, however, and so looked elsewhere. Eventually, in October 1972, the whole of Ellis's operation, including the FFS, was purchased by several Arkansas entrepreneurs who were interested in expanding the commuter services. Ellis stayed on with the new owners for one more year, and then retired late in 1973. By then he had been working in aviation in Fayetteville for over thirty-three years, and during that time he and his wife had never been away from the job for more than three days at a time.

Throughout his airline years in Fayetteville, Ellis was active in civic and community affairs. He served on the boards of directors of the Rotary Club and the Chamber of Commerce and is a past president of both organizations. For seven years he served on the Arkansas State Aeronautics Commission and was chairman of this organization in 1971–1972.

After 1973 Scheduled Skyways expanded considerably, eventually serving an area that stretched from Kansas City to Pensacola and from Dallas to Nashville. In January 1985, it was merged into Air Midwest.

The Ellises settled down to an enjoyable retirement, long overdue, in Fayetteville. In 1982 Ray was inducted into the Hall of Fame of the Arkansas Aviation Historical Society, a well-deserved honor for this true gentleman, who operated one of the earliest successful commuter airlines in the United States.

Profile 8

Roy Franklin
San Juan Airlines

This is the first of two personality profiles from the same airline in the Pacific Northwest. Originally founded in 1947 by Robert F. (Bob) Schoen as the Orcas Island Air service, the company had changed its name to Island Sky Ferries before he sold it in the spring of 1950 after almost three years of truly pioneering work. Later on, with a regional amalgamation, it became Puget Sound Airlines, and finally San Juan Airlines. After forty-two years of service in the area, it went out of business, but during its four decades in the Puget Sound island community, the commuter airline had become an institution, and the credit for achieving the respect of a discerning clientele must go to Roy Franklin, who was in charge of this remarkable operation for most of its life, and for most of his.

Early in 1948, Franklin met Bob Schoen at Bellingham, Washington. Franklin was a flying instructor for Western Washington Aircraft, and Bob needed a pilot to assist him in his "mom-and-pop" operation. Part of the agreement was that Franklin would move to Friday Harbor, at that time a delightful fishing community on San Juan Island (it now doubles as a getaway resort destination), and he has been there ever since. Roy and Margaret Ann Franklin became the Schoens' "other half" at Friday Harbor, and they subsequently became identified as the operators of the leading commuter airline in the Northwest.

When, in the spring of 1950, Dr. Wallace Howarth from Portland, Oregon, now resident at San Juan Island, bought Island Sky Ferries from Bob Schoen, he changed its name to Island Air, and it was operated by Wallace's son Dave, just out of the Army Air Service. The assets of the airline at that time were one Stinson 108 Voyager and Roy Franklin. The Howarths bought a Piper Clipper, a four-place utility aircraft like the Voyager, and for a couple of years Roy shared the flying duties with its owner.

Roy Franklin (photo by Albert Hamilton)

Already an accomplished pilot, Franklin added to his talents by attending an aircraft mechanic school in Arlington, Washington, during the first winter with the Howarths, when the sparse airline traffic did not demand the services of two aircraft. On his return in the spring of 1951, Franklin was soon working for a third owner. Dave Howarth had tired of the airline business and sold Island Air (but not its aircraft) to Harold and Virginia Ferris, who owned the local airfield at Eastsound on Orcas Island. The Ferrises owned a Stinson Voyager, and they asked Franklin to join them in flying it. They changed the airline name back to Island Sky Ferries, built the fleet up to four aircraft, and improved the schedules around the San Juan Islands and to Bellingham.

On 1 June 1953, Roy Franklin bought the airline, including two Stinson 108 Voyagers, from the Ferrises and also acquired a 1948 Plymouth automobile for the Bellingham airport downtown limousine service—a move that was widely acknowledged to be an improvement over the 1926 Whippet first used by Bob Schoen.

During the 1950s, life in the San Juan Islands moved at a more leisurely pace than it does today, and even though Island Sky Ferries could offer improved service to the mainland amenities at Bellingham, its fares had to be set very low to make it competetive with the excellent ferryboat service already in place. Consequently, Franklin sought other work for his aircraft and flew for the National Forest Service on fire patrols at Mount Baker National Forest. This yearly contract was renewed for about twenty years every summer, and the accumulated revenues helped to finance the construction of a new airfield at Friday Harbor to replace the cow pasture that had hitherto sufficed. This airfield project was Roy Franklin's own, and he completed it without any subsidy or other assistance (except verbal encouragement) from the Friday Harbor community.

His experience in operating out of a cow pasture enabled Franklin to make certain scientific analyses relating to cow manure, devising a formula, for example, relating its drying time on a smooth surface (such as an airplane) to the time needed to remove the deposits. His research in another related area revealed that less than a tenth of a second is needed for fresh cow manure to ooze up between the five toes in a lady's open-toed shoe, but that the resultant disbelieving stare occupies almost exactly twenty seconds, as does the withering look at the pilot. Similar expressions of disbelief occur when the assembled passengers, at last comfortably tucked in aboard a Stinson, are informed that the aircraft is stuck in the mud (or other deposits) and asked to get out to lighten the load and—high heels notwithstanding—help to push.

A development of long-term significance for Island Sky Ferries occurred in 1956. On 1 June of that year, it opened service to Seattle, with a schedule that involved all the islands. The Bellingham route, however, was still operated separately, as Bellingham-Seattle direct service via the islands would have competed—very attractively as it happened—with the direct route by West Coast Airlines between those two points.

In 1962 the World's Fair at Seattle encouraged Franklin to obtain a larger aircraft, in the expectation of increased traffic. He went to Texas and bought a twin-engined Lockheed L-10 Electra with ten seats, which made it the fleet flagship, to add to a collection of single-engined six-seat and four-seat aircraft. Unfortunately, Franklin's expectations were not fulfilled. The visitors to the Seattle fair all stayed in Seattle.

Nevertheless, during the 1960s, the San Juan Islands came to the attention not only of the city dwellers of Seattle and Tacoma but also of citizens of urban communities farther away. People started to build vacation and retirement homes in the islands. Real estate and general business activity grew in parallel with this new demographic trend, and Island Sky Ferries grew with it, with air traffic peaking in 1968.

During the latter 1960s, other entrepreneurs took advantage of this environment of fast-growing prosperity, and several other new scheduled air taxi owner-operators established themselves in the Puget Sound area, for example at Whidbey Island (to the south of the San Juans), at Port Angeles, and at Bellingham. They did not compete with Roy Franklin or with each other. Each specialized in providing a service to its own local community.

In 1966, however, an opportunity for cooperation presented itself when the U.S. Post Office finally decided to fly airmail to the islands, replacing the boat service on which it had thus far relied. Traditionally cautious in its dealings with aspiring contractors, the Post Office let out a contract for only thirty days at a time, renewable each month. Franklin, on behalf of Island Sky Ferries, and Tom Wilson, of Skyline Air Service, joined forces to provide the service and formed a separate corporation, Island Mail. By mutual agreement, Franklin took responsibility for the western San Juans (San Juan, Lopez, Shaw, Stuart, and Waldron islands) while Tom took the eastern ones (Orcas, Blakeley, Sinclair, and Decatur). The Island Mail focal point was Anacortes, and service began on 1 July 1966. The partnership lasted until 1979, when San Juan Airlines (which had succeeded Island Sky Ferries) took over the contract; by this time Franklin had sold his business to Jim Sherrell.

In the late 1960s, the owner-pilot fraternity of the small commuter airlines of the Puget Sound area would often converge on Seattle-Tacoma Airport and, over coffee and a little hangar flying, discuss their common problems. Gradually the possibility of a merger took shape. The idea became a reality on 1 June 1969, when, under the name of Puget Sound Airlines, Island Sky Ferries joined up with the others to form a commuter airline consortium. The member companies were Angeles Flying Service, Whidbey Flying Service, Bellingham-Seattle Airways, Bremerton Air Taxi, and Skyline Air Service. The total fleet numbered thirty-six aircraft: Beech 18s, various Piper and Cessna types, and a Stinson Reliant. Yet one of the founding members of the group was sadly absent. Bill Fairchild, of the Angeles Flying Service, had been killed along with his pilot and eight passengers in a Beech 18 while taking off from Port Angeles on 5 February 1969. He had been on his way to rendezvous with his future partners at Seattle to inspect a nineteen-seat de Havilland DHC-6 Twin Otter.

The amalgamated commuter airline group did not succeed in its objective, even though the basic idea—of pooling maintenance and spares, standardizing equipment, and providing mutual support—had made good sense. Puget Sound Airlines closed down in the summer of 1970, during a nationwide shortfall in airline traffic. The ex-partners picked themselves up and resumed their individual careers, mostly in local aviation of some sort. Franklin established a new company, San Juan Airlines, to try to carry on the Island Sky Ferries tradition. He bought back some of the Puget Sound Airlines equipment (some of which had belonged to the old Island Sky Ferries) and kept the Stinson Reliant to carry the mail. Pride of the fleet was a pair of Cessna 206s.

Incidentally, Franklin has never claimed that Island Sky Ferries/San Juan Airlines was the oldest of the commuter airlines, even as it prospered during the 1970s. Although others made such a claim, he respected the historical record and recognized that his new San Juan Airlines was not in direct succession from Puget Sound Airlines in the corporate genealogy, even though some of the aircraft served with both airlines.

Over the following decade, Franklin enjoyed considerable success, achieving it with studied caution. He continued to consolidate the route network on a basic pattern that linked all the islands of the Puget Sound area with all the main cities of the surrounding mainland, from Bellingham in the north to Port Angeles in the southwest. By 1978, he was operating nine round trips a day from the islands to Seattle. During this period, he bought two six-place Piper Aztecs in 1971–1972, two ten-seat Britten Norman BN-2 Islanders in 1973–1974, and two new six-seat Cessna 207s in 1975–1976, directly from the factory. San Juan Airlines, therefore, was in good shape when Franklin sold it, complete with nine aircraft, on 1 May 1979 to Jim Sherrell, a former beer distributor from Dallas, Oregon. At the time, the airline was grossing about $700,000 annually and making a 10 percent profit. Sherrell paid $600,000 for the assets, which included $130,000 for the aircraft and spares and San Juan Airlines' own communications network, centered on a repeater station situated at the highest point of Orcas Island, at an elevation of 2,500 feet.

Franklin still owned the airport at Friday Harbor, and, together with his airline staff, he stayed on until 5 September to ensure a smooth transfer. Sherrell flew the routes, got acquainted with the operation as a whole, and purchased a third Britten Norman Islander. In October 1981, he purchased Pearson Aircraft, which had a permit to fly internationally from Seattle to Victoria, British Columbia, via Port Angeles. He also acquired a Cessna dealership to add to the excellent facilities and good will left behind by Franklin. Sherrell decided to move the headquarters of the airline to Port Angeles, where the installations were arguably better, and he embarked on a program of further expansion, in aircraft and routes, in starting an air freight service and in competing strongly with Harbor Airlines, particularly on an intercity route from Bellingham to Seattle, a departure from the small community service pattern.

In the dynamic airline environment of the deregulated 1980s, Sherrell tried to align San Juan Airlines with changing conditions as the original scheduled air taxi operators lost much of their proudly independent status and the commuter airlines became a cohesive industry, recognized as such by the authorities in Washington. Eventually they grew so vigorously that they were perceived as a threat by the major airlines, which moved decisively in the latter half of the 1980s to put all the best of the commuter airlines under their control through integration of their flights into their computerized reservation systems. San Juan Airlines flirted briefly with United Airlines, outgrew itself, and was forced to terminate operations in 1989.

It died looking nothing like the tiny one-aircraft, husband-and-wife outfit that Bob Schoen had begun in 1947, and that flourished throughout three decades under the stewardship of Roy Franklin.

In an articulate recollection of how he planned the formative years of Island Sky Ferries, Roy Franklin has captured the spirit of the true pioneer and epitomized the attitudes of those commuter airline promoters whose instincts were true and whose convictions were strong as they created the nucleus of this definitive segment of the U.S. air transport industry. Franklin's words are an inspired tribute to a special breed of aviator. They are reproduced as part of the introduction to this section of the book.

Profile 9

Joseph M. (Joe) Fugere
Pilgrim Airlines

Luck is an element of success in most enterprises, and in fashioning a successful commuter airline it can play a significant part indeed. Opportunism, determination, financial acumen—all these and other qualities can combine to make a successful career, but being in the right place at the right time is equally important. Joseph M. Fugere has had his share of lucky breaks, good and bad. The progress of the airline he built was sometimes dependent on the whims of Lady Luck, and although he was adept and resourceful in taking advantage of her smiles, he has also suffered her frowns with equanimity, even cheerfulness.

His was a typical story of faith in an idea, of providing an air service that no one else seemed to want to operate, but for which there was an obvious need. He started with three single-engined aircraft to form Pilgrim Airlines, worked his way to the forefront of the commuter airline industry, and eventually sold his business to another company and took up a second vocation. His career was notable for several accomplishments, not least of which were helping to launch an important airplane on its road to success and opening the first air service to the capital city of one of the neighboring countries of the United States.

Joe Fugere was born at Woonsocket, Rhode Island, on 22 January 1935. He attended Admiral Billard Academy from 1949 to 1952 and the University of Rhode Island from 1952 to 1954. But this latter period of his education lasted only three semesters. The Korean War had just ended in 1953, and Fugere was keen to fly in the services. He signed up as a naval aviator at the naval air station at Jacksonville, Florida, and served aboard a number of aircraft carriers, flying among others the North American FJ-3M, the first fighter to carry the Sidewinder missile.

When he was released from active duty in April 1958 he held the rank of lieutenant in the U.S. Naval Reserve. He returned to the university and "graduated" in June 1960 with a B.A. in economics. Fugere himself

Joseph M. (Joe) Fugere

points out that the term "graduated" is a slight exaggeration; he obtained 144 credits but these did not include the necessary ones in English and the humanities, and he finished up three credits short. In the light of his subsequent life and activities, this shortcoming seems curious, as Fugere has never seemed to lack proficiency in either of these subjects.

Early in his youth, Fugere had attended a preparatory school in New London, Connecticut, and this may have been one of the influences that drew him to join, in July 1960, the New London Flying Service, working as a jack-of-all-trades pilot for a typical fixed base operator. The owner had had a bad Piper Apache accident, there were insurance problems, and he wished to sell his company. Joe Fugere and a partner put up $10,000 in cash each—in Joe's case, borrowed from his parents—plus an extra $10,000 in notes and bought the New London Flying Service for $30,000. Fugere was the new president, and two years later he formed Pilgrim Airlines.

The birth of Pilgrim came about because of an opportunity that was almost forced upon him, and paradoxically, except for an apparent slice of bad luck, it might never have happened. New London Flying Service had been doing a thriving business with the General Dynamics Electric Boat Division at Groton, the submarine capital of the United States. The annual revenue from the service amounted to $150,000, which in 1960 was a very acceptable figure. Unfortunately, more than half of this business was in charter work to Washington, D.C.—those were the days of Admiral Hyman Rickover—and the traffic was sufficient to encourage Allegheny Airlines, then a prominent local service (regional) airline, to start scheduled services between New London and Washington via Philadelphia.

On 1 April 1962, therefore, Pilgrim Airlines was founded almost as an act of desperation after Allegheny had usurped the Flying Service's privileged position as the only air carrier to the federal capital. But Fugere had realized that there was a need to provide a scheduled service to New York, specifically John F. Kennedy Airport. At that time, JFK was the only New York airport at which jet aircraft were allowed, La Guardia's runways not having yet been extended. The geography of the region is such that, from all the populous cities along the Connecticut–Rhode Island–Massachusetts urban corridor, access to JFK is circuitous and often extremely time-consuming, even though several enterprising limousine companies do a good trade in tackling the traffic jams near and on the Whitestone Bridge across Long Island Sound.

The New London/Groton–JFK Pilgrim service was successful from the start. In September 1962, only a few months after opening service with the Pipers, Fugere purchased his first twin Beech 18 (a C-45H conversion), a venerable and veteran aircraft that could be obtained quite cheaply, as there were many war-surplus ones available. It had eight seats—plus the copilot's, if necessary, in busy periods—had two engines (a configuration that was far more acceptable to the clientele), and featured a gross takeoff weight of under 12,500 pounds, which was the maximum weight permitted to air taxi operators at the time.

Pilgrim did a steady business during the next few years, concentrating on its single scheduled route and still building up its fixed base and charter business, in spite of the loss of the lucrative naval account to Washington. Fugere kept his eye open for good airplane bargains and built up his fleet to three Beech 18s, two Piper Aztecs, and various Comanches and Cherokees. Then came a slice of good fortune to compensate for the bad luck in having his best charter route stolen away.

From June to August 1966, International Association of Machinists went on strike for sixty-six days, and although it did not completely paralyze the nation's air transport system, the episode severely affected traffic flows. Air freight was particularly affected, and a New York freight forwarder contracted with Pilgrim Airlines to carry pharmaceuticals, a commodity that was of high value and to some extent perishable, thus demanding rapid distribution. Fugere deployed one Twin Beech on a route from JFK to Chicago via Pittsburgh, Cleveland, and Detroit; another to Atlanta via Charlotte; and a Cherokee Six on an itinerary that took it from JFK to Baltimore and back and then on to Boston before returning to Pilgrim's base at Groton. Pilgrim Airlines made $150,000 net in two months.

With this unexpected windfall, Fugere invested in his first modern commuter aircraft, purchasing a de Havilland Aircraft of Canada DHC-6 Twin Otter for $100,000 cash. The airplane had been built, in traditional de Havilland of Canada style, to succeed the Beaver and the Otter as a bush aircraft to face the rigorous conditions of the Canadian bush and the frozen north. Fugere claims, with some justification, to have been the first to convince the Canadian company that the versatile twin was ideal as a commuter airliner for the United States. The first Pilgrim Twin Otter was delivered in September 1966, and the airline opened the first Twin Otter service in the United States, at 7 A.M. on 1 November 1966. Air Wisconsin, which had also ordered the Twin Otter, missed that privilege by one hour, as its 7 A.M. departure on the same day was one time zone behind.

During the next fifteen years, Fugere and Pilgrim Airlines made steady, if unspectacular, progress. More Twin Otters swelled the fleet to six, and more routes were added, notably flights into JFK from both New Haven and Hartford, meeting the same need as had the New London/Groton link across the Long Island Sound surface transport bottleneck. For two or three years, Pilgrim also provided a mail service from Albany to La Guardia.

In 1974, Pilgrim became an international airline. Using a Volpar Turboliner, a much-modified Beech 18 with tricycle landing gear and Garrett/AiResearch turboprop engines, it began service from Hartford to Montreal. Much of the business on this route came from Pratt & Whitney, which had large manufacturing plants at both ends of the route, and from the insurance business, with such firms as Sun-Life of Canada and the Hartford at each end of the route. In 1977, the Volpar was withdrawn and two Beech 99s, modern fifteen-seat turboprops with better range than the nineteen-seat Twin Otters, were introduced.

As Pilgrim Airlines entered the 1980s, it increased its stature considerably with a remarkable example of initiative. Through his Canadian contacts, Fugere had heard that the dominion capital, Ottawa, "was screaming for service to the United States" but that the CAB had claimed that no U.S. airline was interested in providing it. All the airlines were interested in serving the conurbations of Toronto and Montreal but somehow did not appreciate that the demands of the growing bureaucracy needed to serve a prosperous industrial country had elevated Ottawa, in the manner of Washington, D.C., to the fourth largest population center in Canada.

Fugere flew to Washington, went straight to the CAB, and informed them in no uncertain terms: "you never asked me!" The Board was suitably impressed by his presentation and held a hearing. USAir (formerly Allegheny—the same airline that had tempted away the Groton-Washington charter business in 1962)—and Pan American hastily filed for the route. But Franklin and Pilgrim had done a good promotional job in Ottawa, and the Canadians used their influence with the CAB. Although, with the passing of the Airline Deregulation Act of 1978, the power of the agency was waning, many of the requirements for opening service that it had long enforced still obtained; one of these was the possession of adequate equipment, under the "fit, willing, and able" principle. Fortunately for Pilgrim, in December 1980 it had introduced the first forty-four-seat Fokker F-27 turboprop service, so that nobody could question the airline's ability to serve the Ottawa–New York route.

The service started on 15 December 1981 and quickly proved its worth, becoming the most important single segment of the route network and providing 50 percent of the total revenue. And without the previous CAB-imposed restrictions on aircraft size, Fugere was now free to take the big step and move into jet operations. He negotiated with Fokker once again, as a good relationship had in the meantime developed, with seven F-27s eventually being delivered from the Dutch factory. The new aircraft was a sixty-five-seat Fokker F-28, which had been cocooned since 1980, as Fokker had not been able to sell it. But the F-28 was ideally sized for the New York–Ottawa traffic volumes, had adequate range for the route, and was cheaper than any other twin jet. Not that it came at a knockdown price—the F-28 was one of the top-of-the-line Dash 3000 series. Fugere paid for the airplane on 31 December 1983 and took delivery at the end of January 1984.

But by then disaster had struck. On 13 January, while taking off from JFK International Airport—thus gaining maximum visibility in the eyes of an FAA that was being heavily lobbied to subject the commuter airlines to meticulous scrutiny—a Pilgrim Airlines Fokker F-27 "lost" both engines and was brought down in a crash landing by its pilot. The incident led to an immediate investigation by the FAA and the National Transportation Safety Board, and Pilgrim was grounded pending the results of the inquiry. The new F-28 stayed in the hangar, accumulating interest charges at the rate of $2,300 a day and setting Pilgrim back half a million dollars before it finally went into service on the Ottawa route in September 1984.

During the winter of 1984–1985 Fugere and Pilgrim Airlines worked to restore the company's stature and market share in the Connecticut-centered commuter region. Taking a courageous step, Fugere acquired NewAir, a New Haven–based airline that was operating three Twin Otters, two Embraer Bandeirantes, and two Shorts SD-360s. NewAir was a public company (Pilgrim was privately held), and Fugere traded 20 percent of Pilgrim's stock for all of NewAir's assets, thereby, as he put it succinctly, "knocking out all the competition" on his main route network in the Long Island Sound area and adding Philadelphia and Newark as additional stations.

But this move amounted essentially to a final gesture, a brave attempt to hit a grand slam in the bottom of the ninth when the opposition was ten runs ahead. On 28 February 1986, Joe Fugere sold Pilgrim Airlines to the Marketing Corporation of America, doing business as Business Express out of Bridgeport, Connecticut, and one of the Delta Connection family of code-sharing operators. Business Express (formerly Atlantic Express) had a fleet of five Beech 99s; by its purchase of Pilgrim it acquired six F-27s, an F-28, and nine Twin Otters. Of the $1 million bargain price paid, Fugere received 70 percent, his attorney 1 percent, his three children 3 percent each, and NewAir 20 percent.

This was not much to retire on, compared with the small fortunes made by some of the other commuter pioneers of Fugere's generation. But, just as he always took the rough with the smooth during his airline days, accepting the whims of fortune, so has Fugere taken his exodus from the industry with commendable good humor. While the lawyers are sorting out some of the residual problems stemming from the decline and fall of Pilgrim Airlines, Fugere is getting on with his life, enjoying himself no end by immersing himself in a fascinating occupation—a new vocation and a totally rewarding one. He is now in the business of restoring old New England cottages and houses, transforming dilapidated buildings of rotting wood and crumbling brick and mortar into desirable residences that some would call ancient monuments.

Fugere himself is not ready to admit to being an ancient monument. He is too busy being a craftsman. He keeps his pilot's hand in by flying his own Piper Comanche for pleasure. The airplane is still in his favorite Pilgrim Airlines green and yellow color scheme. These colors could also recently still be seen, faded and weather-beaten, amid the tall weeds of the yard of one of the Fugere restoration projects. They are on an old bus, the one that used to carry interline passengers at JFK Airport. Now used as a dry storage area for timber, it comprises the only other visible remains of one of the true pioneer commuter airlines of the United States.

Profile 10

Richard A. (Dick) Henson
The Hagerstown Commuter and Henson Airlines

Dick Henson is able to claim, with justification, that he was the first of what were then called scheduled air taxi operators to apply the commuter name to his operation when he opened scheduled service between Washington and Hagerstown, Maryland, on 1 October 1962. One of the earliest of the fixed base operators who tried his hand at establishing a regular route, Henson was to expand steadily, always holding his position as one of the larger commuter airlines during the boom years of the late 1960s and the 1970s, and able, by 1989, to rank as the fourth largest regional operation in the United States, with a route network that stretched from Boston to Miami and the Bahamas.

The Henson operation went back a long way, for Henson had founded the Henson Flying Service, one of the early fixed base operators, at Hagerstown, Maryland, in 1931. He had already paid his dues in a variety of aviation-related activities, having bought his first airplane at the age of twenty. Born in Hagerstown on 12 February 1910, he had received a high school education, first at Hagerstown and then later at the Mountain Park Institute in North Carolina in 1928–1929. He started work at the age of twelve, cleaning dental tools, and was earning $13.00 a week when he was sixteen, driving a horse-drawn milk wagon.

His first direct acquaintance with aviation came in 1927, when he found a job at the Kreider-Reisner airplane factory in downtown Hagerstown, but soon after it closed its doors he left to work in the metal shop at the Martin plant at Middle River, Baltimore. He remembers the experience well, partly because of the tough German foreman and partly from riding a one-cylinder Harley-Davidson hand-shift motor bike every week between Hagerstown and Baltimore—not exactly a commute, but nevertheless perhaps a harbinger of things to come.

Having augmented his technical education at Mountain Park, he left Martin, took a temporary job at a Standard Oil filling station at Hagers-

Richard A. (Dick) Henson

town early in 1930, and talked three friends not only into sharing his enthusiasm for aviation but also into sharing an investment in a used airplane. Henson borrowed money from a bank, and together they acquired a $1,500 OX-5 Kreider-Reisner Challenger biplane. He hired an instructor, went "across the Mason-Dixon Line" to Waynesboro, Pennsylvania, where there was a grass field, and spent $35.00 for six hours' instruction for his first solo flight. By the end of the year, he had completed the fifty hours required to obtain a limited commercial license that would permit him to carry passengers for hire, and he started barnstorming to offer joy rides. The following year, he obtained his air transport license, hired a mechanic, and reopened the Hagerstown flying field that had been closed when Kreider-Reisner had folded up a few years previously. By April 1931, the Henson Flying Service was in business, operating out of a small shack on the edge of the field.

Demonstrating ingenuity early in his career, Henson advertised special flights in the Challenger when business was slow. For 50¢ a head, two at a time, he took passengers for a quick circuit—and incidentally took in more cash on the first day of the offer than he ever had before. Nevertheless, this was not a bread-and-butter income, even in the days when 50¢ was worth $5.00 or more in today's purchasing power. So, when the Fairchild Corporation bought out the Kreider-Reisner assets and built the seventy-five-horsepower Fairchild 22, he hired on as a test pilot, on call, at a salary of $5.00 per hour flown and $40.00 per week for a guarantee of on-call availability.

Throughout the 1930s, Henson kept the Henson Flying Service going, and even expanded it, at the same time working almost as a permanent staff member at Fairchild. He contributed substantially to the design of the PT-19 trainer (Fairchild's entry in a U.S. Army design contest to select a new trainer) and took it to Wright Field at Dayton to demonstrate and promote it. He must have done a good job: Fairchild won the competition and sold five thousand airplanes.

In 1939, Fairchild built a large facility at Hagerstown; Henson became the director of flight test,and hired more test pilots. The plant produced hundreds of C-82 and C-119 "flying boxcars," and during World War II the work force peaked at more than 10,000, turning out thirty-two C-119s per month.

Simultaneously, the Henson Flying Service contracted with the FAA under the Civilian Pilot Training Program to establish a Type A Center at Hagerstown, conducting primary, secondary, cross-country, and instructor training. This was a significant move for Henson, as it enabled him to keep two very warm irons in the aviation fire. He might easily have abandoned his fixed base operation in favor of boardroom aspirations at Fairchild; but commuter airline pioneers had one characteristic in common: they could never keep away from the smell of gasoline and grease in the hangar.

Henson thus survived the postwar slump into which Fairchild fell. The company's entire wartime business had consisted of building military transports, but the market for these dried up at war's end, and existing craft contributed to a glut on the used aircraft market in 1945. The company should have recognized the need for a nose-wheel trainer and gone back to the work in which it had previously specialized; instead, in the 1950s, it tried to enter the commercial airliner business by taking a license from the Dutch Fokker company to build the F-27 Friendship twin–Rolls-Royce Dart turboprop. After merging with Hiller to become Fairchild-Hiller Corporation it even developed a slightly larger version, the FH-227, but this aircraft was not a success, as it should have been fitted with the more powerful Series 10 Dart engines to maintain short field performance. By 1964, the Hagerstown plant was down to seven hundred employees. Henson handed in his resignation and concentrated on the Henson Flying Service, which by this time had spread its wings beyond the confines of the normal fixed base operator's horizons.

In 1962, while serving as the chairman of the aviation commission of the local chamber of commerce, he pleaded the case for better airline service to Hagerstown. Approaching Les Barnes, then president of Allegheny Airlines (now USAir), he pointed out that Hagerstown was served only as a "dog's leg" on the Washington-Pittsburgh route via Martinsburg, West Virginia, and that although the two flights a day were operated with a local service airline subsidy, they were not conveniently scheduled for the local residents. But his plea for better service went unanswered.

And so The Hagerstown Commuter was born, starting service on 23 April 1962 with a brightly painted yellow ten-place Beech D-18, purchased for $8,500, and embellished with Horton & Horton interior design and furnishings. The service was operated under the FAA's Part 135 scheduled air taxi regulations. At first it lost money, but Henson improved the service frequency by resizing the aircraft to fit the market.

The introduction of these new aircraft, first a six-place Aero Commander and then a four-place Bonanza, soon put the operation into the black. This early experience with fine-tuning capacity was a lesson that served him well throughout his air carrier career.

The frequency, convenience, and improved equipment made all the difference. Within three years The Hagerstown Commuter was carrying 70 percent of Allegheny's traffic into and out of Hagerstown. Les Barnes responded by locating a Beech 18 at Pittsburgh, but then overloaded it with both equipment and personnel. It was complete with heavy radio gear, copilot, and flight attendant and was not even operating under the more liberal Part 135 regulations. In due course, Barnes called Henson to talk things over. Henson promised, "If you serve Hagerstown properly, I'll get out," to which Les responded that he could not because of the operating restrictions imposed by the full Part 121 transport certificate compared to the Part 135 certificate. So a deal was struck under which, on 15 November 1967, The Hagerstown Commuter became the first Allegheny Commuter, flying into Baltimore (BWI) rather than Washington (National). Barnes guaranteed Henson against financial loss for two years and provided reservations, off-line bookings, and promotion. This was the prototype of an idea that, after a long gestation period, was to become standard practice in the relationship between commuter and trunk airlines.

In naming the victor in this classic case of "if you can't beat 'em, join 'em," a tie would have to be the verdict, for neither of the contestants could have won outright.

To ensure the support of the Hagerstown community, as well as to reassure himself, Henson organized a dinner for twenty-five leading business people and invited Barnes and his staff as guests. The consensus was a clear preference for Henson over Allegheny.

One of the attendees at the dinner was Jack King, vice-president of community affairs for Allegheny Airlines. He persuaded Henson to put two departure and arrival flights into the Salisbury-Washington market as promotional flights, since Allegheny also wanted to withdraw its two flights a day from that market because of financial losses. Henson complied, and his reception at Salisbury was a warm one. Six months later, after he had become well acquainted with the community, he proposed to increase his service to seven departures a day immediately, with the possibility of continually increasing service to a maximum of sixteen flights a day as long as he was breaking even. In return, the community would release Allegheny from its responsibility as a local-service carrier. The program was accepted, and traffic continued to expand and eventually reached the goal. In developing this market, Henson established the basic principle that frequency on short-haul routes, over which there were alternative modes of surface transportation, was more important than capacity.

Henson remained the premier Allegheny Commuter airline during the 1970s. Allegheny, officially designated a local service carrier, eventually rendered the latter term obsolete with its aggressive route expansion program. This involved not only the absorption of other local service airlines but also the expansion of its association with many other commuter operations. Henson continued to serve his own geographical area in the hinterland of the federal capital, concentrating on improving equipment rather than on adding more points to his route map. During most of the decade, an extension to Philadelphia was the limit of his ambitions in route development. But his fleet of seven fifteen-seat Beech 99s and thirteen thirty-seat Shorts SD-330s combined to provide the most efficient service in the Washington-Baltimore hinterland.

Then, in a flurry of activity at the end of the 1970s, Henson moved on all fronts into a higher stratum of commuter airline operations. On 1 June 1979, he started service to link the small communities of the Virginia peninsula with Baltimore and the Norfolk/Newport News tidewater cities; on 15 September 1980 he opened service to the Shenandoah Valley; and on 1 April 1981 he began a route from Richmond to Pittsburgh. For these additions to the network, he introduced the four-engined fifty-seat turboprop, the de Havilland Aircraft of Canada

Dash 7. This aircraft's extra engine power and short takeoff and landing (STOL) capability enabled it to fly into airports with short runways and difficult approaches. These characteristics were very important in the operation at Washington, allowing it to avoid slot limitations by using stub runways off the main runways on a noninterfering basis.

Although the Allegheny Commuter system had been inspired and initiated by Henson, there had always been a certain uneasiness about the terms and the practice of the compromise reached in 1967. As time went on, this uneasiness had developed into outright disagreement, and matters came to a head in 1983. Henson insisted on more independence than Allegheny (by then USAir) was prepared to concede. The regional airline even objected to the prominent use of the Henson name on the aircraft. Henson felt that too much control was being ceded to the planning department at USAir. So, in order to protect the company and his employees (not a single one of whom had ever been laid off for any reason), and at the same time to stimulate them, he asked Ed Colodny, who had taken over Les Barnes's leadership of USAir, to give him a personal contract to run the Henson operation. However, an agreement could not be reached, and on 30 October 1983 Henson switched his regional airline allegiance to Tom Davis's Piedmont Aviation.

At first, Henson tried to persuade Piedmont to adopt the Henson name, subtitling it The Piedmont Regional Airline, as Piedmont itself had also grown considerably. (Indeed, like USAir under deregulation, it had outgrown its own terminology, behaving more like a major trunk carrier than a regional one.) In discussions with Bill Howard at Piedmont, a compromise was reached in the form of a mutual protection plan. Because of his age (which belied his appearance, as he did not look or act his two years beyond the customary three score years and ten), Henson agreed to regular medical examinations as a condition of retaining the chairmanship and control of the Henson operation. But he would surrender financial control over a period of five years, with Piedmont buying him out in five annual instalments of 20 percent each. The result was the establishment, in 1984, of the Piedmont Regional system.

Early in 1985, Piedmont transferred to Henson a number of routes on the northern fringe of its route network, and Piedmont Regional added Boston and several cities in Pennsylvania and Virginia to its flight pattern. In May it took delivery of the first de Havilland Dash 8, a pressurized twin-engined thirty-seven-seat turboprop with good (but not STOL) field performance. It fitted admirably into the size bracket between the thirty-seat Shorts SD-330 and the fifty-seat Dash 7.

During the next couple of years the Henson network moved cautiously southward, establishing on 15 March 1985 a minihub at Charlotte, fast becoming a boom city in the eastern "silicon valley" industrial belt. Florence and New Bern, South Carolina, were added in May, and the prestigious Hilton Head resort in September. By this time, the Beech 99s and the Shorts were gradually being retired as Henson became one of the largest single customers for, and a vigorous promoter of, the Dash 8. By the end of the year, the reconstituted Henson operation, doing business as Piedmont Regional, had three hubs: at Charlotte, Baltimore, and Washington National.

The next step was to inaugurate the Piedmont Shuttle Link on 1 February 1987 in Florida. This was effectively a new intrastate network that covered all of the major cities from Jacksonville and Pensacola in the north to Miami and Naples in the south, with many in between. In addition to the mainland, five points in the Bahamas were served, thus classifying Henson as an international operator.

By the time Dick accepted the fifth and final payment for his airline from Piedmont in October 1987, the Henson name was known from Massachusetts to Florida, and in all the states in between, as it was displayed prominently on the forward fuselage of his Dash 8 aircraft. The operation of "Henson, The Piedmont Regional Airline," into and out of forty-two cities on the east coast made the name something of a household word in the regional air carrier industry.

Having bowed out from direct investment in the commuter airline industry he had helped to create, but still in control of the Piedmont Shuttle Link, Henson came to terms with his arrangement with Piedmont, even recognizing that the solution had been inevitable: "Regardless of what some others may say, marriage to a good major carrier is a fine thing. It's a necessity. . . . I think it's good for the entire industry." Quite obviously, his relationships with Piedmont were built on a sound footing of mutual trust. Each side recognized that it was a specialist in its particular field, and Piedmont's attitude toward Henson had always been "do your own thing and we won't bother you."

In an ironic twist of fate, the Henson operation came full circle and returned to the original Allegheny Commuter system when, on 1 July 1989, USAir finally completed a merger with Piedmont. The two airlines were almost identical in size, but together they constituted a major airline under the deregulated system of airline classification (and would also have been a large trunk carrier under the old CAB-supervised system). Operationally, under an agreement made with Henson on 1 January 1989, the Allegheny Commuter group became the USAir Express. Gradually the Henson name (except possibly on the Delmarva Peninsula, where Henson Aviation, under Dick's personal supervision, kept Salisbury on the airline map) began to recede into airline memory.

In the years since the USAir-Piedmont merger, Henson has focused his energies in other directions and has become heavily involved in community affairs. He still flies his own Citation jet and is building a second home in Naples, Florida, where he is also involved in the boat business. He divides his retirement years between Naples and Salisbury, where he has established the Richard A. Henson Charitable Foundation.

One day, someone might have the inspiration to put up a small plaque at Hagerstown, on the site of Henson's original airfield shack. This would be a fitting tribute to the man who first put into practice the idea of The Hagerstown Commuter, and in so doing gave a name to an entire segment of the airline industry. For fifteen years the word "commuter," first used by Dick Henson to describe a specific operation, would serve the industry during its formative period.

Profile 11

Arthur (Art) Horst
Suburban Airlines

Art Horst was one of the early commuter airline pioneers who actually provided a true commuter service, systematically expanded his airline to match market needs, was flexible enough to seize opportunities or to abandon unsuccessful operations when the time was right, and emerged with a handsome reward when he sold his airline on retirement.

He built up his airline in his native state and wisely concentrated on developing his business from an area with which he was familiar. Born on 18 July 1924 in Palmyra, Pennsylvania, he graduated from high school there and attended Pennsylvania State University at State College for one year before joining the U.S. Army Air Corps in October 1943. After World War II he did some flying that was close in its style to post–World War I barnstorming, and Horst vividly remembers some of wilder experiences in the late 1940s that were reminiscent of the early 1920s.

In October 1952, as a DC-3 first officer, he joined PANAGRA, the Pan American–affiliated airline that pioneered the trunk air route down the west coast of South America. Flying DC-3s among the Bolivian mountain peaks was possibly even more hair-raising than barnstorming in the United States. DC-3 engine-out maximum altitude is 11,000 feet, about 9,000 feet lower than the peaks and even 2,000 feet lower than the airport at La Paz, where "you always took off downhill [at about a 2 to 3 percent gradient] and then 'climbed' downhill for about ten miles along a line of rocks [the tops of which were whitewashed] to a single emergency strip."

When, early in 1954, PANAGRA started to prepare for the jet age and clearly intended to reduce its pilot roster, Horst left; a few months later he got a job as a Beech 18 charter pilot for Reading Aviation Service (RAS). At this time, Reading, Pennsylvania, was served by five scheduled airlines: TWA, Eastern, Colonial, PCA (Capital), and Allegheny, and

Arthur (Art) Horst

opportunities for regular services were not immediately apparent. But Horst perceived that none of these airlines offered a service from Reading to New York that was convenient for visiting businessmen, much less commuters, because the flight times obliged travelers to stay overnight at the destination city.

Accordingly, he persuaded the RAS management to create Reading Airlines, which, under the CAB's Part 298 exemption, started a scheduled service between Reading and Newark—just across the Hudson River from Manhattan—on 1 August 1957. This was one of the first commuter airline routes in the history of the industry to become firmly established, and for about a year and a half Reading's Beech 18s provided the only direct service between Reading, a city of about 120,000 people, and New York. During the 1960s the other airlines deserted Reading, so that the locally based commuter line (or scheduled air taxi service, as it was then called) was able to expand from a well-prepared base.

By now, Horst was attaining a position of influence in RAS, and during the next few years, in company with other similar small quasi-airline operators, he sought an aircraft that was operationally better and commercially more marketable than the veteran Beech 18. He discovered the British de Havilland DH-104 Dove, a neat eleven-seat mini-airliner that was handicapped by the unreliability of its DH Gipsy Queen engine, a six-cylinder inverted in-line design that consumed (and leaked) oil at an astonishing rate and, according to Horst, developed "a porous crankcase" after several years of service. Art fixed it with a welding device for which he obtained FAA approval (the FAA having in the meantime superseded the CAA) and proceeded to replace the Beech 18s with three Doves, one of which was assembled from parts from Miami's famous "corrosion corner," a large area on the northwest corner of the airport where old and obsolete aircraft were parked awaiting sale. (Only seldom were transactions made, and the airframes gradually deteriorated into worthless pieces of scrap metal.) With this modest fleet, Reading Airlines had, by August 1960, opened service to Allentown, Lancaster, Wilkes-Barre, and Buffalo, to establish the foundations of an airline specializing in service to points too small to be attractive to the major airlines.

Wisely resting on its laurels, Reading Airlines resisted the temptation to expand until 1965, when New York's JFK International Airport was added to the network, and the spring of 1967, when service to Philadelphia was introduced. By now a vice-president, Horst had "discovered" Philadelphia, which had better trunk-line service than Newark. (The latter city had to wait until the 1980s for People Express to restore its airport to its prewar position of eminence.) The Doves were supplemented by aircraft such as the Beech 99, the Volpar Turboliner (a Beech 18 with a turboprop engine), and the Lycoming-powered nineteen-seat de Havilland DH-114 Heron. Such a fleet mix was necessary because the scheduled air taxi or "third-level" operators were still awaiting the appearance of a modern aircraft that was properly tailored to their needs.

This came in the spring of 1968 in the shape of the de Havilland Aircraft of Canada DHC-6 Twin Otter. Designed for Canadian bush operations, the airplane turned out to be ideal for the commuter airlines. RAS bought two of them and added a third by the end of 1968. The year was eventful for another reason; for in May RAS bought the Air Taxi Company of Red Bank, New Jersey, which had just renamed its scheduled operations into New York's three airports and to Princeton as Suburban Airlines. Two more Twin Otters came with Suburban, and Horst bought another from Air Wisconsin, to make a total fleet of six. For a year or two, the two scheduled divisions of the merged company operated as the eastern and western divisions, but this arrangement proved unsatisfactory.

Then, in September of the same year, Eastern transferred an important route, to Washington via Lancaster, to Reading/Suburban Airlines.

The transfer was arranged under a progressive contract with Eastern that brought $130,000 in the first year, $65,000 in the second, and $50,000 in the third. This straightforward arrangement had obvious appeal. Simultaneously, Reading terminated its services to Newark and JFK from Allentown. Claimed Horst, "They had operated for seven years without subsidy and never made money."

On 1 March 1970, Art became president of the newly renamed Suburban Airlines. His first act was to shut down the former Red Bank Air Taxi operation, which had never been completely coordinated with the Reading-based one. There had been far too much reliance on inefficient "dead flying," i.e., positioning aircraft for scheduled departures in a nonsequential pattern, and little had been gained through commonality of equipment or installations.

Such decisive action, which owed nothing to tradition or sentiment but much to good business sense, was typical of Horst's pragmatic approach to the commuter airline scene. Possibly because of the success of his 1968 deal with Eastern, he made another vital move. On 1 March 1973 he joined the growing ranks of the Allegheny Commuter system. This was strictly a franchise operation on selected routes: from Reading to Philadelphia, Lancaster, Washington, and Newark, and from Lancaster to Philadelphia and Washington. All the routes were very short—the longest, Reading-Washington, was 125 miles—too short for Allegheny's DC-9s but operationally feasible with Twin Otters.

The Allegheny Commuter transaction was a calculated risk. Suburban continued to operate some routes of its own, linking Philadelphia with Buffalo via Allentown, and this necessitated a separate maintenance base at Allentown. The use of separate fleets, one with the Allegheny Commuter paint scheme, led to integration problems. Possession of the franchise required that Suburban pay Allegheny fees for reservations and passenger handling, and even a fixed amount, irrespective of distance, per passenger boarded. In compensation, however, Suburban became a code-sharer with Allegheny in its computerized reservation system, which was networked with most of the major systems, such as American's SABRE, United's Apollo, and TWA's PARS. Suburban traffic increased by 50 percent almost overnight, and the flight frequency from both Reading and Lancaster to Philadelphia shot up to ten per day.

Progress in route and traffic expansion and in upgrading of equipment was subsequently steady and substantial. The higher traffic volumes led to load factors of 65 percent or more and demanded not only increased frequencies but also larger aircraft. With regulatory restrictions on commuter airlines eased, the first of five thirty-seat Shorts SD-330s went into service in January 1979, supplementing the Twin Otters. The remainder of the Suburban services came under the Allegheny Commuter banner, and on 12 May 1981 the airline made a public stock offering, amounting to $1,782,000. In 1982, following further relaxation of size restrictions, Suburban became the first U.S. operator of the larger—and somewhat handsomer—thirty-six-seat Shorts SD-360. Various changes were made to the route network, the most important of which were the reinstatement of a discontinued route to Washington and the addition of Boston and Pittsburgh as major stations. But Newark was dropped in the face of heavy competition from People Express.

The service into Pittsburgh began on 1 May 1984, with a new, $6 million, fifty-seat Fokker F-27. The F-27 remained the flagship of the line until May 1986, when Horst sold Suburban Airlines to USAir, the renamed Allegheny Airlines parent company of the commuter organization, for $9,742,800. Two more F-27s were promptly leased, so that the Suburban fleet consisted of three F-27s, five Shorts SD-330s, and two Shorts SD-360s. Horst was thus the only one of several commuter airline executives actually to make a success of F-27 operations.

Two years later, Suburban had been completely integrated with USAir, which took over all of Suburban's scheduling and marketing operations and all of its routes. The course of solid but unspectacular route expansion that had characterized Reading Airlines' growth in the late 1950s and thereafter continued. In 1988 Suburban carried 560,000 passengers, and there were almost seventy daily departures from Philadelphia, now its hub. Although all maintenance was done at Reading, Horst could proudly claim that the arrangement did not involve any dead mileage.

Comfortably retired today at Reading and pursuing his hobby of painting—he wields a deft and delicate brush on landscapes, town scenes, and airplanes alike—Horst has been a hardy survivor of the pioneering days of inadequate equipment and operational ostracism. His commuter airline career covered a little more than three decades. He never believed in growth for its own sake, but constantly maintained a levelheaded policy of route and fleet expansion that, by some commuter airline standards, was quite modest. The key to his success was high utilization of fleet installations and staff on routes that had to produce enough traffic to justify their existence. Art Horst operated his own use-it-or-lose-it policy from the start, and his success suggests that his instincts, judgment, and application were sound and a model for others to emulate.

Profile 12

F. E. (Pete) Howe
Rio Airways (To Name but One)

Pete Howe would be the last to claim that his experience as president of a major commuter/regional airline was crowned with as much success as were the careers of those of his compatriots, such as Art Horst or Kingsley Morse, who were able to tuck away fortunes measured in millions when they finally sold their airlines to their dominant code-sharing partners. In his younger days, Howe had been a sportsman of no mean ability, and perhaps the apprenticeship of having to lose gracefully helped him to survive the vicissitudes of his subsequent career. In fact, Howe epitomizes the enterprising airline promotor who carved an important niche in the commuter airline scene and helped to shape the course of the industry, but who, like scores of others, was unable to emerge at the top of the heap when the nationwide auction for trunk airline affiliation occurred in the mid-1980s.

Howe's early years were not marked at first by the familiar fascination with aviation or close association with aviation people. Born at Burgettstown, Pennsylvania, on 30 April 1917, he graduated from the local high school in 1934, excelling as an athlete. His baseball prowess led to an offer from the Pittsburgh Pirates, but instead he took a football scholarship to Monmouth College in Monmouth, Illinois. He soon decided, however, that his future career lay in the business world. The decision may have been influenced by his marriage to Ruth Nelson on 3 February 1938, and the realization that athletic stardom has always been too elusive a target for all but a very privileged few.

Always impulsive in his approach to any challenge, Howe backed this quality with the ability to concentrate with great determination once a course of action had been decided upon. When he began a two-year bookkeeping and accounting course with a correspondence school in 1939, he passed the test in six months. He started work as an accountant with the state tax department at Harrisburg, at $1,380 per year, but soon left to be a traveling auditor with the Singer Sewing Machine Company.

F. E. (Pete) Howe

In 1941 Howe joined his father in a strip mining operation in St. Clairsville, Ohio, but by then he was harboring two desires—to get into commercial aviation—and to live in Florida. He wrote a blind letter to D. G. Bash, the treasurer of National Airlines, then a small three-airplane airline based in Jacksonville. He included with his letter a picture of himself with his two daughters, the only recent picture he had, and Bash hired him for $250 a month on the basis of the picture, not his credentials—Bash loved children! Bash told Howe that he would have to perform an audit immediately upon reporting for work on 1 May 1943. To gain some idea of just how to perform an audit, Howe read J. K. Lassiter's *Internal Auditing* on the bus between St. Clairsville and Jacksonville.

National was operated in buccaneer style by the irascible Ted Baker, who had run into trouble with the CAB over financial matters, and Howe's analysis of the problem and its successful resolution brought not only congratulations from the CAB's Warner Hord but also a doubling of his salary.

He subsequently became involved with the no-holds-barred struggle for routes as the airlines sought favors from the CAB. He well remembers National's bitter rivalry with Eastern Airlines, whose president, Eddie Rickenbacker, did not react magnanimously when, on 13 February 1944, the CAB awarded Baker a share of what had been Eastern's "gravy-run" monopoly on the New York–Miami route. National's entry into the market was modest enough, with a fourteen-seat Lockheed Lodestar. But when, in 1945, National put into service the first new Douglas DC-4 (not a military C-54 conversion), Rickenbacker threatened to kill National by scheduling Eastern flights five minutes before and five minutes after National's.

Such competition was meat and drink to Howe, who thrived on cut-and-thrust challenges. Becoming more and more involved in airline affairs, he left National in 1951 to join the Hawthorne School of Aeronautics at Moultrie, Georgia, to broaden his knowledge. His name must by now have been circulating around the airline fraternity, for on 31 December 1952 he received a telephone call from Keith Kahle, head of Central Airlines of Fort Worth, Texas, one of the original local service airlines established by the CAB during the late 1940s, in a nationwide program to widen the scope of airline service to every community in the United States.

Howe joined Central Airlines on 1 May 1953 and stayed for ten years, until Kahle sold the airline to Jack Bradford, a Texas oilman from Midland. He worked for Caribair, at San Juan, Puerto Rico, for most of 1966, but soon returned to Fort Worth, as he felt that he had no control over what he was doing (even though he had no complaints over his contract with Caribair's owner, Dionisio Trigo). He then served a tour with Transair, a Canadian regional airline based in Winnipeg, as its executive vice-president and later chief executive officer. But once again he moved on, this time, in the fall of 1968, to Atlanta, where a headhunter had convinced him to take over Nationwide Airlines, whose chief stockholder was Bill Evans of Cleveland. Howe immediately changed the name of the airline to Air South as he stepped up service to the Atlantic coastal resorts.

The restless search for a position in which he could fulfil his ambition reached its end toward the end of the 1960s, during a period when the commuter airline industry as a whole was expanding rapidly but individual airlines were booming or busting with equal rapidity. Howe felt that circumstances had combined to give him an opportunity to guide the fortunes of an airline himself and to be on the booming side of the economic equation.

While still working for Air South, on a visit to the Beech Aircraft factory at Wichita, he had met Mark Connell, twenty-one-year-old owner of Hood Airlines of Killeen, Texas, and had agreed to help him run the commuter company. The idea seemed promising, as the traffic base at

Killeen was the largest military establishment in the United States, and its busy connection to the trunk lines at Dallas was a solid base for possible further expansion.

Meanwhile, as part of his restructuring of Air South, Howe had undertaken a program of replacing a fleet of Queen Airs with fifteen-seat Beech 99s, for which he paid the excellent price of $363,000 each. Then, at a company board meeting (which he vividly remembers, as it was held at the Master's Tournament at Augusta, Georgia), the owners expressed the desire to buy much larger equipment, Martin 4-0-4s, from Southern Airways. In Howe's words, he "was not about to write [his] own obituary." Impulsive as ever, he left Air South in July 1971.

In helping Hood Airlines, he won a route to Wichita Falls before the Texas Aeronautics Commission on 15 November 1971, and with his contract with Air South expiring on 31 December, he moved to Killeen. Within a few months, Hood Airlines had taken over Rio Airways, which operated along the Rio Grande Valley but was abandoning its routes. In May 1972, Hood acquired Rio's name as part of the depleted assets.

On 7 March 1973, the new Rio Airways started service to Temple, a city that had found a place on the scheduled air map but that had been successively abandoned by Essair, Pioneer, Continental, Braniff, and then Continental again. On 3 February 1974, Waco was added to the growing spoke network radiating from Dallas, and during the next three years gradual expansion brought in Texarkana, Hot Springs, Little Rock, and Lawton. In 1979, with steadily growing traffic, DHC-6 Twin Otters replaced the Beech 99s, and DHC Dash 7s and Swearingen Metroliners were later added. This a familiar aircraft improvement pattern in the early 1980s, as larger cities such as Memphis, as well as other points in an expanding sphere of influence, demanded larger aircraft.

To demonstrate just how precarious was the life of even a successful commuter airline in the 1980s, two developments occurred that made severe inroads into Rio's traffic base. Austin, the state capital, which was only fifty miles from Killeen, was growing into a commercial center as well as an administrative one, and it began to receive substantial additional trunk line service after airline deregulation in 1978 allowed operators to dispense with long and irritating CAB procedures and objections. Then, when the air traffic controller's strike of 1983 led to emergency measures being taken, Rio found itself at the bottom of the priority list at Dallas and lost 60 percent of its operating slots.

For two and a half years, Rio sought a solution by joining a major trunk airline in what was becoming an essential formula for survival.

Actions taken by the CAB in its twilight years had ordained low priorities on the computer reservation terminals for unaffiliated commuter airlines. Years earlier, the local service airlines had confronted local communities with a CAB-authorized "use-it-or-lose-it" policy. Now the large airlines used their corporate and financial strength to threaten the commuter airlines, warning, in effect, "use our system or lose your livelihood." Rio fell into line by becoming a unit of The Delta Connection on 1 June 1984.

In September 1986, however, Hugh Seaborn bought Rio Airways, and thereafter the connection fell apart. Rio's association with Delta ended on 14 December 1986. On 28 February 1987, the airline declared bankruptcy.

Howe was almost seventy years old by this time, and he decided that three score years and ten were enough. His career in commercial aviation had included tours with no fewer than seven different airlines. While he was able to control affairs, they seem to have prospered, but in almost every case they went downhill after he left. Howe would be the last to say that he was ever a man of compromise, and his refusal to be subjected to pressure over issues on which he felt strongly, especially when the future of his company was at stake, had led to a peripatetic career.

He has no regrets. In his latter years he continues to enjoy life, with an army of friends among his fellow commuter airline promoters. When he retired, three hundred of them gave him a surprise retirement party in Dallas and greeted him with a huge signboard that read "Thanks for 40 Heavenly Years, Saint Pete"—a reference to his annual sponsorship of a "heavenly" golf tournament in which he made all the rules. He may not have made a fortune, measured in hard dollars, but the popularity and respect he holds among his peers could not be bought for a king's ransom.

Profile 13

Milton G. (Milt) Kuolt II
Horizon Air

Meeting Milton G. Kuolt II for the first time is something of a culture shock. At a formal gathering, where most of the assembled company is attired in dark gray suits, Kuolt might be observed wearing casual attire. Ask him a question and you will receive an answer that is not couched in the protective phraseology of politicoindustrial double-talk. These characteristics are an essential aspect of his approach to society, business, and life in general. He does what he feels should be done and allows convention to take care of itself. In doing so, he emanates an aura of honesty and down-to-earth integrity that demands respect. This is the man who, within the span of only six years, built Horizon Air up from scratch into one of the largest and most successful of all the commuter carriers.

There was little sign of this outstandingly successful entrepreneur's potential at the beginning. Born in 1927 in India, the son of missionaries who were stationed in a rural environment in that vast country, he was fourteen years old before he visited a large city. This was at the beginning of World War II, when he was in the United States with his parents, who were on extended leave from their mission field work. He attended Llanerch High School in Philadelphia, where he was voted by his classmates as the one "least likely to succeed."

Kuolt served with the U.S. Navy for eighteen months during World War II and then enrolled in the Bartlett School of Tree Surgery at Stamford, Connecticut. Full of confidence (a quality that has never deserted him), he formed a company immediately after graduation, to put to good use what he had learned. Together with a school friend, he established Gunther and Kuolt, Tree Expert Company, but soon discovered that scholastic expertise did not necessarily translate into a living wage. Practical experience was an essential ingredient for commercial success.

Milton G. (Milt) Kuolt II

Accordingly, he soon followed the time-honored advice and went west, where he found work as a choker-setter at a Weyerhauser Company logging camp near Mount St. Helens in the state of Washington. This position was not very far up the ladder in the Weyerhauser hierarchy, and so Kuolt decided to seek the key to American success by going to college, serving the four-year sentence, and acquiring a degree.

In the summer of 1948, with only $5.00 in his pocket, he walked out of the logging camp and hitchhiked to Seattle, so that he did not have to spend all of his funds on the bus fare. He still owed Weyerhauser for a day's board at the camp, but the timber giant's accountants have to this day not yet sent him the bill. Kuolt's assessment of his ambitions and prospects must have impressed his driver en route to Seattle, for the latter not only paid for his room at the YMCA but also gave him some spending money and bought him a bus ticket to Ellensburg so that he could enroll at what is now Central Washington State University.

Instead of finding a place to lodge for the first few nights in Ellensburg, he took a job at a local corn cannery, working the night shift. He was thus able to live on canned corn and to sleep in a haystack, at least until the college opened its doors for enrollment.

He must have made as good an impression on the registrar as on his philanthropic driver. College regulations normally precluded the occupation of dormitory space until the academic year started. Kuolt stated bluntly, "my objective is not to be a brilliant student, but to get a degree," and such frankness led to his being let in early, so that he could desert the haystack.

Noticing that the many trees on the campus needed attention, he realized that he had the experience, from the Bartlett School, to undertake the necessary maintenance. Normally, ex-servicemen were hired at 50¢ per hour, but Kuolt negotiated a rate of $2.00, enabling him to buy a pickup truck, and the school furnished the tools. He thus demonstrated that entrepreneurship, like an artist's eye or a musician's ear, is quite possibly an inborn ability that no amount of academic learning can match. As he himself has said, "Schools can't teach it. Either you're born with it or you acquire it."

Most of what Kuolt does is invariably unusual, sometimes unorthodox, and occasionally outrageous. But when he emerged from Ellensburg with an economics degree, he did what nearly everyone else does in the state of Washington, other than grow apples: he joined the Boeing Company at Seattle. His initial inclination was to leave as soon as he had built up sufficient equity to start up his own business, but he soldiered on with the aircraft manufacturer for twenty years, partly because he had married and during the 1950s was building up a family (he has six children by his first marriage).

Over his two decades with Boeing, Kuolt rose to become business planning manager in charge of the 737 airliner program, one of the greatest success stories in the history of commercial airliner manufacture. During this time, in 1960, he had already made his first move toward self-sufficiency. A friend had suggested the idea of investing in real estate. Not a man to do things by halves, Kuolt borrowed $1,000 to buy $10,000 worth of land. He paid off the loan as well as the mortgage, worked on weekends on his property, subdivided the land into lots of 2½ acres each, and sold them at $2,000 per acre. With a handsome return on investment, he explored further the idea of land speculation.

As a family man, he was doing quite a bit of camping, but it was often difficult to find space in public campgrounds on the weekends. So he combined business with pleasure, bought 640 acres of land, and in 1969 founded Thousand Trails. He hand-cleared the property and sold the first private campground memberships ever offered at $250. Today a single membership sells for $7,000. And Kuolt owned the land itself until he sold the company in 1980, by which time the enterprise was worth $40 million.

During the period when he was introducing an entirely new approach to the outdoor leisure world, Kuolt developed a disapproval of bankers. He feels they are never prepared to share investment risks fairly with their clients, placing insufficient confidence in individual ability and displaying an inclination to invest in things rather than in people—yet not always assessing the material assets correctly. "Nothing," he says, "is worse than a nervous banker unless it's a gullible banker."

In December 1980, he announced that he was going into the airline business. He had always been convinced that one of the keys to success in any business was providing good service to the customer. He was unimpressed by the airline industry's performance in this respect and felt that, even without previous experience, he could find the proper niche and put his convictions about customer service to the test. He first aimed only to link some of the smaller cities in Washington state, but after founding Horizon Air Industries, Inc. (operating as Horizon Air) as a regional carrier early in 1981, he quickly discovered that his location and timing had been perfect and that the emphasis on service was competitively effective. Former local service airlines were abandoning their routes. The main competition was Cascade Airways, another commuter airline, founded by Mark Chestnutt eleven years earlier; but it was undercapitalized and also operated expensive-to-operate jets and unpressurized Beech 99s, neither of which was suited to the market.

Horizon Air started service on 1 September 1981, on a route from Seattle to Yakima. The latter city is the only one between Seattle and Spokane with more than 50,000 inhabitants. It is also only about thirty miles from Ellensburg, Kuolt's alma mater, and, sentiment aside, he knew the area quite well and was able to assess its market potential correctly. Within a week, he had extended the route to Pasco, another medium-size city in central Washington. His equipment, refurbished Fairchild F-27 forty-seaters, was just about right for the traffic, at least at the time.

In June 1982, he purchased another airline, Air Oregon, a Swearingen Metroliner operator founded in Portland in August 1978. It flew throughout its home state and to neighboring ones, but its main artery connected the north-south corridor of towns from Medford, in southern Oregon, through Portland, and on to Tacoma and Seattle. This acquisition added an important spoke to Kuolt's Horizon network, which was still concentrated on serving points to the southeast of Washington state.

Less than two years later, again by acquisition, the spokes were extended. Transwestern Airlines, also dating from 1978 and operating out of Salt Lake City to points in Utah and Idaho, followed Air Oregon into the Horizon organization in December 1983. The linkage was tailor-made for opportune expansion, so much so that Horizon Air became the successor to West Coast Airlines (later Hughes AirWest and Republic Airlines) as the leading regional airline of the northwestern United States, embracing the states of Washington, Oregon, Idaho, western Montana, and Utah, linking their principal cities and serving the resort areas, especially Sun Valley.

In 1984, Kuolt decided that a substantial injection of additional capital was necessary to consolidate Horizon's position as the recognized regional airline of the Northwest. And another story was added to the Milt Kuolt legend. He entered the sacred portals of his underwriters in Denver wearing a Goofy hat, portraying the famous Walt Disney cartoon character. The brokers and securities analysts may have thought this choice of accessories to be at odds with traditional convention in such situations, but it certainly commanded their attention—and subsequently their financial support. Kuolt went on to augment his fleet with Fokker F-28 sixty-five-seat jetliners and a fleet of de Havilland Dash 8s to expand his network. Pursuing the Kuolt conviction that the public was entitled to good service, and with the details of providing it delegated to the executive team, Horizon introduced hourly departures between Seattle and Spokane and a half-hour shuttle service between Seattle and Portland. Few cities in the world the size of Spokane (population about 170,000) have such convenient access to a nearby metropolis.

Late in 1986, Kuolt formed a loose association with a major carrier, code-sharing with United Air Lines—such a practice having by this time become almost essential for survival in the U.S. airline business. Meanwhile, his chief competitor, Cascade Airways, filed for Chapter 11 bankruptcy and finally closed down on 7 March 1986. Cascade had operated almost entirely over parallel routes, but with too wide a variety of aircraft, some too small and some too big. By the latter 1980s, Horizon dominated the regional routes of the Northwest.

Late in 1986, by which time he had become interested in other service-oriented business ventures, Kuolt surrendered his interest in Horizon almost as abruptly as he had grasped it, barely more than five years previously. The airline was sold to the Alaska Air Group for $70 million, of which Kuolt received a significant portion. Much of his share was reinvested in new enterprises, such as the Elkhorn Resort in Sun Valley, a golf course development in Puerto Vallarta, Mexico, a vineyard in Washington state, and a minority interest in a chain of Azteca Mexican restaurants in Oregon.

He has been awarded the Distinguished Alumnus award by Central Washington University and named Citizen of the Year by the city fathers of Sun Valley. He is on the board of directors of the Pacific Institute and the Idaho Governors Cup and serves on the Board of Visitors for Central Washington University. His rags-to-riches career is even quoted in business case studies.

But these books and distinctions cannot alone serve as lessons for others to follow. Milton Kuolt's ability to build a single route into a company worth $70 million over a period of less than six years is unprecedented in the world of modern airline business. Many other pioneers in the small airline field—including revered and respected men who, for several decades, had shaped the route networks, selected the aircraft, fought the authorities for survival, and become role models for others—never attained the complete and almost instantaneous success of the newcomer from the Northwest. Horizon was the highly successful beneficiary of its promoter's special brand of entrepreneurship. Kuolt's direct involvement, from start to finish, lasted about as long as that of many an aspirant still trying to make up his mind. He came, he saw, he conquered—all in half a decade.

Profile 14

Ross Miller
TAG Airlines

In the chronicle of commuter airlines, one is often overlooked. This is because it was conceived and born in the 1950s, thrived vigorously in the 1960s, and collapsed (through no fault of its own) at the beginning of the 1970s. It had thus passed into history before many well-known companies had developed during the booming 1970s.

Ross Miller had begun service with TAG Airlines in 1957, on a single ninety-two-mile route that no one else seemed to want, and within a few years he was carrying more than a thousand passengers a week, on an on-the-hour, every-hour service. In the October 1963 issue of *American Aviation*, Wayne W. Parrish said of TAG, "It has no connections to offer anyone. It is purely and simply a commuter point-to-point service."

As had been the case with John Van Arsdale's Provincetown-Boston Airline, the CAB did not quite know what to do with this boisterous little company, reluctantly listing it under "other airlines" or "miscellaneous" in its reports and treating Miller with benign neglect as, from 1960 until 1968, he vainly applied for a Certificate of Public Necessity and Convenience. Just as, desperate to break his regulatory shackles, he reluctantly entered into a merger agreement with another airline that could be regarded as a usurper of his birthright, a tragic crash precipitated TAG's abrupt demise.

Miller was born into a farming family in Bridgewater Township, Williams County, Ohio, on 19 January 1910 and graduated from Montpelier High School in 1928. He was very proud of his accomplishment, while in school, of being the champion pig-raiser in the state of Ohio. He was helped by his brother Wesley, and he recalls that "the pigs ate better than I did."

Leaving school, he worked at first for local farmers for the princely sum of $1.00 a day. No doubt feeling that he could do better than this, he went to Chicago and worked at first on the night shift at the Dallas

Ross Miller

Brass and Copper Company, then in a daytime job at Montgomery Ward, "chasing orders on scooters."

Miller came into contact with the oil business in 1930, when he worked for his other brother, Ford, at a gas station in Toledo for $15.00 a week. In 1932, Ross asked for a raise to $20.00 a week. Ford said, "If you think you're worth that, I will loan you $250.00 to start your own business. If you don't make it, I'll take you back at $15.00 a week." Ford lent Ross $250.00, with which he bought his first gasoline, and leased a station in Maumee, thus beginning the enterprise that became the Miller Oil Company in 1935.

During the early 1930s, Ross gradually built up his oil business. "Gradually" must have been the operative word, for he was only making $40.00 a month when he married Erna Trost in 1933. She was working as a bookkeeper and making $149.00 a month.

Miller was, as his subsequent career was to demonstrate, a man of ideas, and willing to experiment. In 1937 he bought his first road tanker, a ten-wheel tractor-trailer, able to transport 3,500 gallons. He bought quantities of a superior kerosene from Leonard Refineries, at Alma, Michigan, and sold it to petroleum products distributors. This special Miller grade was popular with chicken farmers for brooder houses, because there was no odor. Incidentally, in 1938 Bill Berry joined the Miller Oil Company as a driver; he was to rise in his employer's esteem and eventually to become his right-hand man when he branched out into aviation.

Miller had by then become an enthusiastic aviator, and in January 1940 he flew his own Piper Cub to the Panama Canal Zone, where he sold it and returned home by Ford Tri-Motor via Cuba, as far as Miami, and thence by train.

Refreshed by this experience, Ross began to expand the Miller Oil Company. In 1941, he leased an office in downtown Toledo, on South Street. Edna Kumpe, who was eventually to become his second wife in 1983, was at that time his secretary, at $12.50 a week. The next year, he opened his first bulk storage plant for the trucking business, and in 1943 he bought a terminal on the Maumee River in Toledo, close to Lake Erie and the farthest western point to which lake oil tankers could bring gasoline from Ashland Oil at Buffalo. By the end of World War II, in 1945, Miller had thirteen tanker transports.

During this wartime period, after discussion with Leroy Tipton of the New York Central Railroad, he came up with an ingenious idea. For many years, American railroads had granted what were known as in transit privileges. These applied particularly to grain, which was brought in from the Great Plains to such points as Minneapolis, Chicago, or Toledo, where it was ground into flour and then transshipped onward at no extra cost. Miller and Tipton discovered that these privileges could legally be applied to petroleum products.

Thus, if a blending naphtha was railroaded from Big Springs, Texas, to Toledo at 12¢ per gallon, then blended by the Miller Oil Company with natural gasoline (the by-product of local gas plants) to produce regular-grade gasoline, it could be taken by rail to Pittsburgh at no cost because the rate was the same from Big Springs to Pittsburgh. This procedure kept Miller and Bill Berry out of the draft, because they were saving the government as much at 6¢ per gallon, shipping it direct to the east coast terminals, straight into jerry cans.

The war over, the Miller Oil Company continued to operate success-fully, if not spectacularly, for about a decade. Then in 1957, Miller got into the airline business almost by accident. A small company, the Taxi Air Group (TAG) had been operating floatplanes (one de Havilland Air-craft of Canada DHC-3 Otter and two DHC-2 Beavers) on a regular service between Toledo and Cleveland since 1954, but it had not been able to operate during the winter when Lake Erie was frozen and had lost money with the expense of moving the aircraft south. Miller and Berry approached TAG to buy one of the floatplanes but ended up buying the operating company instead and assumed a considerable loss. Their accountants had counted on the $200,000 TAG loss being able to be written off as a tax deduction. But after the deal was signed, the IRS did not agree, and TAG had to take the loss.

By this time Miller must have been intrigued at the prospect of operating an airline. Accordingly, he and Berry bought out the other half of TAG in July 1957, purchased two British eight-seat de Havilland Dove landplanes, and began to operate four round trips a day between Cleveland's Lakefront Airport and the Detroit City Airport. These airports were convenient to the downtown business districts of both cities, in contrast with the municipal airports served by the major and local service airlines, which were located on the outer perimeters.

Miller moved cautiously to expand his new enterprise, by now called simply TAG Airlines. Late in 1957 he signed an agreement with Illini Airlines of Rockford, Illinois, to operate from Rockford to Chicago, at the downtown Meigs Field, and on to Detroit. As part of the contract, TAG bought another Dove and leased a nineteen-seat de Havilland Heron from Illini. Chicago was omitted from this route on 1 April 1958, to enable TAG to concentrate on direct Rockford-Detroit service, taking advantage of the community of interest between Rockford, the tool capital of the United States, and Detroit, the world's automobile manufacturing center. With the same marketing approach, service to Akron's downtown Municipal Airport began on 28 April 1958 from Cleveland, and then on 5 May from Detroit.

In 1959, however, service on both the Rockford-Detroit and the Akron routes was dropped, and TAG settled down to a steady diet of Cleveland-Detroit service. The year-end passenger total of 20,767 in 1959 increased to 44,324 by 1963, and Miller was encouraged to apply to the CAB, first on 1 February 1960 and then again on 8 February 1961, for a Certificate of Public Convenience and Necessity.

This regulatory objective had been considered very carefully by Miller and his colleagues at TAG. Operation under a full certificate would permit, for example, twenty-eight-seat Douglas DC-3 operations. In addition to the heightened traffic, another advantage of the "luxurious 200-mph multi-engined executive airliners," as the Doves were brashly advertised, was that passengers could drive straight up to the airplanes at the downtown airports.

Yet a third application was made to the CAB on 7 August 1964. It was not dismissed; the case was not even heard. TAG immediately refiled, but again got nowhere. North Central Airlines' objection to the application, made on 24 September, may have had something to do with the apparent absence of due process. At the time, TAG was handling 65 percent of all the passengers carried by the small uncertificated airlines.

Further expansion occurred during the mid-1960s. Dove service from Cleveland to Columbus and Cincinnati began on 15 March 1965, and direct service from Detroit to the two Ohio cities followed on 3 May, these latter routes being served by the first of fifteen new Piper Aztecs. Passenger boardings reached a record 83,873 in 1965; part of the increase was attributable to new services into Cleveland Hopkins and Detroit Metro airports, allowing passengers to make connections with other airlines. The next year was one of mixed fortunes, with a new route to Pittsburgh's Allegheny County Airport, but also problems from the pilots' union, whose members inexplicably paraded with signs stating "TAG is unsafe to fly"—before they took the signs off and took off.

During 1966, Miller had discussed with several manufacturers the idea of a new aircraft to seat up to fifteen passengers and fall within the 12,500-pound gross takeoff weight limit. Out of these talks emerged the germ of the ideas for the Beech 99 and the de Havilland Twin Otter. But new acquisitions were soon postponed because of a setback. On 18 May 1967, Gerald E. Weller, a former TAG sales representative, formed Wright Air Lines, which on 27 June started operations on the Cleveland-Detroit route in direct competition with TAG, still frustrated by the CAB in its wish to purchase forty-seat Fokker F-27s. On 1 October TAG was obliged to suspend services on all routes except its own "grandfather" Cleveland-Detroit route. Facing problems with the aging Doves, Miller met with Les Barnes of Allegheny Airlines to discuss the possibility of interline connections. Barnes apparently thought well of the idea, but TAG never became part of the Allegheny Commuter system, which seemed to evolve as a result of that meeting. Meanwhile a third carrier, Air Commuter Airlines, entered TAG's territory but did not last long, merging in March 1968 with Wright.

In the same month, on 8 March, TAG finally received permission from the CAB to operate large aircraft—F-27s, to be followed by FH-227s, were specified—but this time, after protests from Wright, the certificate was revoked, pending another hearing. Finally, after TAG had been incorporated on 28 June in its own right as a separate entity from the Miller Oil Company (which, however, continued to receive excellent advertising rates in TAG's timetables), and after the inevitably drawn-out CAB procedures, Miller received the coveted Certificate of Public Convenience and Necessity, albeit on a temporary basis, on 29 August 1969.

Just as Ross was preparing to purchase three Fairchild-Hiller FH-227s, and just when TAG's competitive position against its challenger,

Wright, looked bright indeed, it was overcome by disaster. On 28 January 1970 a de Havilland Dove, N2300H, en route from Cleveland to Detroit, crashed into the frozen Lake Erie, fifteen miles off shore, into wind-swept, ice-jammed waters. All seven passengers and the crew were killed. Because of the severe winter conditions, with drifting ice and near-zero temperatures, the rescue and salvage operations went on for four months. Thus the incident was kept almost constantly in the public eye, with predictably adverse effects on TAG's traffic levels, revenues, and profit and loss statement. In May 1970, only 881 passengers were carried, as against 4,670 in the corresponding month of 1969. The cause of the crash was later identified as a manufacturing defect—metal fatigue cracks in the right wing. Although the National Transport Safety Board blamed "inadequate safety regulations on the part of the Federal Aviation Administration, not poor maintenance by the airline, . . . for the crash," this finding was not made public until March 1971 and thus was of little consolation to Ross and his much demoralized staff at the time of the tragedy and during the remaining long months of 1970.

In fact, the year was one of drastic retrenchment from a former twenty-seven-airplane fleet. Some Doves were sold, and the operating fleet was down to two, flying ten round trips a day, compared to the forty previously achieved at the zenith of TAG's career. In July the CAB turned down the proposal for a TAG-Wright merger. On 7 August TAG suspended its operation and furloughed all crew members. Then, in an incomprehensible announcement on 24 September, the CAB again rejected the merger proposal, after another review, yet ordered TAG to resume operations. This command to an airline whose passenger boardings had dropped from 58,222 to 9,489 in one year.

The TAG story is a classic "what might have been" saga. In view of TAG's five years of successful operation in the early 1960s, the CAB could have persuaded itself that the TAG route that generated more than two hundred passengers per day could have justified operations by a forty-seat airliner. TAG would have disposed of the Doves by 1966, and Wright Air Lines might never have dared to make its challenge. But would TAG have been able to break even on a ninety-two-mile route with, say, a pair of Fokker F-27s with one in reserve? We shall never know.

What we do know is that Ross Miller was a great standard-bearer for the cause of the yet unborn commuter airlines. It was he who tested the operating environment, stretched his resources to the utmost, and met hardship headon, with no theoretical case study as a guide, no computer software, no mathematical models. He and his attorney, Merrill Armour, set up the Association of Commuter Airlines as early as 1963, to protect the rights of the small airlines against the obstructive practices of their regional rivals. He was often at odds with the Air Line Pilots Association (ALPA), paradoxically because of his efforts to help his pilots earn more money by flying more hours on routes that were not too strenuous for the aircrew and did not seem to require the same kind of restrictions as did the longer intercity routes. ALPA's tactics and methods during these battles were less than creditable, and Miller did not have, at the time, an association of fellow sufferers to give him support.

Miller was the first president of the Association of Commuter Airlines, and none of his peers would begrudge his right to that privilege. But after the Dove disaster, he never returned to active participation in the management of an airline. He still had his oil business and a lovely home overlooking the Maumee River near Toledo. He became something of a celebrity duck hunter, but he suffered a stroke on 29 November 1987, and this curtailed his activities. He died on 28 August 1990.

Because of Miller's reduced participation in commuter airline affairs during the last few years of his life, his name is seldom mentioned at either the official or the informal gatherings of the industry. In its sheer simplicity, TAG had been unique as a "third-level" airline, and it came closer to the collective definition of the essential qualities necessary for successful operation than any other airline, before or since. Ross Miller, a true innovator and the creator of the quintessential commuter airline, deserved a better fate.

Profile 15

Kingsley G. Morse
Command Airways

If some commuter airline pioneers were moved by inspiration, instinct, impulse, or intuition, the same cannot be said of Kingsley Morse. His approach to entering the perilous world of commuter airlines was careful and calculated, methodical and market-oriented. He was probably the only one of his pioneering era who bothered to conduct a proper market survey, a decision due in no small part to the fact that his previous education and training had embraced that field of study.

Morse does not make any claims that his success was a "rags to riches" story, but he might admit to an "off-the-rack to Savile Row" analogy. Born on 30 March 1931, in Pasadena, California, he was one of four children of a successful realtor. He did not waste his educational opportunities, obtaining a B.A. in political science in 1955 at Amherst College in Massachusetts, after a two-year interruption while he was in the armed services as a Marine Corps sergeant. Graduating cum laude, he went on to gain his M.A. in business administration at the Harvard Business School.

During his period at Amherst, he had learned to fly as a private pilot, first on a floatplane on the Connecticut River and then taking to wheels. He had prepared himself well before entering the world of commerce, with an eye toward aviation.

In 1957, Morse went to work for American Airlines in New York City, serving his apprenticeship in the finance and scheduling departments. He gained his first managerial experience in 1962, when he joined the Maxwell House Division of General Foods at White Plains, New York. During 1965 and 1966 he began to "look around for entrepreneurial opportunities" either in the scheduled air taxi industry (as the commuter airlines were then called) or in flight training for the business jet market. Moving right along, he took the precaution of gaining a commercial pilot's license, with instrument rating.

Kingsley G. Morse (photo by Ann Morse)

During March and April 1966, Morse carried out an exercise that was to direct him to the threshold of his career. He conducted personal market research with Red Bank Air Taxi, at Red Bank, New Jersey; Chatham Aviation, at Morristown, New Jersey; Empire Airlines, at White Plains; Mid-Hudson Airlines at Poughkeepsie, New York; Pilgrim Airlines, at New London, Connecticut; and Mac-Aire, at MacArthur Airport, Long Island. After careful deliberation, he approached Ted Lafko of Mid-Hudson and found that Ted was willing to sell out. So Morse took his first big step, purchasing Lafko's assets and paying $40,000 for the goodwill.

The assets consisted mainly of six single-engined three-seat Cessna 172s, one seven-seat Aero Commander 560, and two veteran Beech 18s (C-45s), each fitted with eight seats. The operation fell under FAA Part 135 regulations, i.e., aircraft could not exceed 12,500 pounds gross takeoff weight but could be operated for hire and with a single pilot, without a CAB airline certificate. Mid-Hudson's only route was from Poughkeepsie to New York's Idlewild (now John F. Kennedy) Airport.

On 1 July 1966, Morse bought a cash drawer from the local hardware store and started operations. He changed the line's name from Mid-Hudson to Command Airways, partly to remove the carrier's localized identity and partly to change its image by choosing a name that would inspire confidence and counteract the general impression that the scheduled air taxi operators used old airplanes and employed young (and by inference, inexperienced) pilots. He sold off the single-engined Cessnas and occasionally stood in as one of the aircrew himself.

Two months later, he obtained clearance from IBM, the biggest local employer at Poughkeepsie, to carry its traveling staff, who had been forbidden to use Mid-Hudson to connect with flights out of New York. At the end of the year, he acquired another twin Beech, a refurbished G-18 fitted with nine seats and boasting a tricycle landing gear, and early in 1967 he bought the first of three five-seat Piper Aztecs.

Both of these new acquisitions, however, were sold in 1968, the year when Command Airways commenced turbine-powered operations. Morse acquired the first of three fifteen-seat Beech 99s, fitted with Pratt & Whitney Canada PT6 engines and offering not only faster and smoother flights but also more capacity. They were used mainly for another IBM contract, Poughkeepsie-Burlington, a source of bread-and-butter income that was a welcome supplement to the sometimes fluctuating scheduled business.

In fact, although Morse had entered the scheduled air taxi fray with perhaps more capital and more financial acumen than some of the pioneers, his resources were also limited, and in the latter half of the 1960s he kept afloat by selling company stock to some of his fellow directors. Command Airways badly needed to improve its customer acceptance in the New York market. The Beech 99 was maintaining the image of modernity with IBM, but something better was needed to upgrade the standard of service provided by the old Beech 18s, which, in spite of their respected veteran status, Morse admitted, "were looking tired and worn."

Accordingly, in 1969 he and another director bought a de Havilland Aircraft of Canada DHC-6 Twin Otter and leased it to Command Airways at a favorable rate. This action was a turning point. Although the aircraft could carry up to nineteen passengers, Command restricted it to a more generously spaced fifteen. At the time the traffic potential did not demand the full potential capacity, but the extra legroom was appreciated by a clientele that had, more often than not, just stepped off a big jet. Command had only three Twin Otters, but they performed sterling service until 1983.

Morse's analytical approach to the selection of the Twin Otter in this situation, rather than additional Beech 99s, is worthy of consideration, as it illustrates clearly how two aircraft, ostensibly similar in what they offered to the customer, were in fact suited to different markets. Both had the same engines, Pratt & Whitney Canada PT-6 turboprops. The DHC-6, with nineteen seats, had greater earning power than the Beech 99, with fifteen. But it was slower and had less range, so that for distances of more than, say, 250 miles, the Beech 99 had the edge. However, few commuter routes were that long, and so for average stage distances of 100 miles or so, the Beech 99's speed advantage was of little consequence.

One criticism of the Twin Otter was its somewhat ungainly appearance. Certainly it was not as handsome and sleek as the Beech 99. The late George Parmenter, of Cape and Islands Air Service, described it as "the airplane the Wright brothers forgot to finish." Contrary to popular opinion, however, hard-headed businessmen were unimpressed by superficial appearances. They remembered how Detroit had laughed at the Volkswagen.

The Twin Otter's main advantage, however, was its utter reliability, built as it was to a demanding specification for operations into dirt strips and in the severe climatic conditions of northern Canada. To be able to land and take off from concrete or asphalt was sheer luxury for the Twin Otter, and such pampering made for low maintenance costs.

The Beech 99, on the other hand, was a derivative of the Queen Aire, used for corporate travel and not intended for intensive airline use of up to eight hours per day in the air and perhaps ten or twelve landings and takeoffs during that time. Many of the systems and components needed frequent attention, whereas the Twin Otter, in Morse's terse summary, needed "only kerosene."

Equipped with the trusty Twin Otters, Command Airways began cautiously to expand from an operating area that had hitherto been restricted to that suggested by its original name: Mid-Hudson. In December 1971, it took over the route from Pittsfield, Massachusetts, to New York (La Guardia) from Executive Airlines, which had bought the incumbent Pittsfield scheduled air taxi company, Yankee Airlines. Command assumed responsibility for the route, but not the aircraft, which went to Executive. Morse substituted John F. Kennedy for La Guardia as the New York airport terminus, for the sake of convenient aircraft integration.

The following years witnessed the great fuel crisis precipitated by the Organization of Petroleum Exporting Countries, and in reaction to the sharp increase in the price of aviation gasoline and kerosene, Morse took a bold yet calculated step in aircraft procurement. He realized that, with steady and satisfying traffic increases in the commuter airline business generally, and with increasing congestion at the main New York terminals, an increase in aircraft size was inevitable. In spite of the reliability and satisfactory service record of the Twin Otter, therefore, he moved one more step up the commuter aircraft size ladder and ordered the Shorts SD-330, a thirty-seat aircraft built in Belfast, Northern Ireland. While he awaited delivery of this airplane, Command added two new important city pairs to its modest network: Poughkeepsie–La Guardia (so that both of New York's airports were served) and a White Plains–Boston link. White Plains is geographically situated in the affluent northwestern outer suburbs of New York City, and its Westchester County Airport was ideal for Boston-bound businessmen who lived in the area and who did not wish to endure a long train ride or to hack their way into town to take the Eastern Shuttle.

In July 1976, Command Airways put its first Shorts SD-330 into service. It had been the first airline in the world to order the craft but narrowly missed the privilege of being the first to operate it on scheduled routes. Time Air, a Canadian commuter airline, was able to claim the honor, because of the more lenient certification procedures in Canada.

One disadvantage of being the launching customer—and this applies to all airlines, from intercontinental and domestic trunk lines to commuters—is that early problems can be detected only by day-in, day-out service under real, rather than simulated, conditions. These so-called "teething troubles" have to be remedied by the early operators of the type. The electrical systems on the Shorts were especially troublesome, but in due course Command got the bugs out of the systems, and Morse liked the SD-330 enough to buy seven of them.

During the period 1981–1985, passenger traffic doubled—a healthy rate by any standard, and all the more remarkable in view of the simplicity of the route network. Only two new points had been added: to Albany, the New York state capital, and to Lebanon, the resort center in New Hampshire. Pittsfield had been dropped, so that Morse was in command of only seven commuter airline service stations. But its very simplicity and its ability to resist the temptation to expand into questionably viable markets were two of the secrets of Command's success. Such was the respect attached to it by the business community that when, in October 1983, Morse and his board went public with a stock offering, $6.5 million was subscribed within forty-eight hours, and Command was thereafter listed on the NASDAQ exchange. If this was not enough recognition, in 1985 Command was voted Commuter/Regional Airline of the Year by *Air Transport World* magazine.

As if to demonstrate that the magazine's confidence had not been misplaced, Morse took another step in upgrading the Command fleet. In March 1986, he introduced the Aérospatiale/Aeritalia ATR-42, a forty-two-seat joint Franco-Italian entrant into the commuter airliner sweepstakes. Command was the first U.S. operator, and the third worldwide, of this new airliner, and it eventually purchased five of them.

Shortly afterward, in May 1986, Morse made an agreement with American Airlines to become a component of the American Eagle codesharing system. Such contractual arrangements allowed major airlines and regional feeder lines to share reservations, ticketing, ground servicing, and other closely coordinated services. In almost every such arrangement, the traffic fed from and into the feeder carrier increased significantly, and Command was no exception, although the full effect of the deal was not felt for about a year. The cities of Providence and Hartford were added to the system, and in July 1987 service began to Philadelphia.

Yet another equipment change was made in October of that year, when the Shorts SD-360, an improved thirty-six-seat version of the SD-330, made its debut with Command, which eventually purchased six. The SD-330 had been no beauty, having a box-shaped fuselage with a thin, straight wing on top. It was homely but it was efficient over the short-haul stages that made up Command's taut route system. The SD-360 was not only bigger and even more economical to operate, it was slightly better looking, with some rounded edges on the box.

Just after adding Washington, D.C., to the Command route network in July 1988, Morse rounded off the edges of his own personal success story. On 30 September, he and his fellow stockholders sold Command Airways to American Airlines for a total of $24 million, at $17.00 per share. He was no longer completely in command, but his airline had commanded attention and had carved a niche in one of the most heavily traveled urban regions of the world. With a record of almost continuous progress over a twenty-two-year career with Command, Kingsley Morse may be said to have provided a textbook example of How to Succeed in the Commuter Airline Business.

Profile 16

Raymond A. and David R. Mueller
Comair

Glancing through the 1993–1994 annual report of Comair Holdings, Inc., and observing that it carried 2,735,000 passengers, generated operating revenues of more than $250 million, and made a net profit of $25 million, one is struck less by these impressive statistics than by the fact that this airline was founded as recently as April 1977. Yet it is now among the three or four largest regional airlines—most of the hardy survivors consider themselves too big and too extensive to be labeled commuter airlines any more—and it also ranks, quite astonishingly, as the thirteenth largest airline, measured by passenger boardings, in the United States.

Comair's founders, in fact, came onto the airline scene when many of the pioneers of the commuter airline industry had already been in business for at least a decade, some of them for two; a few of them were, if not actually in retirement, on the point of hanging up their hats. This latter group had watched their segment of the airline business struggle for survival and official recognition, from the early scheduled air taxi operations to the time when they were recognized both by the FAA and by the CAB. They had overcome the indignity of being referred to as the third level of the airline industry as a whole—although this was what they were—and were winning the long battle to be included, like other airlines, in the *Official Airline Guide*.

When Comair was born, however, airline deregulation was only a year away. Statutory limitations in aircraft size were soon to be liberalized in a wave of no-holds-barred competition. Without protection, many of the older, long-established companies fell by the wayside or were forced to merge, simply because they did not operate according to sound business principles and as often as not were run by pilots who knew a lot about flying but not much about accounting and economics. Airline deregulation brought with it a new era in which computerized reservation systems controlled the destinies of individuals, and as inde-

Raymond A. Mueller (left) and David R. Mueller (right)

pendence gave way to partnership agreements, survival of the fittest—
or perhaps the best connected—became a grim reality and a way of life.

Into this competitive arena came Raymond A. Mueller. In an interesting contrast with many an airline entrepreneur who entered the field
because of inspiration from or the encouragement of his father, Mueller
started Comair because of the persuasive influence of his son David,
who, in 1977, was a twenty-five-year-old corporate pilot based in Cincinnati. Mueller had already had a very successful career, in a different
industry, and one that he could easily have regarded as the fulfillment
of a lifetime's ambition. His entry into aviation as the promoter of a
commuter airline at the age of fifty-five is almost unparalleled.

He was born at Bellevue, Kentucky, just across the Ohio River from
Cincinnati, on 26 May 1922. His father was a mechanical contractor
specializing in heating engineering (in the 1920s this meant coal fur-
naces) and, in later years, air conditioning. Mueller thus grew up with a
background of familiarity with mechanical things, and aviation was far
from his thoughts. His education was handicapped because his father
was badly hit by the Depression. Like many young people of his
generation, the need to find work and to relieve the financial pressure
on his parents had to take precedence over the wish to gain a university
education.

Because of a physical disability, he was unable to enter the armed
forces during World War II, but when the war was over, he tried to make

up for his lack of opportunity as a teenager by taking courses in mechanical engineering at the University of Cincinnati. Mueller combined this educational activity, conducted mainly in the evenings, with part-time work for Fairbanks, Morse & Co., a prominent firm in industrial machines; but once again his schooling was curtailed. In 1945, he had married Norma Wellman, and the reality of bringing up a family conflicted with the ideal of attaining academic honors. In 1948, he took his first full-time job, as a sales engineer with Fairbanks, Morse, and was compelled to drop his studies, as the job was in eastern Tennessee.

He was involved in the marketing of an extensive product line, from diesel locomotives to farm machinery, and he must not only have displayed a talent for his work but also discovered his vocation in life, for in 1952, after only four years in full-time employment and seven years in all with the same firm, he decided to start his own business. He founded R. A. Mueller, Inc., to represent the product lines of several manufacturers of chemical processing equipment throughout the Ohio Valley. By 1960, the company had expanded considerably into a full industrial distribution organization. Thus, within twelve years, even with the handicap of having had to abandon a university education, Mueller had fulfilled his determination, as he once expressed it, "to improve myself and make some money without using my hands." Incidentally, R. A. Mueller, Inc., was later sold to Duane Larock, who had married Mueller's daughter Judy. With the sale came a great deal of good will built up in the Cincinnati financial and business community—good will that was later to serve Mueller well when a crisis threatened the existence of Comair.

In 1962, Mueller had learned to fly and had acquired a Piper Aztec for the business; but at that time he still regarded the airplane as simply a commercial necessity; the aviation bug had not yet bitten. Fifteen years were to go by before, at the age of 55, at a time when many men are thinking about taking early retirement, he was talked into forming an airline by his son David.

It was an ideal father-and-son combination. David was a corporate pilot who, like everyone who flies an airplane, was conscious of the potential and opportunity offered by air travel and was no doubt also caught up the spirit and the joy of aviation generally. Ray himself was a self-made businessman who had succeeded in mastering all of the essentials and most of the refinements of good business practice. Therefore, when in January 1977, together with two other investors, they formed Comair at a cost of $60,000, each had, in his own different way, done his homework.

The early development of Comair was the natural outcome of sound decisions on the choice of aircraft and shrewd judgment on the choice of routes. The Muellers began with two Piper Navajos and Ray's private Aztec as a backup, all with seven seats. A small spoke-shaped network radiated from the Cincinnati hub to cities where air service from southern Ohio had been neglected, or even abandoned altogether, by the leading airlines. Comair's grandfather routes were to Cleveland, Akron, and Evansville, and the Navajos were well matched to the as yet modest traffic demand when service started in April 1977. The fleet had grown to eight aircraft within two years, a period during which Ray and David bought out their other investors. Part of the sharp increment in local travel was the direct result of the Airline Deregulation Act of October 1978. When the major carriers pulled out of the medium-size city markets in the Midwest, Comair was poised to fill the vacuum.

Then, in October 1979, disaster struck. A Comair Navajo crashed on takeoff from the home airport, Cincinnati, when it lost power at four hundred feet; the pilot and seven passengers were killed. After little more than two years of scheduled operations, Comair had suffered the fate that all airlines dread: a fatal crash in front of its home spectators. It was a time of trial for the father-and-son partnership and a shattering experience for the nucleus of employees who, until that fateful day, had been enthusiastically confident of spectacular progress, rather than spectacular headlines in the local press.

The Muellers acted promptly and efficiently. The crash had brought with it all the predictable consequences. Adverse publicity aside, lawsuits and settlements ran up bills amounting to $5 million. The bankers withdrew support. David was quoted as saying, "Everyone gave us up for gone." But Ray Mueller's standing in the Cincinnati business community now paid handsome dividends. Together with his own personal funds, he was able to rally enough financial backing to compensate for the adverse effect of the tragedy on revenues. Meanwhile, David, in charge of the day-to-day running of the airline, astutely transferred the hub to Dayton, eighty miles to the north, the center of a large urban population that had been relatively neglected by the big airlines. Amazingly, in less than two years, Comair was back on the upward curve of prosperity. In the summer of 1981, outside stockholders snapped up 40 percent of the stock as the airline went public. And it has never looked back since.

In fact, there was nowhere to go but up, and everything now seemed to fall into place. Even before Comair's name appeared on the NASDAQ list, the Muellers had evaluated the smaller commuter aircraft then available and had ordered two Embraer EMB-110 Bandeirantes. This Brazilian-built eighteen-seater, affectionately known as the Bandit, was a neat solution to matching capacity to demand, and one that had been adopted by many small airlines all over the world. In years to come, the Muellers were to be so satisfied with the product from São José dos Campos that they ordered many more and helped to create a market in the United States for the Bandeirante and its larger successor, the Brasilia.

The Muellers recognized quickly that the days of the old-fashioned independence-at-all-costs commuter airlines were over. Unlike many of the true pioneers, whose roots went back to the struggling times of the 1950s and the early 1960s, Comair was not inhibited by tradition. At the end of 1981, barely two years after the crash, it joined Delta Air Lines' Deltamatic computerized reservation system and proceeded to consolidate its position as the regional carrier of the Ohio Valley, extending its route system to all the cities of the Great Lakes region (except Chicago) and to points in West Virginia.

To supplement the Bandits the Mueller took steps to expand the fleet with aircraft to meet the varied demands of their network. For extra capacity on the more densely traveled routes, Comair introduced the Shorts SD-330 in March 1982. The ungainly looking but effective thirty-seater was the first Comair craft big enough to require flight attendants. Another sign of increased stature was marked, at the same time, by the relocation of Comair's Cincinnati station from Terminal A to Terminal D, adjacent to Delta's facilities at the Greater Cincinnati Airport.

Comair grew steadily and purposefully. In April 1983, it introduced the nineteen-seat Fairchild Metro III. This aircraft was pressurized and had longer range, enabling Comair to enlarge the radius of the routes served from the Cincinnati hub. Simultaneously, it was preparing to reinforce service on the shorter but denser routes, having in February announced the first U.S. order for the Swedish-built SAAB/Fairchild SF-340. When this aircraft came on line in July 1984, its thirty-three-seat capacity obliged Comair to apply to the FAA for permission to operate under Part 121, as this aircraft exceeded the capacity limitations permissible under Part 135.

With a versatile fleet and a route network extending as far as Milwaukee in the north and Birmingham in the south, the stage was now set for a decisive corporate move. On 1 September 1984, Comair became a Delta Connection carrier, one of several such commuter airlines affiliated with the major airline to feed its network. Although Comair adopted the DL reservation code, as did all Delta Connection airlines, it retained its corporate identity, and the aircraft continued to fly under the Comair banner. Opportunities for further route expansion were a natural sequel to the partnership. Only one month later, on 1 October, Roanoke and Richmond brought the state of Virginia into Comair's sphere of influence; perhaps more important, exactly a year later, O'Hare International Airport at Chicago was added to the map.

The tornado that hit Cincinnati on 10 March 1986, which severely damaged the Comair hangar and some of the aircraft, hardly made a dent in the onward progress of the fast-growing airline. In July of that year, Delta strengthened its connection by buying 20 percent of Comair's stock. In 1987, further route expansion occurred. On 1 June, more spokes from the by now reestablished Cincinnati hub were added to points in three states: the Tri-Cities area in Tennessee, Kalamazoo in Michigan, and the Greenbriar (White Sulphur Springs) in West Virginia. But these additions were relatively unimportant compared to the airline's next move, which was to establish a new hub in Orlando, Florida. On 1 November, a separate hub-and-spoke network, to five other Florida cities and to Freeport in the Bahamas, announced Comair's presence in the south.

Consolidation continued as the 1980s drew to a close. In 1989 the Muellers formed Comair Holdings, Inc., a Kentucky corporation, as the parent company for several aviation-related subsidiaries. These included Comair Services, Inc., which oversees nonscheduled operation; CVG Aviation, Inc., a fixed base operation at the Greater Cincinnati Airport that, as Servair, had been purchased in October 1983; the Comair Aviation Academy, Inc., a training center at Orlando; and Comair Aircraft, Inc., responsible for the leasing arrangements through which most of Comair's scheduled and nonscheduled fleet is acquired. These subsidiaries, however, account for only a small proportion of the total fiscal activity. The scheduled airline, Comair, contributes up to 96 percent of all the operating revenues and expenses. And these are impressive. In the year ending 31 March 1994, Comair earned $297 million in operating revenues, with an operating income of more than $47 million. The number of passengers carried was 2,700,000, but more important, the break-even load factor was only 39 percent. This statistic demonstrates that the eighty-three aircraft in the fleet are operated very efficiently over the seventy-eight-location network, and that the two thousand people on Comair's staff maintain the six hundred daily flights with commendable thrift.

The fleet in 1994 comprised sixteen Canadair Regional Jets, nine Metro IIIs, eighteen SAAB SF-340s, and forty Brasilias. This last type, a handsome thirty-seater from the same Brazilian stable as the popular Bandeirante or Bandit, introduced in December 1988, seems destined to become Comair's flagship.

Mueller retired from his position as chairman of the board on 5 June 1990, leaving the company in the good hands of his son David. Seldom has a father-and-son combination been so successful in the aviation or airline business. Only a few years ago, passengers were complaining that Cincinnati seemed to have disappeared off the airline map. Now, thanks to Comair's vigorous campaigning and promotion and to Delta Airlines, which established its own hub in cooperation with its Delta Connection partner, Cincinnati is very much back on the map. There were times when Ray Mueller and son David were thankful for Cincinnati's faith in their endeavors. On balance, the city can conclude that, by connecting Cincinnati firmly with the main arteries of the U.S. airline system, the Muellers have more than repaid this support.

George F. Pickett, Jr.
Atlantic Southeast Airlines

Although he did not make as spectacular an entry into the arena of recent commuter airlines as did, for example, Milt Kuolt of Horizon Air, the achievement of George Pickett—along with John Beiser and Robert Priddy—in building Atlantic Southeast Airlines into one of the nation's largest regional airlines, and winning the Commuter Airline of the Year award after only seven years of operation, was impressive nonetheless. Another feature of his career is that, from the first day, the story of Atlantic Southeast has been one of steady and uninterrupted progress and prosperity. George Pickett's Midas touch became the talk of the entire commuter airline industry. It was felt that he could do no wrong; yet he did nothing that was particularly unorthodox or especially innovative.

Atlantic Southeast, or ASA as it became generally known, just kept doing everything right: expanding the route network around Atlanta; increasing the aircraft fleet to keep pace with the constantly flourishing market; judiciously acquiring one of the few airlines that might have provided competition, had it survived for more than nine months; and, above all, operating with such shrewd efficiency, especially in the matter of schedule and fleet integration, that its break-even load factor was in the low thirties. To be able to make a profit with only one-third of the available seats filled is a feat almost unprecedented in the industry, even for short periods. George Pickett and his team at ASA have managed to do it year after year.

The trio of executives from Southern Airways, the former Atlanta-based local service airline, must have had a premonition that when the merger between North Central Airlines and Southern went into effect on 1 July 1979, the network that Southern had created out of Atlanta would be neglected. The resultant merged company, Republic Airlines, would concentrate on building a nationwide system, and the concept of local

George F. Pickett, Jr. (center), Robert Priddy (left), and John Beiser (right) (photo by Robert B. Tolchin)

service would be forgotten. Showing the courage of their convictions, the Southern trio resigned on 2 January 1979, formed ASA on 5 March, and started service just over three months later on 27 June.

Had Pickett waited two more days, he could have registered the company on his thirty-eighth birthday. He was born on 7 March 1941 in Birmingham, Alabama, and grew up in Childersburg, Alabama, the only child of a salesman and a teacher. He obtained a bachelor of science degree in industrial engineering at the University of Texas and a master's degree in management at Georgia State. With such educational credentials, he was hired straight from college as a reliability engineer at Southern Airways, even though he had no previous experience in aviation. The story of Pickett and ASA from the day the airline started service has been almost monotonous in its litany of repeated successes, year after year. The inauguration was modest enough, with five daily Twin Otter flights from Atlanta to Columbus, Georgia, on 26 June 1979, and only one more route was added in 1980, to Macon. Then the map began to expand more rapidly across the southeastern states: four new destinations in 1981, ten in 1982. In April 1983, one more point was added after ASA acquired Coastal Air Limited, a privately held Georgia corporation operating as Southeastern Airlines; at the same time a new hub was opened at Memphis, Tennessee, to complement the growing intensity of the spoke pattern out of Atlanta. ASA suddenly moved up the commuter airline ranking, based on the number of passengers boarded, to eighteenth place—not a bad performance after only four years in the business.

A year later prospects for even higher status were dramatically improved. On 1 May 1984, ASA became a Delta Connection carrier. The Atlanta-based trunk airline, having acquired Northeast Airlines in 1972, had itself grown rapidly during the post-deregulation years. It had no doubt been following ASA's statistics—from 12,000 passengers in its first year to more than 350,000 in its fifth.

Pickett and his team took the new association, with its code-sharing advantages, in their stride. In the first year, revenues increased by 84 percent, net income almost tripled to more than $5 million, and the break-even load factor was still only 36 percent. The traffic and revenue increases were even greater as ASA leased eight Shorts SD-360s and placed an order for ten Embraer Brasilias to supplement its existing fleet of five de Havilland Dash 7s and fifteen Embraer Bandeirantes. This increase in fleet size permitted an intensive expansion of the spoke route network from Atlanta and the addition, in December 1984, of a second hub-and-spoke pattern at Memphis, to combat Republic's activity at the Tennessee city.

And so the success story continued. In August 1985 the first Brasilia to be placed in service with any airline was delivered to ASA, and yet more stations were opened. By the year's end, ASA was serving thirty-three cities with thirty aircraft and had boarded almost a million passengers during the twelve months of 1985. In December 1986, the Memphis hub was discontinued in favor of a new hub at Dallas/Fort Worth, where the ASA-Delta connection has since built up a formidable spoke pattern to serve fifteen cities in Texas, Louisiana, Oklahoma, and Arkansas. Delta purchased a 20 percent interest in ASA in 1986. The company then ordered twenty-two more Brasilias, and by the end of 1993 passenger boardings on eighty aircraft (sixty of which are Brasilias) at sixty-one cities totaled two million. Revenues were $288 million, and net income was $50 million.

This success has been achieved with no fanfares, no revolutionary gambles, no flamboyant gestures. Sensational headlines in the press have been marred only by a Brasilia crash in Brunswick, Georgia, on 5 April 1991, which attracted more than the normal level of publicity because Senator John Tower was among the twenty-three people killed. The ASA team simply applied sound fundamentals to the operation, introducing the right aircraft to the right routes at the right time and hitching its wagon to Delta, the rising star of the mega-airline fraternity. ASA's road to prosperity has been a textbook exercise on how to run a successful commuter airline.

Profile 18

J. Dawson Ransome
Ransome Airlines

Although he was a little late to qualify as being in the first wave of pioneer scheduled air taxi operators, J. Dawson Ransome, already possessing plenty of flying hours and a load of experience under his belt, did not waste time catching up with his fellow flying entrepreneurs. He was forty-six years old when he founded his airline, having already had two careers, either of which would have been enough for many businessmen or soldiers of fortune—and Ramsone seems to have combined the characteristics of both vocations.

For almost exactly twenty years, he operated an airline, taking it through the periods of infancy and adolescence fairly rapidly, and then rising to rank, during one period, as the largest of all the commuter airlines. He started as an independent, had several romances with other larger airlines without ever actually tying the knot, and finally sold his company to Pan American. He can look back on a distinguished World War II service record, on an illustrious period as a sportsman-pilot, and to a position as one of the leading commuter airline operators. No doubt today, he is still thinking of another aviation role in which to excel.

J. Dawson Ransome was born on 16 November 1920 at Riverton, New Jersey. He came from English stock, his father having been from the same Ransome family whose name is a household word among gardeners in the Old Country, where every garage houses a Ransome lawnmower, if not a car. In the States, the Ransomes linked up with the Gileses to form the firm of Giles & Ransome, specialists in the construction of concrete mixers and large road pavers, and owners of a prominent Caterpillar dealership.

Ransome's introduction to aviation and his early conversion to the cause were a little unusual. At the age of nine, he would join his school friends in riding around the town in a big open touring car, a Packard, owned by one "Sonny" Wright, whose love of kids generally made him

J. Dawson Ransome

enormously popular among the younger generation. In the 1920s, to ride around town in a Packard was like going shopping today in a Lamborghini. Then, one Fourth of July, Sonny Wright arranged for the young Ransome to take a ride in an open-cockpit airplane. Not yet an aeronautical specialist, Ransome never did know what kind of airplane it was. But he does remember that it was a floatplane, that it had a Liberty engine, and that he sat side-by-side with another passenger, with the pilot behind him. In particular, he remembers sticking his arm out of the cockpit, feeling the force of the airflow, and thinking to himself, "Boy, this is for me."

His infatuation with flying took hold to such effect that, in 1936, at the age of sixteen, he made his first solo flight. Three years later, he left high school. He started to fly at Palmyra, New Jersey, working as a mechanic and spending his wages on flying lessons, in a Taylorcraft and a Waco. He attempted—unsuccessfully—to get a job with Chance Vought, test flying the Corsair, and subsequently went to Canada to get into aviation. He soloed in 1938 and acquired a civilian pilot's license. In 1941, he was serving with the Royal Canadian Air Force as a civilian flight instructor, and he later contracted with the United States Air Corps in the same capacity, before progressing to the rank of flight command check pilot. In 1944, Ransome received a direct commission as an officer in the United States Air Corps, assigned to the Air Transport Command.

He was just in time to join the elite group of aviators that was given the task of carrying vital supplies to the beleaguered Chinese army and its supporting American troops and air forces, flying round-the-clock missions from bases in Assam in northeast India, in the foothills of the highest range of mountains in the world. During 1944 and 1945, the intrepid pilots of the Air Transport Command flew Curtiss C-46s and C-54s, Consolidated B24s, and Douglas C-47s over some of the most unforgiving territory on earth, nicknamed the Hump. Emergency landing grounds simply did not exist. Range after range of precipitous mountains, separated from each other by mile-deep canyons, offered no refuge. Ransome survived four engine failures, although an engine failure was normally a passport to oblivion. On one single night thirty-six aircraft, mostly C-46s, went down on the Hump operation. Ransome added more than 1,000 hours of this kind of flying to his logbook and received both the Air Medal and the Distinguished Flying Cross.

Compared with this concentrated aerial activity, the postwar years were relatively quiet, although he was active in the Pennsylvania National Guard as an instrument check pilot, flying Marauders. Although he was involved in the family's business affairs, the aviator inside him was constantly trying to escape, and eventually he decided that he must take the initiative to return to flying as a vocation.

In 1964, therefore, he purchased directly from its designer, Curtiss Pitts, a set of plans for the original Pitts Special aerobatic airplane. To fulfill his desire to own and fly this unique machine, and with the help of his wife Maryann, he built two of them himself, one of the more notable achievements in the home-built airplane world. During the period 1967–1972, he performed aerobatics before audiences estimated to total more than a million. However, this activity, exciting and fulfilling though it was, was in direct contrast to the systematic approach to airline operation that he initiated only two years after buying the Pitts plans. Possibly recognizing the greater challenges of running a successful airline, Ransome retired from aerobatic competition and exhibition and donated one of his Pitts Specials to the National Air and Space Museum of the Smithsonian Institution, where it is on permanent display. As his farewell to sporting aviation, before hanging up his postwar barnstorming hat, Ransome had played a prominent part in promoting the formation of the United States National Aerobatic Team. In 1972 he had the satisfaction, as manager of the U.S. team, of winning in a clean sweep all the events at the semiannual world competition at Selon-de-Provence in southern France.

Ransome never did things by halves. After founding Ransome Airlines in July 1966 at North Philadelphia Airport, as a subsidiary of the

Giles & Ransome organization, he did not take the orthodox course of buying one of the several small types of aircraft then currently popular for air taxi use. One of the best of the available craft was the Beech 18, of which many were on the market, having been converted from war-surplus C-45s. A sturdy nine-seater, if not an outstanding performer, it was twin-engined, which at least gave it a margin of safety, and it was fairly reliable. Ransome, however, went one better. He started operations on 2 March 1967 with the prototype fifteen-seat Volpar Turboliner, a stretched variant of the Beech 18. Reflecting the founder's firm belief that the essence of a commuter operation lay in frequency of service rather than concentrated capacity, the first Ransome Airlines timetable offered eight flights a day between North Philadelphia and Washington, D.C. (National Airport). By the end of the first year, Ransome had carried 6,318 passengers and had a fleet of three Beech 18s.

This passenger count, in fact, was not an outstanding statistic, amounting only to about twenty passengers each day, or ten each way. But it was sufficient to encourage Ransome to seek further fields to conquer. He frankly admits to trying to grow too rapidly and, in expanding the Ransome Airlines network to Richmond and Norfolk and even as far south as Raleigh-Durham, North Carolina, to overreaching himself. "We lost our heads," he recalls. "We were almost broke and the directors were pretty unhappy. I found out to my chagrin how little I knew about business and about the airline business. It was an expensive lesson."

Seeking a solution to his deepening financial problems, Ransome consulted Les Barnes, president of Allegheny Airlines, the successful local service/regional airline of the Atlantic Coast area. Barnes advised retrenchment—an obvious suggestion at the time—and also broached the idea of Ransome joining Allegheny as one of its growing list of commuter airline associates. At that time, Dawson "had to wrestle with the ego problem of taking the Ransome name off the airplanes—not that it's such a glamorous name for an airline." He was faced with the classic decision that almost all commuter airline leaders have had to face sooner or later: whether to compromise with their identity in an effort to survive in the face of overwhelming economic necessity.

At first, Ransome and Leslie Barnes made a mutually agreeable pact on a single route. Early in 1969, Ransome Airlines took over from Allegheny the Trenton–North Philadelphia–Trenton route, where, with low load factors on its Convair 580 forty-four-seat aircraft, Allegheny had been losing money heavily. The permit was a provisional one, lasting for three years, and operated under Part 135 of the FAA regulations, as the Volpar Beeches were below the 12,500-pound gross takeoff weight limit. A few months later, in November, also no doubt as much to Allegheny's advantage as it was to Ransome's, the latter replaced the larger carrier in the important Philadelphia (International)—Washington intercity market. Less than a year later, in August 1970, Ransome became a fully fledged Allegheny Commuter, but Dawson still retained complete ownership. The classic decision resulted in the classic sequel: the Ransome name disappeared from the sides of the aircraft—but after joining the system, Ransome Airlines made its first profit.

Operating on the Trenton-Philadelphia-Washington route, and replacing Convairliners that had been too big, Ransome soon discovered that his Beech Turboliners were too small. By November 1971, the airline was boarding more than five hundred passengers a day, and in December of that year Ransome applied to the CAB for permission to operate larger equipment. He had surveyed the available aircraft types and had decided that the French Nord 262, with twenty-eight seats, was just the right size. With a maximum takeoff weight of 23,370 pounds, it was too big to be operated under FAA Part 135; but in January 1972, the board announced that a special exemption would be granted, in recognition of the special traffic-generating characteristics of this very short-haul market.

In May 1972, Ransome acquired eight Nord 262s from Allegheny, which had inherited them from Lake Central when it had absorbed that Indianapolis-based local service carrier. The aircraft had not been entirely successful, mainly because of the low reliability of their Turbomeca Bastan turboprop engines. The fleet cost $3,200,000, and Ransome did his best to head off some of the problems by simultaneously purchasing a parts inventory worth about $1.5 million. With these aircraft, which had good short-field performance, Ransome and Turbomeca worked to improve the time between overhaul from 1,200 to 10,000 hours, and Dawson gradually expanded the network once again, this time in the opposite direction from his former short-lived excursion to the south. After the network was first extended to Newark, to serve the New York area, and New London/Groton, Connecticut, additional points were carefully added during the next few years. By 1979, Ransome Airlines was serving all three of New York's main airports, plus the outer Long Island suburbs at MacArthur Field; three points in New England (Boston, Providence, and Hartford); and Sullivan County Airport in the Catskill Mountains.

The year 1979 was in fact memorable. More than 600,000 passengers were carried, raising Ransome to the rank of the largest commuter airline not only in the United States but also in the world. The Nord 262 fleet now numbered a dozen, and four of these were converted by the substitution of Pratt & Whitney PT6A-45 engines to replace the Bastans, to be renamed Mohawk 298s. The selection of the name was directly associated with Part 298 of the federal aviation operating regulations, which now allowed aircraft of up to sixty seats.

More significant, however, was the introduction of another aircraft from the same de Havilland Aircraft of Canada stable that had revolutionized the scheduled air taxi business with the DHC-6 Twin Otter, the versatile nineteen-seater that had been such a good breadwinner for many airlines (although Ransome had never owned any). While watching a demonstration of the Canadian company's DHC-7, more commonly known as the Dash 7, Dawson made the decision to buy one. Late in 1979 this fifty-seat, four-engined aircraft, possessing remarkable short takeoff and landing (STOL) characteristics, made its debut in the Philadelphia-Washington market. No agency has ever precisely defined STOL, in terms of runway length required or climb and descent gradients; but had there been an official definition, the Dash 7 would have been the ideal aircraft to meet it. Word had it that, although it needed paved strips, any perimeter or taxi track would suffice in lieu of a runway—and some even claimed that the terminal ramp would do.

Hyperbole apart, the Dash 7's performance was impressive enough for Dawson, and after he made many presentations in Washington, it impressed the FAA too. In 1980, Ransome was permitted to conduct some unprecedented experimental operations, having developed, in cooperation with de Havilland of Canada, the hardware for the world's first three-dimensional RNAV area navigational system, using the DHC Dash 7. In close cooperation with the agency, Ransome worked with de Havilland and Jet Electronics Technology to install the world's first commercial microwave landing system (MLS).

On 20 November 1980, the FAA gave its approval for the system. It permitted Ransome to land its Dash 7s on the secondary runway concurrently with other aircraft on a converging course on the smaller strips at some of the airports. At Washington National Airport, for example, Ransome's aircraft were customarily taking off and landing with only a four hundred-foot roll. Not only that, but Ransome was permitted to fly at lower altitudes on most of its routes, avoiding the mandatory flight paths and holding procedures imposed on commercial aircraft.

This concession cut twenty miles off the Philadelphia-Washington distance and often saved up to half an hour of block-to-block ("doors shut to doors open") time. Quite apart from the obvious advantages to the passengers, and the fuel savings because of the reduced distance, there were also indirect benefits from increased staff productivity resulting from the time saved. On 30 November 1981, at midnight, Ransome made the first RNAV approach to New York's John F. Kennedy International Airport. The experiment was further elaborated when, on 29 March 1982, Ransome began the Service Test and Evaluation (STEP) program, using the MLS. STEP allows aircraft to be monitored from several different directions as they fly into an airport, in contrast with the normal instrument landing system, which channels all aircraft down the same glide path.

By this time, early in 1981, Ransome had started service to Washington (Dulles) International Airport. Possibly Ransome was too far ahead of the times, for the airport had not yet been "discovered" by airlines and was unpopular because the travel time into the city was still too long, and the city had not yet followed a well-established pattern by growing out to the airport. The Dulles service also coincided with the air traffic controllers' strike, and this situation delayed the opening of full service until the fall of that year.

Unfortunately, while Ransome was making technical headlines and attracting much praise for his innovative work, things were none too bright on the business front, specifically in his relations with the Allegheny Commuter system, an association now in its twelfth year. The parent company, Allegheny Airlines, had become USAir and was tightly inhibiting Ransome's route and frequency expansion. Proprietor and staff alike in the Ransome operation had felt frustrated by restrictions on route growth because all decisions on the network shape and pattern were made by Allegheny/USAir. Strike-triggered layoffs were controlled not by Ransome but by USAir. Never one to suffer in silence, and still the owner of the airline (even though, on 1 May 1982, Ransome reservations had gone on-line with USAir's computer reservation system), Ransome abruptly terminated his agreement with the Allegheny Commuter system on 1 June 1982 and resumed operating as an independent airline under his own name, marking the occasion with the introduction of direct service between Dulles and JFK. (The service was suspended, however, on 3 December of the same year.) He also immediately transferred his reservation arrangements from Allegheny to Delta Air Lines.

But the experience had left scars and bruises. Freedom was desirable, but it carried with it some severe handicaps. The Ransome name

on the airplanes once again proclaimed Dawson's spirit of independence, and he was commended for that by his commuter airline peers.
But in splitting with the Allegheny Commuter, he had lost not only the
convenience and distinct marketing advantage of the shared reservation
system, but also the convenience of the use of the Allegheny Commuter
terminal at the all-important Washington National Airport. Within two
years, without the mainline connection, Ransome's passenger boardings
fell from close to 800,000 in 1981 to less than 550,000 in 1983, a 30 percent reduction. From first place among the commuter airlines, Ransome
dropped to tenth.

Yet the airline rode out the crisis, matching its resources to the reduced requirements and even tidying up the fleet in a modernization
program. Some of the Mohawk 298s were sold, leaving only four on line,
but the Dash 7 fleet was increased to eight to replace them. Ransome
also ordered six forty-four-seat Aerospatiale/Aeritalia ATR-42s. His was
one of the first airlines not only to order this new feeder airliner but also
to advise on its development for the U.S. market. Released from Allegheny restrictions on route growth, the New England network was consolidated by new routes in 1983 and 1984, to serve Worcester and
Albany and to establish a direct link to Baltimore from Providence.

Though the freedom from control by a big brother was in many ways
refreshing, by the early 1980s a combination of legislation and reservation system developments had ensured that commuter airline ticket
sales had become irrevocably linked with sales to the big airlines, even
if only by association through the code-sharing practice. For their part,
the big airlines concluded that—with most of the former local service
(regional) airlines now defunct, merged, or, like USAir, grown to become trunks like themselves—feeder networks had to be secured to
compete for the connecting traffic into the major hubs. The year 1984,
therefore, witnessed a crescendo of activity as the former trunk airlines,
now classified as majors, sought partners among the commuter airlines
so as to secure spheres of influence all across the United States.

Dawson Ransome's bid for independence was therefore unfortunately timed, as he was swimming against a tide of adverse marketing
factors. Without a major airline partner, a commuter airline was
doomed, because travel agents would always take the route of least
resistance and book passengers through the most convenient method in
a computerized reservation system—and this was invariably through
the coding of a big airline. Once again Dawson had to compromise, but
this time the terms were better.

When, in June 1982, he had parted company with USAir and transferred Ransome's reservations to Delta, he had already initiated preliminary discussions with Dave Garrett, soon to become Delta's president. In May 1984, Dawson consummated the new association by announcing that Ransome Airlines had become part of The Delta Connection, the newly formed group of commuter airlines linked with the Atlanta major.

The arrangement with Delta was different from the one with USAir. Ransome paid Delta a straight fee for reservation services and airport station handling. Ransome's name was once again on the aircraft, to retain an identity that Dawson felt had been lost with USAir. Route development was carried out and changes were made after constructive discussion, not arbitrarily dictated from Atlanta. Thus the route to New London, on which the traffic volume justified an aircraft of only Twin Otter size, making it incompatible with the fleet as a whole, was dropped. But other routes were added, into Baltimore and to Islip, Long Island. Dawson regarded Delta as an airline "that would allow growth but would also extend a helping hand." The trade-off was that Ransome had to readjust its route pattern so as to avoid duplication with Delta in some markets. The northerly direction of traffic flow was emphasized even more, and Ransome expanded into cities as far north as Vermont and Maine.

Competition among the commuter airlines in the northeastern United States was by now intense. Pilgrim Airlines, from New London/Groton, founded in the early 1960s by old-timer Joe Fugere, had absorbed New-Air, and was itself engulfed by Business Express, a newcomer from Hartford that had been founded only in November 1984, not long after Ransome had joined The Delta Connection.

Which was the cause and which the effect of his next decision may never be known. Possibly Ransome, now in his late sixties, felt that twenty years of battling to create his own airline and keep it viable were enough. In any event, in a surprise move on 1 June 1986, exactly four years after breaking away from USAir, and after barely two years with Delta, J. Dawson Ransome sold Ransome Airlines to Pan American Airways, which had approached him with an excellent offer. The U.S. intercontinental carrier was badly in need of a feeder system to provide the essential traffic-generating spokes to its big hub and international gateway at New York. Accordingly Ransome Airlines became Pan Am Express, and once again the Dash 7s acquired a new paint scheme.

Today, Ransome is taking things easy, splitting his time between his home in Bucks County, Pennsylvania, and his second home on Leeward

Air Ranch, near Ocala, Florida, commuting between the two in his own Piper Super Cub, fitted with full instrument flight rules instrumentation. He seldom performs aerobatics, and he is not yet equipped with full RNAV or MLS, but he logs a respectable number of flying hours every year. He can look back on his airline as one of the most significant of his lifetime of achievements, having attained for a dizzy period the pinnacle of success as the world's largest commuter airline. He has no regrets.

Profile 19

Robert F. (Bob) Schoen
Island Sky Ferries

In this series of special profiles of the men who have done the most to shape the course of the post–World War II commuter airline industry, two are related to the same airline. One is of the original founder and the other is of the man who built it up from a single-route bush operation to one that became a household word in the entire Puget Sound area of northwest Washington state.

The founder sold Island Sky Ferries, primary ancestor of San Juan Airlines, in 1950, many years before the vast majority of today's commuter airlines had even been thought of. His story is important, as it epitomizes the operating conditions and business style of an industry in embryo, one that had no textbook or regulations manual to follow. The founder had to write his own; and he could not count upon support either from government or from state agencies. He even had to prepare most of his own airfields.

Robert F. Schoen, Bob to all who knew him, was born in Seattle, Washington, on 25 March 1919. He wanted to learn to fly even while at the University of Washington from 1938 to 1941, when he was refused entry into the Civilian Pilot Training Program because of an eye problem. This restriction was later to be waived by the CAA. Completing a tour of duty with the U.S. Coast Guard in November 1945, he returned to Seattle, bought a 1939 Aeronca Chief, and obtained his private pilot's license in 1946.

He was married in the same year, and he and his wife Mary spent their honeymoon cruising on a sailboat in the waters of southern British Columbia. On the way home they called in at Orcas Island, one of the San Juan Islands in the north of Puget Sound. They liked what they saw and decided to abandon Seattle city life for the serenity of the islands. Schoen started work at a salmon cannery, and the word soon got around that he had his own airplane. The majority of the residents looked upon

Robert F. (Bob) Schoen

Bellingham, Washington, as their shopping, supply, and social and medical services center. But Bellingham was reached by a two-hour ferryboat ride from Orcas, chief port of Orcas Island, to Anacortes, and thence a ninety-minute drive, whereas Seattle was seventy-five miles to the south of Anacortes, a 2½-hour drive. The idea came to everyone's mind that a regular air service from Orcas Island and other points in the San Juans to and from Bellingham would be a beneficial supplement to the ferryboats.

Subsequent events seemed almost predestined. Schoen began to work on his commercial pilot's license at Western Washington Aircraft in Bellingham in the fall of 1946. That company had just received a 1946 Stinson four-seat Voyager, and Schoen liked it so much that he ordered one. On 28 March 1947, having collected it two days earlier from the factory at Wayne, Michigan, Terry Dalton, the pilot who had taught Schoen to fly, delivered a new red Voyager to Eastsound, where the words "Orcas Island Air Service" were painted on its sides. Schoen became a commercially rated pilot on 8 July 1947 and immediately started to fly his own air service. Dalton had already been flying to and from Bellingham on demand, but this date can be taken as the inauguration of Orcas Island Air Service, the ancestor of what, by some definitions, could be termed the oldest of all the commuter airlines, vying with the Provincetown-Boston Airline or Island Air Lines of Port Clinton, Ohio, for that privilege.

Schoen ran the business with the help of his wife and Terry Dalton. He purchased his fuel from and had his maintenance done by Western Washington Aircraft at Bellingham Airport, a good airfield with three concrete runways. Eastsound, on Orcas Island, had one very poor airstrip. Elsewhere the landings and takeoffs could be adventurous. At Friday Harbor, on San Juan Island, the "airfield" was a square field, and aircraft landed diagonally across it, overcoming a pronounced hump in the middle. At Speiden Island, the strip was on the top of a hill with drops at each end. In contrast, on Stuart Island, the landing had to be made up a hill into a narrow valley. On Lopez Island, the strip was also, like Friday Harbor's, in a farmer's field, and at Waldron Island the choice was between a rough 1,100-foot strip uphill toward trees or, at low tide, the beach. As Schoen recalled, "These were all privately owned strips which people supplied for their own convenience and to help their neighbors. Most of them were short, rough, and narrow, with no possibility of a go-around. It was bush flying at its best."

Schoen's ground organization at Bellingham was, in many ways, an ideal community service, and one that would be commendable for many an airline today. At the Leopold Hotel, the manager, John Pierce, was the unofficial Orcas Island Air Service agent, taking messages and making reservations. Schoen provided an airport limousine, a 1926 two-door Whippet sedan with two-wheel brakes. Schoen admits to it having been "the most dangerous part of the whole trip"; one client took one look and said, "My God, I hope your airplane is newer than your car." Schoen not only flew the airplane, he also drove the Whippet to and from the Leopold Hotel and carried out delivery or pickup jobs in Bellingham for residents of the San Juan Islands. This was in addition to doing all the day-to-day maintenance and checking work on the airplane, including kicking the tires.

The flying was reasonably free of incident, considering the notoriously unreliable weather of the northern Puget Sound area. On the eastern end of the route, i.e., to the west of Bellingham, Schoen could use the radio range "A" and "N" quadrant system and fly along the continuous beam, at least for eighteen minutes, before turning sharp left to Eastsound. On the occasional night trip to Seattle, the lighted airway offered a high-intensity rotating beacon every ten miles. But for the most part, the flying was done visually. If the visibility was bad, Orcas Island Air Service stayed on the ground.

In emergencies, Schoen would call Virginia Ferris, who with her husband owned the airfield at Eastsound, and she would put out some old highway flares, always on the left side of the runway. These flares were primitive in the extreme, just steel containers with wicks burning diesel oil, but they did the job.

During the winter of 1947, Schoen decided to incorporate his airline. Carol Clark of Orcas Island won a free round trip to Bellingham for suggesting the name Island Sky Ferries, Inc., which replaced the Orcas Island Air Service name early in 1948.

At about the same time, Schoen met Roy Franklin, who was an instructor pilot at Western Washington Aircraft at Bellingham. Schoen asked Franklin to move to Friday Harbor on San Juan Island and be responsible for the operation of one airplane based there, while Schoen did the same at Eastsound. Actually the airline staff increased from two to four, as Margaret Franklin doubled up with Mary Schoen in running the office, handling reservations, and answering the telephones.

Schoen had strong convictions about the relative merits of landplanes over floatplanes or flying boats, even operating in an area that was 90 percent water and where the more obvious advantages of operating, say, Cessna 172 floatplanes would appear to have been superficially attractive. He made the decision in spite of being described as "that crazy guy that flies land planes over water in the San Juan Islands." His reasons were succinct and are worth listing, because they represent the carefully considered judgment of a practicing operator—one who owned, managed, maintained, and flew:

a. The cost of floats is much higher than the cost of landing gear.
b. Salt water corrosion considerably increases maintenance costs.
c. Land surfaces are always flat and stable.
d. Lighting is available on land at night.
e. There are no floating objects on landing strips.

Even Bob Schoen, however, might have conceded some reservations about (c) and (d) at certain times. The occasional landing on a gravel road, when Bellingham was fogged in, was accepted as normal, and Western Washington Aircraft would send a car out, headlights on full beam, facing the wind. Once Schoen mistook a farmer's front porch lights for the car, and turned on his own landing lights only just in time to avoid taxiing to a halt in the farmer's front room.

Incidentally, Island Sky Ferries had a flag stop operation—in the true sense of the term. At Waldron, an en route stop between Friday Harbor and Eastsound, the local "agent" would raise a flag on a pole if there was anyone to pick up. If there was no flag, Roy Franklin would simply fly on to Eastsound.

The air service from the islands to Bellingham was very popular, and for good reason. During the late 1940s, typical fares were $4.00 one way (or $7.00 round trip) Eastsound-Bellingham; $5.00 one way (or $9.00 round trip) Friday Harbor–Bellingham; and $2.50 between any two points on the islands. The freight rate was a maximum of $5.00 for a heavy package. Patrons could be in Bellingham by 9 A.M., do a day's shopping or see a doctor or dentist, and be home for dinner. Scenic journey though it was, the trip by ferryboat and road via Anacortes usually took until 10:30 A.M., and the visitor seldom arrived back at the islands before 9:30 P.M.

In spite of such an improvement, however, Schoen could not get a U.S. Post Office mail contract. At that time, for some inexplicable reason (as there had been many precedents, even a historic one in the 1920s in Puget Sound itself), the mail had to go by surface transport: by truck, rail, or boat.

As mentioned earlier, Schoen believed in landplanes, but he and Roy Franklin did, on one occasion, try out a small amphibian, as the harbor at Friday Harbor was right in the downtown area. Schoen bought a Republic Seabee in Lincoln, Nebraska, while Franklin built a floating pier at Friday Harbor, and they tried it out. But, as they had suspected, it proved too expensive to operate and to maintain. Once, Franklin had a hydraulic failure, could not get the wheels down, and "alighted" beautifully in the long grass alongside the landing strip outside the town— until he hit a rock. It was back to the Stinsons.

Schoen has nothing but praise for the Stinson Voyager and its cousin, the Station Wagon. He has asserted, "They were strong, trouble free, and a pleasure to fly. Their advertising states they are stall resistant. I can verify that! You have to work at it to get them into a stall." As a testimony to the airplane's strength he quotes an incident at Bellingham, when a Catholic priest had rented a 1947 Voyager. When it returned two hours later, it had a four-foot length of three-inch-diameter tree branch driven into the leading edge of the left wing up to the front wing spar, the result of flying too close to some trees when the pilot became lost in a fog.

In the fall of 1950, Schoen sold Island Sky Ferries. He had managed to negotiate the purchase of the local Union Oil distributorship on Orcas Island, and decided to concentrate on that. The airline passed to a San Juan Island resident, Dr. Wallace Howarth, originally from Portland, Oregon, whose son was about to leave the Army Air Service and wanted to continue his flying career. Mr. and Mrs. Franklin were included in the purchase.

Schoen's direct involvement in the embryo commuter airline business lasted from the summer of 1947 to the fall of 1949. During that time he missed only ten days of flying because of inclement weather, in a region where fog and unpredictable winds are notorious. He never raised his fares. He said later, "I didn't make any money but the experience was worth millions. I feel very proud to have had the chance to start the first scheduled air service in the islands and see it grow and become what it is today."

Bob Schoen was one of the first and one of the best. In the fine traditions of air transport, he was a true pioneer.

Profile 20

John C. Van Arsdale
Provincetown-Boston Airline

Recognized by his peers as one of the very first pioneers of what are now called the commuter airlines, John Van Arsdale was a true original, a man who, in the classic life cycle of fixed base operator to scheduled airline proprietor, recognized a golden opportunity and methodically seized it. He steadily developed his infant airline to a position of prominence, and for a period his was rated as the largest of all the commuter airlines, measured by the number of passengers carried. For thirty-five years the airline grew steadily, until 1984, when disaster struck and Van Arsdale, no longer connected with the airline, much less in control, had to stand in the wings and watch the airline he had built fall apart. But throughout the trials of recent years, no one has ever pointed an accusing finger at John Van Arsdale, who to this day remains the doyen of the commuter airline industry.

Van Arsdale was born on 4 December 1919, in a Texas farmhouse adjacent to—appropriately—Love Field. His father had been a World War I pilot and was still in the Army Air Corps at the airfield, heading a show called the *Flying Frolic*, which amused the good citizens of Dallas, who could take a train from downtown to Love Field for 43¢. In 1920 the family moved back to their native Massachusetts. John attended the Philips Academy at Andover and then the Suffield Academy in Connecticut. He graduated in 1939 and entered Wesleyan University, where he enrolled in the Civilian Pilot Training Program—during which he now admits to being constantly airsick. After Pearl Harbor, he applied to join the Air Force and was sent to the Massachusetts Institute of Technology (MIT) at Cambridge, where he was an aviation cadet, graduating in meteorology in November 1942 for the U.S. Army Air Corps. After pilot training back in Texas, at Fort Worth, he was posted overseas to England, where he did little flying, as he had been assigned as a meteorologist.

John C. Van Arsdale

Returning home, he wasted no time getting into aviation, but first prudently rounded off his education by completing a degree course at Wesleyan University in Middletown, Connecticut, from which he graduated with a degree in mathematics and economics in February 1946. The same month he leased a field at Marston Mills, Massachusetts, for $1.00 for three years, renovated it to light aircraft standards, and promptly founded Cape Cod Flying Services on 8 May 1946. He acquired a Piper Cub dealership, while holding only a private pilot's license, and bought two Piper J3 Cubs and a Stearman PT 17. Having obtained approval as a flying school to teach veterans to fly, he was taught at his own school under the provisions of the G.I. Bill.

Now aged twenty-seven, Van Arsdale was at full throttle. Within a year he had a fleet of twenty-seven small aircraft, adding Stinsons, Fairchilds, and Cessnas to this first fleet.

In February 1947 the town of Provincetown voted to build an airport, the first one in Massachusetts to draw upon funds through the Federal Airports Act. The Provincetown Airport Commission, whose airport manager had left, asked Van Arsdale to take over. He moved in on 1 October 1948, bringing his operation with him.

There followed the textbook example of how to start a commuter airline. Paraphrasing the three ways of becoming great, Cape Cod Flying Services was not born as a commuter airline, but it certainly became one, and it could claim to have had commuter-type flying forced upon it. People would call in and ask to fly to Boston. Van Arsdale charged a high price at first: $25.00 for one passenger, $30.00 for two. But business was brisk, as covering forty-five air miles in twenty minutes was worth the price given that the only alternatives were either the boat or a 120-mile road journey, both of which took three hours or more.

The popularity of the service was such that the nonscheduled frequency increased to the point that it became in effect a shuttle service, and the volume of traffic permitted a lower fare. The shuttle flights cost $8.50 and Van Arsdale set his own rule: no two flights would be made within two hours of each other. He was doing well. Apart from the Boston service, his fixed base operations thrived, with lucrative charters, including some political campaign trips for a nearby family from Hyannis, the Kennedys.

On 30 November 1949, Van Arsdale founded the Provincetown-Boston Airline (PBA) as an operating division of the Cape Cod Flying Service. The name was chosen for the very sound reason that the public would be immediately informed about where it went. The airline's advertising claimed that "All flights [were made] with multiengined equipment," which was an upbeat way of describing two flights each way per day with a Cessna T 50 "Bamboo Bomber," able to carry four passengers in addition to the pilot.

During the next few years PBA became part of the Cape Cod scene. To Provincetown it was, if not a lifeline, at least as useful as was the ferryboat to Sausalito before the opening of the Golden Gate Bridge—and there was no prospect of a bridge being built to Boston. Quietly prospering—with a contract with MIT to carry people to and from the radar station at North Truro, eight miles away, and with a service from Provincetown to Hanscom Field in Bedford, a Boston suburb—Van Arsdale was able to introduce a special $9.75 same-day round trip "shoppers' special" on the Boston shuttle and to risk operating all year round, even in a Massachusetts winter.

Nevertheless, in spite of special incentives, the traffic was extremely seasonal, with 70 percent of the annual passengers traveling between 4 July and Labor Day. During the busy summer, the volume was such that PBA invested in a twelve-seat Lockheed 10 Electra and consolidated its position in the community by incorporating on 13 February 1953, with John retaining complete ownership.

By this time at least he had overcome the objections of the authorities in Washington, notably the CAB, which had realized that, for about half of the flight from Provincetown to Boston, PBA was operating outside the twelve-mile marine league limit, that traditionally accepted dividing line between home and international waters. Theoretically, and perhaps from a strict legal standpoint as well, PBA should have applied for an operating certificate as a scheduled airline flying over territorial waters. Whether or not Juan Trippe, defending what he considered to be Pan American's inalienable rights to international trading routes, would have raised an objection will never be known, as Van Arsdale was able to settle the matter amicably in a great victory for common sense, by obtaining an exemption from the provisions of the Civil Aeronautics Act.

But common sense would not solve the economic problems of keeping idle airplanes gainfully occupied during the winter, and so Van Arsdale and his wife took off in February 1957 on a Northeast Airlines DC-6B to Tampa, Florida. There he rented a car and explored the west coast of the state, a survey trip that culminated in a meeting with Joe Brown, who was registered as J. L. Brown doing business as Naples Air Service, but was apparently not doing all that much business, at least not by PBA standards. The solution upon which they agreed was obvious. (It was one that had been practiced back in 1921–1923 by Aeromarine, one of the earliest airlines in the United States.) Traffic in Naples was also seasonal, but in the opposite sense from PBA's—the peak traffic was in the winter, when northern tourists flocked to Florida, seeking the sun. Aircraft would be transferred between the two operations systematically so as to provide the maximum capacity when and where it was needed: in Massachusetts during the summer and in Florida during the winter.

Van Arsdale became the manager of traffic and sales of a newly formed Naples Airlines in November 1957 and on 15 December started scheduled service to Miami. The season ran from that day until 15 April, after which the service reverted to a charter operation, as before. In the summer of 1958, Joe Brown's airplanes and pilots migrated to the north, to supplement the PBA fleet when additional capacity was needed most.

A minor crisis occurred the next year, when the city of Naples would not renew Brown's ten-year lease on the airport and the facilities, on the quite reasonable grounds that the rent was twenty-six months in arrears. In December 1959 bids were invited for the renewal lease, and Van Arsdale beat out thirteen other bidders. This time the lease was for only twenty-eight months—the city felt cautious after its previous experience—but good relations were quickly established between the two parties. Taking over the airport on 1 January 1960, Van Arsdale converted Naples Airlines into an operating division of PBA, appointed John E. Zate as general manager, and bought more airplanes. Business was so good that, on 15 December 1961, the Naples-Miami route went on to a year-round schedule, although the seasonal transfer of fleets continued as a basic pattern of operations. In 1962, PBA undertook the construction of a new terminal building, in a deal with the city fathers that converted the short-term lease back to its former term of ten years, running until 1972.

During this period, Van Arsdale guided his dual-location airline through a period of steady growth, not by spectacular route expansion but by intensification of service on the networks centered on Provincetown in the north and Naples in the south. A few new segments were added, from 1968 to 1975, from Naples to Tampa, Marco Island, and Punta Gorda, and when Air New England pulled out of the Boston-Hyannis route in 1979 PBA took over. But the main thrust was in introducing larger aircraft, particularly the Douglas DC-3, of which PBA at first acquired one to cope with the traffic on the Naples-Tampa route and gradually built up to a fleet of thirteen. This fleet included the famous N136PB, which is still recognized not only as the highest-time DC-3, with about 94,000 hours flying, but also as the highest-time aircraft of all time, in any category.

On 1 January 1980, a transformation took place in PBA and in Van Arsdale's career. His two sons took over the airline from their sixty-year-old father. John Jr. became the chairman and Peter the president. The elder John continued to hold the office of vice-president, but the fortunes of the airline were henceforth in the hands of his sons and heirs. He still held the highest percentage of stock, 30 percent. The two sons held 29 percent each, and the rest of the Van Arsdale family held the balance.

The younger generation then proceeded to embark on a program of aggressive expansion, with the thirteen DC-3s plus seven Martin 4-0-4s that had been acquired from Piedmont Aviation starting in 1976. John Sr. soon severed his connection with PBA, and in April 1980 the corporation redeemed his stock at $22.00 per share, for a sum amounting to $660,000. PBA's uninhibited growth continued, and its appetite now seemed insatiable. On 19 September 1983, it made a public offering, estimated by E. F. Hutton to have a paper value of $16 million, to obtain additional capital. Overnight, John Sr. was transformed from the richest member of the family into the poorest, as all his stock had been redeemed.

PBA bought more aircraft and hired more staff. Within a year the fleet grew beyond all recognition, with six Nihon YS-11 sixty-seat turboprops (also from Piedmont) and no less than fifty ten-seat Cessna 402s helping to increase the total number of aircraft to 104.

But pride came before a fall. Two Cessna 402 accidents during the summer of 1984, one in Boston and one in Naples, prompted an investigation by the FAA that led to it abruptly shutting down the airline on 10 November 1984. To fly and maintain its 104 aircraft, PBA had hired many new pilots and flight crew and a host of new mechanics. The payroll now totaled 1,600. Statistically, PBA was now the number one commuter airline. But the FAA ordained that there had been much neglect in training and maintenance, and that PBA had just not maintained tight enough quality control over its operation to ensure safety.

After stringent supervision and praiseworthy effort, PBA was recertificated and resumed service on 25 November. John Jr. stepped down, and Peter took over the management. Demonstrating the "keep 'em flying" determination that so often characterizes airline people, Peter mortgaged his house in January 1985 in order to meet the payroll.

Then one of PBA's Embraer Bandeirantes, Brazilian-built commuter airliners with an excellent worldwide reputation, crashed at Jacksonville on 6 December 1984. The management grounded PBA's fleet of Bandits while suspected defects in the tail were investigated (and, incidentally, never fully explained). This time the curtain seemed to be coming down on PBA, for so long recognized and respected as the granddaddy of the commuter airlines.

This state of affairs came about in spite of a change in ownership when, on 1 February 1985, Hugh Culverhouse, owner of the Tampa Bay Buccaneers football team, took over control of the airline, obtaining a line of credit from the banks and appointing Bill Gregg as the chief executive officer. Culverhouse put up $250,000, which covered one biweekly payroll by a small margin; but this was before he had examined the books closely. Much of his instinctive act of generosity had been based on a long-standing acquaintance with "Old Man Van." But the harsh facts soon appeared in their stark severity.

Many old-timers in the industry had suspected that the younger Van Arsdales were stretching too far and too fast. They were right. The tendency to take up the slack when one of the many small Florida commuter airlines went out of business, without studying *why* it had gone under, was part of the cause of the downfall. On 14 March 1985, PBA filed for bankruptcy under Chapter 11. In a new program of retrenchment, the staff numbers and the fleet size were cut. The large Nihon YS-11s, which had always looked a little incongruous in a commuter airline's colors, were retired in October 1985. PBA was at best treading water, and it grasped desperately at what appeared to be a lifeline when, on 31 January 1986, it accepted an offer from People Express, a post-deregulation airline with maverick tendencies.

But the end of PBA in its own name was in sight. On 15 September 1986, People Express's own balloon burst, and it became Frank Lorenzo's latest acquisition as part of his fast-growing Texas Air empire. The biggest dominion in that empire was Continental Airlines, and PBA was quickly transferred to Bar Harbor Airlines to become, in the fashion that was sweeping the country at the time, a unit of Continental Express.

By this time, John Van Arsdale, Sr. was a disinterested—though certainly not an uninterested—onlooker. To watch his airline disintegrate before his very eyes must have been a great disappointment, but he showed no outward signs of disenchantment with the industry in which he had always believed. He had been one of its pioneers and had left behind a legacy that was perhaps best summed up by George Kean, vice-president of marketing at the time of the bankruptcy: "a brilliant strategist [who] brought that entrepreneurial strength to the airline. He was a risk-taker and he won more times than he lost. We don't have that same capability."

Kean might have mentioned that Old Man Van's risks were always calculated ones. That was the reason why, when he stepped down in 1980, he was still on top.

Profile 21

Joseph C. (Joe) Whitney
Executive Airlines and Air New England

Joe Whitney has alternately enjoyed and suffered through the experience of building two separate airlines that grew and prospered under his stewardship and then watching them collapse after the management of their affairs was removed from his control. He emerged from these substantial stretches of his career perhaps bruised but nonetheless unbowed, and he fortunately had other interests to fall back on to compensate him for a pardonable degree of disenchantment with the regional airline business.

His early life was not particularly oriented toward aviation, and he was already twenty-eight years old before he became seriously associated with what was then called scheduled air taxi operations. Born at Summit, New Jersey, on 14 April 1927, he came from an upper middle class background. His father was in the department store business and his grandfather had been president of the Boston and Providence Railroad. Whitney grew up in Massachusetts and attended the Noble and Greenough School at Dedham, Massachusetts, and the Babson Institute of Business Administration at Wellesley, Massachusetts, obtaining his bachelor's degree after having served a two-year stint in the U.S. Marine Corps in 1945–1946, stationed in the Pacific.

In 1949, Joe Whitney had his first contact with the airline business, working for two years in New York as a salesman for Slick Airways, one of the early all-cargo airlines. During this period he learned to fly at Martha's Vineyard, under the tutelage of Caroline Cullen, who had been one of the original World War II Women's Auxiliary Air Force ferry pilots. He was then a yacht broker for a short while before joining Northeast Airlines, at the time when the Atlas Corporation had taken it over from the original New England owners. Still a salesman, he was based at Hyannis and Boston, until in 1954 he expanded his interests—possibly taking a leaf out of his father's book—by starting his own retail

Joseph C. (Joe) Whitney (photo by Harding-Glidden Inc.)

business, Robin Hood's Barn, a men's and women's specialty clothing shop with branches at Westwood and Edgartown, Massachusetts, and in Florida.

In 1956, having completed his pilot's training, he bought a Cessna 182, used it first as his own executive plane, and then leased it. This latter move was successful enough to encourage him to buy another aircraft, a twin-engined Piper Apache, which he again leased to other operators. In 1959, he decided to take this activity seriously and founded National Executive Flight Service, with a fleet of two Aero Commander 500s and three Piper Comanches. In those days, Whitney recalls, "anybody could operate an air taxi service by going to the FAA and signing a piece of paper. The only real requirements were to own or lease an aircraft and to have a commercial pilot's rating, not even an [instrument flight rules] rating."

On 20 June 1960, National Executive began its first scheduled service, supplementing Northeast Airlines' flights between Boston and Martha's Vineyard. The local service airline's service was not bad—three flights a day in the summer with DC-4s—but, like almost all air taxi/commuter airline operators who found a niche in the airline market, Whitney drew on his knowledge of the local community's needs and offered far more convenient schedules, particularly at the beginning and the end of the business day. The following year, he repeated the performance, with routes linking Boston with Nantucket and Hyannis, and in

1962 he added lines from both Martha's Vineyard and Nantucket to New York.

By this time Northeast was losing interest in serving the smaller communities of New England. It had ceased to operate into Martha's Vineyard, Nantucket, and Hyannis, after trying to upgrade its service with DC-6Bs and even DC-9 jets. Feeling less threatened in his own backyard, Whitney then began to spread his National Executive wings. On 1 December 1964 he established a Florida division, using Piper Cherokee Sixes and starting a route from Sarasota to Tampa.

This move was in a long-established tradition. As early as 1921, Aeromarine, one of America's long-forgotten pioneer airlines, had realized the advantage of transferring aircraft during the winter from the northern climes to the sunny south, where Florida was at the receiving end of a mass tourist migration every year. John Van Arsdale's Provincetown-Boston Airline had done the same starting in 1957, focusing on Naples, Florida. Whitney's service at Sarasota was a success from the start, not least because he offered a genuine shuttle service. One passenger, a shrewd student of the operation, observed: "No matter what the schedule stated, if enough people to fill half a plane showed up at any time, they would run a separate section. During the winter, service could be just about continuous."

In 1966, Whitney bought his first DH-104 Dove—a trim British-built type that had been highly successful on the Detroit-Cleveland trans–Lake Erie TAG Airlines shuttle—and with this aircraft started routes into Maine, again replacing Northeast to some of the smaller cities. There followed a period of reorganization and consolidation during which, in January 1967, he created Executive Airlines as a division of the parent company; in the fall, he replaced Northeast (yet again) on the route from Boston to Lebanon, New Hampshire, and Montpelier, Vermont; and, in the spring of 1968, he purchased Yankee Airlines, based at Pittsfield, Massachusetts, which operated a commuter service to New York. With the Yankee purchase came two more Doves, which were converted to "Riley-Doves," with two Continental eight-cylinder engines replacing the Gipsy Queens, which had been a perpetual source of trouble.

Significant events in Whitney's career followed in 1968. He purchased his first de Havilland Aircraft of Canada DHC-6 Twin Otter (ferrying it personally from Toronto) and almost simultaneously sold the Executive Airlines division to Walter F. Beinecke, Jr., the heir to the S & H Green Stamp fortune who, according to Whitney, with only slight exaggeration, "owned half of Nantucket."

Whitney remained as president and for a while presided over a program of accelerated expansion of the dual-based airline, especially of the Florida operation. The fleet was expanded in short order to comprise ten fifteen-seat Beech 99s and eight nineteen-seat Twin Otters. In the fall of 1968, Executive built a large facility in Sarasota, the first of its kind to be established by a commuter airline to include not only the maintenance installations but also administrative offices, crew quarters, and the reservations department.

This combination of essential equipment, both in the air and on the ground, seemed to be a formula for success, and indeed, in 1969, Executive Airlines was voted "Commuter Airline of the Year" by *Air Transport World* magazine. But then, in a remarkable reversal of fortune, Executive proceeded to plunge into Chapter 11 bankruptcy, having squandered its assets on an overambitious route expansion program, spreading out from Florida, together with uncontrolled staff increases. In 1971 it also purchased Massachusetts Air Industries (Mass Air), a small operator at New Bedford specializing in carrying newspapers to Martha's Vineyard and Nantucket, for which it really had no need.

All this was too much for Whitney, who had a good sense of balance in how far, how soon, and in what direction a small commuter airline should proceed in expanding. In the late spring of 1970, in an obvious personality clash, he parted company with Walter Beinecke and, from the sidelines, watched Executive Airlines part company with its senses. In a piercing commentary, *Business Week* observed, "The company ran through four presidents after Whitney left, and each seemed to have a favorite area that needed a route. One particularly disastrous route was Boston to Monticello, New York, in the borscht belt."

Whitney was appalled at the sight of good market potential in New England going to waste because of inept management by an airline that should have concentrated on plugging the gaps left by Northeast Airlines' abandonment of many of its traditional cities north of Boston. Accordingly, he decided to try to put things right again and reentered the commuter airline arena. He raised $500,000 through some New Jersey investors, including Fairleigh S. Dickinson, Jr., and on 15 November 1970 founded Air New England.

The nucleus of the operation was the old Cape & Islands Air Service, originally founded in 1964 by George Parmenter of Hyannis. As the name indicated, it had specialized in connecting the Cape Cod area with the offshore islands, but Parmenter had retired and sold his fleet of Twin Otters and Twin Beeches to Wiggins Airways of Norwood, Massachusetts, which in turn had sold it to Transair, of Bangor, Maine. Whitney bought Transair's fleet of four Twin Otters and a route network from Maine to Nantucket, changed the name on the operating certificate from Cape & Islands to Air New England, and was back in business.

Whitney observes that, in those days, setting up a commuter airline was relatively easy, as long as the aircraft grossed at less than 12,500 pounds. "The CAB didn't want to know about it, and the operators could do pretty much anything they wanted to." (Today, after airline deregulation, the key dividing line for the FAA is nine seats, excluding turboprops, and the operator cannot publish a schedule unless in possession of a "fitness" certificate from the Department of Transportation.) He then proceeded to compete with his former company, Executive Airlines, still owned by Walter Beinecke but visibly floundering in an administrative and operational mess. It had expanded its fleet to ten Twin Otters, four Beech 99s, and three Convair-Liners, but had failed to appreciate the considerable benefits of the seasonal migration of aircraft to match the summer peak in the north and the winter peak in the south.

By 1970, Beinecke had become disillusioned with his involvement in air transport and had found a buyer. However, he fared no better and soon turned Executive Airlines back to Beinecke. The overexpansion was too much even for an improved management team led by Terry Dennison, formerly of Apache Airlines, and Beinecke thereupon tried to buy Air New England. But by this time, there was not an ounce of goodwill left between the two airlines that had had many an acrimonious dispute over competition on parallel routes. Beinecke had no cards to play. In a perfect world, Executive should have been the surviving airline of a friendly merger, with Whitney, who knew the New England operating environment and was sensitive to its changing character, as its president. Instead Executive Airlines first filed for bankruptcy under Chapter 11 and folded completely by mid-1972. Whitney and Air New England "picked up the residual traffic and none of the headaches, welcomed the routes to Lebanon and Montpelier that came in as extras, and bought Executive's DHC-6-300 Twin Otters from the bank, to replace some of its own older DHC-6-200s."

Whitney then decided that there was a great opportunity to reestablish a full local service operation in New England and that his airline was perfectly positioned as a candidate. After two years of petitioning the CAB, he succeeded. It was the first new local service operator eligible for subsidy to be formed since Ozark Air Lines received its certificate in 1950.

Air New England already had a good working relationship with Northeast Airlines, which had been purchased by Delta Air Lines in 1973. But the CAB had insisted that Delta should receive no subsidy to maintain Northeast's network, and the trunk airline decided to retain only the routes to the main cities north of Boston: Portland, Bangor, and Burlington. This left the field open for Air New England not only to expand, but also to buy from Delta, freshly painted and refurbished, "six fifty-seat Fairchild FH-227s, virtually as a gift," plus spares, for $3 million.

Whitney laid the groundwork for the new local service operator by building a new hangar at Hyannis for FH-227 maintenance and another at Montpelier for the Beech 99s. Cities such as Augusta, Auburn-Lewiston, Lebanon, and Montpelier were transferred from Delta's Certificate of Public Convenience and Necessity to Air New England. And then history repeated itself.

In September 1975, Whitney's contract as president of New England was terminated when the two main investors agreed that one of them, Robert Kanzler, should take over. Kanzler was an absentee president from Detroit, where his father had once been Henry Ford's chief accountant. Within a year, he had handed over control to Charles Butler, but by then Air New England was on a downhill slope and slipping fast. Whitney recalls that "three different unions ate 'em up." But the airline did not go bankrupt. Fairleigh Dickinson purchased most of Kanzler's stock, spent two years liquidating, paid all debts, sold the aircraft for three times their purchase price, and closed the doors in 1978.

As for Whitney, he still had Robin Hood's Barn, the clothing shops, but he could not keep away from aviation. In the spring of 1976, he started Nor East Commuter Airlines, with three Piper Navajos and three Aero Commanders, in the hope of picking up the pieces once again.

But this was not to happen. John Van Arsdale and the Provincetown-Boston Airline (PBA) inherited all of Air New England's routes, even though, Whitney claims, there had been an understanding with Nor East. Shrewdly concluding that this was not going to be a case of third time lucky, Whitney finally got out of the airline business. In 1979, he sold his aircraft and continued as a traditional fixed base operator at New Bedford. He bought a brand new hangar, added extensions, and then acquired every other available installation on the airfield.

Today, Joe Whitney runs a successful real estate business at Edgartown, Massachusetts, and commutes, in his own Aero Commander, to and from his New Bedford operation. Since the embryo years of the commuter airline industry, he has been an active participant in trying to make a go of a New England commuter airline operation. Yet there seems to be a jinx on the area. No airline has ever been a complete success there: neither the local service Northeast Airlines, even with subsidy, nor its successor, Air New England; neither the commuter airline Executive nor its rival PBA (except when operating specialized and extremely localized routes); nor any of today's code-sharing subsidiaries of the major airlines.

Whitney may often review the scene and reflect from time to time on what might have been. Suppose he had stayed with Executive or with Air New England, or if PBA hadn't. . . . He may not have made a fortune but at least he never went bankrupt. As a detached and philosophical observer of the changing scene from his comfortable home on Martha's Vineyard, he can look back with satisfaction on the years that took him from the Barn to the hangar.

Profile 22

Preston H. Wilbourne
Air Wisconsin

Go to any large gathering of people from the commuter airline industry, such as the annual meeting of the Regional Airline Association, and there is certain to be a great deal of convivial conversation about airplanes—what is familiarly known as "hangar flying." Preston Wilbourne is not exactly aloof from these conversations, but he is unlikely to take part in them to a great degree for the simple reason that he is not a pilot, and never has been. Whereas most of the pioneer commuter airline operators were pilots, his commercial aviation career was spent in more down-to-earth activities in those airline departments that make the difference between merely flying and flying for a profit. He is living proof of the point made by C. M. Keys, an airline pioneer of the late 1920s, who declared that "90 percent of aviation is on the ground."

Wilbourne spent the first twenty-three years of his aviation career, with only a couple of years' interruption, working as a station agent, and for 12 years in various jobs in reservations, scheduling, and tariffs, with Piedmont Aviation, the local service airline designated to operate in Virginia and the Carolinas, where he grew up. Born on 25 February 1925 at Duke, North Carolina, he had received his education in the public school systems of that state by 1941, when he joined the National Youth Administration. A year later, he had joined the U.S. Air Force as an airframe and power plant mechanic and flight engineer, working on airframes and engines alike, and attending various schools to improve his grasp of the trade. Although in later years he was to specialize in operational planning and administration, he had thus acquired a thorough grounding in what made airplanes fly, what made them go wrong, and how to put them right. He might not have qualified for hangar flying, but he knew what to do in the hangar.

Moving back to North Carolina after the war, he did not, as did many of today's airline leaders, plunge straight into aviation. From 1948 until

Preston H. Wilbourne

1950 he worked in the steel erecting business, before going into air transport with Piedmont Aviation. In 1950, he married Kitty, who has identified herself with Pres—as he is known to his close friends—and his dedicated approach to systematic planning throughout his career. They have been a true husband-and-wife team.

With Piedmont, he started as a station agent at Roanoke, Virginia, then at Norfolk; another move brought him to Bluefield, a small community on the West Virginia border in the Appalachian Mountains, where he opened up the station. Here he took leave from Piedmont to manage the American Automobile Club travel department at Bluefield, and thus gained some experience in a travel agency. So, by the age of twenty-eight, he was well versed not only in maintenance, but also in station operations and in marketing.

In 1956, Wilbourne rejoined Piedmont and was stationed at Lynchburg, Virginia, for a few months before moving to the airline's headquarters at Winston-Salem, where he was promoted to manager of systems reservations and space control. Within two years he was director of tariffs and schedules, a position that he retained for six more years; during his tenure important steps in the evolution of the airline system were taking place in Washington.

The FAA was formed on 23 August 1958. Under Part 298 of the CAB Economic Regulations, air taxi operators were granted exemption to operate scheduled services, provided that they did not use aircraft heavier than 12,500 pounds gross takeoff weight. This ruling, formally made in 1952, was extended indefinitely in 1965. The operators could begin to fly regularly and publish timetables, as long as they complied with FAA Part 135 regulations for safety and navigation. Formerly they had been required to comply with the full air transport rules (FAA Part 121). Air taxi operators, many of whom did most of their business as fixed base operators, could now qualify as airlines at the bottom rung of the ladder, fly under visual flight rules with only one pilot, and use single-engined aircraft; their pilots did not need a full air transport rating, as long as they had a commercial one.

In line with this development, which was effectively the start of the commuter airline structure that was to evolve during the next thirty years, Wilbourne decided to strike out on his own and become a part of an industry while it was in its infancy. In 1963 he joined South Central Airlines in Charlotte, not more than twenty minutes' flying time from Winston-Salem. Started by a group of investors, it aimed to link the largest city in North Carolina with Ocala, Florida. Wilbourne was put in charge of establishing the tariffs, schedules, and reservation system and writing up all the operating manuals.

This position was just a rehearsal for better things to come. He had been with South Central no more than a year when he was approached by a group of businessmen from Appleton, Wisconsin, where they had incorporated a new airline, to operate under the 12,500-pound limitation, with initial capital of $100,000. Appleton was contiguous with the cities of Menasha and Neenah, on the northern shore of Lake Winnebago; it was close to Green Bay, and Oshkosh was only a few miles to the south. Altogether, there was a thriving community, with much industrial activity (not to mention the famous Green Bay Packers nearby) that was dissatisfied with the air service offered by North Central Airlines— especially when the latter moved to combine all services in the area through a single airport at Oshkosh, starting in March 1966. Furthermore, the Minneapolis-based North Central tended to regard the Fox River Cities (as Appleton and its neighbors were known) simply as one of a selection of intermediate pickup points between the Twin cities and Chicago, and not as a traffic-generating community in its own right.

Wilbourne was appointed general manager of the newly created Air Wisconsin on 8 October 1965. At the age of thirty-nine, his career began to take off—with the involuntary cooperation of North Central, which showed little inclination to study, much less take advantage of, the market potential of the cities in northern Wisconsin.

Air Wisconsin had started service on 23 August 1965, just before Wilbourne arrived. Its first fleet consisted of a single de Havilland Dove, with nine seats. This was a small twin-engined airliner produced in England in the late 1940s. It had clean lines and could have been very successful with more vigorous marketing and had its Gipsy Queen four hundred-horsepower engines been more reliable. It served Air Wisconsin well enough, even though, as Wilbourne ruefully (and with only slight exaggeration) recalls, "you had to change the cylinders every round trip to Chicago."

Air Wisconsin's first step was to link the Fox River Cities with Chicago in the south and later the Twin Cities in the west. The route to the south was the same as North Central's had been, but the service pattern was different, with emphasis on providing same-day round-trip convenience with morning and evening scheduling. This pattern was the basis for many a commuter airline substitution for local service practice.

Service frequency was at first two flights per day, requiring a fleet of four of the Doves, but after two years, in 1966, Air Wisconsin introduced the first of a fleet of seven de Havilland Aircraft of Canada DHC-6 Twin Otters. It claims to have been the first U.S. operator of the type, but Joe Fugere of Pilgrim Airlines in Connecticut started Twin Otter service on the same day and at the same time, although on Eastern Standard Time, and so the issue remains in dispute.

With the Twin Otters, Air Wisconsin grew apace, and not solely in traffic statistics or in route mileage. In fact, Wilbourne never subscribed to the idea that a bigger network, eye-catching though it might be in the publicity pamphlets, was the key to success. Having worked the stations with Piedmont, and having organized tariffs, schedules, and other aspects of the real heart of the airline business, he knew that matching the right aircraft to the market demand and concentrating on the main sources of revenue were the most important strategies in seeking financial viability. And so, with the Pratt & Whitney–powered seventeen-seat Twin Otter, Air Wisconsin came close to breaking even in 1969 and began to make a profit in the following year.

Like many other commuter airline operators, Wilbourne gives high marks to the Twin Otter. It did exactly what he wanted of a smaller airliner, and he would readily echo the remarks of Kingsley Morse of Command Airways, who said that all the Otter needed to keep it happy was regular supplies of kerosene. The Canadian aircraft, though originally built for bush operations, put many a U.S. embryo airline on its feet, and in the case of Air Wisconsin it laid the foundation for future glories.

For six years, Air Wisconsin moved steadily along, with no dangerous sorties into the fields of route expansion, but content to operate a fleet of four Twin Otters, supplemented by three Beech 99s. The 99s were smaller but faster, and thus suitable for the longer segments of the system, and they were powered by the same Pratt & Whitney Canada PT6 engines as the Twin Otter—a big advantage for standardization in maintenance.

Then, on 1 June 1973, the first Swearingen Metroliner service began. This aircraft had nineteen seats (two more than the Twin Otter), was at least as fast as the Beech 99, and was, by comparison, more fuel efficient; furthermore it was fully pressurized. The scheduled time from Appleton to Chicago was cut from sixty-five to forty-five minutes, and the aircraft could also be converted for freight in eighteen minutes. Preston liked this aircraft even more than the old faithful Twin Otter, and he built the Metro fleet up to a round dozen.

Some cautious route extensions were made, but with a strict eye on the profit and loss statement. If a city did not produce, then Preston would soon erase it from the Air Wisconsin map. Although in 1975 the route to the Twin Cities was extended to Lincoln, Nebraska, the routes to Indianapolis, Indiana, and Wausau, Wisconsin, were both dropped. On the whole, however, the line was running smoothly, and Preston felt that the time had come to consolidate his position.

Having studied the possibility for two years, and just before airline deregulation took effect, Air Wisconsin obtained a Certificate of Public Convenience and Necessity from the CAB on 1 October 1978. In issuing this coveted piece of paper, the administrative law judge used phrases such as "If ever a carrier had proved its ability, with a record of accomplished facts."

This elevation to certificated status was accompanied by further moves, including a route extension on 1 April 1979 to Bismarck, North Dakota, in which history was repeating itself, as Air Wisconsin seemed to be following a course of expansion paralleling that of North Central Airlines, the local service carrier, thirty years ago.

On 31 July 1981, the first de Havilland Aircraft of Canada fifty-seat Dash 7 was delivered. It was to have been the first of only three such aircraft—fifty seats was a big jump from the Swearingen's nineteen— but the air traffic controllers' strike declared on 3 August 1981 led Wilbourne, who could juggle scheduling alternatives in his head as well as any computer, quickly to increase the order to five. In a seller's market, at a time when gates and slots were at a premium, he exchanged high frequencies for high seating capacity in his best markets.

By this time, however, traffic was booming on Air Wisconsin's routes to such an extent that even the fifty-seat aircraft were far from being too large. In fact, within two years, on 27 June 1983, Wilbourne raised not a few eyebrows among his contemporaries by introducing the four-engined British Aerospace BAe-146-200 hundred-seat feederliner on services from O'Hare to Akron, Appleton, Fort Wayne, and Toledo, and soon to Green Bay.

The commuter airlines suffered a setback soon thereafter, however, when the CAB ruled to eliminate bias from computer reservation systems. All schedules had to be rigidly displayed in descending order: first, direct flights; second, on-line connections; and third, interline connections. In Wilbourne's succinct analysis, "the federal government commitment to sustain the feeder industry went out the window with that ruling." It set the feeders back twenty years, to the times when they could not get a listing in the *Official Airline Guide*, and "it put us out in left field in the distribution system."

Wilbourne seems to have taken the pragmatic approach of behaving in much the same way as would a major airline, given the circumstances. Late in January 1985, he agreed in principle to acquire Mississippi Valley Airlines (MVA), another large and successful "commuter" airline. He obtained Securities and Exchange Commission approval on 17 May 1985 and completed the amalgamation (actually achieved through the purchase by Air Wis Services, Inc., the parent company, of MVA) shortly afterward, on 1 June 1985.

The two airlines had competed in only a few markets, and both had marketing agreements with United Airlines. The combined company became the third largest operator, measured by airplane movements, at Chicago's O'Hare airport, the busiest airport in the world. Air Wisconsin, ranked fourth among the commuter/regionals, had seven Dash 7s, six BAe-146s, and three BAC One-Eleven twinjets. MVA, ranked eighth, had four Fokker F-27s, six Shorts-SD-360s and six Shorts-SD-330s. Put together, Air Wisconsin's $70 million and MVA's $45 million in annual revenues placed them well over the qualifying level of $75 million to become a national airline. Air Wisconsin had grown from a single-route commuter airline to a carrier of national status in twenty years.

From this time onward, the story of Preston Wilbourne and Air Wisconsin seems almost irrelevant in this book. Shortly after the merger with MVA, United Airlines adopted the common designator system on its Apollo computerized reservation system. Thus Air Wisconsin's flights appeared as United's, sharing its two-letter code, and usually on the first screen. Air Wisconsin had lost a lot of traffic since the CAB's 1984 ruling but now began to win it back. It entered into an expanded partnership agreement with United on 6 June 1986, adopting the United colors on all aircraft and providing a link to distant Dulles International Airport, in Washington, D.C., where United had established a hub. In 1988, it carried 2.4 million passengers, grossed $177 million in revenues, and made a profit of $17 million. The first of a fleet of British Aerospace sixty-five-seat ATPs went into service on 25 March 1990.

On 30 April 1990, Air Wis Services completed the purchase of Aspen Airways, of Denver, Colorado, which continued to operate as a sister company under its own name. Then, on 31 May of that year, Bill Andres, executive vice-president and chief operating officer, was appointed president and chief executive officer of Air Wisconsin. Wilbourne became chairman of the board, finally relinquishing the left-hand seat he had occupied so ably—if never literally.

Part III

Regional Tabulations of Commuter Airlines

One task undertaken by the coauthors of this book was to attempt to compile a complete list of commuter airlines of the United States. Such a list was considered necessary partly to emphasize the amazing diversity of this multifaceted airline industry. Without direction from or requirements set forth by federal or state authorities, with no organization of their own, motivated only by individual initiatives, hundreds of companies, most of them tiny, played their part. The tables that follow illustrate the wide variety of the different companies that, collectively, created a new stratum of air transport. Each deserves to be recognized for its contribution, however small.

This compilation was a daunting task. No single information source covering all the airlines has ever existed, and those directories or listings that have been attempted and made available not only have been incomplete but have often proved to be unreliable. Our regional compilations are therefore based on many different sources: agency directories, magazines and periodicals, newspaper articles, and FAA and CAB listings, but most of all telephone calls and personal interviews, conducted over a period of many years. One source has been the *Official Airline Guide*, but this publication has customarily included only a selection of the commuter airlines that have offered regular service. In the 1960s and early 1970s, it frequently excluded some companies and delayed the inclusion of others for several years after they had begun scheduled services.

The tabulations list all the companies that can be identified as commuter airlines. They have been known variously as scheduled air taxis, third-level carriers, and commuter airlines. The more recent term "regional airlines," though widely used, is not strictly appropriate, as it includes many airlines that are neither short-haul carriers nor operators of small equipment—essential elements in any definition of commuter airlines. The listings do not include scheduled helicopter airlines, nor airlines that have specialized *exclusively* in airmail or air freight.

The tables are divided into thirteen geographical areas, because the characteristics of the commuter airlines differ by region, as described in the individual introductions. Within each geographical listing, the commuter airlines have been broadly classified by the size and importance of their operations. In the first category—those printed in **boldface** type—are airlines that have had a substantial and often permanent influence not only on commuter airline affairs and air traveling habits in their specific region, but in some cases even on the development of the industry as a whole. In the second category—those printed in roman type—are airlines whose influence was more localized and usually not of lasting significance. The vast majority of the companies—those printed in *italic* type—are in the third category, which comprises the "footsoldiers" of the industry. Their influence was usually only localized and frequently short-lived.

In many cases, in the 1960s and earlier, because of the complete lack of systematic record-keeping by any official agency, finding the starting dates for scheduled passenger services was difficult, if not impossible. The "first scheduled service date" noted during this period is often the date when the company received its FAA operating certificate, as this was the only information available. Frequently, the start of actual scheduled services was shortly after (or sometimes even before!) receipt of this certificate. As an example of the confused situation, different FAA publications have been known to show different dates, in which case the coauthors had to select the most likely date.

When available, the airline's two-letter FAA operational code is listed. As already mentioned, U.S. commuter airlines have never been the beneficiaries of continuous and systematic regulation. Thus, many used more than one code during their years of operation, although not simultaneously. Conversely, some codes were used by several airlines, but at different times, as the FAA reallocated them after a previous owner ceased operations.

To include a complete listing of all routes and cities served by every airline would have been impracticable. The objective in this context is to provide a representative indication of the scope of the operation, although where possible the inaugural city pair is shown. This generalization also applies to the fleets of aircraft listed, which are necessarily representative rather than comprehensive; no attempt is made to provide the numbers of aircraft in service, as these have varied continually, sometimes week to week, and even more frequently in some cases.

Some aircraft types are listed in parentheses, to indicate that at the relevant time they required special CAB authority to be operated by the specific commuter airline. This exemption was required because, according to CAB regulations, certain types, such as the DC-3, were considered too large to be operated by a company that did not possess a full operating certificate as a scheduled airline.

The date of the last scheduled service was often difficult to obtain. Airlines do not like to publicize their demise—or have more urgent matters on their minds at the time—and this was especially the case during the 1960s and early 1970s. Many of them did not die; like many an old footsoldier, they simply faded away.

Horizontal lines separate the years of entry into service. This arrangement provides a quick overall visual impression of the ebb and flow of relative prosperity among the commuter airlines. When conditions were favorable, commuter airlines sprang up like mushrooms; when times were bad, they died like flies.

These listings contain a grand total of 1,014 U.S. commuter airlines. Some were so successful that they rose to prominence and were promoted to the ranks of large regional carriers. Some lasted only a few weeks—one lasted for only a day. Large or small, few have survived, but the authors hope that the contribution of each to air travel, however insignificant, is recorded here.

Area 1

Alaska

Any Alaskan will tell you that aviation in the forty-ninth state is unlike that in any of the others, simply because the territory is so vast and so different that it might be another country, rather than part of the United States. In geography, if not political reality, this is true; and but for an episode of timely opportunism, Alaska might well have remained part of the former Soviet Union, inherited from czarist Russia. Certainly, in terrain and climate, and in vegetation and animal life, it has much more in common with northern Canada and northern Siberia than it does with the lower forty-eight.

The differences are reflected in the patterns of human settlement. Until a few decades ago, at the outbreak of World War II, the total population was less than 100,000. The capital, Juneau, boasted about 6,000, and five of the eight largest cities were in the southeastern panhandle. Anchorage, now a city of about 225,000, had barely 4,000 people. The war changed the whole character of the state, and both Anchorage and Fairbanks emerged as cities of substance.

This enormous transformation was further reflected in the patterns of travel, especially in air transport. Before the war, the few companies that could lay claim to being called airlines operated somewhat uncertainly, because of the severe meteorological conditions and the absence of good airfields, navigational aids, or any of the basic infrastructure necessary to support orthodox operations as they had developed in the contiguous states. Most of the airlines flew routes that required the skills and instincts of bush pilots, and the early Alaskan pilots, heroes of the airways in their time, are now revered for their often heroic exploits. Such was their stature in the aviation community that they often formed their own airlines, by incorporating themselves, as an extension of their sporadic flights. These, if all conditions were right, could be described as regular because they served the same places with some frequency—at least most of the time.

The conditions were so bad that the CAB had difficulty in reconciling its regulations, tailored for "normal" operations down south, with the challenges of long periods of subzero temperatures in the north, or long periods of fog and continuous, driving rain in the panhandle. These conditions did not permit the fulfillment of the statutory daily schedules, the publishing of fixed timetables, and the guarantee of punctuality and regularity—all criteria laid down by the CAB for qualifying for airline status. After sending inspectors up to Alaska to see for themselves—a somewhat unnerving experience for Washington-closeted bureaucrats—the CAB granted special privileges to the Alaskan carriers, including relaxed standards for statistical reporting.

After World War II, a hardy group of operators emerged to modify the riskier habits of the somewhat adventurous pioneer airmen into a formula that applied stricter disciplines that were derived from the realities of the environment. The Wien brothers, who maintained Wien Air Alaska; Bob Reeve, who operated in the Aleutian Islands because nobody else wanted to go there; Ray Peterson, who put a number of small outfits together to form Northern Consolidated; Mudhole Smith of Cordova; and Bob Ellis and Shell Simmons, who founded Ellis Airlines and Alaska Coastal Airlines, respectively, all deserve great credit for laying the foundations of the Alaskan airline industry that is today dominated by Alaskan Airlines, itself a distant descendant of the Star Air Service of the early 1930s.

During the 1940s and 1950s, at least measured in passenger boardings, none of these little airlines was as big as even a medium-size commuter airline of today. But they served a vital purpose, providing the only form of transport throughout a vast territory about twice the size of Texas. They were well subsidized, performing as they did a public service in a land where railroads and highways were in short supply. Nevertheless, they had difficulty in making ends meet, and only two companies, Alaska Airlines and Art Woodley's Pacific Northern, had trunk routes to the lower forty-eight that provided a cross-feeding source of traffic generation. Gradually, they were forced to terminate services, especially to the small communities, and this situation gave rise to the emergence of a new breed of airline. Judged by their choice of aircraft, the extent of their route networks, their manner of operation (typically they operated short-haul spoke patterns from a central hub), and their average size (the owner often doubled as the only pilot and his wife often took care of the office), they were much like small scheduled air taxi companies elsewhere in the United States, and they were so categorized by the FAA.

With the deregulation of the airline industry, these small airlines began to proliferate. The accompanying table lists eighty-two that have existed since 1964, and perhaps a third of these are still operating today. As already mentioned, Alaska is, in spite of its growth in the past few years, still sparsely populated. Only Anchorage (225,000 people), Fairbanks (40,000), and the capital city of Juneau (20,000) have populations of more than 10,000. All the rest of the state's population of 300,000 (second smallest of the fifty states) is scattered among hundreds of mostly tiny communities, some of them so isolated that to reach them by any other means involves a hazardous surface journey by dogsled, snowmobile, or boat. Very few towns are linked by the one railroad, and only in the areas around Anchorage and Fairbanks is there a network of roads. Such a distribution of population has created a large demand for local air services, but not a great demand for intercity services—there are just not enough cities.

The service provided by the multiplicity of small air taxi companies (which, for the purposes of this book, can be grouped with, and considered synonymous with, commuter airlines) is phenomenal. In no other region of the United States do tiny villages receive such excellent air service. To Alaskans, as many of whom appear to fly airplanes as drive automobiles, this is as it should be. How else, they point out, can you travel at all? Nevertheless, the facts and figures are extraordinary. To take but one example: Arctic Village, situated on the North Slope mountain range, consisting of only a couple of families, used to receive two flights a week from Arctic Circle Air, to link it with Fairbanks. Today it is still served by that airline's successors. (Of course this history exemplifies another characteristic of the Alaskan breed of commuter airline: most of them do not seem to last very long.)

Because of these demographic realities, most of the airlines have remained very small. This can be discerned by comparing the Alaska tabulation with those of other regions. In the other twelve tables, the larger, well-established airlines often operate fleets of twenty aircraft, and some types seat thirty or more passengers. These fairly large companies have annual dollar revenues of six figures or more, and are shown in boldface. In vivid contrast, in the Alaskan table, only one company qualifies for such selection, although quite a number have been of sufficient influence and good standing for a long enough time to qualify for the second category of medium-size commuter airlines. Yet the vast majority have been very small, and nowhere else in the whole of the United States are so many operators of single-engined aircraft to be found. Typically, they have route networks that are dense arrays in mainly spoke patterns, sometimes of considerable complexity, focused not only on the "metropolises" of Anchorage and Fairbanks, but also on the smaller "cities" of Nome, Bethel, McGrath, and Barrow in the north, and Juneau, Ketchikan, and Wrangell in the southeast.

Because of the nature of the terrain, and the proliferation of small fishing communities in the coastal regions, floatplanes are common. The fleets of Cessnas and Pipers in particular, not to mention the faithful de Havilland Beavers and Otters, are invariably fitted with floats in the southeast, where they provide air ferry service throughout the tortuous fjords and waterways of the panhandle and island communities; in the north, they tend to be converted from float to wheels, or sometimes to skis, according to the changes of climate. Most of northern Alaska is covered in snow in the winter, and the aircraft take to skis as ducks to water. The worst season is the spring, when the thaw melts the permafrost. Unless a community is blessed with a hard runway—a rare occurrence—the aircraft take lessons from the ducks and take to the waters, which comprise most of Alaska's territory during the summer months.

Although the intense activity of the dozens of small operators is unique, and one may suggest that it has no place in this book, there is a curious aspect to at least part of the Alaskan scheduled aviation scene. Some of the small airlines actually do fill a genuine commuter role, in the literal sense of the term. Far from the likes of such airlines as Foster Aviation and, more recently, Olson Air Service, which land on the frozen Bering Strait at Little Diomede Island during the winter months, some of the airlines, such as Southcentral and ERA, do a thriving business actually carrying commuters between Anchorage and the neighboring communities of Homer and Kenai. Alaska has come a long way since Noel Wien carried his first charter passenger in 1924.

AREA 1 (ALASKA)

First Sched. Service Date	Airline and Base	Code	Initial or Typical Route Network	Aircraft Used	Remarks	Date of last service
10 Mar. 1964	Alaska Southcoast Airways (Annette Island)	WJ	Local services, inc. ferry to Ketchikan, Metlakatla	DHC-2 Beaver Cessna 185	Founded by Mark Murdock and Pete Johnson as _Tamgass Aviation_. Changed name in 1969 to _Southcoast Airways_, then to _Alaska Southcoast_.	1974
15 Oct. 1964	Hub Air Service (McGrath)		McGrath-Medfra-Tatalina-Ophir-Flat	various small types		1976
9 Nov. 1964	Safeway Airlines (Anchorage)		Local routes	Piper types		1968
16 Jan. 1965	Fairbanks Air Service (Fairbanks)		Served some villages near Fairbanks	Beech 18 BN-2 Islander DHC-6 Twin Otter	Founded as F.B.O. during World War II. Also operated charters with larger aircraft, DC-3, C-46, L-188 Electra.	1976
1 Mar. 1965	Munz Northern Airlines (Nome, St. Mary's, Kotzebue)	XY XZ	Extensive network in NW Alaska	Aero Commander BN-2 Islander Dornier Do228 Stinson SR-9CM Cessna 206 Aermacchi AL60	First founded in F.B.O. in 1938 by Munz. Became an affiliate of _Wien Air Alaska_. Purchased by _Ryan Air_ in 1983.	1983
30 Mar. 1965	International Air Taxi (Anchorage)		Local services	Cessna types		1970
12 April 1965	Interior Airways (Fairbanks)		Local services	Beech 18, Twin Bonanza	Operated by _Interior Air Taxi_.	1968
April 1966	Glacier Bay Airways (Gustavus)		Juneau-Gustavus-Bartlett Cove; later to Excursion Inlet, Hoonah	Cessna 206 DHC-3 Otter	Founded by Robert Gildersleeve. Exclusive contract with National Park Service to connect with cruise ships.	
1967	Alaska Island Air (Petersburg)	6D	Petersburg-Kake, Baranof, Duncan Canal, Port Alexander, etc.	Grumman Goose DHC-2 Beaver Cessna types	Founded by Lon Marifern as _Lon's Flying Service_. Sold to Dane Roundtree in 1968.	
1967	Peninsula Airways (King Salmon)	KS	King Salmon-Egegik-Ugashik-Pilot Point; K.S.-South Naknek-Levelock. Expanded to Anchorage and Valdez, Bethel, Homer, Dillingham	Cessna and Piper types Piper Navajo Grumman Goose DHC-6 Twin Otter Convair 580 BN-2 Islander	Founded in 1956 as a charter company by Orin Seybert. Began contract work with _Reeve Aleutian Airways_ in 1967.	
24 Oct. 1968	North-Air (Anchorage)	NO OE	Anchorage-Kenai-Soldotna	Beech Volpar DHC-6 Twin Otter		1971
1970	Wings of Alaska (Juneau)	SE	Juneau-Haines, Skagway, Hoonah, Gustavus, Kake, Petersburg, Angoon, Tenakee	Beech 18 Cessna 206 Grumman Goose DHC-2 Beaver	Founded as _Southeast Skyways_ in 1968 by Dean Williams and Billy Bernhardt. Name changed to _Air America_, June 1982, on purchase by Jim Shanks and Jim Lindsey, then changed again to Wings of Alaska on 1 November 1982 when airline bought by Bob Jacobsen, Mike Fenster and Drew Haag.	

AREA 1 (ALASKA) Continued

First Sched. Service Date	Airline and Base	Code	Initial or Typical Route Network	Aircraft Used	Remarks	Date of last service
1970	Southeast Alaska Airlines (Ketchikan)	DE	Ketchikan-Juneau-Petersburg-Wrangell; Klawok, Craig, Hydaburg	Cessna 185 DCH-2 Beaver Grumman Goose	Founded by Jim Webber as Webber Airlines, and merged with Flair Air in 1979 to form Southeast Alaska under Paul Breed. Purchased by Tyee Airlines.	31 Dec. 1982
1971	Alaska Aeronautical Industries (AAI) (Anchorage)	YA YC	Anchorage-Kenai, later to Homer, Valdez, Kodiak, McKinley National Park, etc.	DHC-2 Beaver Cessna types Beech 18 DHC-6 Twin Otter Bandeirante	Cooperative agreement with Western Airlines, Oct. 1983.	22 Apr. 1986
May 1972	Channel Flying Service (Juneau)	IH	Juneau-Angoon/ Pelican/Elfin/Kake/ Haines	Cessna types Grumman Goose DHC-2 Beaver	Founded by Ken Loken as a charter airline in 1964. Operated partly under contract with Alaska Airlines.	23 May 1989
1973	Tyee Airlines (Ketchikan)	KN OF	Ketchikan-Klawock-Craig-Hydaburg, Annette Island; Nanaimo, Vancouver, Metlakatla, Thorne Bay	Cessna 185F DHC-2 Beaver Grumman Goose DHC-3 Otter BN-2 Islander	Founded in 1971 as Coast Air by Stan Hewitt, Art Hack, Terry Wills, succeeding Simpson Air. Sold in 1975 and changed name under Kirk Thomas. Purchased Southeast Alaska Airlines 31 Dec. 1982. Merged with Temsco Helicopters to form Temsco Airlines, May 1986.	25 Jan. 1985
1973	Foster Aviation (Nome)		Nome-Little Diomede Island	Beech 18 Cessna 185 Cessna 207 Cherokee Six	Founded as F.B.O. in 1947 by Neal Foster. Operated seasonal service during winter months to ice runway at Little Diomede, under contract to Ryan Air.	1984
1974	40-Mile Air (Tanacross and Tok)	6M	Tok-Tetlen/Chicken/ Fairbanks, Boundary, and several other villages.	Piper types Helio Courier Cessna types G-21A Goose DHC-3 Otter	Founded by Charles Warbelows. Sold in Sept. 1990 to Warbelows Air Ventures.	1990
1974	Polar Airlines (Anchorage)	PE	Anchorage-Valdez-Gulkana-Big Delta-Fairbanks, Tok Junction Tanacross, Northway	Aero Commander Fairchild PC-6 Piper Navajo Cessna types Beech 18	Lost F.A.A. certificate.	25 Aug. 1980
1975	Coast Air (Ketchikan)		Ketchikan-Craig-Klawock-Hydaburg	Grumman Goose DHC-3 Beaver Cessna types		1977
1975	Vanderpool Flying Service (Aniak)		Aniak-Crooked Creek-Nyac-Kalskag-Holy Cross		Affiliated with Wien Air Alaska.	1979
1976	L.A.B. Flying Service (Haines)	JF	Juneau-Haines-Skagway/Hoonah/ Gustavus/Excursion Inlet, Funter Bay	Piper types, including Cherokee Six, Piper Navajo Chieftain BN-2 Islander Aerostar 601P	Founded in 1956 by Latyon A. Bennett. Scheduled mail service, 1974. Subcontract with Alaska Airlines, 1 November 1984.	
1976	Eagle Air (Sitka)		Sitka-Angoon, Baranof, Hoonah, Tenakee, and other points	DHC-2 Beaver Cessna 185 Piper Navajo Helicopters		1980

AREA 1 (ALASKA) Continued

First Sched. Service Date	Airline and Base	Code	Initial or Typical Route Network	Aircraft Used	Remarks	Date of last service
1976	Alaska Central (Fairbanks)		Fairbanks-Lake Minchumina, Minto, Manley, Tanana, etc.	Nomad Piper types	Founded as Tenana Air Taxi. Operated as Wien Air Alaska.	1984
1977	Air North (Fairbanks)	XG	Fairbanks-Arctic Village/ Fort Yukon/Birch Creek/ Eagle/Galena, and other villages in central Alaska	Twin Pioneer Beech 18 BN-2 Islander BN-3 Trislander Douglas DC-3 Cessna types Piper Navajo FH-227C	Founded in 1967 as Yukon Air Service. Changed name in 1973. Lost FAA operating certificate 1979. Resumed service March 1981. Purchased by Liberty Air, Aug. 1984. Bankrupt shortly thereafter.	4 Sept. 1984
1977	Kenai Air Alaska (Kenai)	XE	Routes from Kenai to Anchorage, Seward, Soldotna, and other points	Grumman Widgeon Piper Navajo Beech King Air Metro	Founded in 1977 by Vernon L. Lofstedt as Kenai Air Service, changing name in 1978. Purchased Southcentral Air, Oct. 1983.	1987
1978	Coastal Aviation (Bethel)		Service to villages around Bethel	Cessna 207 Cessna 402 DHC-6 Twin Otter	Founded 1978 by Terry Yeager. Affiliated with Wien Air Alaska in early 1980s.	Early 1980s
1978	Gifford Aviation (Bethel)		Extensive services from Bethel to surrounding villages	DHC-6 Twin Otter Shorts Skyvan	Founded by Jack Gifford. Wien Air Alaska affiliate in early 1980s.	1985
1978	Kennedy Air Service (Valdez)	KY	Valdez-Anchorage	Cessna types Beech Baron Piper Navajo	Operations ceased when owner disappeared!	Nov. 1979
1978	Hermen's Air (St. Mary's)	2E	St. Mary's-Kotlik, Sheldon Point, Station Point. Developed extensive services from Bethel and St. Mary's to surrounding villages.	DHC-2 DHC-3 Cessna 185 Cessna 207 Cessna 402 Piper types	Founded by Stanley G. Hermens as air charter company in 1974. Wien Air Alaska affiliate. Acquired Galena Air Express 27 June 1989. Became a Markair Express affiliate in 1990.	
Dec. 1979	**Ryan Air Service (Unalakleet, Nome, Anchorage)**	XY 4R	Anchorage-Iliamna, McGrath, Galena, and extensive village services from Nome, Kotzebue, Unalakleet (including routes to Shishmaref, Tin City, Wales for Wien Air Alaska).	DHC-2 Beaver Beech 18 Cessna types Beech 99 Beech 1900 DCH-6 Twin Otter BN-2 Islander Other small types.	Founded in 1950 by Wilfred Ryan as Unalakleet Air Taxi. Changed name in 1979. Bought Munz Northern Airlines on 31 July 1983, and Executive Charter Service on 1 June 1985. Wien Air Alaska affiliate in late 1970s and early 1980s. Alaska Airlines affiliate, October 1983. FAA revoked operating certificate, following B-1900 crash at Unalakleet, 25 Jan. 1988. Ryan resigned and airline resumed limited operations in April 1988. Airline again grounded until 1 October 1988.	
1979	Bush Air (Bethel)		Bethel-Russian Mission, Marshall, Scammon Bay, Tununak, etc.		Affiliated with Wien Air Alaska in early 1980s.	1983
1979	Delta Air Service (Emmonak)		Sheldons Point- Emmonak-Kotlik		Affiliated with Wien Air Alaska in early 1980s.	
1 Jan. 1980	Valdez Airlines (Anchorage)	XX	Valdez-Anchorage, later to Homer, McGrath, Iliamna and other points in western Alaska	Piper Navajo Beech Baron Bandeirante	Operated as Wien Air Alaska affiliate Oct. 1982. Purchased by Liberty Air, Sept. 1984. Bankrupt shortly thereafter.	4 Sept. 1984

AREA 1 (ALASKA) Continued

First Sched. Service Date	Airline and Base	Code	Initial or Typical Route Network	Aircraft Used	Remarks	Date of last service
1980	International Air Taxi (Anchorage)		Anchorage-Skwentna		Affiliated with Wien Air Alaska in the early 1980s.	1983
April 1980	Ward Air (Juneau)		Local routes from Juneau	Beech 18 DHC-2 Beaver Cessna 185	Founded by Ken Ward as Juneau Flying Service.	
1 June 1980	Arctic Circle Air (Fairbanks, Fort Yukon, later to Bethel)	5F	Network of routes to villages in Fairbanks-Fort Yukon area; then around Bethel	Cessna types Bandeirante Piper Navajo DHC-6 Twin Otter	Affiliated to Wien Air Alaska, March 1981. Suspended services Sept. 1986, but resumed and moved to Bethel in 1990 after purchase by a new group.	
August 1980	Akland Helicopters (Talkeetna)		Anchorage-Willow, Talkeetna, Mt. McKinley, Clear, Fairbanks	Cessna 206 Piper Navajo helicopters	Took over routes from Great Northern, August, 1980.	1986
Nov. 1980	Seair (Anchorage)	KJ	Anchorage-Bethel, Aniak, Dillingham, Cordova, and networks around Bethel and Kodiak.	DHC-Beaver Cessna types DHC-6 Twin Otter Convair CV-580 Other small types	Founded as Seair Airmotive as a freight and mail carrier. Also operated as Seair Alaska Airlines. Temporarily suspended service Feb. 1981. Cooperative agreement with Western Airlines, 1983.	18 Jan. 1986
1980	Air Logistics (Bethel)		Routes from Bethel to nearby communities		Operated briefly as Wien Air Alaska affiliate.	1981
Jan. 1981	E.R.A. Aviation (Anchorage)	7H	Anchorage-Valdez, Kenai, Bethel, Homer, and other points in Anchorage area	DHC-6 Twin Otter Convair 580 DHC-7, DHC-8 Cessna 402 Metro	First organized in 1948 as Alaska's first commercial helicopter operation. Associated with Alaska Airlines 31 Dec. 1983 and became code-sharer in 1985. The first route, Anchorage-Valdez, originally operated as Jet Alaska.	
Feb. 1981	Southcentral Air (Kenai)	XE	Kenai-Anchorage, later extended to Homer, Soldotna, and Seward	Cessna types Piper Navajo Piper Cheyenne T-1040 BN-2 Islander	Founded as charter airline in 1967 by Harold and Irene Andersen. Operated briefly as a Western Express carrier, 1986. Purchased by Kenai Air in 1983, retaining name. Codesharing with United Airlines, June 1987-May 1989. Purchased by Kenai Air Alaska, Oct. 1983.	Oct. 1983
1981	Anchorage Airways (Anchorage)			Cessna 404, 441 BN-2 Islander	Merged into Air Logistics and continued to operate separately for a short time until 1983.	5 April 1982
1981	Cape Smythe Air Service (Barrow)	GC	Network of routes in northwestern Alaska; centered on Barrow and Kotzebue	Cessna types DHC-2 Beaver DHC-6 Twin Otter Shorts Skyvan Piper T1020	Founded by Thomas P. Brower Wien Air Alaska affiliate during early 1980s. "America's Northernmost Commuter."	
Oct. 1981	Leconte Airlines (Wrangell)		Wrangell-Yakutat, Petersburg, Sitka, Juneau, Ketchikan	Cessna 185 Cessna 207 Piper Navajo DHC-2 Beaver	Owned by Camps, Inc. Operated some routes for Alaska Airlines.	Nov. 1981
1 Feb. 1982	Air Pacific (Dutch Harbor)	5P	Anchorage-Dutch Harbor, later to Kodiak, Dillingham, King Salmon, Sitka, Seattle	Grumman Goose Cessna 441 Metro F-27, FH-227B BAe-146	Founded as Air Pac, Inc., changing name in Dec. 1982, and operated as an Alaska Airlines commuter of regional airline stature as well as local route status. Filed for Chapter 11 bankruptcy, 11 July 1986.	1986

AREA 1 (ALASKA) Continued

First Sched. Service Date	Airline and Base	Code	Initial or Typical Route Network	Aircraft Used	Remarks	Date of last service
May 1982	Friendship Air Alaska (Galena (and Fairbanks)	4H	Extensive services to many communities in west and central Alaska, especially from Galena, McGrath, Aniak, and Fairbanks	Turbo DC-3 Bandeirante DHC-3 Otter Cessna and Piper types	Founded in 1974 by Harold Esmailka as Harold's Air Service, a mail carrier from Galena. Bought Vanderpool Air Taxi in 1979, and Alaska Central Air, a freight carrier, in 1981. Renamed in Oct. 1986. Wien Air Alaska affiliate in early 1980s. Code-sharer with Frontier Flying Service in 1988.	March 1989
1982	Alyeska Air Service (Anchorage)		Local routes from Anchorage	Piper Cessna	Founded by Ken Triplett. Grounded by F.A.A.	7 July 1989
July 1982	Larry's Flying Service (Fairbanks)	7K	Fairbanks-Tanana/Ruby Galena/Allakaket/ Anaktuvuk Pass and other points	Cessna and Piper types BN-2 Islander Beech 95	Founded by Lawrence A. Chenaille.	
15 Nov. 1982	Bering Air (Nome)	8E	Nome-St. Michael-Unalakleet/Wales, Gambell and other small villages around Nome and Kotzebue, and to Stebbins and Point Hope. Anadyr, Lavren-tiya, Egvikinot, Provi-denya (U.S.S.R.)	Beech 18 Piper Seneca Piper Navajo Cessna 206 DHC-2 Beaver DHC-3 Otter Piper T-1020	Founded as a charter airline in 1979 by Jim Rowe. Operated as Alaska Airlines affiliate from 13 July 1983, code-sharing from1985. Began charter service to USSR points on 12 July 1989.	
1982	Yute Air Alaska (Bethel)	4Y	Network of routes to villages around Bethel	Piper types Cessna types DHC-2 Beaver DHC-3 Otter Grumman Goose Aermacchi AL-60 Evangel 4500 BN-2 Islander	Founded by Philip L. Bingman. Grounded by F.A.A. 27 Sept. 1988 to 12 February 1990	
April 1983	Inter-Valley Airlines (Chugiak)		Anchorage-Whittier, Birchwood, Settler's Bay, and other small villages			
July 1983	North Pacific Airlines (Anchorage)	4N	Anchorage-Soldotna/ Tatalina/Nikolai and McGrath	Beech types, including Queen Air	Founded by Roy Musgrove.	Sept. 1985
Nov. 1983	Ellis Air Taxi (Glennallen)	8L	Gulkana-McCarthy-May Creek-Chisana-Gulkana	Cessna types		Oct. 1986
Nov. 1983	Talarik Creek Air Service (Iliamna)	8T	Iliamna-Nondalton-Anchorage; Iliamna-Kakhonak, Pedro Bay, Port Alsworth and other points	Piper Navajo Piper Saratoga		Aug. 1986
Oct. 1983	Audi Air (Fairbanks)	7E	Fairbanks-Ruby-Galena-Koyukak-Nalato-Kaltag; Fairbanks-Fort Yukon and other points.	Piper and Cessna types	Founded by Walt Audi.	Sept. 1988

AREA 1 (ALASKA) Continued

First Sched. Service Date	Airline and Base	Code	Initial or Typical Route Network	Aircraft Used	Remarks	Date of last service
Nov. 1983	Executive Charter Service (Bethel)	9E	Extensive network of routes to villages around Bethel	Cessna 185 Cessna 206 Cessna 207	Purchased by Ryan Air.	31 May 1985
Dec. 1983	Frontier Flying Service (Fairbanks)	2F	Fairbanks-Bettles-Wiseman-Chandalar-Allakaket, Anaktuvik Pass	Cessna 207 Piper types Douglas DC-3 Grumman Widgeon	Founded by John Hajdukovich. Affiliated with Wien Air Alaska in the early 1980s.	
March 1984	Bellair (Sitka)	5B	Sitka-Angoon-Kake, and ten other villages	Cessna 185 DHC-2 Beaver	Founded by Ken Bellows in 1981.	
April 1984	Tanana Air Service (Tanana)	4E	Fairbanks-Minto-Rampart-Manley Hot Springs-Tanana, etc.	Piper Cherokee Six		
July 1984	Baker Aviation (Kotzebue)	8B	Routes to villages near Kotzebue	Cessna 207, 402 DHC-6 Twin Otter	Founded by Marge Baker. Affiliated with Wien Air Alaska in the early 1980s.	1985
Aug. 1984	Westflight Aviation (Ketchikan)	7W	Ketchikan-Klawock/Craig/Hydaburg/Long Island/Coffman Cove, and other points	DHC-2 Beaver DHC-3 Otter DHC-6 Twin Otter Cessna 206 Grumman Goose	Acquired by Temsco Airlines in 1986.	30 Sept. 1986
Aug. 1984	Liberty Air (Fairbanks)	XG XX	(See routes of Air North and Valdez)	(See fleets of Air North and Valdez)	Formed by purchase of Air North (1977) and Valdez Airlines (1980) by founder of Sunair (Texas) and two former executives of Markair; but quickly went bankrupt.	1984
Nov. 1984	Wilbur's Inc. (Anchorage)	8F	Anchorage-Cordova, later to McGrath, Valdez, Aniak, and other points	Cessna types Piper Seneca Beech 99	Founded as F.B.O. by Joe Wilbur as Wilbur's Flight Operations in 1961, (sometimes operating on scheduled basis, even then).	
Nov. 1984	Flirite (Kodiak)	6F	Kodiak-Old Harbor	Piper Saratoga Cessna 206	Founded by Marilyn L. Buker.	Dec. 1985
1985	Kenmore Air Harbor	5K				1988
2 Jan. 1985	Temsco Airlines (Ketchikan)	KN	Ketchikan-Prince Rupert, Craig, Klawock, Hydaburg, Metlakatla, Thorne Bay, and other points.	DHC-2 Beaver DHC-3 Otter Cessna 185	Formed by Ken Eichner by the merger of a helicopter airline (of the same name) and Tyee Airlines. Acquired Westflight Aviation on 1 Oct. 1986. Became Alaska Airlines Commuter, Dec. 1986.	
Jan. 1985	Armstrong Air Service (Dillingham)	XG	Dillingham-Ekwok/New Stayahok and other points	Cessna and Piper types DHC-2 Beaver	Grounded by F.A.A. 13 Aug. 1988, after accidents. Resumed for a few months only.	Jan. 1989
Jan. 1985	Bay Air (Naknek)	9B	King Salmon-South Naknek-Egegik-Levelock and other points	Piper and Cessna types	Founded by Monte R. Handy.	Sept. 1986
April 1985	Harbor Air Service (Seward)	8H	Seward-Anchorage	Piper and Cessna types DHC-2 Beaver	Founded by Linda K. Pfleger.	

AREA 1 (ALASKA) Continued

First Sched. Service Date	Airline and Base	Code	Initial or Typical Route Network	Aircraft Used	Remarks	Date of last service
July 1985	Iliamna Air Taxi (Iliamna)	LS	Iliamna-Nondalton-Port Alsworth, Kakhonak, and other points	Cessna types Piper DHC-2 Beech Bonanza	Founded by Timothy J. LaPorte.	
1985	Chisum Flying Service of Alaska (Cordova)	6K	Network to small villages around Cordova	Cessna types DHC-2 Beaver	Operated for a few months only.	1985
March 1986	Polar Alaska Enterprises (Fairbanks)	8F	Fairbanks-Anaktuvuk Pass, Nuiqsut-Prudhoe Bay; P.B. - Barter Island	Cessna and Beech types F-27B	Founded by George E. Matz. Changed name to Polar International Airlines, Dec. 1986.	1989
May 1986	Camai Air (Bethel)	3C	Bethel-Scammon Bay-Hooper Bay-Chevak, and other points	Cessna and Piper types	Founded by Joe Angaiak.	
May 1986	King's Flying Service (Naknek)	9K	King Salmon-South Naknek-Egegik-Pilot Point, Levelock, Igiugig	Piper types DHC-2 Beaver		Aug. 1988
Oct. 1986	Galena Air Service (Galena)	AK	Routes around Galena	Cessna 207 Piper Navajo Beech Baron	Founded by Norman Yaeger. Acquired by Hermens Air (see 1978) 27 June 1989.	
Nov. 1986	Haines Airways (Haines)	7A	Juneau-Haines Skagway, Hoonah	Piper Cherokee Six and other Piper and Cessna types	Founded by Reg Radcliff.	
1986	Barrow Air (Barrow)	6Q	Barrow-Wainwright/ Point Lay/Atqusuk	Cessna types	Founded by Jim Pederson.	
1986	Wright Air Service (Fairbanks)	8V	Fairbanks-Anaktuvuk Pass, Arctic Village, and other points	Piper Navajo Cessna types DHC-3 Otter Aero Commander Widgeon		
June 1987	Olson Air Service (Nome)	4B	Nome-White Mountain-Golovin-Elim, Little Diomede Island, and other points	Cessna types	Founded by David K. Olson.	
Sept. 1987	Ketchikan Air Service (Ketchikan)	GS	Ketchikan-Klawock-Craig; Ketchikan-Metlakatla, etc.	Cessna types DHC-3 Otter DHC-2 Beaver	Founded in 1970 by Don Ross, Mike Salazar, Carl Jackson and Earl Lahmeyer.	
Oct. 1987	Taquan Air Service (Metlakatla)	9Q	Ketchikan-Smith Cove-Kasaan-Hollis-Polk Inlet, and other points	Cessna 185 Cessna 206 DHC-2 Beaver		
Nov. 1987	Raven Air (Anchorage)	4R	Anchorage-Seldovia-Port Graham	Cessna types		
Early 1988	Wrangell Air Service (Wrangell)	4W	Wrangell-Petersburg/ Ketchikan, Kake	Cessna types BN-2A	Founded by Dan Baldwin.	Oct. 1990
Mar. 1988	Skagway Air Service (Skagway)	5U	Skagway-Juneau	Piper types BN-2 Islander	Founded by Ben Lingle in 1963 as an air taxi service.	
Mar. 1988	Tatonduk Air Service (Fairbanks)	2F	Fairbanks-Eagle	Piper types	Code-sharer with Frontier Flying Service.	
Mar. 1988	Seagull Air (Bethel)	5N	Bethel-Kwigillingok-Kongiganak-Tuntatuliak, and other points	Piper and Cessna types	Founded by J. Timothy Cracie. Suspended by F.A.A. order after several accidents.	9 Aug. 1989

AREA 1 (ALASKA) Continued

First Sched. Service Date	Airline and Base	Code	Initial or Typical Route Network	Aircraft Used	Remarks	Date of last service
1989	Inlet Airlines (Homer)	4G	Homer-Seldovia-Port Graham-English Bay and other points	Cessna types	Formed as Cook Inlet Aviation by Dennis Rothgeb.	1990
1990	Koyukon Air (Fairbanks)	2Y		Piper types	Took over operating certificate of Brian Thompson Air Service.	

Area 2

Hawaii

Because of the isolation of the fiftieth state of the union, until 1959 a territory, the airlines of Hawaii have always been enterprising and progressive, but they have been limited in their opportunities for route expansion. The pioneering Inter-Island Airways, founded as long ago as 1929, can trace its history in a continuous record of service until the present day. It operated mostly under its new name, Hawaiian Airlines, as a local territorial monopoly until 1946, when it had to compete with a nonscheduled rival. Trans-Pacific Airlines took three years to achieve scheduled status and ten years later, in 1959, it also changed its name, to Aloha Airlines, and it too has operated ever since.

Because of the geography of Hawaii, stretching in a line of islands across four hundred miles of the Pacific Ocean, with the maximum distance between any two islands no more than seventy-five miles, any airline in Hawaii has always been, by definition, short haul. Furthermore, the choice of routes and destinations is strictly limited—from Honolulu, on Oahu, to four other islands—with no chance of further expansion, short of the 2,400-mile "hop" to San Francisco. Until World War II, the only link to the forty-eight states was Pan American's flying boat service, which was expensive and infrequent. Even before the airlines, people traveled in considerable numbers between the islands by ferryboat, some even coming close to commuting regularly, on at least a weekly basis if not daily. As the population of the islands grew (it has tripled since Inter-Island first started), and some of the hitherto rural plantation communities, spread throughout almost the whole territory outside Honolulu, became urban settlements and communities, the need for interisland travel increased considerably.

This expanding local market was certainly helpful to Hawaiian Airlines and Aloha Airlines after World War II. Soon the needs of these local communities were supplemented by the growth of the tourist industry, stimulated by expanded airline service from the U.S. mainland and the discovery that vacations in Hawaii did not need to be spent entirely in Honolulu, the capital. The outer islands—Molokai, Maui, Kauai, and Hawaii (the "Big Island")—gradually became additional tourist destinations in their own right, as Honolulu itself came to suffer from the same problems of overcrowding as all big cities. Molokai and Maui have in recent years come to be regarded almost as outer suburbs of Honolulu. Such was the convenience offered by the many air services that access to the closer islands became almost as easy as that to the outer townships on Oahu, and they were considered as lying within commuting distance.

Strangely, the service offered by the fully certificated Hawaiian carriers does not differ very much, in terms of speed and convenience, from that available from the smaller companies (variously described as air taxis, commuters, or air tour operators) that have emerged during the past quarter century.

The distances are so short that travel times for piston-engined, turbo-prop-engined, or jet aircraft do not vary by more than a few minutes. The longest route, from Honolulu to Hilo, is only two hundred miles. With Hawaiian and Aloha providing frequent service to the main points and competing healthily to provide adequate service, the small airlines have had to scramble to find gaps between schedules, offer cheaper fares, and devise other ingenious ways of combining the airline ticket with other services, such as weekend hotel accommodations. Otherwise there has never been a viable basis for operations additional to those of the incumbent carriers.

Several of the companies combined air tours and regularly scheduled operations in such a way that they were almost indistinguishable; and the fine distinction between the categories would often have eluded the CAB, had it been too closely involved. For its part, the FAA, which was mainly responsible for control, under Part 135 of its regulations, tended to take a tolerant view, and sensibly placed more emphasis on safety and navigational factors.

Bearing in mind the confined territory in which the airlines operate, and the apparent limitations of the market, the number of individual small operators that have lived and died has been quite high during the thirty years since Resort Airways first entered the arena in 1960. Few survived for very long. One notable exception was Hawaiian Air Tour Service, which began service in 1965; however, it has always been more of an individual or group tour operator than a commuter airline. Another was Royal Hawaiian Air Service, which lasted for two decades and closed down only when the airport it served, Kaanapali, near Kona, on the Big Island, was closed down. Kaanapali could accept its Cessnas and Twin Otters but could not take the jets of the large airlines, so that Royal Hawaiian lost its main source of traffic through circumstances beyond its control.

One other airline is worthy of mention. Mid Pacific Air was founded early in 1981, well after restrictions on aircraft size had been liberalized by the Airline Deregulation Act of 1978, and it opened service quite aggressively with sixty-seat Nihon YS-11 turboprops. These were much bigger than the small twin-engined types normally chosen by the commuter airlines, so that Mid Pacific aimed to compete with, rather than to supplement, Hawaiian and Aloha. Its main weapon was low fares, and for a few years they were an attractive enough incentive to draw a substantial number of passengers away from the other airlines, big and small. During the mid-1980s, Mid Pacific ranked as the largest of all the commuter airlines—though in practical terms, it might easily have qualified as the smallest of the national airlines. It seemed to fall halfway between the two classes of carrier. In any event, it was unable to sustain its low-fare competition for very long and ceased operations in January 1988.

There will always be specialized air services radiating east and west from the international Honolulu hub, which is the busy center of a strictly confined spoke system of routes. But these will be few in number and limited in scope. Unlike the markets served by commuter airlines operating in the contiguous states, Hawaii offers no room for expansion, no room for experiments in serving communities that might otherwise be deprived of air service. All the inhabited islands (except little Lanai) have good airports that are already served by the two major intraisland carriers.

During the 1970s, an attempt was made to provide an interisland hydrofoil service, but this failed because the two-airline air service was too good. A resort community such as Princeville, on Kauai, will wish to continue to operate its own air service (or have one operated on its behalf), rather like a hotel limousine connection with the airport. Otherwise new opportunities for a viable commuter airline in the orthodox manner are slim, and the market is likely to frustrate the small airline entrepreneur in the future just as it has in the past.

AREA 2 (HAWAII)

First Sched. Service Date	Airline and Base	Code	Initial or Typical Route Network	Aircraft Used	Remarks	Date of last service
May 1960	Resort Airways (Honolulu)		(Most of the traffic was tour groups)	Aero Commander	Merged with Hawaiian Air Tour Service (HATS) in 1967.	1967
1964	Andrew Flying Service (Honolulu)		(Mainly tours)	D.H. 104 Dove Cessna	Absorbed by Sky Tours., Inc., 1966.	1966
6 April 1965	Pacific Flight Service (Honolulu)			Beech 18 Volpar Beech		1967
8 April 1965	Hawaiian Air Tour Service (HATS) (Honolulu)		Tour services throughout Hawaiian Islands	D.H. 104 Dove D.H. 114 Heron	Absorbed Resorts Airways 1967.	
April 1965	Royal Hawaiian Airways (Honolulu)	ZH	Kona Airport - Kona Village; then extensive network throughout Hawaii	Cessna 310 Cessna 402 DHC-6 Twin Otter	Founded by Woodson Woods and Johnny Peacock as Royal Hawaiian Air Service. Ceased four months after its main traffic source, Kaanapali Airport, closed down.	22 May 1986
28 Oct 1965	Valley Isle Aviation (Kahului)			Beech B-55		1967
3 Dec 1965	Sky Tours Hawaii (Honolulu)		(Mainly tour services east of Honolulu)	D.H. 104 Dove Beech 18	Absorbed Andrew Flying Service and Pan Pacific Aero in 1966. Had agreement with United Air Lines in 1967. Scheduled service as Trans-Isle Airlines in 1969.	1971
16 Aug 1967	Air Molokai (Honolulu)	3R	Molokai - Honolulu; later to Lanai and Kahului (Maui)	Piper Aztec Cessna 402 DC-3	Founded by Hank Younge. Taken over by Air Hawaii in 1978, but resumed independent operations in 1980. Suspended operations for a short period, 1989-1990.	
11 Oct 1967	Air Hawaii (Honolulu)	HI	Honolulu - Molokai, Lanai, Kaanapali (Kona)	DHC-6 Twin Otter	Also called Jet-Air Hawaii; no connection with 1977 airline of the same name.	1970
1969	Trans-Isle Air (Honolulu)			Beech 18	Operated by Sky Tours Hawaii (see above).	1971
12 June 1969	Molokai Aviation (Molokai)			Piper Aztec	Founded by Timmy Cooke.	1971
17 Oct 1969	Hawaii Pacific Airline (Honolulu)	WV	Honolulu - Molokai (Kalaupapa)	Beech 18	Founded by Herman Brandt as Alii Air Hawaii, renamed 1 Jan 1975. Also operated as Brandt Air in 1970.	1979
5 March 1971	Panorama Air (Honolulu)	PV 9P	Honolulu - Molokai	Beech 18 Beech 99	Mainly a tour operator.	Jan. 1972
1971	Island Air (Honolulu)			BN-2 Islander		24 Jan 1972
1973	Kuilima Air Service (Honolulu)	XL	Honolulu - Kuilima Air Park	Cessna types	Founded by Robert Fraker.	1973
16 April 1975	Island Pacific Air (Honolulu)	HP	Honolulu to all main islands of Hawaii	Cessna 402	Founded by Mike Hartley; purchased by Air Hawaii (see below in 1977).	Late 1977
1 Oct 1975	Oahu and Kauai Airlines (Okair) (Honolulu)	YQ	Honolulu - Lihue/ Princeville	Cessna 402	Founded by Robert Fraker; merged into Air Hawaii in 1980.	Jan 1980

AREA 2 (HAWAII) Continued

First Sched. Service Date	Airline and Base	Code	Initial or Typical Route Network	Aircraft Used	Remarks	Date of last service
Late 1975	The Maui Commuter, (Kahului)	GE	Kahului - Honolulu, Molokai, Lanai	Piper Seneca Piper Navajo	Founded by Jack Holzman and Robert Frost as <u>Ananda Air</u>.	1978
April 1977	Air Hawaii (Honolulu)	XK	Hilo - Kona, then throughout the Islands	Beech 18 Cessna 207 Cessna 402 Cessna 404	Founded by Bruce McKenzie (no connection with the 1967 airline of same name). Merged with <u>Island Pacific Air,</u> 1978; acquired <u>Oahu and Kauai Airlines</u> Jan. 1980.	1983
1977	Polynesian Airways (Honolulu)		Molokai (Kalaupapa) - Honolulu	Beech Twin Bonanza Beech 18	Founded by Robert Wittinghill.	
27 Nov. 1979	Paradise Air (Honolulu)		Honolulu - Molokai	Piper Aztec Piper Navajo	Founded by Morris Sakuda as a low-fare airline.	10 Dec. 1983
1980	Tropic Air (Honolulu)	3R DV	Honolulu - Molokai	Cessna types DC-3	Associated with <u>Air Molokai</u> during early 1980s.	Oct. 1989
9 Sept. 1980	Princeville Airways (Honolulu)	WP	Honolulu - Lihue, Princeville; later to Kamuela, Molokai, and Maui	DHC-6 Twin Otter	Owned by the Princeville Development Corp. at Lihue, Kauai. At first, Air Hawaii provided flight and ground crews. Renamed <u>Aloha Islandair</u> in 1989 after having become Aloha feeder on 1 April 1987.	
Early 1981	**Mid Pacific Air (Honolulu)**	HO	Honolulu to all main points in Hawaii	Nihon YS-11 (Fokker F-28)	Founded as a low-fare competitor to Aloha and Hawaiian Airlines. Classified as a commuter airline and during mid-1980s was the top-ranking company in that category.	Jan. 1988
1981	Reeves Air (Honolulu)	RQ	Honolulu - Molokai/ Lanai/West Maui	Cessna 402	Founded by the brothers Doug and Bill Reeves. Shut down by F.A.A.	May 1987
1 Feb. 1985	Maui Airlines (Honolulu)	WW 8M	Honolulu-Kahului	Piper Navajo DHC-6 Twin Otter		Late 1987
Nov. 1985	Big Island Air (Kona)	2L	Kona - Hilo; Kona - West Maui	Cessna 402	Founded by Lew and Shay Mims. Reverted to charter operations.	1 July 1989

Area 3

Northwest

The early commuter airlines in the Northwest were centered mainly around Puget Sound. The small communities across the sound, relatively isolated from Seattle, the local metropolis, together with the San Juan Islands farther north, have provided a natural venue for the operation of small aircraft into small landing fields. This market created a demand for regular service by small airlines, pioneered by San Juan Airlines as early as 1946; almost unbroken service has been provided by many followers ever since.

Later on, other small airlines were able to meet local needs in the Spokane, Portland, and Boise areas, sometimes providing service to winter vacation resorts in the Rocky Mountains, for example to Sun Valley.

The decline of small-city services by the local service airlines from the 1960s onward—a process that began even before the 1978 airline deregulation that accelerated their effective extinction—provided new opportunities to replace discarded air routes, especially those of Republic Airlines (formerly Hughes AirWest, and originally West Coast Airlines and its predecessor companies). This trend gave rise to a different kind of commuter airline, one that effectively replaced the local service operations. Cascade and Horizon were typical of this new breed, and the latter even outgrew its commuter status to become a substantial regional airline, with a large network embracing the whole of the northwestern United States. Today it even offers a no-reservations shuttle service between Seattle and Spokane, and it has become part of the extensive Alaska Airlines system.

In spite of this transformation by an exceptional company, a few hardy survivors among the commuter airlines, as they were originally conceived, still exist, as shown in the tabulation.

AREA 3 (NORTHWEST)

First Sched. Service Date	Airline and Base	Code	Initial or Typical Route Network	Aircraft Used	Remarks	Date of last service
29 March 1947	**Island Sky Ferries (Orcas Island, then Friday Harbor, after 1 June 1953)**		Bellingham - Friday Harbor, via islands in the San Juan group, with later extension to Seattle (1956). Mail routes operated as Island Mail (see below)	Stinson, Cessna Piper types Lockheed L-10	Founded by Robert F. Schoen as Orcas Air Service. Incorp. early 1948 as Island Sky Ferries, Inc. Sold to Dr. Wallace Howarth, Spring, 1950, changing name to Island Air, then to Harold and Virginia Ferris, who changed name back to Island Sky Ferries. Purchased by Roy Franklin on 1 June 1953. Merged with Bremerton Air Taxi, Angeles Flying Service, Bellingham - Seattle Airways, Whidbey Flying Service, and Skyline Air Service on 1 June 1969 to form Puget Sound Airlines.	1 June 1969
2 Feb 1964	Bremerton Air Taxi) Bremerton, Wash.)	KY	Bremerton-Seattle	Piper types Beech 18	Founded by Bob Crowther (Crowther Flying Center). Became part of Puget Sound Airlines.	1 June 1969
8 Sept. 1964	Angeles Flying Service (Port Angeles, Wash.)	XF	Port Angeles-Seattle	Beech 18, Piper Apache/ Aztec	Founded by Bill Fairchild. Became part of Puget Sound Airlines.	1 June 1969
24 Sept. 1964	Bellingham-Seattle Airways (Bellingham, Wash.)	BX BY	Bellingham-Seattle	Beech 18	Founded by Dick Mallberg. Became part of Puget Sound Airlines.	1 June 1969
17 Dec. 1964	Whidbey Flying Serv.(Oak Harbor, Wash.)	WY	Oak Harbor-Seattle	Piper Cherokee Six	Founded by Wes Lupien. Became part of Puget Sound Airlines.	1 June 1969
1 July 1966	Island Mail, Inc. (Friday Harbor, Wash.)		Mail routes in Puget Sound area, mainly the San Juan Islands	Cessna single-engined types Stinson Reliant	Started at Anacortes, Wash., as the mail contract operation of Island Sky Ferries and Skyline Air Service. Moved to Friday Harbor in 1973.	1979
Early 1965	Sun Valley Airlines (Boise, Idaho)	JN VL	Gooding-Hailey (Sun Valley) Twin Falls-Salt Lake City	Beech Queen Air Beech 18 DHC-6 Twin Otter	Began operations from Gooding, Idaho. Joined with Key (Salt Lake City, 1964) to operate as Sun Valley Key during early 1970s.	Early 1970s
1966	Western Aircraft (Gooding, Idaho)		Local services from Gooding	Beech 18		1967
15 Sept. 1966	Eugene Aviation Serv. (Eugene, Oregon)		Eugene-Roseburg	Piper Aztec	Operated on behalf of West Coast Airlines for one year.	Aug. 1967
16 Feb 1967	Skyline Air Service (Anacortes, Wash.)		Seattle-Everett Anacortes	Cessna types	Founded by Tom Wilson. Became part of Puget Sound Airlines.	28 June 1967
1 April 1967	Commute Air (Spokane, Wash.)	ZL	Spokane-Kalispell; Spokane-Moses Lake-Wenatchee-Seattle (Boeing Field)-Everett; Spokane-Sandpoint-Libby-Kalispell-Polson-Missoula-Helena	Cessna 402 Gruman G-44	Founded by Chester C. Johnson "the Northwest's Fastest Growing Air Carrier."	1968

AREA 3 (NORTHWEST) Continued

First Sched. Service Date	Airline and Base	Code	Initial or Typical Route Network	Aircraft Used	Remarks	Date of last service
1 June 1969	**Puget Sound Airlines (Oak Harbor, Wash.)**	WY	Services throughout the Puget Sound area	Beech 18 Piper types Cessna 206 Stinson Reliant Piper Cherokee Six	Created by the merger of six pioneer airlines in the Puget Sound area: Island Sky Ferries, Angeles Flying Service, Bellingham-Seattle Airways, Whidbey Flying Service, Skyline Air Service. Wes Lupien of Whidbey Flying Service, took over leadership of the group.	1 Oct 1970
13 Dec. 1967	Boise Air Service (Boise, Idaho)		Local services from Boise	Aero Commander	Operated by Boise Aviation.	1968
1969	Janss Airways (Boise, Idaho)	JN	Salt Lake City/Boise-Sun Valley			
1969	Northwest Commuter (Everett, Wash.)	WP	Everett-Seattle	Piper Aztec		1969
1969	Trans Magic Airlines (Twin Falls, and Jerome, Idaho)	UE	Boise-Mountain Home AFB-Twin Falls-Sun Valley-Burley-Pocatello-Idaho Falls; Twin Falls-Jackpot-Salt Lake City	Piper Navajo D.H. Heron		1973
1970	**Cascade Airways (Spokane)**	HU CZ	Spokane-Moses Lake-Wenatchee-Seattle; Spokane-Yakima-Olympia; Spokane-Walla Walla-Portland; Spokane-Lewiston-Boise; and inter-connecting routes throughout state of Washington	Beech 99 Bandeirante Swearingen Metro BAe 748 Beech 1900 BAC One-Eleven	Founded by Mark Chestnutt. Expanded rapidly and competed strongly with Horizon. Filed for Chapter 11 bankruptcy, August 1985.	7 March 1986
1 Oct. 1970	**San Juan Airlines (Friday Harbor; then Port Angeles from 1 May 1979)**	YS JX	Routes throughout San Juan Islands, and to Seattle and other mainland points, incl. Vancouver and Victoria, B.C., and Portland, Oregon	Stinson Reliant Cessna types BN-2 Islander Piper Aztec Bandeirante, Beech 99	Founded by Roy Franklin when Puget Sound Airlines ceased operations. Sold to Jim Sherrell, 1 May, 1979.	May 1989
1970	Cross Sound Commuter (Port Orchard, Wash.)	DW	Seattle-Bremerton/ Olympia/Tacoma	BN-2 Islander		1974
1970	West Pacific Airlines(Seattle)	WV	Seattle-Yakima-Pasco-Spokane; Seattle-Bremerton	Beech 99		1971
1971	Air Washington (Seattle-Boeing Field)	WJ	Seattle-Yakima-Pasco	DHC-6 Twin Otter		1972
1971	Eagle Airlines (Port Angeles, Wash.)	GP	Port Angeles-Seattle	Aero Commander		1971
1971	Harbor Airlines (Oak Harbor, Wash.)	HC HG HQ	Seattle-Oak Harbor/ Bellingham/Mount Vernon; Later extension to Vancouver, B.C. (terminated)	BN-2 Islander Bandeirante Piper Navajo Chieftain	Founded by Wes Lupien and Jerry Patterson as Oak Harbor Airlines, changing name in 1974.	
1972	Gross Aviation (Tacoma,Wash.)	HF	Seattle-Tacoma Int. Apt-Tacoma-Olympia		Associated with Cross Sound Airlines.	1973

AREA 3 (NORTHWEST) Continued

First Sched. Service Date	Airline and Base	Code	Initial or Typical Route Network	Aircraft Used	Remarks	Date of last service
1 Feb 1973	Columbia Pacific Airlines (Richland, Washington)	EV	Richland-Seattle-Bremerton; Richland-Walla Walla- Spokane; Richland-Portland	Piper Navajo Chieftain Beech 99	Founded as Execuair, Inc.	Late 1978
1973	Pacific Northern Airlines (Portland)	CG	Portland-Seattle(Boeing Field); Portland-Spokane-Yakima-Medford-Portland	DC-3		1973
1973	Pearson Aircraft (Port Angeles, Wash.)	YE	Port Angeles-Seattle-Olympia	Cessna 207 Cessna 402	Founded by Earl Pearson; purchased by San Juan Airlines after Jim Sherrell took over.	Oct. 1981
1974	Air Idaho (Twin Falls, Idaho)	TJ	Sun Valley-Twin Falls-Salt Lake City	D.H. 114 Heron		1975
1975	Valley Commuter (Eugene, Oregon)	UV	Eugene-Portland	Piper Navajo	Operating division of Eugene Flight Center.	1976
7 April 1975	Sun Basin Airlines (Moses Lake, Wash.)	UO	Seattle-Moses Lake-Spokane	Cessna 402		13 July 1978
Aug. 1976	Air Gemini (Tacoma, Wash.)	FD	Olympia-Tacoma-Sea-Tac Int. Apt; Hoquiam-Sea-Tac	Cessna 207	Also known as Gemini Airlines.	1978
1976	Columbia Airlines (La Grande, Oregon)	QT	La Grande-Baker-Portland-Salem-Redmond Medford; La Grande-Pasco; La Grande-Boise	Beech 99	Division of La Grande Air Service.	Early 1977
Aug 1978	Air Oregon (Portland)	JT	Portland-Seattle; Portland-Salem-Medford and points throughout Oregon. Also to Reno, Boise, Sacramento, and San Francisco	Swearingen Metroliner	Founded as Executive Flight Services, changing name in 1980. Purchased by Justin Colin (owner of Golden Gate Airlines, California) in June 1982. Later sold to Horizon Air.	June 1982
1 Dec. 1978	Gem State Airlines (Coeur d'Alene, Idaho)	GG	Coeur d'Alene-Boise-Pocatello; Coeur d'Alene-Pullman-Lewiston-Boise-Pocatello-Idaho Falls; Boise-Idaho Falls- Salt Lake City; Boise-Sun Valley; Twin Falls-Sun Valley	Swearingen Metroliner	Founded by Tom Soumas, Jr. and James H. Alexander. Operation moved to Monterey, California.	Dec. 1979
Feb. 1979	Mountain West Airlines (Boise, Idaho)	FX	Boise-Salt Lake City-Idaho Falls-Pocatello-Reno	Beech 99 Bandeirante		Early 1981
July 1979	Far West Airlines (Portland, Oregon)		Seattle-Portland; Seattle-North Bend, Portland	Piper Navajo Chieftain		
1979	Fort Vancouver Airlines (Vancouver, Wash.)		Vancouver-Seattle			Early 1980s
Early 1981	Air Olympia (Olympia, Wash.)	OW	Olympia-Yakima-Spokane	Piper Navajo Chieftain		Mid-1981
Spring 1981	Kenmore Air (Lake Washington, Seattle)	5K	Seattle-Big Bay, British Columbia, Seattle-Victoria; Friday Harbor-Roche Harbor; Rosario, Lopez; and to British Columbia	DHC-2 Beaver DHC-3 Otter (floatplanes) Turbo-Beavers	Founded by Robert Munro, as Kenmore Air Harbor. Began operations in 1946 as F.B.O. Purchased OtterAir, 1986.	

AREA 3 (NORTHWEST) Continued

First Sched. Service Date	Airline and Base	Code	Initial or Typical Route Network	Aircraft Used	Remarks	Date of last service
3 July 1981	Lake Union Air Service (Seattle, Wash.)	7L	Seattle (Lake Union)-Roche Harbor; then expansion to points in British Columbia, especially fishing centers, and to the San Juan Islands.	DHC-6 Twin Otter (floatplane) Cessna 206 (floatplane) DHC-2 Beavers	Founded by Hank Riverman as F.B.O. in 1946. Clyde Carlson bought airline on 12 May 1981. Sold to Bruce Leven 9 October 1987.	
1 Sept. 1981	**Horizon Air (Seattle)**	QX UA	Seattle-Yakima-Pasco; Seattle-Portland-Eugene Medford; Seattle-Pullman-Sun Valley; expansion throughout northwestern U.S.A.	Fairchild Metroliner Fairchild F-27 Fokker F-28	Funded by Milton G. Kuolt II as Horizon Air Industries, Inc. Acquired Air Oregon, in 1982. Acquired Transwestern Airlines, Dec. 1983; replaced services of Pacific Express. Affiliated to United Air Lines until late 1986, when it was purchased by Alaska Airlines and continued to operate as an autonomous division.	
1 Jan. 1984	Empire Airways (Coeur d'Alene, Id.)	EM	Coeur d'Alene-Lewiston-Boise; Coeur d'Alene-Seattle	Cessna 414 Swearingen Metro II Fokker F-27	Founded by Mel Stelde as F.B.O. in 1977. "Idaho's Airline".	
1984	Chinook Air (Everett, Wash.)	9C	Seattle-Everett-Mount Washington	Piper types		Mid-1985
Late 1984	Astor Air (Hadlock, Wash.)		Astoria-Portland	Cessna 402	Division of Ludlow Aviation.	Early-1985
Early 1985	Otter Air (Seattle, Wash.)	3Q	Seattle-Victoria; Seattle-Port Townsend	DHC-2 Beaver	Purchased by Kenmore Air.	Dec 1986
Mid-1986	Coastal Airways (Sequim, Wash.)	PN DV	Sequim-Seattle; expanded to several points in the San Juan Islands	Cessna 206	Founded by Jack Sallee. Shut down by F.A.A., August 1990.	June 1990
July 1987	North Pacific Airlines (N P A) (Pasco, Wash.)	NO	Seattle-Portland-Pasco Seattle-Yakima	Jetstream 31	Subsidary of Westair. Formed as United Express affiliated after Horizon purchased by Alaska Air.	
1 Aug. 1988	Chartair (Friday Harbor, Wash.)	5W	Seattle-San Juan Islands; Seattle-Bellingham, Anacortes	Various Cessna types (from 172 to 402). Piper Seneca	Founded by Chris and Jamie Marsden as Air San Juan, after demise of San Juan Airlines.	
April 1990	West Isle Air (Anacortes, Wash.)		Anacortes-San Juan Islands, Bellingham, Bayview	Cessa 172/182 Cherokee Six Cessna 206,210	After Puget Sound Airlines broke up in 1970, John Carabba and Margine Wilson rejuvenated Island Air as a charter operator. After passing to Katie and Gery Rovetto, the business was sold to Jim Burton, who started scheduled service as West Isle.	

Area 4

Pacific

California, and the adjoining states of Nevada and Arizona, have always provided challenging local airline markets. The chief stimulant has been to provide ready access to two of the country's largest metropolitan areas, centered on Los Angeles and the San Francisco Bay Area. As long ago as 1919 the first small airline plied between the Long Beach–Los Angeles harbor area and Catalina Island, and the route has continued to provide an incentive for postwar imitators in this natural market for short-haul air travel. Until the San Francisco Bay Bridge was completed in 1935, people also commuted across the bay by air. In Arizona, the attraction of the Grand Canyon led to the formation of Grand Canyon Airways, which provided a connection with TWA's transcontinental air routes. It was a distant ancestor of Scenic Airways, which still survives today, mainly by carrying people from Las Vegas and (still under the Grand Canyon name) from Phoenix to the south rim of the canyon.

Los Angeles and San Francisco are each surrounded by several medium-size and small cities that are far enough away from the urban centers and from the major airports to require good connecting air service. In the early years of air transport in the United States, during the 1930s, the trunk airlines met the need. They were largely replaced after World War II by the local service airlines which, in turn, concentrated on mainline intercity service, handing down the lesser markets to a host of commuter airlines.

The gambling resorts of Nevada have beckoned small airline entrepreneurs, as have other resort areas in Arizona. Additionally, the urban sprawls of both Los Angeles (about ninety miles long) and the Bay Area have created an intra-urban demand that the commercial helicopter airlines, once thought to be the answer to the problem, were unable to fill.

California in particular has witnessed both the founding and the failure of a multiplicity of commuter airlines. These have sometimes been operated by entrepreneurial individuals and groups whose motivation has been more analytical than the instinctive pioneering spirit and intuitive approach that have characterized airlines in most of the other regions. Yet competition in California has been particularly fierce. Even large commuter airlines, such as Golden West and Swift Aire, fell victim to its intensity. Consequently, and somewhat surprisingly in view of the large numbers, no single airline or individual from this area has qualified for inclusion in the anthology of pioneer profiles in Part II of this book.

AREA 4 (PACIFIC)

First Sched. Service Date	Airline and Base	Code	Initial or Typical Route Network	Aircraft Used	Remarks	Date of last service
27 Aug. 1953	**Catalina Air Lines (Long Beach, Cal.)**	AW	Long Beach-Avalon (Santa Catalina)	Goose (VS-44A)	Founded as Avalon Air Transport, and renamed in 1963. Taken over by Aero Commuter Airlines in 1967.	29 Dec 1967
May 1955	Catalina Airlines (Long Beach, Cal.)		Long Beach-Santa Catalina	DH Dove (DC-3)	(No connection with the Goose operator of the same name).	Nov. 1959
June 1957	**Apache Airlines (Phoenix, Ariz.)**	AP	Phoenix-Douglas, Tucson, Prescott, and other points in Arizona	Beech 18 DH Dove DH Heron	Also had a short-lived operation in Montana; replaced American Airlines at Douglas n 1964, in the first U.S. air taxi replacement agreement. Took over Caravan Airlines in 1967.	1971
24 July 1959	Airtransit (Show Low, Ariz.)	NS	Show Low-Phoenix, Springerville, Holbrook, Tucson	Beech 18 Cessna 205 Cessna 310		1967
15 April 1960	Holiday Air Lines (Pomona, Cal.)		Pomona-Santa Catalina	Beech 18	(Not the same as the 1965 airline of this name.)	10 Oct. 1960
Nov. 1960	Golden Gate Airways (San Francisco, Cal.)		San Francisco-Lake Tahoe	Beech 18	Operations terminated by F.A.A.	Nov. 1961
Aug. 1963	Mineral County Airlines (Long Beach, Cal.)		Long Beach-Burbank-Hawthorne, Nevada	DH Dove DH Heron (DC-3)	Subsidized by a casino in Hawthorne, operated DC-3s after 1964.	1967
1963	North Tahoe Airways (San Francisco, Cal.)		San Francisco-Truckee			1963
1 Oct. 1964	Catalina-Vegas Airline (San Diego, Cal.)		San Diego-Catalina Island, San Diego-Las Vegas	Beech 18 DH Dove	Operated seasonally.	1981
10 Oct. 1964	**Imperial Airlines (Imperial and Carlsbad, Cal.)**	II IW	El Centro-San Diego; Los Angeles, Carlsbad, Bakersfield, San Luis Obispo	Beech 18 Queen Air Bandeirante Shorts SD 360	Founded as Visco Flying Service, Service, a.k.a. Imperial Commuter Airlines; moved to Carlsbad in 1979 after change of ownership.	10 Jan. 1986
16 Nov. 1964	C-Air (Long Beach, Cal.)		Los Angeles-Riverside-Redlands	DH Dove	Parent company C&W Aviation.	1966
10 Mar. 1965	Bank-Air (San Diego, Cal.)		San Diego-Las Vegas	Beech 18 Twin Bonanza		1971
31 Mar. 1965	A-B-C Airlines (Ontario and Fullerton Cal.)		Ontario-Fullerton-Los Angeles	Beech 18 Piper Apache		1966
14 June 1965	Holiday Airlines (Oakland, Cal.)		Oakland-Marysville-Chico-Red Bluff	DH Dove	(Not the same as the 1960 airline of this name.)	1966
11 Nov. 1965	Sierra Pacific Airlines (Oakland, Cal.)		Oakland-Lake Tahoe-Reno	Beech 18	Had interline agreement with Western Air Lines.	1966
Nov. 1965	Air Catalina (San Pedro, Cal.)	FP CT UP CV	San Pedro/Long Beach-Two Harbors, Avalon	Goose	Founded as Catalina Seaplanes and also called Catalina Channel Airlines.	1976
Nov. 1965	Lisle Air Service (Fresno, Cal.)		Fresno-Sacramento	Cessna 206		1966
15 Dec. 1965	Beech Aviation Center (Imperial, Cal.)		Local routes from El Centro, Cal.	Beech 18		1967
1965	Caravan Airlines (Phoenix, Arizona)		Local routes from Phoenix	DH Dove DH Heron	Taken over by Apache Airlines.	1967

AREA 4 (PACIFIC) Continued

First Sched. Service Date	Airline and Base	Code	Initial or Typical Route Network	Aircraft Used	Remarks	Date of last service
26 May 1966	Colorado River Airlines (Long Beach, Cal.)		Long Beach, Burbank, to Bullhead City, Lake Havasu City	DH Dove DH Heron		1968
1 Aug. 1966	Anderson Aviation Sales (Phoenix, Ariz.)		Short routes from Phoenix	Piper types		1968
1 Sept. 1966	Cal-Neva Air (San Jose, Cal.)		Local routes from San Jose	DH Dove		1967
1966	Alamo Airways (Las Vegas, Nev.)		Las Vegas-Tonopah	Beech 18 Cessna 310		1968
11 Jan. 1967	Cable Commuter Airlines (Ontario, Cal.)	KM	Ontario-Los Angeles Ontario-Orange County	Beech 18 Cessna 402 Twin Otter	Founded by Roger Cable. Fleet of 10 Twin Otters when acquired by Aero Commuter Airlines in 1969.	Early 1969
2 June 1967	**Air Pacific (San Francisco, CA)**	IK	First routes Eureka-Sacramento-San Francisco, via Chico, Redding. Then from San Francisco to Merced, Modesto, Chico, Bakersfield.	Beech 18 Cessna 402 Twin Otter Dash 7	Founded as Eureka Aero Industries, Eureka, Cal., with routes from Eureka to San Francisco, Sacramento. Became Air Pacific, late 1979. Merged into Golden State Airlines, 1 March 1980.	1 March 1980
2 Sept. 1967	Priority Air Transport (San Francisco, Cal.)		San Francisco-Salinas, Redding, Sacramento	Beech 18 Cessna 402	Also operated other routes for mail only.	1970
Oct. 1967	Valley Airlines (Phoenix and Safford, Ariz.)	VW	Phoenix-Parker-Lake Havasu City; Phoenix-Safford-Douglas	Beech 18 Pipers		1972
16 Dec. 1967	Sonora Airlines (Reno, Nevada)		Reno-Ely-Lovelock-Winnemuca	Piper Navajo		1969
Dec. 1967	**Golden West Airlines (Newport Beach, later centered on Los Angeles International Airport)**	WH GQ CV GW	Original network of routes throughout the Los Angeles extended metropolitan area, the San Francisco Bay Area, and connecting services between the two, via the coast or San Joaquin Valley. Later restricted mostly to southern California.	Goose Beech 99 Twin Otter Shorts SD-330 Dash 7	Founded as Aero Commuter Airlines at Long Beach. Took over Catalina Airlines, 1967; merged with Skymark and Cable Commuter in 1969. Changed name to Golden West in May 1969, at which time the combined network stretched from the Bay Area to San Diego.	22 April 1983
1967	Cal-Nat Airways (Grass Valley, Cal.)		Los Angeles-Mojave, Fresno, Palm Springs		(Possibly only a mail carrier.)	1969
Feb 1968	Skymark Airlines (Sacramento, Cal.)	EY	Sacramento-San Jose, Oakland, Fresno, Lake Tahoe, Bakersfield	Cessna 402 Beech 99	Merged with Aero Commuter early in 1969.	24 Mar. 1969
1 April 1968	Desert Commuter Airlines (Santa Monica, Cal.)	DC	Santa Monica-Palm Springs	Beech 18 DH Dove	Operating name of division of Los Angeles Air Taxi.	1970
8 April 1968	Golden State Airlines (Burbank, Cal.)		Local routes from Burbank	Beech 18 Lockheed 12A		1969
April 1968	Ambassador Airlines (Las Vegas, Nevada, and Palm Springs, Cal.)	MB	Las Vegas-San Diego, Oxnard, Bakersfield	Beech 18 Aero Commander	Founded as charter airline in 1963.	1968
8 July 1968	Trans-Cal Airlines (Long Beach, Cal.)	ST	Long Beach and/or Los Angeles-Thermal, Bakersfield, Porterville	Queen Air Bonanza	Also called Trans Cal Commuter.	1970

AREA 4 (PACIFIC) Continued

First Sched. Service Date	Airline and Base	Code	Initial or Typical Route Network	Aircraft Used	Remarks	Date of last service
30 Aug. 1968	Trans-Nevada Air Services (Las Vegas, Nevada)		Local services from Las Vegas	Beech 18 Aero Commander		1969
23 Sept. 1968	Air Charter Services (Riverside, Cal.)		Local services from Riverside	Bonanza		1969
1 Oct. 1968	Livermore Air Service (Tonopah, Nev.)		Local services in Nevada	Cessna 206 Cessna 205	Operated jointly with Mustang Airlines.	1970
6 Oct. 1968	Rose Aviation (Hawthorne, Cal.)		Local services in California	Piper Apache Aero Commander		1969
28 Oct. 1968	Nor-Cal Aviation (Redding, Cal.)	CV	Redding-Sacramento, Chico, Red Bluff; expanded to Bay Area, Lake Tahoe, Reno	Piper Navajo Cessna 402	Division of Shasta Flight Service. Initially a mail carrier only.	Jan. 1979
Oct. 1968	Valley Airlines (Oakland and San Jose, Cal.)	HQ	Oakland-San Jose, Fresno, Bakersfield, Santa Barbara	Beech 18 Tradewind	Merged with Ram Airlines to form Pacific Northwest Airlines.	1 Dec. 1974
11 Nov. 1968	Cal-State Airlines (Long Beach, Cal.)	CC	Long Beach-Los Angeles-Bakersfield-Fresno, Santa Barbara	Beech 99 Jetstream		May 1970
Nov. 1968	Sun Aire Lines (Borrego Springs, then Palm Springs, Cal.)	OO	Borrego Springs-San Diego, then Palm Springs-Los Angeles-San Diego, Yuma, Santa Maria	Cessna 402 Metroliner	Founded as Borrego Springs Airlines by the Di Giorgio Corporation. Sold to Skywest 28 September 1984.	28 Sept. 1984
1968	Astro Air (Lompoc, Cal.)	YG	Lompoc-San Francisco Lompoc-Los Angeles	DH Dove Piper Navajo	Operating affiliate of Air Astro Transportation.	1969
1968	Golden West Airlines (Van Nuys, Cal.)		Los Angeles-Palm Springs, Oxnard, Orange County, Santa Barbara	Twin Otter (HFB 320) (Hansa)	After operations terminated, routes were flown by Aero Commuter Airlines, which also adopted the name (see Dec. 1967).	11 Mar. 1969
3 Mar. 1969	**Golden Pacific Airlines (San Francisco)**	GG	San Francisco-Merced-Modesto-Visalia; Santa Rosa, Sacramento, Fresno	Piper Navajo Beech 99 (Convair 440)	In 1971, Golden Pacific was 8th largest U.S. commuter airline.	Early 1973
20 Mar. 1969	**Swift Aire Lines (San Luis Obispo, Cal.)**	IY WI	San Luis Obispo-Santa Maria, San Jose, Los Angeles, San Francisco	Piper Aztec DH Heron Nord 262 Fokker F-27	Founded by Charlie Wiswell Became part of the Golden Gate system in 1981.	18 Sept. 1981
1969	Cal Aero Airways (Van Nuys, Cal.)	EG	Local routes from Van Nuys	Beech 18 Cessna 402		Early 1970
1970	Air Nevada (Las Vegas, Nev.)		Hawthorne-Oakland, San Francisco		(Not the same airline as the one of 1978).	1970
1 Jan 1971	Nevada Airlines (Las Vegas, Nevada)	UD KS	Las Vegas-Grand Canyon; Las Vegas--Tonopah-Hawthorne-Reno-Carson City	Beech 18 DC-3 Martin 4-0-4	Grounded by F.A.A. after a Martin 4-0-4 crash.	June 1980
Sept 1971	**Cochise Airlines (Tucson, Ariz.)**	DP	Tucson-Phoenix, Flagstaff, Kingman	Cessna 402 Metroliner Convair 440	One of the first commuter airlines to receive official C.A.B. certification.	2 June 1982
1971	Sun World Airlines (Burbank, Cal.)		Phoenix-Prescott-Kingman	Cessna 402		1972

AREA 4 (PACIFIC) Continued

First Sched. Service Date	Airline and Base	Code	Initial or Typical Route Network	Aircraft Used	Remarks	Date of last service
Mid 1971	Trans Sierra Airlines (Burbank, Cal.)	XS	San Jose, Burbank, and Los Angeles to Bishop and Mammoth		Reorganized as Sierra Pacific Airlines.	1972
1972	Catalina Seaplanes (San Pedro)	UP	San Pedro-Avalon	Grumman Goose	(Different airline from the one of November 1983.)	Mid 1970s
1972	Sierra Pacific Airlines (Burbank, Cal.)	XS SZ	Burbank-Los Angeles-Fresno, Bishop, Mammoth Lakes	Piper Navajo Cessna 402 Jetstream Convair 340	Founded as Trans-Sierra Airlines and re-organized under new name in 1972. Became a charter airline.	Late 1979
2 May 1972	Baja Airlines (Long Beach, Cal.)	KJ	Long Beach-points in Baja California	Beech 18 Cessna 402	Changed name on 31 January 1975 from Club Baja Airlines.	Late 1976
Late 1972	Westair (San Francisco and Chico, Cal.)	VB OE UA	San Francisco-San Rafael, Concord, Napa, Eureka, Sacramento, Chico, Fresno	BN-2 Islander BN-3 Trislander Cessna 402 Shorts SD-360 BAe Jetstream (BAe 146)	Founded as STOL Air in San Rafael, changing name and base in 1975. Became a United Express affiliate on 1 July 1986, now based in Fresno.	
Mid 1973	Ram Airways (Carson City, Nevada)	FM	Carson City-Reno, Lake Tahoe-San Francisco	DH Dove Piper Apache Piper Navajo	Merged with Valley Airlines (see Oct. 1968) to form Pacific Northwest Airlines.	Mid-1974
1973	Peninsula Airways (San Carlos, Cal.)		Local routes from San Carlos	Cessna 402		1973
1973	Trans Aero-Systems (San Jose, Cal.)		Local routes from San Jose	DH Dove Cessna 207		1974
1973	Trans National Airlines (Oakland, Cal.)		Local routes from Oakland	DH Dove		1974
Mid-1974	Havasu Airlines (Lake Havasu City, Ariz.)	HW YB	Lake Havasu City-Las Vegas	Piper Aztec Piper Navajo	Scheduled operating division of Lake Havasu Air Service. In 1988 operated briefly as YB Express, a code-sharer with Golden Pacific Airlines.	Late 1988
Mid 1974	Catalina Airlines (Long Beach, Cal.)	KG	Long Beach, San Pedro-Catalina Island	Grumman Goose	(Not the same company as the earlier ones founded in 1953 and 1955.)	22 Feb 1981
1 Dec 1974	Pacific Airlines (San Francisco)	US	San Francisco, Oakland-San Jose-Fresno-Bakersfield;-Monterey	Beech 18 DH-Dove Convair 240	Formed by merger of Valley Airlines (Oct. 1968) and Ram Airways (mid-1973) as Pacific Northwest Airways.	1975
1974	Pacific Coast Airlines (Long Beach, Cal.)		Local services from Long Beach	DC-3	Acquired by Pacific Northwest Airways, early 1975, and the short-lived airline renamed again to Pacific Airlines.	Early 1975
Oct. 1975	Pacific Coast Airlines (Santa Barbara)	ID	Santa Barbara-San Jose-Sacramento; Bakersfield; Los Angeles, San Francisco	Beech 18 Piper Navajo Jetstream	Founded as Apollo Airways. Reorganized as P.C.A. on 1 March 1982.	7 Feb. 1986
Oct 1975	California Air Commuter (Oakland, Cal.)	DK	Oakland-Chico-Redding, Oakland-Truckee	Piper Navajo	Operating division of Marin Aviation, also know as Cal Air.	Late 1977
1976	California-Nevada Airlines (Stateline, Nevada)	TQ	Oakland-Concord-Reno-Lake Tahoe; Las Vegas	Aero Commander		1977
Jan 1977	Air Cortez (a.k.a. Air Cortez International) (Ontario, Cal)	AB	Ontario-San Diego-Mexican points on Sea of Cortez. Also to Grand Canyon	Beech 18 Cessna 402 Fairchild F-27		1986

AREA 4 (PACIFIC) Continued

First Sched. Service Date	Airline and Base	Code	Initial or Typical Route Network	Aircraft Used	Remarks	Date of last service
1 May 1977	Inland Empire Airlines(Los Angeles)	LQ CC	Los Angeles-Apple Valley-Visalia-Fresno-San Francisco	Piper Navajo Metroliner	Purchased by Air Chaparral in November 1981.	16 Sept 1983
Late 1977	Baja Cortez Airlines (Los Angeles)	KJ XT	Los Angeles-points in Baja California, Mexico	DH Heron		Mid-1980
1977	Omni Airlines (Las Vegas)	OE	Las Vegas-Grand Canyon/Death Valley	Mooney 20-A		1979
1977	Yosemite Airlines (Columbia, Cal.)	JE	Columbia-Lake Tahoe-San Francisco, Stockton	Queen Air	Operating branch of Tuolumne Air Service.	May 1981
1978	STOL Air Inc. (Santa Rosa, Cal.)	VB	Santa Rosa-Ukiah, Clear Lake, Napa, Concord, Oakland, S.F.		Renamed Westair.	
1978	Eureka Aero Industries (Eureka)	1K	Eureka-Redding-Chico-Sacramento; Eureka-Santa Rosa-Oakland-San Francisco			
1978	Apollo Airways (Santa Barbara, Cal.)	ID	Santa Barbara-San Jose, Santa Maria, Oakland, Sacramento			
Early 1978	Las Vegas Airlines (Las Vegas, Nev.)	TQ GG	Las Vegas-Grand Canyon	Piper types	Reverted to on-demand charter operations.	1987
Early 1978	Trans Catalina Airlines (Orange County, Cal.)	DC	Orange County/Long Beach/San Pedro-Santa Catalina	Mallard Cessna 402		Late 1981
Late 1978	Air Nevada (Las Vegas, Nev.)	LW	Las Vegas-Grand Canyon; Bullhead City, Tonapah	Beech 18 Cessna 402	(Not the same company as the 1970 airline.)	
Late 1978	Eagle Airlines (Long Beach, Cal.)	EB	Los Angeles-Paso Robles, Long Beach, Santa Catalina	Cessna 402	Operating division of Eagle Aviation.	Late 1981
1978	Aviation Services (Reno, Nevada)	ML	Reno-Ely,Elko,Tonopah, Nevada; and San Francisco	Cessna 402		1979
1 Jan 1979	Golden Eagle (Santa Rosa, Cal.)	JO	Redding-Chico-Sacramento-San Francisco	Cessna 402	Absorbed by Westair.	1 April 1979
1 Mar. 1979	Sierra Flite Service (Bakersfield, Cal.)	ED	Bakersfield-Las Vegas	Beech King Air		3 Aug. 1979
15 April 1979	Desert Pacific Airways (Oxnard, Cal.)	TD	Oxnard-Los Angeles, Sacramento, Las Vegas	Piper Navajo		1 Mar. 1980
1 May 1979	C&M Airlines (Inyokern,Cal.)	SM KA	Inyokern-Los Angeles, Ontario, Apple Valley; later to Mammoth Lakes, Edwards AFB	Cessna 402 Beech 99	Sold to Mojave Airlines, 1983; resumed operations, 1 Jan. 1984 Later called Indian Wells Airlines.	Late 1985
June 1979	Golden Carriage Aire (Paso Robles, Cal.)	GD	Paso Robles-King City. San Luis Obispo-San Francisco, Los Angeles	Piper Navajo		Nov 1980
July 1979	Sun West Airlines (Scottsdale, Ariz.)	KY	Phoenix-Gallup-Farmington-Durango	Piper types		1984
18 Aug, 1979	Air Bahia (San Diego, Cal.)	XG	San Diego-Los Angeles, El Centro, points in Baja California	Piper Navajo BN-2 Islander		14 Dec. 1980

AREA 4 (PACIFIC) Continued

First Sched. Service Date	Airline and Base	Code	Initial or Typical Route Network	Aircraft Used	Remarks	Date of last service
8 Oct. 1979	Desert Airlines (Mesa, Ariz.)		Phoenix-Winslow-Gallup-Flagstaff	Piper Navajo	Operating branch of Desert Air Service.	Mid-1981
9 Nov. 1979	**Aspen Airways (Burbank, Cal.)**	AP	Los Angeles-Lake Tahoe, Modesto, San Francisco	Convair 580	California operations of the Colorado company.	Aug 1983
1979	Butler Aviation (San Francisco)		San Francisco-Eureka	Cessna types		1980
1979	Mexico Air Service (Santa Monica)	QK	Santa Monica/San Diego-Mexican points	Cessna types		Mid-1980
Mid-1979	Century Airlines (Eureka, California)	QX	Eureka-San Francisco, Santa Rosa, Eugene, Portland	Cessna 402 Nomad	Originally Six Rivers Air Service "Shut down by tax collectors."	24 Mar. 1981
Late 1979	Shasta Air (Yreka, Cal.)	LU	Yreka-Sacramento, San Francisco; Redding	Piper Seneca		Mid-1983
Late 1979	Desert Pacific Airlines (Sedona, Ariz.)	NP	Sedona-Flagstaff, Prescott, Phoenix-San Diego (Montgomery)	Piper Navajo	Operations suspended after Navajo crash.	Feb. 1981
Jan 1980	**Wings West (Santa Monica, San Luis Obispo, Cal.)**	RM AA	Santa Monica-Mammoth Lakes, San Luis Obispo, Los Angeles, San Francisco	Cessna 402 Beech 99 Metroliner	Founded by Mark A. Morro. Became American Eagle affiliate in June 1986 and purchased by American in 1987.	
16 Jan 1980	**Golden Gate Airlines (Monterey, Cal.)**	GG	Monterey-San Francisco, Modesto-Fresno, San Jose, Los Angeles and then large area in western states.	Metroliner Convair 580 Dash 7	Formerly Gem State Airlines, Idaho, owned by Justin Colin; absorbed Air Pacific, 1 March 1980.	21 Aug. 1981
Early 1980	Ponderosa Airlines (Taylor, Ariz.)	RZ QK	Phoenix-Taylor-Show Low-White River	Aero Commander	Operating division of Ponderosa Aviation; seasonal service.	Mid-1983
Early 1980	Trans-Sierra Airlines (Fresno, Cal.)		Fresno-Bishop	Piper Navajo		Late 1980
11 April 1980	Copper State Airlines (Douglas, Ariz.)	GZ	Douglas-El Paso, Sedona, Prescott, Tucson, Phoenix	Piper Navajo Piper Seneca	Operating division of Go-Flying Inc.	Early 1982
10 May 1980	Magnum Airlines (Van Nuys, Cal.)		Van Nuys-Las Vegas, San Francisco	Cessna 310 Cessna 402		Mid-1981
2 June 1980	Air Chico (Chico, Cal.)	FZ	Chico-Redding; San Francisco, San Jose	Cessna types		Early 1982
13 June 1980	California Amphibian Transport (Long Beach, Cal.)		Long Beach-Avalon (Santa Catalina)	Piper Navajo Mallard	Division of All Seasons Air Pacific.	15 Jan 1982
27 June 1980	Great Sierra Airlines (Oakland, Cal.)	LT	Oakland-Truckee-Reno-Lake Tahoe	Piper Navajo		April 1981
June 1980	Southern Nevada Airlines (Las Vegas, Nev.)		Las Vegas-Grand Canyon	Piper Navajo		Early 1981
July 1980	Sun West Airlines (Phoenix, Ariz.)	KY	Phoenix-Durango, Farmington, Albuquerque	Cessna 414 Pipers	Division of Scottsdale Aviation.	5 March 1985
Mid-1980	Silver State Airlines (Las Vegas, Nev.)	ZG	Las Vegas-Grand Canyon	Bandeirante		Early 1982

AREA 4 (PACIFIC) Continued

First Sched. Service Date	Airline and Base	Code	Initial or Typical Route Network	Aircraft Used	Remarks	Date of last service
4 Aug. 1980	Air Chaparral (Reno, Nev.)		Reno-Winnemuca-Elko, Ely, Tonopah	Cessna 402	Purchased Inland Empire Airlines, November, 1981.	Early 1982
Fall 1980	Pacific National Airways (Burbank, Cal.)	2E	Burbank-Las Vegas-Grand Canyon, and points in Mexico	DC-3	Previously a charter airline.	Sept 1981
18 Dec. 1980	Cal Sierra Airlines (San Diego, Cal.)	QS	San Diego-Lake Tahoe, Burbank	Convair 440		Dec 1981
19 Dec. 1980	Trans California Airlines (El Monte, Cal.)	ZO	El Monte-Las Vegas-Los Angeles	Cessna 402		April 1981
19 Dec. 1980	Pacific Cal Air (Oakland, Cal.)	AX	Oakland-Fresno; Monterey, Sacramento, Burbank, Reno	Metroliner		3 Jan 1984
Late 1980	Air Sierra (Fresno, Cal.)	SI	Fresno-Bishop	Piper	Division of Western Charter Air.	1981
Early 1981	All Seasons Air Pacific (Long Beach, Cal.)	YB	Long Beach-Santa Barbara, San Diego, Burbank, Ontario	Piper Navajo	Also known as ASAP.	Mid-1983
Early 1981	Golden Airways (Sierra Vista, Ariz.)	VF	Sierra Vista-Tucson-Ft. Huachuca	Cessnas Beech 99	Also known as Golden West Air Service.	1983
Early 1981	Arizona Pacific Airlines (Las Vegas, Nev.)	QJ	Las Vegas-Grand Canyon, Flagstaff, Santa Barbara	Convair 440 Convair 580		Late 1981
Early 1981	Royal West Airways (Las Vegas, Nev.)	TT	Burbank-Grand Canyon, Las Vegas	DC-3		Mid-1982
1 April 1981	Air Trails (Salinas, Cal.)		Salinas-Oakland, San Francisco	Cessna 310		14 Aug. 1981
11 Dec. 1981	Interstate Airlines (Burbank, Cal.)		Burbank-Las Vegas	Jetstream		1982
Dec. 1981	Golden Pacific Airlines (Kingman, Ariz.)	2G YB	Kingman-Phoenix, Las Vegas, Prescott, Sedona, Winslow	Cessna 402	Code-shared briefly with Havasu Airlines, 1988.	Early 1989
1981	Valley Catalina Airlines (Van Nuys, Cal.)		Van Nuys-Santa Catalina	Beech 18		Late 1981
1981	Gold Coast Air Hawthorne, Cal.)	HR	Los Angeles-Bullhead City	Cessna types		1982
1982	Arizona Pacific (Las Vegas, Nev.)	QJ	Las Vegas-Grand Canyon	Cessna types		
17 Mar. 1982	Airspur (Los Angeles)	5A	San Diego (Montgomery)-Los Angeles	Arava		Nov. 1982
22 Mar. 1982	Piper Air Center (Long Beach, Cal.)		Long Beach-Santa Catalina	Piper Navajo		1982
1 May 1982	Air LA (Los Angeles)	UE 3D	Burbank-Las Vegas-Grand Canyon, Blythe, Los Angeles	Piper Navajo Cessna 402 Jetstream	Merged with Air Resorts Airlines in December 1990, but the two companies operated separately.	Jan. 1991
Mid-1982	AFS Airlines (Arcata, Cal.)	5E	Eureka, Oakland, Redding, Portland	Piper Navajo	Operating name for Arcata Flying Service.	1984

AREA 4 (PACIFIC) Continued

First Sched. Service Date	Airline and Base	Code	Initial or Typical Route Network	Aircraft Used	Remarks	Date of last service
Mid-1982	Sierra Vista Aviation (Sierra Vista, Ariz.)	7C	Fort Huachuca-Sierra Vista-Phoenix-Tucson	Piper types Douglas		Late 1988
28 Aug. 1982	Desert Sun Airlines (Long Beach, Cal.)	FE	Los Angeles-Twenty Nine Palms, Blythe Riverside, Lancaster Lancaster, Inyokern	Piper types		1987
1982	Golden Valley Aero (Bakersfield, Calif.)		Bakersfield-Fresno-San Jose	Cessna 402 Cessna 404		1982
1982	Mission Airlines (El Cajon, Cal.)	UQ	El Cajon-Los Angeles	Piper types		1982
1982	Western Pacific Express (Westpac) (Van Nuys, Cal.)	GW	Los Angeles-Lancaster-Edwards AFB; Ontario, Palmdale	Beech 99	Resumed operations in 1985 as an all-cargo operator.	Mid-1983
1982	Eagle Aviation (Long Beach, Cal.)		Long Beach-Santa Catalina	Cessna 402		1982
Late 1982	Air Irvine (Orange County, Cal.)	WI	Orange County-Los Angeles, Palms Springs	Piper Navajo Cessna 402	Sold to Dash-Air (see below).	Mid-1983
15 Dec. 1982	Air Resorts Airlines (Carlsbad, Cal.)	UZ	San Diego-Burbank, Carlsbad, Long Beach, Tucson, Santa Barbara	Convair 440 Convair 580	Intermittent operations Also operated in Virgins Islands Ceased operations on 1 April 1984 but resumed scheduled service 14 May 1990.	
Early 1983	Catalina Seaboard Airlines (Orange County, Cal.)	LT	Orange County-Santa Catalina; Bullhead City, Bermuda Dunes	Piper Navajo	Renamed California Seaboard Airlines, 21 Dec. 1983.	Late 1986
Early 1983	Mojave Airlines (Inyokern, Cal.)	KA	Inyokern-Los Angeles	Cessna 402 Beech 99	Purchased certificate from C & M Airlines (see 1 May 1979).	Early 984
April 1983	Air Sedona (Sedona, Ariz.,)	MP UJ	Sedona-Phoenix	Cessna types		
Mid-1983	Dash Air (Orange County, Cal.)	WI	Los Angeles-Orange County, Santa Barbara, Palm Springs, Modesto	Bandeirante Shorts SD-360	Purchased Air Irvine, mid-1983.	13 Sept. 1984
Nov. 1983	Catalina Seaplanes (Long Beach, Cal.)	5D	Long Beach-Avalon, Santa Barbara	Goose Cessna 421		Dec. 1984
1983	Huachuca Airlines (Sierra Vista, Ariz.)	7H	Fort Huachuca-Tucson, Safford, Globe, Phoenix	Piper Navajo		Early 1984
1 May 1984	Connectair (Santa Barbara)	5C	Santa Barbara-Los Angeles, Las Vegas	Fairchild F-27		11 Oct. 1984
Mid 1984	Mammoth Air Shuttle (Mammoth Lakes Cal.)	TB	Burbank-Mammoth Lakes-Orange County Mammoth Lakes	Piper Navajo	Seasonal services only.	Mid 1988
Mid 1984	Alpha Air (Van Nuys, Cal.)	7V	Van Nuys-Bishop-Las Vegas, Mammoth Lakes, and to Grand Canyon	Cessna 402 Beech 1900		
24 Sept 1984	Far West Airlines (Fresno, Cal.)	FV	Fresno-San Jose, Oakland; Burbank-Orange County	Nihon YS-11	Supported by City of Fresno.	13 Dec 1984
Late 1984	Desert Airlines (Hemet, Calif.)	XT	Hemet-Los Angeles, Bullhead City, Lake Havasu City	Piper	Changed name from Air Hemet in 1985.	Mid-1985

AREA 4 (PACIFIC) Continued

First Sched. Service Date	Airline and Base	Code	Initial or Typical Route Network	Aircraft Used	Remarks	Date of last service
Early 1985	Evergreen/Airspur Airlines (Los Angeles)	OT	Los Angeles-Oxnard, Orange County	Twin Otter	Evergreen bought Airspur Helicopter and converted it to a fixed wing operation.	25 Feb 1985
8 July 1985	Westates Airlines (Burlingame, Cal.)	WG	Los Angeles-Santa Rosa	Convair 580		Dec. 1989
Oct. 1985	Golden State Airlines (Newport Beach, Cal.)	GM	Orange County-Las Vegas, Orange County-Los Angeles	Cessna 402	Acquired by Stateswest late in 1986.	Late 1986
2 Dec. 1985	Resort Commuter Airlines (Orange County, Cal.)	MG	Orange County-Palm Springs, Los Angeles, and points in Mexico	Cessna 402 Twin Otter	Affiliated to TWA, 1986-88 as a Trans World Express carrier; resumed as an independent but then became a Pan American Express affiliate on on 1 Nov 1988.	22 Nov 1989
1986	California Seaboard Airlines (Newport Beach, Cal.)	LT	Burbank/Orange County-Catalina, Carlsbad, Ontario	Pipers		1986
Early 1986	Mid-Pacific Air (Honolulu)	HO	Burbank/Orange County-Fresno, Las Vegas	Nihon YS-11	California operations of the Honolulu-based airline.	1986
Mid-1986	White Mountain Aire (White Mountain Lakes, Nev.)		Phoenix-White Mountain Lakes	Piper Navajo		7 Oct 1986
1 Oct. 1986	Stateswest Airlines (Phoenix, Ariz.)	YW	Phoenix-Bullhead City, San Diego, Los Angeles, Las Vegas	Shorts SD-36 Jetsteam Beech 1900	Became a US Air Express carrier, 15 July 1990.	
Late 1986	Sun Pacific Airlines (Long Beach, Cal.)	VL	Long Beach-Calexico	Bandeirante		
Mid 1987	Sierra Mountain Airways (Oakland, Cal.)	HF SI	Oakland, Mammoth Lakes, Fresno, Long Beach, Battle Mountain, Reno	Dornier 228		Mid-1989
Early 1988	Quest Air (Long Beach, Cal.)	7Q	Long Beach-San Diego	Dornier 228		Mid-1988
Mid-1988	Pacific Coast Airlines (Orange County, Cal.)	PQ	Bakersfield-Los Angeles-Ontario	Piper Navajo	Changed name from Holiday Airlines in 1990.	Dec. 1990
1989	Air Vegas (Las Vegas)	6V	Las Vegas-Grand Canyon	Cessna types		
1 June 1989	Pan Am Express (Los Angeles, Cal.)	PA	Los Angeles-San Diego, Los Angeles-Santa Barbara	Dash 7	California feeder operation of Pan American Airways.	1990
1 Oct 1989	Grand Airways (Las Vegas, Nevada)	QD	Los Vegas-La Verne, Grand Canyon, Carlsbad	Cessna 402		
7 Jan 1990	California Air Shuttle (Oxnard, Calif.)	7Q	Oxnard-Las Vegas Sacramento, San Francisco, San Jose	Metroliner	Affiliated with America West Airlines (code-sharing).	Late 1990

Area 5

Rocky Mountains

Airlines in the Rocky Mountain area have traditionally provided a vital transport link between small communities throughout a sparsely populated region of the United States, stretching from the Canadian to the Mexican borders. Even the normally parsimonious CAB has conceded that many communities in the region were "isolated" and therefore qualified for federal subsidy. The terrain is mainly inhospitable, characterized by successive ranges of mountains, interspersed with salt deserts or scrub semidesert. In contrast with routes in some other parts of the United States, the distances are long (Pioneer's nonstop route from Denver to Williston was 594 miles), and, because of the low level of population density, passenger loadings might be expected to be small. This factor, however, has normally been compensated for by the need to shorten travel times over long distances that are often covered only by circuitous surface routes, thanks to the sometimes insurmountable mountain ranges. The region has, therefore, always been a healthy arena for air transport.

Following a familiar pattern, the prewar trunk airlines eventually gave way to the local service airlines, one of which, Frontier Airlines, boasted a widespread network that once embraced about one-third of the area of the United States. Later, with the onset of airline deregulation, the definitions of service patterns became somewhat blurred. Frontier was in the in-between world: too small to compete with the now unrestricted major carriers, yet too big and operating aircraft that were too large to serve the small communities.

A host of commuter airlines had already been formed during the late 1960s and the 1970s; some of these had flourished when, for various reasons, service by Frontier was withdrawn, and some even operated, paradoxically, with that airline's cooperation. During the 1980s, with Frontier's demise, these now found a special niche, so that they effectively found themselves operating the same routes in the 1980s that Frontier and its predecessors had operated in the 1950s and 1960s. Indeed, the network map of Sky West, once a tiny operator in southern Utah, began to look like that of a trunk airline, reaching out to Montana in the north and the Mexican border in the south.

The commuter airlines of the Rockies also met a special demand: that of serving winter resort areas in Colorado, Utah, and Idaho. Almost by definition, the ski capitals, such as Aspen, Vail, and Sun Valley, situated as they are in mountain valleys that are inaccessible to most aircraft, beckoned smaller aircraft types, preferably those with short takeoff and landing capabilities. Because of this technical limitation and because of the seasonal nature of the operations, the certificated airlines were ready and willing to allow specialized companies to do the work, and Aspen Airways was a pioneering beneficiary of this unusual display of magnanimity by the established airline industry.

AREA 5 (ROCKIES)

First Sched. Service Date	Airline and Base	Code	Initial or Typical Route Network	Aircraft Used	Remarks	Date of last service
Late 1940s	Carco Air Service (Albuquerque)		Albuquerque-Los Alamos	Beech Twin Bonanza Beech 18	First F.A.A. Certificate, 1964	1968
1953	Aspen Airways (Denver)	AP UA	Denver-Aspen; later to Gunnison-Montrose, Durango-Farmington-Albuquerque. California division 1980: San Francisco- Lake Tahoe, Los Angeles-Lake Tahoe, then to West Yellow-stone and other Rocky Mountain points.	DH Heron Convair 580 BAe 146 (DC-3)(F-27)	Originally started by Clyde Bonham as F.B.O. Operated under special exemption from C.A.B. Full operating certificate, 9 March 1967. United Express affiliate Sept 1986. Sold most of its routes to Mesa Airlines in February 1990. Airline itself sold to Air Wisconsin, 2 May 1990 but still operated separately.	
1962	Bison Air Lines	BI	Albuquerque-Roswell-Artesia-Carlsbad	Aero Commander		1964
18 Sept 1964	Key Airlines (Salt Lake City)	FS	Ogden-Logan-Salt Lake City, Sun Valley-Salt Lake City, Sun Valley-Boise	BN-2 Islander DHC-6 Twin Otter Convair 440	Started service in Ogden as Thunderbird changing name 1 January 1969. Associated with United Air Lines during late 1960s. Traded as Sun Valley Key during 1970s.	Mid-1979
8 Dec 1964	Severson Air Activities (Great Falls, Montana)	SJ	Great Falls-Conrad-Cut Bank-Shelby	Cessna types		1965
18 Dec 1964	Janss Airways (Salt Lake City)	VL JN	Salt Lake City-Sun Valley-Boise-Burley-Hailey	Beech 18 Piper Apache/ Aztec	Name Changed from Sun Valley Airlines, 27 January 1966.	1968
22 Mar. 1966	Trans Central Airlines (Denver)		Denver-Pueblo-Trinidad-Albuquerque	Cessna 402		1970
13 May 1966	Rocky Mountain Airways (Denver)	JC CO	Denver-Eagle (Vail); Denver-Aspen, later to Steamboat Springs, Cheyenne and other Colorado points	Aero Commander DHC-6 Twin Otter, DHC Dash 7 ATR 42	Founded by Gordon Autry as Vail Airways. Changed name late in 1968. Parent company Rocky Mountain Aviation Inc. First airline in the world to fly the Dash 7. After a short association with United Air Lines, purchased by Texas Air Corporation in May 1986 and became a Continental Express affiliate on 1 July 1986.	
29 Sept 1967	Combs Airways (Denver)	NV FL	Billings-Williston, Cody, Miles City, Sidney, Lewistown, Spokane. Later from Denver to other points in Wyoming and Montana	Aero Commander (Convair 340/ 440) Convair 580	Founded in 1957at Billings, Montana as Combs-Pickens Montana Aircraft Co. Changed name to Combs Airways 15 Sept 1967. Also operated as Montana Air Craft Company. Operating agreement with Frontier Airlines in 1969 to operate selected routes, subsequently moving base to Denver and consolidating the agreement as Frontier Commuter, late in 1983.	14 Jan 1985
1968	Dixie Aviation Corp. (St. George, Utah)	DH	St George-Cedar City-Milford-Delta-Provo-Salt Lake City	Aero Commander Cherokee Six		1970
8 July 1968	Pacific Western Airways (Salt Lake City)	PG	Salt Lake-Provo-Price-Green River-Moab-Monticello-Blanding-Cortez-Durango. Also to Page	Beech 18		1969

AREA 5 (ROCKIES) Continued

First Sched. Service Date	Airline and Base	Code	Initial or Typical Route Network	Aircraft Used	Remarks	Date of last service
17 Sept 1968	Metro Commuter Airlines (Denver)	MF	Denver-Boulder-Greeley; Denver-Laramie-Cheyenne; Denver-Boulder-Fort Collins; Denver-Colorado Springs-Pueblo-Canon City	Volpar Beech 18 Aero Commander Beech Queenair		1970
1972	Western Air Stages (Grand Junction, Col.)	QJ QV	Grand Junction - Vernal-Aspen-Vail, Steamboat Springs	D H Dove Beech Queenair	Also operated as Westair.	1972
19 June 1972	Sky West Airlines (St George, Utah)	QG WA DL	St George-Las Vegas; St. George-Cedar City; Milford-Richfield-Salt Lake City; later expansion throughout western states	Piper Navajo Chieftain Metro III Brasilia	Founded by Ralph Atkin. Bought Sun Aire Lines in 1984. Became Western Express affiliate, 27 April 1986, then The Delta Connection, 1 April 1987. Delta has 20% shareholding.	
1974	Mountain Air of New Mexico (Santa Fe)	UM	Albuquerque-Santa Fe-Taos-Denver	Cessna 402	Generally known as Mountain Air.	1975
1974	Zia Airlines (Las Cruces, N.M.)	ZU	Las Cruces-Albuquerque Santa Fe-Taos; L.C.-El Paso; Las Cruces-Silver City-Alb.; later to Denver, Farmington, Alamogordo	Cessna 402 Jetstream Metroliner	Founded 16 August 1972 as Associated Air Ambulance Service. Changed name to Air New Mexico in January, 1980, when ownership changed.	21 May 1980
1975	Trans Mountain Air, Ltd. (Longmont, Col.)	OW	Longmont-Denver	Aero Commander	Also known as Trans Mountain Airlines.	1976
1975	Ross Aviation, Inc (Albuquerque)	ZD	Albuquerque-Los Alamos	DHC-6 Twin Otter	Primary operation freight and mail.	
1975	Valley Airpark, Inc. (Fort Collins, Col.)	QS	Fort Collins-Denver	Piper Seneca BAe Jetstream	Taken over by Air U.S., 1978.	1978
1976	Hensley Flying Service, Inc. (Havre, Montana)	HI	Havre-Great Falls	Cessna 206	First founded as F.B.O. in 1944 by Walt Hensley; purchased by Jim Stroh in 1974. Certificate sold to Big Sky Airlines, in 1978	1978
1976	Roswell Airlines (Roswell, N.M.)	GZ	Roswell-Albuquerque-Artesia-Ruidoso	Piper Seneca	Founded by Dick Callens, owner of Callens Flying Service.	June 1981
1976	Sterling Air Service (Sterling, Col.)	KZ	Sterling-Denver	Cessna 206		Mid-1980
1976	Trans-American Airways (Denver)	QA	Denver-Cheyenne-Douglas-Casper-Sheridan; Gillette; Denver-Santa Fe	Cessna 402		June 1977
12 Jan 1977	Pioneer Airlines (Denver)	JB CO	Denver-Ogallala-North Platte-Lexington-Lincoln-Omaha; Denver-Sidney-Alliance-Chadron; Denver-Gillette-Sheridan; Denver-Santa Fe; Denver-Williston; points in S.W. Colorado	Cessna 404 Beech 99 Metro III	Operated as Pioneer Airways to 1980. Expanded under presidency of David Forward. Associated with Frontier Airlines when latter withdrew from routes from March 1979. Nonstop Denver-Williston (594 miles) longest segment of all commuter airlines. Became Continental Commuter in January 1983, and went out of business when the agreement ended.	19 May 1986
15 Jan 1977	Bonanza Airlines (Aspen, Col.)	ZA	Gd Junction-Vail-Aspen	Cessna 340 Cessna 206 DC-3	Started by Jim Perry, and changed name from Mountain West Airlines in 1978.	23 Oct. 1978

AREA 5 (ROCKIES) Continued

First Sched. Service Date	Airline and Base	Code	Initial or Typical Route Network	Aircraft Used	Remarks	Date of last service
1977	Airways of New Mexico, (Alamogordo, N.M.)	ES	Alamogordo-El Paso-Las Cruces-Albuquerque	Cherokee Six Cessna 402	Founded by Wayne Nelson and Rober Shook. F.A.A. certificate withdrawn.	11 April 1985
1977	Inter-Mountain Airways(Boulder, Col)	EM	Denver-Durango	Piper Navajo	Flew into Durango's Animas Air Park while Durango airports runways being lengthened.	1978
1 April 1977	Excellair (Riverton,Wyoming)	BH	Riverton-Casper-Denver	Piper Navajo Jetstream	Originally Air U.S., the operating name of U.S. Aviation. Name changed after U.S. Air purchased the rights to the name in January 1984.	May 1984
1977	Star Airways (Denver)	ZR	Denver-Gillette; Denver-Rawlins	Merlin Metroliner Piper Navajo Beech Baron	Airline division of Star Aviation, owned by Lee Hollingsworth.	1980
1977	Colorado Airlines (Crested Butte, Col.)	CS	Paonia-Crested Butte-Denver; Crested Butte-Aspen	BN-2 Islander	Also known as Crested Butte Air Service, Inc. Founded by Ron Rouse.	1979
1978	Crown Airlines (Texico,N.M.)	CC	Albuquerque-Clovis-Carlsbad-Hobbs-Roswell-Lubbock	Piper Navajo	Founded by Bill Davis, to replace Texas International as Essential Air Carrier.	1979
1978	U.S. Aviation (Sheridan, Wyoming)	BH	Sheridan-Gillette-Denver			1979
1978	American Central Airways, (Greeley, Col.)	YX	Greeley-Denver, Ft. Collins-Denver	Piper Navajo		1979
1978	Shavano Air (Poncha Springs, Col.)	ZK	Salida-Leadville-Denver	Cessna 206		1980
1978	Big Sky Airlines (Billings, Montana)	GQ NW	Billings-Butte-Boise; Billings-Helena-Missoula; Billings-Gt. Falls-Missoula-Boise; Billings-Casper; extended to points in North Dakota and Minneapolis	Metro Jetstream Cessna 402	Became part of the Northwest Airlink system on after a short-lived association with Frontier Airlines in 1985. Filed for bankruptcy in 1989 and ended Northwest Airlink connection on 15 July 1990.	15 July 1990
1978	Transwestern Airlines of Utah, Inc. (Logan, Utah)	WZ TR	Logan-Salt Lake City-Provo-Moab-Grand Junction-Blanding; S.L.C.-Sun Valley, Vernal	Beech 99 Piper Navajo	Acquired by Horizon Air.	Dec. 1983
Mid 1980	Air Colorado (Denver)	NY	Aspen-Grand Junction	DHC-6 Twin Otter; Cessna 206		Dec 1980
Dec. 1980	Trans-Colorado Airlines (Gunnison, Col.)	VG CO	Gunnison-Montrose-Denver; Gunnison-Cortez	Fairchild Metroliner	Became a Continental Express affiliate on 1 July 1986 and hub moved to Albuquerque, but filed for bankruptcy in 1988.	25 April 1988
12 Oct. 1980	**Mesa Airlines (Farmington, N.M.)**	YV UA	Farmington-Albuquerque; Farmington-Denver, then extended network in southwestern states, with hub at Albuquerque	Beech 1300 Beech 1900 Beech KingAir Piper Saratoga Piper Chieftain Beech 99 EMB Brasilia	Also known as Mesa Air Shuttle and and Mesa Aviation Services. Took over most of Aspen Airways routes in1990. Affiliated as a United Express carrier, starting in February 1990. In 1991 bought control of Air Midwest.	

AREA 5 (ROCKIES) Continued

First Sched. Service Date	Airline and Base	Code	Initial or Typical Route Network	Aircraft Used	Remarks	Date of last service
1981	Air Link (Denver)	FF	Denver-Steamboat Springs-Vernal; Denver-Fort Collins	Piper Chieftain BN-2 Islander Metroliner	Purchased Fort Collins Flying Service in 1981.	1984
15 June 1981	Centennial Airlines (Worland, and later, Laramie, Wyoming)	BE	Cody-Denver; Riverton-Laramie-Denver; Worland-Denver	Beech 99	Planned purchase by _Mesa Airlines_ did not take place.	Late 1987
1981	Budyer Air (Evanston, Wyoming)		Evanston-Rock Springs-Casper-Salt Lake City	Piper types		1982
1983	Alpine Aviation, Inc. (Provo, Utah)	5A	Provo-Salt Lake City; Provo-Nephi-Salina-Richfield-Kanab; Provo-Mt. Pleasant-Moab-Blanding	Beech 99 Piper Navajo Chieftain	Founded by Eugene Mallette.	
14 Jan. 1985	Greater Southwest Aviation (Roswell, New Mexico)		Roswell-Sante Fe	Piper Cheyenne		1985
16 Jan 1985	Jetaire Airlines (Albuquerque)	3J	Albuquerque-Las Cruces / Carlsbad/Clovis	BAe Jetstream		14 Jan. 1986
Early 1985	Turner Aire Silver City, N.M.)	6T	Silver City-El Paso-Carlsbad			Mid-1985
1985	Mountain West Airlines (Laramie and Cheyenne, Wy.)	9W	Laramie-Cheyenne-Casper	Cessna types		Early 1986
1986	Monarch Airlines (Grand Junction, Col.)	9M	Grand Junction-Aspen-Gunnison	DHC-6 Twin Otter		Early 1987
1 March 1987	Sierra West Airlines (Albuquerque, N.M.)		Albuquerque-Taos	Piper Seneca Cessna 402		
Early 1988	Air Ruidosa (Ruidosa, N.M.)	2R	Albuquerque-Ruidosa	Piper types	F.A.A. Certificate revoked.	Early 1989
18 June 1990	Territorial Airlines (Santa Fe, N.M.)		Albuquerque-Las Vegas, N.M.-Raton	Piper Navajo		17 Sept. 1990

Area 6

North Central

The north central part of the country might be described as Chicago's northwestern hinterland. The term is geographically appropriate, for the city that until recent years was the nation's second largest has always had a magnetic attraction for both commerce and culture. Only nearby Milwaukee and the Twin Cities of Minneapolis and St. Paul are big enough to divert or dilute the main streams of travel from the Windy City. The term is also apt in the airline context, for (following a precedent set by the railroads) the area northwest of Chicago, extending as far west as Montana, has always been the domain of Northwest Airlines.

Founded in Minneapolis in 1926, Northwest has always served the area, pioneering air travel to the small cities of Wisconsin, Minnesota, the Dakotas, and Iowa. The demographics of the area, which is characterized by a dearth of medium-size cities but by a plethora of small ones, have never encouraged large-scale airline route development. Northwest was the last of the transcontinental airlines to reach the west coast, and it had to do so by expanding its line in stages by adding a multiplicity of small stops that few Americans outside the area could place on a map without first consulting an atlas.

Having established its domain, Northwest continued to offer service to small places, almost as a local institution rather than as a commercial, profit-seeking airline; its heritage lasted until the 1960s before its service to small cities was entirely replaced. At that time a local service airline, Wisconsin Central, later renamed North Central Airlines, built itself into one of the largest of such airlines before merging with others to form Republic Airlines in 1979. Effectively, by developing a coordinated network of routes throughout the north central area (and even on to Montana), North Central finished off what Northwest had started.

In due course, North Central itself began to change its marketing goals and route policies, neglecting the small communities in favor of the larger ones, and this change of direction was accelerated and intensified when the merged Republic Airlines sought the status of a major trunk airline.

Throughout this period, from the late 1920s to the early 1970s, the north central region was not a fertile area for the foundation of specialized short-haul or commuter airlines, which depended for their existence, indeed their survival, mainly on hub-and-spoke patterns, rather than the traditional line networks. Eventually, however, certain niches revealed themselves, as Republic began to abandon its least patronized routes.

One of these was the connection between Chicago and the area of Wisconsin around Lake Winnebago. When North Central appeared to be neglecting these "Fox River Cities," in an echo of North Central's own pattern of development, a commuter airline, Air Wisconsin, emerged to provide better service than any of its predecessors, because its aircraft and schedules alike were tailored to the specific market.

In due course, Air Wisconsin expanded to become an industry leader among the commuter airlines and, under airline deregulation, progressed to a level of operation that classified it as a large regional, i.e., an airline with annual revenues exceeding $10 million.

Other airlines, notably Simmons and Mesaba, joined the flurry of newcomers that characterized the late 1960s and early 1970s, but most of the commuter airlines of area 6 have been small, very sensibly concentrating on service from a few rural points to the Twin Cities or to Chicago.

Such specialization has not, however, been a guarantee of success, and the fatality rate of the small airlines of the region has been on a par with that in other regions. Some of them sought diversification by providing flights for enthusiastic fishermen to the many small lakes in northern Minnesota and Wisconsin, but such services were highly seasonal and seldom lucrative enough to support the initiative shown by the commuter airline entrepreneurs.

In recent years, since the passage of the Airline Deregulation Act and, especially, since the evolution of code-sharing agreements between the commuter and major airlines, the wheel has turned full circle. Although a few hardy independents managed to operate for several years, these enterprises have been sporadic and usually short-lived. Mesaba Airlines, one of the Northwest Airlink affiliates of Northwest Airlines, shares the honors with another Airlink airline, Express Airlines One, in dominating the commuter airline scene around the Twin Cities—which ironically are still the home of the airline that pioneered the first local routes in the northwest area.

AREA 6 (NORTH CENTRAL)

First Sched. Service Date	Airline and Base	Code	Initial or Typical Route Network	Aircraft Used	Remarks	Date of last service
1955	Air Activities (Fargo, N.D.)		Fargo-Bismarck-Minot	Aero Commander	Founded by Duane Strand.	1950s
15 Aug. 1956	Illini Airlines (Rockford, Illinois)		Chicago-Freeport; Sterling, Rockford-Madison	D H Dove	Pioneer commuter airline to Chicago's Meigs Field, near downtown area. Purchased by TAG (see Area 9).	Late 1957
14 Mar. 1960	Des Moines Flying Services (Des Moines)		Local services from Des Moines	Piper Types		1968
17 Feb. 1964	Mid-State Airlines (Marshfield, Wis.) Later: Midstate Airlines(Stevens Point, Wis.)	IU	Marshfield-Wisconsin Rapids-Milwaukee-Chicago; expansion throughout Wisconsin and north central states	Beech 18 Beech 99 Swearingen Metro	Founded as F.B.O. in 1946 as Marshfield Airways by Roy and Lois Shwery. Operated at first as Midstate Air Commuter until late 1970s. Sold to Sentry Insurance, whose Bryce Appleton changed name to Sentry Airlines, which purchased Chicago Air, 14 Oct 1986. Unsuccessfully resisted code-sharing.	19 Jan. 1989
16 Sept 1964	Mid-States Aviation Corp.(Chicago)		Local services around Chicago	Cessna types		1965
18 Dec. 1964	Mid-Continent Airlines (Morris, Ill.)		Chicago-International Falls-Winnipeg	DH Dove Beech 18	(Not the same as the airline of the same name at Dubuque, Iowa. See American Central, April 1980.)	1965
2 March 1965	Green Bay Airways (Green Bay, Wis.)	GV HE	Green Bay-Sturgeon Bay Ephram-Gills Rock; Green Bay-Land O'Lakes; Antigo-Eagle River. Green Bay-Madison	Cessnas Aero Commander 500	Division of Green Bay Aviation. Also known as Central States Airlines (HE) from 1978 onwards.	Jan. 1981
23 Aug. 1965	Air Wisconsin (Appleton, Wis.)	WM ZW UA	Appleton/Neenah/Menasha (the "Fox Cities")-Chicago (O'Hare); Appleton-Wausau-Minneapolis; points in Indiana from Chicago; Chicago-Battle Creek-Detroit; extensive expansion to Ohio cities Milwaukee, Flint, New Haven, Lincoln, Neb., and Washington, D.C.	DH Dove DHC Twin Otter Beech 99 Metro BaE 146 DHC Dash 7 BAC One-Eleven	Founded in 1963 as Fox Cities Airlines. Took over routes abandoned by North Central Airlines. Acquired Mississippi Valley Airlines (M.V.A.) on 28 January 1985. Became part of United Express, at Chicago, 26 October, 1986 after previous affiliation at Dulles International Airport, Washington, 6 June 1986. Bought a share of Aspen Airways at Denver, 2 May 1990.	
1965	Isle Royale Airways (Houghton, Michigan)		Houghton-Copper Harbor-Rock Harbor(Isle Royale)	Beech 18 Grumman Goose	Small flying boat operation.	1965
17 Nov. 1965	Commuter Airlines (Chicago)	UU MW	Chicago-Ames-Marshaltown; later Chicago (Meigs)-Springfield, Ill., Elkhart (Ind.), Detroit, Sheboygan, Peoria	Beech Queen Air Beech 99	Founded by Paul G. Delman. Originally based in Sioux City, moved to Chicago in 1967. One of the first to recognize value of hub-and-spoke route pattern versus linear route system.	May 1970
19 Jan. 1966	Midwest Aviation (Janesville,Wis.)		Janesville-Chicago	Beech18		1969
22 June 1966	Command Air (Detroit Lakes, Minn.)	QG	Detroit Lakes-Minneapolis, Detroit Lakes-Fargo-Jamestown-Bismarck, Carrington-Minot	Cessna 411 Aero Commander	Founded at Jamestown, N.D. Merged with Red Baron Airlines in 1969.	1968

AREA 6 (NORTH CENTRAL) Continued

First Sched. Service Date	Airline and Base	Code	Initial or Typical Route Network	Aircraft Used	Remarks	Date of last service
9 June 1967	Sedalia-Marshall-Booneville (S.M.B.) Stage Lines (Des Moines; later, Grapevine, Texas)	MJ	Des Moines-Spencer (Iowa) (also routes in Oklahoma and Texas)	Beech 18 Beech 99	Originally founded as a taxi service in 1920; then as a bus company in 1930. Entered aviation in 1967 as air mail carrier, expanding to air freight in 1968. Became largest air mail contract carrier throughout the Midwest. The Des Moines-Spencer passenger route was operated only for a short time.	1967
26 Aug. 1967	Fleet Airways (or Airlines) (Hopkins, Minn., later Eden Prairie, Minn.)	ZF	Duluth-Minneapolis-Fargo; expanded from Minneapolis to Alexandria-Fergus Falls-Detroit Lakes; Baudette-Roseau	DH Heron		Dec. 1969
1967	Fontana Aviation (Iron Mountain, Mich.)			Beech 18		(Late 1970s)
22 July 1968	**Mississippi Valley Airlines(M.V.A.) (Moline, Illinois)**	XV MT QU	Minneapolis-Winona-La Crosse-Chicago; Chicago-Dubuque-Clinton-St Louis; expansion to Omaha, Kansas City, and cities in Iowa and Upper Mississippi Valley	DHC Twin Otter Beech 99 Shorts SD 330 Fokker F-27 Shorts SD 360	Originally Gateway Aviation, Inc. of La Crosse, Wisconsin. Became M.V.A., Oct. 1969, at first as M.V. Airways. Took over Air Iowa routes, 1974. Moved to Moline, Jan. 1982. Became nation's 8th largest commuter airline before purchase by Air Wisconsin on 28 Jan. 1985, followed by merger in May 1985.	17 May 1985
June 1968	Gopher Airlines (Rochester, Minn.)	OC	Minneapolis-Roseau-Baudette-Chicago(Meigs)	Beech 18 Beech 99	Division of Gopher Aviation operated only 73 flights.	Aug. 1968
1968	Brower Airways (Jacksonville, Illinois)	RE UD	Ft. Madison-Keokuk-Macomb-Chicago; Jacksonville-Macomb-Chicago; Jacksonville-Springfield-St Louis	Beech Baron	Found by Thomas J. Whitman. Originally based at Fort Madison, Iowa, as Brower Flight Service.	20 Feb. 1980
1968	Voyager-Air Airlines (Grand Marais, Minn.)					1968
1968	Gateway Aviation (La Crosse, Wis.)		La Crosse-Milwaukee La Crosse-Chicago			
1968	Apollo Airways (Chicago)			Beech 18		1972
1969	Red Baron Airlines (St Paul)	RR	Minneapolis-Detroit Lakes, Roseau, Park Rapids, and Owatonna. Later to Duluth and Hibbing.	Beech 18 Cessna 402	Merged with Command Air in 1969, retaining the Red Baron name.	June 1970
1969	Midwest Airways (Milwaukee)			Beech 18 Cessna 41		1973
7 July 1969	Chicago & Southern Airlines (Peoria, Ill.)	XX	Peoria-Chicago; Springfield-Chicago; Peoria-St Louis	Beech 18 DHC 6 Twin Otter	Took the name from the former trunk airline purchased by Delta Air Lines which, however, did not protect the right to the name. Service terminated when Beech 18 crashed.	1971
1969	Air Mid-America Airlines (Chicago)	IS	Chicago-Springfield-East St. Louis	(DC-3)		1970
1969	Village Airways (West Chicago)	ZF	Chicago-Omaha Chicago/Milwaukee-International Falls	Beech 99	Mainly an air mail carrier. Renamed Federal Airlines.	1971

AREA 6 (NORTH CENTRAL) Continued

First Sched. Service Date	Airline and Base	Code	Initial or Typical Route Network	Aircraft Used	Remarks	Date of last service
April 1970	Air Illinois (Carbondale, Illinois)	UX QX	Carbonale-St Louis-Springfield; Jacksonville (Ill.)- Chicago; Cape Girardeau; then to Arkansas and to the south, inc. New Orleans. Subsequently reduced network to southern Indiana, Chicago, St. Louis, Memphis.	DHC-6 Twin Otter HS-748 (BAC One-Eleven)	Acquired South Central Air Transport of Natchez, Miss., and expanded to southern states in Dec. 1977. Purchased Decatur Commuter Airlines in 1981. HS 748 crash on 11 Dec. 1983 led to F.A.A. grounding. Resumed service on 11 March 1984 but adverse publicity prevented recovery.	17 April 1984
1970	Manufacturers Air Transport (Peoria)	FC	Peoria-Chicago; Galesburg/Decatur-Chicago			1971
1970	American Carrier Corp.(Chicago)	OX	Chicago-Minneapolis/ Cleveland/Detroit, and to points in the northeast.		Mainly a courier service, but carried some passengers.	1971
1970	Lake Geneva Airways (Lake Geneva, Wis.)	YG LE	Chicago(O'Hare)-Lake Geneva	Beech 18	Served a Playboy Club at Lake Geneva.	1973
mid-1970	Sizer Airways (Rochester, Minn.)	ZS	Minneapolis-Roseau-Baudette; Minneapolis-Rochester	Beech 18	Founded by Orin Sizer. Operated only for a short period. Continued as mail and freight carrier.	End-1970
1971	Air Iowa (Muscatine, Iowa)	BI	Muscatine-Davenport-Chicago (O'Hare)	Beech 18	Routes taken over by Mississippi Valley Airlines.	1974
20 Dec. 1971	Moraine Airways (Waukesha, Wis.)	YW	Fond du Lac-Waukesha-Chicago(O'Hare)	DHC-6 Twin Otter	Started by Jimmie D'Amato Operated for only a few months when airline sold to The Leasing Corp., Boston. Mass.	9 Jan. 1973
March 1972	Air Central (Minneapolis)	CG	Minneapolis-Park Rapids-Detroit Lakes	Cessna types		1973
24 July 1972	Flight Development, Inc. (Minneapolis)		Minneapolis-Fargo		Operated during emergency caused by Northwest Airlines strike.	31 Oct. 1972
7 Aug. 1972	Pro Airlines (Minneapolis)		Minneapolis-Jamestown-Fargo-Bismarck		Operated by Executive Air Transport, Inc., during the Northwest Airlines strike.	31 Oct. 1972
1973	Central Iowa Airlines (Davenport, Iowa)	CW	Minneapolis-Davenport-Ottumwa	DC-3		Oct. 1973
1973	Lake State Airways (New Ulm, Minn.)	NT	New Ulm-Minneapolis-Marshall	Piper Navajo	Started operations as Air New Ulm by New Ulm Flight Service. Merged with Midwest Aviation, 1977 (see below).	9 Oct. 1981
4 Feb. 1973	Mesaba Airlines (Minneapolis)	XJ NW	Minneapolis-Hibbing-Gd. Rapids-Brainerd-Jamestown; Brookings-Huron-Mitchell; Mankato-Fairmont-Worthington; routes throughout north central states	Cessna 421 Beech 99 Metro III Fairchild F-27	Originally founded as a small F.B.O. at Coleraine, near Grand Rapids, Minn., by Gordy Newstrom, who sold business to Halvorson family of Duluth in 1970. Sold to Swensen family of Thief River Falls in 1978. Acquired Ede-Aire, 1978. Replaced North Central Airlines at many points. Public stock offering 1982. Became the first Northwest Airlink operator, 1 December 1984, based additionally at Detroit since 1988.	

AREA 6 (NORTH CENTRAL) Continued

First Sched. Service Date	Airline and Base	Code	Initial or Typical Route Network	Aircraft Used	Remarks	Date of last service
1973	Shawano Flying Service (Shawano, Wis.)		Houghton-Isle Royal	Beech 18	Founded as *Isle Royal Seaplane Service* at Houghton, Michigan. Changed name to Grognet Flying Service, then to Shawano	1986
1974	Hawkeye Airlines (Ottumwa, Iowa)	HI	Ottumwa-Marshalltown Des Moines; Omaha-Sioux City	DC-3		1974
1974	Rynes Airlines (Chicago)		Chicago-Gary			1975
1974	Dakota West Airlines (Rapid City, S.D.)		Rapid City-Brookings-Minneapolis			Sept. 1975
2 June 1975	Silver Wings Aviation (Rapid City, S.D.)	DF	Rapid City-Gillette-Sheridan-Billings	Piper Aztec	Timetable included request "Please be prepared to pay the pilot with cash."	1976
Jan. 1976	Midwest Aviation (Marshall, Minn.)	WV GE	Marshall-Minneapolis; Marshall-Dubuque-Minneapolis; Marshall-Sioux Falls	Piper Navajo	Joint operations, as *Lake State Airways*, with *Air New Ulm* in 1977, and continued independently after L.S.A. merger dissolved.	
1977	Coleman Air Transport Corp. (Rockford, Ill)	LT CH	Rockford-Milwaukee, Moline, Des Moines, Cedar Rapids, Waterloo Detroit, Indianapolis, Cincinnati; Rockford-Detroit	Beech King Air Grumman Gulfstream	Announced DC-9 service, Rockford-New York, 12 Nov. 1979, but lost its operating certificate.	20 July 1980
1978	Ede-Aire (Detroit Lakes, Minn.)	DV	Detroit Lakes-Alexandria-Minneapolis	Piper Seneca	Founded by E.G.D. Domich as F.B.O. Sold to *Mesaba Airlines*.	27 April 1981
1978	Wiscair (Waukesha, Wis.)	FD	Waunkesha-Chicago (O'Hare)	Piper Navajo	Operating affiliate of local F.B.O., Whitman Aviation.	1980
1978	Kenosha Aero (Chicago)		Chicago(O'Hare)-Detroit, Minneapolis, Rochester, Madison	Cessna 402. 404	Founded by Jim Beardsley as an F.B.O. at Kenosha, Wis.	1979
1979	Realwest Airlines (Fargo, N.D.)	KJ	Fargo-Devil's Lake-Minot-Williston-Bismarck-Dickinson-Bowman-Rapid City	Cessna 404	Founded by Wayne Turner as *Turner Aviation Service*.	11 June 1980
1979	PAFCO (Chicago)	NG CV	Chicago(Meigs Field)-Milwaukee	Cessna 402	Division of *Horizon Airways, Inc.* of Kirksville, Mo., with which it shared the code. Originally *Priority Air Freight Co. (PAFCO)*	1979
1 Feb. 1979	Iowa Air Lines (Spencer, Iowa)	BF	Spencer-Pocohontas Des Moines-Iowa City	Cessna 402		1979
1 Aug. 1979	Northern Illinois Commuter Airlines (Plainfield, Ill)	DG	Chicago (Meigs Field)-Peoria, Springfield, Chicago (O'Hare)	Beech 99		1980
1980	Decatur Commuter Airlines (Decatur, Ill)	DK	Chicago(Meigs Field)-Decatur	Piper Navajo	Founded by K.J. Paul, in association with Vercoa Air Service Purchased by *Air Illinois* on 1 December 1981.	1 Dec. 1981
1 July 1980	**Simmons Airlines** (Negaunee, Mich.)	MQ FP	Marquette-Traverse City-Lansing-Detroit; Marquette-Houghton & -Escanaba-Menominee-Manitowoc-Chicago; then through Michigan to Cleveland, Indianapolis, Cincinnati	Piper Navajo Chieftain, Bandeirante Shorts 360, Nihon YS-11	Founded by Larry Simmons. Became part of *Republic Express* system in 1985 Subsequently became part of *American Eagle* system, and transferred base to Dallas, becoming, by 1993, world's largest regional airline.	

AREA 6 (NORTH CENTRAL) Continued

First Sched. Service Date	Airline and Base	Code	Initial or Typical Route Network	Aircraft Used	Remarks	Date of last service
April 1980	American Central Airlines(Dubuque, Iowa)	JR	Dubuque-Waterloo-Cedar Rapids-Des Moines-Omaha; Dubuque-Chicago, Marshalltown, and throughout mid-western states as far as Minneapolis, Detroit, Kansas City	Piper Navajo Chieftain Bandierante	Founded by Terry Hudik and Mike Gedmin as Tri-State Flite Service, dba Mid-Continent Airlines. Changed name in Jan. 1982 as rights to name held by others. Grounded by F.A.A., 8 Dec. 1984. Re-certificated 8 June 1985, but filed for bankruptcy on 9 March 1985.	24 July 1985
25 June 1980	Lakeland Airlines (Rice Lake, Wis.)	YQ	Rice Lake-Minneapolis, Ashland, Eau Claire, Madison, Milwaukee	Cessna 150 DHC-6 Twin Otter	Founded by Steven C. Van Beek. Also operated as Lakeland Commuter.	21 Jan. 1984
1 July 1980	Skytrain Airlines (Chicago)	GO	Chicago (Midway)-Chicago (Meigs)-Lafayette-Indianapolis	Piper Navajo	Also operated as Air Great Lakes.	Early 1982
Oct. 1980	Trans North Aviation (Eagle River, Wis.)	4Q	Chicago (Palwaukee Airport)-Eagle River, Woodruff, Sturgeon Bay	Piper Navajo Chieftain	Founded by Ronald J. Schaberg to serve the "second home" area in northern Wisconsin.	1980s
1980	Alpine Aviation Corp. (Rockford, Ill.)	ZA	Rockford-Detroit	Beech 99		Early 1981
Dec. 1980	North Air (Eveleth, Minn.)	KN	Minneapolis-Eveleth	Cessna 402	Owned by Ed Majerie and Lloyd Gutowski.	Jan. 1981
1980	Burlington Airways (Kenosha, Wis.)	BY	Kenosha-Manitowoc (central Wisconsin), Chicago, Milwaukee	Beech 18 Piper Navajo	Founded by Bernie Golding.	Early 1982
1981	Midwest Aviation (Marshall, Minn.)	WV	Marshall-Minneapolis-New Ulm	Beech types		1980s
12 Oct. 1981	Great Lakes Commuter (Spencer, Iowa)	ZK	Spencer-Des Moines; Spencer-Fairmont-Minneapolis; Spencer Chicago. Detroit-Sault St. Marie, Houghton. Expanded through northern central states	Beech Baron Beech Bonanza Beech 99 Beech 1900	Formed 25 Oct. 1979 by D.G. Voss, I.L.Simpson, W.E. Winger and D.K. Evans, on reorganization of Spirit Lake Airways, formed on 15 April 1977. Associated with Ozark Air Lines, 1 August 1982. Acquired Alliance Airlines, Aug. 1989, which operated as Great Lakes Link.	
Nov. 1981	Northern Airlines (St. Paul)	2N	Minneapolis-Pierre-Brookings-Huron-Mitchell-Sioux Falls-Lincoln-Sioux City	Piper Navajo Nord 262 Nomad	Ceased operations under Chapter 11 bankruptcy, when the Nord 262 was severely damaged at Lincoln.	5 Feb. 1982
Mid-1981	Bemidji Airlines (Bemidji, Minn.)	CH	Bemidji-Minneapolis, Thief River Falls, then to Mankato and Worthington	Beech Queenair Beech 99	Founded by Larry Diffley and Mark Shough. Operated for a while as Great Lakes Link, but resumed under own name in 1986.	
1982	Blue Line Air Express (Dallas, Wis.)	4U	New Richmond-Dallas-Rice Lake, Eau Claire, Duluth, Hayward, Madison, Milwaukee, Chicago (O'Hare), Rockford, Springfield, Indianapolis	Cessna types		Mid-1982
26 April 1982	Air Lincoln (Chicago)	2L	Chicago (Midway)-Grand Rapids-Kalamazoo-Detroit	Piper Navajo	Founded by Linda Pendleton.	18 Oct. 1982

AREA 6 (NORTH CENTRAL) Continued

First Sched. Service Date	Airline and Base	Code	Initial or Typical Route Network	Aircraft Used	Remarks	Date of last service
Late 1983	Northern Airways (Grand Forks, N.D.)	3N	Grand Forks-Fargo-Bismarck	Piper Navajo	Owned by Dave Ramhee and Orvis Kloster, mainly as a mail route.	1 July 1985
Mid-1984	Alliance Airlines (Kenosha, Wis.)	3A	Chicago-Manitowoc-Manistee-Menominee-Sturgeon Bay	Cessna 404	Founded by Jim Beardsley. Affiliated with Midway Airlines as feeder in 1984. Sold to Great Lakes Aviation and operated as Great Lakes Link.	19 Sept. 1988
1 June 1984	West Central Airlines (Minneapolis)	KL	Fergus Falls-Alexandria-Minneapolis	Piper types		May 1985
Early 1985	Tran North Aviation (Eagle River, Wis.)	4Q	Eagle River-Palwaukee Airport (near Chicago)	Piper types	Seasonal only.	
15 Oct. 1985	Iowa Airways (Dubuque)	JT	Dubuque-Cedar Rapids-Des Moines-Omaha; Moline-Ceder Rapids.	Bandeirante Piper T-1020	Jack Schap took over from the original founder, became associated with Tennessee Airways, operating under its certificate, but changing the name. Joined with Fischer Brothers (see below) to form the Midway Connection, but ceased operating when code-sharing ended.	8 Feb. 1990
Dec. 1985	Express Airlines One (Minneapolis)	NW	Minneapolis-International Falls, Hibbing, Duluth, Sioux City, Cedar Rapids and many other points in North Central States	Jetstream SAAB-Fairchild 340	Operated as a Northwest Airlink affiliate, and had bases in Memphis and Atlanta.	
29 May 1986	Chicago Air (Chicago)	ML	Chicago (Midway)-Peoria-Springfield; Chicago-Moline; Madison La Crosse; Green Bay-Traverse City; Eau Claire; Wausau	Fairchild F-27	Taken over by Mid-State Airlines. Operated as a Midway Connection carrier.	14 Oct. 1986
Oct. 1986	Propheter Aviation (Sterling, Illinois)	QS	Sterling-La Salle/Peru-Chicago; Clinton-Chicago	Piper Navajo Cessna 402	Founded by Bob Propheter.	27 April 1990
Jan. 1987	Apex Airlines (Janesville, Wis.)	8M	Janesville-Milwaukee	Piper Navajo	Founded by Randy Pilgreen as the scheduled operation of MST Aviation (F.B.O.). Ceased operations when E.A.S. subsides for Janesville ended.	1 Oct. 1989
15 June 1987	The Midway Connection (Springfield, Ill.)	ML GP	Chicago (Midway)-Peoria; Springfield; Moline-Dubuque; Madison-Wausau-La Crosse-Eau Claire; Green Bay-Traverse City	Dornier 228 Embraer Brasilia	Operated under joint names of the Midway Connection, Chicago Airlines, Iowa Airways (see above). Formerly Fischer Brothers of Galion, Ohio (see area 9).	1991
Early 1989	Prime Air (Carbondale, Ill.)	DE	Carbondale-Louisville, Paducah-Owensboro	Piper Navajo	Grounded by F.A.A.	9 June 1989
17 April 1989	Skyway Airlines (Milwaukee)	YX	Milwaukee-Grand Rapids/ Green Bay/Appleton/ Flint/Saginaw	Beech 1900	Feeder for Midwest Express, wholly owned by Mesa Airlines.	
30 Oct. 1990	Great Western Aviation (Sioux Falls, S.D.)		Sioux Falls-Rapid City	Metroliner	Founded by Rod Skillman.	

Area 7

Central

Traditionally part of the prairie states, the central region encountered early airline activity coincidentally with the oil boom that erupted in Oklahoma and Kansas during the late 1920s. The pioneer airlines found a ready clientele in the affluent oil executives who wished to travel quickly between the oil fields and the big commercial cities in Texas, the Great Lakes, and the Northeast. This vigorous aviation activity also encouraged the birth of several small aircraft manufacturers, notably Travel Air (Beech) and Cessna at Wichita, Kansas.

Throughout the history of U.S. air transport in the region, this community of interest between the local population and the airlines has continued. During the 1930s, the trunk airlines, especially Braniff and Chicago & Southern, provided excellent connecting flights to every city in the region; but in a widespread trend after World War II, local service airlines took over the responsibility of providing service to the smaller places that were scattered across the farming belt of the Great Plains. Later, during the 1960s and 1970s, in a textbook case of history repeating itself, these regional airlines handed over the sparsely patronized routes to the emerging group of scheduled air taxi operators, later termed the third level and finally the commuter airlines.

This somewhat amorphous group was at first composed of small individual entrepreneurs who typically survived only for a few years, and often only for a few months. But the central region can claim the privilege of having spawned one of the first of all the commuter airlines, and one which survived as a trend-setting operator in a segment of the airline industry that has been characterized more by precarious uncertainty than by stable reliability throughout its history.

This airline, Scheduled Skyways, of Fayetteville, Arkansas, deserves an honored place in history for having, through the initiative of its founder, Ray Ellis, identified a window of opportunity for operating small aircraft and maintaining service to small cities that would otherwise have been neglected by the trunk and even the regional airlines. Such communities demanded a special kind of service that was concentrated on their special needs—primarily to have ready access to the nearest large cities for purely local reasons, social and business. Ellis realized that Fayetteville, as the university city of the state of Arkansas, had unique travel requirements, and he set out to meet them. Scheduling, by day of the week and even by hour of the day, was seldom developed by following patterns set by the larger airlines. Scheduled Skyways adapted its entire operation to the needs of its market in a manner that set an example for others to follow, and subsequently, all across the nation, university towns were to welcome the presence of local commuter airlines.

Another airline, Air Midwest, also earned its place in the commuter airlines' unofficial hall of fame. It began in 1965 as a charter airline, primarily to provide air ambulance and air mortuary services. Its major chance to expand came when it began serving as a replacement for Frontier Airlines in the late 1960s, offering substitute services to many isolated small cities in western Kansas. Air Midwest's founder, Gary Adamson, then saw many new opportunities to enter markets being abandoned by local service airlines, a process that accelerated after deregulation, and for some years the company route network stretched more than halfway across the country. Later on, parts of the airline were sold, but Air Midwest still exists as a subsidiary of Mesa Airlines, and still concentrates its services in the Denver–Wichita–Kansas City region—back where it started.

AREA 7 (CENTRAL)

First Sched. Service Date	Airline and Base	Code	Initial or Typical Route Network	Aircraft Used	Remarks	Date of last service
10 Aug 1946	South Central Air Transport (SCAT) (Fayetteville, Ark.)		Fayetteville - Little Rock, Hot Springs, Hope, El Dorado, Harrison	Cessna UC-78	Started by Ray Ellis, of _Fayetteville Flying Service_. Unable to obtain C.A.B. certificate.	End 1947
1 Sept.1953	**Scheduled Skyways (Fayetteville, Ark.) (dba Skyways)**	GM	Fayetteville-Little Rock, Fort Smith, Harrison, Hot Springs, Jonesboro, Texarkana; later to Dallas, Kansas City, Tulsa, St. Louis, Memphis, Knoxville, Mobile, Birmingham, etc.	Cessna UC-78 Cessna 195, Piper Aztec, Beech 99, Metro Nord 262	Founded as _Scheduled Skyways_ by Ray Ellis, of _Fayetteville Flying Service_. Purchased by a group of investors on 1 October 1972. Expanded rapidly and merged with _Air Midwest_ on 17 January 1985, operating as _Air Midwest Skyways_ until 25 June 1985.	25 June 1985
Dec. 1964	Poplar Bluff Airways (Poplar Bluff, Mo.)		Poplar Bluff-St.Louis	Piper Cherokee Six Beech 18	Operated by Radford Air Service.	Dec. 1967
1964	Altair, Inc. (Frederick, Oklahoma)	WR 2U	Altus-Frederick, Elk City, Clinton, Lawton, Dallas, Oklahoma City, Wichita Falls	Cesnna 205	F.A.A. certificated 6 August 1963.	1966
7 Jan 1965	Capitol Airlines (Manhattan, Kansas)	RX	Manhattan-Lawrence, Salina, Topeka, Kansas City (Mo.)	Lockheed 10, Cessna types, DC-6 Twin Otter Cessna 402	Operated by Capitol Air Service. Purchased _Allen Aviation_, 13 August, l975.Operated as _Braniff Express_ from l986	30 Mar. 1989
Nov. 1965	Beeson Aviation (Topeka, Kansas)		Topeka-Kansas City (Mo.)	Cessna types	Absorbed by _Trans-Mo_.	1968
15 May 1966	Henry's Charter Air Service (Concordia, Ks.)		Concordia-Kansas City (Mo.)	Cessna types	F.A.A. certificated 17 August 1965.	1968
June 1966	Pioneer Airlines (Springfield, Mo.)		Points in Missouri	Cessna 205		1968
Sept. 1966	Interstate Airlines (Srpingfield, Mo)		Springfield-Wichita	Piper Cherokee Six		1968
3 Oct 1966	West Central Airlines (Lincoln, Nebraska)		Omaha-Beatrice, Lincoln, Des Moines, Fort Dodge, Salina, Wichita, Kansas City	DH Dove, Piper Cherokee Six	Also operated mail route, Norfolk, Columbus-Omaha. Originally based at Omaha.	1968
Nov. 1966	Trans-Mo Airlines (Jefferson City, Mo.)	XN XU	Jefferson City-Sedalia-Kansas City; J.C.-St Louis; later served Lake of the Ozarks and Cape Girardeau	Cessna types Cessna 402	F.A.A. certificated 11 July 1966. Also traded as Trans-Missouri Airlines.	6 June 1986
7 Dec. 1966	Cannon Aviation (Tulsa, Oklahoma)	CC	Tulsa-Muscogee, Mc Alester, later Albuquerque-Clovis-Lubbock	Pipe Aztec and Cherokee Six	F.A.A. certificated 3 Jan. 1966. Traded as _Carolina Airways_.	1978
3 April 1967	Sun Airlines (St Louis, then Memphis)	YV	St Louis-Kansas City, via many points in Missouri; later expansion throughout central states, from Wisconsin to Louisiana, even to Florida	Beech 18 Lear Jet DH Heron DHC 6 Twin Otter	Founded by George Caleshu. Ambitious expansion, including the first use of a jet aircraft by a scheduled air taxi.	July 1969

AREA 7 (CENTRAL) Continued

First Sched. Service Date	Airline and Base	Code	Initial or Typical Route Network	Aircraft Used	Remarks	Date of last service
April 1967	Air Midwest (Wichita, Kansas)	ZV AA EA BN TW OZ	Wichita-Kansas City; Wichita-Dodge City-Garden City-Pueblo-Colorado Springs Expanded throughout the west central states	Various Cessna and Piper types. Metro SAAB Fairchild 340 Brasilia BAe Jetstream Beech 1900	Founded by Gary M. Adamson as Aviation Services, Inc. Name changed in 1969 First airline to be specifically certificated as a third level (commuter) carrier. Purchased Skyways, 17 Jan. 1985. Associated with Ozark Airlines as Ozark Midwest at St Louis from 1 July 1985, later T.W.A.; and with Eastern Airlines as Eastern Air Midwest Express at Kansas City from 17 June 1985. Began American Eagle ops. at Nashville on 15 April 1986, and sold these to American, 31 Dec. 1987. Code-sharing with Eastern discontinued 18 Sept. 1988, when, affiliated with Braniff until latter's bankruptcy, 28 Sept 1989. Began code-sharing with USAir, 15 Jan 1991. Sold St Louis operation (T.W.A.) to Trans States (q.v.), January 1991. Purchased by Mesa Airlines 1991, but independent operations continued.	
Summer 1967	Altus Airlines (Altus, Oklahoma)	WR JE	Altus, Lawton, Oklahoma City-Dallas, Tulsa, Wichita	Piper Types BN-2 Islander Cessna 402	Began as Altus Flying Service. Services suspended Nov. 1974-1981. Operated as Braniff Express from 1987	
July 1967	Ong Airlines (Kansas City, Mo.)		Kansa City-St Louis and points in Illinois on routes to Chicago	Cessna 402	Operated by Ong Aircraft Corporation	1968
July 1967	St Louis Flying Service (St Louis)		St Louis-Kansas City (Mo.); St Louis-Lake of the Ozarks	Piper Aztec		1967
1967	Southern Aviation Airlines (Lawton, Ok.)	XO	Lawton-Ardmore-Sherman-Dallas	Cessna 206	F.A.A. certificated 15 Sept. 1964. Services suspended 1970-1973	1974
1967	Allen Air Commuter (Topeka, Kansas)	VJ	Topeka-Kansas City (Kansas), Topeka-Kansas City (Missouri) and to Manhattan, Lawrence	Piper types	Operated at first as Allen Aviation. Purchased by Capitol Air Service.	13 Aug. 1975
1967	Executive Aviation (Fort Smith, Ark.)		Fort Smith to points in Arkansas	Beech 18		1968
1968	Smyer Aircraft (Arkansas City, Ks.)	JH	Arkansas City-Wichita	Beech 18 and various small types	Main business with Cessna plants in the two cities. Proprietors killed in accident near Winfield, Kansas, 3 June 72.	June 1972
1968	King's Skyline (Olathe, Kansas)	KT	Olathe-Kansas City-Hutchinson and points in northeast Kansas	Beech 18, Cessnas, Pipers	Operated by King's Flying Service.	1969
1968	Skyway Airlines (Fort Leonard Wood, Mo.)	ZY	Fort Leonard Wood-Rolla-St Louis; Fort L.W.-Lake of the Ozarks-Kansas City; also to Columbia	Lockheed 10 Beech 18 Queen Air, Piper Cherokee Six DC-3	Division of Skyway Aviation, Inc. F.A.A. certificated 18 March 1960, semi-scheduled until 1968. Chicago service in 1969. Also operated as Fort Wood Commuter/Skyway Commuter.	April 1980
1968	Air Executive Airlines (St Louis)		St Louis-points in Ohio	Queen Air		1969

AREA 7 (CENTRAL) Continued

First Sched. Service Date	Airline and Base	Code	Initial or Typical Route Network	Aircraft Used	Remarks	Date of last service
1968	Cardinal Airways (Jefferson City, Mo.)		Local services in Missouri	Piper Navajo		1969
4 Oct 1968	Air Commuter Airlines (Grand Island, Neb.)	CT	Grand Island-Omaha	Piper types	Founded by Norman Anderson.	1970
1968	Mid Continent Airlines (Omaha)		Omaha-Denison (Iowa)-Storm Lake-Spencer-Spirit Lake	Piper Cherokee Six	Operated by Mid-Continent Aviation Inc.	1969
1969	Duncan Aviation (Lincoln, Nebraska)		Local services in Nebraska	Beech 18	Operated in connection with aircraft brokerage/leasing business.	1972
1969	Semo Airways (Malden, Missouri)	VV SM SY	Malden-Poplar Bluff-St Louis; and to Jonesboro, Little Rock, and Memphis.	Beech 18 Cessna 205 DH Heron	Operated by Semo Aviation.	Late 1984
1969	Shawnee Air Commuter (Topeka, Kansas)	KK	Topeka-Junction City-Manhattan (Ks.); Topeka-Kansas City (Mo.)	Cessna types	Operated by Shawnee Air Inc.	1972
1969	Air Missouri (Kirksville, Mo.)	BF	Kirksville-Kansas City-St Louis, Quincy (Illinois), then Spencer-Pocahontas-Des Moines	Piper types Cessna 207	Began as Horizon Airways Inc. Changed name in April 1976.	1978
1970	Sky Harbor Air Services (Omaha)		Local services in Nebraska	Cessna types	Replaced by Trans-Nebraska.	1970
1971	Trans-Nebraska Airlines (Alliance, Nebraska)	YT	Alliance-Chadron, Kearney, Lincoln, Omaha, etc.	Cessna 402	Replaced services by Sky Harbor.	1973
28 Feb 1972	Air Associates Inc. (Wichita, Kansas)	FM	Wichita-Parsons-Joplin-Springfield, Mo.	Cessna types	F.A.A. revoked certificate.	24 Dec. 1972
1972	Ed's Aircraft Service (Bartlesville, Ok.)		Bartlesville-Oklahoma City			1973
1972	Astro Airways (Pine Bluff, Ark.)	JW	Pine Bluff-New Orleans, Little Rock-Memphis	Piper Aztec DH Heron	Operated scheduled services intermittently with charter flights.	1980
1972	Mid-Continent Airlines (Duncan, Ok.)	DG	Duncan-Altus-Lawton-Norman, Oklahoma City, Dallas	Piper types	Operated by Mid Continent Bellanca Sales.	1974
Sept. 1972	Century Airlines (Olathe, Kansas)		Kansas City (International and Downtown)-Springfield-Lake of the Ozarks; K.C.-St Louis	Aero Commander Beech Queen Air	Began operations as S.S. Airways. Still operates air cargo and mail contracts.	1980
1973	Lawrence Aviation (Lawrence, Kansas)	ZQ	Lawrence-Kansas City (Mo.); later to Emporia (Ks)	Piper and Cessna types	Formed as F.B.O. in April 1972.	1983
1973	K.C. Piper Sales (Olathe, Kansas)	BK	Olathe-Kansas City (Mo.)	Piper types	Shuttle service operated within the Kansas City metropolitan area.	1973
1973	Arkansas Aero (Jonesboro, Ark.)		Local services in Arkansas			1973
1973	Twin City, Airways (Texarkana)		Texakana-Dallas			1973

AREA 7 (CENTRAL) Continued

First Sched. Service Date	Airline and Base	Code	Initial or Typical Route Network	Aircraft Used	Remarks	Date of last service
April 1974	Jetstream Commuter (Oklahoma City)		Tulsa-Oklahoma City-Dallas (Love Field)-Waco	Jetstream		July 1974
1974	Stateline Commuter Service (Leawood, Ks.)	ZS	Local services in Kansas City metropolitan area	Aero Commander Piper Cherokee Six		1975
1974	Central Airlines (Omaha)	CN	Omaha-Kansas City	Aero Commander 500		1974
1975	Central Flying Service (Little Rock, Ark.)		Local services in Arkansas			Late 1970s
1975	Aero Southwest (Altus, Oklahoma)		Altus-Oklahoma City	Cessna 206		1975
1 Nov. 1976	Air Arkansas (Eldorado, Ark.)		Eldorado-Little Rock-Shreveport	Cessna 402 Beech Turbo 18	Also traded as _Arkansas Airlines_.	April 1977
15 Nov. 1976	Air Nebraska (Kearney, Nebraska)	DF	Kearney-Denver; Kearney-Omaha, inc. Grand Island, Hastings, McCook; later to Kansas City	Cessna 402 Piper Navajo Bandeirante Nomad	Suspended service to Denver in favor of Kansas City.	July 1981
1 Dec 1977	RAI Commuter (St Louis)	EH	St Louis-Columbia, Jefferson City, Lake of the Ozarks, Springfield	Cessna 402	Operated by _Roederer Aviation, Inc_.	Mid 1982
4 April 1978	Green Hills Aviation (Kirksville, Mo.)	NG	Kirksville-St Louis and Kansas City	Piper Navajo	Took over routes vacated by _Horizon/Air Missouri_.	May 1987
26 June 1978	Air-Plains (Dodge City, Ks.)	WP	Dodge City-Garden City Liberal, Topeka, Wichita, Kansas City	Beech 18	Operated as _4 Sons Flying Service_ until June 1979.	April 1980
June 1978	Air Central (Enid, Oklahoma)	HV	Enid-Oklahoma City, Tulsa, Amarillo, Dallas	Piper Navajo	Served both airports in Dallas. Purchased by _Trans Central_ in June 1980.	1979
Aug. 1978	Arkansas Traveler Airline (Mountain Home, Ark.)	YM	Mountain Home-Memphis, Bartlesville	Beech Baron Piper types	Founded by Thomas L. Fleming Operated until August 1980 as _Mountain Home Air Service_.	Mid 1984
15 Nov. 1978	Royal-Air (Kansas City, Mo)	TR	Kansas City, Columbia, Manhattan, Topeka, Emporia	Cessna types Bandeirante		Jan 1980
2 Jan 1979	Sunbelt Airlines (Camden, Arkansas)	IM	Camden-Memphis; Camden- El Dorado-Dallas; also to points in Alabama, Louisiana, Mississippi	Cessna types, Bandeirante, Shorts SD 360	Operated as _Jamaire_ until April 1982.	9 Oct 1984
Aug. 1979	Omaha Aviation Commuter (Omaha)	LQ	Omaha (Millard Airport)-Kansas City	Piper Navajo Cessna 310		Nov 1980
1979	AAA Air Enterprises (Omaha)	CT	Omaha to points in Nebraska, Kansas City, Sioux Falls, and Yankton, S.D.	DHC-6 Twin Otter Piper Navajo Cessna 404 Bandeirante Metro	Sold to _Mid-Continent Airlines_, 1 April 1985; voluntary bandruptcy, 1986; wound up, July 1987 (see below).	1 April 1985
April 1980	Soonair Lines (Tulsa)	QJ	Tulsa-Dallas	Beech Turbo 18		June 1981

AREA 7 (CENTRAL) Continued

First Sched. Service Date	Airline and Base	Code	Initial or Typical Route Network	Aircraft Used	Remarks	Date of last service
Early 1980	Century Airlines (Kansas City, Mo.)	XE	Kansas City-Salina-Dodge City	Beech types		1980
1 Feb 1980	Gromer Aviation (Versailles, Mo.)	BF	Versailles-Kansas City, Lake of the Ozarks, Sedalia	Piper Navajo and Seneca		Nov. 1980
1 June 1980	Trans-Central Airlines (Oklahoma City)	ZM	Oklahoma City-Little Rock, Dallas, Wichita; later to Memphis, Tulsa, Topeka Amarillo, Midland/ Odessa, Wichita Falls	Piper Navajo Metroliner Nihon YS-11	Purchased assets of Air Central in December 1979.	11 Sept. 1984
1980	Bass Air Corporation (Pine Bluff, Ark.)	SZ	Pine Bluff-points in Tennessee	Cessna 402		Sept. 1980
1980	Jer Don Air Commuter Service (Ardmore, Ok.)	JN	Ardmore-Sherman-Dallas, Ardmore-Duncan-Oklahoma City	Piper Navajo		Dec 1980
11 Mar. 1981	Piasa Commuter Airlines (St Louis)	ZS	St Louis-Kansas City-Johnson County; St Louis-Mt. Vernon-Springfield	Piper Navajo Beech 99		1981
Late 1981	Altus Airlines (Altus, Oklahoma)	2U	Altus-Oklahoma City, then to Lawton, Tulsa, Dallas-Forth Worth, Wichita	Cessna 402	Operated as Braniff Express from 1987 (see also Altus Airlines, 1964-1970).	Late 1987
Mid 1983	Resort Air (St Louis)	9N 7R TW	St Louis-Columbia-Lake of the Ozarks; St Louis-Springfield; Joplin; St Louis-Carbondale, Ill.	Metroliner ATR-42	Became a unit of Trans World Express on 5 Aug. 1985; changed name to Trans State Airlines in June 1989. Bought the St Louis TWA Express operations of Air Midwest in Jan. 1991.	
1 April 1985	Mid-Continent Airlines (Aurora, Colorado)	CT	(See AAA route above)	(See above)	Founded Feb. 1985 Operated routes of AAA Air Enterprises (see above), April 1985. Became Braniff Express carrier, 1 May 1987.	7 Dec. 1989
25 Feb. 1985	Exec. Express (Stillwater, Ok., then Fort Worth)	AD	Essential Air Service (EAS) routes, Tulsa-Enid-Ponca City-McAlester; later hubs in Dallas, Memphis	Piper Navajo Dornier 228	Founded in Stillwater, Oklahoma, and moved to Ft Worth, late 1987. Chapter 11 bankruptcy.	13 April 1988
25 Jan 1986	GP Express (Grand Island, Neb.)	8G GP	Linked six EAS Points in Nebraska to Denver and Omaha	Cessna 402 Beech 99 Beech 1900	Took over EAS routes from Denver-based Pioneer Airlines. In 1990, won a south Dakota state subsidy to operate short-lived intrastate routes as G.P. Express from 8 Oct. 1990.	
July 1986	Springdale Air Service(Springdale, Ark.)		Springdale to points in eastern Arkansas	Cessna 402 Beech 18	Operated some of the routes vacated by Skyways and Air Midwest after their 1985 merger.	1987

Area 8

Texas and Louisiana

In most parts of the United States during the post–World War II era, the early commuter airlines usually emerged in response to the need to provide air service over distances that were so short, and in a market environment so variable, that airlines operating according to standard practices did not provide the service because they could not do so economically. Some of the pioneers, for example, were to be found flying over stretches of water, such as Puget Sound, Cape Cod Bay, the San Pedro Channel in California, Lake Erie, and the Florida Straits. In keeping with its tradition of being different, this was not the case with Texas.

The Lone Star State prides itself on having things and doing things in a big way. Among its sources of pride is Fort Hood, the biggest military base in the United States, occupying the area of a small country and possessing the population of a fair-sized city. It is situated about 150 miles south of Dallas and Fort Worth, about 60 miles north of Austin, and 30 or 40 miles from Temple and Waco, the nearest cities with scheduled air service. But time has always been precious for servicemen, and the need to save time gave rise to the emergence of specialized commuter airlines that catered almost exclusively to the soldiers, flying at times that suited them and not the big airline schedulers. The small airlines set up their own bases at Killeen, a small city next door to Fort Hood.

The pioneer of such operations was Hood Airlines, which started service in 1964 with the then-ubiquitous Beech 18 and made convenient connections from Fort Hood–Killeen to Dallas and Houston at the times when its customers wanted to travel. Trans-Texas Airways, in contrast—serving the nearest cities, such as Austin, Temple, and Waco, with on-line scheduled service—was interested mainly in local traffic within Texas. Had it allocated schedules to suit Fort Hood, these would not have suited its other markets.

Such was the success of Hood Airlines that it soon had a rival, DAL Airlines, but by 1968 the two had merged, and in 1970 they became part of Rio Airways when Hood's owner at the time, Ted Connell, bought that Corpus Christi–based company. Significantly, he considered the Fort Hood market so important that he transferred the airline's base there. Under the vigorous management of Pete Howe, Rio became a major force in the local airline affairs of Texas and became part of The Delta Connection in 1984, but finally terminated service in 1987. Today the tradition lives on: there is still healthy commuter airline service for the soldiers, notably that delivered by Jay Seaborn's Metro Airlines through one of its several subsidiaries.

A somewhat similar development pattern can be traced to scholastic, rather than military, necessity. One of Texas's (and the nation's) largest universities, Texas A&M, is located at Bryan, and because of the importance of this educational establishment, a sister neighborhood—owing its name, no doubt, to the railroad track—became known as College Station. The entire community was heavily dependent on the university, with a large student and teaching population with extensive travel needs, especially at the beginning and end of terms.

Like Fort Hood, Texas A&M needed its own little airline. In some ways it needed one even more, as it was relatively off the beaten track. At least Fort Hood and Killeen were in the corridor of small and medium-size cities between San Antonio and Dallas–Fort Worth, whereas Bryan was comparatively on its own between Houston and Dallas. As the railroads declined and the interstate highways came to Texas, the city of Bryan and Texas A&M were still forty miles away from the freeway. Davis Airlines, founded by L. Thomas Davis in 1965 and also flying Beech 18s, seized the market opportunity and operated for twelve years before being absorbed by Rio Airways in 1970.

During the 1970s, the whole structure of local air service in Texas and neighboring Louisiana changed. Since soon after the end of World War II, Texas had been served mainly by Houston-based Trans-Texas Airways (TTA), which, because of the size of the state it served, was the only one of the officially designated local service airlines that did not need to expand beyond the frontiers of its home state—although it did in its later years. TTA's mode of operation was a grid network of routes serving the vast reaches of Texas, centered on the triangle formed by the cities of San Antonio, Dallas–Fort Worth, and Houston, each one of which has a metropolitan population of more than a million. Dallas is one of the world's banking centers, Houston epitomizes the industrial strength of the oil industry, and San Antonio's economy is dominated by military bases and manufacturing. The three cities generate an enormous amount of air traffic, because they are between 200 and 270 miles from each other, or a half-day's drive on the interstate. Consequently, all the airlines, trunk as well as local service, concentrated on tapping this potentially lucrative market, moved into jet airliner service, and tended to neglect the routes to smaller cities.

Such was the potential of this triangular cornucopia that it gave birth to one of the most successful of all the former intrastate airlines that, before airline deregulation, were able to operate outside the federal restrictions—especially those controlling fare levels—imposed by the CAB. Texas was big enough to sustain such an airline, and in 1971, Southwest Airlines was founded by Rollin King and Herb Kelleher. Eschewing all pretenses of serving small uneconomical air routes, Southwest concentrated on providing cheap service in the triangle, with $40 round-trip tickets between any two points, and offering prepunched IBM-card packets of tickets for commuters, with monthly billing. The red hot pants and orange vinyl hot skirts of its flight attendants might have had something to do with Southwest's initial popularity, but it owed its continued success to the fact that it was literally a commuter airline service. It helped to change the conduct of airlines throughout the southwest, at a time when the operations of the smaller (commuter) airlines were already undergoing the code-sharing metamorphosis.

No longer specialist carriers of corporals and colonels, undergraduates or learned fellows, they now provide service for a more widespread clientele, with networks of routes from El Paso in the west to New Orleans in the east, and from Amarillo in the Texas Panhandle to Brownsville, southernmost point of the U.S. mainland. Like others of their kin, almost all of them have been forced into code-sharing partnerships with the major airlines, and most of the operations have become, like those of their big brothers, intensely hub-concentrated.

Interestingly, by the end of this century, Texas may again be the site of a major revolution in public transportation, one that will affect the shape and charter of all the airlines, large and small. For Texas may pioneer the way in the United States for a return to the railroads, a course of action that all the leading industrial countries of the world have already taken by the introduction of high-speed rail. Pioneered by the Japanese in 1964, with its Shinkansen system of "bullet trains," high-speed rail is now the favored means of transport, for distances of up to 350 miles or so, in France, Britain, Germany, Spain, Italy, and other countries. In the United States, only the New York–Washington Amtrak line even comes close to those systems in terms of efficiency, speed, and travel convenience. But if current plans are translated into action, there will be a revolutionary change in Texas travel habits, with a triangular rail network linking Dallas–Fort Worth, Houston, and San Antonio, with two-hour downtown-to-downtown connections at hourly frequencies. Unless the idea is destroyed by self-serving politicians and industrial competitors, its introduction is only a matter of time. Henceforth, the commuter airline industry of Texas and the Southwest may undergo a subtle change, and it may have to consider the problems of passenger transfers to a surface transport mode as well as to other airlines.

AREA 8 (TEXAS AND LOUISIANA)

First Sched. Service Date	Airline and Base	Code	Initial or Typical Route Network	Aircraft Used	Remarks	Date of last service
27 April 1964	Hood Airlines (Killeen, Texas)	HF HD	Killeen-Dallas Killeen-Houston	Beech 18 Beech 99 Cessna types	Merged with DAL Airlines under direction of Ted C. Connell.	(See DAL)
1964	Wild Goose Airlines (Del Rio, Texas)	WG	Del Rio-Bracketville-Uvalde-San Antonio; Del Rio-Eagle Pass	Piper Aztec		1967
27 Oct 1964	Solar Airlines (Pecos, Texas)	SS	Roswell-Hobbs-Midland-Dallas (Love)-Artesia-Monahans-Ft. Stockton-Alpine-Marfa-Pecos	Beech 18		1965
7 Jan 1965	Southwest Airlines (San Antonio, Texas)	SF	Del Rio-Eagle Pass-San Antonio;-Kerrville	Beech 18	Founded as Wild Goose Flying Service. Herb Kelleher (of the large national airline, Southwest) was a director.	1967
18 Feb 1965	King Airlines (Wichita Falls, Texas)	KQ	Wichita Falls-Abilene, Dallas	Beech 18 Piper types D.H. Heron	Operated by King Flight Service.	May 1971
21 Oct. 1965	Longhorn Air Service(Lafayette, Louisiana)		Lafayette-Houston-New Orleans	Piper types	Moved to Fort Worth in 1967, but did not operate.	1966
15 Dec. 1965	Davis Airlines (College Station, Bryan, Texas)	ZK DV	College Station/Bryan-Dallas-Houston	Beech 18 Piper Cherokee Six	Founded by L. Thomas Davis. Purchased by Rio Airways.	1 Dec. 1977
18 Aug. 1966	DAL Airlines (Killeen, Texas)	DG	Killeen-Dallas Killeen-DeRidder	Beech 18	Merged with Hood Airlines, with Hood as the surviving name, 23 May 1968. Absorbed by Rio Airways 1970.	1970
7 Sept 1966	Aztec Airlines (El Paso, Texas)		El Paso-Las Cruces-Silver City, Douglas	Piper Aztec		1967
14 Feb. 1967	Amistad Airlines (Del Rio, Texas)	YH YL	San Antonio-Del Rio-Victoria-Houston	Cessna 310 Piper Cherokee Six		1980
24 July 1967	Fleetway Airlines (Tyler, Texas)	FZ	Tyler-Austin, Longview-Houston, Dallas, Shreveport, Texarkana, Nacogdoches	Beech 99 Cessna 402		1969
31 Aug 1967	Central Texas Airlines (Killeen, Texas)	VR	Killeen-Dallas. Temple-Waco-Dallas. Lafayette, New Orleans, Lake Charles, Houston	Cessna 402	President: Jim Hadden Certificate revoked by State.	1970
13 Mar. 1968	La Posada Airways (Laredo, Texas)	LS	Laredo-Mc Allen-San Antonio	BN-2 Islander Cessna 402	Owned by Tom Herring, Sr., of San Antonio. Associated with La Posada Hotel in Laredo.	1968
25 Sept 1968	Air Texas (Forth Worth, Texas)	IS	Fort Worth-Austin-Houston	Beech Queen Air Beech 99	Operated by Commuter Airlines.	1970
1968	S.M.B. Stagelines (Des Moines, Iowa and Grapevine, Texas)	MJ	Muskogee-Mc Alester-Paris-Dallas	Beech 18	(See entry in Area 6.)	1976
1968	Miller Aircraft (Waco, Texas)	JJ	Waco-Dallas-McGregor	Aero Commander 500	Founded by Walter S. Miller.	1971

AREA 8 (TEXAS AND LOUISIANA) Continued

First Sched. Service Date	Airline and Base	Code	Initial or Typical Route Network	Aircraft Used	Remarks	Date of last service
1968	Tricon International Airlines (Dallas)	RI	Shreveport-Longview-Tyler-Dallas-Waco-Temple-Austin	Beech 18		1975
1969	**Metro Airlines (Houston)**	HY	Houston Int.-Clear Lake-Houston-Port Arthur, Galveston, Lake Jackson, Victoria; expansion to Dallas and northeast Texas, and later into Oklahoma and Louisiana	DHC 6 Twin Otter, Shorts SD 330, Convair 580 Jetstream	Founded by J.L Seaborn initially to link Houston's southeastern suburbs with Houston International Airport in the north. Operated as Houston Metro Airlines, then Metro Airlines. Acquired Great Plains Airlines on 1 April 1977. Became holding company of five airlines in 1981 (see Metroflight).	
15 Mar. 1970	**Rio Airways (Killeen, Texas)**	XO	Austin-San Antonio-Corpus Christi-McAllen; Houston-Corpus Christi-Laredo, Brownsville. Then Killeen-Temple-Dallas-Wichita Falls; -Waco, Texarkana-Hot Springs-Memphis	Beech 18 Twin Otter Dash 7 Metroliner Beech 1900	Founded at Corpus Christi. Transferred to Killeen, when Ted Connell, of Hood Airlines, bought airline, retaining the name. Vigorous expansion under direction of Pete Howe and Mark Connell. Associated with Delta Air Lines, 1983.	28 Feb. 1987
April 1970	**Royale Airlines (Shreveport, Louisiana)**	OQ	Shreveport-Alexandria-Baton Rouge-New Orleans; Shreveport-Fort Polk-Lafayette-New Orleans; expansion to Monroe, Houston, Gulfport, Jackson, Dallas, and south Texas; and to Pensacola and Memphis	Bandeirante Beech 99 Gulfstream Shorts SD 330 (DC-9)	Founded by D.Y. Smith, Jr. Public stock offering, 1982. Became Continental Commuter, 1 Sept. 1982, leasing a DC-9. Chapter 7 bankruptcy 1989.	Jan 1989
1973	Vanguard Airlines (New Orleans, Louisiana)	VZ	New Orleans-Houma-Patterson-Lafayette	Piper Cherokee		1974
1974	Maverick Airways (Eagle Pass, Texas)	MF	Eagle Pass-San Antonio	Piper Cherokee Six		1976
1975	Magnolia Airways (Alexandria, La.)	ZA	New Orleans-Alexandria-DeRidder/Fort Polk	Piper Navajo		1975
1975	Trans Regional Airlines (Big Spring, Texas)	TB	Midland-Big Springs-Dallas	Cessna 402	Founded by Louis Rosenbaum as El Paso Transport.	Feb 1977
1975	**Metroflight Airlines (Dallas)**	FY AA	Dallas/Fort Worth-Tyler-Longview; expanded to Houston and Oklahoma points	DHC-6 Twin Otter CV 580, SAAB 340	Associated with Great Plains Airline. Original component of Metro Airlines group, formed in 1981. Became the first American Airlines code-sharer in December, 1984.	
1976	Eagle Commuter Airlines (Brownwood, Texas)	EE	Brownwood-Fort Worth/Dallas-Waco-Houston; Brownwood-San Angelo-Austin-Houston	BN-2 Islander Piper Navajo	Founded by Gerald James. Certificated withdrawn for maintenance violations.	Jan 1986
15 Sept. 1976	Chaparral Airlines (Abilene, Texas)	FC	Abilene-Austin, Houston, Midland, Lubbock, Dallas. Later to San Antonio and Alexandria, La.	Beech 99 CASA 212 Gulfstream Piper Navajo Chieftain	Founded by Ollie Higgins and Kent Waddell, of Abilene Aero, Inc. Became an American Eagle affiliate and purchased by Metro Airlines in 1987. Merged into Metroflight.	Mid-1990
1976	Tejas Airlines (San Antonio, Texas)	TB	Laredo-San Antonio-Corpus Christi-Brownsville-McAllen-Waco-Houston-Fort Worth	Metro II Piper Navajo Chieftain		1980

AREA 8 (TEXAS AND LOUISIANA) Continued

First Sched. Service Date	Airline and Base	Code	Initial or Typical Route Network	Aircraft Used	Remarks	Date of last service
Sept 1977	Hammonds Air Service (Houma, La.)	EM	Houma-Patterson-Lafayette-Houston	Piper Navajo Twin Otter Bandeirante	Founded by Charlie Hammond.	Aug. 1984
Late 1977	Big Bend Airways (Alpine, Texas)	JZ	Alpine-Midland-Lubbock	Beech 18		Late 1978
1978	Universal Airways (New Orleans, Louisiana)	UV	New Orleans-Gulfport-Morgan City-Patterson-Laurel/Hattiesburg-Houma Also routes to Houston	Beechcraft Queen Air 80	Operated from the New Orleans Lake Front airport. Survived only a few months.	1978
Feb. 1978	Kitty Hawk Airways (Dallas, Texas)		Texarkana-Dallas	Piper Navajo	Founded by Larry Smith and Ken Dunn.	Oct 1978
1978	Emerald Air (Austin, Texas)	OD	Austin-San Antonio-McAllen-Houston-Corpus Christi-Dallas-Oklahoma City	Fairchild F-27 and FH227 (DC-9-10)	Associated with Pan American Airways as a commuter connector. Filed for Chapter 11 bankruptcy, August 1984, but still operates DC-9-14 charters.	Aug. 1984
Mid 1978	Metroplex Airlines (Ft Worth)	MQ BQ	Forth Worth-Houston	Cessna types		Early 1981
1978	Air Central (Harlingen, Texas)	RF	Harlingen-McAllen; also to Laredo and Monterey, Mexico	Cessna 402		1979
May 1979	Permian Airways, Inc. (Midland, Texas)	FZ	Midland-San Angelo-San Antonio; Midland-Lubbock-Amarillo-Carlsbad	Piper Navajo Chieftain	Founded by John Andrews and David Glover. Ceased operations because of financial problems.	16 Sept. 1982
Early 1979	Alamo Commuter Airlines (San Antonio)	JZ	San Antonio-Eagle Pass	Piper Seneca		Late 1980
11 May 1979	Commutair (Houston, Texas)	QS	Houston (Inter-continental)-Houston (Hobby)-Sugarland-Patterson	DHC-6 Twin Otter		Oct. 1980
1980	Air Texas Airways (Dallas, Texas)	OY FB	Lufkin-Houston	Piper types		Late 1980
1980	Air Texana (Beaumont, Texas)	OJ	Beaumont-Dallas (Love Field)-Dallas/Fort Worth International-New Orleans	Beechcraft Convair		Mid-1981
1981	Southern Skies (Belle Chasse, La.)	HE	Belle Chasse-New Orleans-Lafayette	Piper types		1981
1981	Central Texas Airlines (Brownwood, Tx.)	XT	Waco-Houston	Piper types	Operated as Cen-Tex Airlines.	Late 1983
1981	Texas Star Airlines (Fort Worth)	FD	Austin-Fort Worth	Cessna types		Late 1983
1983	Air New Orleans (New Orleans, La.)	NT	New Orleans-Destin-Panama City, Tampa, then to Mobile and Orlando	Beech 99 Jetstream		1988
1 April 1983	Air Spirit (Dallas/Forth Worth Int. Airport, Texas)	UJ	Dallas-Wichita Falls-Lawton-Waco-San Angelo, Texarkana	Bandeirante	Founded by Troy Post's son-affiliated with Braniff International Airways as a feeder.	1984

AREA 8 (TEXAS AND LOUISIANA) Continued

First Sched. Service Date	Airline and Base	Code	Initial or Typical Route Network	Aircraft Used	Remarks	Date of last service
1983	Wise Airlines (San Angelo, Texas)	4W	San Angelo-Brownwood, Dallas (Love Field), Midland, Austin	Beech 99 Twin Otter	Owned by N.M. Mitchell. Ceased operation under Chapter 11 bankruptcy.	1985
Dec. 1984	Air West (Houston, Texas)	WI	West Houston-Dallas (Love Field)	Twin Otter		15 Oct 1985
Dec. 1984	Forth Worth Air (Fort Worth, Texas)	YM	Forth Worth-Houston, Austin, San Antonio, Abilene, Oklahoma City, Tulsa	Nihon YS-11	Filed for bankruptcy under Chapter 11.	Sept. 1985
Late 1984	Texas Airlines	GL	Austin-Galveston-Beaumont; Lake Jackson-Houston-Beaumont	Piper types		Late 1988
1985	Texas National (San Antonio, Tx.)	GB	San Antonio-Corpus Christi-Del Rio, Laredo, McAllen; McAllen-Monterrey; Dallas-Brownwood, Temple	Piper Navajo Metro III	Registered as Intra-State carrier.	30 July 1988
June 1985	Exec Express (Forth Worth, Tx.)	AD	Stillwater-Tulsa-Enid-McAlester, Ponca City, Dallas/Forth Worth International	Piper Navajo Dornier 228	Founded by Phil Trenary and Gary Varnell in Stillwater, Oklahoma (see Exec Express II, mid-1988).	13 April 1988
Late 1985	Metro Express II (Dallas-Ft Worth)	FY AA	Dallas-Ft Worth-Killeen, College Station, San Angelo, Wichita Falls, Monroe	BAe Jetstream Shorts 330	Formed in 1984 by Jay Seaborn and Edward Henderson to compete with Rio Airways. Owned by Metro Airlines, now a holding company (q.v.).	
14 April 1988	Conquest Airlines (Beaumont, then Austin, Texas)	5C	Austin-Beaumont, Dallas, Corpus Christi	Beech 1900	Founded by Victor Rivas.	
April 1988	Laredo Air (Laredo, Texas)	5L	Laredo-San Antonio, Monterrey (Mexico), Dallas	Convair 440; 580		Late 1989
27 April 1988	Exec Express II (Forth Worth, Texas)	AD	Dallas-Ft Worth-Stillwater, Enid, Ponca City, Brownwood	Piper Navajo Beech 99	Reorganization of Exec Express, which went bankrupt.	
9 Aug. 1989	L'Express (New Orleans, La.)	4X	New Orleans-Shreveport, Alexandria, Baton Rouge, Lake Charles, Monroe	Beech 1900 Beech 99	Founded by Stephen Reed.	
1989	Servicio Aéreo Leo Lopez (El Paso)	8L	El Paso-Chihuahua	Metro	U.S. branch of Mexican independent airline based in Chihuahua.	
15 April 1990	Jet Link (Houston)	RV	Widespread network, focusing especially on Houston, Denver, and Newark	BAe Jetstream ATR 42	Became a unit of Continental Express on 16 August 1990, absorbing some routes of Rocky Mountain Airways of Denver. Other units were Bar Harbor Airlines. Bangor, and Britt Airways, Tere Haute, Ind.	

Area 9

Midwest

The early development of air transport in the Midwest was largely a reflection of the demographic balance. In addition to Chicago, a metropolis that attracted the movement of people and merchandise from throughout the area like a powerful magnet, many other cities were large enough to be regional centers in their own right. In the 1930s the state of Ohio alone could list eight, each with a population of more than 100,000. Predictably, therefore, at the dawn of commercial aviation in the United States, the fledgling airlines made sure that places such as Cincinnati, Cleveland, Columbus, Dayton, Detroit, Indianapolis, Pittsburgh, and St. Louis were on their route networks.

During that period, the feeder traffic into these population centers was well taken care of by the railroads, still at their zenith. Throughout the states of Ohio, Indiana, and Illinois, very few communities were more than a dozen miles from a railroad depot. People could catch a train into the city, or they could take an interurban railway car, for such networks were then quite extensive, reaching intercity status in some areas. With such excellent public transportation available, there was little incentive for prewar local airlines to develop.

The prewar trunk airlines served the major cities in the Midwest partly because these were conveniently placed on the transcontinental air routes, which were the main source of traffic revenue and of federal mail payments and subsidies. The airlines placed little importance on local traffic, and the passenger was obliged to fit his or her plans into the transcontinental schedule—often by traveling in the middle of the night.

After World War II, when Congress supported the admirable (and politically popular) principle that every community in the United States should have the privilege of air travel at its doorstep, local service airlines developed regional networks, each with its own sphere of influence. The Midwest, as defined for the purposes of this book, was served almost entirely by Lake Central Airlines, founded in 1947 at Indianapolis by a group headed by Roscoe Turner, the colorful racing pilot of the 1930s.

All the local service airlines depended upon subsidy to balance their books. Commendable though the objective of air-travel-for-all was, not enough air travelers were forthcoming from the small communities, and the short routes were almost impossible to operate economically. They were expensive to maintain, not least because almost as much time is spent by the airplane on the ground—or in taxiing, waiting, and climbing, circling, and descending—as in flying from point to point. No local service airline in the United States faced a bigger challenge in this respect than did Lake Central.

Trunk and local service airlines alike still clung to the operating custom of line networking, that is, flying aircraft through a combination of stopping points between selected termini at the extremities of the route system. Thus, Lake Central, for all its identification with the local region, had acquired a reputation, not necessarily for poor punctuality or regularity, but for calling at intermediate cities at times when nobody wished to travel.

This combination of circumstances led to the creation of the Taxi Air Group (TAG), founded in 1955. Under the direction of Ross Miller, one of the commuter airline industry's true innovators, TAG seized upon the special circumstances affecting travel between the two large cities in the area. Detroit and Cleveland were only 85 miles apart, but surface transport demanded a 150-mile journey along the shores of Lake Erie, via Toledo. However, the main municipal airports at both cities, as with most cities in the United States, were located out of town, and much of the advantage of air travel was thus lost. TAG solved the problem with a specialized service between the two small downtown airports, the City Airport at Detroit and Lakefront Airport at Cleveland, with flights on the hour, every hour.

For many years, TAG was one of the handful of small airlines that did not fit into any of the CAB's orthodox airline categories, like the Provincetown-Boston Airline in the northeast, Avalon Air Transport in California, and Mackey Airlines and Midet Aviation Corporation in Florida. The big airlines never seriously challenged TAG, because they did not wish to make the special efforts necessary to provide the equivalent service; doing so would interfere too much with their main source of revenue and profit, the long-haul intercity routes.

However, Ross Miller had proved a point, and many attentive eyes were cast on the Detroit City and Cleveland Lakefront airports. During the 1960s a score of small airlines emerged across the fertile lands south of the Great Lakes, often based in small or medium-size cities, such as Fort Wayne, Terre Haute, or Columbus.

During the 1950s, several smaller cities in the state of Michigan had depended on Pennsylvania-Central, later Capital Airlines. But when United Air Lines purchased Capital in 1960, some Michigan routes were dropped from the system, thus providing new opportunities, first for the local service companies and then for their commuter airline successors.

Although the railroads declined as passenger carriers, they were replaced by a specialized network of highly efficient divided highways. The famous Pennsylvania Turnpike was extended all the way to Chicago by turnpike roads, and these were complemented by the massive interstate highway construction program.

Today's commuter airlines of the Midwest, therefore, have inherited few natural advantages to stimulate or justify their existence—no high mountain ranges to impede surface connections, no over-water routes for which the only surface competition is the ferryboat, and no long distances, compared to such areas as the Rocky Mountains or the prairie states. The flat lands of the region encourage the use of the automobile. With the advent of code-sharing and the close association between the commuter and major airlines that occurred during the 1980s, there seems to be room for only a few highly concentrated operators such as Jetlink (Continental Express), Comair (The Delta Connection), Simmons (American Eagle), and Jetstream International (USAir Express).

Other than these, the chances for survival, even of the very existence, of independent commuter airlines in the region are slim indeed. During the 1980s, new entrants have totaled fewer than a dozen, and most have lasted only a couple of years or so. Bill Fischer, for instance, had been one of the partner brothers who, back in the 1950s, had spotted a window of opportunity at Galion and Mansfield, Ohio, off the beaten airways track of all the airlines. When he tried again in 1988, after his former company had folded, he had to accept the inevitable and cease operations in 1990.

The Fischer brothers, with their GCS Flying Service, had epitomized the rise of the midwestern commuter airlines in the 1960s. The demise of GCS Air Service in 1990 seemed to epitomize their fall.

AREA 9 (MIDWEST)

First Sched. Service Date	Airline and Base	Code	Initial or Typical Route Network	Aircraft Used	Remarks	Date of last service
1935	Island Airlines (Port Clinton, Ohio)		Sandusky-Bass Islands Later Port Clinton-B.I.	Ford Tri-Motor Boeing 247 DHC-2 Beaver DHC-3 Otter Cessna types	Founded at Put-in-Bay, South Bass Island in 1929 by Milton "Red" Hersberger, originally as Erie Isle Airways, then as Air Tours. Purchased in 1953 by Ralph Dietrick, of Sky Tours. Moved from Sandusky to Port Clinton in 1962. Changed name when Fords purchased.	
1950s	Midwest Airways (Cincinnati)	DW	Cincinnati-Detroit, Columbus, Cleveland; later to Traverse City, Charlevoix, Harbor Spr.	L-10 Electra	Started by Eddie Lunken from Cincinnati's Lunken Field.	1965
1951	Fischer Brothers Aviation, dba GCS Air Service-Galion Commuter Air Service (Galion, Ohio) moved to Springfield, Illinois, May 1987)	GS GO GP EG NW AL ML	Galion-Marion- Mansfield-Cleveland (Note: GCS derived from Galion- Crestline-Shelby)	Piper Aztec Lockheed 12 Beech 18 DH 104 Dove DH 114 Heron Shorts 330, 360 CASA 212 Dornier 228	Founded by Montford and Wm. Fischer in 1948 as Shelby Sky Haven. Inc. as Fisher Bros. in 1963. Became Allegheny Commuter in 1969, later Northwest Airlink in 1986. CASA 212 crash March 1987. Purchased by Midway Airlines and began operations on 15 June 1987 as Midway Connection with hub at Midway Airport, Chicago.	1991
1 July 1957	TAG Airlines (Detroit)	TO	Detroit(City)-Cleveland (Lakefront). Also to Akron and Chicago (Meigs)-Rockford, and Pittsburgh (Allegheny Apt.)	DH Dove DH Heron (also DHC Beaver and Otter) Piper Aztec	Founded in Cleveland as Taxi Air Group by Wm. Knight in 1955. Sold to Ross Miller in 1957 and started year-round service. Merged with Illini Airlines of Rockford, Illinois, in 1957. Moved to Detroit, July 1958. Dove crash in Lake Erie 28 Jan. 1970.	7 Aug. 1970
12 Nov. 1962	Hulman Airlines (Terre Haute, Ind.)	HU	Terre Haute-Indianapolis, T.H.-Chicago	Cessna types	Founded as Hulman Field Aviation in 1959. Changed name in 1968.	late 1970s
4 Feb. 1963	Fort Wayne Air Service (Ft. Wayne, Indiana)		Fort Wayne-Detroit	Beech 18		1960s
18 May 1964	Detroit Northern Airlines (Alpena, Mich)		Alpena-Detroit	Piper, Cessna types Beech 18 (DC-3)	Founded by Robert C. Welch. Operated by Alpena Flying Services.	1975
29 Sept. 1964	Phillips Flying Service (Conway, Mich.)		Pellston-Mackinac Island and St. Ignace	Piper Cherokee Six	Founded by Alfred Phillips as FBO in early 1940s. Service connected with North Central Airlines at Pellston. Sold to John Guisinger and later to Welch Aviation.	1983
2 Dec. 1964	Miller Airlines (Reed City, Michigan)	YM	Reed City-Grand Rapids-Chicago (Meigs)	Beech 18 Cessna 402	Operated by Miller Airmotive.	1969
1 Mar. 1965	Christman Air System (Connellsville, Penn.)	1J AB SX	Originally (Pitt) a shuttle service between Pittsburgh's two airports Then expanded (as Keystone) local network around Pittsburgh to near cities, inc. Wheeling, Akron etc.	Beech 18 Piper Navajo Beech 99 Bandeirante	Formerly Miller Aviation Center. Then became Pitt Airways, March 1965, changing to Pitt Airlines, 3 Aug. 1967. Renamed Keystone Commuter in 1969. Expanded as Keystone Airlines, and changed name when purchased by Walter Christman in September 1977.	

AREA 9 (MIDWEST) Continued

First Sched. Service Date	Airline and Base	Code	Initial or Typical Route Network	Aircraft Used	Remarks	Date of last service
29 July 1965	Casement Aviation (Painesville,Ohio)		Painesville-Cleveland	Small Cessnas and a Lockheed L-10A Electra	Founded by R.W. Sidley in 1962. Mainly a fixed based operator.	1969
15 Nov. 1965	Shawnee Airways, Inc.(Akron, Ohio)		Akron-Detroit	Beech 18 Lockheed L-12A	Founded in 1958 by Ernest Stadvec as Stadvec Aviation, changed name in 1961 after aircraft collision.	1966
10 Feb. 1966	Air Enterprises (Huntington, W. Va.)		Huntington-Columbus	Piper Aztec	Operated briefly by O.M. Pierce as a connector to TAG Airlines. Became Tyme Airlines when TAG suspended some routes.	1968
16 April 1966	Phillips Airlines (Michigan City, Ind.)	FR PP FQ	Michigan City-Chicago	Piper Apache Piper Aztec	Founded by Joe Phillips as FBO in 1959.	May 1985
1966	Commuter Airlines of Chicago (Chicago)	UU	Chicago (Meigs and O'Hare)-Detroit (City)-Elkhart-Springfield	Beech Queen Air Beech 99	Founded by Chuck Downey. Taken over by Hub Airlines.	Sept. 1970
27 June 1966	**Wright Air Lines (Cleveland)**	FW KC	Cleveland (Lakefront)-Detroit (City). Also to Columbus-Dayton-Pittsburgh, Louisville, Detroit (Metro) Cincinnati, Cleveland, etc.	Beech 18 DH Heron CV440/600/ 640 Shorts 360 DHC-6 Twin Otter	Founded by Gerald Weller, ex-TAG sales manager. Merged with Air Commuter 4 March 1968; with Tyme Airlines, 3 July 1968; and with Aero Mech., Oct. 1983. Weller (who had named company after Wright brothers) left in 1969. Gibby Singerman took over. First commuter airline to go public. Bankrupt 1984. Dropped all routes except Cleveland-Detroit 19 Jan. 1985.	July 1985
25 July 1966	Standard Airways (Pontiac, Michigan)		Detroit-Pontiac-Port Huron-Cleveland (Lakefront)	Beech 18 Piper Navajo		1967
25 Oct. 1966	Trans Aire (Detroit)					1968
21 Dec. 1966	Hub Airlines (Fort Wayne, Ind. then Chicago (Meigs)	XE	Chicago (Meigs)-Dayton-Detroit-Fort Wayne-South Bend	Beech 80 Beech 99	Started by George Bailey. Took over Commuter Airlines of Chicago, 1970. Routes taken over by Skystream Airlines. Associated with Great Lakes Commuter, 1972.	Late 1973
20 June 1967	Midwest Commuter Airlines (Indianapolis)	UM ZB	Indianapolis-Chicago (Meigs), via South Bend	Piper types Beech 99	Taken over by Hub Airlines, then Skystream Airlines.	1974
28 June 1967	Air Commuter (Cleveland)		Cleveland(Lakefront)-Detroit-Columbus	DHC 6 Twin Otter	Founded by Arthur King and F. Jerome Tone. Merged with Wright Airlines.	3 Mar. 1968
1967	Buckeye Air Service (Elyria, Ohio)	UY	Chicago-Detroit-Cleveland	Beech 18		1971
3 Oct. 1967	Tyme Airlines (Columbus, Ohio)		Columbus-Detroit-Cleveland-Huntington Toledo, Portsmouth	Piper Aztec	Founded by O.M. Pierce. Operated in conjunction with TAG Airlines. Merged with Wright Airlines.	3 July 1968
22 Jan. 1968	Time Airlines (Benton Harbor, Mich.)	JI	Benton Harbor-Chicago (Meigs and Midway) - Detroit	Beech 18 Beech 99	Founded by Gene Cramer. Took over Midwest Commuter.	July 1969

AREA 9 (MIDWEST) Continued

First Sched. Service Date	Airline and Base	Code	Initial or Typical Route Network	Aircraft Used	Remarks	Date of last service
1 July 1968	Galaxy Airlines (Cleveland)		Cleveland (Cuyahoga)-Cleveland (Lakefront)-Columbus-Dayton-Cincinnati	(DC-3)	Gained CAB exemption to operate DC-3s.	23 April 1969
25 July 1968	Standard Airways (Port Huron, Mich.)	FD	Detroit-Birmingham-Pontiac-Port Huron	Piper Navajo Chieftain Beech 18		1967
1968	Michigan Trade Winds (Lansing, Mich.)		Lansing-Detroit (City)	Cessna 402	Operated for one summer only.	1968
28 July 1968	**Britt Airways (Danville, then Terre Haute)**	YV RU AL PI PE EA CO	Danville-Chicago, then Danville-Indianapolis, Bloomington, Muncie, Terre Haute, etc.	Beech 18, 99 Swearingen Metro FH-227C BAC One-Eleven DHC-7 Bandeirante ATR-42	Founded as Vercoa Air Service, (from Vermillion Country Airport) at Danville, Ill., July 1956. Became an Allegheny Commuter in 1968. Purchased by Wm. Britt, 1975, changing name to Britt Airlines on 1 June 1976. Sold to People Express Jan. 1986, and absorbed by Texas Air Corp./Continental Express. In 1976, Britt Airways formed to operate non-Allegheny routes. Also operated briefly for Eastern Express at Philadelphia, Piedmont at Dayton and several other alliances. Merged with Rocky Mountain Airways, 15 April 1990. Changed name to Jet Link 15 May 1990.	
30 July 1968	Northern Airlines (St Mary's, Ohio)	NN	St. Mary's-Dayton-Lima-Findlay-Cleveland-Louisville. Also to Bowling Green, Nashville	Beech 18 DHC-6 Twin Otter	Went bankrupt.	16 June 1970
1968	E.F.S. Airlines (Bloomington, Indiana)		Bloomington-Indianapolis			1969
1969	Cincinnati Airlines (Cincinnati)	QH	Cincinnati (Lunken)-Cleveland (Lakefront)	Cessna 402		1970
17 Mar. 1969	Sundorph Aeronautical Corp. (Cleveland)	UQ	Cleveland (Hopkins)-Akron; later to Columbus and Detroit (City)	Lockheed Lodestar Piper Navajo	Founded by Eiler Sundorph, F.B.O. operator. Suspended scheduled service 1970 and restarted on 1 June 1983.	Dec. 1983
17 Mar. 1969	Crown Airways (Falls Creek and Harrisburg, Penn.)	AL PI US	Pittsburgh-Dubois-Franklin	Beech 99 DHC-6 Twin Otter Shorts SD 330	Moved to Harrisburg, Pa., in 1972 to become Allegheny Commuter. Then became division of Brockway Air of Burlington, VT., and a Piedmont Commuter, then US Air Express on 1 July 1989. Sold to Al Beiga and Phil Burnaman, March 1990.	
June 1969	Trans-Michigan Airlines (Traverse City, Mich.)	VZ	Traverse City-Detroit-Flint-Lansing-Marquette, and other cities in Michigan	Beech 99	Succeeded Peninsula Air Transport and was succeeded by Great Lakes Airlines.	March 1970
July 1969	Air Michigan (Kalamazoo, Michigan)	QS	Kalamazoo-Benton Harbor-Detroit-Grand Rapids-Lansing	Cessna 310 Beech 99 DHC-6 Twin Otter	Founded by Dr. Curtis Benson. Known to have hired very short flight attendants for Beech 99 flights.	Jan. 1972

AREA 9 (MIDWEST) Continued

First Sched. Service Date	Airline and Base	Code	Initial or Typical Route Network	Aircraft Used	Remarks	Date of last service
2 Sept. 1969	Hulman Field Aviation, Inc. (Terre Haute, Ind.)	HU	Terra Haute-Indianapolis	Cessna 402	Grew out of cargo and air taxi operation founded by George Johnson.	1971
Nov. 1969	Tri-State Aviation (Huntington, W. Virg.)	JY	Huntington-Columbus, Cincinnati	Aero Commander BN-2 Islander	Founded as F.B.O. by Carlton Clark. Sched. operation started by Ed Hyman and Morris Griffiths.	May 1970
Dec. 1969	Alpha Airlines (South Bend, Ind.)	HP	South Bend-Chicago (Meigs) and Detroit			March 1970
25 Oct. 1970	Air East (Johnstown, Penn.)	AL	Johnstown-Pittsburgh-Altoona	DH Dove Beech 99	Founded by B.F. McKinney. Operated as Allegheny Commuter until a crash at Johnstown on 6 Jan. 1974. Taken over by Clark Aviation (Pennsylvania Airlines).	31 May 1974
1972	MATS Airlines (Peoria, Ill.)	HF	Rockford-Detroit-Peoria-Indianapolis			1973
1 May 1972	Great Lakes Commuter (Flint, Michigan)	VK	Traverse City-Chicago, via points in Michigan	Beech 99	Linked with Hub Airlines for a short period. Sold to Skystream Airlines.	April 1974
1972	Shorter Airlines (Pellston, Michigan)	EO	Detroit-Pellston-Mackinac-Sault Ste Marie	Beech 18 Beech 99 DC-3	Also operated seasonal services in Florida (winter only).	1974
1 March 1973	Apollo Aviation (Lima, Ohio)	AL	Lima-Columbus-Toledo	Beech 99	Operated entirely as Allegheny Commuter by Col. Benjamin Moore, formerly associated with Apollo Space program.	28 Feb. 1974
15 Nov. 1973	Skystream Airlines (Plymouth, Indiana, later to South Bend, then to Chicago, Meigs)	DN	Plymouth-South Bend-Indianapolis-Detroit; to Chicago after Hub takeover	Beech 99	Founded by Cecil Pond, who took over routes of former Hub Airlines. Bought Great Lakes Commuter, April 1974. Suspended service Jan.-April 1975. Took over remnants of Midwest Commuter May 1975. Crash at Meigs Field, 9 June 1979.	14 April 1980
1 Aug. 1974	Chautauqua Airlines (Jamestown, New York)	AL	Pittsburgh-Jamestown-Buffalo, Pittsburgh-Bradford, and points in northern New York state, and to Canada; later to Pittsburgh-Akron and Orlando-Vero Beach	Beech 99 Shorts 330 Metro SAAB 340	Founded by Joel Hall as Allegheny Commuter. Expanded with a Florida Divison 1 February 1979. USAir Express 1 July1989.	
23 Sept. 1974	Air Kentucky (Owensboro, Ky., then Indianapolis, Ind.)	KN AL	Owensboro-Louisville-Paducah-Frankfort-Bowling Green-Evansville-Chicago	Beech 18 Beech 99 Bandeirante Metro	Founded by L.S. Cox as Owensboro Aviation. Became Allegheny Commuter in 1980. Purchased by G.M.F. Investments (parent company of Fairchild, March 1989).	15 May 1989
1974	Eagle Aviation (Flint, Michigan)			Beech 18 Aero Commander		1975

AREA 9 (MIDWEST) Continued

First Sched. Service Date	Airline and Base	Code	Initial or Typical Route Network	Aircraft Used	Remarks	Date of last service
1975	Air Metro Airlines (Traverse City, Mich.)	JB	Detroit-Pontiac-Traverse City; Detroit-Lansing-T.C.-Marquette, Hancock	Beech 99		July 1976
1975	Isle Royale Seaplane Service (Isle Royale, Mich.)		Isle Royale-nearby cities	Piper and Beech types	Service only for one summer season.	1975
10 Sept. 1975	Colonial Airlines (Cambridge, Ohio)		Cambridge-Columbus, Dayton, Akron	Volpar Beech 18	Founded by Novara Nichols.	Dec. 1975
1975	Commut Air of Michigan (Pontiac)	WL	Detroit-Toledo-Lima; Detroit-Pontiac	DHC-6 Twin Otter		1976
1976	Atlas Airlines (Muncie, Indiana)		Cincinnati-Dayton-Fort Wayne	Piper Navajo	Founded by George Wertjes to connect with TWA. Short lived.	Late 1976
Oct. 1976	Seaco Airlines (Detroit)	ZG	Detroit-Lansing-Traverse City/Oscoda-Alpena	Piper Aztec Cessna 402	Operated for a few years, with a mail contract.	June 1980
31 Aug. 1976	Lake Central Av. (Traverse City, Mich.)	FR	Hancock-Marquette-TraverseCity-Lansing-Columbus	Cessna 402		Late 1977
April 1977	Comair (Cincinnati)	OH DL	Cincinnati-Gainsville-Cleveland(Wings); Cincinnati-Dayton-Akron;Cincinnati-Evansville, considerable expansion through Great Lakes states, western Appalachia, and set up new hub at Orlando, Florida	Piper Navajo Bandeirante Shorts SD 330 SAAB SF340 Metroliner Brasilia	Founded as Wings Airways by Pat Sowers and Charlie Fugazzi, starting on 17 May 1976. Bought by Raymond and David Mueller in 1977, and changed name. Became unit of Delta Connection September, 1984, and began rapid expansion, including a second main hub at Orlando, Fla. (see Area 10) on 1 Nov. 1977.	
August 1977	Chippewa Air Commuter (Manistee Michigan)	LW	Manistee-Mt Pleasant-Detroit	BN-2 Islander	Operated for only a few months.	Jan 1978
Oct. 1977	Heussler Air Service(Buffalo)	HQ	Buffalo-Erie-Detroit	Cessna 402 Cessna Citation	Founded by Richard Hammond. One of the few commuter airlines to operate jet aircraft (Citation). Still operates as charter operator.	1983
15 Nov. 1977	Indiana Airways (W. Lafayette, Ind.)	WY	Indianapolis-Lafayette-Columbus	Piper Navajo	Founded by Charles R. Reid, owner of Reid Airways.	15 April 1980
1978	Rapidair, Inc. (Cincinnati)	MC	Cincinnati-Athens-Pittsburgh	Cessna 402		1979
1 May 1978	Air Atlantic Airlines (Centre Hall, Penn.)	OX	State College-Philadelphia, Pittsburgh, Altoona	Piper types	Founded by Russell E. Schleiden, of Penn's Cave Aviation.	9 Jan. 1981
March 1979	Air Great Lakes (Chicago, Ill.)	GO	Chicago-Milwaukee-Minneapolis, Ft. Wayne, South Bend	Corand Commander Piper Navajo	Originally founded by Gil Chcone as PAFCO Airlines (Priority Air Freight Company). Lost F.A.A. cert. Dec. 1979; Purchased by Joe Vallee and changed name to Skytrain Airlines 15 May 1981; then changed name again, to Air Great Lakes 15 Sept. 1981.	May 1982
1979	Indiana Airways (Indiana, Penn.)	GZ	Indiana (Pennsylvania)-Pittsburgh-Youngstown	Piper types		April 1980

AREA 9 (MIDWEST) Continued

First Sched. Service Date	Airline and Base	Code	Initial or Typical Route Network	Aircraft Used	Remarks	Date of last service
Oct. 1979	B.A.S. Airlines (Beaver Falls, Penn. then Youngstown, Ohio)	GS	Youngstown-Detroit (City)-Cleveland	Cessna types	Founded as Skyline Motors Aviation Services. Name changed in June 1981.	Early 1991
1 Oct. 1979	Air Indiana (Indianapolis)	LT	Indianapolis-Danville, St. Louis	DC-3		Dec. 1979
Late 1979	Niemeyer Aviation (Kentland, Ind.)	DK	Valparaiso-Kentland-Indianapolis; Chicago-Kankakee-Kentland	Grumman AA5B Tiger	Founded by Don Niemeyer. Probably only airline to have operated this Grumman type.	Jan 1980
Mar. 1980	Sunbird, Inc. (Murray, Ky.)	FS	Murray, Ky.-Paris, Tenn.-Memphis, Nashville	Piper types	Founded by Dudley Boume.	Dec. 1986
27 April 1980	Freedom Airlines (Cleveland)	CB DN	Cleveland-Flint-Grand Rapids-Lansing-Saginaw	Convair 580 Metroliner	Started as division of Commuter Airlines, Binghamton by Jerry Winston. Expanded to Pennsylvania, Washington, D.C. and Virginia. Ceased operations when Winston died.	14 Oct. 1984
May 1980	Jetstream International (Latrobe, Penn., then to Erie, Penn.)	TF PI US	Latrobe-Pittsburgh-Indiana, then to Erie, Cleveland, Indianapolis, Dayton. Also operated briefly in Florida	Cessna types BAe Jetstream Bandeirante Shorts SD 330	Founded by V. Neal Frey as Vee Neal Airlines at Latrobe, Penn. Changed name 1 Dec. 1983. Piedmont Commuter, 1 November 1985, and sold to Henson Aviation, 1 August 1986. Hubs at Dayton and Baltimore. After USAir merged with Piedmont, closed Baltimore hub and moved it to Indianapolis. Took over many of Air Kentucky's routes when it closed down in May 1989. Now USAir Express.	
May 1980	Emmet County Aviation (Harbor Springs, Michigan)	QQ	Mackinac Island-Pellston	Piper types Cessna 206	Seasonal service, taken over by Michigan Airways.	April 1982
1 June 1980	Terre Haute Air Commuter (Terre Haute, Ind.)	MP	Terre Haute-Lawrenceville	Piper types	Started by William Hubbard and Jack Doub as H & D Aviation; operated as Terre Haute Air Commuter, April 1981.	1 Aug. 1981
June 1980	Penn-Aire (Altoona, Pa.)		Altoona-New York (La Guardia)	Piper Navajo	Founded by W.C. McQuaide.	July 1980
Nov. 1980	Alpine Aviation Corp. (Rockford, Illinois)	ZA	Rockford-Detroit	Beech		Feb. 1981
1980	Erie Airways (Erie, Penn.)	FV	Erie-Detroit, Erie-Pittsburgh	Cessna types	Founded by Bill Connor.	April 1982
April 1981	Direct Air (Kokomo, Ind., later to Ft. Wayne)	UO	Kokomo-Chicago, later to Gary, Ft Wayne, Detroit, Cleveland, etc.	Piper Navajo Beech Catpass 200	Founded by Michael Pittard. Sold to Will Davis in 1991.	
18 Jan 1982	Liberty Airlines (Toledo Ohio)	CK	Toledo-Chicago (Midway), Akron, Philadelphia	Beech Baron Convair 440		May 1983

AREA 9 (MIDWEST) Continued

First Sched. Service Date	Airline and Base	Code	Initial or Typical Route Network	Aircraft Used	Remarks	Date of last service
May 1982	Michigan Airways (Pellston, Mich.)	QQ	Pellston-Mackinac Island; later Alpena-East Tawas-Saginaw-Detroit	Piper Navajo DHC-6 Twin Otter 300	Formerly Emmet County Aviation (see above). Purchased by James van Sickle and Robert James Smith. Changed name to Drummond Island Air, July 1989, after purchase by James C. Bailey and Bruce Varda.	Jan 1991
2 Dec 1982	Swift Air (Sout Bend, Ind.)		Sturgis-South Bend-Chicago (Meigs)	Piper Navajo		1984
1 Aug. 1983	Trans Midwest Airlines (Columbus, Ohio)	7T	Columbus-Lima, Dayton Cincinnati, Huntington, Charleston	Piper Navajo	Founded by Tom Koehler. Originally intended to be a TWA Commuter, but operated as an independent.	April 1985
March 1985	West Penn Commuter, (St Mary's, Penn.)	BB	St Mary's-Pittsburgh	Piper types	Founded by Mike Cardimone and Leo Angevine as Bradford Air Transport. Changed name March 1986.	April 1986
1987	Welch Aviation (Alpena, Mich.)		Alpena-Detroit (Metro)	Piper Navajo	Founded by Robert C. Welch. Operated for six months, until Simmons entered market.	End 1987
March 1988	G.C.S. Air Service (Galion, Ohio)	GP 7R	Mansfield-Cleveland	Beech Queen Air	Founded by Wm. Fischer, after Fischer Brothers Aviation (see above, 1951) sold to Midway Airlines.	Feb. 1990
2 May 1988	Enterprise Airlines (Cincinnati)	BE	Cincinnati-Columbus-Milwaukee; Columbus-Cincinnati-Baltimore, later to many points in northeast, incl. New York, Boston, Memphis	Cessna Citation	Founded by Pat Sowers. Sold 51% stock to Chicago West Pullman, June 1989. Began Boston-New York (JFK) as British Airways Commuter, 1 June 1989, connecting with Concorde flights. Later operated Hartford-Boston.	14 Nov. 1990
Nov. 1989	Central States Airlines (Cleveland-Cuyahoga)	PS	Cleveland (Cuyahoga)-Cincinnati (Lunken), Pittsburgh, Detroit (City)	BAe Jetstream	Founded by Thomas Small and partners.	11 Oct. 1990
7 March 1990	Northcoast Executive Airlines (Dayton-General Airport)	5N	Dayton (General)-Detroit (City); Chicago (Midway)-Flint	Metro III	Founded by Cal Humphreys. Link with Midway Airlines at Chicago (Midway), Sept. 1990.	23 Jan. 1991

Area 10

Southeast

Air activity in the six southeastern states has, since the beginning, been concentrated in Florida. The inheritance by the commuter airlines of that state's historic role as the cradle of commercial aviation in the United States therefore comes as no surprise. In 1914, Florida witnessed, with the debut of the St. Petersburg–Tampa Airboat Line, the world's first scheduled airline service; in 1920 it hosted Aeromarine West Indies Airways, the first airline in the United States to survive for more than a few months. In 1936, Florida Airways was the first to open contract airmail service (though this was not sustained), and in 1927, Pan American Airways inaugurated the first tentative route of what was to be the world's first truly transocean, globe-encircling airline, while Miami became the aviation gateway to Latin America. Considering Chalk's Flying service, there is some credence to the claim that Florida also produced the first small operator, because "Pappy" Chalk, who started operations in 1919, always maintained that his was America's oldest airline, albeit with a broad interpretation of the true functions of an airline.

This last assertion depends on one's definition of an airline, and by all the normal criteria Chalk's claim does not stand up. For almost the entire period of operation before World War II, Chalk's service was offered on demand only, and there is scant evidence that he ever kept to a timetable, much less published one, even though there was usually a flight to Bimini at around breakfast time. Regular, punctual, and dependable service is an essential qualification for recognition as an airline. After World War II, however, on 21 November 1947, Chalk successfully applied to the CAA for a certificate as an irregular air carrier, and so from that date onward his service could legitimately be admitted to the airline ranks, even though his flights were customarily intermittent.

Another issue to be taken into consideration is whether or not Chalk's could be defined as a U.S. commuter airline, for he never operated within the United States, only on foreign routes to the tantalizingly close Bahamas. But this ruling would apply also to dozens of other southeastern operators, many of whom flew within Florida and to neighboring states as well as to the British (and later independent) neighboring islands.

The state of Florida has, for several decades, been among the fastest growing of all the states of the union. Its welcoming beaches, its consistently warm climate, its proximity to the Caribbean, and, since the advent of air transport, its relative convenience to the highly populated and seasonally chilled Northeast—all these factors have combined to encourage prosperity and spectacular growth, based on a vigorous tourist industry and, more recently, marketing of the state as an attractive area for retirement homes. The size and shape of the state have also contributed to the popularity of air transport. Its airlines have joined those of California, Texas, and a few other states in being big enough to sustain themselves wholly within a state boundary, and therefore able to operate outside the rigid federal control of the CAB. The surface journey between the main centers of population—Miami, Tampa, Jacksonville, and more recently Orlando, with Disney World—is long enough and unattractive enough, in the absence of a passenger railroad system, to stimulate air traffic.

And so, in the early years of the commuter airline boom of the 1960s (when they were still called scheduled air taxi operators), most of the small airlines of the southeastern corner of the United States tried to exploit these often lucrative markets. Two of the most successful companies, Naples Airlines and Executive Airlines, followed the precedent set forty years earlier by Aeromarine Airways. Founded and based mainly in the Boston–Cape Cod area of Massachusetts, John Van Arsdale and Joe Whitney each moved some of their operations south to Florida in the early 1960s to take advantage of the annual winter traffic surge.

This is not to suggest that commuter airline traffic in the southeast consisted entirely of intrastate Florida traffic, Bahamas connectors, or routes along the Florida Keys. Airlines have been founded, have even occasionally prospered, in other southeastern states; but because of the polarized population distribution, and the different balance of urban versus rural inhabitants, the same incentives provided by the multiple cities of Florida were not as great in Georgia, Alabama, Mississippi,

Tennessee, or South Carolina. An exception was the emergence of Atlanta, not only as a metropolis in its own right, but also, because of its geographic location, as a major airline hub. Delta, a major trunk carrier, and Southern Airways, a local service operator, had created intensive and dynamic airline spoke patterns long before the mid-1980s, when the hub-and-spoke system of route and schedule planning became the essential feature of airline operating practice throughout the land. With such excellent service as those two airlines provided throughout the postwar era, until the advent of airline deregulation in 1978, the need for competing or supplementary airlines hardly existed. The average income level in the region was also low, so that the sparse distribution of commuter airlines across a broad belt from the Mississippi to the South Carolina coastline was no accident.

Nevertheless, the way in which the commuter airline balance evolved during the 1970s and 1980s was based far more broadly than on Florida demographics and geography alone. Some of the earlier pacesetters somehow lost their way, mainly by outgrowing their own strengths or, as many an airline in the higher echelons has done, by trying to expand too quickly, too soon. The classic example was the downfall of Naples Airlines/Provincetown-Boston Airlines which, after various reorganizations and changes of ownership, built up the biggest fleet in the industry and then went bankrupt in only a year or two of sensational headlines.

After 1968, dozens of airlines came and went, but few survived beyond the mid-1970s, as other aspirants took their place and, in turn, lasted only a few years. The big airlines started to consolidate their position as godfathers to the smaller ones, who were forced into code-sharing arrangements and obliged to surrender their independence in favor of partial, if not complete, ownership by their larger brethren. Those that defied extinction were either close associates of the major airlines or "express" carriers created by the major airlines themselves.

Atlantic Southeast Airlines (ASA) was one of the most successful and, against the traditional trend, was based in Atlanta. Founded by George Pickett and two other former Southern Airways executives, it inherited many of the spoke-patterned routes from that city that had been abandoned or neglected by Republic Airlines (formerly Southern), which had in turn been taken over by Northwest Airlines. ASA became an important arm of The Delta Connection group of satellite carriers and grew rapidly to rank as one of the largest, and one of the most profitable, of all the commuter airlines. Another Delta affiliate, Comair, from Cincinnati, also established a division at Orlando, concentrating on the vacation traffic that was the inevitable sequel to the establishment there of the outstandingly successful Disney World.

Intensely leisure-oriented, the commuter airlines of the southeast have always tended alternately to prosper and fade in tune with the rise and fall of the economy and the resultant fluctuation in discretionary incomes. But Florida as a state, and Atlanta as a southern metropolis, are both now of such stature as traffic generators in their own right, for year-round business and social travel, that with good management the continued success of the commuter airline industry in the southeast is assured.

Prospective airlines should, however, be careful not to follow the lead of Sunair, of Fort Lauderdale, whose grandiose ambitions and sensational advance publicity were unsupported by careful planning or adequate financing, staffing, or experience. Sunair managed to exist for only twenty-four hours, March 17–18, 1981, and it left behind debts estimated at upward of $1 million.

At least Chalk's is still flying, albeit now as Chalk's International, and its Grumman flying boats are among the few waterborne aircraft in the world still plying their trade in the airline business. So the Southeast holds the record over the years for having nourished among its commuter airline fraternity both the longest- and the shortest-lived. And there were a great many in between.

AREA 10 (SOUTHEAST)

First Sched. Service Date	Airline and Base	Code	Initial or Typical Route Network	Aircraft Used	Remarks	Date of last service
21 Nov. 1947	Chalk's International Airlines (Miami)	OG BK	Miami-Bimini, Miami-Nassau, and other destinations in the Bahamas	Grumman Goose, Grumman Mallard, Grumman Turbo Mallard	Has always claimed to be the oldest airline in the world. Chalk's, formed by Arthur ("Pappy") Chalk in 1919, has operated regularly since that time, but only intermittently on any kind of fixed schedule, and continuously only since after the end of World War II, when it was controlled by Resorts International. Known as Chalk's Flying Service until it opened its Watson Island terminal in 1936. Took over operations of Paradise Island Airways in December 1989, but reverted to independence again on 1 January 1991.	
1 Jan. 1960	Naples Airlines (Naples, Florida)	PT CO	Naples-Miami; Naples-Marco Island; Miami-Marco Island; Naples-Tampa, Naples-Ft Myers	Lockheed 10A Piper Aztec Douglas DC-3 Cessna 402 Marin 4-0-4 Bandeirante	Established as subsidiary of Provincetown-Boston Airline, when it transferred equipment seasonally to participate in Florida's winter traffic. Sold to People's Express May 1986, which in turn was taken over by Texas Air Corporation in April 1987. Reorganized as the Southern division of Bar Harbor Airlines, April 1987, itself a unit of Continental Express (see Area 11).	6 Sept. 1988
6 July 1960	Air Sunshine (Key West)	AV AG QH YI	Miami (and adjacent cities)-Key West; Tampa-Key West, Miami-Marco Island (1972, from Executive Airlines) Ft . Lauderdale-Marathon-Sarasota	Piper Aztec Cessna 402 Beech 99 DH-114 Heron	Founded as American Air Taxi (or A.A.T.) Airlines at Opa Locka and Fort Lauderdale. Also operated as Key West Airlines. Changed name to present one in 1974.	
25 Sept. 1962	Southeast Airlines (Miami)	SL	Miami-Marathon-Key West; later Miami-Freeport (Bahamas)	Beech 18 Grumman Goose Metroliner (Douglas DC-3) (Fairchild F-27) (Martin 202A)	Developed route after National Airlines abandoned the route to Key West. Founded by Irving Jones and Donald Sittman. Grew to acquire the status of an intra-state.	1976
July 1964	*South Central Airlines (Ocala, Fla.)*	*OE*	*Ocala-Gainesville-Jacksonville*			*1965*
30 Oct. 1964	Florida Airlines (Sarasota)	FA FE FV	Tampa-Fort Myers; Tampa-Ocala-Gainesville-Jacksonville; Tampa-Sarasota. Expanded to Macon when Eastern suspended service in 1979 and briefly, to Columbus, Ga., when Delta suspended. Ceased operation 11 Jan 1980 but resumed.	Beech 18 Piper Aztec Cessna 402 Beech 99 Douglas DC-3 Martin 4-0-4	Founded as Florida Air Taxi which in the 1970s developed into an intra-state airline. Amalgamated with Air South late 1975, and associated with Shawnee Airlines and marketed as "The Connection."	1981
7 Sept. 1964	*Albany Air Service and Athens Aviation (Albany) and Athens, Georgia)*	*ZN*	*Albany-Atlanta, Athens-Atlanta, Athens-Jefferson-Winder-Gainesville-Atlanta; Auburn-Lanette-La Grange /Pine Mountain-Atlanta*	*Beech 18 Piper Apache Piper Cherokee Six*	*Operation at first under both names from the two bases, respectively, but service to Albany discontinued. Operated in 1968 as Cherokee Airways.*	*1970*

AREA 10 (SOUTHEAST) Continued

First Sched. Service Date	Airline and Base	Code	Initial or Typical Route Network	Aircraft Used	Remarks	Date of last service
1 Dec. 1964	**Executive Airlines (Sarasota)**	EX	Sarasota-Tampa, and network of routes in Florida	Piper Cherokee Six, Aero Commander Beech 99	Originally Executive Flight Services, founded by Joe Whitney (see Northeast Area 11), and renamed in January 1967.	1973
25 June 1965	East Coast Flying Service (Jacksonville)			Beech 18		1966
20 Oct. 1966	Gold Coast Airlines (West Palm Beach)	GM	West Palm Beach, Ft Lauderdale-Miami; W.P.B-Boca Raton-Miami	Beech 18 Piper Cherokee Six	Founded as Gold Coast Air Taxi changed name in 1968.	1968
1 Sept. 1966	Tennessee Airmotive (Chattanooga)	EH	Chattanooga-Nashville	Piper Aztec Piper Navajo		1968
1967	Coastal Airways (Orlando)		Orlando-Tallahassee, Tampa, Nassau, Freeport, West End	Grumman Goose, Beech 99	Founded as Coastal Aviation, operating from Herndon Airport at Orlando.	1969
1967	Nationwide Airlines Southeast (Atlanta)		Atlanta-Albany, Augusta, Birmingham, Charlotte, Greenville	Beech Queenair	"Gets You To The Jets On Time."	1968
1967	Skyways Aviation (Orlando)			Cessna 310	Very short-lived operation.	1967
March 1967	**Mackey International Airlines (Fort Lauderdale)**	MI	Fort Lauderdale-Miami-Treasure Cay-Marsh Harbour (Bahamas); Ft Lauderdale-Fort Myers. Also as far as the Turk Islands.	Piper Navajo Beech 99 DHC-6 Twin Otter Convair 440 (DC-6)	Began operation as Mackey Air Taxi, then Mackey International Air Commuter. Founded by Col. Joseph Mackey, who had sold Mackey Airlines to Eastern in 1966.	1981
July 1967	Crest Airlines (Atlanta)	KW	Atlanta-Dalton, Calhoun, Tifton	Aero Commander		End 1967
Jan. 1968	Air South (Atlanta)	NJ FE	Atlanta-Birmingham-Nashville, and local points in Georgia, incl. St. Simons Island resort, and Greenville, South Carolina	Beech 99 Beech Queenair	Founded as Nationwide Airlines Southeast in August 1967. Changed name, December 1968, after F.E. "Pete" Howe took over management. Amalgamated with Florida Airlines, 1975.	1980
Early 1968	Florida Atlantic Airlines (Fort Lauderdale)	FL	Ft Lauderdale-Freeport, Miami-Freeport-; Ft Lauderdale-Miami	Beech 18 DHC-6 Twin Otter	Claimed to operate most flights over a longer period of each day from Florida to Freeport	1969
12 July 1968	Shawnee Airlines (Orlando, later Ft Lauderdale)	WB XW	Miami-Orlando-Gainesville; Tampa-Ft Lauderdale-Freeport, and extensive network throughout Florida STOL service to Walt Disney World in 1971.	Beech 99 DC-3 DHC-6 Twin Otter DH Heron FH-227	Founded by David D. Latham. Subsidiary of the Root Co. of Daytona Beach. Strong competition from Mackey to Bahamas and from Florida Airlines led to decline.	1980
15 Aug. 1968	South Atlantic Airlines (Myrtle Beach, S.C.)	SE	Hilton Head-Columbia-Raleigh; Jacksonville-Savannah-Hilton Head-Charleston-Raleigh	Aero Commander	Affiliated with Sports-by Air, Inc.	1969
1969	Dixie Air (Tuscaloosa, Ala)			Cessna 310		1970
1969	Hawkins Airways (Jackson, Miss)	HQ	Jackson-New Orleans	Piper Cherokee Six Beech 18	Airlines division of Jackson Air Center.	1977

AREA 10 (SOUTHEAST) Continued

First Sched. Service Date	Airline and Base	Code	Initial or Typical Route Network	Aircraft Used	Remarks	Date of last service
1969	Montgomery Aviation Corporation (Montgomery)			Beech 18		1970
1969	Mid-Continent Airlines (Memphis)	DR	Memphis-Blytheville-Jonesboro; Memphis-Dyersburg-Union City-Paducah; extended to serve 21 cities	Cessna 402		1970
1969	Sun Air (St Petersburg)	YX	Lakeland-West Palm Beach-Miami; Lakeland-Gainesville-Jacksonville	Cessna 402		1978
1969	Florence Airlines (Florence, S.C.)	DY YF	Florence-Charlotte; -Myrtle Beach; -Winston-Salem	Piper Aztec Piper Cherokee Six	Originally operated as _Air Taxi_.	1974
1970	Georgia Air (Atlanta)	GP WQ	Atlanta-Rome	Cessna 402		1972
1970	Volusia Air Service (Daytona Beach)	VQ	Daytona Beach-Disney World-Tampa		Division of _Volusia Aviation_, and also know as _VQ Airlines_.	1973
1971	Gulf Coast Airlines (Gulfport, Miss.)	UU QR	Gulfport-New Orleans, Gulport-Jackson	BN-2 Islander	Division of _Gulf Coast Aviation_.	1975
1971	Volunteer Airlines (Chattanooga, TN)	HE	Chattanooga-Nashville-Memphis-Huntsville-Birmingham; Chattanooga-Spartanburg	Lockheed L-10 BN-2 Islander		1973
1971	Southeast-Commuter Airlines (Mobile)	YC	Mobile-Montgomery-Birmingham; Mobile-Pensacola-Dothan-Montgomery	Beech 18		1971
1971	Del Airways (Valdosta, Ga.)	DG	Valdosta-Jacksonville	Beech 18		1971
1971	South Central Air Transport (SCAT) (Natchez, Miss.)	CG	Natchez-Jackson, New Orleans; Tupelo-Columbus-Jackson-New Orleans; New Orleans-Montgomery, Mobile, Ft. Walton Beach, Panama City	BN-2 Islander DHC-6 Twin Otter Handley Page Jetstream		1978
1972	Clarksville Flying Service (Clarksville, Tenn.)					1975
1972	Aerie Airlines (Clarksville, later Nashville, Tenn.)	FZ	Clarksville-Nashville; Clarksville-Owensboro, Ky.-Evansville, Indiana, and to Louisville	Beech 18		1977
1972	Catawba Air Transport (Charlotte)	WJ	Charlotte-Hickory-Wilkesboro			1973
1972	Valdosta-Phoenix Airlines (Valdosta, Ga.)	XZ	Valdosta-Atlanta	Cessna 402		1973

AREA 10 (SOUTHEAST) Continued

First Sched. Service Date	Airline and Base	Code	Initial or Typical Route Network	Aircraft Used	Remarks	Date of last service
Oct. 1972	Marco Island Airways (Opa Locka, Florida)	LS	Miami-Marco Island	Martin 4-0-4 Beech 99	Subsidiary of Deltona Corportation, which built a planned community on Marco Island. Sold to Provincetown-Boston Airline (P.B.A.) 5 Oct. 1984. Operated some routes as an Air Florida Commuter.	5 Oct. 1984
1973	Vero Mommonin Airlines (Vero Beach)	VM	Vero Beach-Tampa, Miami, Melbourne, Orlando		Southern division of Monmouth Airlines (Area 11).	1975
1974	Cannon Aviation (Hickory, N.C.)	OY	Hickory-Charlotte		Operated by Carolina Airways, Inc.	1974
1 Aug. 1975	Southeastern Airlines (Atlanta)	WH	Atlanta-Auburn-Tuskegee	DH Dove BN-2 Islander	First operated as Coastal Air, then as Southeastern Commuter Airlines.	1983
1975	Air Carolina (Florence, S.C.)	FN	Florence-Hickory-Charlotte; Florence-Augusta, Ga.	Beech 99 DHC-6 Twin Otter	Purchased by Atlantis Airlines in 1980.	1980
1976	Bankair (Columbia, S.C.)	JA	Routes from Columbia to about a dozen points in South Carolina			1986
1976	Coastal Airways (Gulfport, Miss.)	NG	Gulfport/Patterson/Hattiesburg-New Orleans	Cessna 402	Also operated as Southern Flyer.	1978
1976	Commutaire International Airways (Miami)	VN	West Palm Beach-Boca Raton-Ft Lauderdale-Miami; Miami-Key Largo	BN-2 Islander		1977
1976	Nelson Airlines (Alcoa, Tennessee)	VZ	Tri-Cities-Nashville-Chattanooga; Tri-Cities-Knoxville-Nashville	Cessna 402	Operated by Nelson Aviation, Inc.	1978
1 Jan. 1977	Ocean Reef Airways (Key Largo)		Ocean Reef-Miami		Operated year-round charters, but scheduled in winter only.	1977
15 Mar. 1977	Appalachian Airlines (Blountville, Tenn.)	DI	Tri-Cities-Wise-Bluefield;Charleston, W.V.,-Wise-Bluefield	Piper Navajo	Founded by King Rogers.	15 Mar. 1980
1977	Charter Airlines (Gainesville, Fla.)	HO	Gainesville-Tallahassee; Gainesville-Tampa-FT. Lauderdale-Marsh Harbour	Cessna 402	Operated by Charter Air Center and at first as Charterair.	1979
1977	Alair (Anniston, Alab.)	KB	Anniston-Birmingham	Piper Navajo		1978
1977	Panhandle Airways (Pensacola, Fla.)	DH	Pensacola-Panama City-Tallahassee-Tampa	Beech 18	Operated only 3 days per week.	1978
1977	Air Miami (Miami)	VW MC AF	Miami-Tampa; Miami-Fort Myers-Cape Coral	DH Heron	Operated some of Air Florida's commuter routes.	1981
1977	Central Air Transport (Nashville, Tenn.)	OX	Nashville-Indianapolis	Beech Queen Air		1978
1977	Trans Air Express (Enterprise, Alab.)	YJ IX	Enterprise-Montgomery-Atlanta	Piper Aztec		1979
1978	Coastal Plains Commuter (Hilton Head, S.C.)	KA	Hilton Head Island-Charleston; Hilton Head Island-Savannah			1979

AREA 10 (SOUTHEAST) Continued

First Sched. Service Date	Airline and Base	Code	Initial or Typical Route Network	Aircraft Used	Remarks	Date of last service
1978	Aerosun International (Clearwater, Florida)	MF	St Petersburg-Key West-Cayman Islands	Douglas DC-3	Founded as _Red Carpet Flying Service_, and also operated as the _Red Carpet Airline_ until 1981.	1982
1978	Southeast Airlines (Jackson, Tenn.)	RM	Jackson-Memphis; Jackson-Corinth, Miss.	DH Dove	(Not the intra-state operator based at Miami.)	1979
1978	Argosy Airlines (Ft. Lauderdale)	VJ	Ft. Lauderdale-Great Harbour Cay	Douglas DC-3		1979
1978	Tennessee Airways (Alcoa, Tenn.)	ZN JT	Knoxville-Tri Cities; Knoxville-Nashville; Nashville/Knoxville-Chattanooga-Charlotte	Cessna 402 Bandeirante	Temporarily suspended service, 1988-1989.	
1978	Airbama (Sheffield, Alab.)	JN	Muscle Shoals-Chattanooga-Knoxville/ Nashville; Muscle Shoals-Montgomery	Handley Page Jetstream		1979
1979	Trans Air (Ft. Lauderdale)	GO AT PI	Ft Lauderdale-Bahamas, (about eight destinations); Also Melbourne-Ft. Lauderdale-Miami	Cessna 402 Piper Seneca	Started as a charter operator, _Trans Island Airways_, which started scheduled operation, adding _Trans Inland Airways_ as a division intra-Florida. Changed name to Trans Air in 1981.	1987
1979	Golden South Airline (Fort Pierce, Florida	SI	Ft Pierce-Orlando; Ft Pierce-West Palm Beach-Orlando	Piper Navajo		1980
1979	Vale International Airlines (Nashville)	ZA	Nashville-Indianapolis; Nashville-Lexington-Columbus, Ohio	Piper Navajo		1980
1979	Atlantis Airlines (Florence, S.C.)	EA	Myrtle Beach-Greensboro, N.C.,-Tri-Cities (Tenn.); M.B.-Charlotte-Tri Cities; Charlotte Columbia-Hilton Head. Later expansion to Atlanta, Knoxville, and other points in Georgia	DHC-6 Twin Otter Swearingen Metro Piper Navajo Chieftain BAe Jetstream	Claimed to be the first airline to be formed after the 1978 Airline Deregulation Act, based first at Myrtle Beach. Bought _Air Carolina_ in 1980, moved to Florence. Acquired by _Eastern Express Airlines_, 15 Feb. 1989.	15 Feb. 1989
1979	Knight Airlines (Miami)	FO	Lakeland-Miami	Piper types		1980
27 June 1979	**Atlantic Southeast Airlines (ASA) (Atlanta, later also in Dallas)**	EV DL	Atlanta-Columbus, Ga.; then expanded rapidly serving many points in spoke network from Atlanta to Florida, North and South Carolina, Tennessee,and Miss. Later added a similar network from Dallas	DHC-6 Twin Otter Shorts SD 360 Bandeirante Brasilia DHC Dash 7	Founded by George Pickett, John Beiser, and Robert Priddy. Expanded rapidly, and acquired _Southeastern Airlines_ on 1 April 1983. Became a unit of _The Delta Connection_ on 1 May 1984.	
1979	Dodge Air Charter (Miami, Springs)	VF	Miami-Cape Haitien	Douglas DC-3		1980
1979	Sunbelt Airlines (Rome, Georgia)	ZS	Rome-Atlanta	Cessna types		1980
1980	Phoenix Airlines (Atlanta)	JW	Jacksonville-St Simons Island-Savannah-Atlanta	DH Heron	Based at Peach Tree Airport, Atlanta.	1980

AREA 10 (SOUTHEAST) Continued

First Sched. Service Date	Airline and Base	Code	Initial or Typical Route Network	Aircraft Used	Remarks	Date of last service
1980	Florida Commuter Airlines (W. Palm Beach)	PG	West Palm Beach-Kissimee-Gainesville; Tallahassee, Daytona Beach, Melbourne	Piper types	Founded as <u>Red Baron Air</u>, then known as <u>Southern Airlines</u>.	1981
1 Oct. 1980	Sunbird Airlines (Nashville)		Nashville-Murray	Piper Cherokee Six		1980
1980	Chautauqua Airlines (Orlando)	AL	Orlando-Ocala, Lakeland, Vero Beach	Beech types	Southern division of Chautauqua of Jamestown, NY., an <u>Allegheny Commuter</u> operator.	1981
1980	Walker's International (Ft. Lauderdale)	XW	Ft. Lauderdale-West Palm Beach-Walker's Cay	DHC-6 Twin Otter	Originally <u>Walker's Cay Air Terminal</u> and, in the early 1980s, <u>Walker's Cay Airline</u>.	1990
1980	Key West Airlines (Boca Raton, Fla.)	WY	Key West-Ft Lauderdale/ Miami	Cessna types		1981
1980	Aero International (Homestead, Florida)	ZS GD	Fort Lauderdale/Miami-Bimini, later (as Air South)-Marathon, Marco Is.	Beech types BN-3 Trislander	Formerly <u>Bahamas Caribbean Airlines</u>, and <u>Air South</u> (not the same as the 1968 airline).	1987
17 Mar. 1981	Sunair (Fort Lauderdale)	FN	Fort Lauderdale-eight Florida cities (Made one flight)	Bandeirante	Founded by A. Wayne Lackey, who had purchased a charter airline of that name. Grandiose plans but equally grandiose debts, amounting to an estimated $1,000,000. Chapter 11 Bankruptcy 24 March.	18 Mar. 1981
1981	Air South (Mobile, Alabama)	HS	Mobile-Pensacola; Mobile-Gulfport-New Orleans	Metro		1982
1981	Pompano Airways (Ft Lauderdale)	MG	Ft. Lauderdale/Miami-Treasure Cay, Marsh Harbour, North Eleuthera, West End, Club Cay	Cessna types	Promoted "Love at First Flight," was an Air Florida Commuter.	1985
1981	Proair (Miami)	SZ	Miami/Ft Lauderdale-Key West, Marathon, Marsh Harbour, Treasure Cay	Cessna 402 Douglas DC-3 Martin 4-0-4		Mar. 1988
1981	Slocum Air (Miami)	MB	Miami-Ft Lauderdale-Ft. Myers; Miami-Melbourne-Vero Beach; Miami-Melbourne-Orlando	BN-2 Islander		1984
1981	State Airlines (Ft Lauderdale)	OY	Ft Lauderdale-Sarasota, Ft Myers, Bimini, Freeport, Treasure Cay, Marsh Harbour, North Eleuthera	Piper types		1984
1981	North American Airlines (Miami)	GG	Miami/Ft Lauderdale-Marathon;-Ft Myers-Tampa;-W. Palm Beach-Titusville-Daytona Beach	CASA 212		1985
1981	Sunbird Airlines (Denver, NC)		Charlotte-Raleigh-Rocky Mt; Greenville, Kinston, Fayetteville-Wilmington; Florence, Columbia, Jacksonville, Hickory-Atlanta			1982

AREA 10 (SOUTHEAST) Continued

First Sched. Service Date	Airline and Base	Code	Initial or Typical Route Network	Aircraft Used	Remarks	Date of last service
1981	Trans Air (Dania, Florida)			Cessna types	Originally Trans Island Airways— see 1979.	1981
1981	Gulf Central Airlines (Opa Locka, Florida)	BJ	Miami-Ft Lauderdale-Melbourne-Orlando, Jacksonville, Tallahassee; Miami-Key West	Piper types	Founded as Devoe Airlines; connected with Republic Airlines at several Florida cities.	Early 1984
15 Dec. 1981	Dolphin Airlines (Tampa)	DV	Tampa-Orlando-Jacksonville-Savannah-Charleston; Tampa-Miami; Tampa-W. Palm Beach; Tampa-Sarasota-Ft Myers-Miami; Tampa-Tallahassee/Panama City-Pensacola; later to New Orleans, Key West.	Bandeirante	Founded as Dolphin Airways, changing name in May 1983. Purchased Tampa Air Center in 1982. Assets sold to PBA.	20 Jan 1984
Early 1982	Aero Coach (Ft Lauderdale)	DF	Ft Lauderdale/W. Palm Beach-Georgetown, Marsh Harbour, Bimini, Treasure Cay and to other Bahamas destinations	Cessna 402 Bandeirante	Operated by Aero Coach Aviation International.	
15 May 1982	Atlanta Express (Atlanta)	FX	Atlanta-Macon, Columbus, Anniston; Charlotte-Chattanooga, Raleigh, Florence	DHC Dash 7 Shorts SD-330	Founded by American Financial.	1983
1982	National Florida Airlines (N F A) (S. Daytona, Fla.)	XQ	Daytona Beach-Tampa; D.B.-Ft Lauderdale, Miami; Ft Walton Beach-Orlando-Ft Lauderdale	Piper Navajo Chieftain, Metroliner	Connected with Republic Airlines.	1984
15 June 1982	Southeastern Airlines (Huntsville, Alabama)	WH	Huntsville-Gadsden-Atlanta; Huntsville-Memphis, Nashville; Atlanta-Auburn; Memphis-Tupelo-Columbus	GAF Nomad Cessna 402 Bandeirante		1983
1982	Finair Express (Miami)	ZE AF	Miami-Lakeland/Gainesville	Piper types	Operated for a while as Air Florida Commuter until 15 May 1984.	1984
1982	National Commuter Airlines(Miami)	DC	Miami-Sarasota-Tampa	Nord 262		1984
1983	Caribbean Express (Miami Springs)	WH	Miami-Treasure Cay, Marsh Harbour, North Eleuthera, Governor's Harbour, Rock Sound, George Town	Cessna types	Filed for Chapter 11 bankruptcy in 1988.	mid-1988
1983	Gulf Central Airlines (Melbourne, Florida)	BJ	Melbourne-Orlando-Fort Lauderdale; Melbourne Miami	Piper types		1984
1983	Gull Air (Miami)	JI	Miami-Freeport; W. Palm Beach-Treasure Cay; Jacksonville-Orlando-W. Palm Beach-Nassau	Cessna 402 CASA 212	Florida operations of the Hyannis, Massachusetts-based company. Operated first as an Air Florida Commuter, then as a Continental Express affiliate.	March 1987

AREA 10 (SOUTHEAST) Continued

First Sched. Service Date	Airline and Base	Code	Initial or Typical Route Network	Aircraft Used	Remarks	Date of last service
2 April 1984	**Eastern Metro Express (Atlanta)**	EA HY QO	Atlanta-Chattanooga, Tri-Citites, Asheville, Augusta, Albany, Columbus, Panama City, Ft. Walton Beach, Dothan, Montgomery	BAe Jetstream	Wholly-owned subsidiary of Metro Airlines, Inc., owned by Jay Seaborn, based in Houston. Approached by Frank Borman, of Eastern Air Lines, and created first dedicated code-sharing agreement in the U.S. Bought Atlantis Airlines, 15 Feb. 1989. Collapsed with Eastern in 1991.	18 Jan. 1991
1984	Southern Express (Miami)	ZE PI	Ft Myers-Tampa-Tallahassee; Tampa-Key West; Miami-Marathon; Miami- Ft. Lauderdale-Sarasota-Tampa-Jacksonville	Bandeirante	Operated as a Piedmont Commuter in 1986.	1986
1984	Skyway Commuter (Ocala, Florida)	9S	Ft. Lauderdale-W. Palm Beach-Tallahassee	Beech 99	Began as Skyway of Ocala, and operated as an Air Florida Commuter associate.	1985
June 1984	Southern Airways (Jackson, Miss.)	EC	Jackson-New Orleans; Jackson-Greenwood-Memphis, Jackson-Oxford-Tupelo	Beech and Piper types	Founded in 1977 as Flight Line by Miller-Wills, an F.B.O. Changed name in 1985. Also known as Southern Express.	1987
1985	Eagle Airline (Auburn, Alabama)	DN	Auburn-Atlanta	Piper types		1986
1985	Trans Southern Airways (Florence, S.C.)		Florence-Atlanta; Florence-Charlotte		Associated with Tennessee Airways.	1986
1 June 1985	Republic Express (Memphis, Tenn.)	RC	Memphis Monroe/ Columbus(Miss)-Green-ville, and extensive network radiating from Memphis	BAe Jetstream	Registered as Express Airlines I to code-share with Republic Airlines.	
1985	Central Airways (Ft Lauderdale)	ZA	Fort Lauderdale-Sarasota	Cessna types	Briefly was an Air Florida Commuter.	1985
1985	Airways Inter-national (Miami Springs)	HO 4A	Miami-North Eleuthera/ Governors Harbour/ Rock Sound/Marsh Harbour	Cessna types		
1985	Galaxy Airlines (Ft Lauderdale)	9G	Fort Lauderdale-Miami	Cessna types		1987
15 April 1986	**Air Midwest (Nashville, Tenn.)**	AA	Extensive network centered on Nashville	Metro SAAB 340	Established American Eagle oper-ation when American started a hub at Nashville. Sold to American on 31 Dec. 1987.	31 Dec. 1987
1986	Prime Air (Clarksville, Tenn.)	DE	Clarksville-Nashville	Piper types		1987
1986	Southern Airways (Jackson, Miss.)	EC	New Orleans-Baton Rouge; Jackson, Miss.	Piper T-1040	Code shared with American Airlines.	1987
April 1987	**Bar Harbor Airlines (Miami)**	EA CO	Extensive network throughout Florida and to six point in the Bahamas	Beech 1900 CASA 212 SAAB 340	Bar Harbor had become a unit of Eastern Air Express in 1986 (see Area 11). When Texas Air Corp. acquired 50% share of Provinceton-Boston Airline (PBA) in April 1987, it transferred that company's Florida operation (Naples Airlines) (see 1960) to Bar Harbor, as Eastern Express.	18 Jan. 1990

AREA 10 (SOUTHEAST) Continued

First Sched. Service Date	Airline and Base	Code	Initial or Typical Route Network	Aircraft Used	Remarks	Date of last service
1 Nov. 1987	Comair (Orlando)	DL	Extensive network from Orlando throughout Florida, and to Birmingham, New Orleans, and the Bahamas	Bandeirante Brasilia	Southern division of Comair of Cincinnati.	
1 Jan 1988	Nashville Eagle (Nashville, Tenn.)	AA	Extensive network centered on Nashville	Metro SAAB 340	Wholly-owned subsidiary of AMR Corp. (parent compay of American Airlines). Purchased assets of Air Midwest (see 1986)	
1988	Key Largo Airlines (Homestead, Florida)		Miami-Club Cay			
1989	Panama Airways (Panama City, Fla.)	6A	Panama City-Tampa-Orlando; Panama City-Pensacola-New Orleans	Piper Navajo		Early 1991
15 May 1990	Pan Am Express (Miami)	PA	Feeder network radiating from Miami	DHC Dash 7	Sold to TWA when Pan Am went out of business.	1991
Dec. 1990	Gulfstream International (Miami)	3M	Miami-several points in the Bahamas			

Area 11

Northeast

If Florida could be described as the cradle of commercial aviation in the United States, this area could be described as the nursery. There could be endless arguments about which was the first individual U.S. commuter airline (and there could be many firsts, simply by varying the precise definitions), but as a group, the northeastern states, especially those of New England, provided the ideal conditions for the emergence of commuter airlines as an identifiable segment of the airline industry.

Throughout the history of air transport, the northeastern United States has presented contradictory opportunities. On the one hand, ready markets have been provided by the many population centers. The whole corridor of dense population between New York and Boston contained several medium-size cities, all of which required quick and frequent transportation links with the two great metropolises. The railroad system was not outstanding. Even today, over a route only 185 miles long, the New York–Boston trip takes four hours by rail, a situation that would not be tolerated in any other industrial country in the world.

But there was a paradox. The area south of a line from Boston to Albany and north of New York, a rectangle no larger than one hundred by fifty miles, contained nine cities, each with a population of more than 100,000. Yet north of the line, except for such northern Massachusetts cities as Lynn and Lowell (effectively part of the Boston conurbation), the states of Maine, New Hampshire, Vermont, and northern New York were quite sparsely populated.

Those routes, therefore, that could be served by a short-haul airline in the New England–Hudson Valley area fell into two categories: they were either of high market potential but too short to be economically viable by air, or they were long enough but served only communities of insufficient market potential (with the exception, perhaps, of Portland,

Maine, or Burlington, Vermont), and thus did not encourage airline development.

Aggravating this feast-or-famine situation was the seasonal nature of much of the traffic. The sparse winter traffic conditions of northern New England could be mitigated by some imaginative scheduling and route transfers. This strategem actually went into effect in the early 1920s, when one of the great pioneering airlines, Aeromarine, transferred its business from the New York area in the summer to Florida in the winter. But Aeromarine disappeared in 1923 when it could not make ends meet; and when the United States began seriously to develop an air route system in the late 1920s, the planning was based on mail contracts allocated to specific routes that did not have the flexibility of being transferred.

Thus the airline that won the mail contracts for the New England area, Boston-Maine/Central Vermont, was burdened with a multiplicity of short-haul routes, a large number of small cities to serve north of Boston, and the problem of appalling winter conditions. The airline, which later became Northeast, was backed by three local railroads, and the operating challenges were so severe that even the CAB tolerated their retention of control well into the 1940s, an exceptional case of that agency permitting as an expedient the maintenance of interlocking relationships between different transport modes. Northeast is possibly the only airline that ever fitted snow chains to the tires of its aircraft, such were the snow and ice hazards of the primitive fields up north.

Two small airlines in the area, Mayflower and the Airline Feeder System, tried to start in the 1940s, but these were doomed from the very beginning. Mayflower suffered partly from bad luck, as its route, connecting Boston with the offshore islands of Nantucket and Martha's Vineyard, was one of considerable potential. These growing resort areas were served by surface transport involving train and/or road, plus a ferryboat, and the trip from Boston or New York took most of a whole day. But, unfortunately, wartime restrictions on civilian travel were particularly applicable to the area.

Northeast was never successful, and it always struggled for survival. Only the intense loyalty of New Englanders provided the necessary support that enabled it to last until 1972, when it was taken over by Delta Air Lines—which promptly dropped many of the thinner short-haul routes. It was one of many airlines that suffered from the CAB's reluctance to recognize that not even the most efficient organization could make money with an average stage distance of less than two hundred miles.

Some fixed base operators pondered the new opportunities for developing air travel, perhaps with the thought that Northeast had just not done things correctly. John Van Arsdale was the first to match his thoughts with action, as early as 1949. His Provincetown-Boston Airline, named ingenuously—or ingeniously—because it flew between Provincetown and Boston, was an early prototype for hundreds of small short-haul airlines in the United States that subsequently found (or thought they had found) a missing link or two in the chain of line networks discarded by the trunk and local service airlines. Although not geographically so, Provincetown was essentially an island in relation to the major city of Boston, and the flight distance between the two was uneconomically short. Van Arsdale bought a small airliner, a Lockheed 10 Electra, considered to be out of date by the certificated airlines, and tailored the operation precisely to the route. Others in the eastern Massachusetts area, headed by Cape and Islands Flight Service and Executive Airlines, followed in providing specialized services to the offshore islands.

Meanwhile, during the early 1960s, a rash of small airlines grew up around New York to take advantage of the special urban situation. A large proportion of the inhabitants of this teeming conurbation of perhaps eighteen million people live to the west across the Hudson in New Jersey and to the north in the outer suburbs beyond the Bronx and Connecticut; but the main airports served by the major domestic and international airlines are to the east, on Long Island. Even with freeways—and these were often congested, especially at rush hour times—the journey to the airports could often be a nightmare. Within a few years, a spoke pattern of short-haul air routes radiated from the New York airports to places like Poughkeepsie (Command Airways); Red Bank, New Jersey (Air Taxi); New London (Pilgrim); and even Pittsfield, in western Massachusetts (Yankee).

The very size of New York reflected the paradox of urban transport during the period of intense population growth of the mid- to late twentieth century. Airports were built on the edge of the developed areas, but the problems of reaching them intensified. No city suffers as much as the Big Apple, with the Hudson River, the East River, and other waterways, not to mention the crippling traffic jams and the congested subways in the concrete cordillera of Manhattan that houses the commercial heart of the city.

North of Boston the problem was different, as previously explained, with sparser populations and a highly seasonal pattern of demand. But in the early 1960s, the attractions of the northern New England states as both summer and winter vacation areas also began to register in the traveling consciousness. Air taxi airlines were quick to meet this special travel requirement, and the opportunity to serve vacationers also emerged in the New York area, with airlines in the Catskill and Pocono Mountains following the trend.

However important were these specialized operations—the island air ferries, the New York spokes, and the resort services—the fundamental need in the northeastern states continued to be for short-haul airlines whose equipment and resources were properly matched to the characteristics of the region, dictated by the manner in which the urban population was distributed.

This was evident in the highly populated Boston-Washington (Boswash) corridor. It was also true along the Mohawk River Valley, where a succession of airline participants can be traced as a textbook example of the different periods of evolution of U.S. air transport: from the late 1920s, when Colonial Western Airways dominated the region; to the 1930s, when Colonial was absorbed into American Airlines; to the post–World War II years, when the local service carrier Mohawk Airlines relieved American of some of the responsibility of serving this "milk-run" route. Then, as the local service airlines concentrated on jet operations, the commuter carrier Empire Airlines took over in 1975, and it grew so quickly that within a decade it was purchased by a national airline, Piedmont, itself once a local service airline, to set up a local hub.

In recent years, as almost every one of the commuter airlines has been engulfed by the major carriers (who eventually realized that the routes they had once despised were essential to their well-being as feeders), another independent voice was heard in the Mohawk Valley, as a new Mohawk Airlines, based at Syracuse, rose, phoenixlike, to maintain the undying spirit of individuality that has always been the mainspring of the commuter airline industry. But sadly—as if to prove a point—the second Mohawk collapsed in August 1991.

AREA 11 (NORTHEAST)

First Sched. Service Date	Airline and Base	Code	Initial or Typical Route Network	Aircraft Used	Remarks	Date of last service
30 Nov. 1949	**Provincetown-Boston Airline (PBA) (Provincetown, Mass.)**	PT	Provincetown-Boston; expanded to Naples and points in Southern Florida in 1960; further expansion to points in Massachusetts and New York State in 1981. Substantial expansion in eastern U.S. after 1985	Lockheed L-10A Douglas DC-3 Martin 4-0-4 Bandeirante YS-11A Cessna 402	Founded as Cape Cod Flying Services, an F.B.O., in May 1946 by John Van Arsdale, Sr. Started as commuter airline as Provincetown-Boston, on 30 Nov. 1949. Services from Naples, Florida, 15 Dec. 1957. Re-organized 1 Jan 1980; shut down by F.A.A. 9 Nov. 1984, but Bandeirante crash led to Chapter 11 bankruptcy, March 1985. People Express rejuvenated airline on 13 May 1986 but absorbed into Bar Harbor Airlines, which became a Continental Express carrier when Texas Air bought People Express.	6 Sept. 1988
April 1951	Cape & Islands Flight Service (Hyannis, Mass.)	IK	Hyannis-Nantucket, and local services in eastern Massachusetts	Beech 18 DHC-6 Twin Otter	Founded by George Parmenter Agreement with Northeast Airlines, 16 June 1969, to operate local routes. Bought by Airspur early in 1970, then Air New England.	1970
1955	**Command Airways (Poughkeepsie, N.Y.)**	MI DD	Poughkeepsie-New York; later to Albany, Boston, White Plains, Lebanon, N.H., and later to Providence, Hartford, Philadelphia, Washington (National), and Burlington	Beech 18 Beech 99 Shorts SD330 ATR 42	Formed as Mid-Hudson Airline, an F.B.O., in 1951. Purchased by Kingsley D. Morse and changed name on 1 July 1966. Purchased Pittsfield-New York route from Executive Airlines, December 1971. Public stock offering, October 1983. Became American Eagle operator, 27 April 1986, and purchased by American on 30 September 1988.	
2 Dec 1958	*Aeroflex Corporation (Andover, N.J.)*		*Andover-New York*	*Beech 18*		*1968*
May 1960	*Princeton Aviation Corp.(Princeton, N.J.)*		*Princeton-New York,*	*Beech 18 Piper Apache DHC-6 Twin Otter*	*Founded by Webster B. Todd and Lawrence Tokash. Participated in the Metro Air Service,in association with American Airlines, Sept. 1965.*	*Early 1969*
20 June 1960	**Executive Airlines (Boston, Mass.)**	EX	Boston-Martha's Vineyard, then to Nantucket and Hyannis. Florida routes from Sarasota, in 1964,expansion north of Boston to points in Maine, New Hampshire, and Vermont in later 1960s	Aero Commander Beech 99, D.H. 104 Dove DHC 6 Twin Otter	Founded by Joseph C. Whitney in 1959 as National Executive Flight Service. Established Florida Division, 1 Dec. 1964, and changed name in January 1967. Acquired Yankee Airlines, July 1968, and Massachusetts Air Industries (Mass Air) in 1971. Whitney left in 1970 to establish Air New England. Largest of all commuter airlines in 1969, but bankrupt in 1971, and ceased operations, July 1973.	July 1973
8 Dec. 1960	*Air Taxi Company (Red Bank, N.J.)*	TI	*Red Bank-New York Washington, Allentown-Reading-Lancaster, Philadelphia, Buffalo*	*BN-2 Islander*	*Founded by James Loeb. Participated in the Metro Air Service, in association with American Airlines, Sept. 1965. Merged with Reading Aviation on 29 July 1968 to form Suburban Airlines.*	*29 July 1968*
19 Mar. 1962	*Yankee Airlines (Pittsfield,Mass.)*	YK	*Pittsfield-New York (La G.)*	*DH 104 Dove*	*Division of Greylock Airways, a fixed base operator, founded in 1953. Sold to Executive Airlines.*	*July 1968*
28 Mar. 1962	*Mac-Aire Aviation Corp.(Ronkonkoma, N.Y.)*	RL	*East Hampton, Islip, Bridgeport, New Haven-New York*		*Founded by Jim Keena.Participated in Metro Air Service, in association with American Airlines, September, 1965.*	*1968*

AREA 11 (NORTHEAST) Continued

First Sched. Service Date	Airline and Base	Code	Initial or Typical Route Network	Aircraft Used	Remarks	Date of last service
1 April 1962	**Pilgrim Airlines (New London, Conn.)**	PM	New London/Groton-New York (Idlewild); New Haven- N.Y.; Boston-N.Y.; later expansion to Hartford, Albany, Montreal,Ottawa. Also to Oxford, Ct.	Beech 18 DHC-6 Twin Otter Fokker F-27 Fokker F-28 Beech 99	Founded by Joe Fugere. First U.S. operator of the Twin Otter. Operated first direct service from New York to the Canadian capital, Ottawa. Acquired New Air in February 1985. Sold to Business Express, 28 February, 1986.	28 Feb. 1986
July 1962	Pocono Airlines (Mt. Pocono and Wilkes-Barre, Pa.)	PL 8P 4P	Mt Pocono-New York, later to Wilkes Barre-Hazelton, and to Philadelphia	Beech 18 Metroliner Beech 99 Nord 262 Metro III	Founded by Walter Hoffman. Became Allegheny Commuter, 1968, but affiliation ended on 1 July, 1988, when it filed for bankruptcy. Resumed in March, 1989 as TW Express.	5 Jan 1990
14 July 1963	*Montauk-Caribbean Airways (Montauk,N.Y.)*	*YL*	*Montauk-New York, and to islands in Long Island Sound, later to East Hampton and Fisher's Island*	*Cessna types BN-2 Islander, DH-114 Heron, Beech 99*	*Seasonal operations, moving to Florida during winter. Affiliated to Long Island Airlines, which took over all operations in 1985. Also operated with Ocean Reef Airways.*	*1985*
1963	Air North (Burlington, Vermont)	NO OY AL	Burlington-Massena-Ogdensburg-Watertown-Syracuse; Saranac Lake, Rutland, Albany,and throughout New England	Beech 18 Fokker F-27 Shorts 330 Gulfstream	Founded by E. Andrew Deed II, of ANA Ltd., as Northern Airways, taking over routes in northern New York state from Mohawk Airlines. Became part of Allegheny Commuter group in 1970, and changed name. First carrier to operate under E.A.S. subsidy, 1978. Purchased by Brockway Air, 1 October, 1983.	Nov. 1983
11 May 1964	*Empire State Airlines (Syracuse, N.Y.)*		*Syracuse-Ithaca-Elmira-Binghampton, then to New York and Washington*	*Beech18 Learjet*	*Founded as Flight Service in 1953. One of few commuter airlines to use Learjet.*	*13 July 1966*
12 Oct. 1964	Commuter Airlines (Binghamton, N.Y.)	CR CB	Binghamton-Washington; later to Boston, New York, Utica, Ithaca, Elmira, White Plains	DH 104 Dove Beech 18 Metroliner CV-580	Founded by Jerry Winston. Merged with Freedom Airlines in 1980.	1982
5 Nov. 1964	Trans East Airlines (Manchester, N.H.)	ST ES EE	Manchester-New York, via New Bedford, Hartford; Manchester -Lebanon-Albany; Manchester- Portland, Albany- Portland	DH 104 Dove DHC-6 Twin Otter	Founded as Statewide Airlines, changing name when purchased by Walter S. Blandford. Bought Buker Airlines, contract air mail carrier, on 29 August, 1968.	1971
17 Nov. 1964	*Massachusetts Air Industries (Mass Air), (New Bedford, Mass.)*	*IM*	*New Bedford-Nantucket*	*Beech 18 Cessna 402*	*Founded by E. Antony & Sons. Name changed when purchased by Ottaway Newspapers, 1 Feb., 1966 Purchased by Executive Airlines in 1971.*	*1971*
23 Nov. 1964	*Monmouth Airlines (Monmouth County Airport, N.J.). Briefly also known as Vero Monmouth Airlines (Vero Beach, Florida)*	*VM*	*Monmouth County-New York (JFK)-Wilkes-Barre; M.C.-Washington. Short-lived operations from Vero Beach, Florida*	*Piper types, Beech 99 Piper Navajo*	*Founded by Ed Brown as Air Taxi Associates, changing name to Eastern Air Taxi on 23 Feb., 1965. In 1966, Tom Hartford, William(Bill) Piper's son-in-law, set up the Castanea Corp., which took over E.A.T. and called it Piper Twinair, operating in cooperation with T.W.A. Sold in 1968 to Charles Robertson, who changed name to Monmouth Airlines. Later, in 1979, changed name again to Ocean Airways. Bankrupt in 1980.*	*1980*

AREA 11 (NORTHEAST) Continued

First Sched. Service Date	Airline and Base	Code	Initial or Typical Route Network	Aircraft Used	Remarks	Date of last service
Nov. 1964	Chatham Aviation (Morristown, N.J.)	XV	Morristown -New York	Cessna types	Founded by Jack Cullen as Lemco Flying Service. Participated in Metro Air Service, in association with American Airlines, Sept. 1965 Flew as Chatham Airlines.	1970
12 Dec. 1964	Newport Air Park (Newport, R.I.)	NU NB NF	Newport-New York (La Guardia); Newport-Providence	Aero Commander Cessna Types	Later operated as Newport Aero. Also operated MassAir to Boston, Martha's Vineyard, Nantucket (sea above). Later operated as EJA/Newport.	1981
27 Dec 1964	Viking Airways (Westerly, R.I)	VK	Westerly-Block Island; also to Newport, R.I., Providence	Cessna and Piper types, BN-2 Islander	Founded by Thomas Corwin, who purchased Travel Air Service of Block Island, 24 February 1967 changing the name.	June 1970
3 May 1965	Aroostook Airways (Presque Isle, Maine)	QK	Presque Isle-Augusta-Portland-Boston, and intermediate points	Piper types	Founded as P. & M. Flying Service by John C. Philbrick. Changed name in 1968.	1972
13 Jan. 1966	Hartford Airlines (Plainville,Conn.)		Plainville-Hartford-New York (La Guardia)	Aero Commander		1966
6 May 1966	Catskill Airways (Oneonta, N.Y)	KF	Oneonta-New York (La Guardia); later to Newark and Boston.	Beech Baron Beech 99 Beech Queenair	Founded by Steve Low. Moved to Utica in 1988 and sold to Robert Peach, Jr., of Mohawk Airlines.	1988
8 June 1966	Raritan Valley Air (Manville, N.J.)		Manville-New York (La Guardia)	Beech, Piper		1968
13 Jan. 1967	Vermont International Airways (Morrisville, Vermont)		Local service in Vermont	Beech 18 Cessna 402	Founded by John McDonald.	1969
May 1968	Downeast Airlines (Rockland, Maine)	XY DE KN	Rockland-Boston; Wiscasset-Boston; Augusta-Boston	Piper Navajo DHC-6 Twin Otter	Founded in February 1960 as Mid-Coast Airways. Changed name in June 1968. Sold to Bar Harbor Airline in 1980.	15 May 1980
1968	Anjill Airlines (Forty Fort, Pa.)	JB	Wilkes-Barre/Scranton-Teterboro, N.J.	Piper Navajo		1970
1968	Hunter Aviation Corp. (Fitchburg, Mass.)	HV	Fitchburg-Boston	DHC-6 Twin Otter	Operated as Time-Air.	1969
June 1968	Winnipesaukee Airlines (Laconia, N.H.)	WW ZM	Laconia-Boston; Laconia-N. Conway, Worcester	Piper types		Jan. 1980
1968	**Bar Harbor Airlines (Bar Harbor, then Bangor, Maine)**	QO EA CO	Bar Harbor-Bangor, then to Boston, Portland, points in New England, and to Albany, New York, and Philadelphia. Also operated to Quebec, Canada	Cessna 310 Cessna 402 Beech 99 Convair 600 CASA 212 Beech 1900 SAAB 340	Founded as F.B.O. in 1946 by Tom and Joe Caruso. Purchased Downeast Airlines in 1980 and Valley Airlines in 1986. Cooperative agreement with Eastern Airlines (System-One reservations) in 1981, and became a unit of Eastern Air Express in 1986. Acquired Provincetown-Boston Airline (PBA) in April 1987, in association with Texas Air Corp. When latter acquired 50% share of Bar Harbor, which then became a Continental Express carrier.	

AREA 11 (NORTHEAST) Continued

First Sched. Service Date	Airline and Base	Code	Initial or Typical Route Network	Aircraft Used	Remarks	Date of last service
1969	Mountain Airways (Saugerties, N.Y.)	MC	Kingston-Newburg-New York (JFK)	BN-2 Islander		1970
1970	North American Airlines (Windsor Locks, Conn.)	ON	Hartford-Montreal	Beech 18	Pilgrim acquired the rights to Montreal.	1971
12 Aug. 1970	New England Airlines (Block Island, R.I.)	EJ	Block Island-Westerly Block Island-Providence	Cessna 172 Piper Cherokee Six Piper Aztec BN-2 Islander	Founded by William Bendokas as "Block Island's Resident Airline."	
1 Nov. 1970	Air New England (Boston)	XQ	Hyannis-Nantucket, then to New York, Boston, New Bedford, Augusta, Portland, Martha's Vineyard. Later to points in Maine New Vermont, Hampshire, and ultimately to Cleveland and Rochester	Beech 99 Aero Commander Douglas DC-3 DHC-6 Twin Otter Convair 580	Founded by Joseph C. Whitney and former employees of Executive Airlines, and George Parmenter, of Cape & Islands Flight Service. Backed by Robert Kansler of Detroit, and Farleigh Dickinson, Jr. On 24 January 1975, certificated by C.A.B. as a regional air carrier, the first (and the only) one to be so certificated since Ozark in 1950. All services suspended on 31 Oct. 1981.	31 Oct. 1981
1970	Holiday Airways (Monticello, N.Y.)		Sullivan County Airport-New York (La Gaurdia)	Beech 99	Also known as Catskill Holiday Airlines.	1970
1970	Morris Air Transport (Morristown, NJ)	UM	Morristown- New York	BN-2 Islander		1971
1971	New England Commuter (Manchester, NH)	NP	Manchaster-Lawrence-Newark	Cessna 402		1971
1972	Cherokee Airlines (Flushing, NY)	HW	Islip-New York (JFK)-Wilmington	Beech 18		1973
1972	Hudson Valley Airways (White Lake, NY)	XW	Monticello-Scranton-Buffalo; Monticello-New York			1973
July 1972	Downtown Airlines (New York)	DR	New York-Philadelphia-Washington	Piper Aztec DHC-6 Twin Otter	Operated with floats between downtown riverfront locations.	1975
1973	Rainbowair (Keene, NH)	ER	Keene-Hartford; Keen-Boston; Nashua-Boston	Cessna 402	Previously operated from Bridgeport to Cape Cod and the Islands.	1974
1973	Centurion Air Service		Greenville-Bangor-Augusta	Cessna 402		1973
1973	Mall Airways (Albany, NY)	FH	Albany-Binghamton-Ithaca-Elmira; Albany-Newark, Providence, Syracuse, Rochester, Montreal,	Beech 99 Piper Aztec	FAA Certificate withdrawn, 1988 but resumed operation and sold to Business Express, Sept. 1989.	1 Sept. 1989
1974	Manhattan Airlines (Syracuse, NY)			Beech 18 DC-3		1975
1974	Air Speed (Bedford, Mass.)	WP	Bedford-New York, Boston	Beech 99		1975
19 Feb. 1975	Atlantic Central Airline (Bangor)		Bangor-St John, N.B.	Beech 18		1976

AREA 11 (NORTHEAST) Continued

First Sched. Service Date	Airline and Base	Code	Initial or Typical Route Network	Aircraft Used	Remarks	Date of last service
1 May 1975	Gull Air (Hyannis, Mass.)	JI	Hyannis-Nantucket and Martha's Vineyard; Boston-Nantucket and M.V. Later to Florida, local routes including some for Air Florida	Beech 18 Cessna 402 CASA 212	Founded by Robert Welch at Nantucket. Purchased by Iyanough Management Corp. in 1983 and expanded to Florida. Associated with Texas Air Corp., March 1986.	10 Mar 1987
16 June 1975	Merrimack Airways (Bedford, Mass.)	ZE	Lawrence-Boston, Springfield, White Plains, New York (La G), Boston-Burlington	Piper Navajo Chieftain	Founded as Merrimack Air System at Lawrence, Mass. Moved to Bedford and changed name in 1978.	1979
22 Sept. 1975	**Empire Airlines (Utica-Rome, NY)**	UR	Utica-Syracuse; Utica-Newark, Buffalo, Boston; Syracuse-New York and throughout New York State, New England, and to Washington and Montreal	Piper Navajo Metro II (Fokker F-28)	Division of Oneida County Aviation, Inc. Obtained full C.A.B. certificate, Oct. 1979 Considerable expansion under presidency of Paul Quackenbush. Purchased by Piedmont Airlines, 2 October 1985.	2 Oct 1985
1975	Federal Carriers (White Lake, NY)	MF	Monticello-New York	Beech 18		1978
1975	Lebanon Airport Devt. Corp. (W. Lebanon, NH)	XW	Lebanon-Whitefield, N.H.	Aero Commander		1976
1975	Flying Dutchman Corp. (Amherst, NH)	YV	Manchaster-Washington (Nat.)	Piper Navajo		1976
25 May 1976	Rutland Airways (Rutland, Vermont)	RQ	Rutland-Keene-Boston	Cessna 402	Originally an F.B.O., founded by Al Greenwood. Sold in 1975 to Larry Healy. Ran into financial problems.	17 Jan 1977
1976	Air Atlantic (Danvers, Mass.)	HO	Manchester-Boston Syracuse-Utica-Boston	Beech Queen Air		1976
1976	Seaplane Shuttle Transport (NY)	SX	New York-Philadelphia	Twin Otter (floatplane)	Connected downtown floatplane bases.	1977
1976	Business Commuter (Bridgeport, Conn.)	TT	Bridgeport-Philadelphia, Albany, Farmingdale; seasonal service to Nantucket and Martha's Vineyard	Piper types	Operated by Business Aircraft Corporation.	1980
1976	Island Air (New York, NY)	YN	Farmingdale-New York; New York-Philadelphia-Baltimore	Douglas DC-3		1976
1976	Alector Airways (Newburgh, N.Y.)	US	Newburgh-New York	Piper Navajo		1977
1976	Executive Airlines (Cambridge, Mass.)	WP	Boston-White Plains	Beech 99 Beagle	Not related to the earlier Executive airlines of 1960.	1977
1977	Nor East Commuter Airlines (Boston)	YN	Boston-Hyannis, Nantucket, Martha's Vineyard, New Bedford	Piper Navajo	Founded by Joseph Whitney, formerly founder of Executive Airlines of 1960.	1981
1977	Albany Air Service (Albany)	YU	Albany-White Plains-New York	Beech 18		1978
June 1977	Precision Airlines (Springfield, Vermont, and Manchester, N.H.)	RP	Boston-Springfield, Rutland, Keene, Manchester, later to New York (La G) from Rutland and Pittsfield then points in New Hampshire and Vermont and to Philadelphia	Piper Navajo DHC-6 Twin Otter Dornier 228	Founded by Walter Faucett. Affiliated as Eastern Express carrier on 1 May 1986, but changed to Northwest Airlink in May 1989, after Eastern ceased operation. Sold to Northeast Express in 1989, but independent operations continued.	

AREA 11 (NORTHEAST) Continued

First Sched. Service Date	Airline and Base	Code	Initial or Typical Route Network	Aircraft Used	Remarks	Date of last service
13 July 1977	Air Hyannis (Hyannis, Mass.)	YB	Hyannis-Boston-Worcester; Boston-Nantucket; Hyannis-Nantucket; Providence-New York	Piper Seneca Cessna 402	Began as Hyannis Aviation.	1981
13 Feb. 1978	Princeton Airways	PN	Princeton-Newark, later to Washington and Boston	Piper Navajo Chieftain BN-2 Islander Nomad	Founded by David E. van Dyke, of Princeton Aviation Corp.	
June 1978	Susquehanna Airways (Sidney, N.Y.)	FR	Sidney-Syracuse	Piper Aztec	Founded as Forde-Aire by Bernard Forde. Changed name to Susquehanna in December 1979. Sustained two crashes in 1984, and F.A.A. revoked certificate in April 1985.	15 Jan. 1985
16 Oct. 1978	New Air (New Haven, Conn.)	NB NC	New Haven-Islip; New Haven-Baltimore; then to Philadelphia and Washington	Piper Navajo Bandeirante Shorts SD 360	Organized by Don and Frank Santacroce in 1962 as F.B.O. Began schedule service as New Haven Airways. Changed name on 18 July 1980. Acquired by Pilgrim Airlines in 1985.	Feb. 1985
1978	Sound Air Aviation (Ronkonkoma, NY)	KK	Islip-New York (La G)	Aero Commander		1978
1978	Cosmopolitan Airlines (Farmingdale, NY)	HX	Farmingdale-Boston, Atlantic City, and Albany	Convair 440	Founded by Peter and George Garrambone, as affiliate of Cosmopolitan Aviation. Also operated as Coastal Airways. Bankrupt.	1985
1978	Nitlyn Airways (Shirley, N.Y.)	YJ	Westhampton-Shirley-New York (JFK)	Piper Navajo Chieftain		1979
1979	North Central Airways (Lincoln, RI)	VF	Providence-Block Island	Piper Navajo Chieftain		1979
April 1979	Green Mountain Airlines (Warren, VT)	VS	Montpelier-New York (La G)	Cessna 402		Late 1980
May 1979	East Hampton Aire (East Hampton, L.I.)	IN	East Hampton-New York (La G) and Boston; and briefly to Washington	Piper Navajo Beech Baron Beech 99, 1900	Founded by Frank Lavigna. Certificate withdrawn by F.A.A. Changed name in 1990 to Business Wings.	Feb. 1991
April 1979	Air Vectors Airways (Newburgh, N.Y.)	ZB	Newburg-Poughkeepsie-Binghampton; Newburgh, Newark-Morristown, Boston, Poughkeepsie-Washington (Dulles Int.)	Piper Navajo	Founded by Jim Aspin.	1985
1 June 1979	New Jersey Airways (East Orange, N.J.)	OY	Atlantic City-Newark Atlantic City-Trenton	BN-2 Islander	Later combined with Merrimack Airlines.	1980
1979	Aerotransit (Beverly, Mass.)	YV	Beverly, Mass.-New York (La G)	Beech Queen Air		1980
1979	Sair Aviation (Syracuse, N.Y.)	JR	Syracuse-Toronto/Ottawa	Piper Navajo Chieftain		1980
Sept. 1979	Courtesy Air Service (Glens Falls, NY)	QQ	Glens Falls-New York (La G), Saranac Lake-New York (La G)	Beech 18 Navajo Chieftain	Founded by Ted Zoli. Provided service for Winter Olympics, 1980.	Aug. 1980
Sept. 1979	Air East Airlines (Westfield, Mass.)	JW	Westfield-Hartford-New York (La G)	Piper Navajo Chieftain	Founded by William Blamey and Edward Davis.	1980

AREA 11 (NORTHEAST) Continued

First Sched. Service Date	Airline and Base	Code	Initial or Typical Route Network	Aircraft Used	Remarks	Date of last service
June 1979	Holiday Airlines (Newark and Morristown, N.J.)	JO	Montgomery, New York-Newark; Newark-Atlantic City, Hyannis, Martha's Vineyard	Piper types DHC-6 Twin Otter		18 Dec. 1989
1979	Southeast Air (New Bedford, Mass.)	HO	New Bedford-New York; New Bedford-Martha's Vineyard-Nantucket			Late 1979
1980	Danbury Airways (Danbury, Conn.)	VS	Danbury-New York (La Guardia and JFK)	DHC-6 Twin Otter	Founded by John Dunning.	1981
1980	Transtate Airways (Oxford, Conn.)	ZO	Oxford-New York (La G)-Atlantic City	BN-2 Islander		1980
1980	Bard Airlines (Cortland, N.Y.)	NB	Erie-Newark	Piper types		1981
1980	Will's Air (Hyannis, Mass.)	WA YW	Boston-Nantucket; Hyannis-Nantucket	Piper Aztec Piper Navajo BN-3 Trislander DHC-6 Twin Otter	Founded by William Welsh. "The Little Airline with the Big Heart."	Feb. 1986
Jan 1981	Astec Air East (Farmingdale, N.Y.)	JJ	Farmingdale-Bridgeport, New Haven, Hartford, Albany, Providence	Piper Navajo Chieftain Piper T-1020		June 1982
1 April 1981	Clinton Aero Corp. (Plattsburgh, N.Y.)	CA SS	Plattsburgh-Burlington	Cessna 172 Piper Aztec Beech 99, 1900	Founded by Mary and Jim Drollette, later with Anthony Von Elbe. Purchased by Brockway Glass (Aviation) 1 August 1983. 23-mile route across Lake Champlain one of world's shortest.	1983
13 Oct. 1981	**Business Express (Bridgeport, Conn.)**	4A HQ	Bridgeport-Philadelphia; Bridgeport-Martha's Vineyard-Nantucket. Then (after change of name) to Boston, and expansion throughout New England, and to Montreal, Toronto, and Washington	Piper types then Beech 99 Beech 1900 SAAB 340 Shorts SD 360 Fokker F-27	Founded as Atlantic Air. Purchased by Marketing Corporation of America in November 1984, changing name to the present one. Bought Pilgrim Airlines on 28 February 1986. Became a unit of The Delta Connection, 22 April 1986. Purchased Mall Airways 1 Sept. 1989.	
13 Oct. 1981	Atlantic Air (Bridgeport, Conn)	HQ	Bridgeport-Philadelphia; Boston, Bedford; White Plains-Bedford-Nantucket, Martha's Vineyard	Beech 1900 Beech 99	Purchased by Marketing Corp. of America in November 1984 to form Business Express (q.v.).	Nov. 1984
2 Nov. 1981	Valley Airlines (Frenchville, Maine)	FZ 2V	Frechville-Presque Isle, Augusta-Portland	Cessna 402 Beech 99	Founded as F.B.O. in 1974. Intermittent operation until purchased by Bar Harbor Airlines in 1986, but continued as separate operation. Renamed Northeast Express Regional Airline on 18 Sept. 1989, and became a Northwest Airlink carrier on 5 Feb. 1990.	
1981	Northern Airlines (Martha's Vineyard, Mass.)		Nantucket-Martha's Vineyard-New Bedford-Newark	Piper types		1981
1981	New York Air (Farmingdale, N.Y.)	TB	Nantucket/Martha's Vineyard-New York (La G)	Bandeirante Cessna types	No connection with the New York Air jet operator of Texas Air Corp. Later merged with Trans East International and Southeast Airlines.	1984

AREA 11 (NORTHEAST) Continued

First Sched. Service Date	Airline and Base	Code	Initial or Typical Route Network	Aircraft Used	Remarks	Date of last service
Dec. 1981	Air Vermont (Stowe, Vermont)	MV	Burlington-Boston, Albany, Hartford, New York (JFK), Washington, Portland; Hartford-Islip-Wilkes-Barre	Piper Aztec, Seneca Piper Navajo Chieftain Beech 99	Founded by Gene Kazlow and John Porter. Burlington-Boston frequency up to 12 round trips daily, but forced into Chapter 11 bankruptcy by a local fare war.	20 Jan 1984
Early 1982	Kobrin Airways (Princeton N.J.)		Princeton-Philadelphia	Piper T-1020	Founded by Bernie Kobrin. Short-lived.	Late 1982
1982	Silver Kris Services (Bradley Field, Conn.)		Bradley Field (Hartford) to points in Vermont	BN-2 Islander Piper Navajo Chieftain	Founded by Bill Kingson.	1984
1982	Trans East Int'l (Farmingdale, N.Y.)		Bridgeport-Nantucket, Atlantic City, New York	Cessna 402		1982
1982	National Air (Marston Mills, Mass. and Newport, R.I.)	OW	Hyannis-New Bedford-Newport-Providence-New York (JFK)	Cessna 402 CASA 212	Became a subsidiary of the U.S. CASA distributor.	30 Sept 1984
1982	Maine Air (Bangor, Maine)	SM	Bangor-Portland-Boston	Piper types		1983
17 Jan. 1983	Atlantic Express (E. Farmingdale, NY)	QD	Boston-Farmingdale (Syracuse-Albany-Farmingdale)	Metro III		1983
1983	Bangor International Airline (Bangor, Maine)	IL	Bangor-Houlton	Cessna types inc. Type 206		Late 1987
1983	Air Marc (Farmingdale, N.J.)	NP EK	Albany Park, N.J.-New York(JFK)	Cessna types	Founded as Eastman Airways, changing name in November 1984.	1985
1 Aug. 1983	**Brockway Air (Burlington, Vermont)**	SS	Combined networks of Clinton and Air North to consolidate routes throughout New England and northeast states, as far west as Rochester and as far south as Washington	Beech 1900 F-27 Shorts SD-330	Founded when Brockway Glass Co. purchased Clinton Aero Corp. (see above, 1981) and, on 1 October 1983, Air North (see 1963) and also purchased Crown Airways. Became Piedmont Commuter affiliate on 15 March 1986. Purchased by Owens Illinois Inc., of Toledo, spring 1988. Sold to Metro Airlines, Dallas, as Metro Airlines Northeast 7 April 1989. US Air franchise (formerly Piedmont) transferred to Trans World Express in July 1989. Bankrupt 30 May 1991.	7 Feb 1991
1983	Tri-State Airlines (White Lake, N.Y.)	ZQ	Albany-Newark; Harrisburg-Newark	Piper types		August 1984
1984	Island Air (Farmingdale, N.Y.)	WS	Farmingdale-Martha's Vineyard-Hyannis; New York (La G)-Nantucket-Martha's Vineyard	Cessna types		Dec. 1984
1984	Action Airlines	XQ	New London-Block Island, Fisher's Island, East Hampton, also to AtlanticCity	Piper Cherokee Six Piper Navajo Piper Seneca	Founded by John Rutledge. Operates year round to Fisher's Island, others seasonal.	
1984	Gulfstream Airlines (S. Windsor, Conn)	7G	Atlantic City-Hartford	Piper types		

AREA 11 (NORTHEAST) Continued

First Sched. Service Date	Airline and Base	Code	Initial or Typical Route Network	Aircraft Used	Remarks	Date of last service
1984	Cape Air (Hyannis, Mass.)	EK 9K	Hyannis-Martha's Vineyard-Nantucket; Providence-Boston	Cessna 402	Founded by Dan Wolf. Operated briefly in 1984 but resumed on 16 October 1989, after purchasing the Martha's Vineyard route from Edgartown Air.	
1984	Express Aire (New Bedford, Mass.)	FX	Hyannis-Nantucket	Cessna types		
1985	Long Island Airlines (East Hampton, L.I.)	YL	East Hampton-New York (La G)	Piper Navajo DHC-6 Twin Otter	Founded by Robert O. King. Sold in 1985 to Michael Perregine, who absorbed Montauk-Carribbean Airways (see 1963), to which it was already affiliated. Chapter 11 bankruptcy, October 1990.	Oct. 1990
1986	Sakonnet Air Charter (Middletown, R.I.)	9S	Providence-Newport	Piper Navajo		1987
Spring 1987	Princeton Air Link (Princeton, N.S.)	IV	Princeton-Newark; later to New York (JFK), also to Allentown from JFK	BN-2 Islander	Founded by Jack Hoyt. Bankruptcy, Sept. 1988.	Sept 1988
1 April 1987	Tri Air (Hyannis, Mass.)	8T	Hyannis-Nantucket; Hyannis-Martha's Vineyard	BN-3 Trislander		Aug. 1989
June 1987	Nantucket Airlines (Hyannis, Mass.)	DV	Hyannis-Nantucket	Cessna 402	Founded by Charles Harris High frequency shuttle service.	
1988	Spectrum Airlines (New Bedford, Mass.)		New Bedford-Hyannis-Martha's Vineyard-Nantucket	Piper Navajo		1990
26 Sept. 1988	Westover Air (Chicopee, Mass.)	IN	Chicopee-New York (La Guardia)	Beech 99, 1900	A division of East Hampton Aire, Long Island, New York.	5 Jan. 1989
Jan. 1989	Edgarton Airways (Martha's Vineyard, Mass.)	3D	Martha's Vineyard-Hyannis, M.V.-New Bedford; New Bedford-Nantucket	Piper Navajo Chieftain BN-2 Islander	Founded by Mike and Nikki Madeiros, formerly an F.B.O at Katama field, Martha's Vineyard.	
20 Mar. 1989	PAC Air (Provincetown, MA)	7F 3N	Provincetown-Boston	Piper Navajo Chieftain	Operated by Pearson Aviation Corp., owned by Arthur Pearson.	14 Oct. 1989
1 Aug. 1989	CommutAir (Plattsburgh, N.Y.)	US	Network of routes in the northeast, feeding USAir at Albany, Syracuse, Burlington, etc. from Buffalo in the west to Boston in the east	Beech 1900	Founded by Jim Drollette (see also Clinton Aero, Brockway) and Anthony von Elbe as USAir Express Affiliate when Metro Air Northeast lost that franchise.	
1 Oct. 1989	Mohawk Airlines (Syracuse, N.Y.)	ZO	Network of routes radiating from Syracuse, as far as Boston, New York, Buffalo	Beech 99 Beech 1900	Founded by Robert Peach, Jr., son of Robert Peach, Sr., who was president of the first Mohawk Airlines (1945-1972).	1991
June 1990	Valley Air, Inc. (Burlington, VT.)		Burlington-Rutland-Albany	Piper Navajo	Operated by Valley Flying Service.	Aug. 1990
12 July 1990	Travelair (Newark, N.J.)	8T	Newark-Hartford, Newark-Nantucket-Martha's Vineyard	Shorts SD-330		Oct. 1990

Area 12

Mid-Atlantic

During the formative period of what were to become known as the commuter airlines of the United States, there was much activity in the coastal region and its hinterland that extended as far south of New York as North Carolina. Conveniently described here as the mid-Atlantic area, the region contains several large cities, such as Philadelphia, Baltimore, and Washington; several medium-size cities, such as Norfolk, Richmond, and Charlotte; and many more population centers, including a chain of urban communities stretching for about two hundred miles across North Carolina. Throughout the whole area, the larger cities have in the past enjoyed good air service from the trunk and local service airlines, but the smaller towns or cities have received service that was too often dictated only by the geographical or operational convenience of the certificated airlines, and which, in the postwar years, became only sporadic and of deteriorating quality. The rise of commuter airlines was therefore predictable, for demographic reasons if for no other.

One such airline, in fact, was one of the earliest of all the scheduled air taxi operators, as they were at first called. It got under way as a small scheduled airline operating out of the city of Reading, Pennsylvania, which was one of those communities that the trunk and local airlines had regarded as only marginally viable. Recognizing both the problem and the opportunity, a fixed based operator, founded in 1946 as Reading Aviation Services by Sime Bertolet, started Reading Airlines in the summer of 1957. Its main mission was to provide a scheduled line to Newark (serving New York), and it later extended routes to Philadelphia, Buffalo, and other points in the region. Still later, it merged with the Air Taxi Company of Red Bank, New Jersey, to form Suburban Airlines in 1968, and under the vigorous direction of its new president, Art Horst, grew in strength and stature before becoming an Allegheny Commuter affiliate in 1973.

This was the forerunner of several scheduled air taxi/third-level/ commuter companies that were being established in the area during the major growth period of that airline category, and which prospered in the area during the 1960s. For reasons that are only partially explained by the demographic factors referred to previously, several airline entrepreneurs emerged with a collective vision that ran parallel with, and even extended beyond, that of the pioneer company at Reading. Richard A. Henson in 1964, Roy Clark in 1965, J. Dawson Ransome and Angelo Koukoulis of Clarksburg, West Virginia, in 1967—these men founded Henson Airlines, Pennsylvania Airlines, Ransome Airlines, and Aero-Mech Airlines, respectively, to provide scheduled air services based at Hagerstown, Maryland, Harrisburg and North Philadelphia, Pennsylvania, and Clarksburg, West Virginia. All these points were by this time receiving inadequate service, or had seen their air service evaporate altogether, as the certificated carriers abandoned community service in their search for higher status, prestige, and profits. (North Philadelphia was a special case, serving an area of that large city that was remote from the main airport.)

The five airlines thus briefly summarized were so successful in establishing their own spheres of operation that they were able to withstand the threat, real or imagined, of the reintroduction of normal scheduled service by the certificated airlines. Indeed, as recounted elsewhere in this book, the main local service operator in the mid-Atlantic region, Allegheny Airlines, decided to recruit the smaller airline services into a partnership rather than to compete with them as rivals. Through the initiative of Richard Henson, working with Les Barnes, the president of Allegheny, The Hagerstown Commuter became the prototype of the now-familiar partnerships that proliferated throughout the United States. This was as long ago as 1967, and in due course in the late 1960s and early 1970s, AeroMech, Ransome, Suburban, and Pennsylvania Airlines all joined the Allegheny Commuter organization, together with other airlines farther to the west. The mid-Atlantic region, therefore, can be regarded as the birthplace of the commuter–major airline partnership practice that is one of the cornerstones of the interwoven air network of the United States as we know it today.

The Allegheny Commuter cooperative system worked well, although there were occasional dissenting voices. It survived the scramble for commuter airline partnerships that evolved in the 1980s and enabled the renamed USAir to ward off competitive threats to most of its traffic catchment area. However, some airlines outside the Allegheny/USAir protective umbrella were not so lucky. Altair, for example, established a hub at Philadelphia, but it tried to run before it could walk and collapsed in a heap of debt in 1982.

Later on, other airlines of some significance emerged, particularly as Piedmont Aviation began to withdraw from the smaller cities in Virginia and the Carolinas. Colgan Airways in 1971 and Air Virginia and CC Air in 1979 all made their presence known, but after initial success, they too had to become code-sharing affiliates of the major airlines.

Many smaller companies flitted, mothlike, across the scene. Quite a few of them were located in the Delmarva Peninsula, which is all but cut off from the mainland by Chesapeake Bay. The fixed based operators in the area catered to their market's needs very efficiently, and some, like Henson, flourished.

In recent times, the airlines of the mid-Atlantic area have faced competition that is unique to the region. The Amtrak line from Washington to New York, the only truly high-speed railway line in the United States, has diverted some local traffic away from the commuter airlines, as well as from the end-to-end commuter traffic on the New York–Washington air shuttle services.

The Amtrak trains stop at Baltimore, Wilmington, Trenton, and Newark among other, smaller places. New construction, modern technology, and sensible intermodal connecting arrangements are again making the trains an acceptable alternative to the very commuter airlines that once usurped their traditional role. Just as Dick Henson's Hagerstown Commuter was a key player in developing the role of the airline in local community affairs, so might an expanding rail network in the hinterland of the New York–Philadelphia–Baltimore–Washington–Richmond–Norfolk corridor bring about another transportation revolution.

AREA 12 (MID-ATLANTIC)

First Sched. Service Date	Airline and Base	Code	Initial or Typical Route Network	Aircraft Used	Remarks	Date of last service
1 Aug. 1957	**Suburban Airlines (Reading, Pa.)**	RE UQ TI AL US	Reading-New York (Newark) then to Philadelphia, Allentown, Buffalo, Wilkes-Barre, and other points in the northeast.	Beech 18 DH Dove DHC Twin Otter Beech 99 DH Heron Shorts 330 Shorts 360 DHC Dash 8	Started operation as Reading Airlines, operated by Reading Aviation Services, F.B.O. founded in 1946. by Sime Bertolet. In August 1968, merged with Red Bank Air Taxi (see Area 11) and adopted present name. Arthur M. Horst president 1970. Allegheny Commuter, March, 1973. Bought by U.S. Air Group in 1986.	
12 Nov. 1963	East Coast Commuter (Cambridge, Md.)	HO	Washington-Baltimore-Cambridge-Salisbury-Wallops Station-Ocean City	Cessna 310	Operated by East Coast Air Taxi, Inc.	(1970)
1 Oct. 1964	**Henson Airlines (Hagerstown, Md., then Salisbury, Md.)**	HC PI US	Hagerstown-Washington, Salisbury-Washington, then to Baltimore, Newport News, Philadelphia, and later to Shenandoah Valley, Pittsburgh, New York	Beech 18 Aero Commander, Beech 99 Shorts 330 DHC Dash 8	Founded by Richard A. Henson as The Hagerstown Commuter. On 15 Nov. 1967, became the Allegheny Commuter, the prototype for the now-familiar commuter-regional/trunk partnerships. Transferred to association with Piedmont in 1983, to retain independence, and adopted Henson name. Separate route network established in Florida (see Area 10). Became part of US Air Group on 1 July 1988.	
21 Nov. 1964	Maryland Airways (Easton, Md.)		Easton-Washington/Baltimore	Beech 35		1968
15 April 1965	**Pennsylvania Airlines (Harrisburg, Pa.)**	HR EB AL US	Harrisburg-Washington, Harrisburg-State College, later to Pittsburgh, Allentown, Johnstown, and Philadelphia	Beech 18 DHC Twin Otter Beech 99 Nord 262 Shorts 330 DHC Dash 8	Started as the Harrisburg Commuter, a subsidiary of L.B. Smith Aircraft Corp. Operation purchased by L.W. (Roy) Clark and registered as Pennsylvania Commuter Airlines on 29 January 1970. Associated with Eastern Airlines 1968 and became an Allegheny Commuter unit on 1 October 1973. Dropped the "Commuter" in 1980.	
1965	Southern Jersey Airways (Atlantic City)	6J AL CO	Atlantic City-Newark-Monmouth; Atlantic City-Cape May-Millville-Philadelphia	DHC Twin Otter DHC Dash 8	Founded by Don Young, Senior and Junior. Sold to Richard Olsen, 1987. Became Allegheny Commuter briefly but became Continental Express affiliate on 13 May 1989.	Oct. 1990
19 Nov. 1965	Walter Faryniak (Allentown, Pa.)			Pipers		1968
15 Feb. 1966	General Airlines (Reading, Pa.)		Reading-Baltimore-Washington	Beech 18	Changed name in 1967 from General Aviation Service.	1968
25 Feb. 1966	Air Shannon (Fredricksburg. Va.)		Fredricksburg-Washington (National)	Pipers		24 April 1967
16 Mar. 1966	Cumberland Airlines (Cumberland, Md.)	NQ NT	Cumberland-Washington, later to Baltimore, Ocean City. Pittsburgh, Latrobe	Piper Aztec Piper Navajo Beech 99	Changed name from Nicholson Air Service in 1969.	
4 Nov. 1966	Altair Airlines (Philadelphia)	XD AK	Philadelphia-Scranton, Richmond, White Plains, Albany. Later expansion to many points in north-east, the Carolinas, and ultimately to Florida.	Beech 99 Nord 262 (Fokker F28) (Douglas DC-9)	Airlines expanded ambitiously but filed for bankruptcy under Chapter 11.	10 Nov. 1982

AREA 12 (MID-ATLANTIC) Continued

First Sched. Service Date	Airline and Base	Code	Initial or Typical Route Network	Aircraft Used	Remarks	Date of last service
2 Mar. 1967	**Ransome Airlines (Philadelphia)**	RX PA AL RL RZ	North Philadelphia-Washington, Richmond, Newark; then expansion to Boston and New England cities	Beech 18 Volpar Beech 18 Nord 262 DHC Dash 7	Founded by J. Dawson Ransome. Became an Allegheny Commuter in 1969, but terminated agreement 1 June 1982 to be independent. Then associated with Continental Express, and then The Delta Connection. Sold to Pan American, 1 June 1986 when it became Pan Am Express.	1 June 1986
11 June 1967	Horizon Airlines (Charlottesville, Va.)		Lynchburg-Charlottesville-Richmond	Piper	Initially based at Lynchburg.	1969
12 Sept. 1967	Dovair Air Transport (Dover, Delaware)	DE	Dover-Wilmington-New York-White Plains	Cessna		1968
1967	AeroMech Airlines (Clarksburg, W.V.)	KC RZ AL	Clarksburg-Pittsburgh, Morgantown, Charleston Washington; later expansion to Cincinnati, Columbus, and other points in Allegheny region	Beech 99 DHC Twin Otter Bandeirante	Founded by Angelo C. Koukoulis Temporary contract service for Lake Central in 1964; became an Allegheny Commuter in 1968. Separated from USAir (successor to Allegheny) in 1980. Merged with Wright Airlines, October 1983 (see Area 9). Bankrupt 1984.	1984
16 Sept. 1968	Shenandoah Airlines (Charlottesville, Va.)	DW	Lynchburg, Charlottesville Washington (Dulles)-Baltimore. Roanoke-Shenandoah-Charlottesville.	Beech 18 Beech Queenair	"Your Personal Airline."	1969
20 Sept. 1968	Washington Airlines (Baltimore)	WV	Baltimore (Friendship)-Washington (National)-Washington (Dulles)	Dornier Skyservant	Formed by Butler Aviation This attempt at a STOL(Short Takeoff and Landing) operation failed because of lack of traffic.	Sept. 1969
1 Oct. 1968	Cardinal Airlines (Lynchburgh, Va.)	DH CD	Lynchburgh-Washington (Dulles) Washington (Nat'l) Charlottesville	Britten-Norman BN-2A Cessnas, Pipers Beech 99	Sold to Rodney Jaeger, who operated an F.B.O. Flight America, at Lynchburg. Jaeger later formed Air Virginia.	1976
1968	Washington-Baltimore Airways (Washington, D.C.)		Baltimore-Pittsburgh; Martinsburg-Cumberland; Charleston; Bluefield-Bristol, Reading, and various cities throughout Pennsylvania.	Piper Aztec Beech		1970
1969	Pioneer Airlines (Washington, D.C.)					1970
1969	Travel Air Aviation (Morgantown, W.V.)					1972
1969	KMK Airlines (Arlington, Va.)	XU	Washington National-Williamsport, Pa.	Cessna types		1970
1971	Colgan Airways (Manassas, Va.)	MC CJ CO	Manassas-Washington (Dulles)-Binghamton; Manassas-Raleigh; Raleigh-Washington Poughkeepsie	Beech 99 Shorts 330	Founded by Charles Colgan, Democratic Senator. Operated as New York Air Connection, Nov. 1985. Purchased by Presidential Airways, 13 August 1986. To Continental Express, Feb. 1987. Filed for bankruptcy, 2 December 1989.	2 Dec. 1989

AREA 12 (MID-ATLANTIC) Continued

First Sched. Service Date	Airline and Base	Code	Initial or Typical Route Network	Aircraft Used	Remarks	Date of last service
1972	Superior Air (Fairmont, W.V.)	VL	Fairmont-Pittsburgh-Wheeling	BN-2 Islander		1973
Summer 1972	Downtown Airlines (Philadelphia)	DR	Philadelphia (Penn's Landing)-New York (Wall Street Pier 8). Briefly extended to Washington.	Piper Aztec DHC-Twin Otter	First inter-city floatplane service by a commuter airline.	1975
1973	Pinehurst Airlines (Pinehurst, N.C.)	PF HI	Pinehurst-various points. Later Greenville/ Spartanburg-Atlanta	DC-3 YS-11	Founded by Lewis C. Burwell, Jr. as a specialized resort service at Pinehurst, N.C. Moved to Greenville, S.C., in 1979.	1982
1973	Shamrock Airlines (Easton, Md.)	WR	Easton-Baltimore			1974
August 1973	Wheeler Airlines (Raleigh, N.C.)	WR UZ	Raleigh/Durham-Greenville-Norfolk; Raleigh-Charlotte-Asheville-Augusta and Huntington, W.V.; later to New York, Washington	Beech 18 BN2-Islander Fairchild F-27	Founded by Warren Wheeler as the Wheeler Flying Service. One of the few airlines in the U.S. founded by a black citizen. Filed Chapter 11 bankruptcy in 1985, but continued operations. WRA Inc. (q.v. 1987) took over routes.	1987
1973	AirExec (Ocean City, Md)	EE MD	Ocean City-Georgetown, Washington, D.C., Philadelphia, and Baltimore	DHC Twin Otter		1975
1974	Crown International Airlines (Norfolk, Va.)	RL	Hatteras, N.C.-Manteo, N.C.-Norfolk	DH 104 Dove	Seasonal service.	1979
1974	Flightways Av. System (Philadelphia)	FO WQ	Philadelphia-New York (JFK) and Wilmington, Del.	DH 114 Heron	Operated by Flightways Corp.	1975
1975	Skyline (Winchester, Va.)	XQ	Winchester-Baltimore, Newport News-Norfolk, Washington-Ocean City, Richmond	Beech 99	Operated by Skyline Aviation.	1976
1975	Air Carolina (Charlotte, N.C.)	FN	Florence-Charlotte; Greenwood, S.C.-Anderson, S.C.-Atlanta	Piper Navajo		1980
1975	Cannon Aviation (Hickory, N.C.)	OY	Hickory-Charlotte	Cessna 402		1976
1975	Mid-South Airlines (Southern Pines, N.C.)	VL	Pinehurst-Raleigh/Durham; Pinehurst-Charlotte;-New Bern-Rocky Point;-Washington Newport News, Richmond, Danville	Piper Aztec Cherokee Six, Navajo Chieftain Beech Bonanza, King Air Bandeirante Shorts 330	Started as Resort Commuter Airlines. "Carolina's Wings to the Future". Sold to Air Virginia 1983.	1983
1976	Dovair (Dover, Del.)	VJ	Dover-Philadelphia	BN-2 Islander	Began as Baltimore Airways.	1977
1976	Perkiomen Airways (Reading, Penn.)	RY	Reading-Allentown-New York (La Guardia)	Piper Navajo		1979

AREA 12 (MID-ATLANTIC) Continued

First Sched. Service Date	Airline and Base	Code	Initial or Typical Route Network	Aircraft Used	Remarks	Date of last service
1977	Southern Maryland Aviation (California, Md.)	SF	St Mary's, Maryland-Washington	Piper Aztec		1978
Feb. 1977	Wings Airways (Blue Bell. Pa.)	WQ	Blue Bell-Philadelphia; also Philadelphia-Dover, Del, Millville, N.J., and Washington	BN-2 Islander BN-3 Trislander	Operating name for Pennsylvania Aviation. Suspended scheduled Service with onset of Gulf War.	Early 1991
1978	Trans Penn Airlines (T.P.A.) (Reedsville, Pa.)	PF	Reedsville-State College-Pittsburgh; State College-Baltimore-Atlantic City	Piper Navajo	Operating name of Trans Pennsylvania Airlines.	1980
1978	Air Atlantic (Centre Hall, Pa.)	OX	State College-Philadelphia	Piper Seneca		1981
19 Mar. 1979	Air Virginia (Lynchburg, Va.) AVAir after 1 November 1985	CE AA	Lynchburh-Washington-Baltimore;Lynchburg-Charlottesville; Roanoke, Richmond; expansion to many points in Mid-Atlantic states from New York to Charlotte.	Piper Navajo BAe HS 748 Metro III	Founded by Rodney Jaeger (see Cardinal Airlines). Bought Mid-South, 1983. Sold to Dimitri P. Nicholas, Oct. 1984. After brief association with United Airlines, became part of American Eagle System, 15 May 1985. Renamed AVAir, 1 Nov. 1986. Declared bankruptcy, 15 Jan. 1988 and bought by Nashville Eagle operation of American Airlines.	1988
1979	ISO Commuter (Kinston. N.C.)	IV	Kinston-Raleigh/Durham-Washington, N.C.	Cessna types	Operating division of I.S.O. Aero Service.	1980
1979	New Jersey Airways (Trenton, N.J.)	OY	Trenton-Newark	BN-2 Islander	Later known as Merimack Airlines-New Jersey Airways.	1980
15 Nov. 1979	CC Air (Charlotte, N.C.)	ED PI	Charlotte-Raleigh-Rocky Mount; Charlotte-Hickory; later expansion throughout N.Carolina, Tri-Cities, Norfolk, Atlanta	Cessna 402 Beech 99 Shorts 330 BAe Jetstream	Founded by Roy Hagerty as Sunbird Airlines, at Denver, N.C.. Merged with Hagerty's Air Transportation, 11 July 1984 and moved from Hickory, N.C. Associated as a Piedmont Commuter, 1 May 1985 and changed name to C.C. Air on 1 Jan. 1986, then to U.S.Air Group on merger of U.S. Air with Piedmont.	
1980	Eastern Carolina Aviation (Rocklands, N.C.)	VJ	Wilmington, NC-Jackson-ville, NC; Wilmington-Charlotte and Raleigh.	Piper types		1981
1980	Air-Lift Commuter (Raleigh-Durham, NC)	AJ 3L	Raleigh-Rocky Mount-Wilmington; Raleigh-Greenville	Piper types	Airline division of Air Lift Associates.	
15 April 1981	Air Pennsylvania (Philadelphia)	ZY	Philadelphia-Reading-Hazleton	Piper types		1982
15 June 1981	Williams Air (Mount Holly, N.J.)	YX	Burlington Country Airport-Philadelphia Int'l	BN-2 Islander		1983
1982	Asheville Flying Service (Asheville, N.C.)	2 F	Asheville-Raleigh/Durham	Piper types		1983
1982	Resort Airlines (Baltimore, Md.)	RY	Baltimore-Dover/Atlantic City/Ocean City/Washington	Piper types		1986

AREA 12 (MID-ATLANTIC) Continued

First Sched. Service Date	Airline and Base	Code	Initial or Typical Route Network	Aircraft Used	Remarks	Date of last service
15 Dec. 1982	Waring Air (Charlottesville, Va.)	7W	Carlottesville-Charlotte	Beech 18		1983
15 Mar. 1983	Americair (Washington)	DE	Washington (Dulles)-Baltimore, Washington (National)-Richmond	Cessna Crusader Piper Aztec BN-2 Islander	Founded by Dave Sullivan "Airlink to the Nation's Capital." Close association with British Airways.	1984
1984	Pegasus Air (Washington, D.C.)	8P	Philadelphia-Washington (Dulles)-Fayetteville, N.C.	Piper Navajo Chieftain		1984
1984	Mountain Air Commuter (Denver, N.C.)	7M	Washington(National)-Baltimore	Cessna types	Organized by Sunbird Airlines of Denver,N.C.	1985
1985	North American Airlines (Atlantic City, N.J.)		Atlantic City-Boston			1986
1985	Bader Express (Atlantic City, N.J.)		Atlantic City-Washington (National)	CASA 212		1986
1987	WRA Inc. (Morrisville, N.C.)	8R	Roanoke-Richmond	Piper types	Intrastate affiliate of Wheeler Airlines. Took over Wheeler's routes in 1987 when that company liquidated.	
1987	Catawba Air Transport (Hickory, N.C.)		Hickory-Charlotte			
1987	Chester County Air (Coatesville, Pa.)	2D	Coatesville-Philadelphia	Mitsubishi Mu-2		1988
1988	Jet Express (Newport News, Va.)	JI TW	Atlantic City-Charlottesville, Islip, Morgantown, Clarksburg, Washington	CASA 212	A TW Express affiliate of TWA. Founded at Atlantic City but on 17 July 1990, moved to Newport News after purchase by Smith Air Express.	
15 Dec. 1989	Atlantic Coast Express (Washington, D.C.)	NO UA	Washington (Dulles)-Allentown, Islip, Knoxville, Lynchburg, Newport News, Raleigh	BAe Jetstream EMB Brasilia	Established by Westair, a California-based United Airlines Code-sharing affiliate.	

Area 13

Caribbean

Like all island groups throughout the world, those known as the Greater and Lesser Antilles, which form a chain encircling the northern and eastern perimeter of the Caribbean Sea, have attracted the attention of airline promoters. During the 1930s Pan American Airways regarded the islands, from Cuba to Trinidad, as convenient stepping-stones on its route from Miami to South America. The larger islands, especially Cuba, had their own air services, but not until just before World War II did any U.S. company seek to establish a local air route system.

This company, Caribbean Atlantic Airways (Caribair), was established in San Juan, Puerto Rico, in 1939, and during the 1960s it built up a small network, using DC-3s and later Convair 340s. Its main route was to the island of St. Thomas in the U.S. Virgin Islands, a very popular resort destination for American vacationers. The ninety-mile route took only about twenty-five minutes in a forty-seat Convair-Liner.

Caribair was classified by the CAB as a territorial airline, and like its mainland local service compatriots, was subsidized quite generously for providing what was considered to be an essential transport service to the public. Caribair's Convairs, however, were integrated into its larger operational schedules, and the San Juan–St. Thomas route often had to fit in with other requirements. The frequency, therefore, was barely adequate, and in the view of many residents of St. Thomas—for whom San Juan was the local center of all kinds of business and social activities—this was not enough. Over at St. Croix, even farther away from San Juan, the service was also considered to be unacceptable for local needs, even if it suited Caribair.

Thus some small companies began to emerge as local entrepreneurs, realizing that an opportunity had presented itself for providing specialized air services. Already one or two fixed base operators had extended their activities into operating air taxi flights between the islands, and—

again in a familiar evolutionary process—these evolved partly into scheduled services.

In the mid-1960s, however, two vigorous newcomers entered the market of the two U.S. Caribbean territories, Puerto Rico and the Virgin Islands. Each one in its own way carried the element of specialization nearly to perfection. The two rarely competed with each other, and each carved a niche for itself that will long be remembered, not only by the islanders themselves but also by students of airline history. Each, in its own way, developed a style of scheduled airline business that, while it lasted, has never been emulated in its widespread acceptance and popularity.

The first of these was Antilles Air Boats, which started service between St. Croix and St. Thomas early in 1964. This remarkable operation was started by Captain Charles F. (Charlie) Blair, a retired Pan American Airways veteran who had had considerable experience with, and had acquired a great love of, flying boats. He realized that the harbors of Christiansted, in St. Croix, and Charlotte Amalie, in St. Thomas, offered ideal anchorages for small craft such as the Grumman Goose, and that he could offer a half-hour service between the two points, a saving of two and a half hours over the landplane service between the airports. Furthermore, with the smaller planes, he could develop a more frequent service. The Goose could be there and back twice, or even three times, before a passenger could make the journey via the airports or the ferryboat.

Charlie Blair built up his waterborne commuter airline service until, by the late 1970s, Antilles Air Boats ranked as one of the nation's largest and was carrying more than a quarter of a million passengers each year. But the spirit of innovation and adventure that had been the motivation for forming the airline eventually led to its downfall, for a fatal accident in 1978, in which Charlie Blair himself was killed, led to a scathing analysis by the National Transportation Safety Board, and the airline closed down a couple of years later. But Antilles Air Boats is remembered with affection for a time when "the Goose" was as much a part of the Virgin Islands scene as cable cars are a part of San Francisco's today.

The second airline, based in San Juan, was founded at the same time as Antilles Air Boats, by Jaime Carrión. At first called Ponce Air, because it plied between San Juan and Puerto Rico's second largest city, it changed its name to Puerto Rico International Airlines, or Prinair, in 1966, when it too jumped on the St. Thomas commuter bandwagon. Prinair's specialty was the British de Havilland DH-114 Heron, a small fourteen- to sixteen-seater that had the advantage of having four engines, which gave it good engine-out performance and an aura of "four-engined safety." Carrión improved its performance by installing three hundred-horsepower Continental engines, increased the seating to nineteen, and proceeded to buy every Heron in captivity.

The size of the airplane was just right. By 1970 Prinair was operating eighteen round trips a day on the twenty-five-minute trip to Ponce, and twenty a day to St. Thomas, plus many second sections. In 1972 it ranked, by the number of passengers boarded, as the largest commuter airline in the world. New routes were added to other islands in the Antilles, and Prinair claimed to be flying to the territories of seven different flags, from Santo Domingo to Guadeloupe.

The company was sold to the Union Corporation of Pittsburgh in 1973 and continued to flourish. The frequency to St. Thomas increased to thirty-six round trips per day. But then Prinair's fortunes changed rapidly. Several factors combined to sap its strength. The Heron aircraft eventually had to undergo complete overhaul and "re-lifing," which was a costly program. Traffic as a whole took a downturn, reflecting general economic sluggishness. A new highway from San Juan to Ponce cut further into that traffic. Then, almost as an echo of Antilles Air Boats' experience, a fatal Heron crash at St. Croix in 1979 added to the decline. Prinair finally went out of business in 1985.

Following Prinair's demise, a variety of other companies have maintained American-flag commuter air service in the Puerto Rico–Virgin Islands area. In fact, since the 1960s dozens of companies have appeared and disappeared, reflecting the general pattern that was experienced so commonly on the mainland. A few of these airlines have used flying boats, but the majority have relied on such proven landplanes as the Cessna 402, the BN-2 Islander, the DHC-6 Twin Otter, and the venerable DC-3.

Since the 1980s the code-sharing revolution has also come to the Caribbean. But with many potential light-density routes to smaller islands and towns, the code-sharers have not been as dominant as they have been elsewhere. With its scattered markets in a very favorable over-water operating environment, this area can be expected to continue to offer many opportunities for everyone—code-sharers and independent commuter airlines alike.

AREA 13 (CARIBBEAN)

First Sched. Service Date	Airline and Base	Code	Initial or Typical Route Network	Aircraft Used	Remarks	Date of last service
Late 1963	Virgin Islands Airways (St Croix, V.I.)		St. Croix-St Thomas-San Juan	Beech 18 DH 114 Heron Aero Commander	Founded by Bill Bohlke, Sr. (see also Caribbean Air Services).	1968
June 1964	Trade Winds & Western Airways (San Juan, P.R.)	WQ	San Juan-Mayaguez, St Thomas, Ponce, Viequez, St. Croix, St. Thomas-St. Croix	Beech 18 Aero Commander DHC-6 Twin Otter	Founded as a charter operator, Trade Winds Airways, in 1959. Acquired Western Air Services, 1968.	1970
4 July 1964	**Prinair (San Juan, P.R.)**	PQ	San Juan-Ponce, St Thomas, St Croix, Beef Island, Mayaguez.	DH 114 Heron Convair CV-580 CASA 212	Founded as Ponce Air; changed name to Puerto Rico International Airlines (Prinair). Acquired large fleet of the de Havilland four-engined feeder airliner changing the Gipsy Queen engine with Continentals. For many years was the largest U.S. commuter airline, operating the San Juan-St. Thomas route as a no-reservations shuttle service.	1985
2 Sept. 1964	*Western Air Services (Mayaguez, PR)*			*Beech 18*	*Merged with Trade Winds Airways.*	*1968*
21 Oct. 1964	*Inter-Island Airways (San Juan, PR)*		*St Thomas-Tortola*	*Piper types BN-2 Islander*	*Founded by Jack Chapman.*	*19 Mar. 1980*
21 Oct. 1964	*North Cay Airways (San Juan, PR)*	JV	*San Juan-Aguadilla, St Thomas, Mayaguez, Ponce, Calebra, Vieques, St. Croix*	*Piper Cherokee Six BN-2 Islander DC-3*	*Operated to both of San Juan's airports: International and Isla Grande.*	*1973*
Oct. 1964	Crownair (Dorado, PR)	KW	Dorado-St Thomas-Virgin Gorda-San Juan (British Virgin Is.)	Piper Aztec and Apache Piper Navajo BN-2 Islander BAe Jetstream DHC-6 Twin Otter	Formerly Dorado Wings, founded as an affiliate of Rockresorts (see also Area 10). Changed name to Crownair on 2 Nov. 1981. Purchased assets of Prinair, 1985.	1986
5 Feb. 1964	**Antilles Air Boats (St Croix, V.I.)**	AD	St. Croix-St Thomas Fajardo(PR)-St Thomas	PBY-5A Grumman Goose Grumman Mallard (VS-44) (Short Sandringham) (All flying boats)	Founded by Charles Blair, former Pan American pilot. The airline became one of the best-known operations in the Caribbean. Suffered a tragic accident on 2 Sept. 1978, when Blair was killed. Sold to Resorts International in April 1979.	10 Sept. 1981
27 Mar. 1965	*San Juan Air (San Juan, PR)*			*Piper Cherokee Six Piper Navajo Cessna 310 BN-2 Islander*		*1971*
Sept. 1967	Air Indies (Santurce, PR)	QE	San Juan-St Thomas, St Croix, Ponce, Mayaguez	Beech 18 Beech 99 DHC-6 Twin Otter, DC-3	Originally formed to operate scenic flights from Miami to the Bahamas.	1973
Early 1968	Caribbean Air Services (CAS Air) (St Croix, V.I.)		St Croix-San Juan, and to other Virgin Islands points	Beech 18 Aero Commander DC-3	Founded by Bill Bohlke, Sr. Sold to John Stuart-Jervis and also flew C-46s on air cargo charters.	Early 1980s
1969	*Caribbean Executive Airlines (San Juan)*	ER	*San Juan-St. Thomas*	*Beech 18*		*1972*

AREA 13 (CARIBBEAN) Continued

First Sched. Service Date	Airline and Base	Code	Initial or Typical Route Network	Aircraft Used	Remarks	Date of last service
1969	International Sky Cab (San Juan)	SI	San Juan-St Thomas, St Croix, Ponce, Viequez, Mayaguez	Piper Navajo Piper Cherokee Six	Operated from both of San Juan's airports:International and Isla Grande.	1970
1970	St Thomas Tax-Air (San Juan, PR)	QH ST	St Thomas-San Juan	Beech 18		1976
19 Dec. 1970	Virgin Air (St Thomas, VI)	ZP	St. Thomas-St Barthelemy (French Guadeloupe)	Beech 18 Piper Apache/ Aztec Cessna types BN-3 Trislander	Founded by Paul and Margaret Wikander.	
1971	Air Best de Puerto Rico(Isla Verde, San Juan, PR)	YB	San Juan-St Thomas	BN-2 Islander		1973
1971	Caribbean Island Airlines (St. Thomas,VI)	RQ	San Juan-St. Thomas	Beech 18 DHC-6 Twin Otter		1975
May 1972	Vieques Air Link (Vieques, PR)	VI	Vieques-Culebra, San Juan, Humacao, St Croix; later to Fajardo, PR	Piper Cherokee Six BN-2 Islander BN-3 Trislander	Started as a charter airline in 1965.	
1972	Pan Island Air Tours (San Juan, PR)	XF	St Thomas-San Juan, Vieques	BN-2 Islander		1974
1973	All Island Air (St Croix, VI)	AJ	St Thomas-Tortola- Virgin Gorda-Tortola- Anegada (British Virgin Islands)	Piper Apache/ Aztec BN-2 Islander		1980
1973	Trans Commuter Airlines (San Juan)	TJ	San Juan-St Thomas	Beech QueenAir	Purchased by Oceanair (see below).	1979
1974	Eastern Caribbean Airways (St Croix)	EL HR	St Croix-St Thomas St Croix-Nevis (St Kitts-Nevis)	Beech 18 Piper Seneca DHC-6 Twin Otter	Founded in 1960 by Ruth and Bill Bohlke, Jr., as Virgin Island Flight School. Route to Nevis purchased by Coral Air (see below).	1980
1975	Palmas Air Corp. (Santurce, PR)	PF	San Juan-Humacao	BN-2 Islander		1977
15 Nov. 1975	Air Mont (Vieques, PR)	HD	Vieques-San Juan Vieques-Culebra	Piper Seneca	Founded by Capt. Yves Dumont.	1980
Dec. 1975	Air Caribbean (Isla Verde, San Juan, PR)	ZF	San Juan-St Thomas	DC-3	Owned by Old South Air Service.	1979
Late 1975	Clipper Air International (St Croix, VI)	ES	San Juan-St Croix- St Martin/St Maarten (French/Netherlands Antilles) San Juan- Tortola (British V.I.)	Piper Apache/ Aztec Piper Seneca Beech 18	Founded by J.S. Jervis.	1976
1976	Valley Air Service (St Thomas, VI)	GQ	St Thomas-Anguilla (British Virgin Is.)	BN-2 Islander		1978
4 Mar. 1977	Aero Virgin Islands (St Thomas, VI)	QY	St Thomas-San Juan St Thomas-St Croix	DC-3	Founded by Joe Cranston. Reduced operations when its aircraft were destroyed or severely damaged by Hurricane Hugo, 17 Sept 1989.	
1979	Marshall's Air (St Thomas, VI)	HS	St Thomas-Tortola- Virgin Gorda (Brit. Virgins)	BN-2 Islander		1980

AREA 13 (CARIBBEAN) Continued

First Sched. Service Date	Airline and Base	Code	Initial or Typical Route Network	Aircraft Used	Remarks	Date of last service
1979	Sun International Airways (Isla Verde, San Juan)	RY	San Juan-St Thomas-Aguadilla; St Thomas-Vieques-Culebra	Beech types	Associated with Perkiomen Airways, Pennsylvania (Area 12).	1982
8 Nov. 1979	Oceanair (San Juan, PR)	TJ	San Juan-St Thomas-St Croix	DCH-6 Twin Otter Fairchild F-27 Queenair	Purchased assets of Trans Commuter Airlines (see above).	1984
May 1980	Coral Air (St Croix, VI)	VY	St Croix-San Juan, St Thomas, Tortola (British Virgin Is.)	Nomad DHC-6 Twin Otter Shorts 330	Founded by J.S. Jervis (see Clipper Air, above). Changed ownership, 6 August 1982.	1985
1980	Caribbean International Airlines (Santurce, PR)	XQ	St Thomas-San Juan	DC-3		1981
1980	Carriba Air (Carolina, PR)	YV	St Thomas-San Juan	DC-3		1981
1981	Flamenco Airways (Culebra)	FK	Culebra-San Juan, Vieques, St Thomas	BN-2 Islander Cessnas		
15 Mar. 1982	**Virgin Islands Seaplane Shuttle (St Croix)**	3G TW	St Croix-St Thomas-St John-St Croix-Tortola (Brit. V.I.)-St Croix-San Juan-St Thomas-San Juan	Grumman Mallard (flying boat) DHC-6 Twin Otter	Founded as Sea Air Corp. dba Virgin Islands S.S. (later under own name). Replaced services of Antilles Air Boats, buying some of its aircraft. Became a Trans World Express carrier, 1 June 1988. Ceased operations after fleet destroyed by Hurricane Hugo, 17 Sept. 1989, and bank would not advance further credit. Chapter 11 Jan. 1992.	12 Oct. 1989
5 July 1982	Sunaire (St Croix)	5S OY EA	St Croix-St Thomas-Tortola-Virgin Gorda; St Croix-Vieques-San Juan; San Juan-Mayaguez, San Juan-St Maarten	Piper Seneca DHC-6 Twin Otter SF-340	Founded by Stephen Milden, 1981. Div. of Aviation Associates. Became an Eastern Metro Express carrier, 15 Nov. 1985. Renamed Sunaire Express on demise of of Eastern 19 Jan. 1991.	
1982	Coastal Air Transport (St Croix)	DQ	St Croix-Anguilla (Brit. Virgins), St Croix-Barthelemy (French Antilles) St Croix-Nevis (St Kitts-Nevis)	Beech Baron BN-2 Islander Cessna 402	Founded by Mike Foster.	
1985	Air Puerto Rico Airlines (San Juan)	FD	San Juan-Ponce, Mayaguez San Juan-St Thomas, St Croix	Shorts 330	Operated for only about six months.	1986
1985	**Executive Air Charter (San Juan)**	NA AA	San Juan-Ponce, Mayaguez, San Juan-St Thomas. Expanded after American Eagle status throughout the Antilles, inc. Santo Domingo, British Virgins, Guadeloupe, Martinique, St. Lucia.	DH Heron DHC-6 Twin Otter CASA 212 ATR 42/72	Founded by Jose Facundo and Joaquin Bolivar as Executive Air Charter. Became American Eagle affiliate, Sept. 1986. Saved fleet from Hurricane Hugo, 17 Sept. 1989 by flying it to the Dutch Antilles. Purchased by American (AMR Eagle) in 1989.	
1986	LAPSA (San Juan)		San Juan-St Thomas	BN-2 Islander Shorts 330 DC-3		1989

AREA 13 (CARIBBEAN) Continued

First Sched. Service Date	Airline and Base	Code	Initial or Typical Route Network	Aircraft Used	Remarks	Date of last service
1988	Air Anguilla		St Thomas-St Croix	BN-2 Islander DHC-6 Twin Otter	U.S. Part 135 operator despite its name.	
1990	Royal Caribbean International (San Juan)		San Juan-St Thomas and St Croix	GAF (Australia) Nomad		1991

Appendixes

Appendix 1

Commuter Aircraft Specifications and Characteristics

Early Piston-Engined Scheduled Air Taxi

Manufacturer and Type	Engines			Dimensions (ft.)		Pass. Seats	Cruise Speed (mph)	Gross Weight (lb.)	First U.S. Service		Total Number Built
	No.	Type	h.p. ea.	Span	Length				Date	Airline	
Cessna 180	1	Continental IO-470	230	36	26	5	140	2,800	1953	Island Sky Ferries	6,207
Piper PA-23 Aztec/ Apache	2	Lycoming 0-320/0-540	250	37	28	5	200	4,800	May 1960	Princeton Aviation	6,976
Beech 18	2	P & W R-985	450	50	35	9	185	9,900	Feb. 1940	Wiggins Airways[1]	7,020[2]
De Havilland D.H. 104 Dove	2	Gipsy Queen 70 Mark 3	400	57	39	8	180	8,950	1955	Midway Airlines	544
De Havilland Canada DHC 2 Beaver	1	P & W R-985 Wasp Junior	450	48	30	6	130	5,100	July 1957	TAG	1,692[5]
De Havilland Canada DHC-3 Otter	1	P & W S3H/S1H Wasp	600	58	42	9	130	8,000	July 1957	TAG	466[5]
Aero Commander 500B[3]	2	Lycoming IO-540	380	49	42	8	225	8,500	1955	Air Activities	2,079[4]
Beech 50 Twin Bonanza	2	Lycoming GO-435/480	295	46	32	6	170	6,300	1953	Carco Air Service	1,072

1 Wiggins was one of the first Local Service airlines which used Beech 18s extensively, pre-dating the widespread deployment with air taxi companies.

2 Number includes more than 5,000 built for the U.S. armed forces, mostly C-45s.

3 Many different versions of the Aero Commander were built. The one described here was among the most popular.

4 Total of all piston-engined Aero Commanders. 751 Turbo Commanders were also built but seldom used by the commuter airlines.

5 Used almost entirely in Alaska.

Developed Piston-Engined Air Taxi ("Third Level")

Manufacturer and Type	Engines			Dimensions (ft.)		Pass. Seats	Cruise Speed (mph)	Gross Weight (lb.)	First U.S. Service		Total Number Built
	No.	Type	h.p. ea.	Span	Length				Date	Airline	
Cessna 206	1	Continental IO-520	300	36	28	5	160	3,600	May 1964	Mustang Airlines	7,020[5]
Piper PA-32 Cherokee Six	1	Lycoming O-540	300	33	28	5	160	3,400	1965	East Coast Air Taxi	4,373
De Havilland DH 114 Heron	4	Gipsy Queen 30 Mark 2[1]	250	72	49	19	180	13,500	June 1957	Illinois Air Lines	149
Cessna 402	2	Continental T510-520	300	40	36	9	230	6,300	Feb. 1967	Peninsula Air Transport	1,540[4]
Cessna 404	2	Continental GTS10-520	375	46	39	8	229	8,400	Nov. 1976	Air Midwest	397
Piper PA-31 Navajo	2	Lycoming IO-470/ T10-540	310	41	33	7	200	6,200	Aug. 1966	West Coast Airlines[2]	1,785
Piper PA-31[3] Navajo Chieftain	2	Lycoming T10-540	350	41	35	8	220	7,000	1973	Harbor Airlines	1,825
Britten-Norman BN2 Islander	2	Lycoming IO-540	260	49	36	9	150	6,300	Jan. 1968	La Posada Airways	1,270[6]

1 Most Herons, particularly the large fleet used by Prinair, were re-engined with 260hp Continental IO-470s, 300hp Continental IO-470s, or 290hp Lycoming IO-540s.

2 West Coast Airlines was a Local Service airline, and one of the first to make an agreement with a small air taxi operator.

3 Later versions from 1980 were called simply "Chieftain."

4 404 Cessna 401/401A/401B were also built.

5 Excludes Cessna P206 Super Skylane.

6 Still in production as Pilatus Britten-Norman PBN2. Also includes military variants.

Small Turboprops (Up to Twenty Seats)

Manufacturer and Type	Engines			Dimensions (ft.)		Pass. Seats	Cruise Speed (mph)	Gross Weight (lb.)	First U.S. Service		Total Number Built
	No.	Type	h.p. ea.	Span	Length				Date	Airline	
De Havilland Canada DHC-6 Twin Otter[1]	2	P & W Canada PT 6A	620	65	52	20	200	12,500	Oct. 1966	Pilgrim Airlines Air Wisconsin	844
Beech 99	2	P & W Canada PT 6A	680	46	45	15	280	10,900	May 1968	Commuter Airlines (Chicago)	239
Swearingen/ Fairchild Metro	2	Garrett-AiResearch TPE 331	715	46	59	20	280	12,500	March 1973	Commuter Airlines (Binghamton)	204[2]
British Aerospace Jetstream 31	2	G-AiR TPE 331	940	52	47	19	280	15,300	May 1983	Atlantis Airlines	350*
EMBRAER EMB-110 Bandeirante	2	P & W Canada PT 6A	750	50	50	18	230	12,500	Dec. 1978	Wyoming Airlines	500
Fairchild Metro III	2	G-AiR TPE 331	715	57	59	20	300	14,500	1981	Pioneer Airlines	242[3]
Beech 1900	2	P & W Canada PT 6A	1100	55	58	19	280	16,600	March 1984	Bar Harbor	274
Dornier 228	2	G-AiR TPE 331	715	56	54	19	230	13,670	June 1984	Precision Airlines	205[4]*

1 Purchased by the Boeing Company in 1988, then by Bombardier (Canada) 1992.

2 Number includes Metro II and Metro IIA's.

3 Number includes P&W Canada PT6A-engined Metro IIIA's.

4 Number includes Indian-built aircraft by Hindustan Aircraft (HAL).

*Still in production.

Larger Turboprops (More Than Twenty Seats)

Manufacturer and Type	Engines			Dimensions (ft.)		Pass. Seats	Cruise Speed (mph)	Gross Weight (lb.)	First U.S. Service		Total Number Built
	No.	Type	h.p. ea.	Span	Length				Date	Airline	
Nord 262	2	Turboméca Bastan VII	1,065	72	63	29	230	22,930	31 Oct. 1965	Lake Central Airlines[1]	111
Shorts SD3-30	2	P & W Canada PT6A	1,198	75	58	30	227	22,900	Aug. 1976	Command Airways	133[5]
De Havilland Canada DHC-7[2]	4	P & W Canada PT 6A	1,120	93	81	50	265	44,000	3 Feb. 1978	Rocky Mountain Airways	113
Shorts SD3-60	2	P & W Canada PT 6A	1,424	75	71	36	230	27,100	1 Dec. 1982	Suburban Airlines	165
De Havilland Canada Dash 8 (DHC-8)[2]	2	P & W PW121	2,000	85	73	40	300	34,500	24 April 1985	Eastern Metro Express	320*
SAAB 340[3]	2	General Electric CT7	1,735	70	65	37	300	28,500	1 Oct. 1984	Comair	280*
EMBRAER EMB-120 Brasilia	2	P & W Canada PW 118	1,800	65	66	30	330	25,350	Oct. 1985	Atlantic Airlines Southeast	260*
Aérospatiale-Aeritalia ATR 42	2	P & W Canada PW 120	1,800	81	75	50	290	36,800	17 Mar. 1986	Command Airways	224*
Aérospatiale-Aeritalia ATR 72	2	P & W Canada PW 124	2,160	89	89	74	300	47,400	Jan. 1990	Executive Airlines (Am. Eagle)	56*
CASA C-212 Aviocar	2	Garrett-AiResearch TPE 331	900	62	50	28	215	16,420	June 1978	Air Logistics	450[4]*

1 Local Service Airline.

2 Purchased by the Boeing Company in 1988, then by Bombardier (Canada) 1992.

3 Formerly SAAB-Fairchild.

4 Includes Indonesian-built Nurtanio-CASA models.

5 Includes military variants.

*Still in production.

Appendix 2

Statistical Record of the Commuter Airlines

Number of Operating Companies

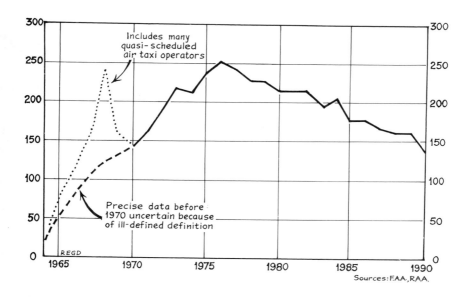

Includes many quasi-scheduled air taxi operators

Precise data before 1970 uncertain because of ill-defined definition

REGD

Sources: F.A.A., R.A.A.

Total Passengers Carried (Millions)

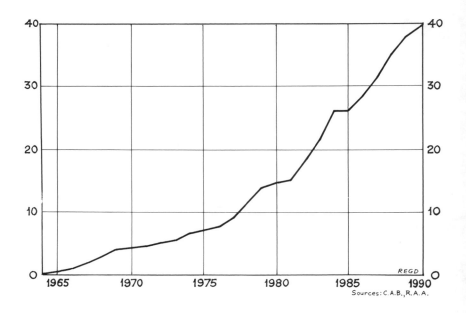

Sources: C.A.B., R.A.A.

Average Airline Size (Passengers Carried per Airline [Thousands])

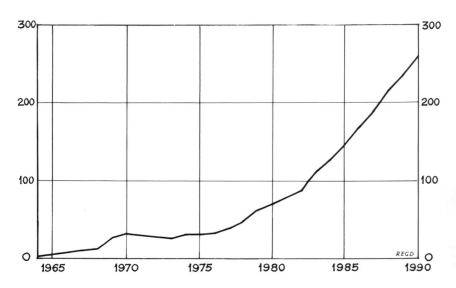

Aircraft Fleet (Industry Total)

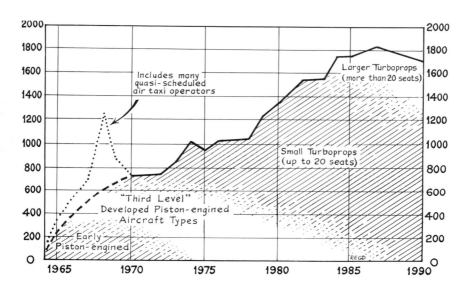

Average Individual Fleet Size

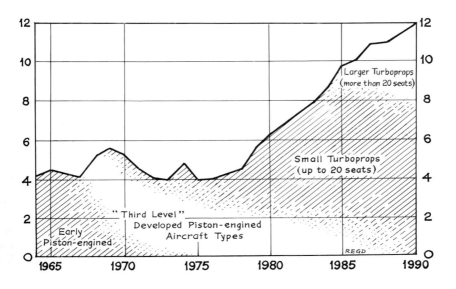

Bibliography

Air Transport World (Cleveland, Ohio: Penton).

Aviation Week and Space Technology (New York: McGraw-Hill).

Civil Aeronautics Board, *An Analysis of Scheduled Air Taxi Operations* (Washington, D.C: Civil Aeronautics Board, 1969).

———, *Part 298 Weight Limitation Investigation: Brief of the Bureau of Operating Rights* (Washington, D.C.: Civil Aeronautics Board, Bureau of Operating Rights, 1971).

———, *Analysis of Certificated Carrier and Commuter Air Carrier Service and Traffic Between Major Hubs and Points Within 200 Miles* (Washington, D.C.: Civil Aeronautics Board, Bureau of Operating Rights, 1972).

———, *Service to Small Communities* (Washington, D.C.: Civil Aeronautics Board, Bureau of Operating Rights, 1972).

———, "Commuter Air Carrier Traffic Statistics" (Washington, D.C.: Civil Aeronautics Board, various dates).

Commuter Air (Washington, D.C.: Airline Publishing Group).

Commuter Airline Association of America, *Annual Report: The Commuter Airline Industry* (Washington, D.C.: Commuter Airline Association of America, various dates).

Commuter Regional Airline News (Arlington, Va.: Airline Media Associates).

Commuter World (Burnham, U.K.: Shephard Press).

Cover, Virgil D., "The Rise of Third Level Air Carriers," *Transportation Journal*, Fall, 1971, pp. 41–51.

Creedy, Kathryn B., *Regional Airline Review and Questions for the Future* (Alexandria, Va.: Global Airline Enterprises, 1989).

Davies, R. E. G., *A Report on U.S. Third Level Airlines* (Hatfield, U.K.: Hawker Siddeley Aviation, Sales Engineering Department, 1966).

———, *Airlines of the United States since 1914* (Washington, D.C.: Smithsonian Institution Press, 1972).

DeLoff, James L., *Commuter Airlines* (Hicksville, N.Y.: Exposition Press, 1979).

Eads, George C., *The Local Service Airline Experiment* (Washington, D.C.: The Brookings Institution, 1972).

Elliot, Timothy S., "Development of Third Level Air Transportation," *Journal of Air Law and Commerce*, Vol. 29, 1963, pp. 182–204.

Endres, Günter, "Third Level Airlines," *Flight International*, 14 February 1974, pp. 199–216; 13 February 1975, pp. 245–271.

Federal Aviation Administration, *Scheduled Air Taxi Operators as of* [various dates] (Washington, D.C.: Federal Aviation Administration, 1965–1968).

———, *Commuter Air Carrier Operators as of* [date varies] (Washington, D.C.: Federal Aviation Administration, 1969–1971).

————, *Commuter Airlines and Federal Regulations, 1926–1979* (Washington, D.C.: Federal Aviation Administration, January 1980).

Feldman, Joan, *The Ransome Airlines Story* (Philadelphia: Ransome Airlines, 1977).

Flight Magazine (Dallas, Tex.: Air Review).

Kasper, Daniel M., *The U.S. Regional Airline Industry to 1996* (London: The Economist Publications, Special Report No. 1985, 1987).

Mayer, Jonathan D., "Local and Commuter Airlines in the United States," *Traffic Quarterly*, April 1977, pp. 333–349.

Molloy, James F., Jr., *The U.S. Commuter Airline Industry: Policy Alternatives* (Lexington, Mass.: Lexington Books, 1985).

Official Airline Guide: North American Edition (Chicago: Official Airline Guides).

Pickering, E. H., "Needed: A Third Level of Air Service," *Flight Magazine*, August 1961, pp. 28, 29, 44; September 1961, pp. 62, 64, 66; October 1961, pp. 36, 37, 38; November 1961, pp. 58, 60; December 1961, pp. 68, 78; January 1962; pp. 34, 39, 40; February 1962, pp. 54, 66; March 1962, pp. 48, 55.

Quastler, I. E., *Swift Aire Lines, 1969–1979: The History of an American Commuter Airline* (San Diego: Commuter Airlines Press, 1979).

————, *Air Midwest: The First Twenty Years* (San Diego: Airline Press of California, 1985).

Regional Airline Association, *Annual Report of the Regional/Commuter Airline Industry* (Washington, D.C.: Regional Airline Association, 1981–1991).

Taylor, John W. R., and Gordon Swanborough, *Civil Aircraft of the World* (New York: Charles Scribner's Sons, 1974).

Waldo and Edwards, Incorporated, *The U.S. Commuter Airline Industry—Its Current Status and Future Outlook* (Newport Beach, Calif.: Waldo and Edwards, 1970).

Index

Entries suffixed by an f denote citations within figure captions; those suffixed by a t, within text tables. The page number for the summary description of each airline within the regional tabulations in Part III is printed in *italics*. (Note that more than one airline may have the same name.) All references to aircraft types are listed under the general entry Aircraft.